MARGARET STORM JAMESON

MARGARET STORM JAMESON:

A Life

JENNIFER BIRKETT

OXFORD
UNIVERSITY PRESS

OXFORD

UNIVERSITY PRESS

Great Clarendon Street, Oxford ox2 6DP

Oxford University Press is a department of the University of Oxford.
It furthers the University's objective of excellence in research, scholarship,
and education by publishing worldwide in

Oxford New York

Auckland Cape Town Dar es Salaam Hong Kong Karachi
Kuala Lumpur Madrid Melbourne Mexico City Nairobi
New Delhi Shanghai Taipei Toronto

With offices in

Argentina Austria Brazil Chile Czech Republic France Greece
Guatemala Hungary Italy Japan Poland Portugal Singapore
South Korea Switzerland Thailand Turkey Ukraine Vietnam

Oxford is a registered trade mark of Oxford University Press
in the UK and in certain other countries

Published in the United States
by Oxford University Press Inc., New York

British Library Cataloguing in Publication Data

Data available

Library of Congress Cataloging in Publication Data

Data available

Typeset by SPI Publisher Services, Pondicherry, India
Printed in Great Britain
on acid-free paper by
CPI Antony Rowe, Chippenham, Wiltshire

ISBN 978–0–19–955820–9

1 3 5 7 9 10 8 6 4 2

For Stan

ACKNOWLEDGEMENTS

I should like to thank the University of Birmingham, the Arts and Humanities Research Council, and the British Academy, for the funding for research leave and travel to archives and libraries without which this book could not have been written. The librarians and staff of all the institutions I visited and consulted have been unfailingly kind and helpful. I am especially indebted to the expertise and patience of Michael J. Boggan at the British Library; Patricia Fox and Richard Workman at the Harry Ransom Center; Chantal Morel, former Assistant Director of the Médiathèque de l'Institut Français du Royaume-Uni; Erin O'Neill at the BBC Written Archives Centre; the Macmillan Archivist, Alysoun Sanders; Christopher Sheppard, Head of Special Collections at Leeds University Library, and Mark Shipway, formerly University Archivist; and Bernard Horrocks and his colleagues at the National Portrait Gallery.

In the course of the project, I have received advice, information, support and encouragement from many quarters, for which I have been most grateful. Special thanks go to Margaret Atack, David Bradshaw, Margaret Callander, Martyn Cornick, Alex Danchev, Syd and Wyn Donald, Alison Harvey Wood, Sarah Hesketh and her predecessors and colleagues in the Office of English PEN, Mark Jacobs, Mary Joannou, Judy Kistner, John Lucas, Edward Mendelson, Alan Munton, Joseph Pridmore, the late Josephine Pullein-Thompson, and Zara Steiner. Collaboration with the enthusiastic and indefatigable Chiara Briganti on an edited book of essays on Jameson helped energise the final stages of my writing-up. Tim Farmiloe, now retired from Macmillan, originally suggested, when I first began to write about Storm Jameson, that a biography was both needed and already overdue. Andrew McNeillie's warm support and enthusiasm for my text were greatly appreciated, and I have been fortunate in the advice and help of his colleagues at OUP, Jacqueline Baker, Fiona Vlemmiks and Tom Chandler. Christopher Storm-Clark has been most generous in allowing access to his Private Collection of Jameson's letters, documents, photographs and book collection, regaling me with information and anecdotes, and putting me in contact with other family members. His support and encouragement made this book a pleasure to research and write.

My own family—my mother, Elsie, my sister and brother-in-law, Gillian and Michel Gegout, and my nieces, Catherine and Nathalie—have borne with me patiently during the years of its gestation, and kept the food, drink and cheerfulness flowing. My godmother, Edna Cutts, has been a bountiful source of homemade fruit-cake. Stan Smith first brought home Jameson's *Journey from the North*, in the Virago edition, from a bookstall at one of the Essex Conferences, in the mid-1980s. We now dispute ownership of a near-complete and much-read collection of her work, gathered from the shelves of second-hand bookshops throughout the UK. A working partnership is the best kind, and I recall how Jameson wrote in her Preface to Guy's memoirs of drawing thoughtlessly on his learning, his familiarity with worlds to which she came new, the sweep of his reading and his pleasure in travel, which heightened her own: 'He made all other company a little dull.'

CONTENTS

PART II

Socialism and Internationalism:
the English Road to Europe

PART III
Europe At War

PART IV
Going Home

Contents

LIST OF ILLUSTRATIONS

All items are from the Private Collection of Christopher Storm-Clark, and appear here by kind permission of Christopher Storm-Clark. Every attempt has been made to trace other copyright holders; where known, these are indicated below.

Front cover: Margaret Storm Jameson. W. D. and H. O. Wills: Cigarette card series 'Famous British Authors (17/40; *c.*1932).

Back cover: Margaret Storm Jameson, Scotland, 1972.

Pictures in text

ABBREVIATIONS

BL	British Library
CSC	Private Collection of Christopher Storm-Clark
DCBCLUL	Dobrée Correspondence, Brotherton Collection, Leeds University Library
DSIF	Denis Saurat Archive, Archives of the Institut Français du Royaume-Uni—French Institute in London
HRC	The Harry Ransom Humanities Research Center, The University of Texas at Austin
JN	*Journey from the North* (London: Virago, 1984).
JK-CSC	Collection of letters belonging to Judy Kistner, held in CSC.
IR-CSC	Collection of letters from Storm Jameson to Irene Rathbone, held in CSC.
LHC	Liddell Hart Centre for Military Archives, King's College London
MABL	The Macmillan Archive at the British Library (3rd Tranche)
MSJ	Margaret Storm Jameson
NTLP	*No Time Like the Present*
Survivor	Guy Chapman, *A Kind of Survivor. A Memoir*, ed. MSJ (London: Gollancz, n.d.)
TLS	*Times Literary Supplement*
UALUL	*University Archive, Leeds University Library*

COPYRIGHT AND PERMISSIONS

The author and publisher would like to thank the copyright holders for kind permission to reproduce extracts from the following copyright material:

The unpublished correspondence of Storm Jameson and the unpublished typescript of *Journey from the North* (© Storm Jameson). Reproduced by permission of PFD (http://www.pfd.co.uk) on behalf of The Estate of Margaret Storm Jameson.

Letters, documents and photographs held in the Private Collection of Christopher Storm-Clark. Reproduced by permission of Christopher Storm-Clark.

Letter from Phyllis Bottome, in Correspondence and papers of and concerning P. Bottome and Capt. A. E. Forbes Dennis 1882–1972, held in the British Library. Reproduced by permission of Georgia Glover on behalf of David Higham Associates.

Letter from John Galsworthy held in the Private Collection of Christopher Storm-Clark. Reproduced by permission of Christopher Sinclair-Stevenson on behalf of the Literary Estate of John Galsworthy.

Letter from A. R. Orage, in the Private Collection of Christopher Storm-Clark. Reproduced by permission of Mrs A. R. Orage.

Letters from Dorothy Pateman, held by Christopher Storm-Clark in his Private Collection. Reproduced by permission of Judy A. Kistner.

Letter from A. D. Peters in the Storm Jameson Collection at The Harry Ransom Humanities Research Center, The University of Texas at Austin. Reproduced by permission of PFD (http://www.pfd.co.uk).

Letter from Irene Rathbone. Reproduced by permission of Mrs P. Utechin.

Dossiers in the Denis Saurat Collection held in the Archives of the Médiathèque at the Institut Français du Royaume-Uni—French Institute in London. Reproduced by permission of Dr Chantal Morel on behalf of the Institut.

Material held in the BBC Written Archives Centre, Caversham Park. Reproduced by permission of Erin O'Neill on behalf of the Centre.

Introduction

Writing and Politics: Life Lived at the Double

From her childhood in Whitby to her long old age in Cambridge, Margaret Storm Jameson lived many lives in one. The aptly titled *No Time Like the Present*, the first of her autobiographies, published in 1932, elicited from her friend Bonamy Dobrée intense admiration for the gift for vivid writing, and vigorous living, that turned her own vision of the world into the mirror of a generation:

[H]er life is in a sense my life, and your life, too, ungentle reader! It is because it is an amazingly vivid, astonishingly honest autobiography that it has this effect. [...] It is literature because it is life seen through the lens of a mind intensely alive.[1]

Jameson was a prolific writer, and her writing, especially her novels and short stories, was the form in which contemporaries over several generations knew her best. She was also, and equally, a political activist, fighting the great causes of her day in everything she wrote, as well as in committee rooms and on public platforms, driven by a thirst for social justice and a commitment to freedom. Some of the colour of her commitment changed with age: she started off reading *The New Age*, and ended up taking the *Times*. But she never gave up her hatred of capitalist values, or of the politicians, businessmen, factory owners, and financiers who drew their power and place from a system that denied ordinary people the chance to live decent human lives.

Journey from the North, the last of her autobiographies, published in two volumes (1969–70), is a map of the many roads she travelled, and the cultural bridges she crossed—and constructed—from Whitby to Warsaw and Washington. Born in Yorkshire, for many years she held Whitby, the harbour town of her birth, to be the heart of Englishness; the stubborn individualism of the Yorkshire moors, and the endurance of the miners and factory-workers of the North, were for

1

her a bulwark against the apathetic indifference of a Southern England grown rotten in the tooth. She had no nostalgic delusions about a region where isolation could easily turn into parochialism, with its associated vices: the selfishness, cruelty, and violence of the closed mind. From industrial Leeds to literary London, she travelled her own fiercely libertarian socialist path, on the fringes of feminism, through the Labour Party, into working alliances with Communists and fellow-travellers, and into the centres of pacifist organisation. A member of the London PEN Centre (Poets, Essayists, Novelists) from the early 1930s, and then wartime President of English PEN—one of the most hard-working and charismatic personalities to hold the office—her zeal for free speech, the free passage of ideas across frontiers, and the freedom and dignity of the writer and the common man, carried her into the heart of Europe, and beyond.

Her writing had by then already taken her own ideas across frontiers. From the 1920s, thanks to her work in the London office of A. A. Knopf, her novels were published in the United States as well as in England. America continued to welcome her work at least as warmly as England, with the high point, arguably, the well-paid serialisation in 1955 of her novel *The Hidden River* in *The Saturday Evening Post*. She spent a year in Pittsburgh, just after the war, with forays to New York (where her sister Winifred had a flat and a job), Washington and Vermont, to give talks or to holiday with PEN contacts and close friends. From the mid-1930s onwards, and especially the Second World War, she and her second husband, the historian Guy Chapman, counted numerous American journalists, publishers, diplomats, and academics among their friends.

Only a couple of translations into European languages appeared in the early days of her career, and it was the PEN connection that enabled Jameson to take her socialist convictions onto that wider stage. Cultural historians most readily remember the rescue mission she helped conduct for refugee writers, and the propaganda contributions that she helped PEN make to the Allied war effort. These were in one sense ancillary undertakings to the larger defence of freedom of thought with which PEN under her leadership became indelibly associated. Following the path established by H. G. Wells, Jameson pushed and steered the association through the difficult period in the late 1930s when the defence of intellectual freedom of expression, one of its primary principles, clashed with the equally hallowed doctrine that PEN's effectiveness depended on its detachment from overt political commitments. Her firm insistence that writers must defend their fellows who in the name of freedom of conscience were resisting the policies of their own national governments, as well as international oppression, was crucial in rallying members to stand up against fascism (and, after the war, against Stalinist Communism). From the start of the war, she used the platform of PEN to speak out for the need to plan for a different form of social organisation after the war, both at home and throughout Europe. PEN, for Jameson, was to be one of the gateways to the creation of a new Europe, beyond national differences, based on social justice.

Between her commitment to politics and her commitment to writing, there was no conflict. Jameson's distinctive genius was to produce novels that married her passion for political change to her passion for writing. The best of her writing is a materialist project, exploring the questions of the day in the landscapes and language of their making. She wanted to understand how history was felt and thought by the new kinds and classes of individuals who were emerging from the melting-pot of a new Europe, where populations were moving from the country to the metropolis, and from land to factory. She wrote about what she knew, and what she didn't know, she researched. She read voraciously, and she worked, talked, dined, and corresponded not just with writers but with journalists, politicians, and political activists of every stamp, academics, military men, and diplomats from all countries: Harrison Brown, Helen Kirkpatrick, Nye Bevan and Jennie Lee, Philip Snowden, R. H. Tawney and Harold Laski, Basil Liddell Hart, the Czech leaders Eduard Beneš and Jan Masaryk, and John Winant, American Ambassador to London during the war. The novels she wrote from the 1930s to the 1960s, the period over which Britain came slowly to acknowledge its changed place in the European and transatlantic order, are structured and styled by a depth of historical and political knowledge, and by unmatched sharpness and sophistication of insight, deceptively simple in its clarity. In the *Mirror in Darkness*, the trilogy on the 1920s that presents the origins and collapse of the General Strike of 1926 (*Company Parade, Love in Winter, None Turn Back*), as in the long sequence of novels that tracks the nightmare of war in Europe, and its resonances for Britain (*In the Second Year, Europe to Let, Cloudless May, Before the Crossing, The Black Laurel*), she carefully picked apart the threads of individual greed, craven political leadership, and the brutality of the military-industrial complex, that go to make the social web. After the war ended, between *The Green Man* and *Last Score*, she explored the consequences for individual lives of the long decay, at home and abroad, of Britain's imperial glory, and its squalid attempts to hang on to colonial power. Her writing, which mirrors her own life-experience, mirrors also the long, convulsive remaking of Europe and the West throughout the twentieth century.

Virginia Woolf declared herself 'bewildered' by James Joyce's *Ulysses*: 'We don't pretend to say what he's trying to do. We know so little about the people.'[2] Jameson, from time to time, had her own reasons for attacking Joyce's writing; but she certainly knew all the people, across the whole social spectrum, and was concerned that each should come to know the others. The individual, for her, was the meeting-point of many voices, a production of experience that is always both personal and generic, a part of the common stock; and her great concern was the disappearance of local and national community, and the sense of mutual responsibility, that protects individual freedom against the bureaucratic uniformity generated by an over-active State. She identified, and sometimes foresaw, the key issues of her day, which are ones that are still compelling for our own contemporaries: the real and ideal relationships of individuals to their communities; social justice; cultural heritage and memory; freedom of ideas and people; imprisonment and torture; exile; cruelty and kindness. To her discussion of all these, she brought her innovative insights into newly forming geopolitical categories of social and cultural identity. Exploring the European dimension of Englishness, from the early 1930s, she came to see in the fostering of European loyalties and European structures, beyond the deadly straitjacket of national identities, the chance to create a new and better community for the future.

Understanding politics was not enough. Understanding had to be communicated back to every level of this new world, to shape it into a new community. Jameson was obsessed with aesthetic form, and her obsession was driven by the desire to impress her analyses, simply and clearly, on the widest possible range of readers. Surface appearances here are deceptive, and the realist mode in which she writes is not simply mimetic. The mirror of her representations of the parade of humanity, over the highroads and by-roads of England and Europe, fuses the aspirations of Stendhal for the novel ('[un] miroir qu'on promène le long des chemins') and Victor Hugo for the drama ('[un] miroir de concentration'): a concentrating lens that inscribes in its images of observed reality the shaping power of the artist's eye and brain. Jameson evolved her own version of stylised realism, both in tune with her times and in advance of them, in which the forms of 1930s social documentary, fiction and film, were married to the different modernities of Stendhal, Flaubert, Baudelaire and the Symbolistes, Giraudoux, Eliot, and Auden.[3] *No Victory for the Soldier*, perhaps the most brilliant of her novels, published in 1937 under the pseudonym of James Hill, is an evocation of the quest of the modernist artist. The musician

John Knox, in search of innovative forms that will ally the energies of modern European cities to the deep-rooted knowledge and community spirit embedded in Europe's diverse landscapes, learns finally how to speak of reality from the frontline of European conflict, simply, and in the name of the common man, out of the anguish of the Spanish Civil War.

Jameson's formal achievements were never in her own time fully recognised. And at the moment in the late 1950s when she seemed at last poised for recognition, appreciation of the distinctive nature of her writing was blocked by the waves of new creative and critical fashion that surged through the metropolitan journals. Only recently have the limitations of the categories and boundaries imposed by the methodologies of 'scientific' criticism on twentieth-century artistic production (realist, modernist, structuralist, poststructuralist, postmodernist) begun to be recognised, and the return begun to kinds of criticism that can read the relations of cultural forms to cultural practices, and recognise the particular operations of particular texts. A cultural community that can feel its way below the apparently clear surface of Jameson's writing, and read all the levels of her work, is perhaps at last in process of formation.

Writing the Landscape: Culture and Identity

Jameson's life and work, fallen out of sight in the early 1970s, came back briefly into the public eye in 1984, with the re-issue by Virago of *Journey from the North*. Even then, one of the most significant themes of that text, cultural identity, went unrecognised, as it had on first publication of the work. Long before Raymond Williams began his investigations into the forms of culture and society, the link between individuals and culture, and the definition of 'culture', as a complex phenomenon that must include both 'high' culture and the lived experience of the everyday, was under discussion at the London School of Economics in the 1930s by R. H. Tawney and his colleagues. They influenced the work of Jameson's second husband, Guy Chapman, and Jameson herself, and she committed a series of novels in the late 1930s and the 1940s to exploring the link between the material of culture and the materiality of language. Her distinctive mode of stylised realism, which brought together insights into the nature of Symbolist poetry and realist prose fiction, culled from a variety of sources, was an attempt to find a form of writing that could remake

5

connections between elite culture and the culture of everyday life. Through that mode, she was also able to bring to a wide audience her own innovative insights into the geopolitical categories of cultural identity. The strict observance of national differences had tumbled Europe, in her own lifetime, into two world wars. Future citizens of Europe would be defined by their triple cultural heritage: the regional, the national, and the European. Tracing the process by which Jameson developed these insights is one important aim of this book.

Before the narrative begins, it will be worth looking closely at a distinctive feature of Jameson's cultural vision, which is the intimate connection of landscape and identity. *Journey from the North* alerted readers to the challenge that faces all those who want to write about the intangible nature of selfhood:

> The pain and ecstasy of youth, the brief happiness, the long uncharted decline, can be summed up in the tune of a once popular waltz, of no merit, or the point in a country lane where the violence and hopelessness of a passion suddenly become obvious, or the moment when a word, a gesture, nothing in themselves, gave the most acute sensual pleasure. None of these can be written about.[4]

But write about them she did. As her writing matured, there were the French Symbolists to show the way. Baudelaire is an obvious literary echo in the 1930s novel *Love in Winter*, where the opening of a drawer in a Chinese cabinet is the focus for Hervey Russell's evocation of the multiple associations of memory, and its transformative effects on past and present:

> No doubt it is the simplicity of my life then [in the country outside Liverpool], hard though it was, which charms me and has been preserved in my memory of the country, much as pulling open a drawer in the Chinese cabinet at home gives me back the whole of my early life at once and more than that, the life of Danesacre when it was still alive and lovely, one of the ports of England and familiar to men living as far away as Odessa or Archangel and even China.[5]

Or, some pages before, Hervey tries to fix in writing how moments of transcendent vision, summoned up by layered memories, bring a rare and piercing awareness of selfhood. The coarse grass of Danesacre, piercing the cobblestones, transports her to a grassy field on the ramparts of Antwerp, and

> Again, just as in the Antwerp field, I felt my whole being transported with bliss, and each time I visited the street in those years the sense of strangeness and beauty returned. I believe that the two moments, separated by years, were parts of a secret I have not understood—as when, passing along a street, we hear spoken a few words, too few to grasp the meaning of the sentence, only enough to seize its unmistakeable importance

for us, so that we can never rest this side of understanding. Meaning or no meaning, time or no time.[6]

From Jean Giraudoux, from T. S. Eliot, and later from a fellow Yorkshireman, W. H. Auden (and behind them all, the French Symbolists), Jameson pieced together the techniques for evoking, how through words, the flickering intuitions of self-consciousness find embodiment in remembered space.

This understanding is the dynamic of her most creative prose. Through the forms of landscape she was able to evoke the thrill of an acutely perceived identification of self as a body among other bodies. She could take her own experience of the intimate and living connections of sight, sound and place, and communicate them in writing, in the language of the tribe—she shared Mallarmé's aim, without sharing his elitist obscurity. The writer may claim to despair of finding the words to write such deep knowledge. But she knows that 'the tune of a once popular waltz, of no merit' is always waiting in the wings, one of the familiar, transient harmonies of a culture held in common, ready to be called into service to carry the passion and the delight that, in a world of prefabricated experience, can still be felt. Such prose is deeply political. Places, addressed through the imaginative powers of hearing and vision, are cultural productions, and can become key sites of interaction for the renewal of individuals, and of community.

Journey from the North offers in its opening pages a distillation of this perception.[7] Beneath the easily accessible realist prose is a highly abstract model of how the sound and light of landscape can be invoked to define the shared experience of a generation, one that is both generic and intensely personal. Jameson summons up a cluster of earliest childhood memories of things seen: the sunlit deck of a ship, the sheets on her crib ('a crevasse, its walls densely white'), a field of marguerites. These blur into an image of fierce white light undifferentiated and ungraspable: '[T]he whiteness seared, dazzled, blinded, a naked seething radiance, whiter than all whiteness, running out of sight.' The dazzlingly blank page of human experience is cut through by three distinctive sound-notes. Two of them are the fundamental notes of the human condition, the paradoxical desire both for the security of home and the challenge of the unknown. The deep note of the Whitby bell-buoy, fixed in its original place, reverberates its warning of invisible depths and currents; the piercing voices of fishermen's children, swallowed into the screech of gulls, is a call for departure, 'Ah-wa-a-ah!' 'Away!' In between lies all human speech, taking different forms in different times. The note that defines Jameson's personal difference, the one that dominates, is the voice of the mother, coming out of nowhere to fill memory, and the page, with its authoritarian timbre. Apparently nurturing, essentially hostile, this is the keynote of the child's struggle for self-definition: 'Nonsense. Children don't have headaches.'

Jameson's writing life was a long struggle to give forms to this insight into the functioning of the image, and the interplay of sound and light through which individual perception can be transformed into generic experience. Its best illustration is *No Victory for the Soldier*, where music is the model for writing, and the avant-garde musician John Knox is trying to write the harmonies of the modern world. His Paris Symphony is to be an artistic production composed out of his own body, but accessible to all bodies, with multiple points of entry, using forms that model the natural rhythms of men and women moving in their own experiential space. Jameson's text emphasises the difficulty inherent in both composing and receiving a work constructed out of such determination to abandon conventional vision, and presenting objectively the multiplicity of relationships that constitute the modern city:

He worked very slowly—all the ease and fluency he had delighted in had left him, and with it all his pleasure in writing. He was the more driven to write. Everything in his days, all he saw, a child, a leaf, an old woman so nearly finished that she scarcely twitched any longer, all his thoughts, if they were only of bread, became music. But this torrent of sounds pouring in on him came against a frightful resistance; he had to force himself past it on to the level where these things were no longer part of himself. He must walk about his own deepest experience as if it were a separate city, *another* Paris, because only in this way could he throw it open to others, with its confusion and horror, its cruelty, indifference, its Seine, its fountains, hospitals, noise, sunlight, ecstasy, gardens, death. The lucidity of this music is almost terrifying: it disconcerted its hearers at the one performance (a bad one)—'brutally detached, cold, over-elaborate.'
'What did they want?' Knox said: 'To be able to drive about it in a taxi?'[8]

Journey from the North is the generic journey of the twentieth century. The Odyssey of Daisy Jameson takes her from her starting point of Whitby, and its harbour, moors, and sea, to the industrial townscape of Leeds and the cityscape of London, and from there to the towns and fields of France, and finally of all Europe, learning to live, and learning to write. Where she ends is where she began, in the unspeakable place of origins where all the threads of history, culture and tradition meet and tangle, and create common humanity: 'a continuous present in which the dead, and the little I know about them, jostle the ghosts of the living.'⁹ The difference between beginning and end is that the blindingly empty space, dominated by the mother, becomes dark with diversity, crammed with uncountable bodies and voices.

In this continuous present, the sounds in the landscape, turned to articulate speech by their human perceivers, speak of a shared culture of humane, aesthetic, and political values, and of a common destiny. Sitting on the edge of a lake in the United States in 1949, Jameson produced a distillation, in that shred of landscape, of how it felt in such a time and place to be English, the displaced inheritor of the European mind. In her perception, past, present, and future were blended: 'the antique chorus of frogs listened to in March 1935 in Spain is—at the same time—distending the darkness above a lake in northern New York State fourteen years later.'¹⁰ The past—a European past—is a radical one. Aristophanes' frogs croak their challenge to the city-state, and the Spaniards stand poised to fight for their Republic. The present is American, the smooth surface of a lake that could be European, but has depths that no European can see. The future is Europe in an American voice, a monstrous unknown evoked in the rhythmic croak of a phrase bringing no clear knowledge, only 'distending the darkness'.

Writing Herself: The Woman and the Masks

The writer described above is not the Jameson known to most literary historians. Her name is not generally associated with complex questions of symbolic form or cultural identification. She is more usually classed with contemporaries such as Vera Brittain, Winifred Holtby, Phyllis Bentley, and Phyllis Bottome, or even J. B. Priestley, and treated as an inheritor of the popular realism of Arnold Bennett and John Galsworthy. For this very mistaken impression Jameson herself was partly to blame, having opted in the 1930s to associate herself vociferously with the documentary realism in which many of her politically committed contemporaries engaged. The need to build a recognised profile in a competitive publishing market helped keep her confined to this category. In her novels, recurrent characters and dynastic families encouraged a regular readership, who could be further reassured that they 'knew' their author by the highly personal, autobiographical element in many of her fictions. She wrote good stories, with rounded characters, and plenty of 'human interest', and on this basis could sell her writing to the book market, the tabloid press, women's magazines, radio, and eventually television—and thus to a middle-brow, and even popular audience.

A clear voice tells of herself in all her texts—vivid, witty, mordant, attractively self-deprecating. Rather too clear, perhaps, to be always convincing. Friends who read the first draft of *Journey from the North* complained that she laid on the guilt too thick, and indeed, in that version, her excessive self-flagellation indicates a degree of seething resentment, imperfectly repressed, that was almost eradicated in the published text. She certainly worked from life, in her autobiographies and in her fiction. But more accurately, she worked on life.

She controlled her public image. She did her best to reduce the amount of paperwork she left behind. She kept manuscripts and typescripts for a long time, storing them in trunks with Harrods as she and Guy traced their long periplus through countless flats and hotels. Some she gave away in the war, as a thank-you to America, and afterwards to American academic hosts. Others she sold in the 1960s, when she needed the money.[11] She made a point of burning letters.

As invasion looked increasingly likely at the start of the war, many letters were destroyed if there was material in them that could incriminate a PEN officer who figured on the Nazi blacklist, or that could endanger her contacts. She was known in any case for destroying correspondence. Returning her letters after their final quarrel, Vera Brittain decided she would have copies made, to ensure the content survived for publication after both their deaths.[12] Other people kept them too, for less polemic purposes, either in the jumble of their personal papers, or, in the case of individuals corresponding in an institutional context, such as PEN, more or less carefully filed away. In the early 1960s, writing her autobiography, Jameson said she had few letters left, from a lifetime of correspondence.[13]

The collection she left at her death contains probably more than a hundred letters from that time, used when composing *Journey from the North*, but not many more. However, there is also much correspondence from the years after the autobiography was published, received from old friends while she was in Cambridge, which is often illuminating about the past as well as the present.

The collection consists of three box files of personal letters. A note in her handwriting is pasted into the lid of Box 1, addressed 'To my Executor' and explaining that these are 'a minute portion of many thousands of letters received and answered in my long writing life'.[14] She had destroyed many letters, she said, often because there was such a lot of travelling and house-moving, and books were already a problem; and sometimes because the writers had been very frank, in the expectation they could trust her. She wasn't a hoarder. The letters still left were personal to her, so she didn't want them read even by friendly eyes. The biggest portion was from family, and those should be given back to the writer. 'I hope', she said, 'I have left no letter which, if read, could harm or vex its sender.' There was an envelope in the wardrobe cupboard containing the few letters left from well-known people, which she left to her Executor's discretion. There was one final note:

When, during the almost fifty years of our marriage, Guy and I were separated, we wrote to each other daily. In the later years we were not separated. After he died, I burned the large pile of my letters to him, keeping back his to me—to be burned by a close friend after my death.

Her grandson and literary executor, Christopher Storm-Clark, according to her instructions, burned a sealed box. He had to open it to burn the papers properly, and the top few items he saw, but didn't read, were in Guy Chapman's handwriting. She added later to her covering note, in red ink: 'These letters represent, I think, the only biographical material I am leaving.'

Anyone reading in this collection must be intensely aware of Jameson's presence, actively constructing her own persona to the end and beyond. Among the correspondence is a letter from a research student asking for information on one of Jameson's contemporaries. The student sets out her sense of intrusion as she read in her own subject's archive things that were not meant for her eyes, and her recognition that, in her own study, some things must remain unsaid. It's a sharp nudge.

In the closing movements of Jameson's last novel, *There Will Be a Short Interval* (1973), the middle-aged narrator is preparing himself for the risky operation he has finally decided to face. He goes through the drawers of his desk, tearing up photographs, letters from friends, and letters from his wife and his son, as a child. There are not many, because all through his life he has had

something of a mania for destroying the documents—letters, papers, scribbled notes, engagement books—he considered entirely private. Private to himself or others. He tore up every personal letter as soon as he had replied to it, even letters that might be of interest to excavators of the distinguished dead. There are too many embalmed half-truths littering the world.[15]

To be excavated is arguably preferable to being overlooked, especially for someone who conducted the greater part of her life in the public sphere. Those who lived and worked alongside her have been surprisingly reticent about the parts she played. The number of autobiographies of literary lions where there 'should' have been traces of her, and aren't, are legion. Vera Brittain blotted her out of her autobiographies and diaries, except for occasional hostile comments, and the original dedication to her from *England's Hour* is absent from some later editions. There are glimpses of her in the work of other writers and friends, such as Amabel Williams-Ellis and Irene Rathbone, but they are all too brief. An index reference in Frank Swinnerton's *Autobiography* produces only a mention of 'my dear friend Storm Jameson' on a short list of 'interesting people' of whom 'I shall say nothing whatsover'.[16]

There is something deeply puzzling in the fact that a woman who was so well known, and popular in so many circles, could have slipped so completely from view. It can't have been merely metropolitan antagonism to her provincial connections. When she began writing, numbers of Northerners were making their way to London in search of their fortunes, and the regional novel was in vogue. Her interest in Europe was not widely shared before 1939, but her work with PEN and the refugees from Central Europe gained her considerable general respect, and many people shared her admiration for France, and her interest, after the Second World War, in the idea of a united Europe led by an Anglo-French coalition. Her perspectives on class politics, whether flamboyantly socialist in her student days, or Tory revolutionary in later years, under Guy Chapman's influence, made her both friends and enemies. The same was true of her attitudes to feminism. She was a firm believer in women's rights to a career as well as their responsibilities as mothers, and a loud disapprover of political correctness. Never rigid in her positions—her switch of allegiance from pacifism, in particular, antagonised important friends—she never managed, or wanted, to settle into allegiance with one single group. She worked with many groups, for many causes, but identified herself finally with none. One reviewer of *Journey from the North* pegged her, with some exaggeration, as 'a loner', and asked who, if you were playing literary snap, you could possibly pair her up with?[17]

For many years, her association with PEN was the one that counted most for her. She exhausted herself with the drudgery of committee work. She enjoyed the parties and lunches more than she often admitted, and said after the war that she suspected she could easily become a habitual committee-member, enjoying the committee intrigues and dagger-work. She was a brilliant and inventive organiser, and a charming manipulator, who could make people make things happen. But after her first two years as President, serious illness as well as the demands of her own writing career made the commitment hard to sustain, and she was not always frank with the PEN International Secretary, her great friend Hermon Ould, about her willingness to carry on. Ould, in his turn, was not always fair in the pressure he put on her to stay. She was still surprised at the speed with which, after her resignation from the Presidency, she vanished from the sight of literary London. She didn't, perhaps, try hard enough, or care enough, to maintain networks and contacts. As she wrote her autobiography in the 1960s, she was conscious that her kind of novel seemed irrelevant to the writers and critics now making their names, ruefully telling her friend Basil Liddell Hart that they were making her a scapegoat for her generation.[18]

Her personality was not an easy one to deal with, but nor was the world in which she had to live. She cared deeply for people, in the general, and as individuals. But she could, as she recognised, be suddenly thoroughly selfish, and unkind, to everyone but Guy. Her sister Dorothy recognised the absolute priority she gave to her writing career, and for that reason was adamant that if she was killed in the war (as she was), she would rather her children stayed in the States with their American foster-parents than came home to an aunt who could give them everything money could buy, but not all the time and attention that a mother would.[19] She felt constant guilt at leaving her son Bill in boarding schools while she pursued her career, but she still left him. *Journey from the North* shows her punctilious in her concern for her grandson after Bill's first marriage broke up—and always eyeing him warily, expecting to be judged for the failures in love for which she always judged herself.

She berated herself for her exploitation of people in her writing. Her brilliant dialogues are always observed from the real. After her quarrels with her first, faithless husband, she reported, she went back to her room and wrote it all down; and the same exchanges and phrases recur in novels and short stories, as she writes out but never exorcises her jealousy and her humiliation. No one person is ever a single source for a character, but many of her characters are composites of words, gestures, and attitudes garnered from herself, family, friends, and acquaintances. To Basil Liddell Hart, she explained the process,

13

not a direct transplant of the living person, which would not, she felt, be a decent thing to do, but a kind of 'blood transfusion':

So, for example,—I need an unusually intelligent or an unusually civilised character for some situation or some theme of a novel: I try to imagine, when I'm writing a scene in which this person must act, how Basil Liddell-Hart [sic] would act in such a situation, what he would say, how he might feel. The character's role in my novel, his appearance, upbringing, etc., are probably quite wildly unlike anything I know about the life of Basil L.-H. Hence what comes through is a sort of essence of B.L.H., his voice speaking in this imagined figure.[20]

The process could also operate in the negative, to produce a character who was consciously the opposite of the source. And sometimes, indeed often, the transfusions became pastiches and parodies. Priestley and Auden fared badly at her pen, in *Company Parade* (William Ridley) and *The Green Man* (Acker) respectively, as did Ethel Mannin, who forced Jameson to tone down and distance the portrait she thought she recognised in *Delicate Monster*. But this is, as Jameson recognised while preparing *The Road from the Monument*, another of her autobiographical fictions, how all writing works, a 'positively evil' misuse of others' emotions. And yet: 'It may not be only evil. Nothing is pure or single; there might be compassion in the impulse as well as coldness and inhumanity.'[21]

The novel *There Will Be a Short Interval* appeared just after *Journey from the North*. The two together offer a kind of ironic commentary on the nature of the self of fiction, and the fictions of self. The narrative of the autobiography and the narrator of the fiction speak with one voice of a life that seems to have been a failure, and a search for the 'truth' of oneself, which can never get beyond the mask:

God damn it, he thought sharply, you should be able to see through yourself now. Almost your last chance. The truth is, my friend, that you were quite simply incapable—too restless, too impatient, too intractable, too gauche—of insinuating yourself into influential circles. Incapable, even had you been given the chance, of making yourself felt there. Nobility my foot. In the circumstances, what could you do except become a disinterested man? What sort of reputation, except for honesty and unsubservience, had you the slightest chance of deserving?[22]

A reputation for honesty and unsubservience is not a bad one to end with.

PART I

The Little Englander

1

A Yorkshire Childhood

[P]rimitive or underworld images, voices out of sleep, out of a lost harbour, which are mine. They may indeed be the only things I ever, in the positive sense of the word, hear or see.[1]

Margaret Ethel Jameson opened her eyes in Whitby in March 1891, and for a while saw and heard nothing to speak of.

There was, however, much going on, and much waiting to be seen. Whitby was a town preparing itself to enter the twentieth century, while still clinging determinedly to the habits of a long history enshrined in the narrow streets and tight-packed houses tumbling down the hillside, from the great ruined Benedictine Abbey founded by St Hilda, onto the quays of the busy harbour and port. This was the view from the window in the first house Jameson could remember from her childhood, 5 Park Terrace, on the North bank of the river Esk.

Daisy Jameson grew up in a landscape where thinking and working went side by side, in a close-knit community bustling with the best and the worst of the new age.[2] Everything she would do in later life, however much driven by the burning ambitions she freely acknowledged, was attuned to awareness of the surrounding press of others, and the needs of a crowd of faces, each with the challenge of their own individuality. The fishermen, women, and children who stare boldly into the camera of the local photographer, Frank Meadow Sutcliffe, well-fed and robust despite their tattered clothing, left their mark on her imagination.[3] The children's seagull cries punctuate her adult writing, and close her last autobiography, *Journey from the North*. Their more frightening avatars are the dreams of the evil

17

Figure 1 The view across the Esk, across Whitby harbour, from the North Bank.

dwarfs in the streets that haunted the little girl until her adolescence: 'one touch from them would horribly twist your body, if not kill you.'[4]

Nightmares and all, the Whitby that appears in Jameson's autobiographies and autobiographical fictions, retrospectively invented, is the writer's ideal place of origins: a past into which the present is projected, in order to identify the seeds of the future. The view out to the sea, to the northern coasts of Europe, promised open ways and different paths to those experienced by many Englishmen and women of her generation and class. At the back of the house, the road to the moors led to secret places, easily defended against metropolitan intruders. The town itself was the ideal place of belonging, where the path to home travelled confidently through streets trodden by the feet of familiar others, past and present. When in 1919 the faceless crowds of London overwhelm Hervey Russell, Jameson's alter ego, she flies for refuge to the Danesacre that is Jameson's Whitby, and the aching consolations of the home that was always whole, and always lost:

The loveliness of Danesacre hurt her, because she thought of all the women who had walked in its streets, of whom through their eyes it had become part, until they died and saw it no more.[5]

Whitby, in Jameson's books, is the place of beginnings, a source of energy, and a passport to identity. It was a good place to start from—and, she soon decided, an even better place to leave.

18

Figure 2 A picture postcard, with a note on the back in Jameson's handwriting: 'Whitby before the fish quay spoiled the sand.'

Around Town

The little world of Whitby in the 1890s was a busy place, opening its eyes to the modern world, but more confident of its past than concerned with making its future. The whaling industry was long gone except from folk memory, and shipbuilding had decreased almost to vanishing point, though at the start of the decade there were still twelve ship-owners, two shipbuilders, and five boat builders.[6] By the time Jameson was noticing things, only the skeletons of two old yards remained.[7] But the harbour was still full of boat traffic: local fishing boats, the Cornish fishing fleet that called every year in September and October, sailing ships, steam luggers, collier brigs, yachts, and paddle steamers with day-trippers. The open quays were still lined with fisherwomen's stalls. There were two coach-builders, two breweries and 167 jet manufacturers, making jewellery and ornaments out of Whitby's famous local stone. Most of all, there were fifty-four hotels and inns, two private hotels, and 168 lodging-house keepers. Tourism was the growing business.

Discriminating visitors had long appreciated the picturesque aspects of the port and its streets, the light from the sea, filtered through the mist, and

19

the smoke from the fishermen's cottages, and the relative quiet of a town less well-frequented than fashionable Scarborough, where the Sitwells lived, or even Filey, which, not long before, had been the favoured haunt of German and English aristocracy. Literary visitors who gave cachet to the place included Mrs Gaskell, George du Maurier, who regularly brought his family, and Bram Stoker, whose *Dracula* appeared in the year Jameson was born. The American James Russell Lowell, poet and essayist, and a former United States Minister to England, visited Whitby every summer in the 1880s and lodged with two Misses Gallilee, recording in 1888 that 'the badness of their cookery is equalled only by the goodness of their intentions', and in the following year, his ninth visit, noting the changes that tourism was bringing to the local landscape:

Whitby is coming more and more into the currents of civilisation. We have a spas-modic theatre and an American circus that seems a fixture. [...] One other amusement is the Spa, where there is a band of music bad enough to please the Shah. It is brilliantly lighted, and at night it is entertaining to sit above and watch the fashionable world laboriously diverting themselves by promenading to and fro in groups, like a village festival at the opera. The sea, of course, is as fine and irreconcilable as ever. Thank God, they cannot landscape-garden HIM....[8]

Jameson too considered the creation of the Spa, formerly called the Saloon, and a simple collection of grass, paths and steps twisting down the West cliff, the first step towards Whitby's ruin. And like Lowell, she was to express her faith in the power of the North Sea to stand out against 'progress', resistant to all change except the changes of its own moods: 'the milky blue of summer, [...] the savagery of winter, [...] suave, icy, gentle, enticing, treacherous, charg-ing the air with splinters of light [...]'.[9]

The heirs of St Hilda valued the things of the mind. Bulmer's Directory lists eight booksellers and stationers, eight printers, and nineteen schools and academies.[10] They took their religious responsibilities seriously, if in something of a factional spirit, with Congregationalists and members of the Church of England in fierce competition. Eliza Ashton, Jameson's grandmother, tricked her daughter-in-law, who had recently joined her pious sister Jenny in what were considered the lower-class ranks of the Congregationalists, into baptis-ing the new grandchild into the Church of England. She promised a generous christening present, but baptism over, the baby received an egg, a pinch of salt, and a silver threepenny bit.[11] Unsurprisingly, the spiritual side of religion passed Jameson by. It would never matter much in later life, except for a period in and shortly after the war and its anxieties, when her friendship with PEN colleagues Hermon Ould and David Carver stimulated an interest in astrology and in fashionable contemporary forms of mysticism. She was an avid reader of horoscopes throughout her life. But the austere ethics of both communions contributed to the rigid moral values of the local community, which marked her long beyond childhood, both in the sexual repression that came into play in her most liberated moments and in her inordinate propensity for guilt: 'I emerged from the hands of formal religion with no definite beliefs indeed, but with an indefinite regret for its passing. [...] but I am bound hand and foot by the repressions of a traditional race-morality.'[12]

Political issues played a much smaller part in most people's lives. Local politics in the 1890s was dominated by unquestioning conservatism. The Member of Parliament for the Whitby Division was a Tory, who had obtained his seat at the General Election of 1885, the first held after the passing of the Franchise and Redistribution Bill, and increased his majority at each election until in the 1895 election he was returned unopposed.[13] The tide of reform turned slowly, with the turn of the century. In 1918, Jameson herself made a small contribution to the local anti-Tory vote, sitting on one of Osbert Sitwell's platforms in the Khaki Election. He failed to win, but she remembered her Tory mother's pride in seeing her share a platform with the local aristocracy.[14]

Home and Family

Whitby in the 1890s was a close community, and the local boast then, as now, was that everyone was related. In 2004, the Church Maid in St Mary's Church, asked for directions round the old pews by the present writer, was pleased to declare herself probably some sort of relation of Jameson's, and point to the name of Ann Gallilee, painted on the old wooden board listing the Church's benefactors, whom she thought must be a mutual ancestor. In the 1881 census, the town was registered with a population of 15, 212, a tidy number, but small enough for everyone of consequence to know everyone else.[15] The tally included Jameson's awe-inspiring maternal grandfather, George Gallilee, a ship-owner, and his first wife, Hannah Jameson, whom he had married in December 1872. It also included his wife-to-be, Eliza Ashton, whom he married in September 1886 when Hannah died, to look after his seven children. Another imposing, sharp-tongued figure, Eliza was the only grandmother Jameson knew, being also her grandmother on her father's side. Neither Jameson's mother, Hannah Margaret, nor her father, William Storm Jameson, was aware of the connection when they first met, and neither was especially concerned or surprised by it.[16] There was a crowd of aunts on her mother's side, who was the youngest but one of the seven siblings. Mary, Ann, Jenny (Jane, the youngest sister, who was twenty-four at the time of the 1901 Census), and two uncles, George and Will, are all mentioned in Jameson's autobiographies. Jenny, Hannah Margaret's favourite sister, lived the longest, and Jameson returned regularly to Whitby to visit her.

The Jameson house at 5 Park Terrace is still standing, on the West side of the town, up the hill, at the point where the River Esk tips into the harbour, and overlooking the railway line that in 1836 brought Whitby the first connections to its hinterland. The terrace was one of a sequence of newly built streets, occupied by middle managers and ranking merchant sailors: professional men on the way up.

William Storm Jameson had been indentured to the merchant navy at the age of 13, and his indentures were among the papers his daughter preserved until her death.[17] Shortly after she was born, he was promoted to captain. Even with the promotion, the little family did not have much money, and this was a cause of friction between Jameson's parents. Her mother, mindful of the standards appropriate to a Gallilee, was extravagant, and loudly critical of her husband for his failure to provide for her as she thought he should. Money was short, and the family's social position was precarious, as the child came early to realise.

William's occupation at least produced a degree of adventure and opportunity. A sea-captain was allowed to take his wife with him on his voyages, and Jameson often went with them, long after she had ceased to be the only child. She recalls in *Journey from the North* the thrill of departures, the long boring days at sea, and the excitement of ports, especially Antwerp and Bordeaux. One particular incident, when they stepped ashore onto a husk-strewn wharf to the excited accompaniment of the news of the death of Queen Victoria (in 1901, when Daisy was ten), lodged indelibly in her imagination a thrilling and distinctive association of journeys with death—the source, perhaps, of her lifelong ability to enjoy endings as places of resurgence, and the talent for beginning again that she would later associate with her adopted motherland, France. She had never heard of Victoria, Jameson wrote in her autobiography, 'but a sense of her importance and the strange husks underfoot started up in me such a crazy excitement that to this day voyages and death resemble each other in my mind as one harbour is like another in another island'.[18]

Jameson's recollections of childhood are crammed with instances of such neurotically intense responses to physical stimuli. They say, of course, less about Daisy's childhood sensitivities than about how the grown-up writer, in the 1930s or the 1960s, reimagined her younger self. The husks crunching through the syntax of her disembarkation in 1901 owe more to Eliot and Giraudoux than to precocious insight. In the forms of her recollection, though, there are still kinds of historical truth. Former neighbours who wrote to her in 1969 when the first volume of *Journey from the North* appeared recognised the accuracy of her descriptions of the intimate landscape of growing up in Whitby—the games, the reading and story-telling, play on the seashore, country walks, marketing, and all the ritual of annual holidays and birthdays—and probably their recognition came all the easier for the sudden moments of intensely focused vision that from time to time blaze through Jameson's narrative, bringing a personal moment of self-recognition into the world held in common. In the lanes near the house where she played, a hedge smothered in white convolvulus, the dazzling whiteness of a field of marguerites, and the sharp, hard clarity of summer evening light in Mulgrave Woods, designate the Whitby of Jameson's first ten years as the idyllic place where a child first came to see. These are the originary moments of the writer's long self-training in perception, a blend of sensuous response and analytical reasoning which she would later describe as France's great gift to the European cultural heritage.

Not everything in that landscape was Edenic. Rousseau's writing borders too closely on the wilful and the irrational for him to earn a mention in Jameson's pantheon of French models, but her own autobiographical accounts often recall his *Confessions*, in the way they chart the stages of her awareness of selfhood through moments not only of piercing pleasure but also of fear, humiliation and pain. The Whitby she grew up in was a brutal world, where the violence that threatened on the streets had its counterpart behind middle-class doors, and parental authority could easily turn into tyranny. The terrors of a not-very-distant past leak out into Jameson's earliest fictions, sometimes disguised as dark secrets of the moors, and sometimes paraded on the open streets of Danesacre itself. Violence was endemic.

Jameson left out of her published autobiography an explicit indictment of what she described in her draft as her mother's sadism, and her account of her own slowness in coming to understand that pattern of calculated cruelty, alternating with equally calculated kindness and consolation, that left her a ready victim for her first husband and insecure in relationships for the rest of her life. She left out too a paragraph describing how the family next door heard her screams when she was beaten, without intervening. She included a learned memory of 'the persistence of a six-months-old child in climbing stairs she was beaten for climbing, six attempts, six beatings, before her baffled mother threw her into her cot to sleep it off.'[19] She left in the published version a string of less shocking accounts of early memories of running away from her mother's thrashings, hiding from the threat of her grandfather's, and of being whipped at the Misses Corneys' nursery school, in the house next door, for filling her brother's shoes with water.[20]

Children were as cruel as adults. At 8, she was almost strangled by an unknown 16-year-old boy while out playing.[21] In Miss Lily Ingham's school, which she attended from the new house on the West Cliff where the family moved in 1903, playground games were an opportunity to torment the new girl.[22] No less painful was the mockery and spite the older girls practised on each other, using friendship as a weapon. Writing novels, she later thought, might have been the 13-year-old's defence mechanism:

I remember that when a little blue-eye bandy-legged girl whose ready chatter and skill in typing [sic] a ribbon round her long yellow hair I admired and envied—what would I not have given to be more like her?—told me, smiling, that her brother said I was a freak, I said carelessly that I was writing a book about her and the others. This at a time when I could no more write an original line than make myself attractive in the dancing class.[23]

If there was hostility from children outside the family, inside it the situation was more mixed. Jameson had difficulty coming to terms with the displacement that is the lot of all first children. She was 4 when her sister Winifred was born in March 1895. A brother, Harold, appeared the following year, and much later, in December 1906, a second sister, Dorothy. All shared, she wrote in her autobiography, a profound sense of family feeling, a bond of duty that transcended any individual antagonisms.[24] But her memoirs and letters are still shot through with confessions of rivalry and resentment, and the beautiful, gifted heroines of her earliest novels have vast circles of admiring friends, and no brothers and sisters.

Winifred was never a threat, though often a nuisance. She was not a happy child. From the age of 3, she regularly tried to run away from home, and was as regularly carried back.[25] Despite another unsuccessful attempt to escape at the age of 17, Winifred was eventually to find herself left in Whitby taking

Figure 3 Margaret Ethel Jameson in 1895, with a note on the back
in an unknown hand: 'Daisy at 3½ years'.

Figure 4 Hannah Margaret Jameson and her three daughters. Storm Jameson is on
her mother's right, and Winifred on her left; Dorothy is seated, front.

Figure 5 Jameson's brother Harold in his R.F.C. tunic, back from the Front [summer 1916], in Whitby (*JN* I: 101).

care of her parents, dutiful and unappreciated, until her mother's death. Jameson, feeling always a little guilty at having abandoned her, was equally always aware how little they had in common. Reading *Journey from the North*, in 1969, her old friend Archie White was to point out reprovingly the near-total absence of Winifred from the text.[26] She had already been written out of the fictional recreation of the family in *Farewell Night, Welcome Day*. Jameson did her best to help her sister after their mother's death, and was perhaps instrumental in her getting a job in New York.[27] But visits to Winifred in the States, or visits from Winifred to England, frequent from the 1960s, were purgatory for Jameson, though she did her best to make her sister feel welcome. They had nothing in common. Winifred was tactless and insensitive, and she talked too much.

She was far fonder of her brother Harold, whose shoes she had filled with water, but even then a familiar self-judgement ('She did not love enough') opens her account in *Journey from the North* of his adolescent struggles to make something of himself in the world, in which she saw a cloudy reflection of her own.[28] After a disastrous first apprenticeship on the same merchant ship line as his father, and then on his father's ship, made worse by William's brutal lack of sympathy, he went on his own initiative to Manchester to register with the Royal Flying Corps as a wireless operator. After that, the war gave him his chance. He trained as a pilot in France in June 1915, after receiving the DCM (Distinguished Conduct Medal) for wireless work under fire. In peacetime, there would have been no money to pursue such an ambition. Then came the French Médaille Militaire and the Military Cross, and the week before he was killed in action, on 5 January 1917, he had been promoted to Flight Commander.[29] Tucked into Jameson's own copy of her autobiography is a photograph of the 18-year-old Harold in uniform, dated 1915, taken in Frank Sutcliffe's studio, some notes on his career, the original of the *London Gazette*, announcing his death, a postcard of Poperinghe cemetery, a few miles direct west of Ypres, where he was buried, and a photograph of his grave.[30] Jameson's account of the arrival of the telegram, six months after the event, evoking the visceral wrench that is the loss of family, is no less painful for the conscious literary reference to the pain of Antigone, which lifts the personal experience into universal tragedy.[31]

Of Dorothy, the youngest sister, Jameson said little of their relationship in their early years. Dorothy was her mother's favourite, and Jameson's jealousy ran close to the surface. The two were to grow close in the 1930s, when Dorothy joined her older sister in London to take a magazine job; tough, quick-witted and practical, she tackled life with a gaiety and confidence Jameson could only wonder at.[32] Keeping house for her older sister when their two families moved to live together outside Reading, as the bombs begin to fall, and relieving her of the domestic responsibilities that cut across her writing, Dorothy was to become the mother Jameson would have liked to have. But the competitiveness remained to the end.

Jameson's sympathy for her father was of longer standing and went deeper than the scanty references in *Journey from the North* might suggest. He was not often there in her childhood, being away at sea on behalf of his employers, the Prince Line. What might have been a more traumatic absence in Spring 1916, when his ship, the Saxon Prince, was sunk by a German cruiser, and he wound up in a concentration camp for civilians in Brandenburg, passed relatively painlessly.[33] The children, taking their tune from their mother, who never forgave him for his treatment of Harold and the privations of her own life, hardly missed him, and he returned unharmed. He was cold-shouldered by his wife after he insisted on retiring, at 74, in 1929, and her rage doubled

Figure 6 Captain William Storm Jameson, with the inscription
'Best love, from Daddie'. 'Not until he died did I see that he,
too, was to be pitied and respected' (*JN* I: 35).

when, in the 1930s, the shipping line was taken over by Furness Withy, who
promptly slashed his pension.[34]

The older Jameson was less of a participant in her mother's hostility than
appears from her autobiography. Indeed, she was conscious and resentful of
her mother's attempts to come between her husband and children. Fathers
in Jameson's earlier novels are distant, but unthreatening and sometimes sad
figures.[35] In later novels, pairs of good and bad fathers are at least as frequent
as pairs of good and bad mothers, though the good fathers are as much
based on the many father-figures Jameson adopted in the course of her
career, especially R. H. Tawney, with perhaps some elements of her redoubt-
able grandfather George Gallilee. The selfish, failed father in *There Will Be a
Short Interval*, trying on the eve of a dangerous operation to make a connection with the son he had never loved enough in life, is Jameson herself. From
the beginning, she developed a mixture of masculine and feminine identifications that defies categorisation in terms of conventional gender roles and
models—and with them, that blend of personal ambition and a sense of

nurturing responsibility for others that made her adult career so rewarding, and so difficult.

Mothers in the first two novels that Jameson wrote are dead. In *The Pot Boils* (1919), Athenais's mother dies after her daughter graduates with a first from Leeds, and is replaced by the more attentive and better-connected mother-figure who is her employer and patron in London. In *The Happy Highways*, Margaret's mother dies at her daughter's birth and her father some time afterwards, leaving her with plenty of money and a rich uncle as her guardian. The novels Jameson wrote after the war, and after her mother's death, figure increasingly pairs of good mothers who are dead, or powerless to help, and bad mothers who neglect and exploit their children and project into them their own thwarted ambitions. In *Last Score*, for example, the last exchange between the selfish and emotionally atrophied Governor of the colony, Richard Ormston, and the mother he idolises, rehearses the confrontations that Jameson should have had in her mother's lifetime. What the son once saw as his mother's cool self-control he now understands is inherent coldness. He accuses her of regretting marrying beneath her, and blaming him, because if he hadn't been born she could have put right her mistake. He finally provokes her to the admission Jameson always feared: '[I]t's true. I never liked you. I never wanted you.'[36]

And yet Hannah Margaret Jameson was the idol lodged in her daughter's head, whom she needed to please by her successes, and compensate for the career and the luxuries her children had stopped her enjoying.[37] The damage was done long before Jameson was born, by George Gallilee, who took his daughter away from school and forced her into domesticity.[38] Emblematically, she merges with Jameson's Whitby of imagination, the home of nostalgic desire and the place you most need to escape from. She was a flamboyant, overwhelming figure. Jameson wrote: 'Behind my own memories of Whitby are my mother's, and sometimes I forget which is which.'[39] Her mother's tales and memories, she went on, were more riotous, and of higher and merrier times. In contrast, 'I was a stolid, literal-minded child'.

Whatever her motives, Hannah Margaret saw to it that her eldest daughter had everything she had missed. There was money for music lessons, and money to support her through the Cambridge examinations, and send her to the Municipal School at Scarborough to prepare the County scholarship examinations that would finally take her to University. From the start, the daughter 'was eaten alive with ambition',[40] and learned the characteristics that enable ambitions to be realised—endurance, persistence, violence, and self-control:

I have the gross strength of my original hunger. Punished sometimes justly—I get up and start again, always with less ease. I know whom I have to thank for my power of resistance, for the habit of enduring, the habit and pleasure of defending myself by any means—dissimulation, lies, tricks.

And (make no mistake about it) the violence I have spent my life disguising in myself, the freedom I denied myself or was denied, are essentially—what is the word I want?—fastidious.[41]

Jameson's move to the Municipal School in Scarborough was recognised by mother and daughter as a watershed for both of them. This was the moment when she left her family, and entered the brother-clan who became Class 1914.

The Harlands

In a hand-written note on a bundle of carefully preserved letters from her oldest and closest friends, the Harlands, Jameson indicated the importance of a friendship that introduced her to the political and intellectual enthusiasms that were to last her a lifetime:

The two Harlands, Sydney (Pip), now a distinguished FRS, and Oswald, an underrated novelist, are, with Archie White, VC, my three oldest friends. I lived with them in digs when I was working on my MA thesis in London in 1912–13. A brief account is in Vol. I of *Journey from the North*. One of the formative years of my life.[42]

Before that formative year in London came the even more important year in Scarborough, about which Jameson's autobiographies say little. Sydney's autobiography is more forthcoming:

One morning in September 1907, the Headmaster came in, accompanied by a girl. She looked about 16, shy and uncomfortable, but there was something about her—I can't describe it; I can only say she shone. She sat down, put her books on the desk and began to work rapidly and with great concentration. She was Margaret Storm Jameson from Whitby. She had come to the school to work for a County Major Scholarship, which she was quite sure of getting, so she said.

Oswald and I took her in hand to educate her privately—that is, to put revolutionary ideas into her head. [...] Oswald and I were red-hot socialists. She listened, but said very little. Out of school we hardly saw her. Most nights we were too busy working to go gallivanting about. Nevertheless, we became close friends, and I confided in her about the girls I was interested in.[43]

The Harlands' family was probably the closest Jameson got to the moors people of North Yorkshire, on whom she bases her first representations of the character and attitudes of working men. Sydney was born in the village of Snainton, on 19 July 1891, and his brother Oswald in 1892. There were three other children, who play no part in Jameson's story. Distant family antecedents included the Harland who founded Harland and Wolff, the Belfast shipbuild-ers, whom Sydney took as a model for his own ambitions to 'make it' in the world outside the North Riding. His paternal grandfather, from a relatively comfortable family of tailors, was a strict Primitive Methodist. His paternal grandmother was a hard-working, sharp-tongued woman, who spoke a pure North Riding dialect. His father sold insurance and later second-hand furni-ture, and the family was always poor. His mother, an orphan, had been fos-tered out to work for a farming family. She was an avid reader, determined to put all her children through a good education, a convinced republican, and fiercely hostile to aristocracy. Sydney's home background, he wrote to Jameson in 1973, telling her about the autobiography he too was writing, was much better, and warmer, than hers.[44]

At the turn of the century, the family lived in 'an appalling slum house' in Huddersfield. In 1901 they moved to Scarborough. Around the age of 12, thanks to the devoted coaching of his primary school, Sydney won a scholar-ship to the Scarborough Municipal Secondary School. He took up his place in September 1903.

The School had been founded in 1899 by the Rt Hon. A. H. D. Acland to provide education for working- and middle-class boys and girls who would normally leave school at 14. There was a special commitment to teaching sci-ence; Acland was a friend of Richard Burton Haldane, the uncle of the geneti-cist J. B. S. Haldane, who later became one of Sydney Harland's friends. It had rapidly acquired a reputation for turning out excellent and successful students, including numbers of future university lecturers. The Headmaster, Arthur Tetley, whom Jameson too praised as a great headmaster, was a history gradu-ate from South Wales. The education Sydney described was both broad and advanced. He himself specialised in Chemistry, but there were tutors to spark a lifelong interest in art and art criticism, and to introduce him to the nature-writer Richard Jefferies. The school library was good, and the adjacent library in the Mechanics Institute offered a vast range of the most up-to-date cultural magazines including the *Strand, Pearsons, Harpers, Atlantic Monthly, The Fort-nightly Review*. The young intellectual was also a self-confessed 'delinquent', who made stinkpots in the school Chemistry laboratory and organised a group to drop them in the aisle at a Conservative party meeting. He deliberately, he says ('accidentally', according to Jameson), set fire to the heather on the moors near Snainton. To his amazement, the Headmaster and the town Education Officer, a former Headmaster of the School, gave glowing testimonials to his character and school record, and he was simply bound over for twelve months. It was the year after that episode that Jameson arrived.

Sydney was by then an 'avowed socialist', converted by Robert Blatchford's popular version of William Morris's socialism, *Merrie England* (1894) and H. G. Wells's Fabian pamphlet of 1907, *The Misery of Boots*.[45] Socialism was unpopular in the school, but Jameson was a willing disciple who embraced all Sydney's enthusiasms. Margaret, in *The Happy Highways*, shares her political innocence: 'She had never heard of the social problem but she accepted his socialism unquestioning.'[46] The greatest discovery was A. R. Orage's *The New Age*, to which Sydney introduced her that year. Orage's journal, an existing title bought with the help of George Bernard Shaw and a Leeds Theosophist banker, Lewis Alexander Wallace, and relaunched as a New Series in May 1907 with an explicit commitment to present a socialist perspective on politics, literature, and art, was exactly pitched to appeal to these new cohorts of bright young people from poor families, crossing the threshold to education and the promise of career opportunities their parents had been denied.

His socialist commitment, Sydney emphasised, was always principled, and never personalist: 'With no feeling of envy, I used to watch the Sitwell children—Robert [sic], Edith and Sacheverell—riding their ponies on the beach on Saturday mornings. Edith had long yellow hair.'[47] Daisy was doubtless equally principled in her commitment, but, under her mother's influence, more acutely aware of the personal dimensions to class difference. At any rate, when opportunities offered themselves in later life to meet Oswald and Edith in political and literary circles, she would register with pleasure the change of circumstances.

Sydney left the Municipal School in July 1909, in his own words, 'a socialist, a revolutionary and an agnostic', with extensive knowledge of English literature and history, a talent for writing, fluent French, an ambition to be a research scientist, and a place at King's College London. His studies had been helped in his last school year by a Student Teacher's Bursary, in return for which he taught at an elementary school near the harbour, attended by some fishermen's children but mostly by children from the slums, 'filthy, lousy and ragged. [...] When I looked at my pupils, I thought the whole social system had to be changed.'[48] He also had a King's Scholarship of £30 a year to attend a teacher training college or a University with an Education Department, and a £20 grant from the Scarborough United Scholarship Foundation. He didn't especially want to teach, though he was good at it, but it was the only way to get a university education. Oswald, the future minor novelist, would follow him to London a year later, also with the help of a scholarship.

There was some talk of Jameson being sent to Newnham, but neither she nor her mother thought it financially possible. In September 1909, she left home for Leeds University, with a County Scholarship of £60. She was growing up emotionally—she had had her first experience of serious passion, with H.C., a handsome, unintelligent boy of 16—and she had caught from the Harlands intellectual enthusiasms and political commitments that would stay with her for the rest of her life.[49]

2

The Student in the North

How convey the spirit of these north-country universities? Oxford is in another world. [...] As I walked about Leeds I felt around me and under my feet the pulse of a vast machine. I might be in a university library bent over an Anglo-Saxon grammar but five minutes' walk brought me to the place where, through a gap between houses, I stared at the ring of factories closing in the town on three sides. By day hideous, at night flames writhed from the chimneys—that was indescribably beautiful and exciting.[1]

Being young in Leeds, in 1909, with a £60 scholarship, a confident manner, an attractive appearance, and a capacity for work equalled only by a capacity for play, was very heaven. Surrounded by the raw energy of a city hurtling into industrial modernity, and joined, behind their protective rampart of books, to the riches and privileges of inherited culture, Jameson and her contemporaries stood before doors that seemed to open as they approached. There was an imperative to succeed that students at more privileged institutions, or from more moneyed backgrounds, would never feel; for most of them, a degree was the only way to a better life. At the same time, as they broke new ground for their generation and class, innocence or ignorance of the obstacles that lay ahead brought a gaiety that carried all before them. Jameson wrote:

The Harlands and I emerged from our three starveling years with a lighthearted confidence that we were conquerors; we had none of the slightly sour grudge against society which today is usual: not only did we want nothing it could give us, but we felt certain of being equals in any social class.[2]

34

Not long before, the dream of Oxford had done for Thomas Hardy's obscure working-class intellectual. Published in 1896, *Jude the Obscure* appeared at the beginning of that period of major national investment that was to send so many bright working-class and lower middle-class students to university, training them to train the skilled workforce that was urgently needed to restore Britain's economic standing. But in Leeds in 1909, a lively woman with a Gallilee for a mother, a sea-captain for a father, and, thanks to her mother's snobbery, little trace of a Yorkshire accent, was well placed to make her way in the world. Being a woman was not the handicap it would have been a generation earlier. Her class would have been a disadvantage at Oxford, but in this University, she was fairly high up the social order. Her Scarborough education and the Harlands' tutelage had given her more knowledge and a more open mind than the average teacher trainee. Leeds would be the ideal preparation for the tougher fights to come.

The Academic

Formed by the union of Leeds School of Medicine and Yorkshire College, a constituent college of the federal Victoria University, Leeds University had received its Charter in 1904. Jameson and the institution grew up together. The number of women students was expanding, though they were still relatively few. In her second year, 1910–11, with 183 women registered, as against 718 men, the University established its first Hall of Residence for Women Students, most of them trainee teachers, in De Grey Road.[3] In 1912, as Jameson's degree course drew to an end, the University site was being further enlarged, and more academic posts were being created to cater for growing numbers of students.[4] When she began her studies, Sir Nathan Bodington was coming to the end of his time as Vice-Chancellor. As they ended, the great liberal educationalist and administrator Michael Ernest Sadler took up the post, and the institution underwent a sea-change.

Margaret Ethel Jameson, from Ryedale House, Chubb Hill, Whitby, signed the Register of Students for Session 1909–10. She was Student No. 7135, one of 116 enrolments, and she paid an entrance fee of one guinea.[5] She had arrived on the 5th October, she was eighteen and three-quarters, a North Riding Major Scholar, and she gave her proposed occupation as 'Teacher'.

She registered for Honours in English Studies, which also required the study of one classical and one modern language. Jameson signed up in her first year for classes in Latin, English Language and Literature, French, and European History. In session 1910–11, half her programme was in English Literature, with one course in English Language, one in Philosophy (Ethics), and one in French. In her final year, she followed five courses in English (one in English Language), and one in Modern Philosophy. The French subsidiary courses she followed in French focused on Classicism and Romanticism, and seem not to have reached beyond the French novel of 1850. On that course, however, it seems likely that she embarked on her lifelong love affair with Stendhal.

The Professor of English Language and Literature was Charles E. Vaughan, from Balliol, who also served as a notoriously hands-on Dean of Arts. Vaughan was a wide-ranging researcher interested in things European, and according to the students' journal, *The Gryphon*, a stimulating if terrifying lecturer. He disliked women, and though this seems not to have affected Jameson during her course, her treatment after graduation in June 1912 at the top of her year, with a First Class Honours degree in English Language and Literature, was very different from that accorded to the man who had carried off the laurels in the previous session.[6] H. B. Charlton had been awarded a University Fellowship, and was working in Berlin on an edition of Castelvetro's *Poetica di Aristotile*, with his academic career assured. In Summer 1912, the man who came second in their class of five, George Herbert Cowling, was offered a lectureship, while Jameson was 'fobbed off' with the John Rutson research scholarship, to be held in London University.[7] At the time, she claims, she felt no disappointment, not realising the implications for her ambitions for an academic career.

Jameson cut lectures—though not Vaughan's—and worked on her preferred topics at her own speed, without any challenge from her tutors. The English syllabus was dull and crowded, 'not so much a training as an endurance test'.[8] Carlyle and Browning were as modern as it got until her final year, when Eliot, Swinburne, and Morris appeared to strike some very different notes. A course in the History and Theory of Criticism, from Aristotle to Shelley, was fascinating, although it left her devoid of 'even the beginnings of a critical sensibility'.[9] She found consolation in George Saintsbury's *History of Criticism*, whose wide-ranging enthusiasms and provocative, highly personal opinions, challenging the blandness of received academic ideas, thrilled a generation newly come to the cultural heritage. Even at the end of her career, she was still cherishing the desire to rewrite and update her mentor.[10] The Final Examination papers that were set for session 1911–12 point to the kind of circumscribed learning that characterised institutions up to the 1960s, and dampened all but the most robust students: 'Give some account of the condition of English prose in the first forty years of the eighteenth century, and characterise the styles of Swift and Addison.' Though given Jameson's own later obsession with landscape, she must have welcomed one invitation: 'What difference do you find between Thomson and Cowper in the manner of representing scenery? State and defend your preference.' There was at least the chance to write an independent thesis. She chose to work on William Blake, spending one summer researching in the excellent collection of the Leeds Public Library, and then writing up her material at home in Whitby, producing eighty thousand words. For an aficionado of *The New Age*, Blake, with his distinctive blend of mysticism and revolutionary socialism, was an obvious point of attraction.

By the end of her course, she had decided that English had been the wrong subject for her:

My mind was a chaos of ideas gathered from books, from the *New Age*, from the economics I read struggling to understand. I knew now that I had been wrong to take the English schools. [...] I should have done better to study economics or biology.[11]

When she wrote that in the early 1930s, she was clearly thinking both of Sydney Harland, whose studies in biology and genetics had long since taken him off to the West Indies, and her second husband, Guy Chapman, who was about to enrol onto a degree course at the London School of Economics. But the breadth of her English syllabus, and the scope it left for independent thinking and personal reading were precisely what had given her room to read *The New Age*, and absorb the distinctive blend of economics, aesthetics, and politics that was to provide a lifetime's inspiration. Guild Socialism was a bizarre and backward-looking bundle of contradictions, as its co-founder, G. D. H. Cole, later acknowledged, but its vigorous correlation of individualism and the demands of social justice appealed to her imagination more than any dry academic course in economics, or biology, could have done. And no course could so effectively have opened her mind to the newest enthusiasms of avant-garde art and politics, from social realism to imagism, and from Nietzsche to H. G. Wells.[12]

Socialite and Socialist

In any case, the course at any university is always less than half of the real experience. Living independently was a delight, and she made friends easily. There was no Women's Residence when she first arrived, and she welcomed the chance of freedom. Women's lodgings were supervised and regulated, but she was on good terms with all her landladies, and coming home in the early hours was never a problem. When in her second year, she fell in love with the man her autobiographies refer to as 'K', or 'C', Charles Douglas Clarke, the third-year Classics student she was later to marry, she often returned after sunrise from their summer evening walks into the country.[13] In her first year, the records show, she paid 16 guineas to live at 6 Hall Grove. In her second year, her room at 8 Warwick Place cost her 13 guineas; in her last year, for ten guineas, she lodged at 15 Mount Preston.[14]

Little of her activity in student societies reached her published memoirs, in which the most interesting exploit she narrates is her purchase of a carpet, as Secretary of the Women's Representative Council of the Union, without the approval of the Union Treasurer.[15] But from the start, she was making far more significant marks on the social and political scene.

Her career in student politics at Leeds was not as interesting as that of Athenais, the heroine of her first novel, *The Pot Boils*, part-satire and part-celebration of her student experiences in Leeds and London. The narrative opens with an account of the wave of 'Socialistic thought' that swept through an unnamed university, in the period 1895–1910, 'in the wake of the crude Liberalism of wool-merchant's sons and the missionary circles of the women students. The few existing Socialists, alarmed by their sudden popularity, became further uneasy as the newborn babe burst from its swaddling clothes an unmistakeable changeling.'[16] Students devouring Marx, especially the women, challenge the outdated scholarship of the Professor of Economics. A Society for Social Work is formed, and men and women students visit workhouses and factories. Jameson pokes savage fun at the neophytes, women who have swallowed whole William Morris's *News from Nowhere*, and men pretending to be feminists to catch the girls. True socialists fled into a renamed Society for Fabian Study, which fifteen years on was well established, and run by the men. The account is finally brought up to date with an account of a rowdy meeting of the Fabian Society dominated by the challenges of the Irish revolutionary Desmond, with Athenais at his side.

Real life in Leeds was a more prosaic matter of registering a presence on the approved student committees of the University. The *University Calendar* for 1910–11 recorded the active presence of Miss D. Jameson in two societies. She was an ordinary member of the Women's Representative Committee, one of five annually elected by the women students. The WRC controlled the Women's Common Rooms and appointed representatives on the University Union Committee and its sub-committees.[17] The business dealt with, detailed in the *Yorkshire College WRC Minute Book* (1902–14), was the intensely important trivia of student communal life: choosing a journal (the choice was between *Englishwoman* and *Votes for Women*, and the former won), putting up a new notice-board for the Christian Union and the Debating Society, fining people for leaving books around, and discussing whether women students might with propriety talk to men in corridors and the library. The following session, her third year, she was Honorary Secretary of the WRC, and one of three student representatives on the larger Student Union Committee. She was also on the *Gryphon* Committee, the Entertainment Committee, and the Dance Committee. As Honorary Secretary of the WRC, she was asked to write to the Vice-Chancellor about students' difficulties in crossing the road to lectures; and she was in communication with him again on matters of bicycles and telephones.[18]

She does not figure in the *University Calendar* as a committee activist in the Women's Discussion Society, newly formed in session 1910–11 for the discussion of social, economic, and political issues affecting women, especially 'the conditions under which women work and [...] their economic position'.[19] The Society organised, for example, talks on 'Girls' Clubs', and 'Women's Work in Factories', which she must have attended, and she certainly spoke there herself.[20] Miss D. Jameson was however joint Secretary with Mr. A. Moody of the Society for Social Study, 'formed for the purpose of obtaining a good understanding of social questions and schemes of social reform by means of lectures, discussions and other methods'.[21] In the next session, she was the Society's Vice-President. Feminist and socialist activity ran side by side in Leeds, as everywhere else in the country, and perhaps more so: Isabella Ford, who in 1890 founded the Leeds Women's Suffrage Society with her sister Bessie, had also in 1893 been involved in forming the Leeds Branch of the Independent Labour Party. By the time she became the full-time organiser of the Women's Social and Political Union in Leeds in 1906, Mary Gawthorpe, future co-founder of *The Freewoman* in 1911, with Dora Marsden, had lost faith in the willingness of male socialists to support the cause of women's suffrage. But others were still prepared to work together; in 1913–14, the University Women's Discussion Society was to amalgamate with the Society for Social Study.

The most informative source about what students in Jameson's day were really saying and doing is their own magazine, *The Gryphon: The Journal of the University of Leeds*. Excellent value for sixpence, *The Gryphon* combined reports of undergraduate scandals, lampoons and spoofs with serious accounts of the activities of clubs with a well-developed social conscience, concerned with local employment and working conditions, especially those of women and young people.

The year before Jameson arrived, the Society for Social Study was already in full swing. *The Gryphon* carried a report by 'K' (perhaps her future husband, and perhaps not) on a talk on 'Work in an East End Settlement', together with his plea for more students to join the society.[22] An Editorial in the next issue, March 1908, was most preoccupied by Senate's reception of a student deputation anxious about the half-day holiday, but it also found room to refer to a Union debate on Women's Suffrage.[23] 1908 was the year in which Mrs Pankhurst addressed a mass meeting of suffragettes on Leeds' Woodhouse Moor. K. published another report, this time on a talk on juvenile crime. In Jameson's first two years, the Society's programme schedules included A. Mansbridge, speaking on 'Workers and the Universities', C. S. Locke, on 'Poor Law Reform', Mrs Sydney Webb, on 'The Philosophy of the Minority Report', a talk on 'Tariff Reform and Socialism', a lecture on 'Industrial Peace' by the Mayor of Huddersfield, and a talk on 'Juvenile Employment' by Mr Keeling of the Leeds Labour Bureau.

In later life, Jameson often claimed to be a poor speaker, and to hate speaking in public. According to *The Gryphon*, she made her voice heard in a range of clubs, on socialist and feminist issues, almost as soon as she crossed the University threshold. In her first term, she spoke in the Debating Society on the motion: 'That a system of separate Universities for women is desirable.'[24] After Christmas, she was on her feet again, seconding the opposition to the motion that: 'Socialism tends to destroy the moral fibre of a nation.'[25] At the Society for Social Study, after a lecture on 'Women's Work and Wages', it was reported that:

Miss Jameson, opening the discussion, outlined the chief reasons why Trade Union movements amongst women are most desirable at the present time. Before resuming her seat, this speaker yielded to a temptation with which she is often met, and appealed for 'Votes for Women.'[26]

At the Union Debating Society in her second year, she proposed the motion in favour of 'Women's Suffrage on the lines of the Conciliation Bill', which was won by 65 votes to 36.[27] In the issue reporting the vote, the Editor also printed a letter from Miss A. M. Cooke, Chairman of the Women's Discussion Society, insisting that theirs was not a Suffragette Society. His editorial commiserated with her for having to write this disavowal, which he attributed to University policy against 'partisan' societies.

Policy or not, the continuing student interest in feminism was acknowledged a few months later by *The Gryphon* in an article on 'The Modern Maiden', who apparently consisted of 'brains, hairpins and corsage—mostly inferior corsage'. After this unfortunate beginning, the writer recuperated his position by declaring modern women, though still in a transitional stage, to be more intelligent, less enslaved to the idea of marriage, and less dedicated to seeking male approval. Men too were getting better: '[T]here are those who would prefer a sensible companion to a domesticated or a fashionable doll.'[28]

The Pot Boils records a state of affairs in which socialist male students, demonstrating a misogyny of a very traditional kind, blamed women who worked, rather than the employers, for the problem of low wages that bedevilled the economy and threatened social stability. Denarbon, the activist and painter, rants against the modern maiden:

They've forced their way into industry and cut men's wages down to starvation level: such of them as have attained a degree of intellect affect an insufferable conceit and spread their imitated ideas all over literature. They're in the way; man made society in the past; how is he going to remake it, hampered by woman in search of a soul?[29]

The narrative commentary underlines male contemporaries' obsession with the issue:

They could not keep off the question of women and women's work. But they shut it out as much as possible. [...] The men who spoke affected an enthusiasm or a violent misogyny which they did not feel. They were surprised to find themselves talking like lyrical feminists, or else in a discourteous and blatant scorn of women. The women themselves were either silent, or voluble and arrogant.[30]

Jameson was among the voluble. In spring 1912, the Women's Discussion Society advertised a forthcoming talk by her on 'Infant Mortality', part of a programme that had already included talks on the health of working women, and the Industrial Laws and how easy it was to evade them.[31] She may also have been among the arrogant. Some of her audience were certainly sceptical of her qualifications to speak on some of the topics she took up with such enthusiasm. A commentator on 'Forthcoming Lectures' declared that:

The announcement that Miss M. E. Jameson is to speak to the Social Study Society on 'How to keep a family on £1 per week' provokes the following suggestions for topics and speakers:
    How to dress on 2d per month—F. M. R.-W.
    How to make an evening paper interesting.—The Editor of the *Gryphon*.[32]

In her last year, as Trade Union unrest throughout the country reached its peak, and Leeds saw a major strike in the tailoring industry, Jameson records taking tins of cocoa to the families of strikers in the slums and asking what she deemed, with hindsight, unacceptably patronising questions. She went in the company of her latest passion, one of the theological students from the College of the Resurrection at Mirfield, Charles having gone down the previous year with a not very good degree, to prepare a diploma in education in Cambridge.[33]

Not all students, of course, shared the enthusiasms of their socialist contemporaries. In the summer term of 1911, while the Society for Social Study took itself off to Leeds Steel Works, the Literary Society made a more conventional trip to Grasmere.[34] And whatever regard Jameson and her friends might have for the radical thought of H. G. Wells, one jaundiced reviewer of *The New Machiavelli* (1911) was clear about the real priorities, complaining that Wells's politics ('organised communism') had wrecked his novel writing.[35] However, those who, like Jameson, chose the radical route were, if not in the mainstream, then riding a tide that would take them to new areas of opportunity, and their enthusiasm did them no harm with academic staff who were often themselves deeply concerned about the local community in which their institution was embedded.

The Sadlers: The Road to London

Jameson's final year saw the arrival in Leeds of the new Vice-Chancellor, Michael Sadler, whose interests and connections were to prove among the most important of her future career. She says nothing about the contact in her own accounts of Leeds life, but the bright young student will not have passed unnoticed. There was the sequence of letters on bicycles and telephones to keep her name in the Vice-Chancellor's mind, and if that wasn't enough, there was always *The Gryphon* to provide a link. On graduation day, in its end-of-session send-up, 'Popular Plays and Books of Prominent Persons', two names figured large: 'The V.C. The Man of Destiny [...] Miss Jam-son. The Bohemian Girl.'[36]

Michael Sadler's political convictions were far to the right of Jameson's. Antagonistic to what he considered 'anarchy', he saw in working men's strikes the potential for unwanted revolution. In 1913, after Jameson had left for London, he helped break a municipal strike, and as a result earned much dislike in both the University and the town.[37] But he brought to Leeds a reputation as a reforming educationalist. He had been active in Oxford University Extension from 1885 to 1895, and since then had contributed to the national expansion of secondary, continuing and technical education. He oversaw the transformation of his new charge from a technical college to a modern civic University, and he extended his activities from gown to town.

Fascinated by avant-garde painting, and especially devoted to Kandinsky, he threw his weight behind the continuators of Orage's projects to bring contemporary European art to the citizens of Leeds.[38] He was co-opted onto the Board of the Leeds Art Collection Fund, run by Frank Rutter, the Director of the Leeds Art Gallery, and shared Rutter's interest in the Post-Impressionist painting that had swept into fashion in London in November–December 1910, with Roger Fry's celebrated exhibition at the Grafton Gallery on 'Manet and the Post-Impressionists'. An anonymous critic in *The Gryphon* in March 1912 on 'Post-Impressionism' boasts of making a valiant attempt to treat fairly the artists involved in the latest exhibition, even though the rest of Leeds had uttered 'howls of derision'.[39] In the issue of May 1912, a satirical but sympathetic piece, 'The Reality of Life', pokes gentle fun at academics who are committed to bringing the light of Art into working men's lives.[40] It opens a debate on how much art, and of what kind, the working man wants and needs, that continues into the next couple of issues. 'Post-Impressionism Again', an article by T. Huffington, opposed the new cult fashion, and was scathing about the support given it by Sadler. Such devotion, he noted, runs in families: 'the organ of the latest art is a production called *Rhythm*, to which [his son] Mr. M. T. H. Sadler regularly contributes.'[41] Had Huffington known that the Vice-Chancellor himself had put money into the journal, he would have been even more censorious.[42]

The following year, *The Gryphon* published 'In Defence of Post Impressionism' by Michael T. H. Sadler.[43] Sadleir (shortly to add the 'i' to distinguish

43

himself from his father) had gone straight from Balliol into London art and publishing circles. He came to Leeds to lecture on 'Post-Impressionism and Public Galleries' on 12 June, in order to help launch a major Post-Impressionist exhibition at the Leeds Arts Club, for which he also wrote the catalogue.[44] By the time Sadleir's piece appeared, Jameson would be away in London, enjoying the opportunity to see for herself the Vice-Chancellor's favoured artists—and in passing, to note their irrelevance to ordinary people's lives in terms not far removed from that of *The Gryphon*'s reviewer.[45] But it seems unlikely that the growing reputation of the Vice-Chancellor's son, and his increasing importance in London publishing, will have escaped her. When she speaks in her autobiography of discussing the publication of *The Pot Boils* with Michael Sadleir, she presents it as a first meeting. It must however have at least been facilitated by Sadleir's recognition, in her text, of the Leeds University connection; and the chances of the two not already having met at some University function, in the small world of that time, are pretty remote.

It is usual to think of Jameson's removal to London from Leeds, after her degree, as a difficult transition from the provinces to the intimidating metropolis. But in fact Jameson was moving into territory already, effectively, colonised. The Sadlers, father and son, were connections whose importance would not be tested immediately, but the Orage connection was significant from the start. *The New Age*, its editor, and the heady mix of socialism, feminism, and avant-garde aesthetics that was in ferment in Leeds, were also well-established in London, and backed by the Fabian Arts Group that Orage and Jackson had founded, with the help of H. G. Wells and Eric Gill, as an alternative to orthodox Fabian Socialism. Jameson's intellectual transition in that respect was a seamless one. Most of all, the Harlands, last seen in Scarborough Municipal, were already there to prepare a welcome.

3
London 1912–1918

Student Freedom

Jameson arrived in London in September 1912, with a first-class degree in English, an old flame in Cambridge, and money of her own. The John Rutson Scholarship, worth £70, was for one year in the first instance, and renewable for a second. She went to work with Professor Walter Ker, University College, on a masters thesis on pantheism in French and German literature. She graduated in 1914 with a study on Modern European Drama, inspired perhaps by the combination of the *New Age*'s interest in English theatre and the example of her critical mentor, George Saintsbury, who in the context of fiction-writing had written urgently of the need for modern English writing to be informed by the example of the French.

1912 saw the beginning of her long love affair with London. The city provided her with a second idea of home, a landscape that would at times interpenetrate with that of Whitby, and at others stand in stark contrast. The view from Whitby windows, onto the sea or the moors, was an opening to one kind of freedom, in the form of escape into an undefined and open horizon. The view from a London hotel window out onto crowding rooftops and streets carried the even more thrilling freedom that comes of being in a place already crammed with possibilities. In this hotch-potch of jostling classes and cultures, high and low, the epitome of Englishness before the Great War, Jameson was in her element. The sights and sounds of the galleries of modern art, theatres, variety halls, the scent of London's parks in all their seasons, the noise and movement of the streets round Piccadilly and the poor streets of the suburbs, light flickering on the dark, coiling depths of the Thames, all seized hold of her imagination, and made their way into the forms of the writing that was to come.

Life began, once again, with the Harlands. While Jameson was following her English course at Leeds, Sydney Harland had been attending King's College, in the Strand, as a King's Scholar in the Day Training Department, working for a degree in science and at the same time preparing his Teacher's Certificate. He attended lectures at the London School of Economics—an experience expropriated by Jameson for Athenais, in *The Pot Boils*. He joined the Young Fabians, and became familiar with the most important faces, including Ramsay MacDonald, Philip Snowden, the Webbs, and George Bernard Shaw.[1] He stood on a soapbox to speak on Socialism.

Oswald joined him a year later to read for a degree in arts, specialising in English and History. Between them, they explored London's museums, art galleries and theatres, and accumulated a wealth of experiences ready to be shared with Jameson. In his third year, Sydney became Secretary of the University Fabian Society, attended a debate between Shaw and G. K. Chesterton, chaired by Hilaire Belloc, and took Shaw out to tea.[2] In his second and third year, he came into contact with the suffragettes, then 'on the rampage':

Their headquarters were in Adam Street, not far from the College. When they came into the Quadrangle of King's, the hose was turned on them. I once helped Adela Pankhurst in a meeting when the crowd turned hostile. I brought a half brick in my briefcase and hurled it through the big plate glass window. In the smashing of glass there is great joy.[3]

Jameson's account of those first London years in *The Pot Boils* and *The Happy Highways* might well, one suspects, draw as much from Sydney's accounts of his exploits as her own direct experience. Sydney certainly borrowed a copy of *The Happy Highways* before settling down to write his own memoirs.[4]

Jameson shared their rooms at the top of Herne Hill, in a small street of new houses. Archie White, Sydney's friend and fellow-lodger since their second year as undergraduates, was to become another life-long friend. Archie too was a Yorkshireman, from Boroughbridge, who was to make up for a poor degree by a brilliant Army career, winning the Victoria Cross in the First World War and later becoming a Fellow of King's and then Principal of the City of London College.[5] She held Archie in enormous respect, much admired his cool, reliable, and bitter Yorkshire wit, and was immensely proud of the Army medals he collected.[6] Quiet and supportive, though never uncritical, there is probably much of Archie in Joy, the blind soldier who is the narrator of *The Happy Highways*, who keeps to himself his love for Margaret, until the final pages.

In her first and last autobiographies, *No Time Like the Present* and *Journey from the North*, Jameson vividly evokes the excitement of walks and cheap

Figure 7 Archie White, with whom the Harlands and Jameson shared
rooms in London. On the back, in Jameson's handwriting, 'Photograph
of Colonel Archie White, our close friend'.

bus-rides with her three young men round a London now long-vanished,
seeing the sights, visiting art galleries, music-halls and Promenade Concerts,
and puzzling over the gulf between the high and popular cultures of the day,
in both of which she felt equally at home. Neither text mentions the suffragette
marches that appear in *The Happy Highways*, but they appear in a much later
essay as a high-point of a feminism whose victories by the 1930s were beginning to turn sour:

This cherished and precious independence of ours—for which we fought, bit policemen (yes, this I did, in Hyde Park, of a fine Saturday afternoon in the year before the

Great War), cut off our hair, grew it again, drove omnibuses, entered Parliament, and walked all day in the rain, carrying a change of clothing, with bare knees and untidy hair—must it be marked down to a doubtful bargain?[7]

Talking late into the night, they enthused over Nietzsche, and admired Orage, Wells, Freud, and the iconoclastic wit of Anatole France.[8] *The New Age*, 'the Bible of our generation', guided their discussions.[9] Volume 12 of Orage's journal, covering the period from November 1912 to April 1913, includes articles on Nietzsche's influence in England, the first articles on Freud to appear in England (by Alfred Randall), regular drama reviews by John Francis Hope (a pseudonym of Alfred Randall), and a translation of the correspondence between Nietzsche and Strindberg.

She was interested in Spinoza, and she was delighted to discover Strindberg,[10] who would figure prominently in her masters thesis, despite (or because of) his misogynist and anti-feminist perspectives. The talk went on. They discussed death (there was no life after it), love (could you write about love without experiencing it?), sex, new writing, including modernist writing (Jameson bought a copy of *Rhythm*), and how to create a world without war and poverty.[11]

Her friends were almost all in the academic world. She abandoned University College because the classes were too big, there were too many women students, and the boys said it was 'no better than a cram-shop'.[12] Instead, she frequented King's, especially enjoying the lectures by Professor Israel Gollancz, Oswald's English tutor. King's was the home of the Eikonoklasts, who met in the men's Common Room. After her first month, she was allowed in, to listen and watch,[13] and in 1913, she recalled, the group welcomed enthusiastically the copy of the Tauchnitz edition of *The New Macchiavelli* that she had bought in Antwerp.[14]

In her own reminiscences, there are no references to Sydney's Fabian activities. Rather, she declares: '[W]e disliked and distrusted Fabians, partly because those we saw and heard were middle-aged, even elderly, an order of brahmins. And, worse, smelled of a bureaucracy.'[15] By this time, Orage's *New Age*, wholeheartedly given over to Guild Socialism since 1909, had disowned and been disowned by its former Fabian friends, and the student household wrote a collective 'jeering letter' to *The New Statesman*, Orage's new competitor.[16]

Jameson did however venture outside the university world to teach for a year as a volunteer at the Working Women's College in Earl's Court, run by Mrs Bridges Adams.[17] This experience informs the account in *The Happy*

Highways of a highly successful scheme for workers' classes that started in January 1913.[18] There were some surprises to be had in those fictional classes, not least the discovery that biology, literature, and art were what the workers wanted, not politics, especially Marxist politics, but the results overall were heartening: 'I believe that there exists in the intellect of the working class a vigour and freshness that may well bring forth a new Renaissance. For generations crushed under the industrial slavery, I believe that it will move when it does move, with a mighty bound.'[19]

And then Daisy got married. Mostly because her mother forced her to, but partly because she herself recognised, responding to an unexpectedly deep vein of Whitby conventionality, that that was what young women did.

Charles Clarke, the undergraduate she fell in love with her in her second year at Leeds, visited her in Herne Hill in 1912. The boys didn't like him, but she didn't discourage him. From the first, she had made her mind up: 'I felt firmly that we should marry and be happy.'[20] Though she did remember later that she had not been particularly happy with him in Leeds, except at the start, and had often felt 'puzzled and disappointed' by him. Sydney, who had graduated in the summer of 1912 with second-class Honours, and then in September passed his MSc in Geology, had decided there was no future for him in England, and applied for jobs abroad. In January 1913, the night before he left for a teaching post in the West Indies, he urged her not to get married; partly because she was too much of a bully, and more than her future husband could deal with, and partly because she should identify her ambitions for herself, and not give in to her desire for an easy life.[21] But none of them would explain why they disliked him, and in 1969, reading *Journey from the North*, Archie White wrote to her apologetically that they should have expressed their disapproval more explicitly. What she had written in her autobiography, he thought, was fair and not unkind; the man was a fantasist long before he and Jameson met.[22]

The affair might have blown itself out, but her mother had seen his letters and been shocked by them.[23] She told relatives in Whitby, announcing her daughter's imminent marriage, that it was a pity, when she could have had a career, and a waste of an education. There may have been some satisfaction in seeing her successful daughter turned into the same dead end as she had entered at George Gallilee's behest.

They were married on 15 January 1913.[24] The marriage certificate is not to be found among the papers Jameson left with her grandson, though the certificate for her second marriage to Guy Chapman is carefully preserved, and on it her designation as divorced wife of Charles Douglas Clarke. By the late summer, they were living together in Caxton Street, Shepherd's Bush, in a squalid room on the north side of the green. What he was doing is not recorded, but she was finishing her thesis in the British Museum, trying her hand at journalism, and still loving being at large in London. They were very poor, she lunched regularly on plums, and they squabbled bitterly. She tried to commit suicide with an overdose of phenacetin, and he was deeply unsympathetic. She fell ill at the end of the year and went home to her parents in Whitby, while he moved in with his Quaker parents in North London.[25] In Whitby, she completed her thesis, sent it to Leeds in April 1914, and was awarded her MA.

The Land of Lost Content

For the next few years, the road to London would effectively be barred to her, though the city remained fixed in her imagination as the land where, whatever the poet might say, she was determined to come again. Before leaving London, she had made her first foray into journalism, and she worked hard to maintain the fragile lifeline.

Her first essay for Orage's *New Age* was out in March 1913, having been sent off at a venture and accepted with the generosity to new writers for which Orage was famous. The month before, he had published in his 'Pastiche' column Sydney Harland's aptly titled 'Raving of an Immature Science Student', which prophesied (without much fear of contradiction) that the human race would end in the next million years.[26] Two other essays were written over the first years of her marriage and the birth of her son. The content of all three essays is of interest for the formation of her political ideas, but of equal interest is the context in which they appeared. What Jameson read in the *New Age* at this time shaped her thinking and writing through the 1920s and early 1930s, up to the time of her meeting with the thought of Tawney and his heirs at the London School of Economics. Most immediately, the multitude of views on art and politics to which Orage cheerfully gave house-room would feed directly into the bubbling mix celebrated in *The Pot Boils*.

Jameson became a contributor at a turning-point for the journal, at the conclusion of the long series of articles that set out the principles of Guild

Socialism against State-regulated, rationalist socialism on the Fabian model. Guild Socialism, in the anti-industrialist tradition of Carlyle, Ruskin, and Morris, purported to invest control over production in the workers, organised into Trade Unions operating like medieval Guilds. In fact, it was biased towards employers, and paternalistic. A regular series of articles by J. M. Kennedy ('Notes on the Present Kalpa'), written from an ultra-conservative Catholic perspective, explored the effects of the economy on social life, developing themes that would be central to Jameson's fictions: the inhumane nature of life in industrialised society, under the rule of the financier, and its deforming effects on the individual and social relationships. In Kennedy's pieces, an effective critique of social conditions was married to a poor grasp of modern economic realities, and a nostalgia that made no secret of its political allegiance:

The wealth of England, as of every nation, lies ultimately in its agriculture, not in its city factories; and the unit of agricultural life [...] is the parish, including, one may presume, the much-derided parish pump. Around it the village Hampdens still foregather, pheasants permitting; and these ears of mine have heard more common sense in its immediate neighbourhood than they heard at any time in the House of Commons. [... The parish pump] is real, conservative, Tory and Catholic.[27]

This Tory paternalism found its way into *The Pot Boils*, in a satirical version that indicates Jameson's ability to establish her own hierarchy of political preferences out of the rainbow coalition of Orage's contributors. Equally, that novel, and others that followed, showed her not unresponsive to the temptation to the pastoral.

Feminist questions were regularly addressed in the journal, with a decided lack of sympathy for the suffragettes and the men who supported them. Morley Seymour's 'The Male Suffragist' appeared in the same issue as Jameson's essay, to argue that:

To imprison the militant suffragette for smashing panes of glass, or assaulting policemen, has so far proved useless, as she is too illogically minded ever to see how unreasonable, childish and futile such conduct is. No, we must go to the root of the evil, and the root of the evil is the male suffragist.[28]

He went on to advocate the importance of trade union action by women, in terms that Athenais was shortly to embrace:

Lately THE NEW AGE pointed out that for 50 years seven millions of men have failed to better their economic status in the least degree by means of the vote. It has been trade unions that have raised wages, and it was a long and arduous fight before workmen secured recognition for trade unions. Let the women combine. If a very small part of the energy that has been given to the illusory vote had been devoted to the forming of a Woman's League for the advancement of women's interests and influence in social life, much might have been done.

Jameson's first two essays for the *New Age* were direct attacks on Fabianism. The first, 'The End Thereof', came out of her thesis, and criticised Shaw's plays for their poor characterisation and for the half-baked ideas that came from his yielding to 'the Fabian tentacles':

Mr. Shaw's connection with the Fabian Society, the apotheosis of political futility, dates back to within a year of its formation. In that Society a number of opinions, worthless in themselves, and harmful as applied to the body politic, are established on the firmest foundation, that of invincible smugness. [...] Here Mr. Shaw found a first necessity of his nature, convictions ready-made, requiring and brooking neither question nor research, and here satisfied the desire for power in the delusion that with the Webbs he formed one of the controlling forces of social progress.[29]

Her second essay, in April 1914, which could charitably be described as an exercise in Swiftean irony, was a lampoon of Fabian rhetoric and the Fabian cult of bureaucratic rationalism. 'New Statesmen. A Bill Providing for an Economic Basis of Marriage' begins:

Disgust unspeakable assails us as we think of the over-breeding, the wanton matrimonial untidiness of the poor. In the ultimate, this squalid overplus of children is the cause of our vast national poverty and Labour discontent.[30]

The Bill proposes a set of income levels at which it will be both legal and compulsory for men to have more than one wife, or share wives with others: '[S]ix labourers earning £1 a week or less will be permitted to join in the support of one woman. This system of connubial co-partnership necessitates the erection of blocks of model buildings. The housing problem solves itself.' A system of State officials will oversee the scheme (themselves being exempt). There will be lethal chambers for the removal and disposal of weaklings. Poverty will be eradicated, and the Woman Question will be gone, since marriage (there is some personal bitterness here) will be compulsory. The labour problem will be resolved: 'The State is provided with healthy men for its armies, its workshops, its police.'

Her final contribution appeared in September 1916. 'A Plea for the Arbitrary Limit' is a curious piece, a collection of *New Age* clichés, with little obvious motive for its writing but the need to keep her name in front of metropolitan readers.[31] *The Pot Boils* was finished, and she was looking for a publisher.

A lament against the 'steady crushing of the individual craftsman' that came with the end of feudalism and the installation of 'the conception of a man as a mere appanage to a machine' was followed by an attack on 'the cant of equality' practised in a culture that works to maintain inequality, and another lament for the disappearance of individualism and the cult of excellence. She attacked 'the growth of a spurious internationalism', and wrote her first and last patriotic paragraph in praise of national boundaries and partisanship: 'The most deep-rooted instinct of a man is the love of one particular place and a desire to glorify it above the rest of the world.'

Jameson was less successful with the connection she would have liked to build with Dora Marsden. Jameson and Marsden had much in common, and a generation of difference between them. Marsden, another Yorkshire-woman, born in 1882, was a pupil-teacher who had funded herself on a scholarship to Owen's College, Manchester, in 1900. She was an activist in workers' education, and was prominent in the Pankhursts' Women's Social and Political Union in the period 1908–11. Like Jameson, she had no time for feminist gestures, and thought votes for women were less important than women's economic independence, which brought abstract rights directly into the structures of everyday life. Her journal, *The Freewoman—A Weekly Feminist Review*, proposed that: 'Woman is a distinct entity...she must be taught that she is not an adjunct to man...in an ideal condition she would be released from the narrow conditions of the household and free to make her contribution to the labour of mankind in that sphere to which she had a bent.'[32] These ideas were embraced wholeheartedly in *The Pot Boils*, as were cognate questions about the connections between personal and sexual life and radical social change. Marsden's interest in the anarchist individualism of Max Stirner, a voluntarist philosophy, left no room for the concern with the relations of behaviour to social environment that interested Jameson, but her vigour and drive would have appealed to the younger Nietzschean.[33]

The Freewoman was always controversial, and always struggling for cash and readers. It appeared first on 23 November 1911, survived for six months as a weekly, and then staggered on for a further five months to its last issue on 10 October 1912. It became *The New Freewoman* in August 1913, supported by the money and editorial talents of Harriet Shaw Weaver, and employing as assistant editors Ezra Pound and Richard Aldington. It became *The Egoist* in January 1914, Aldington was called up to serve in the trenches, and T. S. Eliot took his place. This was the point when Jameson entered its ambit.

Jameson had met and been impressed by Marsden at the end of 1913, while living in London with Clarke, just before illness and lack of money drove her home to Whitby. In a letter dated 1st January 1914, she offered reviews for *The Egoist*, and placed two pieces of drama criticism.[34] Harriet Shaw Weaver invited her to work on the journal for £2 a week. She first accepted excitedly, and then turned the invitation down, yielding to her mother's wish for her company at home. The post was offered to Rachel East (Rebecca West), and helped establish her career. Jameson never forgave either her mother or herself. She made efforts to regain a foothold in the journal, and Dora Marsden for a time seemed ready to help, though its finances gave her little leeway and Jameson was unreliable. In April 1914, Marsden, telling Shaw Weaver that she was about to write to Jameson, added that: 'I didn't mention her latest statement as to her possible movements because, to speak the truth of her, she *does* seem the subject of extraordinarily rapid changes of circumstance.'[35]

Another cash crisis in October 1915 had Marsden considering closing down the magazine for three months and starting again with lighter, brighter personalities than her poets and Egotists. They should, she thought, start by securing Rebecca West, after which they might find the right place for Storm Jameson.[36] In November 1915, Jameson published a long review, 'England's Nest of Singing Birds', denouncing the deplorable state of contemporary drama and poetry (including Imagism, Pound and Aldington, the *Egoist*'s house geniuses). In September 1916, a review essay debated Emma Goldman's ideas on free love and marriage. But nothing more came after that.

This was however for Jameson an important intellectual contact with a different breed of modernists from those who figured most frequently in *The New Age*, especially Eliot, for whom she developed a lifelong admiration, in whose poetry were naturalised the innovations of the French Symbolists that she later drew on for her own prose. Aldington, a regular contributor to Orage's journal, was responsible for the appearance in *The Egoist* of the work of Remy de Gourmont, the great French student of the physiology of style, and the only writer who at that stage, Jameson said, 'put under my eyes the case for the experimental novel, for the growing impulse to break the traditional mould, achieve a new fluidity, new and personal symbols for human experience'.[37] In her first novel, she recorded the thrill of so many jostling, unsorted new ideas, and Dora Marsden, the lost patron, fed into the Margaret Destin movement in whose literary–political circles Athenais met everyone who mattered.

Extraordinarily Rapid Changes of Circumstance

In April 1914, still in love, Jameson joined her husband in Kettering, where he had got a teaching job, and they lived in a small commercial hotel near the station.[38] She began writing *The Pot Boils*, cramming into it all the laughter and talk of London, and ideas borrowed from *The New Age* and Anatole France, Allen Upward's *The Divine Mystery*, and J. A. Symonds's *History of the Renaissance in Italy*.[39] A subscription to The Times Book Club kept her in touch with the latest metropolitan thinking. But increasingly, impoverished domesticity took its toll. She wrote to Archie White confiding her problems, but there was little any old friend could do. It was worse when Charles got a job in Liverpool as a junior classics master at the end of May 1914. They moved into a raw new house in Liverpool Garden Suburb in December, and for the next two years she felt 'biologically trapped'.[40]

Bill (Charles William Storm Clark) was born in Whitby, in her mother's house, on 20 June 1915. After six weeks, she took him back to Liverpool. The First World War passed almost unnoticed as she struggled to cope with this new

Figure 8 A Whitby tradition: mother and new baby (Storm Jameson and Bill), photographed in Sutcliffe's studio, 1915.

Figure 9 Jameson, Charles Clarke, her first husband, and the baby, in Liverpool.

responsibility. Between pages 94 and 95 in Jameson's own copy of *Journey from the North* is a little photograph of herself, and presumably Charles, with a small baby Bill, the model of a happy family. On those pages are accounts of their poverty, her hunger, the impossibility of writing, her manic gaiety, sullenness, and sarcasm, Charles's touchiness, their fights, and one icy winter night in 1916 when he threw her out of the house for several hours. They were both, she later realised, reacting in their different ways to a feeling of being trapped.

Writing in 1935 to thank James Hanley for the copy of *The Furys* he had just sent her, she was especially appreciative of his characterisation of Stoker Bush:

Reading about Mrs Fury I was not without some experience to help me. I have been very poor, and hungry for weeks at a time, and I have scrubbed floors with the desperation of utter weariness. But the forces that make a Chris Bush what he is, that work in him, that make him beat his wife, and that dictate the attitude of the other people to this action of his, are alien to me. I could not for myself imagine them. Now reading your book I have lived these things, and since I have been mercilessly beaten myself though not in such circumstances, I do now understand things I didn't before.[41]

In March 1917, Charles was in uniform, and training (on her brother Harold's advice) as an Equipment Officer in Reading. She followed him round the country, living in rooms, to Bradford and Lincoln, and finally to Stockbridge, in Hampshire. In October 1917, he was posted to Chattis Hill, and they had rooms in a farm in Broughton village. The landscape was consoling, but not enough to make up for a marriage that was falling apart, and financial problems made worse by her husband's selfish improvidence.[42]

But she had started writing again. In Whitby with the baby, at the end of 1915, she had returned to the manuscript of *The Pot Boils*. She finished it in Liverpool in the spring of 1916. It was rejected by Duckworth and then by Fisher Unwin, and finally accepted by Michael Sadleir, for Constable, in November 1917.[43] She went up to London to dine with Sadleir and his wife, who from then on were both important contacts and loyal friends, and started straight away on her next novel, *The Happy Highways*. She made fresh overtures to Dora Marsden, who however had had enough of her former protégée, writing to 'My dear Josephine' in January 1918 of the 'commonplace unrelieved stodginess' of the latest material Jameson had sent, adding:

You know Constable's are bringing out her book (novel) and have paid her £10 in advance? I will read it and unless there is something radically different in that I shall say we've been 'took in'. I'm sorry. I hoped she would turn out rather good.[44]

On 11 November 1918, Jameson hopefully renewed her seven shilling subscription to Marsden's journal, but to no purpose.[45] Even when *The Pot Boils* eventually appeared, in the following year, Marsden was to express no more than mild interest: 'Have you heard lately from Miss Jameson. She said she was going in for journalism and had thrown up the Carlton business. I haven't written to her. Grace has absconded with the book.'[46]

The couple were still living on the farm in June 1918 when Charles brought home the Texan Captain and Commanding Officer of an American Air Force squadron based at Chattis Hill, Jesse Fry, with whom she fell passionately in love.[47] He appealed, she wrote in her autobiography, to the 'gross, violent' side of herself she had always been at pains to hide from her friends.[48] His father was a wealthy businessman. Fry paid for Charles and herself to spend a week in London at the Piccadilly Hotel, and made a pass at her, which she rejected. Michael Sadleir knew him—they may have met when the Texan returned for three days to London, in the summer of 1919, when he proposed marriage.[49] She thought afterwards of her refusal as the moment when she rejected her 'violent self'. Lilo Linke, reading the episode in the draft of *Journey from the North*, was less admiring of what Jameson had considered her self-restraint:

Figure 10 'Best Regards from Two Texas Steers "Abroad" 1918'; on the left, Jesse Fry, Jameson's American Air Force Captain.

'there's a word for women like you'.[50] Certainly, her writing-up of the episode later in a short story is disturbingly smug.[51] They stayed in touch while he wrote letters to her from China, South America, and Texas (she destroyed them all), and sold arms to both sides in the Sino-Japanese war. Fry inspired the character of Jess Gage, Hervey's suitor in *The Mirror in Darkness*, the figure of superior American money, oil, and arms, who manipulates and patronises Thomas Harben, the British capitalist. [52] Gage laughs at the puny idealists and socialists that Hervey defends, 'all the highminded buzzards and their League of Nations', who are blissfully unaware that 'John D. Rockefeller and Thomas Harben had it squeezed into a ball between them'.[53]

At the end of October 1918, Charles was posted to Canterbury, and Jameson moved back to Whitby. He made no attempt to send for her and Bill, and refused to let her have any of his October pay. When the Armistice came, he was unable to find a job, so she got one instead, with the Carlton Agency, an advertising firm in Covent Garden. She went back to London at the end of December, leaving Bill with a Miss Geeson, in the village of Ruswarp, a mile outside Whitby. Her sense of guilt was tremendous, but it was far outweighed by her need to move on.

4

London 1919–1924

The New Novelist

The London Jameson returned to in January 1919 had nothing in common with the student paradise she had lived in before the war. When she looked back on it in 1961, she described it as a shoddy and ungenerous city, which had rapidly and deliberately repressed every trace of the sacrificed generation that had bought its survival: 'millions of fresh young bodies pushed hurriedly into the ground, their eyes and supplicating hands, out of sight.'[1] In 1934, she described in *Company Parade* the frenetically gay streets and noisy cafes where only Hervey Russell, up from the country, was prepared to confront the lost eyes of the lonely ex-serviceman, and the memories of the trenches that lay behind them. Lodging in north-west London in the house of a 'slightly louche' officer's widow who later became the model for Hervey's blowsy friend Delia Hunt, Jameson began to learn the business of writing advertising copy with the Carlton agency. She did it embarrassingly well.

The Pot Boils came out in the spring of 1919, and, with publishing still in the doldrums, received a creditable number of reviews. Literary London had not lost all memory of the idealism buried with the war, and her book, raw and crudely written as it was, anticipated a need to look again at the dissatisfactions and ambitions that had driven Class 1914. G. H. Cowling, her former rival from Leeds, praised its prescience, welcoming

a new kind [of novel], the novel of opinions, or intellectual novel—a kind which our modern *intelligentsia* will probably write when they have finished with the psychological novel, and particularly the study of abnormal psychology.[2]

Without naming the *New Age* and its Fabian competitor, he situated it in their ambit:

It is an attempt, by a mind which knows something of mysticism and (despite the novel's lack of human interest) something of drama, to express its presentation of the notions of that portion of the English cultured classes which calls itself the *intelligentsia* ('brains agin' the Gover'ment')—the Fabian, the feminist, and the dissatisfied artist. Though her criticism of life and human institutions is often shallow, sometimes even cheap, yet it does produce an effect.

The Pot Boils was an account of the first coming together, just before the war, of well-connected metropolitan middle-class progressive intellectuals, the new crowd of poor young socialists up from their provincial universities, and the occasional member of the working classes whose lot they were out to improve. The public narrative was held together by a private fantasy: Jameson's dream of what might have happened in the metropolis if her mother hadn't intervened, curtailing her attempts at sexual liberation and a career in journalism. Athenais is Jameson herself, physically ('her face seemed wholly childlike in its round smoothness. Not even the broad forehead and an unexpected squareness of jaw took much from the prevailing youthful roundness') and morally ('a Socialist, but through instinctive hatred of injustice rather than through knowledge or experience. She listened.')[3] Unlike her creator, she was well-connected, had an influential patron, and had studied not English but economics. She proposed to write a corrected Marx, and to put right both the Fabian technocrats and the lecturers at the LSE, all convinced of the sanctity of capitalist economics and more interested in statistics and theory than in their human material. Athenais was a model for a generation of new women, making the first significant breach in the men's world of professional work.

Women's sexuality is a central theme. At this stage, Jameson's analysis took mostly negative forms. Women sit silent on the fringe of men's political talk, accepting their role of sexual object. The great set-piece of the novel, a debate on the best form of communal life, is framed by a fight between two of the men over a woman. From the artist Denarbon, Athenais learns her socialism, and how to distinguish between the different forms on offer. In their northern university, he teaches her to despise the Fabians. Later, in London, he introduces her to the Pioneers, a group working in Hammersmith, working men and middle-class men who are workers, and who are demanding freedom as well as bread. They are the new tool of change, imperfect, but one that will cut.[4]

Athenais's socialist education is gained at the cost of a feminist commitment. She listens quietly while Denarbon mocks women's career ambitions in the language of the *New Age*, attacking the 'male feminists' who support them.[5] At times, the narrative seems to share his criticisms. The Fabian Summer School held in a country house near Scarborough is full of caricature feminists: the enthusiasts for motherhood, the androgynous haters of men, the fanatical opponents of prostitution.[6] The salon hostess, Elsa Carey, is the first incarnation of a figure who recurs frequently in Jameson's fictions: the pretentious woman writer, an arrogant power-broker with no talent.[7] Later, Athenais complains about the militant suffragists taking over the socialist paper she writes for, wasting the time and energy of the activists it commands: 'As if they had the right, while there is one ill-paid, ill-fed working-woman in England.'[8] But she draws the line when Denarbon criticises working women because they undermine working men's struggle for better conditions. She challenges him with an account of women's situation that describes Jameson's own, trapped in Liverpool, looking after Bill:

I know there is something wrong when [...] the only alternative to offices and factories is life in a suburban rabbit-hutch—baking, cleaning, washing, nursing the child, and waiting for the man to come in and be fed. [...]

[Y]ou've got to see, and I've got to see that not only have [feminists] wrought such spiritual changes that the mental outlook of women and of men on women—will never be the same again, but that they're not alone in making and clamouring for change. Behind them are the thousands—the hundreds and thousands of women—some in suffrage and socialist societies, some not out of college, and some—like me—just females at large, who can never get back into kitchens, never be satisfied again with the four walls of Nook Rise and Fairview.[9]

Like Dora Marsden, Jameson is convinced that women need careers, and liberation from 'the pressure of modern villa drudgery': 'You'll have to make your plans for a re-made society on the basis of feminine labour alongside masculine.'[10]

Denarbon leaves the country to work abroad, and is replaced by Richard Thurlow, a humbler admirer from student days, who is happy to play the new man to Athenais's new woman. Thurlow's idealist profession of faith in common service to the community, dismissed by Denarbon as 'syndicalist', is not far removed from Guild Socialism. He respects the commitment to the community, in their different ways, of the Church of England and men of science, and he advocates a working alliance of the New Tories, the Suffragettes, the Socialists and the working class:

[The working class] must demand the control of their own labours [...], so that they may serve the community worthily. And this they will do, not as a state within a state, but in conjunction with the other classes whom they serve, and within proper safeguard, to be fixed by the whole community. Am I clear? And I say also that there is no hope for the middle classes till they take control of their professions in somewhat the same way, and are prepared to serve with brains and hands, and to accept the full responsibility for their service to society.[11]

He, like Orage, blames the problems of society on the death of the feudal system of crafts and guilds and its replacement by the Manchester school of industrialism, and calls for a new breed of economists that doesn't identify workers with their machines. He urges Athenais to join him and abandon the *New Macchiavelli*, the *Blue Weekly*, the *New Statesman* and the New Tory Party, for 'the grime and filth of the East End, or Leeds or Liverpool'.[12]

His final conclusion, like Jameson's own, is that the best contribution intellectuals can make is to expose the cant that is creating the current shambles: 'If we can't be the masons of the new State, we can be the men who come with a great hose before dawn and flush the streets. In every shape and form we can fight cant—the cant of politician, economist, feminist, priest—not omitting to keep an eye open for our own.'[13] In this way, young men from the colleges can swell the ranks of the workers as 'an army of iconoclasts—men that can write and men that can talk, a new brand of experts—honest ones'.

Thurlow expresses Jameson's enduring commitment to freeing working people to create their own destiny. At university, he had mocked the patronising Fabian.[14] Athenais refuses to work for Margaret Destin's movement because of its patronising attitudes to the poor: 'a wretched lay figure on which a thousand itching brains and fingers satisfy their need to interfere and rule.'[15] Her position is echoed by Jameson's inspired character Poskett, the working man who denounces the Board of the *Beacon* for their scheme to replace increased wages for men by tickets for meals and clothes. The metropolitan version of the independent Yorkshireman, Poskett has a native grasp on all that is best in socialism, but no access to any organisation that can help him engage effectively with the ruling powers of the modern world. The final hope of the novel is that Athenais and Thurlow, married and recuperating in Whitby, will one day go back to London, and help form a new alliance between northern intellectuals and the London working class.

The Bohemian Girl

Life in London became much more pleasant with the publication of Jameson's first novel. She moved into a flat in St John's Wood with John Gleeson, a former Eikonoklast with whom Sydney Harland put her in touch, and his beautiful wife Elizabeth, sister to the writer Stephen Graham.[16] There followed a glorious period of Bohemian poverty and disorder, referred to in a letter she wrote to Ethel Mannin in the 1930s that challenged Mannin's claim to be the first inventor and best-known exponent of 'free love':

This 'philosophy' was not invented by you, nor are you, by millions, its sole exponent. When I first went to London, in 1919, I lived in a set which held and practised it without any fuss and without feeling that they were doing anything startling.[17]

In *The Happy Highways*, Margaret is said to have discussed free love with Michael (Sydney Harland) at school, as part of the bundle of socialist knowledge he was concerned to impart. In London, Margaret defended to her fellow-lodgers her free love relationship with Keith (Charles Clarke). The novel's narrator, Michael's brother, without referring to free love, characterises the new idea of women they had gathered from living alongside the thoroughly emancipated Margaret:

I think it rather an important thing—our freedom from the obsession of a romantic sex ideal that keeps bursting out even now in books by men on the Soul of Woman, or thrusts up in a strange, perverted form as a bitter antagonism to all that savours of feminism.[18]

Much later, Jameson would record listening with some embarrassment to a conversation in Naomi Royde-Smith's salon, some time in 1920 or 1921, about the correct way for a young wife to deal with a mistress her poet-husband had brought into the household.[19] She didn't, she said, join in to express her own views.

In the early autumn of 1919, having read *The Pot Boils*, Frederick Thoresby contacted Jameson with an invitation to join him on the new penny weekly he was about to launch, *The New Commonwealth*.[20] As a sub-editor at £50 a month, working from an office at 133 Salisbury Square, just off Fleet Street, she oversaw proofing and printing and wrote a substantial part of the paper's content: drama criticism, brief essays, and political notes and reviews. Politics in the paper covered both domestic and international affairs, and in the latter showed a strong animus against America's post-war undermining of the League of Nations. Writing to Alfred Knopf in 1981, looking back on that moment, she recalled a London that felt open, exciting, and above all, safe:

The first job I had in London, when I was very young, as the totally inexperienced sub-editor of a weekly journal owned by an elderly eccentric semi-millionaire, involved me once a week in working until two or three in the morning in a large printing works in Fleet Street. Then I used to walk back to my lodgings, right across London, through silent empty streets, without the slightest fear. None of the fatherly printers who had been giving me cups of dreadful tea, imagined that I might be running any sort of risk. Nor was I. That decent England died some time after the Second War, some time in the fifties. It no longer exists. How could it, now?—the lengthening dole queues, the extremely ugly riots, the overall cynicism, are the thin skin over a frightening barbarity and callousness.[21]

The first issue of Thoresby's weekly, published on 1 October 1919, proclaimed itself a rallying point for workers and 'the black-coated workers' (lower middle-class clerks), advertised its intention to found a National Union of Citizens, and declared in its first leader that strikes were not only inevitable but neces-sary. Thoresby's position on strikes was timely. On 5 October, the railwaymen secured a highly favourable settlement of a two-week strike that had been pro-voked by the Government and conducted against an extraordinary barrage of Press hostility.[22] Arthur Henderson wrote a Supplement for the first issue on 'Brotherhood and the World Unrest'. Supplements were to become a major feature of the journal. In the first three months, the theosophist Annie Besant, much admired by Thoresby, produced a four-issue sequence on 'The War and the Future', G. D. H. Cole wrote on Guild Socialism, and George Bernard Shaw on Socialism and Ireland.[23]

Jameson contributed to the first issue a column on 'Divorce', an issue of both general and personal interest, which argued all proceedings should be conducted in private, the children's welfare should be taken into account, and if a couple could not be reconciled they should be allowed to divorce quietly. She attacked with relish the 'indecency' of the divorce laws, and 'the present-day spectacle of grave and reverend judges squatting on their judicial heels to peep through bedroom keyholes [...] stripping the very sheets off the adulter-ous bed'.[24] Athenais had the platform she had always wanted.

In later issues, Jameson was the source of at least some of the numerous items on women's politics. [25] Her own initials appeared under the column on 'Divorce', a column on 'Profiteering', and another on 'America', which pointed out how different were Americans, and evoked 'an American race with hardly a drop of British blood in its veins', frontiersmen and dollar fiends, in contrast to old England: 'We inherit an old and subtle civilisation: we respond to calls and whisperings in the blood that are mute, or never were at all, for those others across the world.'[26] The item may well have had something to do with her meeting with her Texan in the summer, and his marriage proposal, as well as President Wilson's recent failure to give support to the League of Nations in its attempts to bring unity in Europe. Pieces initialled M. I. are in her style: 'A Woman's Thoughts. The Political Situation', for instance, which demanded on behalf of the soldiers returning from the front a better peace, better living conditions, and no war with either Russia or Ireland, and the piece that appeared in the following week, 'Wages for Wives'.[27]

The issue of 29 October had a distinctive European dimension, both literary and political. The interest of avant-garde English and Anglo-Irish writers in French experimental writing had been continuous from the 1890s, and the first decade of the 1900s had seen interest in French literature expressed in a number of journals aimed at the wider public. The *Times Literary Supplement* made an early start on keeping its readers up to date with the latest publications from Paris, but Jameson gives no indication of having read it. She did however read more idiosyncratic publications. The readers of Orage's *New Age* were generally more familiar with the ideas of Nietzsche, but they heard a lot about French culture, from the satirical novels of Anatole France, the champion of free thought and free speech, to Stendhal's coolly analytical prose. A translation of *L'Amour*, serialised in 1915, is probably the source for the distinctions between three kinds of love that Jameson was scribbling in the 1920s, in her search for a modern language for the representation of modern feeling.[28] The *New Age* was selective in its recommendations, preferring the French realists, and warning readers against the French pretentiousness from which most Englishmen, it thought, would want to keep a distance. It was left to the likes of the *New Freewoman* and *The Egoist* to introduce Jameson's generation to the forms of French Symbolism.

In 1919, it was the stylish realists who were holding her attention. Jameson will probably have commissioned for *The New Commonwealth* the lengthy review by EAB of the second volume of George Saintsbury's *History of the French Novel*, published on 29 October, which emphasised the parallels between those who on both sides of the Channel were 'the sober philosophical or critical delineators of ordinary life'. In England, the reviewer pointed out, there was a tradition of social realism running from Austen to Bennett, Wells, and Walpole, while in France:

> Parallel with these, we might make out a list from Balzac and Beyle, through George Sand, Flaubert, Maupassant, Zola, the Goncourts, Daudet and Huysmans, to Fabre, Rod and the novelists of today. [...U]ntil we have watched Balzac labouring at his colossal scheme of the Human Comedy; or Flaubert, with his infinite patience, striving to reproduce in his transparent medium the very figure or type, we shall never realise the vast extent and multifariousness of the possibilities in the novel, as an interpretation of human life.[29]

The *TLS* had similar things to say about French writers, but *The New Commonwealth* provided a context that was distinctly more controversial. In the same issue as EAB's review, the column of news in brief, 'Through Our Periscope', included a note of the manifesto published in the Communist *L'Humanité* against the blockade of Soviet Russia, signed by Anatole France, Victor Margueritte, and Henri Barbusse. Barbusse, celebrated for his great naturalist novel of the first world war, *Le Feu*, and more controversially, founder of the pacifist association *Clarté* and its eponymous journal, funded by the Communist Party, was regularly reviewed by Aldington in the *TLS*, praised for the quality of his writing, and denounced for his Bolshevism.

In the 1950s, as temperatures dropped in the Cold War, Jameson asked Macmillan's publicity department to drop her brief period with *The New Commonwealth* from her published biographical details ('It doesn't matter much, but it was rather an absurd little paper, as I look back on it').[30] In the 1960s, writing her autobiography, she was prepared to include it, but disavowed any personal commitment to its radical positions, saying that she reserved her real passion for her polemic pieces on the children starving in Austria and Germany as a result of Anglo-American indifference, her first intimation of the darkness gathering on the other side of Europe.[31] In 1919 though, she responded with enthusiasm to the ferment of ideas in the paper, and it certainly stimulated her own creative production. Thoresby serialised *The Happy Highways*, introducing it with a generous interview and a photograph.[32] She published her first short story, 'A Cloke for Two', a scandalous tale of a daughter covering for her mother's adultery,[33] and under the pseudonym George Gallilee wrote a column of childhood memories, 'A Philosophy of Youth'. These first attempts at autobiography offer sharp insights into the moral baggage she carried with her from her Yorkshire childhood into the larger freedom of the metropolis. Dealing for example with the issue of sex education for children—unnecessary, in her view—she indicated the shift of moral criteria she had observed in her generation from religious to social imperatives:

We [my generation] do respond—in a hesitating, half-conscious fashion—to the older racial impulse that punished adulterers not for their crime against a God, but for their crime against the tribe. [...] None of these racial impulses are fiercer or deeper-rooted than those which reach back, however tortuously, to the basal [sic] sex instinct. The child is asked to respect the religious taboos: he does not have to learn respect for the taboos of sex. They are rooted in his mind with the instinct of self-preservation and the impulse towards co-operation.[34]

From 19 March, the New Commonwealth became a monthly, and Jameson did regular theatre reviewing. She now shared reviewing with Thomas Moult, the Derbyshire novelist, author of anthologies and editor of a poetry journal. In April 1920, in 'A Special Literary Supplement Containing Reviews of Current Literature by Thomas Moult and Storm Jameson', she put her name to a polemic essay on 'The Modern Novel', where she attacked the Georgian novel for its 'bloodlessness', designated Virginia Woolf's characters in *Night and Day* 'humourless', and 'dull dogs', dismissed James Joyce and Dorothy Richardson as rubbish, and named Michael Sadleir as the only decent novelist around.[35] In October 1920, an anonymous reviewer—probably Moult—provided a full page review of *The Happy Highways*, describing it as an important novel of ideas, and a ringing indictment of modern society.[36]

Her creative writing was already becoming known. She was making a name not just as a novelist but as a short-story writer, helped by Michael Sadleir. In 1919 she had begun publishing short stories in Basil Blackwell's series, *The New Decameron*, with a mixture of established and coming writers such as Compton Mackenzie, D. H. Lawrence, Dorothy Sayers, J. D. Beresford, Michael Sadleir, Vita Sackville-West, Edgell Rickword, L. A. G. Strong, and Blair.

The New Age reviewed the first two collections, and picked out both her contributions, though not for praise. The reviewer was particularly censorious about 'The Woman Doctor's Second Tale. A Player Perforce',[37] a complicated narrative of frustrated love and humiliation: 'There is evidently a youthful intention to shock their elders in some of the stories; the imagination of Mr. Basil Blackwell and Miss Storm Jameson does not even respect death—and apart from the "shock" that their stories are intended to give, they seem to have no point.'[38] The point was often to work through Miss Storm Jameson's experience of the unhappy marriage that was dragging relentlessly on. In 'The Tale of the Solitary English Girl. The Pitiful Wife', crammed with bodice-ripping rhetoric, she wrote up for the first time her recent escapade with the Texan, her rejection of his offer of marriage, and her discovery immediately after that rejection of Charles's infidelity with a secretary.[39] Her fourth and last contribution was the Bureaucrat's Tale, 'Monotony', in which a middle-aged Russian princess and her English husband, at dinner on her estate deep in the Russian forest, sit drinking the last bottle of Imperial Tokay as the starving serfs burst in, rape the princess and kill them both. The bloody and respectably salacious conclusion is ironically calculated to fit the frustrations and repressions of the Bureaucrat, but these are also at this time very much Jameson's own.[40] The public took to the collection as a whole, and the back leaf of volume 4, where the Russian melodrama appeared, cited a *TLS* reviewer's comment that: 'It assembles some of the most notable names of the younger school of British authors.'

The *TLS*, in the person of Orlo Williams, had been less kind to *The Happy Highways* when it was published by Heinemann in 1920 (Sadleir having turned it down for Constable). It was, Williams said, a lecture rather than a novel, 'a deluge of talk on every controversial subject in modern society', with 'Mr' Jameson 'writing down a flood of memories, lest he should forget them, for the satisfaction of his own soul.'[41] Mr Jameson seemed to have registered every hit possible on the political and metropolitan prejudices of Williams, who declined all interest in these 'violent young people from Yorkshire', who were 'as garrulous and argumentative as Russian students'. On the same page, he recommended to the reader's attention a translation of a German novel, high in murder and love interest, for its vivid passages evoking Bloomsbury boarding-house types and suburban middle-class life. John Galsworthy also found in the novel too much talk and philosophising for his taste, but was much taken by what he saw as an excellent evocation of discontent, heartache, and youthful ambition.[42] Writing to Jameson in October 1923, thanking her for sending her new novel, *The Pitiful Wife*, and hoping young Bill was over his diphtheria, he reiterated how much he had liked her second novel, not for the style, but for its innovative documentation of the energies of young people before the war—very different, he thought, from the drifting youth of the present.[43]

It was a document on a disappointed generation. With its epigraph from 'A Shropshire Lad', the novel struck from the start a note of nostalgia and regret, very different from the upbeat hopes on which Jameson had ended *The Pot Boils*. It presented the period from 1910 to the end of the First World

War as a trajectory from 'Irresponsibility' (Book I) through socialist dreams ('Eikonoklasts', Book II) to the puncturing of those dreams by the brutality of history ('Chaos', Book III). A generation of young people, excited by the new worlds that English society seems ready to offer them, is turned back at the threshold by irreconcilable class conflicts, ignorance of the cloudy European horizon, and finally, the advent of the Great War. Debates on free love, and romantic episodes, add spice to the rudimentary plot, but the real centre is socialist and feminist politics. Margaret, stumbling along the path of love, marriage, and divorce, is a more credible character than Athenais, and more critical of the passions that saw her predecessor engaged in feminist struggle in the London Spring of 1913. Jameson catches the violence and the fear of suffragette marches, mounted police charges, rallies in Hyde Park, and battles with policemen, in which Margaret 'accidentally' finds herself caught. Asked to speak in Hyde Park, she finds that speaking makes her excited and angry. The police twisted her wrists and took her by the throat, and she kicked and bit. She reports afterwards to her fellow-Eikonoklasts: '"I understand now what makes them fight policemen and kick stewards of meetings and chain themselves to railings. It goes to your head—like—Wagner," she finished vaguely.'[44] By now she is angry with herself, and dismisses suffragist action as a 'silly game'.

All the same, this heroine is far less in thrall to the superior wisdom of her male contemporaries. The Harland brothers play their historical roles, but as more dependent figures, Margaret's admirers as much as her mentors. The narrative voice of the novel, Captain Joy, is besotted with Margaret, and in the closing pages it turns out that he was blinded in battle and is now totally dependent on her. This tragic hero is the first of Jameson's mediocre male narrators.

The critique of London socialism undertaken in *The Pot Boils* is reinforced in this novel by the Yorkshiremen sitting in the farm kitchen, who, like Margaret and her friends, looked for something more vital and practical than young Fabians could offer. The men of the moors are not without experience of the socialist movements of their time, and not unsympathetic to idealists. One man, who was in Paris just before the Commune, is forgivingly dismissive of the 'Communist' [sic] leaders he encountered:

'They meant well', he said, 'but they were nobbut daft oits. [...] honest fools.....There bean't noa honest socialism. 'Tis all folly and self-seeking. I doan't say but that some on 'em mens well, reet well, but they knaw namore o'life than yon owd bitch.'[45]

Jameson, who has experienced both cultures, the blinkered regional and the self-regarding urban, is alarmed by the antagonisms her society has bred between town and country: 'It is wrong and wicked beyond belief that a child should be born and bred out of sight of the meadow grass and sound of the homing birds.'[46] Even more alarming is the failure of London socialists to recognise the barriers that prevent them bringing the men of the moors into line with 'the workers of the busy outside world'.[47]

Widespread ignorance of the great internal splits in British society is matched by an equally culpable ignorance of foreign affairs. Even to the Eikonoklasts, news of the Austrian ultimatum was a bolt from the blue: 'For all our deep social preoccupation, we had never lifted our eyes beyond the limits of our island society, its injustice and its shortcoming.'[48] In the long run, recognition of the European horizon to British politics, hammered home by this most brutal of wars, was to make all the difference in the world. In the short term, the novel acknowledges bitterly how little change war brought to the barriers between classes. In the winter of 1915, the conversations of wealthy women in a Bond Street cafe stand in even sharper contrast to the destitution of the poor in the streets outside.[49]

The Happy Highways is a farewell to youthful dreams. There might have been an artistic renaissance, inaugurated by the new Post-Impressionist art that 'leaped upon us in the Exhibition of 1912', offering forms that could have swept away all the prohibitions the old men had established to keep down the young, but the old men's war put a stop to that.[50] There might have been personal happiness, but though the closing pages see a divorced Margaret living with Joy, she is clearly more nurse than lover. Joy still dreams of a future for the working-class Kersent, Poskett's heir, but can only speak about men's continuing alienation from each other—the subject of the ironic poem on 'The Brotherhood of Man' with which the novel closes. Joy's generation, from the radical Kersent to the Tory socialist Chamberlayn, did not die for the nation, but they did die for a national vision of freedom, justice, and equality, which will never be realised: '[Chamberlayn] and his comrades, whether they knew it or not, died for a dream.'[51]

In December 1920, Jameson's masters thesis on *Modern Drama in Europe* was published. Jameson's reviewing of contemporary London plays for the *New Commonwealth* will have helped encourage Collins to take it, though it was based purely on her research in the British Library in 1912–13, topped up by a fortnight's extra reading at the end of the war.[52] It shocked most of the drama critics by its iconoclasm. The *TLS* reviewer, however, gave a well-weighed assessment, praising the range of her knowledge and the depth of her thinking but regretting the narrowness of her preferences and her prejudice against writers such as Masefield and Galsworthy who focused, he said, on real-life conditions and lower-class people. He praised her chapter on Nietzsche's influence on the drama, and commented on her admiration for Strindberg's passionate and exceptional characters, noting astutely that: 'Strindberg's dread of women and dislike of "feminism" chime in with Miss Jameson's.'[53]

Jameson's attack on feminist positions in her study was certainly as striking as that she had offered in her novels. She defended Strindberg's misogyny, arguing that the modern feminist should recognise she and men were both victims of industrial society. She attacked Ibsen's Nora for abandoning her children in order to be 'free'. She praised Oscar Wilde's *A Woman of No Importance* for attacking current cant about women, and reproduced approvingly Wilde's aphorism to the effect that women were certainly less developed intellectually at the moment than men, but that their potential was stupendous.

Settling In

Under the aegis of Michael Sadleir, with her novels, stories, and journalism to give her credibility, and a certain reputation for iconoclastic outspokenness, Jameson made her entry into the London literary world at the Thursday evening gatherings held by Naomi Royde-Smith in the flat in Queen's Gate she shared with Rose Macaulay.[54] She dismisses Royde-Smith's circle in *Journey from the North* as a sober, Establishment, urbane backwater, out of touch with all progressive currents and all the people she would have really liked to meet, from T. S. Eliot to Raymond Mortimer. The latter is mentioned very much tongue-in-cheek, and she made her own contacts later with Eliot. But she did meet there some interesting and influential figures: Rose Macaulay, Arnold Bennett, 'Eddie' Marsh (later Sir Edward, Winston Churchill's private secretary (1906–29) and the friend and editor of Rupert Brooke), Harold Monro, Siegfried Sassoon, Robert Graves, St John Ervine, and Frank Swinnerton.[55] More contacts followed. At a party given by the science fiction writer J. D. Beresford, she met Walter de la Mare and John Middleton Murry.[56]

She complained later that the socialising she engaged in at this time was meaningless, but some genuine friendships began here.[57]

None of this success was going to help consolidate her marriage with Charles Clarke, who had been demobbed (reluctantly) in late 1920, and came to live with her in two rooms in North-West London. A note of quiet triumphalism appears in her autobiographical account of a period in which she was acquiring a new self-confidence, while he was struggling to find work, and frequenting what Michael Sadleir called 'the third-rate Fleet Street set'.[58] What Charles felt about the account of their relationship she had given in *The Happy Highways* is not recorded. He had failed dismally to find work for himself, so in March–April 1921 she handed over to him her sub-editor's job with the *New Commonwealth*, with some relief at having more time for her own writing. She was not ready to end the relationship, and was still struggling with the complexity of her feelings—some attachment, a lot of irritation, and a great fear of loneliness. Other family matters also clamoured for attention. She went to Whitby to see 6-year-old Bill, whom she hadn't visited for a few months, and was concerned and guilt-stricken by his reported fits of rage. But with a hardness inherited from her mother, she refused to stay with him, setting instead the pattern for their joint future. Bill stayed with her occasionally, or she visited him, paying with guilty over-compensation for the freedom she needed to make her writing career.

Back in London, she was still a political enthusiast. A correspondence in July 1921 with John Galsworthy shows her inviting him to join twelve men of letters in signing a letter to be drafted on the Irish situation—in what, he politely pointed out, seemed to be incoherent and simplistic terms.[59] Replying the next day, and thanking her for her 'charming' letter, he straightened her out:

The really serious thing about Ireland is, or has been, Governmental adoption and justification of reprisals, involving the innocent; that is a question of world-ethics, against which the voice of Letters should be raised.

The rest—including as it does the Ulster minority rights, and the strategic safety of England and Scotland and Wales—is too complicated, and too much a matter of give and take to be dealt with in the way suggested.[60]

Jameson was also preoccupied with other matters. She was trying to finish her third novel, *The Clash*, and undertaking additional assignments to keep afloat financially. In July–August 1921, she undertook some research on birth control statistics for Margaret Sanger, the American crusader (whose pamphlet on 'Family Limitation' would in two years' time come before the courts for indecency).[61]

At the height of that blistering hot summer, in a state of nervous exhaustion, she found a collar-box full of letters with evidence of her husband's continuing unfaithfulness. Her reactions, which she could still describe in detail forty years later, were to spill into numerous novels and short stories.[62] Humiliation was the chief. She made copious notes on all her contradictory feelings, all the phrases that she hurled at Charles, and all the invented phrases she found as she re-rehearsed their confrontations. She took steps to initiate divorce proceedings, and then gave way to her husband's appeals they should try again.

The marriage trailed on. They visited the Gleesons together, and Elizabeth, to her friend's disappointment (though not, perhaps, surprise) took Charles's side. The *New Commonwealth* closed down, but Charles's family came to his rescue, with funding for him to study for a doctorate at Oxford. Glad of the freedom, Jameson nevertheless went to visit him in the Spring of 1922, and was pleased to have his undergraduate friends pay her court.[63] The confident young woman painstakingly constructed by her hard-won successes at university and on the London career scene had been displaced and the insecure adolescent, the 'freak', was back.

Published in the summer of 1922, *The Clash*, whose heroine Elizabeth enjoys a string of extra-marital affairs with officers, including an American, Jesse Cox, probably also helped to reassure its author of her own sexual attractiveness. But the reviews were bad, and the novel lent itself easily to malicious summary and quotation. The *TLS* reviewer noted that Elizabeth's black-browed conquest, Major de Wend, in Jameson's own words, 'flew drunk rather than sober', and women adored him 'for his innate courtesy and for his eyes, which were the blue of rain-wet hyacinths'. Her book was lumped in with a host of other fashion-following novels dealing with the 'sex problem', including several by authors who would later acquire substantial reputations: Grazia Cosima Deledda's *The Woman and the Priest* (the translation of *La Madre*, with an introduction by D. H. Lawrence), Jane Mander's *The Passionate Puritan*, and James Hilton's *Storm Passage*.[64] Michael Sadleir liked it immensely, and wrote to say so, blaming Charles's connections with the second-raters in the popular press for its poor reception in the better papers.[65] Winifred Holtby saw stylistic promise: 'Her descriptions are exquisite, wonderful. Her people are queer, sinister puppets, with the strange life of puppets. They move in a sharp, uncanny light like the light under the sea. They talk with disturbingly clever talk, such as one never really hears, and it's all shockingly, disquietingly alive.'[66]

Reviewers were readier to welcome *The Pitiful Wife*, published in July 1923, where the young heroine appeared in more conventional terms as the victim of her husband's philandering.[67] Orlo Williams liked the Yorkshire setting, and the melodramatic characterisation that it apparently legitimised. Both Jael and Richard, he noted, brought to their marriage 'an inheritance of tumultuous Yorkshire blood, with all its individualism, its sensuality and its power of bitterness'.[68] Jameson herself eventually came to agree with Raymond Mortimer who said in his review that it was the silliest novel he had ever read; though she also thought that as a male intellectual he was ill-equipped to appreciate what she saw as the only 'real fragments' in it, the dialogue between the husband and the jealous, immature young wife.[69]

The writing is certainly very bad. In this first attempt to use description to set an emotional as well as social landscape, the changing seasons of the North Riding moors that open the novel are painted in romantic purple, with lavish adjectives and rotund syntax. In winter the moors are bleak and wild, with 'louring' hills, while in summer 'The fruitful mists drop fatness'. There is nothing to signal the multi-layered signifying landscapes that are the context of Jameson's mature fictions. Passions are never less than melodramatic. Jael's unhappy mother beats her daughter, and then walks out of her second childbed to die in the winter ice and wind. Her sadistic old husband, humiliated by his young wife's contempt, takes revenge by humiliating and tormenting Jael and her brother. Jael grows up nevertheless in remarkable rustic innocence and marries her childhood sweetheart, who returns wounded from the War to become a failed sculptor. What works best is the later part of the novel, written in a simpler, even stark style, where Jameson explores the motivations beyond the sensual that define Richard/Charles's need for his mistress—his sense of failure, disappointment, and entrapment—and his contradictory feelings towards Jael of love, guilt, and resentment. The last section tracks in excoriating detail the wife's discovery of her husband's affair and the long repetitive sequences of recrimination and self-loathing that followed, and examines with brutal honesty feelings that conventionally remain unspoken. Jael, bending with hatred over her sleeping son, 'the sign and symbol of the shame to which she had delivered herself,' almost kills him with the venom of her resentment.[70]

In real life, Jameson's own relationship with her son had become closer. From the beginning of 1923, on the strength of a £100 advance from Sadleir for her novel, and an unexpected £50 from Charles, she had been living with Bill, then aged 7, in rooms in the village near Whitby where he had been boarding. In July, when the novel came out, she was nursing him through a serious attack of diphtheria. In November, the two of them moved to her mother's house, where she herself fell victim to the epidemic and was nursed back to health by her sister Winifred.[71]

Before then, seeing no prospect of making her own way financially, she had reluctantly promised to go to Cornwall with Charles, who in July 1923 had given up his thesis and taken a teaching job in Launceston. But in September 1923, everything changed.[72] On Michael Sadleir's recommendation, she was interviewed by Alfred and Blanche Knopf, of the American publishing house, who wanted a representative to open a London office to net books and authors. They offered her the job, and she moved to London, abandoning Charles with all the less compunction for having discovered that he was still carrying on his affair. A light-hearted squib, *Lady Susan and Life: An Indiscretion*, published at the end of the year, restored her to full favour with the *TLS*.[73] In January 1924, she was settled in Norham, St Mary's Road, Weybridge, in Surrey, only forty minutes from London by train, and boasting a suitable school for Bill, recommended by Sadleir. She wrote to her new employer in high excitement:

I appreciate profoundly your generosity over my contract. I only hope to the Lord I can justify three hundred pounds worth of generosity: I do not mind how much work I have to do to do that. I understand also the way you wish to limit your list, and I think that I ought to be able to weed things out much more rigorously in future without running too much risk of missing things. There are also a few people—e.g. Michael Arlen and Rose Macaulay—whom I can continue to 'nurse'.

The extraordinarily generous letter you have written to the publishers will certainly help to strengthen my position in more ways than one. Thank you very much: you are most kind. My position will be further strengthened when I come to London—as I shall do.[74]

In the same month, she met Guy Chapman, and entered a new life, and a new world.

5

London 1924–1928: Publishing, Passion and Politics

Passion and Publishing

Guy Chapman, born on 11 September 1889, was 35 when he met Margaret Jameson, and she was 33. The relationship that began in 1924 lasted for almost fifty years until his death on 30 June 1972. Her Introduction to his autobiography, *A Kind of Survivor*, which she brought to press from the rough handwritten drafts and notes he had left, evokes not only deep affection but the delight of an intellectual collaboration whose value she fully acknowledged:

How thoughtlessly […] I drew on his learning, on his familiarity with worlds in which I am blind or deaf or ignorant, on the sweep of his reading, on his knowledge of music and architecture. It is only now that I realise how sharply my pleasure in travel was heightened by his lively memory for places.[1]

His mother's father had been a partner in a big shipping firm, Gellatly & Gellatly, which disappeared in a financial crash, and Guy inherited his grandfather's taste for travel and good claret.[2] His barrister father, G. W. Chapman, came from country gentlefolk. His paternal grandfather had bankrupted himself in publishing, but the rest of the family were still wealthy people. Guy's father took the family every year on a visit to Kingussie, inspiring his life-long love affair with the Scottish countryside. Guy followed his father to Westminster School and then to Christ Church Oxford (1908–11), which he left with a Third because his father insisted he read Law rather than History, his first love. He shared his staircase with Ralph Hodder-Williams, the future head of Hodder and Stoughton, and Adrian Boult, a contemporary at Westminster. Of the same generation as Jameson, Chapman's social position was completely different. He and his friends went to war as officers, and most of those who came back slipped relatively easily into high places in public life. Jameson enjoyed the entrance he gave her into London's establishment, and the change of lifestyle he brought, though her pleasure was shaded by feelings of guilt. At the end of *Love in Winter*, Hervey Russell's entry with Nicholas into the sunny flat on Primrose Hill coincides with the death of the child who has been struggling to survive in the London slums, the protégé of the ascetic socialist David Renn, who is the last of the Eikonoklasts.

Chapman's autobiography never speaks of any reciprocal benefit that came to him through Jameson's networks, more often complaining of the burden of being roped in as a PEN delegate to faraway places, or the tedium of dealing with the refugees and exiles who frequented their London flat during the 1930s. Yet he enjoyed the pleasure of sitting next to Arthur Koestler at PEN dinners, and of leading delegates to the famous places of Venice and being praised for it by Auden, while scorning the poet for his wartime derelictions.[3] A famous wife meant shared invitations to lecture tours and to interesting and well-set dinner-tables.

It wasn't perfect bliss. He will not have enjoyed the moments when she was earning money for both of them to survive, or, later, to ensure that his wine and his linen were always of the quality he expected. In her turn, she was often irritated by the disruption his wartime postings or peace-time academic moves brought to her writing career. But by the end, none of that mattered. He was her mentor, her inspiration, and the centre of her existence. They were perfectly matched, and when he died, the zest of life was gone:

We went to places, obscure ruined monasteries, small provincial art galleries, the house in which a dead philosopher spent his life, salt marshes, trout streams, some turn in a rough nameless road which offered a view of a smiling valley and a line of hills, because, although he had not seen them, he knew they were there.

He made all other company a little dull.[4]

When they met at the end of January 1924, in his office at Chapman & Dodd, they had already been in written contact. He had read one of her novels, and asked her to write a book for the firm. They had quarrelled over the proposal ('Written from Yorkshire, her answers to my short-tempered letters amused me, but I thought her conceited and hard'), but on meeting, he had quite a different impression:

She was wearing a heavy coat over a faded pink knitted dress, and a hat which did not suit her, and she smiled at me. She was rather lovely, with long cool grubby fingers, and

Figure 11 Guy Chapman, Jameson's second husband, in Germany after the
Armistice, sitting in the front row, second from left. A note on the back
from Guy's cousin, Peter S. Chapman, who sent the photograph after Guy's
death, indicates '17 Royal Fusiliers at Hoffnungstahls, July 1919'.

she held herself badly: she made me think of a well-bred foal, unbroken and enchant-
ingly awkward. Something she said at that first meeting, I forget what, made me laugh
with pure pleasure.[5]

Chapman's career was progressing slowly, and like Jameson, he had problems
from a first marriage. He had stayed on voluntarily in 1919 in the Army of
Occupation, to get promotion and better pay in order to support his wife,
Doris May Bennett, married on 26 November 1914 in Kensington Register
Office.[6] Demobilised at the end of February 1920, with the rank of major, he
returned to the publishing house he had worked for before the war. He was
offered a small poorly-paid job, all that was available, and his wife was engaged
in an affair and asking for a divorce.[7] To save her future husband's career in the
Foreign Office, he agreed to be designated as the guilty party, and also to go
on living with her in their flat as cover for her reputation. He eventually got a
job in 1922 as manager for a new London branch of an Irish publishing firm,
Chapman and Dodd, in Denmark Street, Soho. Slowly learning his trade, he

had some successes, and moved in the following year to new premises opposite the *New Statesman*, where he became friendly with Desmond MacCarthy.
A lifelong member of the Savile Club, a literary club situated at 107 Piccadilly,
he made further interesting connections there, from W. B. Yeats to the young
Brendan Bracken (Minister of Information in the Second World War, who
would be an important contact for both Jameson and PEN). By July 1924, he
had started his own firm in an office in the Adelphi, at 8 Buckingham Street,
with a small legacy from an aunt, and in partnership with Hamish Miles, who
introduced Osbert Sitwell.[8] Sitwell apart, the firm's authors were not neces-
sarily chosen among the best-sellers of the day. Chapman printed the sort of
books he liked, not the ones the market would snap up, and between 1924 and
1928 he was beset with financial problems and always fearful of failure.

Jameson in the meantime was doing increasingly well. Knopf published *The
Pitiful Wife* in the United States (and picked up nearly all her books thereafter
until 1935, when she went to Macmillan, and then to Harper's). She began
writing her fifth book while enjoying single life in Weybridge and by 1928 had
finished two more (*Three Kingdoms*, and *The Lovely Ship*).

She enjoyed working for the Knopfs. An impractical sort of man, Alfred,
like Guy, only published writers he liked and had little sense of the market, but
he had the money to indulge himself. She respected him tremendously, and
he in turn recognised the benefit that came to the firm from her energy and
acumen.[9]

From her sickbed in Whitby, Jameson began writing her characteristically
charming letters to authors, critics, and publishers, from John Buchan to Middleton Murry, and receiving in return pleasingly friendly replies.[10] Once settled
in London, she found her social life rapidly expanding with Knopf's money
and influence. She told a correspondent in the 1980s:

I knew, through talking and writing to [writers]—on behalf of A.A.K.—about their work,
and through standing them lunch at the Carlton Hotel where A.A.K. had arranged for
me to sign the bill, many of the up and coming writers of that time, many more indeed
than I cared to meet. Some of them became and remain my friends, close friends.[11]

Her confidence was returning. About the time she first met Guy, J. W. N. Sullivan,
who wrote on mathematics and music, had proposed they have an affair. She
wrote entertainingly about his drunken advances in her autobiography, using
extracts from three letters she 'accidentally' kept, and describing herself as
'too calculating and fastidious' to take him seriously.[12] In 1932, in Orage's *New*

English Weekly, reviewing *But for the Grace of God*, an autobiographical fiction, she praised the honesty with which Sullivan discussed his three great interests, Beethoven, mathematics, and sexual desire, and on the latter, spoke feelingly: 'In personal relations he is incurably stupid; there seems to be absolutely no communication between his mind and the mind of the other person.'[13]

The relationship with Guy developed quickly if unevenly. On her side, there was intense passion, and on his, need. He was often cold and distant, exhausted, she thought, by his wartime experiences and the struggle to succeed in the post-war world.[14] They met two or three times a week, he wrote to her in Weybridge, and in the spring of 1924, Charles found his letters. Some time in late summer, after some stormy months, he agreed to a divorce.[15] Margaret and Guy were designated the guilty parties, and Charles in return agreed to relinquish all claim on Bill. After that, Charles more or less disappeared from her life, making only intermittent, increasingly strange appearances. On 3 November 1937, for example, the day after the emergency meeting of the Peace Pledge Union that followed Dick Sheppard's death, he visited her in her Reading flat, in Guy's absence, for the first time in four or five years. He was riding in a chauffeur-driven Rolls Royce that he said belonged to his employer, and claimed to be working for Intelligence, on behalf of three important Labour leaders. She dropped the incident from her published autobiography, together with her note that as she was writing, in May 1964, she didn't know if he was still living.[16]

In the autumn of 1924, she moved to Sloane Street, into a big first-floor room in a large house owned by a friend.[17] Noel Streatfeild, then an actress, leaned over the banisters from the floor above, watching Jameson's furniture arrive and making mocking comments to her friends. The two became great friends, though for long stretches they met only intermittently.[18] She was visited there by Edith Sitwell, and visited her in turn, sometimes for lunch. On one of those occasions she met Peter Quennell, whose adoration for the old literary lioness is probably one of the sources of her later satirical portraits of the gender politics of London literary life.[19] At the end of 1924, Gerald Bullett and J. B. Priestley often came to tea. She admired Bullett immensely. Priestley, in whom she saw her mirror-image, was too close to her in his Yorkshire temperament (though, as she often pointed out to family and friends, he was one of the loud-mouthed vulgarians from the West Riding, not the civilised North), and too much of a rival for the same markets, for either of them to get on easily with the other.[20] Part-model for the figure of William Ridley in *None Turn Back*, Priestley attracted her merciless criticism for his aspirations to write great social novels. Reviewing *Faraway*, in 1932, with a waspishness that even for her went too far, she quoted mercilessly his attempts at Lancashire dialogue, his abuse of descriptive passages, and the superficiality of his analyses, commenting: 'In San Francisco William bites into a luscious-looking pear only to find it woolly and flavourless. The reader's experience of this book is very similar.'[21] In *None Turn Back*, William Ridley refuses to sign a letter on behalf of the miners, arguing that writers should stick to writing and steer clear of politics. The 'nerves' of his writing, Hervey notes, are missing.[22]

She kept out of the bundle of letters marked for burning after her death a few of those that Guy wrote to her at this period, as matters of business sent them travelling in different directions—she to Nice in September, he to Scotland in October. Early uncertainty has gone, his 'beloved' has transformed his life, and he is 'utterly in love with you, enchanted'.[23] By the end of 1924, Guy and Margaret were living together in the flat she had found at the top of Primrose Hill.[24] The following Easter, she moved Bill to live with her mother and attend school in Whitby, and in May, Guy took her to Aviemore for two weeks, to introduce her to his beloved Scotland.[25] Guy was still moody, divorce negotiations with Doris dragged on, and she continued to feel guilty about abandoning Bill, but life was relatively happy until the autumn, when Guy's financial problems made it impossible to carry on his business, and Jameson turned to Alfred Knopf for a solution. The couple went over to New York in January 1926, for ten days. Guy hated it; everything, he thought, from the traffic to the exchange of ideas, moved too quickly and relentlessly. Hard work in the office by day was followed by opera, theatre, and dinner parties in the evening. He was struck though by what he saw as America's racial tolerance: 'In the literary and musical circles we touched there was no anti-semitism, no racial tension: it was fashionable to entertain at home black singers with lungs of brass, and to visit Harlem night clubs—Carl van Vechten's overrated *Nigger Heaven*.'[26] Jameson's grandson recalls playing to her while he was at university George Gershwin's *Rhapsody in Blue*, which he wasn't sure she would like: yes, she did, she told him, and she remembered hearing it for the first time played by Gershwin himself, one evening in the Knopfs' flat.[27] In such proximity to the interesting and famous, and the apple of the Knopfs' eye, Jameson enjoyed herself much more than Guy, but she was still glad when it was time to go home to England.[28]

Knopf bought out Guy's firm and set up his English publishing house. He insisted that Jameson was part of the bargain, on a half-time basis that in practice became full-time. From 1926 to the middle of 1928, when they parted amicably, her name appeared with Guy's on the headed notepaper as joint manager. She would have liked to give up publishing altogether to concentrate on an increasingly promising writing career. But like her mother ten years before, Guy needed her to be there. This time, her career didn't go on hold, but the drain on her energies was considerable.

In their memoirs, neither mentions the day of their marriage. It took place on 1 February 1926, at the Register Office in Chelsea. Guy Patterson Chapman was 36 years old, and Margaret Ethel Clarke (formerly Jameson), was 35.[29] Guy's autobiography speaks of 'my new wife' and her spendthrift nature—she had no idea of saving money, and was reckless and disrespectful of it.[30] (That this worked often to his advantage was not an idea that seemed to occur to him.) There were more serious matters to disrupt their first married days together. Doris Chapman, whose own affair was not running smoothly, wrote incessantly to her former husband and his new wife. Twenty years later, when Irene Rathbone wrote to say she had just met Doris's former lover, Jameson recalled a long period of unpleasantness:

She wrote filthy and quite cracked letters about me, too, every day, for weeks and weeks, months. Although I did not meet Guy until she had been living apart from him for three years and there was no question of their ever living together again. Anyway, Guy's life was permanently twisted by the whole thing. Felix Cross is probably less of a cad than one thought, and less innocent than he now believes. Doris Chapman was so egotistical as to be not quite sane, but she spoiled her own life too. It all seems to belong to another planet now, and Felix need not mind Guy if they meet. Or me.[31]

In the new well-staffed office in Bloomsbury, at 38 Bedford Place and then in Bedford Square, Guy's inability to judge the English market was compounded by that of his new employer. Knopf produced Max Brod, Bruno Frank, Alfred Döblin, and René Schickele, and the Chapmans arranged to have them translated, but for English book-buyers the French were still the only foreigners worth reading.[32] Wyndham Lewis almost left in a huff, but Jameson flattered him into staying. Edward Thompson's novels of India sold well, and she was pleased, because she admired in him an integrity and sense of loyalty that later reminded her of R. H. Tawney.[33]

They moved house a lot. The flat in Primrose Hill was reclaimed by its owner, and they spent 'months' at The Spreadeagle in Thame, as guests of the eccentric John Fothergill. He had taken over the establishment in 1922, booted out its local customers, and rapidly acquired a fashionable London and then Oxford clientele, including Augustus John, Arnold Dolmetsch, H. G. Wells, Osbert and

Sacheverell Sitwell, George Gordon, the President of Magdalen, the undergraduate Evelyn Waugh, Maurice Bowra, and John Betjeman. He was known for his snobbishness, his hostility to any working-class customers who innocently wandered in, and the quality of his food and wines. The Chapmans were welcome visitors: 'A lovable couple and a good blend. [...] Where she is masculine, he is feminine, and vice versa.'[34] In 1931, she was happy to contribute a short story to his anthology of eighteen tales by famous clients, and his Introduction thanked her for her help and encouragement in putting it together.[35]

After that, there was a year's tenure of a large flat in Belsize Park, and then another year, from spring 1927 to summer 1928, spent in a flat in a wing of a big house in Harrow Weald Park, near London. Bill came to live there, and attended a nearby prep school as a day-boy. Then Margaret and Guy went back to London, and Bill back to Whitby.[36]

In all this activity, the General Strike of May 1926 came and went unnoticed. Like their wedding, it merits no comment in either of their memoirs. Naomi Mitchison, in hers, would at least note that it had taken place, and describe frankly the lack of connection she and her husband felt at the time with the workers:

[W]e did not really know what it was about. My father certainly supported the Samuel Report but probably did not go so far as totally to support the miners. I at least was more worried about the children than anything else and also somewhat envious of our strike-breaking friends who were doing gorgeous things like driving real trains.[37]

Jameson's previous professions of socialist commitment left her with far less excuse, as her self-lacerations for backsliding in *The Mirror in Darkness* indicate. Strikes are a theme in *The Lovely Ship* (1927), but the author's sympathies seem equally divided between the starving workers and the struggles of young Mary Hervey, head of Garton's shipyards, to keep afloat a business struggling to survive against international competition, and the pressures of the technological switch from sail to steam, and wooden ships to iron.

Publishers, Essayists, Novelists

On all counts, at this period, Jameson was perfectly qualified for membership of PEN. PEN (Poets, Essayists, and Novelists, or Publishers, Essayists, and Novelists, or even, someone suggested, *Paix entre nous*) was the brainchild of

C. A. Dawson Scott, known to her admirers as Mrs Sappho, who envisaged a Literary Dining Club, on the American model. John Galsworthy was invited to be first President, in preference to H. G. Wells, because 'He hasn't an enemy. He is charming, delightful, a pleasant speaker, has infinite tact. And he's a gentleman. H. G. isn't.'[38] Hermon Ould was invited to be the first Secretary, and forty-four writers and journalists came to the Foundation Dinner on 5 October 1921 and became Foundation Members. They included Ould, Rebecca West, May Sinclair, Violet Hunt, Marjorie Dawson Scott, Sappho's daughter, Fryn Tennyson Jesse, and of course Galsworthy. The first Executive Committee consisted of Austin Harrison, Rose McLeod, Rebecca West, Elizabeth Craig, Horace Shipp, C. S. Evans, and Louis Golding. Galsworthy remained President until his death in January 1933; by then, the times were changing, and the ungentlemanly Wells would be the choice to replace him.

The earliest dated record of a PEN connection for Jameson is in February 1925. A letter to Ould records her tearing up a diary and finding in it a note of an appointment for that month with Czarnomski, a member of the Polish Legation.[39] At an unrecorded date, she wrote to Ould with a request to attend the December dinner and sit with Amabel Williams-Ellis. On 1 December 1926, she accepted an invitation from Ould to be a hostess at a PEN At Home, and subsequently she accepted more invitations to carry out similar small duties.[40]

With Amabel (Mary Annabel Nassau) Williams-Ellis, John Strachey's red-haired sister, and daughter of St Loe Strachey, founder of *The Spectator*, only two years older than herself, she struck up a lifelong friendship. Amabel, an ardent socialist, had followed her adored brother John into the ILP. She was a VAD (voluntary ambulance driver) in the War, assigned to duties in England, and afterwards, like Jameson, had been angered by Britain's greedy claims for reparations from Germany, and by the slow pace of post-war social reform at home.[41] During the General Strike, she enthusiastically addressed envelopes for the unions (as did Hervey Russell, in *None Turn Back*). In January 1928, she went with John to Russia, to look at coal-mining. She will have been delighted to see John elected as a Labour MP in 1929 and joining with Nye Bevan to draft a radical programme to end unemployment in Britain. Equally, she must have been disturbed when he turned in his disappointment in 1931 to Oswald Mosley's New Party. In 1913, she had married Clough Williams-Ellis, a committed socialist architect who wanted to create private housing schemes for working-class people. He was sensitive to environmental concerns, hostile to modern technology, and determined to build houses for 'the natural needs of soft little animals—us—not machines'.[42] He founded the village of Portmeirion in 1925, with a hotel designed for the 'well-to-do intelligentsia', a restricted but regular clientele which included the Mitchisons, Bertrand Russell, and the upper ranks of Hampstead socialism. For the Chapmans, Portmeirion would always provide a welcome and a refuge.

Jameson's novels were now appearing regularly. In 1926, Constable published *Three Kingdoms*, which drew heavily on her own experience, its heroine a woman whose energies were divided between her husband, her child, and her career as managing director of an advertising company. Marjorie Grant Cook was pleased, she said, to see a novel where both men and women had brains.[43] More important, in 1926 Jameson was writing *The Lovely Ship*, the first of her trilogy on the changing fortunes of shipping in the North-East from the mid-nineteenth century, and the life and personality of Mary Hansyke. It was published by Heinemann in April 1927, and she wrote self-deprecatingly to a friend that:

The Lovely Ship is not worth your reading. I have a *Family Herald* mind, madly allied to a debased Smollett sort of imagination. The result has to be read to be believed—but need not be read again.[44]

Like the next two novels of the trilogy, *The Voyage Home* and *A Richer Dust*, *The Lovely Ship* was an experiment in writing social and historical fiction, the back-story for Jameson's 1930s trilogy on the interwar years, in which the novelist Hervey Russell is Mary's granddaughter.[45] The parallels between the fictional characters and members of Jameson's family (her mother, and the awe-inspiring George Gallilee) are obvious; but with hindsight, Jameson decided that the result of her work was more of a museum reconstruction than the evocation of a living period. Orlo Williams was of the same mind. The characters, he thought, were better than the historical narrative, which was undigested documentary.[46]

But Jameson was starting to make a name as an analyst of modern feeling, and the novel brought her to the notice of other young women writers. Vera Brittain wrote in her biography of Winifred Holtby that:

In April 1927, Winifred wrote me that she had just interviewed Storm Jameson, whom she had not previously met, for the 'Women of the Day' series in the *Yorkshire Post*. In my reply from America, I enclosed for *Time and Tide* a review of Storm Jameson's new novel, *The Lovely Ship*. I added that I was probably going to have a baby.[47]

85

It wasn't a very positive review, and was marked by a certain envy of Jameson's success.[48] Jameson wrote to Brittain in September to say she hoped they might meet up, and apparently they did, but no sparks were struck. In contrast, after the *Yorkshire Post* interview, according to Brittain, Jameson and Holtby became friends. They didn't write very often, but their meetings were always easy and enjoyable. With Jameson, as with another Yorkshirewoman, Phyllis Bentley, Winifred formed a commonality from which Brittain clearly felt excluded: 'They understood Yorkshire reticences, Yorkshire dignity, Yorkshire inhibitions, because they not only shared them, but experienced, like Winifred, secret moods in which the inhabitants of the rest of England appeared shallow, fussy and unreliable.'[49]

The relationship between Chapman and Jameson at this time was difficult and stormy, complicated by the demands of the partners from their previous marriages. Once again, Jameson turned to fiction to work out her feelings. In *The Lovely Ship*, historical displacement allows her to be graphically explicit about the rawness of her emotions. *Love in Winter*, in the 1930s, would rework the same material in its contemporary context, and show more discretion in the discussion of both partners' responses. *Journey from the North*, for all its autobiographical profession, is far less frank about what each of them felt. Guy made no comment, in public at least, on this soul-baring, but he must have been equally surprised by the sexual frankness of the novel of 1927 and the cold analysis in *Love in Winter* of his indecisiveness, and the frustration it caused his new wife.

The narrative of *The Lovely Ship* is in fact well conducted, and the historical context unobtrusively and dramatically set. The story begins in the summer of 1841 with Mary's birth, and traces the fortunes of her uncle's shipyard in Danesacre (Whitby). In the 1860s, the great swing-over from wood to iron and sail to steam is accomplished, and Mary takes over Garton's. By the end, in the 1870s, with the Suez Canal about to be purchased, Disraeli talking in Berlin of Peace with Honour, and the freight industry at an all-time low, Mary, alone of her owners' generation, foresees the imminent displacement of iron ships by the steel vessels some entrepreneur must now engineer. But Orlo Williams was right to say that the characters are the most interesting part of the tale, and the key section is the segment where Mary and her engineer-manager lover, Gerry, travel together on one of Mary's clippers to Tonnay-Charente, to pick up a cargo of cognac. In a restaurant, they are astounded to be confronted with Gerry's destitute wife, Mercy, who demands Gerry honour his promise that he would always take her back. Gerry does so, being both highly moral and riddled with guilt at having been, as Mercy repeatedly told him, a failure as a husband. Mary recognises that Gerry is a fool, but she is infatuated, and will do anything to make him happy. Her anger is vented on his wife, and through Mary's eyes Jameson delivers a portrait of a monster, once beautiful, now still handsome but battered, 'old and tired and dreadfully knowledgeable'.[50] On the first night of the voyage back to England, Mary must share her cabin with Mercy. Jameson lingers over a flesh-creeping scene of humiliation, intensely sensuous:

Mercy Hardman moved uncomfortably on her couch, but she was too hardy to be quelled. A wish to assail Mary's innocence seized her and pushed her past caution. She began to talk to Mary of her life, forcing on the younger woman knowledge that sickened her, and all the time Mary brushed her long hair with a steady motion, neither answering nor checking the flow of Mercy's malice. Mercy talked herself out and lay down between the blankets, her face turned despitefully towards the room. She knew that Mary loathed the thought of undressing in front of another woman, and kept her dark eyes widely open.[51]

On their return to England, Mary hands the couple her own home to live in—Jameson's resentment at Doris Chapman's intrusions into her life was acute.

The visceral revulsion inspired by Doris Chapman, and more importantly, by Guy's insistence on putting her welfare before their own, is less intense in the novel Jameson wrote ten years later. *Love in Winter* covers the court-ship of herself and Guy in the early months of 1924, and works a way out of the resurfacing insecurities of her childhood. Writing is presented there as the means of creating a salvific distance. Hervey Russell is writing a book using the same material Jameson used for *The Lovely Ship*. It will be a 'rubbish book', a potboiler, she tells Nicholas Roxby, her cousin and lover, but she sells it triumphantly in the closing pages for a great deal of money.[52] Alongside the composition of this book, Hervey writes notes for her own satisfaction about themes of more importance, ones that Jameson was developing at that time: a Stendhalian analysis of feeling, echoing *De l'Amour*, and the significance of layered memories in landscape. In a disturbingly uncanny turn, mirroring her author's mirror-techniques, Hervey invents a surrogate self about whom she tells herself stories as a means of self-protection:

In one of the many endless fantastic stories she told herself when she was bored, or at night before she fell asleep, she had made a doll which was her double and went everywhere while the real Hervey stayed safe at home. Once, at a trying dinner party, she pretended she was this doll and succeeded so well that she grew frightened and pricked herself with a knife to make sure.[53]

What Jameson was protecting herself from, at the same time as she confessed it, was the frightening truth about her feelings for Guy, whose self-absorption was by the 1930s arousing her increasing resentment. This novel is more bitter than *The Lovely Ship*, and ready to express not only anger over his dithering about his divorce and their marriage, but envy at the privileges of class and money he had enjoyed.[54] She began to forgive him for that only as she became more successful.

Pen for Hire

By early 1927, Jameson had begun writing features for the *Daily Mirror*, where she figured as the house-trained *enfant terrible*, a tractable representative of the socialism and feminism which had once again become hot news. She was not in entirely disreputable company. Alongside such exponents of popular romance as Ethel Mannin, Baroness Orczy, and Clemence Dane appeared the names of J. B. Priestley and Edith Sitwell. And there was something to be said not only for the size of the cheques, but for the availability of a platform to address a popular audience.

The popular picture newspaper had been bought by Lord Rothermere in January 1914, and he kept it until 1931, after which it moved left. Rothermere also owned the *Daily Mail* and the *Evening News*, which supported Oswald Mosley until July 1934 and Hitler and Mussolini long after that.

When Jameson joined the paper in 1927, Britain was fighting in Shanghai, and the pages were filled with photographs of troops and ruined houses. Nationally, anti-trades union legislation was being drafted to mop up the elements of resistance left over from the General Strike. The *Mirror* regularly quoted approvingly the advice that came to workers from Labour's Philip Snowden on the uselessness of general strikes. From April 5th, it published regular reports of drastic strike law changes proposed in the Trade Disputes and Trade Unions Bill that had just been published. In the Bill, for example, peaceful picketing was sharply defined, strikes coercing Government or any substantial part of the community were declared illegal, and restrictions were placed on unions' operation of a political levy. From May, the paper ran a strong campaign against union activity, socialists and 'Reds'.

Less to the editor's taste were more liberal measures coming from the Government on women's civil rights. In March, the paper followed through the debates in Cabinet over whether women of 21 should have the vote, and the leader on 11 April 1927 sent out a call to 'Stop the Flapper Votes Folly'. On 13 April 1927, reporting the Cabinet decision to introduce a Bill to that effect, the paper was shocked, and noted that women voters would be in the majority in practically every constituency if it became law. The Conservatives didn't want it, was the editorial line, nor did the young women. It printed letters from young women who said so, as well as a feature by the leader of the Women's Anti-Suffrage Society. Issues were filled with music-hall jokes about women, debates about whether policewomen were up to the job, and whether women could think. Eventually, the editorial line softened, and more favourable accounts of 'modern woman' began to appear. Jameson's first feature article, 'Problem of Sex in Public Life', appeared in March after a long-running controversy on the feminine cigar, and shared the page with a half-page advertisement for a Silk Stocking Competition, for a prize of one hundred pounds, with a tasteful sketch of a woman in camisole and French knickers reclining on a cushion.[55]

Subtitled 'Strange Antagonisms and Rivalries that Divide Men and Women', and by-lined 'By Storm Jameson, the well-known novelist', the article was a response to a declaration by Hugh Cecil that men and women could not work together. It was a light, funny piece, which played knowingly to readers' prejudices and, with the help of a charming photograph, read like a ticking-off from a delightfully contentious favourite grand-daughter. She was forgiving: 'Ten years ago I might have joined in the indignant shouts of "Reactionary" which greeted this latest Cecil pronouncement, but not today. I am not now nearly sure enough for indignation—on either side.' She was challenging: 'Many a man has not the moral courage of a hen in dealing with his feminine colleagues and subordinates.' On the issue of sexual attraction, she advised that the best mode for a 'really sensible' woman to adopt with a male colleague was arm's length and strictly non-confrontational:

She should learn to avoid choking at butter and wincing at a bullying voice.

And she should acquire as quickly as possible that orderly room tradition which allows a man to remain on excellent terms with another man who has recently slanged him severely.

On 23 May 1927, 'the eminent author and feminist', pictured in an even prettier photograph, presented another piece entitled 'Nothing Wrong with Modern Woman', graced by a subheading from a less than subtle copy-editor: 'Only sceptical of a man-marred world—complete answer to her misanthropic critics.'[56] On 17 May, Austin Harrison, the *Mirror*'s resident ranter, had asked, 'Is Modern Woman Losing Her Ideals?' Jameson thought not. Despite her declared affection for Harrison, who had, she began, encouraged her early essays in criticism, she tore systematically into his assertions that women choose their clothes only to attract men, they copy men, they don't vote and they don't think. She had some sharp comments to make about the lighter, freer clothes worn by modern women, and their stark contrast with men's heavy suits and stuffy shirts (a current talking-point in the paper). But the thrust of her attack was on the political side, where she wrote first as a feminist—a woman earning her own living—and then warned of the imminent challenge to the world men had made:

If [modern woman] no longer gets excited when a Labour man turns Liberal or a Conservative Government exhibits its heart on the wrong sleeve it is not that she does not understand, but that she is becoming sceptical of man's parliamentary gestures. [...]

It is not to be supposed that in a quarter of a century—less than that—modern woman could have made the least impression on this age-old chaos. She has first to discover for herself a code of living suitable to her changed conditions. The rules of conduct that were useful to a protected woman in her drawing room are not in the least useful to me.

I am not being tenderly cared for in a drawing room. I am down among the dust and the shouting with the other bread-and-butter fighters.

She had, she said, as a modern woman, a lot of thinking to do on the personal level before she could address the question of her political ideals.

But you wait, Mr. Harrison. Wait until I've learned my own private lessons. Then I shall have something to say about the way men have mismanaged our world.

[...] But it does not help me—in my efforts to catch up—to be cursed for my knees and my morals. I like my knees as they are, and my morals, as long as they interfere with no other person's happiness, are my own business.

Her writing was fresher, more substantial, and far funnier than that of her fellow-contributors, and in May she was asked whether she would like to write a serial for the paper.[57] The invitation was not followed through to completion, and given the standards set by the current serial writers, this was probably as well.

Figure 12 Valentine Dobrée, writer and painter.

The tumult of those years is captured in Jameson's letters to the writer and painter Valentine Dobrée, wife of Bonamy Dobrée, a friend of Guy's from army days.[58] Bonamy had served in the First World War with the artillery, in France, Egypt, and Palestine. In 1925, the couple had just moved to London, where Bonamy had been appointed lecturer at East London College, part of London University. Between 1926 and 1929, they were in Cairo, where he was Professor of English at the Egyptian University. Valentine, a pupil of the Surrealist André Derain, had exhibited her paintings in the early 1920s with the London Group, and at the Salon des Indépendants. She was a popular figure in London's Bohemian circles, and a friend of Roland Penrose and Dora Carrington. But she first began to acquire celebrity as a writer, hitting the headlines with her treatment of incest in *Your Cuckoo Sings by Kind*, which Jameson edited for her at Knopf.[59] Jameson was godmother to their daughter Georgina, born in 1930, and for many years the two couples exchanged mutual support, advice on writing, publishing contacts, and help in finding jobs.

Jameson's friendship with Valentine was very close. From a holiday in Mullion, Cornwall, regretting the Dobrées' imminent return to Egypt, she wrote that: 'I am going to miss you horribly—and curse Bonamy.'[60] Separation meant a lot of letter-writing, and Jameson wrote freely to her friend of her many frustrations, her constant money worries, and her domestic tangles. In May 1927, she was in Middlesex with Bill, at Harrow Weald Park, while Guy was in Paris, and she complained of domestic life and the Knopf job.

The work was depressing and frustrating for both of them, but she was sternly practical: 'Guy says he must, must, MUST "get out", and at once. I won't let him "get out" until I've saved a thousand pounds.' The *Mirror*'s invitation to write a serial was most welcome in the circumstances, and 'though I may not be able quite to hit that level, I shall try'.[61] A couple of weeks later, the pressures had increased, and Jameson complained she was unable to write anything, not even her *Daily Mirror* serial.[62] Nothing was said of the intermittent pain she was also suffering, which in July 1927 would need an operation.[63]

Things got worse. An invitation in February of the following year to join the Dobrées in Marseilles had to be refused. Alfred and Blanche Knopf had raised some difficulties, and were planning to come to London in April or May. Guy intended to resign his manager's job, and Jameson saw the two of them reduced to living in a cottage in Wiltshire. But she was clinging on to the prospect of joining Valentine in Egypt in a year's time.[64]

The longed-for journey to the East was never to be realised. The Chapmans parted peacefully from the Knopfs in the autumn of the year, having made a new friend in the firm, Philip Jordan, who had just joined.[65] Before they went, there was time to enjoy a few days' holiday relaxing with the Dobrées at their Suffolk house.[66] After that, in November, they spent a couple of weeks at the Spreadeagle and then moved to Whitby. Jameson still couldn't write anything but short stories for the Sunday papers.[67]

Guy's divorce from Doris Chapman finally came to court, and Jameson wrote to Valentine that: 'The last four days I have spent entirely in the Divorce Court, as a witness and sponge-holder, and I am still exhausted by strain, and stunned by contact with a vocabulary and a moral standard that I simply did not know existed.'[68] Guy had sent in his resignation to Knopf, and she had been writing furiously:

I have sent in my shocking novel and written a lecture entitled 'The Georgian Novel and Mr. Robinson'.[69] Also an article entitled (though not by me) 'Can a wife say: "You Shall Be Mine?"' And another called 'Inefficient Wives'. And another (unpublished) called 'The Damnation of Storm Jameson'. Why in the name of God have I no self respect?

The 'shocking novel' she had just finished was *Farewell to Youth*.[70] Nineteen-year-old Nathaniel Grimshaw, an Oxford student sent down in 1914 for a term for a prank, spends the time in London pursuing a girl he secretly marries. She is vain and frivolous, goes out with other men, and asks him to let her divorce him when he comes back from the war, so that she can marry his friend George who's chosen to sit out hostilities in the Foreign Office.

The personal drama—the Chapmans' own, thinly disguised—is framed in a detailed historical narrative. The characters were still actors against a back-drop—Jameson had yet to resolve the problem of embedding the political in the personal—but the political issues raised were acutely contemporary, and carefully analysed, and they represent the beginnings of the larger European historical vision Jameson would display by the end of the 1930s in *Europe to Let*.

In its opening pages, the narrative charts the long European run-up to the First World War. Nathaniel's father James, the first Minister in a new Department of International Intelligence, is an expert in Balkan politics and Franco-German rivalries. He had frequented Bismarck, Clemenceau, Poincaré, and Jaurès, and was sympathetic to exiles, refugees, and revolutionaries such as Kropotkin, Delcassé, and Keir Hardie. But though he knew many great men, he did not believe that they were the makers of history, and his view of history's true agents is echoed in all Jameson's later novels:

[T]he real tale of life came in the end to a peasant stooping over the wrinkled earth, on whose surface the activities of these others made as little mark as did the bodies of the men who had died fighting over it in forgotten centuries and been buried where they died.[71]

In this book, Jameson at last hit her stride in the recovery of historical land-scapes, figuring the life of pre-war London in an atmospheric evocation, through Nathaniel, of the noise and smells of its streets in the gathering dark of the day's end, life evaporating into the scent of decay:

Dusk was thickening in the streets when he had walked as far as Leicester Square, a London dusk in summer, composed of scent, petrol, sweat, lamplight striking up through dusty branches, lengthening shadows falling east out of Piccadilly, noise of motors hurrying between restaurants, clubs and theatres, murmur of voices squeezed thin by the heat of the day, light-shod feet on hot pavements, odours of food, garlic and *vin de maison* escaping from little cafés, scent of roses in the emptying baskets of flower-girls, of women's bodies, of fruit exposed all day on barrows, a mingled incense ascending to the veiled sky of crowded life, corruption and death.[72]

The war—Guy's war—has a section of its own, with graphic accounts of the trench warfare at Beaucourt-sur-Ancre, in November 1916, the vividness it brought to being alive, the comradeship it fostered, the 'protective love' the officer felt for his men, and the revolutionary political sentiments the soldiers of all ranks brought back, to challenge an indifferent nation.[73] For the Second World War, Jameson's landscapes of conflict (in *Cloudless May*, for example), are sites of inherited culture, and the blood that is shed in them has a purpose, which is to save civilisation. In this war, there is no civilisation to save, only a mindless, animal struggle. Like the corrupt and decaying London that sent her sons to war, the landscape of battle is full of stinking bodies, dissolving into another form of corruption:

There was a stench, the breath of corruption, a mixed smell of exploded picric acid, gas, blood, rotting bodies and broken bricks. A murdered house has its own smell.[74]

This is Jameson's first attempt in fiction to understand Europe and its nationalist antagonisms. At a dinner-table of chemists, men from seven nations try and fail to broker a business deal. None of them wants war, and none of them can stop it, though James has always done his best.[75] Precursor of the socialist idealist Henry Smith (*None Turn Back*), James is familiar with the suffering that crowds the roads of blood-soaked Europe, and knows that to be European is to be a participant in exile and death:

The very roads themselves, that must know by heart the pressure of refugees' feet and the cries and tears and blood of the harried, the wounded, and the dying, know no more than he did. He knew every time the armies of the Great War opened an old wound and pressed on old graves. There were moments when it seemed to James that the whole tale of Europe might be compressed into one picture of a peasant dead across his own shattered threshold.[76]

For the first time, too, Jameson explores the triple allegiance of Europeans to their continent, their country, and their locality, and begins to elaborate her vision of the modern European as of necessity both traveller and the creature of home. 'Home' is an increasingly elusive concept. Sitting on the downs about Saints Rew, Nat's family estate, Nat evokes for Ann, his new lover, all the varieties of Englishness that are embodied in all the downs of England, with their wildly different histories. A common English culture has generated radically different landscapes of experience. The downs about Saints Rew remember the Roman legionaries, the Middle Ages, and generations of pilgrims, pedlars, and merchants; they are places of openness, and passing through. At the other extreme, Yorkshire's moors embody recalcitrance and seclusion, a certainty of being and belonging that looks only inward, and closes its doors to the outside world:

Yorkshire was, of all English counties, that one which most obstinately keeps its secrets and wears its English rue with a difference. It savours of itself; harsh, soft, arrogant, tender, teeming, empty, it keeps no memories but its own.[77]

A generational difference is emerging in the identifications that Englishmen choose for themselves. James, despite his protestations, is English before he is European: 'England had perhaps been his only illusion.'[78] His dream of England is lodged in the family home, and he has sacrificed the welfare of both wife and son to keep it going. With the ground of history shifting under his feet, Nat cannot share this fantasy of stability. He is ready to turn his back on Saints Rew, and go his own road.[79]

For Nat, it's enough to have a job, a wife, and the prospect of a son. He doesn't need the old house: and yet, in a strange conclusion, the house still speaks to him. The persistence of the house of tradition, the interplay of home and the road, and the inclusive embrace of the English landscape, are themes that persist in Jameson's fictions through to the 1950s, culminating in her great family saga, *The Green Man*. There the translation of Englishness into the space of the twentieth century will achieve its most substantial representation, between the industry-scarred moors of the North and the horizon of Europe. England's homeland is inward-looking, while Europe offers a more ambivalent destiny. In Europe, there is the closure that comes from the peasant spirit of competition and possessiveness, expressed in the stalemate of the battle-fields. But there is also the star-studded, limitless horizon of the European mind, the shared inheritance of centuries of culture that promises an unending journey towards a shared future.

The Utopia of *The Green Man* was still in the late 1920s a long way beyond Jameson's envisioning, and for the moment, like Nat, she was more than content to travel light.

6

London 1928–Yorkshire 1931: 'Trying to be Superwoman'

Fleet Street Rubbidge

In 1928, the issue for Jameson was one of survival. In October, another contract to supply feature articles for *The Evening News* was a welcome source of extra income. It was a less prestigious commission than the weekly book column offered to J. B. Priestley, that began on 12th October, and that was irritating; but Dorothy Richardson, D. H. Lawrence, and Robert Graves were fellow-contributors, and her reputation, though not enhanced, was not damaged.

She was proudly presented by Rothermere's paper as 'Our contributor, Storm Jameson, one of the most candid and resolute critics of modern ways'.[1] As before, she began systematically turning her own life into copy, but whereas in her fictions this had, at its best, generated an understanding of the deep-seated problems of the age, in her features the tone was that of an entertaining but shrill-voiced guest, swapping clichés around the dinner-party table. 'Bored Wives' attacked housewives who made no attempt to develop independent interests and personalities. 'What Are You Going to Do with Your Boy' sparked a lively correspondence on the relative merits of boarding school and day school. A picture of herself and young Bill accompanied an article on the impossibility, at 35, of successfully combining motherhood and a career ('Which Would You Choose?'), subheaded in the manner that never, apparently, dates, 'Trying to be Superwoman'. 'Who'd be a Woman' was wryly comic about the tyranny of the home and the travails of the modern wife, worn away to 'one quivering ear and an understanding smile'. This is 'The Golden Age of Spinsters', who can go to work, as writers or surgeons, travel, and if they wish, foster children. It's the married women who have the problems, trying to be both married and free.[2]

Figure 13 Jameson and Bill, pictured in *The Evening News*: combining motherhood and a career.

These squibs were redeemed by the last of the whole series, 'The Soul of a Modern Woman', published on 7 January 1929, which was a thoughtful summary of her feelings about her own marriage, and its relation to her current ambitions. Jameson set out her conviction that a woman's priority should be her marriage. She believed, she said, in loyalty, kindness between husband and wife, and service, and thought that a wife working for her husband's success was happier than one working for her own. The sentimentality was undercut by the acid comment that very few men are good enough to generate this degree of loyalty. She expressed her gratitude to 'those early feminists who fought my battles for me before I was born, and battered themselves to weariness on barriers that no longer, thanks to them, exist for me.' She expects high standards from women, but these should not include needless self-sacrifice. The woman with no children owes no duty to an intolerable husband. She should 'leave [her duty] wrapped up in a piece of newspaper with the cold remains of Sunday's dinner and fly for her life'.

She strikes a confessional note that, for all their problems, indicates how completely marriage to Guy had resolved her old insecurities:

When one is very young, it seems immensely important to be right with the world, to be admired, to succeed, to write a book, to be well spoken of. I used to suffer agonies of humiliation at the thought that I had made a fool of myself in company, talked too much or been dumb, or said the wrong things. Life is much simpler now that I can hope, if I am lucky, to be important to one person in my lifetime. But not to more than one. And that, in fact, nothing matters except to be approved of and of supreme moment to one other person. It is terrible to be lonely and to have no refuge. I cannot bear to remember that there are friendless people in the world.

Success is bought at the price of the fatal disease of 'making contacts'. 'It means running about seeing people—preferably people of your own craft—haunting parties and societies, talking and being talked at, keeping yourself under the eye of your world' until 'in the end, distraction sets in, followed by coma and the death of the real self'. More important are 'the essential things –the love of children, the kindness of married love, the warmth of homes, the friendship of books, the healing of sleep in a quiet house. I would sell all I have if I could buy in exchange quietness, and time to live.'[3]

The pitch at the values of the paper's readers is obvious, but it was also what she felt as she wrote, burdened by deadlines and financial pressures. For the moment, 'making contacts' was the only way any writer, however devoted to her marriage, could live.

That devotion had been constantly tested over those past months. While Jameson was writing her potboilers, Guy worked hard at his detested job, lamented his failure as a businessman, and made four or five trips up to Edinburgh's Register House, reading the letters of an old love, the eighteenth-century diarist William Beckford.[4] He took Jameson with him on one of these trips, a week after he left Knopf, in November 1928, and she sorted manuscripts for him while he read more letters.

Around that time, because of her familiarity through Knopf with the London literary scene, she was invited as a prospective witness to give evidence at the trial of Radclyffe Hall for the alleged obscenity of *The Well of Darkness*. She had already signed the letter of protest organised by Arnold Bennett and E. M. Forster, which never reached the press because Radclyffe Hall objected to its emphasising the legal aspects of censorship rather than the literary merits of the book.[5] But she told Radclyffe Hall's biographer, Michael Baker, that she didn't know much about either the writer or her writing, and she couldn't remember whether she had met her before the case. She remembered a few things, like going to meet Virginia Woolf for the first time, to be reassured that the witnesses would not be required to say that Radclyffe Hall's book was great literature. And:

I had a conversation with Radclyffe Hall at the Old Bailey, between the evening and afternoon sessions, of which I only recall that she alarmed me by saying in a powerful voice: I stand for perversion, mental and moral. All the same I felt a genuine respect for her forthrightness and plainness. Una Troubridge—whom I am certain I never saw again—struck me as abominably overdressed and over-made-up.

She had even less information to offer about the literary world of Radclyffe Hall between the wars:

Your letter suggests—forgive me if I mis-read it—that Radclyffe Hall was not the only lesbian writer of that time. (I had not the faintest idea how lesbians amuse themselves— nor have I now) but they can't have been much in evidence. What in fact at the time was the particular literary world Radclyffe Hall inhabited? A world, a small world, of what used to be called immoralists? If it in fact existed I didn't notice it: I'm infinitely less interested in the moral habits of my friends than in the books they write or their other talents or their good or difficult tempers.[6]

It is hard to believe she was completely unaware of the proclivities of such as Sackville-West and Royde-Smith, but her declaration that she cared more about her friends' books than their moral habits rings true. The most memorable part of the affair for her would seem to have been that first meeting with Virginia Woolf, of whom, in deference to Valentine Dobrée, who revered her work, she had begun to speak respectfully, but still with reservations. She liked *Orlando*, she wrote to her friend on 17 November, from the Spreadeagle at Thame, but despite its loveliness and strangeness she felt there was something missing from the book. At the end of the letter, she added, as an afterthought, that Radclyffe Hall had lost her case.[7]

The following month, she had her own problems. Guy discovered that the secretary he had brought with him to Knopf's firm, a Mrs Boyce, had been defrauding him and then the Knopfs for years. Jameson wrote in horror to Valentine from The Spreadeagle on 8 December that Mrs Boyce had stolen £300 from Alfred Knopf, and all the money Guy had. She had deliberately messed up the books, and had lost them all their credit. Guy's book on Beckford had been 'sandbagged', even though it was written and the contract signed with Constable: because of the scandal, the trustees of the Hamilton estate had refused him permission to use the papers. Jameson couldn't afford to go to Egypt, and she must work even harder to straighten things out: 'I shall have to do more journalism. (Just when I was staggering to the end of my Evening News contract!) Oh Valentine. I could cry. [...] I feel so beaten and defeated and <u>burdened</u>.'[8]

By the beginning of January, things had calmed down and the Chapmans were ready to forgive Mrs Boyce. She wrote more cheerfully:

I've finished the Evening News writing the last article (The Soul of a Modern Woman!) on Christmas Day. I have three to do for Britannia, one now and two later, but I have been trying to write a story for a book that is being done for the Prince of Wales for the British Legion. I wanted to write a good one, and I have been at it now for ten days and written 2000 words. It is like digging in wet clay with a blunt spade. Do you suppose my brain is quite gone or merely buried under Fleet Street rubbidge.[9]

But money was now a terrible problem. In the course of 1929 she wrote twice to Hermon Ould, notifying him of her frequent changes of address and apologising for missing a PEN subscription payment—they had needed the money.[10] They lodged uncomfortably in Kent for a few months, at the Spa Hotel in Tunbridge Wells.[11] She was still very much in touch with her London publishing contacts, trying, for one thing, to persuade her editor at Heinemann, Charley Evans, currently publishing *A Richer Dust*, to take on Valentine's book, *The Emperor's Tigers*. Whom failing, Victor Gollancz was a possibility; but in May she wrote reconsidering that idea: 'I am nervous about Gollancz for you. He is such a sharp Jew. I might die, then who would protect you from his fangs?'[12] The casual anti-semitism of her discourse sits strangely, to contemporary ears, alongside the devotion to Jewish refugees Jameson displayed in the war years, but by no means undermines it; throughout their lives, Jameson and Guy spoke without thinking, like the rest of their generation, the language in which they had been brought up.

In the spring or summer of 1929, Jameson bought a house in Whitby, in, Guy said, 'one of her somewhat desperate attempts to settle us'.[13] 'Mooredge' was a small house on the edge of town on Mayfield Road, which led to Aisalby and the moors. Guy found the countryside pleasant but felt himself an alien in the community, and would rather have been in Scotland. Jameson, for all her protestations of affection for her Yorkshire roots and the inspiring view from her study window of the hard line of the hills against the sky, was, by the autumn, at least as unhappy: 'I hate living up here, so far from any civilised voice. As soon as Bill goes to Cambridge (or Oxford) I shall sell this house and fly for my life. I can't stand it. Guy likes it.'[14]

What with autobiographical hindsight could appear as a peaceful interlude of three years, with time to develop her writing, felt then like frustrating isolation, compounded by the difficulties she experienced, from a distance, in getting her latest novels accepted by publishers. To Bonamy Dobrée in November, thanking him for the dedication of a book, she lamented that Heinemann had turned down her last three novels. Constable now being barred to her (Sadleir was still a friend, but by this time, it must be assumed, tired of being played off against other publishing houses), she might now try Chatto, or even Gollancz: 'Gollancz is good, but such a Jew of the Jews.'[15] She wrote to him again on 28 November, telling him facetiously that she was currently writing a new book, a novel influenced by Hemingway and Andrewes, 'in words of one syllable and leaving everything out'.

The Meretricious and Fading Rewards of Novel Writing

The Voyage Home, the second volume of her shipbuilding trilogy, appeared in January 1930, to polite reviews.[16] The fairly conventional format is enlivened by sections evoking the changing relations between workers and employers in the 1880s, with a new spirit of independence among the men, and Mary's own son advocates consultation with them. After a lock-out and a strike, Mary finds herself building a ship the firm can't afford to make sure that the workers' children can eat.[17]

Jameson confided in Bonamy Dobrée her money difficulties, and her growing depression:

[T]he thought of all the things—insurances, school fees, and shoes—I have to squeeze out of my inadequate novels has begun to block the light, until I have scarcely enough left to write so I think I shall try to get a job, but I can't face journalism again. If I'd stuck to an academic life I might have been a professor by now. Dr Jameson sounds well. What a fool I was to run after the meretricious and fading rewards of novel writing. Now I can't even write novels. I shall change my name to Williamson and write about my emotions during a brutalising school life. It should be easy.[18]

Together with Ernest Boyd she published a collection of translations of Maupassant's short stories for Cassell and Company.[19] But expenses still outstripped income. Bill, aged 15, came home in the summer of 1930 from his new public school looking thin and tired, and there was talk of a threatened lung, so she sent him to an expensive English school in Switzerland. He was to stay there till early 1933, when she sent him briefly to Göttingen.[20]

Somehow at this period, she found the time and energy to produce her strange little book *The Decline of Merry England* (1930). Clinging still to the values of the Guild Socialism disseminated by the *New Age*, the text was also influenced by Guy Chapman's interest in economic and cultural history. The book is dedicated to him, and the Preface acknowledges an immense debt to his scholarly help, and to the thought of R. H. Tawney. Tawney's *The Acquisitive Society* (1921) and his *Religion and the Rise of Capitalism* (1926) are both referred to in the text. The celebrated historian wrote on 18 September from his home in Mecklenburgh Square to thank her for the copy she had sent him, and then again, this time from China, on 20 February 1931, to apologise for the brevity of his first note. He had been on the point of leaving for China when the book arrived; he had now read it twice, he said, and found it excellent.[21]

Jameson's book is a history of the Civil War, its personalities, and its religious conflicts. It is a highly personal mixture of ideas and assertions couched in an overblown rhetoric that Guy, a stern critic of her style at this time, can hardly have approved, whatever he thought of the content. Its aim was to show that the Puritan ideal, together with the advent to power of the middle classes after the Civil War, was the source of all the ills of modern society, and the end of happiness in England: 'The city conquered the country.'[22] The outcome was the collapse of a society that had been a smoothly functioning united commonwealth of interdependent persons, classes and institutions, King, Church, and Council. It was shattered by the demands of individual rights and consciences, and by the beginnings of industrialisation and the drive for trade. The world that replaced it was energetic, industrious, disciplined, orderly, and uniform. Traditions were ended, repression installed, and self-interest, money-worship, and mutual contempt between classes replaced the old values: 'Unconsciously, the economist, the moralist and the employer of labour were beginning to look upon the lower classes as not only separated from themselves by a gulf, but as a species of quite a different order in nature.'[23] Jameson's hope is that 'the mediaeval ideal of the commonwealth' might be on its way back.[24] But the former Eikonoklast has little to offer to cure repressions and conflicts apart from a rambling, rose-coloured vision of the life, loveliness, and energy of rural England in Elizabethan times, its rituals and its mirth. In two years' time,

Guy would be registered at the London School of Economics, and she would acquire along with him a more rigorous and realistic understanding of the relationship of culture and the economy, and the nature of rural life.

Looking back was the keynote of her writing in 1930. On 25 October, she began a new novel, *That was Yesterday*, narrating the early years of her first marriage, from Kettering in 1913 to London at the end of 1918.[25] She changed the order of events, left some material out, and wrote in the third person, but didn't, she said, try to hide her humiliations and her flaws. She wanted to know what had become of her during those five years.[26] Guy's influence appeared in her determination to write 'with unromantic plainness'; what she didn't realise at the time was that her change of style was going to lose her one market before she'd got the attention of another, 'my equals'.

The PEN connection was a lifeline. She was flattered by Hermon Ould's invitation to sit on the Selection Committee for the International PEN prize, and the chance it offered to come up to London for meetings.[27] She and Guy were both writing steadily, and she felt that she was learning a good deal about her craft, not least from Valentine Dobrée. She studied Valentine's short stories, and praised the directness of her vision, her easy, sharp and witty style, the economy of her detail, and her vivid precision. In contrast, she said, 'I am so clumsy and when I seem to be precise it is by an effort like an elephant balancing on a bottle in a circus'. But at least, she thought, she had now learned to read well.[28]

But *A Richer Dust* was selling badly. She was increasingly anxious, and determined that if her next book was a failure, she would give up writing and find a job.[29]

She drove herself to finish *That was Yesterday* in June, and found she disliked it intensely. She had been experimenting with a 'modified and un-Joycean' stream-of-consciousness mode, which she had dropped because it was pretentious, but there was, she told Valentine, enough left to be awful.[30] When it appeared, in March 1932, reviewers liked it: 'It does not spare us sordid details and dreary patches but is always alive and sincere.'[31] The voice is relentlessly revelatory, far more in this fiction than in any later avowedly autobiographical text. A selfish, contemptibly weak-willed Penn hits his wife and steals from her. The affair with the American is recounted in detail. Hervey Russell, Mary Hansyke's granddaughter and Jameson's closest and best female persona, makes her first appearance.

As soon as she had finished the novel, she began work on two articles on Man. 'Man the Helpmate' appeared in April 1932, in a collection of essays alongside work by E. M. Delafield, Sylvia Townsend Warner, and Rebecca West. Echoing the harrowing fictional account she had just written of her personal situation, supporting Charles (and, though she would never say this, Guy) in his ambitions and projects, it was a heavily ironic plea for men to take back some of their traditional role of supporting women, and for some more equal division of functions. Women should not be assigned the labour of maintaining material life for both sexes, leaving men alone free to develop their artistic and scientific creativity:

[W]e must practise until it becomes as much in nature for a woman to fly to Australia, compose a symphony, or idle away a month over a single play of Shakespeare's, as it is now for her to run large businesses, argue in Parliament, and combine to reform the world. [...] We must become less competent that men may become more; we must idle, in order to persuade them to work.[32]

Tears of Watery Blood

Guy was unhappy. He still couldn't get Grierson to release the copyright permissions for his life of Beckford.[33] He had finished, in 1930, *A Passionate Prodigality*, his brilliant memoir of the First World War, and no one wanted to publish it. He had editorial work to do for Eyre & Spottiswoode, and had returned to the passion for history that his father had stopped him developing at Oxford. But he was missing London's libraries and its intellectual life. To Valentine, Jameson wrote that: 'Guy is sunk in gloom, and I am writing a novel so gloomy that it positively drips. Tears of watery blood ooze from the page.'[34]

There were certainly times when Guy could rightly blame their lifetime failure to settle down on his wife's 'restlessness',[35] though it's likely that if they could have afforded a cleaner and a cook she would have happily lived in a house rather than hotels. This time, however, she was making progress on a new way of writing, with her novellas, *A Day Off* and *Delicate Monster*.[36] The view from her study window was helping her renew acquaintance with the values she lodged in the world of her childhood, and strengthening the foundation from which she would shortly start writing the *Mirror in Darkness*, with its satires of metropolitan modernity. But his discontent infected her—and perhaps in any case, she herself now needed to be back in London to make public her new directions.[37] At her suggestion, he applied to read economic history at the London School of Economics.[38] It was a decision that would transform both their lives.

Not all was misery. In April, just after the abdication and flight of the King of Spain, she was with Bill in the Basque country, visiting the flooded caves near Sare on the Spanish frontier.[39] There were the pleasures of commitment expressed in local politics. At a moment when the future of the Labour Party was at a crossroads, she became the reluctant chairman of the local Labour Party:

The mainstay of this derisory branch of the party was a family called Reynolds, magnificent people, the salt of the earth—and of the Party: short on doctrine, they had long memories of days when a well-known socialist and his family were more likely than not to go hungry. I loved and respected them. In 1931 we fought that catastrophic election, without help from headquarters [...] and for the first time in that constituency, bottom of the poll though he was, the Labour man did not lose his deposit.[40]

The catastrophic election was that of 27 October 1931, when Ramsay MacDonald and his National Coalition were returned to power with 554 seats to Labour's 52. In the Autumn, Jameson was in Scarborough at the Labour Party Conference, with everyone cast down at having had to swallow Ramsay MacDonald's betrayal.[41] *Journey from the North*, while expressing distaste for Arthur Henderson, the new leader of the Labour Party, includes no details of Henderson's manipulation of Conference. (According to Allen Hutt, he brushed aside discussion of the circumstances that led up to the Government's crash, and complaints of 'the lack of contact and confidence between the Executive and the membership on the one and between the Parliamentary Party and the Cabinet on the other [...]'. Hutt suggests that Henderson would himself have supported a national coalition had there been better consultation.)[42] Instead, Jameson writes about the people she met, vivid embodiments of the political styles and positions now emerging in England and Europe.

Against the smug selfishness of the Labour leadership, she could set a glimmer of hope. Lilo Linke, poor, beautiful, and a fiery socialist, brought with her from East Berlin a contempt for old men and an enthusiasm for change that reminded Jameson of her own iconoclastic youth. They immediately became close friends. Lilo for Jameson was the 'Younger Brother' of fairytale, brimming with life and enthusiasm, always successful, and always loved. In every sense: *Journey from the North* evokes her advocacy of free love, and in the uncut version Jameson speaks of Lilo's 'intense sexuality' and the lovers she found across Europe. In Berlin, there was an affair with her editor, Gustav Stolper, sanctioned by his wife, and later, in London, a violent and stormy affair with Thomas Balogh, the Hungarian-born economist.[43]

The final months of 1931 saw the beginning of a contentious exchange with Ethel Mannin, the popular romantic novelist, whose life and career to this date might be considered a sunnier version of Jameson's. In December, a letter from Chatto and Windus, who were preparing to publish *Delicate Monster*, expressed fears of a possible libel claim from Mannin.[44]

Libel was a fashionable concept. On 3 March 1927, the Daily Mirror reported that Lord Gorrell was moving in the Lords the second reading of his Law of Libel Amendment Bill, and that: 'In recent years members of the reading public had begun to see that it was possible to make money out of the chance circumstance that some character in a story a play or a poem applied to themselves, and writers had been threatened with libel actions.' For a writer like Jameson, whose characters were always syntheses of physical and moral traits, words and phrases, drawn from people observed in her family or social circles—a kaleidoscopic, or prismatic mode of creation—it was inevitable that resemblances at some stage might be noted and challenged. It was still disconcerting. Her first draft of a reply to Harold Raymond at Chatto almost admitted poking fun at Mannin's 'philosophy', which, she argued, was in any case hardly an exclusive one. But the version she finally sent said unequivocally that she had tried hard to avoid all resemblance to anyone, and her heroine was simply a type. She asked whether she should show Mannin the proofs of the story, and tell her that it had been thought that the heroine's views on education might refer to hers. She didn't herself think that was necessary.[45] This seems to have satisfied Raymond, who wrote back setting out advances and royalties.[46] Jameson sent her proofs to Mannin's home on Wimbledon Common, and was stunned by the ferocity of her response.

With more force than tact, Jameson wrote back, beginning 'My dear Ethel, I honestly think you're mad', and denying all the similarities Mannin had found in the text.[47] The following day, she wrote in calmer mood, and addressed Mannin's complaint that Jameson's heroine, like Mannin herself, had a lover who committed suicide, by referring her to a first version with *four* suicides in it, and noting her own accidental overdose of phenacetin at college. She listed changes she was prepared to offer, but robustly refused to change her references to her heroine's advocacy of free love; that too came from her own experience.[48]

Mannin suggested that Jameson rewrote her material, and the text be published with a prefatory exchange of letters setting out their opposing views on Mannin's 'philosophy'.[49] Jameson requested the return of her proofs, and as soon as she got them refused all Mannin's suggested revisions and suggested their common friend May Edginton be asked to arbitrate. Mannin refused to bite. With American publication now imminent, Jameson notified her that she would revise her text in accordance with the changes she had offered in her letter of December 29th.[50] On the same day, she wrote to her friend A. D. Peters ('Peter') to say that Mannin had rejected her request for a preface to the book

for a reason I ought to have thought of myself. 'Why should she use her real and increasing reputation to bolster up my lesser one?' She says I'm the clearest case of sexual frustration she knows of except Rose Macaulay and she means to clear the writing world of all such jealous withered ghosts. I do think this belongs to the Ho Hum department—although I feel very old I don't feel disembodied.[51]

It was, by the end, quite a pleasant little spat, in which Jameson clearly felt she had come off best. No libel writ emerged.

PART II

Socialism and Internationalism: The English Road to Europe

In the past there have been little Englanders (one has a pen in her finger writing the words), in love with an England which never was but could be, and, as if opposing them, internationalists of a country no smaller than Europe. It is time for the two dreams to grow together [...] a settled Europe, with England at its heart. [...] It is therefore our duty, and it should be our pleasure, to assume the responsibility, and show the bogged and strayed nations of Europe a road to follow.[1]

7

London 1932–1934: New People, New Politics

The 1930s was to bring a complete transformation of Jameson's intellectual and political horizons. Her ideological commitment to the virtues of the North would be as firm at the end of the decade as at the beginning. The cataclysm that rocks the world in *The World Ends*, the apocalyptic novel she wrote in 1937 under the pseudonym of William Lamb, leaves untouched one small height in the Yorkshire Dales, just outside Thirsk, from which civilisation will—perhaps—start again. She began the 1930s fighting the lost cause of 'real' Labour against the Ramsay MacDonalds. She would end it still fighting for social justice, against the official leaders of the Labour Party and the Trades Unions as much as against bosses and financiers. But by the end of the decade the platform from which she spoke would be wider and higher, and she would be addressing the world from the heart of PEN, alongside the liberal left gathering in London from every country in Europe, on behalf of European intellectual freedom and social reform.

It was a decade of intellectual journeys, inspired by the academic circles Guy enrolled in at the London School of Economics, the new political and journalistic connections they both made, the European writers Jameson encountered through PEN, and a younger generation of engaged English writers. She rediscovered the excitement of her youth before the First World War, meeting at last a later generation of younger men and women who could join hands and ideals with Class 1914. It was also a decade of real journeys, with travels in France and Germany, Spain, and Central Europe, which was the frontier, she wrote, of European civilization. Vienna is 'as far east as an Englishman can go without losing touch completely with a tradition, only partly Christian, which holds in one and the same hand even countries hostile to each other'.[2]

In this renewal of old ideals, a lot of her old innocence had gone. The more she saw and thought about Europe, the more she saw and feared the approach of another war. The continuing derelictions of European leaders threw into relief—if relief were needed—the oppressive and repressive complacency of England's rulers, accepted without demur by a public that preferred, for the most part, to keep its eyes and minds shut. She might dream of peace and justice in an England at the heart of a just and peaceful Europe. She saw and wrote about the reality, the growing 'moral stench' at home and abroad: 'On one side Dachau, on the other the "distressed areas" with their ashamed workless men and despairing women.'[3]

Europe at the Edge

In January 1932, the Chapmans went to Berlin and stayed there through to the end of March.[4] Early visitors to the Weimar Republic, they joined a few other observers, mostly journalists, including their friend, the freelance journalist Harrison Brown, who wrote for the *Evening Standard* and the *News Chronicle*. All were looking for insights into the mood of a deeply divided Germany, in the weeks before Hindenburg's first-round success in the Presidential election of 13 March (confirmed by the second round on 10 April) tipped a delicate political balance. Guy described in his memoirs a society living in extremes and contradictions: 'bloody quarrels between socialist workers and Nazis [...] high unemployment and hunger, and at the same time all urban pleasures on offer at a low price.'[5]

Alfred Knopf, in Berlin on the lookout for new Weimar authors, bought them an expensive lunch at Horcher's, later to become famous as Goering's favourite restaurant, surviving under his protection until late in the Second World War, when Goebbels finally managed to close it down. Jameson refused to feel guilty about enjoying such indulgence, and took the chance to make a new contract for her novels.[6] They stayed in a large attic room in a pension on the Kurfürstendamm, run by a Frau Doktor Broesike, strident in her dislike of Hitler, and Lilo Linke showed them round a very different Berlin from that inhabited by American millionaires. They attended with her the election meeting for Thälman, the Communist candidate. Guy thought it was all empty rhetoric, though he also acknowledged feeling the 'sense of menace' on the streets.[7] Lilo took them one evening to the home of some impoverished Communist friends, and argued vehemently the social democratic case for supporting Hindenburg, who she was confident could keep Hitler in check.

An invitation to dinner from Lilo's editor Gustav Stolper and his wife Toni, along with the American journalist Edgar Mowrer (all three became great friends of the Chapmans), and a banker and an industrialist, saw no one but Stolper convinced that Hitler was containable. But another old-fashioned musical evening, with Schiller, Bach, and the rituals and courtesies of half a century ago, suggested the persistence of another Germany in which Hitler might still prove irrelevant. Jameson was left, as she later ruefully admitted, with the impression of a country fragmented, chaotic, and feverish, which was no threat to the rest of Europe.[8]

Only one year later, the balance of the situation would change. John Lehmann, staying with Christopher Isherwood in Berlin in February 1933 during the elections that put Hitler into power, noted how rapidly he had captured the support of those respectable, traditionalist middle classes. He recalled how, a few days before the flames of the Reichstag lit the Berlin sky:

All over Berlin, especially in the middle-class shopping and residential districts, huge pictures of Hitler were displayed at night in windows illuminated by devout candles. As I wandered along the streets with Christopher, muffled up to the eyes against the flaying wind, the crude likenesses of the Man of Germany's Destiny, row upon row above us, were like altars dedicated to some primitive demon-cult, and seemed to menace far more terror than had been conceivable in the rational, easy-going atmosphere of London.[9]

Lehmann tried, as Jameson would do later, and with as little success, to alert a British public lulled by the damaging complacency of the BBC and the press:

[W]hen a broadcast by Vernon Bartlett on the new Germany was reprinted in *The Listener*, I wrote a letter in which I denied all his hopeful and comforting conclusions and said roundly that Hitler's success meant war sooner or later and we should very quickly find the treaties torn up in our faces. From that moment, it seemed to me desperately urgent to do all in one's power to help build some kind of dam against this torrent that was sweeping down towards war, and in spite of governments if governments were too half-hearted about it. [...] I experienced for the first time the strange paradox of life maintaining its smooth and smiling surface while out of sight thousands were being tortured and broken, and edifices of political liberty that had taken generations to build up were being sent crashing to the ground.[10]

Vernon Bartlett, a journalist on the *Daily Mail* and the *Times* as well as a regular broadcaster on the BBC, friend of Léon Blum, Ernest Bevin, and Beaverbrook, had for ten years, in the 1920s, been director of the London office of the League of Nations. He had been far less hopeful when he spoke to the Chapmans, in the late summer of 1932. On a walking holiday in Yorkshire, he had called in shortly before they moved to London, to say that: 'The next six months will say whether we're to have another war or not. If the Disarmament Conference fails and if we fail over Japan there isn't a shred of hope left.'[11] The Geneva Disarmament Conference, which had opened in February, did fail, Germany left it on 14 September, and Japan moved on from its annexation of Manchuria into invasion of China, in the teeth of international protest. But there were still six months to go before the advent of the terror that opened Lehmann's eyes, if not Bartlett's, and for the time being, the Chapmans had their own nearer concerns to occupy them.

The London School of Economics

Guy took up his place at the LSE in the Autumn of 1932, and the couple left Whitby in September for a small flat in St John's Wood that Jameson had taken on a three-year let. 139 New Abercorn Flats, Abercorn Place, London NW8, was a service flat with a restaurant downstairs, ideal for residents with no time or inclination to cook. The house in Whitby was kept on until halfway through Guy's last year at the LSE. It was the place they spent the long vacations, where Jameson could write in peace.

In 1917, Athenais had found economics lectures at the LSE disappointingly conservative, and written her own Marxist versions. In 1932, the tone of the institution was set by the charismatic political scientist Harold Laski, an ardent socialist far to the left of the Labour leadership and an energetic and vociferous opponent of all things Conservative. Naomi Mitchison describes him turning up to Dick Mitchison's first outing as a Labour candidate in the 1931 General Election, at King's Norton, one of many candidacies he supported at that important moment, and telling her: 'You just press a button and I make a speech.'[12] In this world, Jameson was totally at home, as she made plain to the Leeds student who interviewed her for *The Gryphon* in November 1936:

I am a Socialist because I believe that the capitalist system is no longer capable of using the technical and scientific achievements of our age as they should be used [...]. But I do not know that my socialism is altogether in favour with the present leaders of the

Labour Party. I should like every student to read a pamphlet by Professor L. Hogben, professor of Social Biology at the London School of Economics. It is called 'The Retreat from Reason,' costs 2/-, and is published by Watts.[13]

Guy Chapman was registered in the Economic History department, where Richard Henry Tawney had taken up the Chair in 1931, the year he published *Equality*. Tawney, Guy was pleased to recall, had recommended his admission after an interview in his room in Mecklenburgh Square, arranged by W. E. Williams, an influential figure in adult education, later to become Secretary of the Arts Council.[14] Williams, together with his wife, was a close and helpful friend to both the Chapmans, and provided important institutional contacts in both adult education and cultural politics. Tawney had worked for the Workers Education Association since 1905, and been its President since 1928. Like Guy, he had fought in the War (as a Sergeant, in the 22nd Manchester Rifles), and he had been wounded at the Somme in July 1916.[15] He was delighted by the vigour of Jameson's writing ('She writes like a devil', he commented on *A Day Off*),[16] and she transferred to him the admiration that twenty years before she had given to Orage. A close and affectionate friendship soon developed, and the Chapmans often stayed with Tawney and his wife Jeanette, William Beveridge's sister, in their Cotswold cottage, on the road between Stroud and Birdlip.[17]

The radical shift in Guy's political commitment, evoked in Nicholas Roxby's conversion to socialism in *Love in Winter*, was a response to Tawney's idealism. Tawney was, Guy said, 'the only man who moved me to a serious belief in distributive socialism: it may be humanly impossible, but it is the only human dream worth dreaming. An aristocrat of the oldest English stock, [... he] hated inequality. He hated it with the involuntary distaste of a Christian gentleman for the vulgarian and self-seeker—"class privilege, the gross inequalities of wealth on which it exists, are not only a hideously uncivilised business, but an odious outrage on the Image of God".'[18] Tawney would shortly, merged with Laski, become the R. B. Tower of *In the Second Year*, the radical socialist intellectual in London University that even the National State Party dared not touch. And as late as 1957, his commitment to workers' education would feed into the figure of Mr Thorgill, the old organiser who maintains the English socialist tradition that still endures when Communism has revealed its totalitarian face (*A Cup of Tea for Mr Thorgill*, 1957).

To Tawney's influence was joined that of the economic historian Eileen Power, a medieval specialist, who often came with her husband to dinner at

Abercorn Place, and the French scholar, Wilfred Pickles. It was Pickles, Guy said, who first made him understand the distinctive nature of the French economy, whose forms were still shaped by older ways of life: '[France's] agriculture and industry, and the persistence in it of the traditional life of town and country, which changed everything I was thinking about.'[19] This was an important insight also for Jameson. It provided the intellectual substance behind the nostalgic vision of France that would develop in her writing throughout the 1930s, and through to the end of the coming war.

This France was an icon of organic community. It preserved a sense of wholeness, of respect for the simply human, and an appreciation of simple everyday life that had vanished from an England sold out to 'modernity'. In May 1930, sitting in a copse by Whitby, the place she had thought the safe centre of her Englishness, Jameson had experienced her first moment of dryness as a writer, and she immediately associated that with the damage being done to English literature and society by industrial and commercial values, marketing and advertising, and her growing sense that the civilisation she knew was about to collapse into another war.[20] She needed a new landscape to sustain her creative imagination. The process of its discovery had already begun in *The Triumph of Time*, which embedded in Whitby's shipbuilding past scenarios of flights to France, to Bordeaux and Dieppe, based on recent visits with Guy and old memories of visits as a child, with her mother. The next war would complete the process. By 1945, Jameson had merged her inherited Whitby landscape with her adopted landscape of France, where even after the war organic community seemed to resist the depredations of industry and commerce. In the *Journal of Mary Hervey Russell*, the prehistoric caves of Vézelay, the flickering light of the Loire, and the old towns on the river's banks, are the frame in which old England, and the ghosts of her English family, are brought back to life, to join her in the hopeful vision of a new beginning.

In *Parthian Words*, at the end of her writing life, she would confess that this was a 'romantic notion' of France. But in the early 1930s, it was a lifeline, representing a mode of living with the modern world that was arguably economically and politically achievable. As the next war drew closer, France was the vital symbol of values that had to be defended. In the late 1960s, when she cut radically the typescript of *Journey from the North*, tipping its balance from autobiography into memoir, the heart of the text would become the imaginative constructs she created in the 1930s, to represent the rival challenges offered to Europe by two polarised national cultural landscapes. Against

Weimar Germany, represented by the urban energies of Berlin in 1932, collapsing into the violent cruelties of Vienna in 1938, stands the unchanging rural peace of France. This retrospective refocusing in the 1960s was of course again dictated by political context: this time, contemporary debates over the construction of a new European order.

The Chapmans' insights into the politics behind the news extended radically in the early 1930s. Around 1933, Guy joined a group of journalists and foreign correspondents who lunched together regularly in the Commercio restaurant on Mondays, right up to 1940.[21] Most of them were destined for glittering careers in different areas of foreign affairs. Among journalists, besides Vernon Bartlett, there was the Francophile Bill Casey, a member of the foreign leader-writing staff of *The Times*, who would shortly take a stand with fellow-journalists against *The Times*'s notorious appeasement of Hitler. In 1941, he would become deputy editor of the paper, and in 1948, its editor.[22] Gerald Barry, celebrated for his stand against Beaverbrook in 1930 in the name of independent journalism, was then editor of the *Week-End Review*, soon to merge with the *New Statesman and Nation*, at which point he joined the board of directors. In 1934, he became features editor of the *News Chronicle*, for which Jameson occasionally wrote, and in 1936 its managing editor.[23] Clifford Norton was in the Foreign Office, private secretary to the powerful Robert Vansittart, then Permanent Under-Secretary of State, who would become Chief Diplomatic Adviser to the Foreign Secretary from 1938 to 1941. Norton himself was to be nominated to Poland as chargé d'affaires in 1938–9, Ambassador to Bern in 1942, and in 1946, Ambassador to Athens.[24] Philip Jordan was one of the party, the old friend who had joined them at Knopf in their last year. His exemplary socialist credentials would shortly earn him consignment to the concentration camp in Jameson's novel *In the Second Year*.

'London at that time was a listening post for the ambiguous voices coming out of Europe', and a multitude of voices collected in the Chapmans' service flat in St John's Wood.[25] Two different social circles developed there. Guy's account in his memoirs distinguishes between talk with 'our' friends, foreign correspondents, English and foreign, liberal journalists and Left politicians, including Aneurin Bevan, to which Jameson formed a silent but appreciative audience,[26] and the visits of the refugees and exiles who came to see his wife from 1933 onwards, after Hitler came to power. The latter were Social Democrats and Communists, some sent by Lilo Linke, some coming through Jameson's PEN connections, some perhaps also coming through the LSE, to which many

Jewish academic refugees gravitated. These Guy left her to feed and console while he retreated to his study, acknowledging fretfully her generosity:

> During those years she poured away her energy, of body and mind, like a woman care-lessly emptying out a bowl of water. The physical squandering was the less important, she was astonishingly resilient, but the other was pure unforgivable irreparable waste. [...] I doubt that I could have checked her if I had tried: she was, as she is, incapable of the saving egoism of your dedicated writer.[27]

Guy himself seems to have been allocated a healthy dose.

The Politics of Pacifism

While this was going on behind the scenes, Jameson's public political activity in the early years of the 1930s was most attached to the cause of pacifism.

The period from 1931 to 1932 was the 'pinnacle of pacifist political optimism during the interwar period'.[28] With apparently hopeful prospects of collabora-tion with the League of Nations and disarmament movements throughout Europe, pacifism seemed to be the most effective rallying-point for reforming British intellectuals. It was not a point where harmony reigned, and still less so, unity. Following Germany's walk-out from the Geneva World Disarmament Conference, and the important demonstration for disarmament organised by the League of Nations Union (LNU) at the Albert Hall on the 15 November 1932, the movement was divided between the socialist pacifists, concerned '[to] relate their views to what the 1931 political crisis had led them to believe was an incipient revolutionary situation in Britain', and the rest:

> [...a] heterogeneous collection of 'extreme' pacifists—Gandhi (or, more accurately, his British disciples), Ponsonby, Einstein, the Peace Army, and popular intellectuals such as Nicholls, Joad, and Storm Jameson—who were either enthusiasts for the as yet largely unexplored orientation of non-violence or spokesmen for the still surprisingly neglected humanitarian inspiration for pacifism, or both.[29]

Within these, Ceadel puts Jameson with the humanitarian pacifists, describing Beverley Nicholls, Cyril Joad, and herself as the best-known converts of 1931–2.[30]

Jameson had always seen a case for pacifism. In 1919, presenting in *The New Commonwealth* the forthcoming serialisation of *The Happy Highways*, she had discussed one of her pacifist characters: 'I come [...] of a fighting family. I lost my brother during the war, and naturally all my inclinations are on the side of those who took part in it. But there is everything to be said for the honest paci-fist.'[31] In that novel, the pacifism of the working-class Kersent was sympathetically treated, especially when he died in prison as a conscientious objector, but pacifist arguments from feminists and Christians were dismissed with contempt, as self-aggrandising positions. The novel's sympathy was with Captain Joy, the narrator, who acknowledged that war is wicked, but still said justice had to be fought for.

Jameson's pacifism was not simply humanitarian. Her socialist convictions were always part of her pacifist perspectives—though equally certainly, she could not be associated with the members of the Communist Party who urged workers to resist going to war on behalf of right-wing governments whose greatest antagonism was to Soviet Russia. She was clear-sighted in the distinc-tion she made in her account of an early meeting she attended of the Writers' Committee of the Anti-War Council, in October 1933 or 1934, in a flat close to Buckingham Palace:

Every person in that shabby room was against war and against Fascism. Only the middle-aged Communist with the nose like a spiral of discoloured flesh separating his tired eyes knew that this was a contradiction in terms.[32]

Her own socialism had nothing to do with defending Russia, as she frequently insisted. It came from a larger conviction that workers should not be delegated to fight wars conducted on behalf of profit.

There was, of course, a strong emotional dimension to Jameson's pacifism, and Ceadel is right to point out how her first attempt at autobiography, *No Time Like the Present*, published in 1933, unexpectedly turned into 'an out-spoken anti-war polemic'.[33] This was not, Bonamy Dobrée pointed out in his review, a fault, but rather a key structural element, an indication of the pas-sion of the autobiographical subject that made for compelling and challenging reading.[34] The passion was political as much as emotional, or humanitarian, as Sylvia Townsend Warner recognised:

It is a book Communists should read. Even if they disagree with some of the matter, they can learn good lessons from the method. [... It is] written with a white-hot appear-ance of coldness, with a fury of the intellect, with an intolerance of half-measures, with no politeness whatever.[35]

Jameson recalls that she started on her memoir '[to] convey the spirit of my generation, subtle (because we were the last children of a social order founded on peace and expanding markets), and easily pleased'.[36] One-third through the book, the description of a generation logically leads to an urgent explanation of why it matters how they were, and what they thought and did, and then to an indictment of what a corrupt present is making of their innocent, heroic past. Sorrow for the loss of the dead, and sympathy for the anguish of the survivors, generates an outpouring of personal feeling in which the keynote is the desire for social justice that was the hallmark of Class 1914. The iniquity of child poverty and the disarmament talks in Geneva in that same year (1933), where England failed miserably to push disarmament through, are two sides of the same coin. Simply disarming, or proliferating pacts, will never end war:

War is only made less probable by changing the social conditions in which the seeds of wars are nursed to maturity. If the governments were to pay more, and more intelligent and unprejudiced attention to settling in a new spirit the problem of poverty and its results in social and economic instability at home and less to debating with each other on the quantity of the destructive weapons in their hands, the chances of another war would really recede.[37]

The emotion finds another channel, in an attack on the hypocrisy of contemporaries—Churchmen, and bellicose intellectuals—who advocate wars they expect others to fight. There is increasing fury in her tone, fuelled by the guilt of the survivor, and, more cogently, the non-participant: 'Here someone looked over my shoulder to see what I had written and said: "You keep talking about war as if it were the end, but we did, you know, survive the last." '[38] The 'someone' will have been Guy, whose quietly heroic *A Passionate Prodigality*, completed in Whitby in 1930, was at last published in 1933, and who later noted that the fear of war 'filled a larger place in her mind than in mine'.[39] But it's only just, she argues, that Churchmen and intellectuals will probably also die in the coming war, and civilians be subject to bombing raids and chemical attacks: 'War is more decent when we are all [...] involved in it and not sheltering behind the young men we push and encourage to fight for us.'[40] The focus of attack switches to capitalism, and the profits nations make from armaments. Jameson was lining up for her forthcoming attack in the *Mirror in Darkness* trilogy on the William Garys of the world, the businessmen who pay the scientists who make the gases and bombs. Women's collusion is addressed, and Jameson is equally offended by the women who hand out white feathers and the 'feminists' who claim their equal right to fly planes and drop bombs. The final question she addresses is a personal one: whether, if war were to break out next year, she would tell her son not to fight. But the answer is political.

Yes, she would, because war does not advance socialism; it produces the breakdown of civilisation. After the last war, none of the promised brotherhood of the trenches found its way onto factory floors. What is needed is not war, but 'a social order which does not require war as a solvent'.[41]

What Jameson wrote in her autobiography in the 1930s was far stronger in socialist terms than the account she would give of herself in the 1960s. In *Journey from the North*, it is her personal, emotional response to the approach of war that is highlighted, as she tracks moments of private terror: waiting in Berlin in 1932 for Hindenburg to win the election, hearing the note of fear in Lilo's letters from Berlin after February 1933, following Hitler's accession to power, listening to Harrison Brown back from Berlin in 1933, in the Café Royal, talking about Hitler's plans for the Jews—and, equally chilling, about *The Times*'s refusal to print his reports—and finally, watching the refugees arrive.[42] But whether a son should be required to fight was not yet a real issue. Bill, 17, was still at school in Germany, in Göttingen, and the question was, more simply, whether he should be brought home in view of the unrest. She wrote to express her concern to Vernon Bartlett, and seek his advice; and in the next sentence, she invited Bartlett to dinner. The edge of a mother's anxiety was not especially sharp.[43] She indicated no anxiety at all in the letter she wrote to Valentine Dobrée the following day, and Bill came home safely, with no stories of Nazi persecutions to tell.[44]

History, like historians, has a habit of requiring subjects to shape themselves to fit tidy categories, or take sides, when day-to-day reality is generally a matter of messy choices on the way to a vaguely-defined goal. The goalposts may not always shift, but the field of play often does. In the 1930s, Jameson's political ideals had to come to terms with the confused and compromised nature of everyday experience. She later admitted to long vacillation after 1933 in her pacifist commitment, and blamed it on a divided mind and a desire not to offend people she liked and respected, whether pacifists or supporters of the League of Nations: 'My only immoveable conviction was my loathing of war.'[45] Such honesty is welcome, and she certainly never spared herself in active work for the cause; but it could make her seem duplicitous and shallow, in comparison with contemporaries who built their pacifist careers on the profession of more absolute principles.

One of the latter kind was Vera Brittain, with whom Jameson now formed a close friendship—one that brought her as close as she ever came to the inner circles of interwar feminism. The two exchanged letters in September 1932, after Jameson published an extract from the forthcoming *No Time Like the Present*, in *The New Clarion*, and a period of joint log-rolling began.[46] Jameson reviewed Brittain's *Testament of Youth* in the *Sunday Times* in September 1933, and said that as a representation of war from a woman's perspective 'its mere pressure on mind and senses makes it unforgettable'.[47] The following month, she wrote a warm letter in Brittain's defence in the *New English Weekly*, provoked, she said, by a sense of the journal's unfairness in having allowed two reviewers, in consecutive weeks, to attack the book. Its only fault, according to Jameson, was to portray a generation of deluded patriots, who learned pacifism too late. The book was 'honest, unsparing of the writer, and, surely, inspired by pity and a horror of war'.[48] Brittain returned the compliment the following year by including a mention of *No Time Like the Present* in her essay 'Can the Women of the World Stop War?' The answer was that by and large they are too lethargic to try, although:

A few organized women, such as the members of the Women's International League, are working nobly and continuously. One or two women writers—Miss Storm Jameson, for instance, whose brilliant *No Time Like the Present* was one of the outstanding books of 1933—constantly urge upon their readers the waste and futility of war.[49]

Brittain was one of the contributors roped in for the collection of essays, *Challenge to Death*, that in the Autumn of 1933 Jameson agreed to edit for Philip Noel-Baker.[50] Her experience in advertising, and in netting authors for Knopf, proved invaluable in lining up contributors. She kept two letters of refusal, one from Hugh Walpole, who pleaded ignorance of economics and inability to write propaganda, and another from Aldous Huxley, who said he had no time, and did not think that intellectual arguments for peace could win over anyone not already convinced. The thrills of hatred supplied by nationalist ideologies, such as Nazism, compensations for those who felt themselves inferior, had no equivalent, he thought, in the kindnesses of pacifism.[51]

Vernon Bartlett, who since January 1934 had new responsibilities as diplomatic correspondent for the *News Chronicle*, tried to resist. A letter from Mooredge swept him into compliance, with the mixture of hyperbolic flattery and stern efficiency which characterised Jameson's organisational style:

My dear Vernon, quite honestly I don't know who else could write that chapter. This is apart from (1) my personal wish to have you in my book and (2) the glory of your name, which I want for the book. The technical side of Disarmament need not be in any way emphasised. We'll probably get too much of that from P.N.B. [Philip Noel Baker]. You deal with principles.

I shall wipe from my mind all your reservations and write your name on the Draft, with the others. You have the 2-3 months to write it. I do think it is worth doing, and it is a good team of writers. And even if we are fighting a lost cause it is something which has to be done.[52]

Bartlett's reward for his efforts was an even more effusive letter of admiration and gratitude:

To be able to think with such lucidity, and to write so compressed and impressive a chapter in the middle of the strain in which you must be working—it is amazing. [...] It is much the best of the 10 chapters I have had, and you wrote it hanging by a foot to a giant wheel. I am deeply grateful.[53]

Challenge to Death appeared in 1934, carrying in its front pages a pair of advertisements for two other Constable publications, which between them show how eclectic were Jameson's networks at this time. Anna Eisenmenger's *Blockade: The Diary of an Austrian Middle Class Woman, 1914–1924,* was accompanied by an extract from a review in the *Manchester Guardian*, which made much of the difference between narratives of trench warfare and this tale for the human heart, arguing that: 'If war is to be abolished it will probably be by women, who alone have the courage to take risks and the fanaticism needful for the great missionary enterprise.' *Regiment Reichstag. The Fight for Berlin, January 1919*, with its Introduction by Michael Sadleir, a tale of heroics rather than the human heart, was accompanied by an extract from Jameson's own review in the *New English Weekly*, praising the publisher for making available 'German books and novels of this importance'.

The list of contributors reflected the diverse networks Jameson could now call on for support. Alongside herself and Guy Chapman figured the names of Vera Brittain and her husband George Catlin, Winifred Holtby, Rebecca West and Mary Agnes Hamilton, Philip Noel Baker, Gerald Barry and Vernon Bartlett, Edmund Blunden, Ivor Brown, Gerald Heard, Julian Huxley, and J. B. Priestley. Viscount Cecil's Foreword successfully harmonised the range of positions represented, arguing broadly against nationalism and in favour of co-operation and collective action, led by the League of Nations, and the 'common system of international justice' for which the League stood.[54] He did not rule out the possibility of war, but it would be a war conducted under the aegis of the League of Nations, to prevent an individual national aggressor from turning to force to secure its own interests:

If the nations are to agree to co-operate for the maintenance of peace and the advancement of prosperity it is evident that some measures must be arranged to deal with a nation that breaks away from its agreement and tries by violence to force its neighbour to accept its demands. Questions may arise as to the nature of the pressure to be exercised against the covenant-breaking aggressor. But whatever it may be, it must be the result of collective and not individual action.

Jameson's opening contribution, 'The Twilight of Reason', was in line with Cecil's sentiments. Something of a rant, it piled up clichés. Germany's resentment was the natural consequence of the humiliation forced on it by the Treaty of Versailles, whose terms were the natural consequence of the Acquisitive Society (Tawney's term), general disrespect for reason ('The philosophy of Bergson, the novels of D. H. Lawrence, the infection of every country by jazz, are all in their different degree symptoms of this disrespect, and furtherers of it'),[55] the fashion for unrepressed emotion, and most of all the drum-beat of nationalism, with its refusal to submit to the laws of the international community. She touched in lightly the idea of an armed League, favoured by both Cecil and Noel-Baker, recognising the clash with pacifist idealism, but seeking to reformulate the issues at stake: 'Let us not say: "Will you choose war or peace?" Let us say: "Will you choose the sovereign independence of your country, armed to enforce its rights, or will you choose peace?" '[56]

Her closing essay, 'In the End', was sharper and better. The psychology of war, she said, was best explained from a socialist position, that would take account of different class perspectives: 'Even to a man who experienced it with reluctance, war can seem more decent than to be living in the purlieus of a mechanical civilisation with its trail of half-fed children and men "economised" into misery. [...] The Acquisitive Society perpetuates the existence of irresponsible classes. War is the final solution of their mindless and irresponsible activities, and their wasted or unsatisfied passions.'[57] She proposed a different solution. Taking up a new position, uniting the dreams of both little Englanders and internationalists, would destabilise the economic interests currently vested in nationalist politics, and create 'a settled Europe, with England at its heart'.[58]

For Jameson, this was an important and prescient book, which identified Europe as the working horizon for her generation, and made 'an eloquent plea for a united Europe'.[59] War was drawing closer, but the company she was keeping was full of enthusiasm and vitality:

I should be lying if I pretended that I spent much time feeling anxious. Incidents like these were icy jets rising to the surface from an underlying terror. The surface itself was as lively as a June sea, splinters of light piercing the water, leaping, breaking, re-forming. What I remember about unnumbered evenings at this time is, first of all, an immense liveliness and gaiety.

I have never been so gay since, in any society.[60]

8

London 1934–1936:
Expanding Horizons

Socialist and European

The politics Jameson was engaged in now was at a different level from the Labour Party campaigning of her Whitby years. She still maintained her Whitby Labour Party connection, and in 1933 had been the Whitby delegate to the Labour Party conference in Hastings, sitting alongside Philip Noel-Baker, who was shocked to see her voting for workers' control in factories, and watching Arthur Henderson turn away timid requests for help from beleaguered Trades Unionists in Berlin. Old George Lansbury spoke kindly to her, and Bill Mellor, and a handful of others, had tried to sing the Red Flag, but all revolutionary impetus had gone.[1] The politicians she could approve of were all concentrating on the long-term, apparently insoluble issue of unemployment. At a dinner in her flat in 1934, Aneurin Bevan told stories of his attempts in early 1931 through the Parliamentary Labour Party, working with Oswald Mosley and John Strachey, to persuade Ramsay MacDonald to call a conference to address the appalling problem, and MacDonald's obduracy, that had provoked Mosley and Strachey to break with Labour.[2]

She was still profoundly attached to the ideals and ideas of A. R. Orage, and promptly contacted him when he reappeared in London in the spring of 1932. He invited her to a meeting—their first—and she accepted his invitation to review for him in his new journal, the *New English Weekly*. The arrangement lasted, without pay, for two years, from April 1932 to December 1933, and when pressure of work forced her to resign he wrote a letter of gratitude which she preserved carefully among her papers.[3] They stayed in touch until his death in November 1934.

126

In July 1934, Orage wrote to her with a string of suggestions for topics for the pamphlet she had agreed to write for him. 'The Common Heritage' could be 'an attempt to show that *everybody* contributes to it, and always has. For example,—language, morals,—not to say needs,—are conditions of inventions, productions, etc.'[4] Or she could talk about how to encourage the right use of leisure, or tackle the problem of how to get personal service if no one needed to work for money, or discuss 'The Arts under Social Credit', or 'Women in a Social Credit Community'—his list was endless. The idea of the common heritage might have been expected to attract Jameson, and doubtless his enthusiasm reinforced ideas that were coming through to her from the LSE. In the late 1930s and early 1940s, these would feed into her explorations in fiction of the relations of culture and society, and after the war would produce further meditations on the exiled writer's relationship to his own language and the language of his adopted culture. For the moment, however, she settled on 'The Soul of Man under Leisure', which Orage greeted with pleasure and an allocation of 5,000 words.[5] In the same letter, with a complete lack of self-consciousness, he noted he had stayed with the Dobrées, and all of them had agreed that Jameson did too much for nothing.

Her pamphlet was published in 1935, the year Stanley Baldwin returned to power as the Conservative Prime Minister of another National Government. It followed a wonderfully eclectic sequence including C. H. Douglas on 'The Use of Money', Ezra Pound on 'Social Credit: An Impact', and Herbert Read on 'Essential Communism', and came just before Bonamy Dobrée's 'An Open Letter to a Professional Man'. Jameson's contribution was a faithful representation of Orage's social philosophy. Society, she argued, had fallen prey to a small elite of profiteering financiers, served by their middle-class dependents and by workers whose minds had been enslaved by the machine-culture that claimed to liberate them. To be restored, the nation must find again those links with the past that had been severed by industrialisation and the introduction of mass production. Everyone must have equal shares in drudge-work and cultural activity. She argued for an end to serfdom, a classless society, and the revival of regionalism—then everyone could lead happy lives. It was, Jameson said later, perhaps more an expression of what she knew Orage thought than of her own convictions. Writing to Irene Rathbone in 1937, discussing the novel (*They Call It Peace*, 1936) in which Rathbone had set out the case for Social Credit, she admitted her own reservations: 'I wish Orage had read this book. I'll make a confession. When he was alive I smothered my doubts. Since he died I haven't been able to.' By this time, despairing of peaceful reform, she could see no hope for socialism except through revolution:

I feel that the vested interests in this country are cleverer, stronger, deadlier than anywhere in the world. I feel that they will bring us all down. [...] That there will be perhaps war, perhaps civil war, one or the other certainly—and after that the sort of society we shall get will not have much use for sanity. This is not defeatism really. The effect on my mind is to make me feel that nothing is worth working for but socialism, since credit reform is an integral part of any socialist state. I have no deep hope that socialism can be put across in this country without the revolution that would twist it to some bloody shape. But I have a better hope of it than I have of putting across social credit in time. I give my support therefore to the Popular Front, and to the United Front, in the hope that if this government were got rid of there might be a return to sanity in international affairs—which might just save us and give us time.[6]

And besides, she said later still, Guy had assured her that Social Credit was 'economically impossible'.[7] In 1936, in *None Turn Back*, the exemplary ILP organiser Henry Smith, who is the workers' best hope for the future, rules out all prospect of cooperation between classes for the common good: 'On the day you persuade yourself that there is good in common between William Gary and locked-out desperate miners you cease to be a socialist.'[8] Jameson had remained loyal to Orage's philosophy longer than many others, including G. D. H. Cole, its co-founder, who wrote its valedictory in an essay in *New English Weekly* in September 1934, a month before Orage's death.[9] Guild Socialism, Cole explained there, had originally been conceived as a way of putting an end to poverty by better sharing of resources without recourse to the mechanisms of the State, which would simply replace the rule of the owners of capital by the rule of bureaucrats. In 1911 and 1912, trade unions had been militant, and were better placed than Labour politicians to bring about the transformation. Economic power, Guild Socialism argued, preceded political power, and what was envisaged was a new form of economic citizenship. But in 1934, the advent of mass unemployment had destroyed all those hopes. The way forward, Cole now thought, was through parliamentary socialism, but it was up to the young to achieve it.

There was however always more to Orage than Social Credit. Any journal he edited put its readers in direct touch with the important intellectual and political debates of the day. Jameson's thinking about Europe, and especially

European integration, was substantially fed by Philip Mairet's essays. 'Patriots of Europe' introduced the concept:

Genuine demand for European integration, in the name of culture and human welfare, is all too weakly expressed both here and on the Continent. Not only is it swallowed up in the clamour of desperately urgent national issues, but it has certainly been both diluted and misled by the vague world-ambitions of the League of Nations, so that true and realistic European patriotism is but a still, small voice. Nevertheless, it is a voice of reason, and in some sense must finally prevail.[10]

Mairet reviewed the most important recent contributions to the debate. Christopher Dawson, in 'The Modern Dilemma', made the cultural case for European federation, and also emphasised its political urgency 'in view of the vast size of the coming world-powers'. The USSR, China, India, and the USA, Dawson argued, had already achieved unification, profiting from ideas that had their origins in European thought. F. McEachran's pamphlet, 'The Unity of Europe,' offered an important elucidation of the European ideal of individuality, and quoted Ortega y Gasset's insight, that the strength of a community lay more in a sense of a common future than a common past. From Czechoslovakia, he noted Beneš's speech on 'Le Dilemme Européen'. He concluded his account with a point of his own, which Jameson's essay 'In the End', as well as her Mirror in Darkness trilogy, was to echo. The obstacle to European integration was the proliferation of nationalist feeling, and the hijacking of internationalism by Supercapitalism—which sought to exploit both, indiscriminately, in order to achieve 'a super-state control'.

Six months later, Mairet's review article drew readers' attention to A League of Minds, the first book produced by Paul Valéry's consortium, the International Institute of Intellectual Co-operation, which was sponsored by the League of Nations. This was an international collaboration between European intellectuals, seeking to set aside political interests and work together to put the cultural heritage at the service of society.[11] The list was impressive: Valéry himself, Henri Focillon, Salvador de Madariaga, Miguel Ozorio de Almeida, Alfonso Reyes, Einstein, Freud, and Gilbert Murray. Mairet recalled Allen Upward's frustrated initiative twenty years before 'to found an intellectual co-operation of the elite of Europe', which was now, he felt, come to fruition in this collection of correspondence, 'the first sketch of a plan to audit the intellectual assets of our culture, with a view to exploiting them in the interest of mankind'. Mairet was not however impressed by the confusions inherent in the consortium's claim to be 'non-political'. Intellectuals in his view must have political views; it was their responsibility to 'get a grip on reality'. He welcomed the dissenting voice of Alfonso Reyes, who spoke out for active participation in 'the social unrest of our time', and argued that the League should be the context of that participation. Valéry's initiative, with Mairet's socialist inflections, caught Jameson's imagination. It would provide the model for her wartime ambitions for PEN, and enable her to see the possibilities, after the war, in linking PEN into the work of UNESCO. In her post-war saga *The Green Man* (1952), Richard, struggling to keep intact the crumbling English manor house his family has occupied for four centuries, holds the key to renewal for both England and Europe in the European networks centred on his corresponding journal. By the 1950s, Richard's network would represent an alternative form of European integration to the Communist internationalism whose bankruptcy the novel also explored. In the 1930s, for Jameson at least, European integration and socialist ambition were not mutually exclusive.

The Rise of Fascism

There was already a darker side to European integration, to which Orage's famously open publishing policy also gave a platform. In the spring of 1933, the essay by Quintus on 'Germany and the Jews' was a chilling indication of the emergence of a different kind of intellectual network, which laid out its own claim to the European inheritance. Claiming to deplore 'the Jew-baiting in the Germany of today', the writer in fact sought to justify it. Anti-semitism, he claimed, was a symptom of mass disgust with present-day values, in a country where 'the panders of Plutocratic vulgarity', the media and the stock exchange, were largely under Jewish control and ownership:

Can we not sympathise with the Nazi hatred of naked dancing in hot night clubs before overfed profiteers, with their dislike of that strident negroid jazz music which assaults our ears in nearly all public places. They denounce such music as unsuitable for the Teutonic stock. Is it suitable for any of us Europeans, who are the heirs of Bach and Mozart and Beethoven?

　　[...] If we think what Europe means and has meant, of the essential qualities which unite such diverse European buildings as the Parthenon and Santa Sophia and Chartres Cathedral, or such different writers as Homer, Cervantes and Goethe, or such varied painters as Botticelli, Velasquez and Turner, we can feel that spiritual unity which is Europe and we can realise the disgust with which any of these great architects or writers or painters would have regarded those aspects of the present age which are condemned alike by the enthusiasm of the Nazis and by the scorn of Lawrence and Aldington.[12]

By this time, Jameson was already working from the London PEN Centre in defence of European colleagues, and for the development of the right kind of Europe. In January 1934, she began to deluge Hermon Ould with letters urging him to mobilise PEN on behalf of Ludwig Renn, the left-wing writer and journalist, whose novel *Nachkrieg*, about the Spartakist Rising, had been published in 1930, and who had lectured at the Marxist workers' school in Berlin. A vociferous opponent of Hitler, Renn had been arrested in 1932 and charged with 'literary treason'. His name was raised at the May 1933 International PEN Congress in Dubrovnik, along with others such as Carl von Ossietzky, Erich Muehsam, Sigmund Freud, and Heinrich Mann, and much publicised in *The Times*. The German Branch had left PEN after having been censured at the Congress for their failure to speak out on the banning of their colleagues and Hitler's Burning of the Books, but Jameson thought that they should still be urged to try to secure leniency for Renn, and that Wells and other English writers should be urged to do the same.[13] It could so easily happen in Britain, she told Ould:

In 1931 I talked to three mildly Socialist writers in Berlin, who laughed and said: 'Who would want to harm us: we're too obscure and harmless.' One has now committed suicide, and the others are both in exile. [...] I know that the Ambassador is being spoken to about it privately and if this is not followed up he and others will think no one cares but a handful of wicked Left intelligentsia.[14]

She was, she wrote next, receiving information on developments from an influential politician whose name she couldn't give, since his Left opinions must not become known. He had advised PEN write privately to Dr Ernst Hanfstaengl, Hitler's English expert, and to Goebbels, as Minister of Propaganda and Public Enlightenment, suggesting that leniency towards Renn would have a favourable influence on the attitude of English writers to the Nazi regime—she added that she had choked over that last point.[15]

Wells declined to approve any letter from PEN, and proposed individuals should write. She sent her own letter for Ould to forward to Goebbels, but warned him only to send it if other well-reputed writers were sending at the same time: 'I feel [...] that I am the wrong person to beg for them. My friends are all Left and further Left than I am, and therefore less respectable.'[16]

Her engagement with the pacifist movement, and indeed with PEN itself, was taking her further into Left-wing circles. Amabel Williams-Ellis, who described Jameson as being in the early 1930s 'a political mentor of mine' was now enthusiastically fellow-travelling down the Communist road that her brother had already taken.[17] John Strachey, having declined to follow Mosley into the British Union of Fascists in 1932, would soon be joining with Victor Gollancz and Harold Laski, to found the Left Book Club (1936). Working alongside the Communists was, Amabel wrote in her memoirs, a key step towards Left unity, a view shared, she said, by the Webbs and Shaw: 'I was one of those who found it possible and necessary to work with the Communists [...] the failure of the German Left to unite was for me a terrible precedent.'[18] She belonged to a group that met in a pub in Fitzrovia and included Edgell Rickword, Ralph Fox, Hugh MacDiarmid, Bert Lloyd, and Tom Wintringham; this group set up the Society for the Defence of Culture and the Revolutionary Writers group, and then founded *Left Review*,[19] of which Amabel was an editorial board member.[20] For the first number, which appeared in October 1934, she wrote a report on the First Soviet Writers' Congress in Moscow, where she was the only British delegate (she didn't, according to later critics, understand much of what was on the agenda).[21] She was actively involved in setting up the 1935 London Congress of Peace and Friendship with the USSR, and the 'awed fellow-writer' at whom Jameson raised an eyebrow when she approved of Soviet writers being ordered to write in praise of a factory was probably Amabel.[22] The red-haired novelist Sophie Burtt in the internment camp of *In the Second Year*, viciously beaten by the women guards in a sadistic little scene, is certainly her.

Eyebrow-raising against repression in the USSR was at this stage as much as Jameson was prepared to do. There was far worse going on in the West, and in June 1934, she listened with chill terror to Dorothy Thompson's account of the Night of the Long Knives.[23] A month later, on 7 July, like others on the left, including Aldous Huxley, Vera Brittain, and Dick Sheppard, all like herself future founding members of the Peace Pledge Union, she attended the meeting at Olympia organised by Oswald Mosley.[24] She wrote to the *Daily Telegraph* to describe the scene:

A young woman carried past me by five Blackshirts, her clothes half torn off and her mouth and nose closed by the large hand of one; her head was forced back by the pressure and she must have been in considerable pain. I mention her especially since I have seen a reference to the delicacy with which women interrupters were left to women

Blackshirts. This is merely untrue....Why train decent young men to indulge in such peculiarly nasty brutality?[25]

These events formed the background to the composition of her trilogy, *The Mirror in Darkness. Company Parade* had been finished in November 1933, but the writing of *Love in Winter* took almost the whole of 1934.[26] Lord Rothermere eventually withdrew his support for the BUF, on the grounds of its increasing commitment to dictatorship, anti-semitism and the corporate state, after which the movement had to seek publicity through even more brutal confrontations, and increasingly lost support.[27] In Jameson's *None Turn Back*, Marcus Cohen, the newspaper proprietor whose role in relation to the proto-fascist Economic League reflects Rothermere's support for the BUF, fails to make a break, and the text understands his motives.[28] The cancer attributed to Cohen's wife Sophie is a displaced condemnation, with a brutality of its own.

An End to Dithering

In August 1934, Jameson gave in gracefully to Henrietta Leslie's urging and stood for the PEN Executive Committee.[29] Mrs Dawson Scott herself, the founder of PEN, had encouraged her nomination, on the grounds that: 'She *really has* done things that are international.'[30] After her election at the AGM in October, she had to send several apologies for missing meetings, up to June of the following year, for illness, or being out of London.

That same autumn, Bill went up to Trinity College, Cambridge, to study Mechanical Sciences. He had been at home for a year, living in the Abercorn Place flat and occupying his mother's bedroom while she slept on the daybed in the living-room. They left the Whitby house for good in January 1935, and she expressed bitter regret at abandoning her past, the view from her study window, and all her primordial images.[31] Guy was delighted: 'This was not my place (nor, except on a sunken level of her life, hers).'[32] In March, they went to north-east Spain for the last vacation before Guy's Finals, to Tossa, then still a small fishing port, unchanged since the Middle Ages, and a fashionable haunt for English painters and writers.[33] Jameson probably saw the regular advertisement in the *New English Weekly*:

The beautiful Tossa, Spanish Mediterranean coast, with its mountains and forests, the wonderful sand-beach, its quietness and simplicity, the place for your holidays. Full board in German-Swiss house (running water in all rooms, baths, first-class cooking) Ptas. 12 (6/-). Cheap travel by special arrangement. Information catalogue at Casa Steyer, the Guest-House of Foreigners. Tossa de Mar (Gerona), Spain.[34]

They were there for five happy weeks, from March to April, living on taste-less meat, bread, and coffee made with goat's milk, sharing the village with a handful of German refugees and a band of English female artists. There was just the one hotel, run by a Swiss and a German Jewish exile, a quiet headland, harbour, stony soil, empty streets, and the sea covered with fishing boats.[35] Guy read his notes for Finals, preparing for the First he would be awarded in June. She found the image that inspired *In the Second Year*, the account of English fascism she had wanted to write since hearing Dorothy Thompson's account of Hitler's murderous despatch of his rivals. The homosexual tension binding together two Spaniards, caught in the lamplight at their table, was the per-fect representation of the relationship between her English dictator and the soldier friend who brought him to power.[36] The same hotel scenario, with the same characters (English artists, quiet shabby German-Jewish refugees, and an unassuming clerk) reappears almost twenty years later in *The Green Man*, inhabited by Andrew and Robert, the young men who discover in Republican Spain, in the late spring of 1935, what life is really about:

A hard simple sensual happiness of warm sand after cold battering waves, the scent of herbs and wood smoke, the scorching light, the darkness and its chorus of cicadas and frogs. They lived, completely content, in their bodies—it was as if, in this light, bodies became porous to the least vibration of the air.

There were other vibrations here—of poverty and anger. They got those clearly enough. A selfish instinct turned both young men away from them. Time enough for that. It was enough to feel that the men they drank with in the small dark wine-shop by the harbour had not been distorted by anything they had learned with their heads. In the hard bareness of their lives they played out like a rope their whole selves.[37]

They feel the vibrations of a conflict that hasn't yet become theirs, but the lines are being drawn:

A sun-blackened fisherman asked Robert abruptly if it was true that England and Germany were allies. 'No, a lie,' Robert said.
'A good thing,' the Catalan said drily.[38]

Discussion goes no further, but Robert will return to fly planes against Franco.

The writer Ralph Bates, who had been a labour organiser in Spain, and was a Communist Party member, was brought round to dinner in London by Lilo

Linke one evening in 1934, to join Philip Jordan and Nye Bevan and enlighten them about Spain, the only country, he said, where the movement still thrived. 'Poverty and hard living—that's the secret. You won't see any labour leaders there stuffing themselves in the Ivy.'[39] Until then, Jameson knew Bates only through his collection of short stories (*Sierra* appeared in 1933). She saw a lot of him subsequently, admiring his books and disliking his gluttony.[40] He visited the Chapmans while they were in Tossa, and ate with them in their hotel, where he told them about the imminence of civil war, 'a workers' war', and offered to find a role for her: 'We shall need a few writers outside. Money and arms more, of course, but—.'[41]

Why they needed to be told is something of a puzzle. According to Roy Campbell, the coastal area around Tossa was a notorious hotbed of Republican and Communist activity. In his autobiography, the pro-Franco poet describes living in 1934–5 by Altea, close to a coast 'full of Germans, mostly Jews, fleeing from Hitler', who got funds from the Komintern and had established 'sex-clinics and Communist cells' in the village:

Now all those veiled forces of socialism, the base self-seeking greed, which is at the bottom of all modern reform and egalitarianism, began to come to the top. Bombs went off every day, hurting or killing innocent people. Murders were committed in broad daylight. Discontent and hatred seethed everywhere.[42]

The Chapmans seem to have missed it all—though there was a connection to come later, through Guy's friend Peter Chalmers Mitchell.

After Guy's Finals, he needed a rest before starting on his next project, which was to be a study of the socio-cultural and political consequences of the economic change that took place in the eighteenth and nineteenth centuries: the transition from a subsistence economy to one offering variety and leisure to larger numbers of people. He was interested in what might be extrapolated from that study to address the problems of the declining birth-rate that colleagues in the Social Biology department of the LSE were forecasting for the 1960s. *Culture and Survival*, published in 1940, would acknowledge in the Preface its debt to Dr Enid Charles and her co-researchers in the Department, as well as his thanks to Tawney, Jameson, and Wyn Griffith for their comments.

On the recommendation of their friend Bjarne Braatoy, London correspondent of two Norwegian newspapers, they went in June to Holmsborg, a small island in a fjord to the south of Oslo, and then at the end of July to a hotel in Oslo.[43] Guy may have been resting, but Jameson was working hard.

They needed the money. She told Valentine Dobrée that she had put aside *None Turn Back*, the third volume of her trilogy, to start writing *In the Second Year*:

I have been doing a crazy thing. I abandoned my half-finished Vol 3, and I have been working from 9 to 3 every day, typing a short novel. [...] The product is queer, too. It has no depth but all hard brittle surface (like a biscuit). When it is finished I shall have written, I mean typed 80,000 words in six weeks. It is nearly worthless. Theme— semi-Fascist England. Time—1942. No one will like it. But it was so very necessary that I should write two novels this year, that I just had to do it.

Almost as an afterthought, she added that Guy had got his First—with the same degree of interest with which she also reported that Bill had taken up with a fat girl, and she herself was reading Bonamy's book on the mutiny.[44] She didn't mention that the 'fat girl', who had joined them on their holiday, having travelled together with Bill through a barrage of obstructive Nazi officials, was Barbara Cawood, Bill's future wife; nor did she mention her unkindness and rudeness to Barbara, or her refusal to allow the couple to become engaged. Barbara only discovered on arriving on the island that Mrs Chapman had been told nothing by her son of their plans for the future, and, as she reported to her mother in a letter home, she was astounded by the weakness he showed.[45] She was far more robust than he, determined, she told her mother, to enjoy the holiday regardless, and even coped with being sent home by herself while Bill travelled with his parents; she hadn't enough money for her ticket, and had to cable her father for funds.

That summer had a sad end. In September, responding to Ould's invitation to become a Vice-President of PEN, Jameson wrote to say her attendance would probably be too irregular, since they were leaving London this year to live somewhere—they didn't know where—in the country. She pleaded also her hopelessness as a chairman, and then went on to apologise in advance for missing a PEN dinner on 1 October: Winifred Holtby was dying, and she had promised Vera Brittain that she would take her away for a few days after it was all over. Two days later, she wrote again to accept the Vice-Presidency, adding that for Winifred, now, it was only a question of days, perhaps hours.[46]

On Tawney's recommendation, Guy applied for a lecturing job with the Workers' Educational Association, and they found a flat close to his work on the outskirts of Reading at 68a Shinfield Road, near his London friends and Oxford libraries, and close to Jameson's sister Dorothy. Dorothy had left university after her second year, gone to secretarial college in London, and married a scientist,

Robert Pateman, whom she had known at university. She kept her job in London, and they got a little flat in Reading, where Robert was manager in a factory, until Hannah Jameson helped them with the money to build a house. (Jameson was chagrined to hear that, though it was, she writes, because of the injustice to her other sister, Winifred, whose life was devoted to looking after her parents.)[47] The Chapmans stayed on in Shinfield Road when, in 1936, Guy found another WEA job in Yorkshire. He drove up there every Monday and back on Friday, lodging in Leeds, where Bonamy Dobrée now held the Chair of English at the University, and travelling round to Goole, Scarborough, Selby, Saddleworth, and East Ardsley. The job was harder work than the middle-class constituency he had served at Reading, but, he felt, more rewarding.[48]

While Guy was driving up and down the country, Jameson's commitment to PEN was increasing, artfully fostered by Ould. She wrote to him from Oxford in November 1935 to give him her address for the rest of the month (23 Merton Road) until her return to Reading, telling him she was shortly to leave for Whitby and the annual Scarborough meeting of the League of Nations Union, to deliver a speech—something, she claimed, she did consummately badly.[49]

The next month, she was apologising for a missed Committee meeting, where discussions had focused on the situation of Carl von Ossietzky, at that time still held in a concentration camp at Esterwegen-Papenburg for his anti-Nazi activities, and offering her support.[50] The discussions will presumably have been linked to the letter-writing campaign organised by the journalist's colleagues in the German League for Human Rights, which ended in the award of the 1935 Nobel Peace Prize. In February 1936 came the first invitation to be a PEN delegate, to the forthcoming Congress in Argentina at Buenos Aires. She was overworked, she said, and in panic at the prospect of making a speech, and she wondered whether Guy might come too, although not yet a PEN member ('He jolly well ought to be—he's the author of a very good war book').[51] She was very excited, but foresaw problems:

I seem to have to settle the lives of an army of people before I can go away by myself, dropping all responsibilities into the sea. I swear to let you know by the end of the week, and to come if it is possible. I do want to come. I never seem to go anywhere.[52]

Finally, it was decided that she could indeed go, and on the 3 March, at Ould's request, she sent a biographical note:

Born at Whitby in Yorkshire in a seafaring and ship-owning family. (As a young child the name of Buenos Aires was familiar to me—it was pronounced Bonnus Airs by the sea captains of those days. And we spoke of going out to 'the Plate', too.) […] Author of too many books, as follows […].

She selected twelve titles from her record, including eight lengthy novels, from *The Lovely Ship* to *In the Second Year*, and her first autobiography, *No Time Like the Present*, and concluded:

That's all I've done, except to work and write against war and fascism, which I shall do until forcibly prevented.[53]

The 'all' was already a list to be proud of.

9

Fiction and Form

Since the move to London, Jameson's political activity and her writing had been mutually enriching. Her frustration with the collapse of the Labour Party's commitment to social justice, and her anxiety at the rise of anti-Semitism and fascism, poured into the three major novels she had completed by the middle of the 1930s, evoking the parallel derelictions and betrayals in the previous decade and their culmination in the General Strike, where businessmen and politicians had artfully combined to crush the gathering forces of workers and radical intellectuals. With hindsight, and the comforting knowledge of the contributions she was now making, she faced up to her personal part in the failure of the Strike. Locking themselves away into their own private concerns, relationships, and careers, she and others like her had created the social unrest that was now contributing, at home and abroad, to larger and more terrible conflicts. *In the Second Year*, her coldly horrific vision of England in 1942, ruled by an authoritarian government, with all dissenters consigned to concentration camps, was an attempt to warn of the disaster ahead. The narrator of that text, the writer who stands at the margins of society but is connected, by a vast range of threads, to every member of its ruling establishments, fills the same structural space as Jameson herself: horrified at what he has helped to create, near-powerless to put things right.

Throughout the 1930s, Jameson wrote, her attention was fixed on 'the spectacle of Europe', and the many scenes being played out simultaneously on this complex stage.[1] Her writing now had two aims. One was to tell the English what was happening in Europe, which was also what was happening at home. The other was to find forms to drive home to a nation trained by its leaders to be blind and deaf the true implications of all these dramatic events.

Staging the Spectacle

Europe, as the mirror in which England can achieve self-knowledge, and recognise the public dimensions of 'private' life, hardly figures in the trilogy, which is, after all, a 'Mirror in Darkness'. But it is no accident that at the beginning of *None Turn Back*, Hervey is reading Jean Giraudoux's novel of 1926, *Bella*, filled with the voices of the young dead of the First World War; and that at the end, as she sinks into dream under the surgeon's knife, she has just put aside Stendhal's *La Chartreuse de Parme*. Stendhal's Fabrice, the man who lived out his private passions in a quiet little duchy, oblivious of the Napoleonic struggles tearing Europe apart, is crossing a field when he is almost trampled to death by the thundering hooves of the cavalry at Waterloo, where the last breath of European revolutionary fervour is expiring in a clash of empires. Like Fabrice, Hervey is a character on the margins of the great struggles, yet all her 'personal' choices have made their contribution to the ruin of her world. Unlike Fabrice, she recognises her responsibility. All wives and mothers, like all the soldiers of Class 1914, are the conscripts of capital. Their dreams and disappointments are spun into the same web—'the economic web, the social web'.[2] Recovering from her operation for cancer, and still not strong enough to read much, she folds into the pages of Stendhal's novel a letter from T. S. Heywood, an old friend from Class 1914, who has sold his scientific genius to the producers of poison gas.

Teaching the reader to understand is the key to a trilogy that Jameson frequently disowned. She wrote to Valentine Dobrée: 'Don't praise *Love in Winter*. I know how unworked it is, the materials for a novel rather than a novel.'[3] But her engagement with the persona of the reader, her treatment of characters, and especially, her deployment of landscape, give the lie to her modest disclaimer. The materials are carefully worked out across the three texts, to incorporate the reader into Hervey's vision, from the opening section in Chapter xxviii of *Company Parade* headed 'I am you reading', to that final acceptance of oneself as the sick citizen who must prepare for a personal and collective convalescence.

The readers thus addressed are not exclusively those who enjoyed Jameson's popular romances in the 1920s. But that wider, unpoliticised audience was certainly likely to be drawn in by the familiar autobiographical dimension to the central characters in this saga. Jameson's struggles with Charles, and then with Guy, are the basis of Hervey's private romance. *Company Parade* covers

140

Jameson's marital problems from January 1919 to June 1923. *Love in Winter*, set in 1924, follows faithfully her love affair with Guy, up to their moving in together in Primrose Hill, and *None Turn Back* lifts her continuing annoyance with his neurotic dithering into the perspective of the greater commitment to social justice they both discovered in the 1930s. But the readers initially attracted by familiar romance would soon find these figures operating on another, generic level, as social functions. These are individuals finding their place not just in relation to each other, but in the larger interconnections of the politics of the modern city.

Contemporary society in the trilogy is not a constellation of private romances, but a public spectacle, whose stage is the metropolis. The action of these novels is street theatre, moving from the frenetic carnival of post-Armistice London, the serial experience that is the lot of the unselfconscious and uncommitted (*Company Parade*), to the groups of workers and owners coalescing to change the march of history (*None Turn Back*). The crowd is the most significant actor on the stage, and Hervey Vane, the writer in formation, is its mediator. Hervey's job is to learn how to configure her own angles of vision to penetrate and communicate the varieties of individual experience that form the many hinterlands of the collective. The refinement of Hervey's aesthetic awareness—a key motif—effects a political progression from fear of the crowd, as faceless collective monster, to identification with it as the sum of its individual members. It is ignorance that creates the monster. In the Lyons Teashop, the space par excellence of alienated community, where the eyes of waitress and customers connect only in the business of consumption, the crowd seen by a Hervey fresh arrived from the North is composed of rootless, featherlight individuals, whose collective form is a murderous mass:

They drifted into the room, clung for a time to one of the tables, and drifted away, into streets and rooms she could not imagine, more than a million of them, squatting and pressing on the earth, pressing out grass and trees, killing the roots of many living things, so that these rootless creatures could exist.[4]

A few years later, in *None Turn Back*, a more experienced Hervey pictures the Londoners thronging the streets during the miners' strike as a joyous crowd, liberated from the treadmill of capitalism, in a holiday mood that is not simply carnival but a more sacramental celebration, the promise of a better future: 'These people felt no grudge against the miners who were making them walk, nor sympathy for them either. They walked. It was a new feast of the Passover.'[5]

Finding a form to characterise the crowd, the trilogy indicates, is the greatest challenge confronting the contemporary political novelist. Hervey struggles, but her male counterparts fail completely. They are too obsessed with their own vision to surrender themselves to that of others. Like T. S. Eliot, whose forms they imitate, they can draw the surface of the drama, but cannot touch the human potential sleeping below.[6] For William Ridley (J. B. Priestley, with a touch of Wyndham Lewis), the simple careerist, devoid of genuine feeling, the crowd is an eyeless or many-eyed monster, a secretion of the cityscape.[7] David Renn, the passionate socialist, can only recreate, in fragments that recall both Eliot and John dos Passos, his own despair before the fragmented landscape of human endeavour.[8] To begin with, Hervey's inexperienced eye produces too much abstraction. Listening to the tale her American lover spins of their present and future together, she finds that the forms of his discourse jar with her reality:

The room, the discreet orchestra, lights, waiters, diners, unfamiliar tastes and odours, formed in her mind a picture which bore scarcely any resemblance to the reality. It changed and fell to pieces momently—now the tables were radial lines with a vast bare arm filling the foreground, now a bar of music took shape as a street with lit windows, or an eye, and dominated the pattern.[9]

But by the end, she has abandoned the attempt to enforce simplistic, abstract patterns on reality. Only a whole-body engagement in the production of form, combining artistic detachment with experience from the inside, can accurately convey the complex smells, sights, and rhythms of modernity. Returning to London after a six-month interlude in Danesacre, she tumbles into a physical and syntactical engagement with the crowding images of the streets:

She reached London after dusk and spent the evening walking with herself, in an indescribable excitement squeezed from the crowded irregular streets, the lights and darkened doorways, the gaiety, the furtive faces, the misery, the colours running pell-mell over restaurants and theatres, the smells, all that whirl of stone and cataract of bodies caught in the forms they assumed for one moment one evening in February 1923, once and once only, then and only then.[10]

Regenerated in that hard-won artistic matrix, the kaleidoscopic fragments of seemingly disconnected individual lives fall together, and produce a coherent vision of the contending groups to which those lives belong, and the intricate choreography of their relationships. On the one side, the Economic Council is the meeting place of an unholy alliance of capitalists. Thomas Harben, who owns the shipyards that used to belong to Hervey's family, is a man under threat. In *Company Parade*, the threats he identifies come from his global competitors, America and Japan, and his workers at home, striking, and demanding nationalisation.[11] In *None Turn Back*, all his hatred and fear is focused on his workers. The unions are his enemy, and wages and ownership the only issues he recognises.[12] Like his wife Lucy, old aristocracy devoted to 'her' land and 'her' people, he has set his face against change.[13] The real threat to them both is the man Harben thinks is his ally, William Gary. Made impotent by a shell fragment in the trenches, unable to found a family of his own, Gary is driven by the need to make a different kind of mark on history. He wants to make a 'better' world, in his own image, and to do that he will buy up fellow-capitalists, and turn workers into cogs in his schemes.[14] Julian Swan, another cripple, who runs the Economic Council, is his right-hand man. Swan's mainstay is Tim Hunt, a former commander in the Black and Tans, who organises Swan's Special Service Corps, a khaki-shirted volunteer defence corps whose watchwords are 'authority and obedience', 'leadership and discipline'.[15] Swan's anti-Semitism, increasingly violent, joins with his virulent anti-Communism and his sadistic misogyny; these are the black energies of a decaying society, frustrated by its own impotence, and ready prey for Gary.

Ironically, Gary's other important lever of power is Marcel Cohen, the Jewish newspaper proprietor modelled on the Rothermere who employed Jameson on the *Daily Mirror* and the *Evening News* (in the novel, the *Daily Post* and the *Evening Post*), at the end of the 1920s. The portrait Jameson builds up of him represents an important recognition by her, in the 1930s, of the dangers of her generation's casual anti-Semitism. There is sympathy for the Cohen who as a child suffered abuse for his poverty and his race, as well as contempt for the war profiteer: 'He reflected that if peace had come in 1916 he would have been poorer by half a million pounds. The rat underneath the joists saw a balloon of swollen profits go up from the battlefields.'[16] This is the man who printed the Zinoviev letter, at Harben's request, but he is also, for Hervey, a fellow-exile, and fellow-survivor: 'It gave her pleasure to match her mind against the mind of the shrewd worldly Jew and be more Jewish than he was. Her life had taught her these tricks. [...] the old wealthy Jew had a generous root in him.'[17] Part of that generosity is an attachment to England far more genuine than that of his allies in the Economic Council.[18] The last element in the capitalist alliance is the established Church of England. The Church Commissioners own the Deptford slums, leased to one of Harben's companies, where the workers live alongside the rats, and their children die of tuberculosis and malnutrition.[19] Swan's visible acts of terrorist violence are an important part of Gary's armoury, but his most powerful weapon is the invisible systemic violence he can take for granted, the living conditions by which the workers' opposition is perpetually undermined.

Against the power of capital, Jameson lines up its victims. For the most part, they are faceless, and consigned to darkness. Most visible are the unemployed. Hervey puts a penny on the tray of an old beggar, glances away from the gulf of poverty behind his eyes, and walks on. Least visible are the miners, the slave caste tunnelling away underground, on whom the modern city depends: 'The architects of the modern city of the world buried a living man under the first stone. It is an old custom.'[20] But as they gather in the strike committee room, they become individuals, as well as representatives. Henry Smith is William Gary's counterpart, the child from the Cardiff slums who has become an organiser for the ILP. He spent four years in Spain and Germany as labourer, lorry-driver, and waiter, from 1919 to 1923, shocked by the slums of Barcelona and Hamburg, and watching Germany's Nationalist Socialist Party rise to power through the failures of the Social Democrats.[21] The workers of London appear in the person of the ex-soldier Joe Bradford, the union organiser, and Frank Rigby, the engineer and staunch union man. Their official representative is the Labour MP, Louis Earlham, struggling to be all things to his voters and his Party hierarchy, and finding it easier to deal with William Gary or Ramsay MacDonald than the strike committee. Smith understands that socialism must take the form of antagonism between the classes.[22] The likes of Hervey and Nicholas, the middle-class intellectuals, find a provisional place alongside the strikers, and Nicholas is especially welcome, by virtue of the former comradeship of the trenches. But in the end, while the slum children die, they survive, Hervey sells out to Cohen's 'rag', and the ghosts of Class 1914 gently criticise their falling away.

The stage of this unequal conflict is itself already sold-out to capital. The provincial landscapes of post-war Britain are being bought up by William Gary and his collaborators:

[Gary] inherited his mines in Scotland in the same year he was wounded. He joined them to other mines, north-east to Stirling and Fife, east to the Lothians, south and south-west to Lanarkshire and Ayrshire; burrowing under the shires like a mole he saw the sun again in south Yorkshire. If you travel to the north, look out for trucks painted with the names Harben and Gary (names covering the ranks of back-to-back houses marching crazily from Field Bottom to Steep Row, covering burning heaps of ash eating into the soil, covering wheels and hoists, the pithead anatomy, covering cage, galleries, roads for men and ghosts in the heavy earth.[23]

In the cityscape of London, the landlord is in possession, and everything is rented—a hotel or hostel room, a room in a slum, a seat at a cafe table, a seat in a cinema. No one in the crowd has security of tenure. On the edges of the city, the new suburbs promised homes for heroes. Instead, the likes of Frank Rigby, the ex-soldier trying to scratch a living for his family from his coffee-van at the road's edge, are pushed aside and dispossessed by the speculative builders of estates, turning homes into profit.

An even more disturbing account of the politics embedded in landscape is to be found in the volume Jameson wrote to one side of the trilogy, breaking off from *None Turn Back* to complete it. *In the Second Year*, published in early 1936, holds against the dark mirror of the past the unforgiving light of the future.[24] Jameson wrote it as Stanley Baldwin came back to power in England with another National Government, Laval became Premier in France, and Tomáš Masaryk resigned the Presidency of Czechoslovakia. The Popular Front was slowly building in Europe, but in England the larger community of resistance was already gone. Extrapolating trends to the near future of 1940, Jameson imagined an England that had elected a proto-fascist Government, where Left politicians, Communists and Socialists, Trades Union organisers, and dissident intellectuals vanished into concentration camps, while everyday life continued in the blindness of apathy and self-interest.[25] The academic R. B. Tower (Tawney) divides the blame between liberals, who had hoped for gradual reform ('there is no half-way house, but only brief rests between a caste society and one in which there are no classes except of individuals, of like mind'), and socialists like himself, who had failed to see the growing despair of the middle-classes, whose traditional expectations were frustrated by social changes that they didn't understand:

We used to talk a great deal about the irrational forces in society. Certainly they exist— the brute in us that was afraid of any further civilising of the world—say, the formation of a united Europe. The thoughts of civilized men were feeling slowly toward that— hence the need to deny thought. Chamberlayn [...] was able to count on the brute, and on the spiritually immature, and on the despair of men without a future.[26]

In this context, Jameson explores the bond between city and country, and finds that the alternative perspective that in *Company Parade* had been Hervey's life-line, the road to the moors, has vanished. The cancer that has eaten away the substance of society has reduced London life to mere performance. The long night at the opera, a brilliant set-scene where singers, critics, and audience are all playing to the dictator, is the simulacrum of life left to London. But in the country too, reality has been laid waste. In the opening chapter, the moors and the manor-house garden are a moonlit stage, where the dictator and his friend strut through the final moves of their private drama, with its homosexual undercurrent of mirror-love and deadly rivalry. As the story unfolds, the moors are revealed as a dumping-ground for the unemployed, cast out of the big cities, and at their heart is the concentration camp where dissidence is beaten into submission. By the end of the 1930s, the dark powers of a capitalism in crisis have filled the English landscape, transferring to it all former human agency:

> Perhaps there are times, in the history of a country, when naked forces take charge, needing only the covering of flesh as the hand needs the white glove. They rise from the ground, from the fields left unploughed by the farmer, from the spoiled orchard, from streams poisoned with oil, from dry wells. [...] The tongue moves but the words are given.[27]

In the early 1930s, Jameson approached the depiction of landscape in the mode of Eliot, using it as a screen on which to project a character's thoughts and feelings. For *In the Second Year*, the influence was that of Eliot's protégé, W. H. Auden, and the balance was reversed. Landscape is no longer the projection but the producer of feeling and action, and Englishmen mere actors in the spectacle, speaking lines given them by forces they do not control.[28]

For the protagonists of this drama, only two spaces seem still to offer escape. Outside is the European horizon, in the shape of the Norwegian coast. Inside, there is the bleak West Riding, rough countryside spattered with the closed and close-knit communities of the pit villages. Lying either side of the modern arterial roads that carry Gary's profits north and south, the North of the miners enjoys a neglectful isolation that might yet prove, Jameson hopes, to be the nation's salvation.

Taking the Pulse of Modern Fiction

The three novels of the *Mirror in Darkness* and *In the Second Year* bear witness to significant developments in Jameson's writing of political fiction. She would say later, in *Journey from the North*, that after leaving Whitby in 1932 she had—to her later regret—become a writer interested in social significance, for whom 'the crisis' was the only subject. She had, she said, in that context abandoned the formal experiments of *That Was Yesterday*, and the novella *A Day Off*, with their Joycean streams of consciousness and inner landscapes, and replaced them with a neo-naturalist style. She had felt that to start with form as her main preoccupation would end in 'sterility and the breakdown of communication'.[29] But when she wrote that self-critique in the 1960s, the literary scene was totally different from that of the 1930s, and the sterile novelists she had most in mind were the *nouveaux romanciers*.

In the early 1930s, though the whole issue of 'committed' writing certainly focused for her the need to be intelligible to a wide readership, and her public statements became increasingly polemic, she never abandoned her recognition that it is careful and creative use of language that produces the most effective political statements.[30] In the same section of *Journey from the North*, noting that she was 'genuinely fascinated by the spectacle of a society in transition and convulsions', she refers to the French models for her trilogy, Balzac and Proust. They start from different points (Balzac from characters, Proust from images and ideas), but they both have something vital to say. Their combined influence might make her books appear inchoate, devoid of a clear centre, but, she thinks, they still have good in them. French nineteenth-century social realism, in its many guises, is as much the inspiration for her desire to turn her writing into 'a receiving station for voices' as the modern technology, radio and film, that inspired that image, and she was incapable of working from observed fact without addressing the question of the language by which the 'fact' is created.

She was learning in the early 1930s from friends and fellow-writers. She took to heart Guy's strictures about making her writing less florid, and the prose of his *A Passionate Prodigality* was to influence dramatically her own style. In Valentine Dobrée's writing, she found a similar economy of expression, precise vivid detail, and direct vision in the manner of the William Blake on whom she had written her undergraduate dissertation almost twenty years before.[31]

The reviews she undertook for Orage's *New English Weekly* from April 1932 to March 1933, many of which she collected and published in *Civil Journey* (1938), enabled her to take the pulse of modern fiction, and to observe some of the techniques with which other contemporaries were experimenting. She knew what she was looking for: a form for the novel that could speak across the cultural divides in society, bridging the gap between popular and elitist literature. Society needed: 'a novelist great enough to see the whole of his age and controlled enough to present and interpret it as a whole. [...] an English novelist of this size is not writing or has not yet been born.'[32]

Novel-writers seemed to have a new aim: 'The growing end of the novel to-day is in the minds of those novelists whose intention can be put something like this: "I'm not interested in making up, I want to get at something real." Whatever else it is, this is not the story-telling impulse, though a story may serve its purpose.'[33] In Francis Stuart's first novel, she went on, the pleasures of story-telling (always one of Jameson's own strengths) were replaced by the pleasures of a prose that was economical, simple, analytical and precise, and without artifice: '[H]e has worked to give his prose the concentration and intensity of poetry.' The sensuous apprehensions conveyed in Stuart's novel were sharply formulated, to convey the larger significance of a real that isn't just 'the look of things'. Hemingway and Faulkner, in contrast, she rejected for their artificiality, their leaning to literary conventions, and the 'tricks' with which they replaced the real. In another review, she praised Dos Passos's *Nineteen nineteen* for the exciting experiments with fragmentary narrative form that take the reader below the surface of the contemporary world, reproducing 'its disintegration, its stale disillusion'. Violent transitions in the narrative uncover the cracks in the social fabric. Dos Passos's writing was however limited, she thought, since it suggested no end to decay, and no new road forward.[34]

The Jameson who reviewed for Orage required the novel to perform a double function, to offer a critique of society and also hold out the prospect of its renewal. Her 'real' must have an idealist edge. Edward Thompson's war novel, *Lament for Adonis*, understood that; Thompson deployed 'feeling and intelligence' not just to lament the traditions endangered by a mechanical civilisation, but also to express hope for renewal.[35] Winifred Holtby's savagely comic *Mandoa Mandoa* was a model of how to show the necessary connection of passion and politics—in which passion, for the novelist, must always come first: 'It is a complete picture of any of those upheavals—from a lawsuit to a war—in which passions are exploited by interests and while seeming to obey them are fulfilling laws and needs of their own. It is the ambiguity of these conflicting passions which astonishes us in life [...].'[36]

She left it to others to review the fictions of a James Joyce. But she devoted three pages to taking apart J. B. Priestley's *Faraway*, for its banal thematic, but even more, its contempt for form that she saw as contempt for his readers: 'In reading [*Faraway*] we do not feel that we are in contact with anything more discriminating than a movie camera or typewriter.'[37]

These reviews hardly acknowledge the appearance of the proletarian novel (later designated 'that abortion').[38] She was however in regular contact by letter with James Hanley, from June 1933. She wrote to thank him for *Captain Bottell*, saying she always looked forward to a new book from him (she had recently read *Boy*) and was glad to hear he had liked her own *No Time Like the Present*.[39] To begin with, she said, she had found the dialogue of *Captain Bottell* excessive for captains and engineers, but by the end she recognised that the stylised language contributed to the power of the climax.[40] At the end of the year, she had advice to offer on the manuscript of *The Furys*. The tempo needed to be broken up, he shouldn't hammer the reader so continuously. This, she thought, could be 'the book we have all been waiting for—the great novel to do for the mass what has been done over and over again for the classes, but never with this power'; and in Mrs Fury, she saw both an individual and a character larger than life, a type from Greek tragedy.[41] When the first volume was published, she was fulsome and detailed in her praise of this promising start to 'that "epic of working-class life" which has been promised so many times and is so very badly needed to fill a gap in our literature'.[42] She sent a positive reader's recommendation to the New York offices of Macmillan, who accepted it for publication.[43] In September, thanking Hanley for the character of 'Stoker Bush', she assured him that no other English writer had his ability to force readers to share lives beyond their own experience. Only the Americans—James Farrell and the author of *Somebody in Boots*—had that same skill.[44]

In tune with the times, she expressed her criteria of literary excellence as a lively, distinctive voice, enthusiasm, passion, and the ability to change the reader's life. Bonamy Dobrée had always taken that line, but now the Leavises came on the scene, to make it their own. She invoked Queenie Leavis's denunciation in *Fiction and the Reading Public* of the betrayals of the best-seller writers, and her requirement that a novel should both criticise false and decaying values, and create states of mind to enable better values to replace them.[45] Too many novels, Jameson thought, were written for women: 'Deep calls to deep, and the writer's thought is sucked into the immense vacuum created in women's minds by a civilisation in which they have either nothing to do or too much (too much machine-minding).' It was better to read novels that talked to men. In the same review, she recommended a new quarterly called *Scrutiny*, which had just appeared. In March 1933, in her last piece for Orage, 'Culture and

Environment', she drew together Norman Angell's *The Press and the Organisation of Society* (describing the rabble-rousing skills of the Beaverbrooks, Bottomleys and Rothermeres), *How to Teach Reading, Culture and Environment*, by Frank Leavis and Denys Thompson, and Ezra Pound's *How to Read*. These books together, she wrote, revealed the disintegration of contemporary culture, and all argued that sensitivity to good style, and the ability to judge the values underlying public rhetoric, were two sides of the same coin:

It is not possible for a mind able to detect falseness in a poet's expression of emotion to fail to detect it where it exists in current modes of life. Thus the school-training of taste (where such training ought to begin) cannot confine itself to training a pupil to distinguish between the sound and the pretentious in writing. It must enable him to pass a like judgment on current values as exemplified in the press, the cinema, the pronouncements of public men, in brief, all those voices which, as soon as he is out of school, din in his ears and seek to exploit his emotional responses for their own ends.[46]

School-training must nowadays replace writers' proper engagement in the creation of better writing, alongside the return to humane values. For the time being, the models of good engaged writing were only to be found on the Continent:

In this country there is no *enthusiasm* of the kind which made Charles Péguy's bookshop the forcing-house for a new spirit in literature. It is impossible to suppose an English Péguy having so much influence. When writers cling together in this country it is rarely evidence of a pure and ardent love of letters. You can therefore expect no help from writers as a body in any effort to change by criticising them the conditions, material and intellectual, in which they find themselves comfortable.[47]

For Jameson, too many English novels were blind and parochial, productions of 'an England which has maintained itself until now by ignoring everything it disliked and did not understand, and is perhaps about to die of what it ignored.'[48] She found room in her reviews to pick out new work coming from Germany, offering vivid accounts of the political confusions, and the passions, of the post-war nation. J. M. Frank's *Fever Heat*, for example, depicted a country where community was being torn apart by the quarrels of Nazis, Communists, and Republicans, in the aftermath of defeat and a cruel Peace.[49] But most impressive, and meriting a review to itself, was Hermann Broch's *The Sleepwalkers*, in the Muirs' 'superb' translation. Jameson praised its brilliantly coherent account of the stages in social and spiritual disintegration of Germany between 1888 and 1918, the larger disintegration of humane values in Europe from the Renaissance to the present day, the sense of futility and conflicting values that marked the present—and its heroic attempt to show new community emerging from the fragments:

[I]n place of one coherent and comprehensive value-system there are now any number of unrelated and conflicting systems: the bankers, the soldier, the business man, the writer, live each by his own code and none can relate his private good to another's, since there is no universal term of reference, no supreme value in which all men believe [...]. Silence isolates each of us, 'each in his prison Thinking of the key.' (That is Mr. T. S. Eliot, and it is a very curious experience, and one which I suggest to you, to read 'The Sleepwalkers' and 'The Waste Land' side by side.) [...] Now a new process must begin, the creation from the atoms of the old of a completely modern synthesis.[50]

Broch's sleepwalking figures and Eliot's landscapes of decay fed directly into the unresolvable conflicts depicted in the *Mirror in Darkness*: 'We, men living in 1932, are the sleepwalkers.' The English, stirring uneasily in their sleep, were about to wake up to the nightmare of lost community that Germany and Russia already knew. Jameson was preparing to explain to them their participation in European politics; and for that, the forms of European writing were to prove invaluable instruments.

10

1936–1938: Waking up to War

From Pacifism to Popular Front

On 7 March 1936, Hitler marched into the Rhineland. In the Café Royal, all the talk was of the League of Nations' debates on the Rhineland issue, and the likelihood of war. Thomas Balogh passed on to Jameson his insider knowledge of the role of European finance in the crisis. He had seen French and Swiss bankers in June, in Paris and Geneva, and he reported that the French bankers had deliberately created the crisis in the franc to frighten the politicians into economies and wage cuts; they did it badly and frightened everyone, including themselves. He had heard a Swiss banker swear to defend the virginity (the banker's own word) of the Swiss franc, and blame England for violating the pound and wanting other currencies to be reduced to the same state.[1]

She left Balogh to meet up with Guy, Philip Jordan, and a Foreign Office official, who was a friend of Philip's. She burst out that someone ought to assassinate Hitler, and thought: 'If I believe that concentration camps, the torture of Jews and political opponents, is less vile than war, I must say so plainly, not pretend that the price is something less….' She couldn't say it; she felt physically sick. Guy, more straightforward, declared himself ready to enlist at once, to fight for France.[2] After her outburst, she was full of silent self-recrimination:

Is this a way for a convinced pacifist to feel? Think, woman, think…None of the others knew or remembered that I was a sponsor of the Peace Pledge Union. I had joined Dick Shepherd when he started it, in October 1934. Then, I was absolutely certain that war is viler than anything else imaginable…Do I think that now?[3]

Like this confession, an extensive section dealing with events in the PPU at the end of 1937, and the effect on the movement of Dick Sheppard's death on 31 October, was dropped in her published autobiography. In the draft, she described her fear, as well as her grief, at the loss of the man whose certainties had been a bulwark against her own wracking doubts.[4] Two days later, on 2 November, there was an emergency meeting of PPU sponsors in an upper room in 96 Regent Street, including George Lansbury and Canon Morris. She finally acknowledged to herself she no longer thought that the pacifist movement could stop the war. But she couldn't confess that, and even after Munich, she still couldn't bring herself to make the break.[5]

Back in 1936, Jameson's writing was not going well. After finishing *None Turn Back*, she experienced a sense of dryness, feeling she was writing against the grain of her real talent, and also that she could not produce her particular vision of contemporary England unless she abandoned politics, family, and friends to concentrate on her writing.[6] She had moments of unbelievable fatigue, crying alone in the flat. She should, she told herself, have listened to Gerald Bullett and H. G. Wells, who had admired *Delicate Monster*, and told her to stop writing and wait until she had solitude to think and write, and not try to cram politics into a crude aesthetics.[7] She partly resolved her predicament by adopting pseudonyms to undertake more radical formal experiments without compromising her new image. As James Hill, she began *Loving Memory* on 10 March 1936, and quickly finished it. William Lamb's *The World Ends*, an apocalyptic fantasy, written over the summer, was finished on 11 October.[8]

Guy's work was going even less well, and he had become dispirited by a winter spent travelling in pursuit of his WEA commitments. At Jameson's suggestion, he left for Malaga at the start of the summer to stay in a villa belonging to a friend (Sir Peter Chalmers Mitchell) and travel with him around Spain— managing again, apparently, to remain oblivious of the civil war that was to break out in July.[9] In his absence, she followed with passionate interest the course of politics in France, where the Popular Front had come to power in May; and she was angered by an editorial in *Time and Tide* that claimed that in England there was no common cause on which a Popular Front could be built: 'In this country Fascism is placed among the Curious Cults, and a "popular front" that combined on the basis of war would soon split on the ingrained pacifism of Left opinion in this country.'[10] Her response, pointing out the editorial 'misconceptions' of the character of a Popular Front, which could never be merely an alliance of the leaders of Left groupings (in France, 'it was in effect forced on the Socialist leaders from below'), followed up her criticisms in her novels of Trade Union and Labour Party leaders, and the 'apathy and active opposition' they demonstrated towards the idea. She contrasted the failure of British action in 1926 and the current successes in France, and spelled out the collaboration with the Communist Party that was now necessary to oppose fascism.

A coalition of leaders, she said, was futile. What was needed was a rallying point for the strong anti-fascist feeling in the country, which the Labour Party should be providing, and wasn't. She proposed:

The reanimation of the Labour Party—by (1) a change in its constitution. The statement that the Labour Party is ruled by the Trade Unions is delusive. As constituted, it is ruled by a narrow oligarchy of Trade Union leaders, as much out of touch with their rank and file as is the executive of the Labour Party with the Party rank and file. (2) An alliance, on the basis of an exactly defined programme, with the progressive Liberals, I.L.P. and Communist Party, as distinct from a shabby vote-catching agreement between leaders—is a preliminary step towards the only form of Popular Front worth voting for.

Apart from a people's front, what indeed is there to hope for in the political future? And without it, what hope of averting the eventual triumph of reaction by the default of the Labour Party?

She ended by drawing readers' attention to a recent series of articles in the Labour Monthly, written by MPs and Labour Party members, setting out the Party's views,

as distinct from the inscriptions on the official tombstones. The current issue, containing the very candid advice of Mr. Aneurin Bevan, and a clear and careful analysis of the Popular Front, is required reading for any understanding of the problems involved.[11]

She also busied herself with plans for the coming PEN Congress in Buenos Aires, determined that the English delegation would take a stand for freedom. She wrote to Hermon Ould that she would have nothing to do with a mealy-mouthed American resolution: 'I don't mind saying publicly that when I want to "maintain relations of friendship and cooperation with writers in countries etc. etc." I can do so outside the countries in question, since all the writers of importance are exiled from them.'[12]

In June, dragged reluctantly into a PEN conference called in pursuit of a scheme for an encyclopaedia of European culture, she described gleefully to Valentine Dobrée how she had cut through the fog of French rhetoric:

The best thing was the speech by Benda, who is perfectly charming. Then Malraux made an impassioned speech about the cultural heritage—Amabel said they had

been talking about it ever since they began—and only a reference to the encyclopedia. [...] They would have gone on doing it all Sunday again, but I led a private revolt
and said I'd go home if they didn't get down to brass tacks, so a furious Ehrenbourg
was postponed, and after we'd drunk some tea, Malraux went at it again, and told
us about the encyclopedia. H. G. Wells was sitting beside me, perspiring madly, and
very angry with every one, and when Malraux ended his account of what would be a
monstrous project, taking years and years, he got up and said it would cost as much
as three battleships and where please was the money coming from? The French were
much displeased at this display of coarseness. Malraux seemed not to have any idea
that the whole teaching profession of this country was not to a man able and eager to
collaborate in subscribing to the project.[13]

This is the event described in *Time and Tide*, which took place at the Second
Congress of the International Association of Writers for the Defence of Culture, held in London on the weekend of 19–21 June, though in the official
version it sounds grander and more productive, and H. G. Wells's explosion is
differently turned:

The Congress, at which Ernst Toller, Ralph Bates, Gerald Heard, and André Malraux
in turn presided, and Rebecca West, Ilya Ehrenbourg, Rose Macaulay and other eminent authors spoke, paid homage to the memory of Maxim Gorky, whose conception
of a world Encyclopaedia, organized by the writers of the world, they had met to
discuss. [...]
  'The *Encyclopaedia Britannica*,' said H. G. Wells, 'is a contemptible performance in
regard to the needs of today. We are wasting an enormous amount of energy through
inaccuracy. This Encyclopaedia is urgently necessary. It will cost £30,000,000 (thirty
million pounds) as much as three battleships....'
  To which challenge André Malraux replied: 'The project is already going forward
in Europe. If we could spend as much money on this encyclopaedia as the whole British Fleet costs, we should be able to make an even better job of it. For our ultimate
objective is to eliminate all battleships.'[14]

The letter to Valentine also reported excitedly on Bill's university career. His
second year was proving something of a failure, but he was enjoying the flying
lessons his mother had paid for. Her work was back on track. She was writing
two books together, one in the morning and one in the afternoon, and preparing for her trip to Buenos Aires on 15 August.
  Then everything went awry. Her mother had been unwell while staying
with her in May, in Reading, and she had missed a few PEN meetings in consequence.[15] In August, Hannah had a heart attack. Buenos Aires was out of
the question. Jameson stayed in Whitby for some weeks, then went back to

Reading, Guy, and her unfinished novel.[16] She fell ill herself, sending repeated letters of apology for missed PEN meetings in September and October, and as her illness looked set to drag on over the end of the year, offered to resign from the Executive.[17] The offer wasn't accepted. She was summoned back again to Whitby in February 1937, where her mother had fallen unconscious. Two or three days later, her mother was dead.[18]

Guy resigned from the WEA in April 1937, physically exhausted, and his idealism worn thin.[19] In June, they went to France to recover.[20] Guy was still writing *Culture and Survival*, which he would finish in early 1939. As he wrote it, his new lifetime project for a study of the Third Republic was taking shape, and with it he was developing the themes that would inform Jameson's novels of the late 1930s and 1940s: the political and economic importance of the peasant, the interrelated interests of the wine-growing areas and the industrial regions, the 'enmity' between the industrial worker and the peasant or craftsman who is his close relative, the revolutionary legacy of liberty and equality—fraternity, he says, never caught on in France—and authoritarianism and violence.[21] His expression of affection for the French peasant, on the occasion of their visit to France the following summer, chimes closely with Jameson's cult of the men of the Yorkshire moors:

I confess I like peasants in spite of their covetousness, greed and petty economising, their dirt and their unambitious traditionalism. Tradition may be a slow and stupid god: it certainly has been. On the other hand the tradition of the family is not a false god, and may still save us from being wiped off the planet.[22]

As the Chapmans had failed to register the revolutionary allegiances of the peasants in Spain, so the Communist loyalties of the peasants in a number of departments (not least their beloved Gironde) slipped their notice. In Royan, a resort at the mouth of the Gironde, Jameson made notes for a new book by James Hill, *No Victory for the Soldier*. They drove home to Shinfield Road in July.

Bill, aged 22, had graduated from Cambridge in June with a rather poor degree in Engineering and the affections of Barbara Cawood, the young Yorkshire-woman who had clashed with Jameson in Norway in August 1935, and whom he was soon to marry. Barbara had, in the words of a neighbour from Shoreham-by-Sea, where they settled after their wedding, the dark good looks of the film actress, Margaret Lockwood.[23] In Cambridge, where the two had met, she owned and ran two restaurants, bought for her by her father, and like Bill frequented

Figure 14 Bill in the 1930s.

Marshall's Aerodrome; she acquired her pilot's licence about the same time as Bill. (Bill's second wife, Ruth, nicknamed Patchen, was a Ferry Pilot in the Second World War, as well as an airline stewardess.)[24] Jameson was still not pleased with the match, and the more she learned of Barbara's background, the less she liked it. Barbara's mother, Hilda, came from Skelmanthorpe, a village near Huddersfield, built on mining and textiles. Her father, Frederick, was a self-made businessman from Sheffield, where he had founded his fortune pioneering hire-purchase for motor-cars; in the 1930s, he had built a large Lutyens-style house at Fyling Hall, near Robin Hood's Bay. Barbara was a cultured woman, educated at Malvern Girls' College and at a finishing school in Switzerland, and unlike her parents, she had little or no trace of Sheffield in her accent, but Jameson was never going to find a West Riding woman culturally or socially good enough for Bill.

Jameson arranged for Bill to train at Hamble as a civilian air pilot, at considerable expense. By the following year, he would be employed by Olley Air Services, flying de Havilland Dragon Rapides from Shoreham to the Channel Isles. The couple were married on 14 June 1939, at the Register Office in Dorking. They spent their honeymoon in Germany, Austria, Switzerland, and

Figure 15 Bill and his first wife, Barbara Cawood, walking down
a street in Cambridge in the 1930s.

Italy. In Germany, Bill was arrested for refusing to give the fascist salute at the
end of a cinema performance, and in Italy, Barbara was held in gaol overnight
for taking pictures of planes on an airfield.[25]

As the summer of 1937 drew to a close, Guy went back to Spain to stay with
Peter Chalmers Mitchell. Jameson spent September in Paris with Lilo Linke,
in attic lodgings on the rue de l'Abbé de l'Epée, enjoying the excitement of
the metropolis, and the recaptured thrill of youthful freedom, that she would
shortly evoke in the pages of *No Victory for the Soldier*.[26] They met a wide range
of people: Lilo's friends, mostly Jewish refugees, Henriette and André Buffard,
the latter a lycée teacher and a keen socialist, who became a lifelong correspondent, and, at the other end of the spectrum, members of 'the other France', partisans of Hitler. They finally left Paris at the end of October. James Hill's book was
not yet finished, and would not be completed until September 1938.[27]

Guy turned down a teaching job in Leeds, and accepted a part-time job
instead as a reader at Jonathan Cape's, from November 1937. She didn't want
him to take a post that would pin them down in England, but he thought
it better, given her improvidence, that he should have a job and earn some
money. She, he thought, was a much better writer than she gave herself time to
be, and her time and energy were increasingly heavily committed.[28]

158

In November, Jameson launched into a self-education programme on Surreal ist poetry and painting, of interest partly because it enabled her to express her growing hostility towards the cult of the irrational, and partly because of its relevance to her accounts of contemporary music in *No Victory for the Soldier*. Surrealism, she told Valentine Dobrée, was 'on a level with the false neo-classicism of some modern musicians'.²⁹ Political prejudice probably played a part in her judgements; in *The Novel in Contemporary Life*, published in the States in the following year, she made plain her dislike of the Surrealists' insistence on the impor- tance of Freud and Marx.³⁰ She disliked Paul Eluard, possibly because his Commu- nism was uncompromising, and found André Breton more interesting. In painting, she liked Picasso, but not Max Ernst or de Chirico.³¹ Much later, in *Parthian Words*, a parting attack on Surrealism would repeat her hostility to the irrational, and argue the impossibility of attacking disorder with disorderly language.

The year ended on a mildly entertaining note. Jameson received a letter from Bertrand de Jouvenel (the philosopher and political economist, Colette's stepson, and the *Chéri* of the novel), written on notepaper borrowed from a Westminster Member of Parliament, and introducing the Countess Paule de Beaumont and Horace de Carbuccia, the notorious owner of the extreme right-wing French journal *Gringoire*. They were eager to translate and publish *Love in Winter*, and would launch the work in *Gringoire*, with a portrait of Jameson. *Gringoire* was, Jameson considered, a slander sheet, and Carbuccia was violently pro-Nazi and anti-English; her friend in the French Foreign Office, an elegant ultra-conserva- tive, described him as a scoundrel. Jameson replied to de Jouvenel that as a socialist she could have nothing to do with *Gringoire*. She refused permission for a translation, but offered Carbuccia a lunch invitation, to a restaurant, which he turned down. She wrote to her French agent, telling him to make sure her photograph did not appear in *Gringoire*, adding '*Gringoire*, ça pue' ('Gringoire stinks'). The letter was inadvertently forwarded to Carbuccia, who reportedly said that Madame Storm Jameson should go to hell.³²

Approaching Apocalypse

Of the novels she published in 1937, two were of minor interest, but reason- ably well reviewed. *In Loving Memory* (1937), published under the pseudonym of James Hill, was a fairly simple romance. *The Moon is Making* (1937) was a more interesting mixture of the political and the personal, exploring the madness of lives led in the feudal fastnesses of Yorkshire, in and around a town not unlike Whitby, by those who hadn't had the sense, or the opportunity, to escape to London. It could perhaps be thought of as a study of the situation created by contemporary capitalism for those who live on the edge of society; if so, it showed Jameson confronting the dark side of her nostalgic vision of Yorkshire.

The best of that year's production was her second dystopia, written under another pseudonym. William Lamb's *The World Ends* explored the death of Europe's nations, civilisation, and culture.[33] A mountain in the Alps falls into a narrow valley and triggers global catastrophe. After the cataclysm, the writer–hero, Richard Blake, wakes to find himself alone on a small tongue of moorland, with the sea around him, flooding the plain of York. He takes refuge in the one remaining house with a family of farmers.

The story is written out of deep rage. It opens at Blake's middle-class dinner-table, where polite conversations about writing, painting, pacifism and war mask deep resentments and selfish interests, lust, jealousy, and violence. Everything wrong in England is represented here, and Blake attacks it all, from the complacent self-interest of statesmen that allowed Hitler to take the Rhineland, and the gesture politics of pacifism that had given such statesmen such power. Then the narrative confronts the unthinkable for which Blake, and his creator, secretly long. Suppose this civilisation based on machinery and industry were to vanish. Could there be a new society, and a different kind of culture? What would survive of the cultural heritage; and what use would that heritage be to people living on the edge of survival?

Guy Chapman's study of *Culture and Survival*, still being written, will have supplied some of her answers. His definition of culture lodged it not in the conscious productions of high cultural activity, but in the habits and mindset acquired through the class-based institutions of everyday life. It was 'that congeries of habitual thoughts and actions which are derived from the material circumstances, traditions and conventions of the average man in relation to his class rather than his conscious behaviour in relation to his society'.[34] His exploration of the link between the nature of culture and the economic base of a society set out stages which Jameson uses in her novel as the scaffolding for the recovery of civilisation. In the beginning, collective survival in a peasant economy requires lots of children, harnessed to work the land. Only once a basic level of existence is assured is there scope to look for comforts, and then amusements. A culture grows as it slowly becomes child-conscious, and in the end, its focus of concern is the right kind of education for its children. Chapman identified three factors that drive both survival and culture: independent thinking, concern for the next generation, and concern for the survival of the race. In his conclusion, he emphasised the resistant force of civilisation: 'Before the outbreak of this new war, men used to say: "The next war will end civilization." That is unlikely—unless we have gone so far back on the way to barbarism that extermination is sanctified. No: our defeat will be mean and slow.'[35]

Jameson offered in her novel an imaginative exploration of cultural collapse, and the human potential for survival and revival. In a brilliant interplay of the natural landscapes of disaster with the remembered landscapes of a highly structured civilisation, she celebrated the recuperative powers of the European mind, while confronting the limits of individual human memory. There is a clear process: remember, reformulate, make new, apply, hand over, and let go. Whether the process ends in defeat or triumph depends on the perspective you choose.

Richard Blake stands at the centre of the process, in Jameson's own position. He is the representative of what the middle class has learned to call culture: the artist, created by and owner of the high European cultural heritage. Knowledge of certain kinds is valuable, and may speed the way back to better ways of life. But high culture has limited usefulness. After the cataclysm, Blake's money will buy nothing, and he is too weak to work effectively in the fields. He has lost his copy of Palgrave's Golden Treasury, and he can't remember the poems. He can't remember Paris. He can best remember the small things and spaces that are the habits of home, part of the culture of everyday: 'a road curving over the brow of a hill; his room in his mother's house; a friend talking to him across a table, the flames of the candles frozen in the dark surface—all small things, pressing lightly on his mind, as a seed blown by the wind.'[36]

When his place in the relations of production is transformed, a writer must develop a different working relationship to things. When he needs it, a little of Blake's former reading comes back, and the rest he must make up. He tells stories to console a sick girl, he finds a remedy to cure a sick boy, he invents a winnowing technique, and he is finally allowed to teach the children. The brutal, illiterate farmer, who despises the intellectual's weakness, can only do what he has always known how to do, while Blake can always think of something different. Memory and improvisation are the tools that create culture, and rationalist method is another powerful instrument. He keeps records, and maintains a calendar. Though the books have gone, he can remember themes and narrative models, and he can tell their stories in his own words. Stories catch the children's imagination, and open for them the possibility of different and better ways of living.

As he grows older, and more forgetful, Blake is increasingly distressed by his awareness of how much he has forgotten, and how many memories will die with him, of so many lovely things. Initially he rehearses, obsessively, the list of things he regrets he can't remember. Reconciliation to his individual condition comes as he begins to remember not the cultural object but its impact, especially the emotions he and his generation brought to its appreciation: the poor of Vienna crowding to catch a concert, and the casual beauty of London limes.[37] He dies at the age of 60, recognising that there will be a future of which he will not be part, angry at first, and then reconciled to his moment, flicking through fragments of memories that suddenly return: *Pilgrim's Progress*, the shrieks of gulls and the scent of lilac, and the Third Brandenburg Concerto. On that last note, he dies, and the text declares the absolute loss from which the collective can be saved, but which is every individual's destiny: 'I shall never hear it again, he said to himself.'[38]

Against Blake, and hard-won civilisation, stand the men of the moors, England's last peasants. Jameson abandoned in this book the nostalgic and romantic figures of her earlier texts. Before the cataclysm, Blake shared her earlier illusions. Sitting late at night in an inn on the edge of the moors, he listens to the quiet country voices, communing with one another, the trees, the crackling fire, and the house itself:

For all the differences of pitch, they were as alike as the sounds made by a group of trees, or as sticks crackling in the fire, and their slow speech, never altering its accent, seemed to come from the old walls or to rise from the stone flags under their feet. It was the voice of this country.[39]

But this is a poetic construction of rural community, a sophisticated verbal invention of continuity and unity, drawing together wildly disparate entities and concepts—trees, speech, the walls, the country, men. The reality is violent, and ugly.

These are Zola's peasants, blindly committed to survival, bound to the land. They survive as a family, the minimal form of community, held together by need and instinct. The father is brutal and domineering. The mother reproduces and nurtures. Children work the land. The only moral imperative that joins them all is survival, and survival justifies incest, and murder. The farmer's older son, Philip, is the child most drawn to Blake's memories of the past, but his younger brother is a greedy, robust animal, who murders Philip in order to possess his wife, their sister. Their mother condones what he has done, because the family must go on.

And yet, in Jameson's version, all the children have an instinct for knowledge—a pleasure in seeing things—and out of peasant endurance will eventually come a new collective subject. Philip's son learns by himself how to sing, and for him Blake, at the end, puts together 'The Child's Book', with all he can remember of the drowned culture: 'This thin thread, he thought ironically, may hold until daylight.'[40]

This is a motto that Jameson takes for herself. However fervently she argues during the war years, and afterwards, for the need to preserve the values of the European mind, her underlying conviction is that the civilisation she has known is bankrupt and cannot survive. The unknown children, teaching themselves what they want to know, are the best chance for a humane future, and all that can be done is to hand them the best and strongest thread that will hold them until they find their own light.

Excursions and Invasions

In the spring of 1938, an American tour was proposed. Carol Hill, Jameson's American agent, wrote to A. D. Peters that Jameson was considering moving to America, being profoundly depressed by the failures of the peace movement, and in search of a better life for herself and her family. Hill had finally persuaded her to sign a lecture contract for the following January, and expected both herself and Jameson to do well out of it financially.[41] Guy too might have been invited, except that Peters cautioned against it:

He has nothing like the mental calibre or the charm of his wife. [...H]e has done various things, none of them successfully, except, perhaps, a good book about the war. He is, in a way, a war victim: not physically but mentally. [...] He belongs to the type which is well known to both of us: that is, the husband of a successful female novelist.[42]

In June 1938, Jameson was, she said, too busy writing the lectures for America, as well as two books, to accept an invitation to write a book for a new Liberal

Book Club series.[43] But the visit eventually fell through, partly because her PEN commitments were too heavy, and partly because of Guy's responsibilities at Cape. They were, as she had feared, pinning themselves down in England.

Larger political concerns may also have come into consideration. On 20 May 1938, just before Jameson's sister Dorothy gave birth in the nursing home to her second baby, Judy, Hitler had moved troops to the Czech frontier.[44] He claimed that he was defending the Germans in the Sudetenland from discrimination by the Czechoslovakian government, which wanted a fully assimilated state. The Czechs called up their reserves. Towards the end of May, the British Ambassador and the French Foreign Minister, having forced concessions out of the Czechoslovakian government, had warned Germany that France and Britain would fulfil their pledges to come to the defence of Czechoslovakia. Hitler, briefly, reduced the pressure.

The warning was not backed by action. In June, Paul Reynaud asked Britain to send land reinforcements of 60,000 mechanised troops. The troops were not sent.[45] When Jameson and her fellow-delegates arrived in Prague that same month for the PEN Congress, they did their best to reduce Czech expectations. Wells and the International President of PEN, Jules Romains, talked to Beneš in private, and Wells warned the President not to trust too much to British promises. Romains, Jameson recalls, in public at least, offered a high level of rhetorical support, entrancing his local auditors, especially Jiřina Tůmová, the secretary of the Czech Centre. She paints in her autobiography a portrait of silver-tongued treachery.[46] Her original sketch was fuller and harsher, recalling how when Romains was originally elected President at the Congress in Buenos Aires there had been a second candidate, Karel Čapek, the Czech novelist and friend of Masaryk. Romains had telegraphed to his rival telling him to withdraw, and he did. Jameson commented: 'He had been an admirable President, serving the PEN by making it serve his ambitions, which were unbounded.'[47]

Romains's speech was certainly well-judged, one that could satisfy all its hearers without committing Romains to anything that might alarm his government back home. He refused, pleading PEN policy, to get behind any State and national positions, or to pass judgement on the Austrian *Anschluss* (though he came close to it, commenting that it was only natural for people to wish to follow their affinities of origin, language, and culture—hardly the most tactful thing to say with the threat to the Sudetenland on the horizon). He did however declare that for Raoul Auernheimer, former president of the Austrian PEN Club, to be in a concentration camp, and Freud and Mann in exile, was an undesirable state of affairs. A magnificent closing peroration praised Masaryk and Beneš, and urged all Czechoslovakians to be moderate but firm, assuring them that the world was watching.[48] It certainly wasn't doing much else.

In Bratislava, as guests of the Slovak PEN, the English delegates met Marina Pauliny, its chairman, who a year later would be a refugee in London, and a frequent visitor of Jameson's in 1942.[49] Jameson struck up a close friendship with Otakar Vočadlo, a professor at the Komensky university, who would later write to her the letters describing the Nazi occupation of the right bank of the Danube, after Munich, which she quotes in her autobiography, and which she kept among her papers until her death.[50] They were all confident of their allies' support, and she assured them fervently of her own, convinced they were going to be let down, and racked with guilt. This was the beginning of her close relationship with Czechoslovakia and its writers, based on a sense of personal trust that remained constant on both sides as the allied politicians fell away.

After the conference, she began the fact-finding journey in Central Europe, travelling to Vienna and Budapest, which later fed into her novel *Europe to Let*, and later still closed the first volume of *Journey from the North*. This confirmed, depressingly, what she already knew of the terrible consequences hanging on the refusal of the liberal nations in the 1920s and 1930s to acknowledge the terror building beneath the smooth surface of Europe. She gained first-hand insights into the effects of the Nazi threat in Central Europe, the internecine hostility it fostered among the little nations, the plight of the Jews, everyone's scapegoats, and the gatherings of whole populations, preparing to move over Europe. She saw the crowds besieging the British Consulate in Vienna, and the peasants thronging in the station in Budapest. The cultural connections that she, and her PEN connections, had fondly hoped might still hold between peoples were stretched to breaking-point by violent political reality. In Budapest, she met the journalist Alexander Baneth, who could not report to the *News Chronicle* the persecution of the Jews by the Hungarians, for fear of his own persecution. The Czechs in the garden room of the palace in Prague, who had staged Shakespeare for the PEN delegates, as a tribute to their shared European heritage, were about to be rudely awakened. In Vienna, she stayed with Toni Stolper's sister, Anna Jerusalem, and saw the Jewish family preparing to leave, and Anna's farewell to her household possessions—she was later to see the same look in her sister's eyes, as England prepared for invasion.[51]

It was a relief to meet Guy in July, in Basle, where he had driven to meet her. They spent ten reinvigorating days in Annecy, across the frontier in France.[52]

165

11

1938–1940: Crossing the Rubicon

On 7 September 1938, noted Basil Liddell Hart in his *Memoirs*, the leader in *The Times* recommended that Czechoslovakia should cede the Sudetenland to Hitler.[1] Jameson's autobiography remembers the date as the 5th, marked by an embarrassing lunch with her friend Helen Kirkpatrick, the American journalist, who was contemptuous of Britain's failure to stand up to Germany.[2] She wrote the same day to Valentine Dobrée that war, according to her American correspondents, was imminent.[3] The shame and guilt of Britain's handing over her Czechoslovakian friends and colleagues to Hitler would remain with her for the rest of her life, as the beginning of the end of European civilisation.[4]

The collapse of Anglo-French promises came quickly. On 12 September, Hitler demanded self-determination for the Germans in the Sudetenland. 15 September, Chamberlain began shuttling to Munich to see Hitler at Berchtesgaden, and came back convinced he would be satisfied with the surrender of the Sudetenland. From 19 September, the British and French governments were indicating to the Czechs that they must hand over the Sudetenland or they would be defending themselves alone. Czechoslovakia agreed to Hitler's demands, and then on the 21 September he further demanded that German troops be allowed to occupy the territory. The Czechs, and then the British, began to mobilise. But Chamberlain came back from the Munich conference at the end of the month with the surrender of the Sudetenland agreed, and Britain and France having assured Hitler that they would make no intervention. President Beneš resigned on 5 October and took refuge in England.[5]

Poets to the Battlefront

In the days after Munich, Jameson finished James Hill's second novel, *No Victory for the Soldier*, published in the same year, and well received by critics.[6] The summary she gives of the book in *Journey from the North* says only that it is a portrait of the 1930s, showing many scenes in England and Europe. It is one of her best books, perhaps the best of all; untouched by despair at the derelictions of governments, and full of hope in the transformations individuals might bring to their world. It is the only book in which she addressed the tragic heroism of the Spanish Civil War,[7] and it is a brilliant evocation of the capacity of modernism—the Auden generation—to speak for a new kind of future.

No Victory for the Soldier, begun in 1936, explored the scope for producing socially progressive art in a modernist mode. Publishing under a pseudonym gave Jameson the freedom to experiment with a different kind of writing, joining her central character, the musician John Knox, in the search for new forms to capture the fractured rhythms of modern European sensibility, and the distinctive taste and smell of Europe's great cities. Knox is a child of European cities, unburdened by the regional nostalgias that bedevilled his creator. He is only touched by the countryside when he reaches Spain, and finds there the energies that, reconnected to those of the cities, might yet drive the creation of a better world.

The language they were looking for was already being invented by Jameson's fellow-Yorkshireman, W. H. Auden. Jameson's interest in Auden's writing, reinforced by the example of political commitment he set in the 1930s, began with the appearance of his first poems. What she wrote about them after the war still has the ring of her early excitement. In *Poems 1930* she saw 'a young gravity and steadiness in their identification of feeling and image', and 'imagery [...] of an extreme sharpness and concreteness'. In the writing of the young Auden, the 'Factory and power-station' that other poets deployed with self-conscious clumsiness were fully assimilated.[8] His understanding of the poetic function of landscape, as already indicated, was replacing that of Eliot in her imagination as she wrote *In the Second Year*. His departure for America in January 1939 was to be a tremendous blow. It raised the whole issue of the writer's relation to his cultural heritage, and the way in which the forms of his work spring from the landscapes of his origins, and it cut across Jameson's hopes for some collective artistic endeavour to reconfigure the relations of language, society, and individual minds and bodies. Auden's departure, said Jameson, in the *Journal of Mary Hervey Russell*, in the voice of the dead soldier-poet Green, was a denial of

something we had in common, which was valuable, which we ought to have guarded, with all we had, if it was necessary with our minds and our precious—I mean it seriously—bodies. I can't describe to you what this something is since it must take a different form for each of us. For me it was the curve of a road I could see from my bedroom window, crossing the side of a hill to a group of trees.[9]

Knox is not Auden, but rather a composite figure of the artistic visionary who was needed, Jameson felt, to remake the links of individuals with the spaces history had given them collectively to inhabit. The clearest biographical connection is a tabloid headline: Knox abandons his work to drive an ambulance in Spain, as Auden was reported to have done. Unlike Auden, he dies at the wheel of his ambulance, fleeing with his Basque comrades before the German advance, shot dead by a nervous anarchist.

But the real likeness is in their experiments with modernist form. Knox's friend Andrew responds to the musician's first concert in terms similar to those in which Auden's poetry was discussed in the 1930s. Profoundly moved, he recognises a condensation of meaning, so intense that it almost defies understanding, drawing on the artist's own experience, but at the same time forcing its auditors to recall buried feelings and repressed knowledge of their own:

[E]ach phrase was almost shattered by the meanings packed into it, pierced by knives it made and turned against itself. The music did not lack feeling, but it was not the feeling of a very young man, nor of an old one. It forced Andrew to recall certain moments of the past three years he had decided to forget. Yet he knows nothing of all that, he thought, startled, shivering.[10]

The James Hill book expressed hopes for the future of people and politics which, as the German tanks moved towards the Czech frontiers, were already being disappointed. The bullet that cut short Knox's brilliant career, already put on hold while he made his contribution to a gloriously futile cause, foreshadowed the bullets of the coming war, which was to put a stop to Jameson's own most radical formal experiments.

Her following book, *Here Comes a Candle*, was written to make money, and in the hope that it might be taken up as a film.[11] The intention shows in the form, intensely visual and oral: a variety of techniques, from stream of consciousness to dialogue, and simple third-person narrative description, generates a chorus of voices, speaking within a shocking but gripping story-line. *Here Comes a Candle* explored the condition of the working people of contemporary London. The old tenements of New Moon Yard are home to the flotsam of a capitalism in long-drawn-out crisis, with no social conscience. Refugees, Jews, Italians, whores, poor young families, young couples with ambition, old people abandoned behind the closed doors of single rooms, jostle each other on the edge of survival. In those conditions, people make a living as well as they can, and self-preservation leaves no room for altruism. A pair of arsonists canvasses the occupants of the tenement, offering to burn it down so that they can collect on their insurance. Behind the gritty drama and the search for spectacular effects is a clear allegorical warning. New Moon Yard is a microcosm of an England on the edge of conflagration; and England itself is a microcosm of a Europe already in flames.

As Jameson later acknowledged, the only decent writing in those years was that which recognised the spectacle of a Europe on the edge of the pit.[12] When Auden left Europe, her model became André Malraux.

The Rallying of Class 1914

In the middle of September 1938, Jameson met with her old friend Sydney Harland, back from Peru after a long absence. Together, they talked, and as they talked, fellow-Eikonoklasts slipped back into place beside them. So said her Introduction to *Civil Journey*, dated 22 and 23 September, drawing together the essays on politics and fiction she had written throughout the 1930s and assigning them new meaning in the waiting-time before Munich.[13] Harland, she reported, said he was shocked by the spirit of conformity he found in the young writers and scientists he met in London. No one wanted to talk about writing, or science, only politics—nothing wrong with politics, of course, but the current kind was mere jargon, all deference to authorities and dogma. Jameson recalled their own generation's creed. It was the writer's duty to be critical of authorities and doctrines. A writer must be committed, and a committed writer must take orders from the political leaders he has agreed to support. But he is still obliged to judge and criticise whatever he is told to do. Voltaire, the rationalist and sceptic, was still their icon, but to Voltaire they now added André Malraux and Tawney.

The cultural battle-lines, Jameson continued, were being drawn up across Europe. The new barbarians were burning books and driving writers into exile, but even behind the parapets of traditional European culture there was growing contempt for the things of the mind. Paul Valéry's initiative under the aegis of the League of Nations, the *Institut International de Coopération Intellectuelle*, which had been reported in the *New English Weekly* in June 1933, was about to come into its own. Jameson noted the report of its conference that had appeared in July 1937, *Le Destin prochain des lettres*, and advised: 'It is worth reading for other reasons than the interest of knowing the mind on this question of such men as Valéry, Romains, Madariaga, Huizinga, Duhamel, Forster.' The 'other reasons' were the nationalist positions that were emerging on freedom of thought:

There were no German writers. The Italians found offensive the words *liberté de pensée* in the text of the resolution. On the whole, the balance inclined to pessimism in the minds of the French and the English—from which you may suppose either that we are more afraid or that we see more clearly.[14]

The idea that another Dark Age, or a new Deluge, was imminent brought a quotation from William Lamb's *The World Ends* (Jameson didn't admit her authorship). She urged writers to hold on to whatever they could recall of whatever they had read. The writer's memory could be the last repository of the European heritage.

Civil Journey, written out of the ideals of the young born before the First World War, and addressing the generations who would have to fight the next, was a timely manifesto for the new President of PEN. The collection is not merely an account of a journey concluded, but a map for the future. Its orientations are clear and simple. It reasserted the responsibility of the writer to defend freedom of thought, and justice, and it set out the European dimension of Englishness:

I am a Little [...] Englander on one side (the left—the side of the heart), and on the other I try to be a good European. Much good it will do us now to talk of Isolation, standing on the edge of a continent which can be overrun in a few hours by air. [...]

My pride and belief in England are such that I would rather she took more, not less, part in the business of Europe, interfered more often, and spoke—with the certainty of being listened to—in a less lawyer-like and equivocal voice.[15]

The political alignment is more of an imperative here than the cultural connection, but developing both was one of the most important tasks to which

Jameson would commit PEN. In constitutional principle, PEN was above politics. But in fact, as Jameson acknowledged in the 1960s, in *Journey from the North*, every national Centre was 'wormholed' with its own kind of literary politics. In Paris, politicking was a question of career and personal ambition (the original draft indicated acidly that this was especially true for such as Jules Romains). In some countries, where the right to nationhood was a matter of continuing struggle, literary politics was, rightly, 'ferociously nationalist', and the writer was as accountable for his actions as anyone else.[16] The English had no skill in literary politics, only in 'disorganised struggles, vanities'. By the end of the war, English writers, in PEN at least, were better organised, they were rebels, and their minds were European. And the European mind, for Jameson, was French.

PEN Prepares for War

The description in *Journey from the North* of Jameson's contribution to the wartime work of PEN is a radically condensed version of her original draft. That, in its turn, could only show the tip of the mountain of letters, drafts, and dossiers that piled up in the files of PEN and its officers throughout the war. With hindsight, she wrote in her autobiography, she regretted bitterly the time lost in work for PEN from her development as a writer. But for Hermon Ould, she would have found a reason to resign after the first year. She made several attempts to relinquish the post, justifiably pleading the illnesses its responsibilities exacerbated. Ould regularly kept her to it, both by refusal to accept her resignation and by the example of his own dedication, his total absence of egoism, and his willingness to sacrifice his own unwritten plays and poetry.[17]

She became President at the height of the Munich crisis. On 28 September 1938, Harold Nevinson had presented his resignation to the Executive of the London Centre of PEN. The question of a successor was discussed, and Jameson's name was put forward by the Secretary and warmly supported by the President and others.[18] Not everyone was convinced that she was totally suitable. Jameson wrote ruefully to Hermon Ould after a meeting held shortly afterwards: 'I felt horribly sorry last night that I was a woman, thus bringing dissension into the Club by the hand of Henry Simpson and some others. I must work harder to remove this awful stigma.'[19] The meeting of 28 September drew

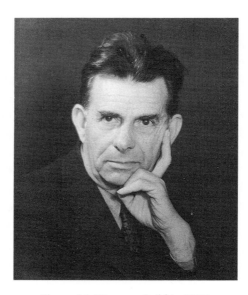

Figure 16 Hermon Ould in 1946.

up contingency plans in case war broke out before the next meeting. The Secretary would draft a resolution reaffirming the principles of the PEN and calling on members to counteract attempts to inflame national hatred.

The kind of peace Chamberlain brought back from Munich on 29 September 1938 was welcomed by many. The International President of PEN, Jules
Romains, sent to London copies of the three letters he had written to Georges
Bonnet (the French Minister for Foreign Affairs), Edouard Daladier, and
Beneš, all dated 2 October 1938, thanking them for the role they had played
in the current crisis. To Beneš, he added his admiration for the way the statesman's love of peace had enabled him to conquer his national and personal
pride. In his covering letter to London, written on the same day, he indicated
he would like to write to Chamberlain in similar terms but wanted first to
know if London agreed. There is no record of a reply; if there was one, it will
not have been supportive.[20]

For advice, Jameson turned at the beginning of October to Basil Liddell
Hart, who predicted to her that Hitler's next move would be to invade Czechoslovakia, in March 1939. (He was right: German troops entered Prague
on 15 March.) Britain, he said was powerless to stop him. In *Journey from
the North*, Liddell Hart appears in the closing pages of the first volume, as

172

the one honest, clear-sighted figure in the political confusion; against him, Jameson sets her sister Do and herself, representatives of a wilfully ignorant public, not wanting to hear the truth.[21] Liddell Hart described war as near-certain. Jameson's letters to Hilary Newitt Brown at the end of 1938 are full of rumours of disaster and betrayal. The 'nice American woman who runs The Whitehall Letter' told her that the Cabinet was sharply divided on whether or not to stand up to Hitler. Spain was 'on the mat now'. Stories were coming through of the treachery of the French politicians over Czechoslovakia, and the corruption of French Trade Union leaders. A 'shocked' member of the TUC had told her that 'The only T. U. leaders in France who were willing to fight were the Communists. The others, the ones who came over here to see our people, were as determined not to fight as Chamberlain himself.' She went on bitterly:

Oh, you can break your jigsaw puzzle of France and England into the smallest bits. It's no use any longer looking for any wide stretches of soundness, it is all in small pieces and most of them are rotten. I'm talking about the officials, of course. The poor bloody infantry is still sound, but it isn't up to defeating these people who are selling it in advance.[22]

Jameson and her sister took out a joint lease in November on Heathfield, a large Victorian house in Mortimer, eight miles outside Reading, with a large garden that would ensure the children could be fed. The Chapmans were to move there in the spring of 1939. The place was perfect, a relaxing refuge, but by no means out of the mainstream of things, and in easy travelling distance of London. For the same reasons, the Society of Authors was later to move its headquarters there. Their friends Aneurin Bevan and Jenny Lee lived in a nearby village. The Chapmans visited them there in October 1939, to be told of Nye's expectations that the war would be over in December, which Jameson thought nonsense, and hear his analysis, which she appreciated more, of the venal ambitions of the Labour Party and Trade Union officialdom to share power, rather than seize it on behalf of the workers.[23]

In the meantime, there was practical action to be taken on behalf of PEN. The writers from Germany, Poland, and Hungary who had taken refuge from Hitler in Czechoslovakia were in flight again, this time to France and England. Jameson wrote to Ould from Shinfield Road on 13 October 1938 that expressions of sympathy were all very well, but money was what the Czechs needed, and they must open a fund:

I see before us a future of opening fund after fund, as one country after another goes down, until the moment when our own fate is so close that we go to the bank to draw out the last two shillings to buy ourselves a ticket to the moon, and the law, probably Henry Simpson in the uniform of a special constable, arrests us for sedition with the 2/- in our hands.[24]

A flood of instructions followed. They must send a letter to the weeklies, *Time and Tide*, the *New Statesman*, *The Spectator*, the *New English Weekly*, and to the *Daily Telegraph*, *The Times*, the *News Chronicle*, *The Herald*, the *Yorkshire Post*, the *Manchester Guardian*, and any other papers they could think of, especially the good provincial ones. She would draft it for him to correct. It should be signed by the three ex-presidents, Hermon and herself. She would write to Priestley. They must ask the Society of Authors to associate themselves with it. They must send roneoed copies to members and typed copies to non-members—to Duff Cooper, Harold Nicolson, Charles Morgan, Bonamy Dobrée, F. L. Lucas, Winston Churchill, Brigadier General Spears, Edward Thompson, Phyllis Bentley, and Lettice Cooper.

At the same time, PEN's own funds needed reinforcement, and she had been talking to W. E. Williams, then Director of the British Institute of Adult Education, and a member of the British Council subcommittee.[25] He had told her to try to make personal contact with Lord Lloyd, the Chairman of the British Council. She would do that. Hermon must tell Intellectual Liberty (the Communist-organised group, whose office was up the stairs from PEN), what PEN was engaged in, and make them keep off the shared phone line. She concluded:

What with the Japanese taking South China, and the prospect of a sort of Boer War in Palestine, and the colonies screaming against being given back to Germany, and Dr Funk pocketing all the trade from Prague to Istanbul, and more money wanted for arms, it looks as though this would be the last fund we'd get money into ever![26]

In the first instance, they collected £1,000. She wrote towards the end of October to Valentine Dobrée, to tell her about the fund and to report that they had already helped two Germans out of Prague. There were others still there, and she expected that the pure Czechs would be coming soon, as well as more Germans:

The lot of the Germans is very bitter, since these fled there from Berlin years ago, some of them after having been in concentration camps as socialists, pacifists, liberals, and whatnot. Now the wave has overtaken them again. Europe as a spectacle is nearly unbearable.[27]

She added that she had just seen Picasso's 'Guernica' in Paris.

From this initiative, PEN raised almost three thousand pounds. It was not a great deal, Jameson thought, but these were not famous writers, and moreover 'they had been victimized by their own people, a suspicious circumstance'.[28] Most of the famous writers, then and later, would head for America, leaving the London Centre to hold the stage for European culture, with the under-studies and supporting cast.

In her autobiography, Jameson mostly confines her account of PEN's achievements with the refugees to their impact on individuals' lives. She passes over in silence the important connections her work was helping PEN establish at that time with the British Council. Since the middle of 1935, the British Council had changed and extended its functions under the direction of Lord Eustace Percy, who in a letter to the Foreign Secretary in 1937 set out the change:

The Council is no longer expected merely to rescue British prestige from neglect; it has to defend that prestige from deliberate attack. The political motive has become over-whelming [...]. It is supposed (to mention only one aspect of its work) to be doing at least something towards making good the ground of British influence in Egypt, in the Eastern Mediterranean and in Portugal against Fascist cultural penetration; and it has to perform these tasks with resources no more than sufficient to enable it to conduct Pleasant Sunday Afternoons for Anglophils in Gothenburg and Helsingfors.[29]

Under Lord Lloyd, the process of extending British influence was accelerated. Its best-remembered activities today are probably those described in the East-ern Mediterranean, familiar to readers of Olivia Manning's novels, *The Balkan Trilogy* (1960–5) and *The Levant Trilogy* (1977–80). PEN's activities made a substantial balancing contribution to the defence of British cultural prestige in Western and Central Europe. Lloyd's description of the Council's strategies is closely attuned to the lines Jameson took in PEN. Political success, he argued in one of his speeches, would be a matter of personalities and ethics:

Our cultural influence is, in fact, the effect of our personality on the outside world...What most interests the outside world, beyond the fact of our power, is the use to which that power will be put. The answer to that question lies deep in our national character—a character which many, even of our friends, have misunderstood, and our opponents have been concerned to misinterpret. All the more reason that we should give the world free access to our civilisation, and free opportunity to form its own judgement on our outlook and motives [...] Everywhere we find people turning with relief from the harshly dominant notes of totalitarian propaganda to the less insistent and more reasonable cadences of Britain. We do not force them to 'think British', we offer them the opportunity of learning what the British think.[30]

The relationship between PEN and the British Council was often one of rivalry (as was that between the British Council and the Ministry of Information), and the extra political edge it brought worried, or annoyed, some PEN members. It was however a key part of PEN's effective functioning in the wartime years.

Jameson first took the President's chair at an Executive Committee meeting of London PEN on 26 October 1938. The meeting was attended by Richard Church, Eleanor Farjeon, Nora Heald, Henrietta Leslie, Owen Rutter, Irene Rathbone, Ellis Roberts, Horace Shipp, L. A. G. Strong, Noel Streatfeild, Mrs Arthur Watts, Alec Waugh, and Hermon Ould. It approved the election of two new members, Lilo Linke and Ll. Wyn Griffith. It learned that the Viennese Centre had been dissolved, and that Rudolf Olden, Secretary of the German PEN Club in Exile in London, had written to ask whether an Austrian Group should now be established, or Austrian writers-in-exile be absorbed by the German Group.[31]

On 15 November, Olden wrote to Jameson that twelve people in Prague had got British visas, five had already left, and the rest would follow at the end of the month. They would arrive in England penniless, and he expressed his relief that she had been so farsighted as to arrange for PEN to set up its fund.[32] The work of the fund expanded rapidly. Grants were originally 20 shillings for a single person, and 25 shillings for a married couple, but as numbers grew, these figures had to be halved. In addition, PEN looked for volunteers to provide full hospitality for the refugees, so that the money grant could be used to help them to write and publish. On 24 November, Doreen Marston wrote to Rudolf Olden to tell him she had taken over the administration of the fund in a separate department, working from 59 New Oxford Street, in order to release Ould and Jameson for the actual work of the PEN Club.[33] Later, Janet Chance took over the work.

That still left a lot of tasks that only the President and the International Secretary could deal with: expanding the organisation of the refugee work, helping refugees obtain visas, compiling lists for the authorities of those most endangered, and increasingly, dealing with the political problems they posed for the British authorities, who were suspicious of the socialist enthusiasm that in Britain had so successfully been marginalised. Rudolf Olden expostulated to Ould on the treatment of a German publisher denied entry to Britain, on the suspicion, Olden thought, of Communist leanings. Jameson reprinted his letter in her *Journal of Mary Hervey Russell*, but omitted (this was 1945) his defence of the Communists:

What kind of political tendency do the British authorities expect of refugees from Germany? Certainly not a Nazi tendency. Consequently there will always be ties to Communists. For the anti-Nazi opposition has the shape of the Popular Front. This is not our invention but it has been created by Herr Hitler himself who persecutes Communists, Socialists, and Liberals.[34]

He copied his letter to Jameson, and asked that PEN take action. At the end of December, he reported that Friedrich Burschell had been elected to represent the refugees from the German Reich coming through from Czechoslovakia. Burschell was helping those who were still waiting for travel permits. A hundred visas had just been granted, but there was much competition for them; so it would be useful if Jameson could write to the Layton Committee, which met at 5 Mecklenburgh Square, underlining the especially dangerous situation these writers were in.[35]

Contacts with other creative arts associations were developing. In December, for instance, Stanley Richardson, Secretary of the Arden Society for Artists and Writers Exiled in England, wrote to agree to collaborate with PEN in the work with exiles. He mentioned in his letter that he was about to leave for Spain to see Casals about a concert, for which Jameson had already agreed to be a patron.[36]

Most exhausting for Jameson, and most appreciated by the refugees, were the personal contacts at PEN's social events, and the morale-raising speeches she gave. No one else, wrote one member, expressing her deep gratitude, understood so well what the bitter crisis of sudden exile must mean, for writers.[37]

The plight of those left in Czechoslovakia was again brought to Jameson's attention in December 1938, by a letter from the President of the Prague Pen Club, Madame Tilschova, regretting deeply the banishment of the refugee intellectuals and expressing surprise at the absence of any expression of sympathy for them from the Paris Centre.[38] On the other hand, the writer commented, the International President, Jules Romains, had managed to thank enthusiastically the English and French statesmen whose policies had procured the tragedy. The London Centre was asked to approach the French and English governments on behalf of all the PEN Clubs and ask them to offer asylum to these victims of appeasement. Preserved in the same archive folder as this letter are two typed foolscap pages, headed 'Le Sensible Jules Romains' ['The Sensitivity of Jules Romains'], dated from Lidové Noviny—Brno, 28 November 1938, and written in response to a circular from Romains, as International President, received on 19 November, which had asked all PEN Clubs to speak up on behalf of Jewish writers experiencing persecution. The author (perhaps the Secretary of the Czech Centre, Jiřina Tůmová, whom Guy Chapman had seen in Prague during a business trip for Cape in December 1938)[39] declared the request, coming from Romains, was grotesque. His speech at Toulouse, the writer went on, which thanked the leaders of France and Britain for preserving peace at the expense of Czechoslovakia, was only equalled by the two speeches he had made in Hungary twelve and six years earlier.[40] The Prague Centre had telegraphed a protest at that time, and Romains had replied that he was speaking not as the International President of PEN, but as a French citizen. Czechoslovakia, the document ended, was now full of refugees from Germany, Poland, and Hungary, who needed to be allowed into France and England.

In the following year, the pressures increased. On 22 February 1939, the London Executive Committee received an appeal sent from Toulouse, from a Monsieur Obiols, who was accompanied by thirty-one members of the Catalan Centre in flight. Ould was delegated to go to Paris and interview any who had arrived there, and plans were made to raise funds for them. Jameson gave a report on the situation of the political refugees arrived from Prague, and those who were still in Prague without permits, on whom it was increasingly difficult to get information. A representative needed to be sent, but money was a problem.[41]

By March 1939, the money problem was on its way to being resolved with the foundation of the Arts and Letters Refugee Committee, which pooled the efforts of the Actors' Refugee Committee, the Architects' Refugee Relief Fund, the Arden Society, the Artists Refugee Committee, the Czecho-Slovak Journalists Relief Fund, and the PEN Refugee Writers Fund.[42] On 31 March 1939, the Co-ordinating Committee of the new body received the draft of an appeal to the Baldwin Fund, which included details of each organisation's activities. PEN reported having spent the money it had raised to date (£1,000) on grants of 10s. a week (in addition to hospitality arranged by Committees) to over forty writers, to help them become self-supporting. Credentials had been examined in all cases. The PEN offices were used daily for help for refugee writers, including help with visas; there was an Advice Bureau to assist writers to become self-supporting; there was help with access to libraries, social contacts, and English lessons. To these services would shortly be added a fortnightly advice bureau on publishers, agents, and translators, run by Robert Neumann, President of the former Austrian Centre in Vienna. The Trades Union Congress was heavily involved, and refugees had free membership of the Trade Union Club.

Janet Chance's regular typed reports to Jameson and Ould kept them in touch with the formation and progress of this umbrella Committee. On 10 February, she warned that if substantial sums were requested, PEN might end up vetting and looking after all refugee writers in Britain, dealing with extra work in the office, and setting up a board of referees for each country; but she still thought they should go ahead. On 14 February, she reported plans to seek representation for the new body on the Co-ordinating Committee for Refugees, based in Bloomsbury House. L. A. Berry from the Czech Journalists group would be their representative, with herself as substitute.

Shuttling between London and the flat in Reading, Jameson wrote strings of letters to the PEN office, with instructions about letters to be passed on to Hermon Ould, the Refugee balance sheet, and circulars for members about a memorial tribute for Lorca, for which she would pay the postage, as her personal tribute to the poet.[43] On 15 March 1939, the Germans marched into Prague. The original thousand pounds in the refugee fund collected from writers was nearly gone, and on 20 March Jameson signed a new circular appeal, to be sent to newspaper editors and PEN Centres in the Dominions and America.[44] In May, she was writing to the office with instructions on how to handle the contributions.[45]

She was also building up her personal connections with colleagues in the French PEN Club. She spent five weeks in Paris, in April and May 1939, and was taken by Benjamin Crémieux, of the International Committee, to watch Louis Jouvet in the dress rehearsal of Giraudoux's *Ondine*, and to meet the writer whom she had long admired. Afterwards, over supper in an expensive restaurant, Crémieux described the behaviour of the diners after Munich, and their loud expressions of gratitude to Daladier. Crémieux, whose humanitarianism and idealism she would later incorporate into the figure of the patriotic left-wing Jewish editor in *Cloudless May*, commented that too many of his compatriots were less afraid of the Nazis than of socialism. Jameson, out of politeness, she later wrote, told him they had their English counterparts, and kept to herself the thought that the English, at the end of the day, were more likely to stand up and resist.[46]

From Paris, she wrote to encourage Valentine Dobrée to take advantage of an opportunity to send her daughter Georgina, Jameson's goddaughter, to safety.[47] She told Valentine Paris was nervy and on edge. She had money problems. PEN refugee activity was encountering obstacles; and she had still to fulfil her personal commitment to help rescue the parents of a young couple she had met in Prague.[48]

The Chapmans moved into the big house in Mortimer with Do and Robert and their two children at the end of May. In June, there were arrangements to be made for the delegation to the Stockholm Congress. Jameson was pleased that E. M. Forster would be one of the delegates, but anxious about the speech she would have to make, telling Ould she was only doing it out of concern to hold up the London end against Romains.[49] In the same letter, she raised the possibility of getting the committee to discuss, in her absence, extending the PEN presidency from its current one-year term. She suggested that PEN might take over the international symposium, the Entretiens de Pontigny, and told him of her cheerful refusal of the chairmanship of Margaret Rhondda's Six-Point Group:

> The Six-Point Group is the Great Feminist haystack built by Lady Rhondda and *Time and Tide* and now running on its own, with all the war-horses of feminism. Two years ago they asked me to be a vice-president. I agreed on condition that they did not expect me to attend a meeting or pay a subscription. I have neither attended a meeting nor paid as much as a shilling to the funds. So why they picked on me to be Chairman I can't imagine. I refused joyfully.[50]

PEN commitments were hard work, but clearly she felt them more congenial, as well as more useful. The London Executive Committee was responding with enthusiasm to her leadership. Irene Rathbone sent an admiring letter of support, enclosing her attempt at a declaration of intent for the PEN (the 'homework', she joked, that Jameson had asked them all to do at the last meeting):

> If you want us to go more political, I'm with you. Politics have become ethics nowadays. Certain happenings, states of affairs, are ethically to be condemned. We can't, just because we're a club for 'culture' or whatever, *not* condemn. We're on this ghastly earth with the rest. And you, for your misfortune, happen to be at the head of us at just this time. Take your line. For myself, I trust you so completely—as human being, 'scribe', president—that whatever line you took would be right.[51]

At the end of June, the Chapmans went back to France and spent the last pre-war summer in Saumur, by the Loire, and in Bordeaux.[52] On her return to

England, Jameson was confronted with the news of Chamberlain's attempts at economic appeasement. She wrote to Harrison Brown: 'His dread of war is a dread of revolution, of course, and has consequently all the force of a really deep terror behind it—a business of man's fear for his money. Also he is inspired by God—an awful combination.'[53] Her dealings with the rising tide of refugees took on a tinge of desperation: 'It seems absurd to be trying to get people to guarantee an elderly Austrian writer, with the world rocking as it is. Perhaps it will rock over this autumn, and then everything will be impossible.'[54]

On 24 August 1939, the Minutes of the London Executive recorded an urgent debate on whether the Stockholm Congress should be cancelled. Wells thought it should go ahead, as a demonstration to the world that intellectual workers were not to be dictated to by political dictators. It was reported that Henry Nevinson had written to protest against a poem published in the Bulletin of the Rome PEN Centre, which had glorified Mussolini's destruction of the Abyssinians, and described them as black ants. A statement was prepared by Jameson, Ould, Wells and E. M. Forster, reminding members throughout the world of their responsibility to rise above nationalist prejudice and speak out for the truth:

We the members of the English Centre of PEN call the attention of all centres to the fact that in the event of war, or if the international tension becomes worse, great pressure will be put on writers to place their skill at the disposal of a government policy: in such a situation the individual writer must decide for himself where his duty lies, but we remind members that their pledge forbids them to disseminate hatred in any cause; that they owe a duty to truth and reason and that if they allow truth to be destroyed and hatred to triumph they will be betraying their own countries, other countries, civilisation itself.[55]

On 28 August, an Emergency Executive agreed to encourage the Stockholm Congress to go ahead. Jameson was unhappy with the decision. In the draft of her autobiography, she records hearing from Philip Jordan that a friend of Nevile Henderson, the British ambassador in Berlin, had been assured it was safe to holiday in Austria in August, on two conditions: 'one, that the English newspapers ceased to be provocative, and second that "our Polish friends" (the inverted commas were Nevile Henderson's) were not too exigent.'[56] This could, Jameson thought, portend another Munich at the Poles' expense. She had no intention of finding herself in Sweden and not knowing what was happening to Bill. Chamberlain finally solved the problem. On 3 September, Britain and France declared war on Germany.

PART III

Europe at War

12

1940: Vile Betrayals

PEN at War

The refugee operation changed gear. More help was needed to establish individuals' identities and allegiances. Jameson contacted a fellow-Yorkshireman, the writer and high-ranking civil servant Humbert Wolfe, and she and Ould used him unsparingly to help obtain visas and work-permits for refugee writers.[1] Refugee members were drafted in to help. Robert Neumann and Rudolf Olden were asked to join a new PEN Committee which would identify reliable anti-Nazi refugees, and tell such persons that PEN was willing to help them.[2] Other members included Otto Pick and Bernhardt Menne, Chairman of the Thomas Mann Group of the Czech Refugee Fund (the German writers who had fled to Prague in 1933, and were later forced to flee again, to England). The first meeting was planned for 7 December, in Noel Streatfeild's house. A separate letter of 28 November, to Olden, asked for advice on letters of denunciation that had been sent in from the Czech Trust, which accused certain members of the Thomas Mann Group of being Gestapo agents.[3] PEN was entering dirty political waters.

At the end of September, a different kind of political problem had arisen. A statement had been received from the International President, Jules Romains, with a request for it to be circulated to all Centres as a message from the International Executive.[4] The London Executive declined to do so, on the grounds that passages in it, apparently urging PEN members to identify themselves with their national governments, were in contradiction of PEN principles. With malicious pleasure, Jameson wrote a polite letter to the great Frenchman, expressing her reservations, and saying the International Executive needed to be consulted.[5] Eventually, she secured the approval of the Paris Centre for a joint communiqué with London, sent out in May 1940, which told members that governments were not to be supported uncritically, and that a very clear political position must be taken against the current threat.[6] In his speech to the PEN Congress in Nice after the war, 17 June 1952, 'Un essai d'une politique de l'esprit' ['Towards a Politics of Mind'], Romains later set out his claim to have been the first International President to lead PEN to political activism.[7] He waxed ironic at the expense of colleagues who, he said, had complained of his lack of consultation with the members of the International Committee, and blocked his call for writers to mobilise. He claimed that their counter-message was a call to neutrality. He went on to defend his self-exile to America in June 1940 as a self-sacrifice to preserve freedom of speech for PEN's International Presidency, to win over America to support the war, and to save from the Nazis PEN's dossiers of letters received from clandestine opponents of the regime in occupied countries.

That was all to come after the war, and in the meantime, it was Jameson who headed PEN's call for writers to take up their arms, and gave it her own distinctive orientation. The article she published in the *TLS* that October, on 'The Writer's Place in the Defence Line', gave a firm steer towards the liberal ideals that such as E. M. Forster had argued in the mid-1930s, while adding a strong dose of the socialism of Class 1914.[8] She pointed to the traditional role of France and England as the joint defenders of European civilisation, and gave her definition of that civilisation, something still to be fought for: 'the reflection of a precise idea of human dignity'. She pinned her flag to the mast: writers must be against anti-Semitism, class oppression, authoritarianism, the suppression of free speech, and nationalism. At the centre of her piece, she quoted Tawney's letter from 'a soldier', printed during the previous war (in *The Spectator and Nation*, October 1915), attacking the betrayal at home of the soldiers' fight for a just society. It was, she said, the writer's duty to stop that happening again, and to fight to maintain the free transmission of ideas across frontiers:

A modern dictator who is able to turn ideas back at the frontiers of his State does civilisation a far worse turn than if he merely destroyed roads. Anything that a writer can do, to cheat the dictator's police, he ought. [...] This is not asking him to be, in the glib phrase, internationally-minded—no writer has ever been more deeply and fully English than he whom the Germans call 'unser Shakespeare'. But it requires him to be certain that civilisation is sinking in Europe because the communications have broken down, that his duty is to restore them everywhere; that his fellow-countrymen are Čapek,

Unamuno, Einstein, Rilke, Freud, Mann, rather than some he went to school with. Even this phrase is misleading, since he must have gone to school with these too.

Writers, soldiers, and peasants, all represent the common man, and in their collective name she attacked the evil of simple-minded nationalism:

A correspondent in *The Times* wrote lately: 'We have no other aim than to destroy Hitlerism [...].' The writer cannot allow himself to share this comforting simplicity. He cannot think in terms of destroying Hitlerism, but only of saving the Europe of which England is a part, of imagining for Europe a future from which the poison of nationalism has been drawn.

This double challenge—saving Europe, and saving England—was to mark all her political work and her writing in the years of war. In January 1940, she published a major article in *The Fortnightly*, with some very timely proposals for an economic federation of Europe that would put an end to the current disorder and waste of life and resources. These were, she said, familiar ideas, but

[t]he form given them by the English Society for Federal Union and in Streit's *Union Now*, and their eager acceptance in this crisis of Europe by people of all sorts, are new. Streit's book, and an excellent Penguin book, *The Case for Federal Union*, by W. B. Curry, provide the material on which people may form their own judgement.[9]

Bringing an end to 'the disease of economic nationalism' and establishing peace would involve very specific and radical steps towards institutions of economic co-operation, beginning with the limitation of sovereignty:

The power to control trade and finance, to deal with other States and groups of States, to control and limit armaments, to enforce respect for international law, to control the use of raw materials, to govern and educate in colonial territories and to prepare them for self-government, to reconstruct and develop certain social services in Europe (e.g. communications, medicine), should be handled by a federal European Council, or Parliament—what does the name matter?[10]

The United States should not be involved at this stage (presumably because of its negative influence in the League of Nations after 1918), but the self-governing Dominions of the British Empire should have a role. Federal union could best be achieved by stages:

A basis exists in the Oslo Group, and in the re-created mechanism for Franco-British co-operation. It is not utopian to make plans for the common economic and social organization of Western Europe, including Norway, Sweden—and Germany. Germany cannot be left outside, and we ought to agree that we are fighting this war to compel her to come in.[11]

Europe Abandoned

Jameson began writing her novel *Europe to Let: The Memoirs of an Obscure Man* in the middle of the Czech crisis, and finished it in November 1939.[12] Colleagues and friends wondered at her stamina. In Irene Rathbone's novel of 1952, *The Seeds of Time*, the novelist Camilla, invited to a country-house party, is a standing reproach to friends seized belatedly of the consequences of appeasement:

Figure 17 Irene Rathbone in Venice in the 1920s. On the back, 'Margaret from Irene', and in Jameson's hand, 'Irene Rathbone'.

'Camilla, stay on here a bit. You've put a lot of toil and ardour all winter into good causes. You've somehow finished a book too—I don't wonder your friends call you "the fastest hack in London". You deserve to laze. M'mm. And it's nice spring weather.'

From her friend, kneeling on the hearthrug, head averted: 'This spring of disgrace. [...] Two republics, two small, intrepid peoples, ardently friendly to us, sunk into night with our contrivance in the same spring. [...] As though by these vile betrayals we could keep safe ourselves for even six months longer. What's the alternative left to us but general war? A cowed, foetid and brutalized planet.'[13]

For her new book, Jameson drew on more than twenty years' experience of Europe's nationalist struggles, and the collective failures of nations and individuals—among whom she included herself—to make interventions that could have brought reconciliation and peace. The self-flagellating guilt that drives the narrative is the same that drove her work in PEN, plucking victims from the catastrophe, as she saw it, too late and too few.

Europe to Let is the nightmare spectacle of the end of the high civilisation of the West. The Mediterranean culture of rationalism and humanism is being devoured by an older, monstrous inhumanity waking on Europe's northern and eastern borders. The first three *nouvelles*, covering the period from the French occupation of the Rhineland in 1923 to the fall of Czechoslovakia in 1938, follow the journeys of Captain Esk, a commander in the First World War, now turned writer, to the sites where the derelictions of England and France made war in Europe inevitable. These landscapes are heavy with an inescapable political history. In Vienna in 1937, Esk walks through a world where space, time, and human endeavour, long frozen together, are slowly awakening into something shapeless and beyond control:

The whole of Central Europe must have been ice-bound, a dry frozen plain under the black bubble of the sky, with a few lights of villages and cities scattered in it like seeds of thistledown in a field. A lifeless snake, the Danube, lay in this field. [...I]t was like watching the North Sea at night—nothing is stable, there are no forms, no limits; anything may be shaping itself in the darkness, and it may be any hour of any century.[14]

The last *nouvelle*, 'The Children Must Fear', is set in Budapest, on the frontier between Europe and Asia, the edge of 'new country' which is another black space. This is the irrational, barbarian underside of Europe's history, of which modern Europe never speaks—which Esk, like his creator, is beginning to discover, is also an unconfessed monstrosity repressed in himself. Jameson's novel is a brilliantly understated evocation of the

189

psycho-history of Europe. The Christian communion celebrated in the images of eating and drinking, in the cafes and homes of ordinary Europeans, is a far-off reflection of primitive rites of sacrificial violence. In the surreal landscapes of night-time Budapest, doorways are portals into some other, crueller reality:

> In the narrower streets there were no lights, and the fronts of the houses were dispersed and split open by the darkness. A doorway blinked like an eye which appears, for no reason whatever, except that the painter saw it there, in a corner of the canvas. [...] I understand at these moments how provisional and insecure is the shape, the timing of reality that we have agreed upon. Even I myself have to reckon with another I. My flesh knotted under my clothes, I am resistant and irresponsible. What is happening to the men and women clinging to Europe as to a raft does not move me. [...] I am uncouth, defensive, full of hidden malice.[15]

Esk himself is drawn into the city's hallucinations. Walking by the Danube, he smells in the river's stinking breath the fetid breath of another life, and the return in himself of long-repressed, debilitating emotions. Jameson's struggles with her sadistic mother run below the surface of the text. Named after the river that ran past her childhood home, Esk is another Jameson persona, who, like her, has been forced to confront in Budapest the double stream of good and evil that is in every European's blood, uniting states, families and individuals:

> Budapest stinks of death and violence. An invisible other keeps step with me, to my left between the unappeased Danube and its old woman's chuckling gossip, and my hand. What a breath from this river! What an old woman's acid breath. If I lean towards it I shall get in my face such a whiff of memory it will make me uneasy. And why should I feel an anxiety about this month, or this year, or any year? For what mistake as a child am I being punished by these reminders of guilt—too many of them?[16]

Esk flees from such self-knowledge, and in so doing he abandons to their fate all the oppressed of the city, from the self-effacing Jewish fellow-journalist who has been his guide to the frightened boy glimpsed among the milling peasants at the station, abandoned, and with 'nothing to hold on to'.[17]

The novel was posted off to the contracted publisher, Cassell, who declined to publish it. Desmond Flower claimed there was a problem of obscenity—there were, he said, three unprintable words in the text—and a sentence that might be a libel on Lord Runciman (Runciman had been sent on a mission to Prague to persuade the Czechs to abandon their resistance). Whatever the objectionable words were, they slipped into the edition

published by Macmillan in America, proofed, Jameson said, without reference to the author, while the subsequent battles over English publication
continued to rage.[18]

Europe to Let marked a watershed in Jameson's publishing career. An introduction from Vera Brittain to Rache Lovat Dickson at Macmillan led to an invitation
from Lovat Dickson to show him her current book and her contract with Cassell.[19] After some three months' acerbic discussions with Cassell, in which Nancy
Pearn, of Pearn, Pollinger, and Higham ('my broken reed of an agent')[20] was, as
ever, no help, Jameson took over her own negotiations[21] and became a Macmillan writer. In Lovat Dickson, she found not only a most sympathetic editor, who
organised efficiently the distribution and publicity of her books, but a lifelong
friend, who offered over the years much good advice and practical help. The
connection with the Macmillan family was equally helpful, and much to her
current taste. In answer to a request from Lovat Dickson for autobiographical
details, she produced an account that showed how far the Eikonoklast had come:
'I have written too many books, I travel as often as I can, I admire the French
and love the Czechs, I study foreign politics, my own are what you might call a
revolutionary conservative, or a conservative revolutionary.'[22] She was in contact
with Harold as well as Daniel Macmillan (though more often the latter). She
would shortly be rejoicing in Chamberlain's success in the May election, since it
indicated that Harold Macmillan might soon have a role in the government.[23]

As 1939 drew to its end, the situation in Europe grew darker. Jameson wrote
to the Paris Centre asking for news of colleagues who had vanished into prison
and camps. H. G. Wells and Beatrix Lehmann had both expressed to her their
concern for the novelist Jean Giono and the philosopher Alain. Eventually, letters of reassurance that both had been released came back from André Gide,
left in charge of the Paris Centre (and addressing the London President, dis-
concertingly, as 'Monsieur').[24] Vacillating politicians continued to weaken the
Allies' position. Around the end of January 1940, with Finland about to be
invaded, Jameson found herself sitting between E. M. Forster and the First
Secretary of the French Embassy, Monsieur de Charbonnières, at a PEN lunch
held at the Café Royal. Charbonnières, outspokenly pro-Polish, shared with
her his anger at the tales of German atrocities coming from Poland, for which,
to her surprise, Forster gently asked for evidence; she felt herself reproved
by his scrupulous sense of justice.[25] She reported to Charbonnières a remark
made by Harold Macmillan when she met him to discuss *Europe to Let*: 'What
frightens me about Chamberlain, Hoare, Simon, is that, like very old men, they

can't decide anything, they change their decisions about Finland from day to day, almost hour to hour.' Charbonnières had sympathised: 'You have been no more fortunate than we have in your parliamentarians.'[26]

The Germans made their military breakthrough in France in the May of 1940, and Jameson recorded the buzz of voices at a reception at the Chinese Embassy on that day. There was a hubbub of left-leaning intellectuals, journalists, writers, and politicians, discussing the German advance and evaluating dismally their prospects in the event of the invasion of England.[27] Victor Gollancz said he would take poison; he couldn't go to America or all his work would be discredited. A 'don turned publicist' said that *The Times* had been right to advise Britain to make friends with the Germans. He, Jameson commented, saw himself as a power behind the throne in left politics, supported by his rich wife; he would help the Germans administer the country in the event of a British defeat.

Germany's invasion of France resolved Jameson's hesitations over her pacifist commitment. Along with many others, including Louis Mumford and Bertrand Russell, she resigned her PPU membership in May.[28] Vera Brittain remained, and later joined the PPU Executive. As British forces were being evacuated from Dunkirk, Ould and Jameson persuaded the London Executive Committee on 31 May 1940 to issue the 'Appeal to the Conscience of the World' that Jameson had drafted the previous September. Dated 24 May 1940, and sent out to all Allied countries, it urged respect for the enemy alongside defence of freedom of speech and the free movement of ideas, and told writers 'to repeat, if necessary to die repeating that any word, any act, any treaty which debases the dignity and freedom of the common man is evil and to be rejected'.[29] Centres in neutral countries were specially adjured to remember their responsibilities. The Macmillan office in New York distributed the appeal throughout America, and it appeared in local and national journals and newspapers from Washington to Tennessee. In *The Nation*, published in New York, it figured prominently on 27 July 1940 on a page full of letters challenging American isolationism.[30]

Europe to Let turned out to have an important role to play in the Allied war effort. On 17 August 1940, the novel was the centre-piece of the BBC's Czechoslovak programme.[31] The month before, on 3 July, Beneš had been recognised by the British as the head of a provisional Czechoslovak Government, and the process of rebuilding confidence between the two countries had begun. The presenters of the August broadcast began with general information about the many English books of fiction, journalism, and politics, and English films, that had appeared in the last two years on Czechoslovakian issues, all of which demonstrated, they said, England's determination to question its conscience after its excess of trust in Hitler, and share the sacrifices of the Czechoslovakian people. In particular, *Europe to Let*, published in April, was praised for its admission of England's betrayal of the Czechs, and for understanding the need to explain Europe and its nations to the English. The novel was greeted as the most powerful evocation of Czechoslovakia in English that had appeared within the year, and its author was described as one of the greatest living English writers. The speakers praised Jameson's deep understanding of European countries, and her ability to draw naturally and convincingly characters from each different nation. Her book wrote in detail the epic of recent Czechoslovakian history, projected into the macrocosm of pan-European crisis, and the microcosm of the fate of individual people in particular nations; and it showed how clearly the sympathies of the English man-in-the-street were with the people of Czechoslovakia.

The broadcast also had a secondary purpose, of building bridges with France. The novel, it was pointed out, certainly described the ugly defeatism of certain French circles, but it was also at pains to show the decency and courage of ordinary Frenchmen.

These conciliatory moves towards France were as important for England as for Czechoslovakia. In the summer of 1940, counter-arguments were urgently needed against German and Vichy propaganda efforts to foster Anglophobia in post-invasion France, after the apparent abandonment of France by Britain at Dunkirk and the shelling of the French fleet by the Allies at Mers el Kébir (July 1940). Dealing with the resentment of the British public at France's collapse was another issue.

Internment

June brought a new set of problems for PEN's work with the European refugees in England. In September 1939, there had been over 60,000 German and Austrian refugees and around 8,000 Czech refugees in Britain. As soon as war broke out, a large number of Nazi sympathisers and a few leftists and Jews had been promptly interned, and thereafter all other 'enemy aliens' classified by tribunals: 'A', subject to internment; 'B', restricted in their movements; or 'C', the majority, allowed to move freely. From mid-May 1940, after the debacle in France, all

'B' class aliens were rounded up. On 10 June, Mussolini declared war on France and Britain, and on the same day Reynaud's government abandoned Paris for Bordeaux. The Germans entered Paris on 14 June. In Britain, by 20 June, authority was given to bring in any 'C' class Germans or Austrians felt to be doubtful, and after 25 June, all 'C' class men under 70 were subject to internment.[32] Ould and Jameson, who had been dealing with the authorities from the start over the classification of 'their' refugees, now found themselves writing new letters to get them out of the camps. A joint letter appeared in *The Times Literary Supplement* in July, spelling out the cruel illogicality of the official position:

> The work of such writers as Rudolf Olden and Robert Neumann since they came here has been that of active opponents of the Nazi regime. Now that we ourselves are at war with this regime these representatives of the true German culture are discovered by the authorities to be a danger to the country, and their intelligence and experience are hurriedly interned. [...]
>
> It should be possible, even now, to retrieve from the camps those German and Austrian writers who are known by their works as bitter opponents of Nazi Germany. It is not only that they can be useful, and want to be useful. We need for our own sake to make it clear that the principles those writers hoped to assert in exile are as actively to be defended as our homes.[33]

Robert Neumann was in Mooragh Camp, in Ramsey, on the Isle of Man. He chafed at the slowness of the authorities, who, he said, were giving priority to workers (these were workers needed in agriculture and industry), but keeping behind the barbed wire proven enemies to Hitler, many of whom had already been in German concentration camps.[34] He asked Ould for PEN International Membership cards, signed by himself and Jameson, to hand out in the camp, and urged them to prioritise release efforts for political internees, who would be most vulnerable in the event of an invasion. There were no cards to send, Ould explained. They came from Paris and there was no one left there to sign them; Romains had gone to New York, and the situation of the Paris Secretary, Benjamin Crémieux, was a cause for anxiety.[35] Neumann asked for help obtaining a visa for America, but none could be obtained, despite Jameson's best efforts.

Neumann telegrammed to Jameson to inform her of his release on 25 August 1940, urging her to get Rolly (Franziska) Becker out. She was his partner, but since the two were not married, she had not been released automatically with him, even though the decision to intern her had been made solely on the basis of their relationship.[36]

Rudolf Olden and his wife Ika, with whom Jameson had developed a warm friendship, had an even harder experience of internment. Olden was interned on 25 June 1940 at Warth Mill Internment Camp, near Manchester, a derelict cotton factory infested by rats. On 13 June, Ould had written to the Home Office asking for a decision on Olden's petition for naturalisation, which had been submitted in January 1939. Ould explained that Olden and his wife had been in England since November 1933. Mrs Olden's mother was British, and her father Russian. They had one child, born in the United Kingdom. Olden was not German; he had been deprived of his German nationality in 1936, for writing against Hitler. The two had been guests of Professor Gilbert Murray at Boars Hill, Oxford, since coming to England, and Olden lectured at Oxford University. He was active in PEN, as organiser of the group of German writers who had become victims of the Nazis, and his wife did ARP work.[37] Jameson joined in the struggle to extract his papers and secure his release. Kept in verminous conditions, and demoralised by the refusal of the Home Office bureaucracy to recognise his desire to share in Britain's fight, Olden was seriously ill by the time of his release in August 1940. Jameson wrote to Valentine Dobrée:

I went on Tuesday to see Rudolf Olden, who was released about ten days ago, but he was too ill to see me. His wife told me that he was in a disused cotton mill. 1500 of them where 400 would have been too crowded, nothing but bare filthy rooms, no latrines, no beds, not even straw, the food so disgusting that few of them cd [sic] keep it down. It has nearly killed poor Rudolf.[38]

He was offered a professorship at Columbia, but hoped to the end to stay in Britain. Both he and Ika wrote Jameson sad little farewell notes, before they sailed for America, which she kept to the end among their other letters to her.[39] They were on the *City of Benares*, crammed with children being evacuated to America, when it was torpedoed. Rudolf was too ill to get into a lifeboat, and Ika refused to leave him.[40]

Not all the numerous cases documented in the PEN archives could receive such close attention from the President and the Secretary, but the overall responsibility was theirs, the situation dragged on painfully, and it was about to get worse. Preserved in the PEN archive in the extensive dossier of the Thomas Mann Group, alongside the separate pages on individual internees, is a short statement on the condition and needs of interned writers in the winter of 1940. The situation, it reported, was better than in summer, when many were sleeping in factories on wet floors. But people now needed warm clothing, better food (they were living almost entirely on porridge, beans, rice, potatoes, margarine, salted herrings and kippers), tobacco, paper, and books.

Pacifism: A Personal Quarrel

While some writers in England were suffering from confinement in the camps, others were suffering on principle. The Appeal to the Conscience of the World brought Jameson into conflict with the uncompromising pacifists on the PEN Executive Committee. On 31 October 1940, Horace Shipp argued that the Committee's Appeal to the Conscience of the World was not in the original PEN spirit of friendliness between nations. He said he had contacted two of the original signatories, one of whom was Vera Brittain, querying their approval of the Appeal, and had discovered they in fact agreed with him. The officers closed ranks, and Jameson refused to give any weight to the opinions of two persons, 'one of whom had signed the Appeal without reading it, and the other without agreeing with it'.[41]

A clash with Horace Shipp was unimportant. But the disagreement with Vera Brittain was the beginning of the end of a relationship that both women had valued. On 6 September 1939, Brittain had asked Jameson to act as a guardian for her two children, John and Shirley, and on 24 September, Jameson was named as one of the people who provided proof corrections for *Testament of Fortune*.[42] At the end of that year, by introducing Jameson to Macmillan, Brittain had effectively transformed her career. In *Testament of Friendship*, published in January 1940, she made several warm references to the friendship between Jameson and Winifred Holtby.

Brittain's friendship was not however without its drawbacks. Jameson wrote to Irene Rathbone in August 1940 about a commission she had accepted to research and write a booklet on women working in arms factories:

The Ministry of Supply have drawn up a list of factories for me to visit, to write them a stinking little booklet—most dangerous, I consider it. The very idea of visiting arms factories, Woolwich, Cardiff, etc etc [sic] in the middle of a Blitzkrieg! [...] I do wish I had boldly refused to do it.[43]

She went on to confide a malicious, or perhaps simply childish gesture on Brittain's part. Denied permits to visit factories and off-limits areas for *England's*

Hour, Brittain had written to the Home Office to tell them that Jameson was a Sponsor of the PPU and ask why she should be given permits, if Brittain was refused them. Jameson's permits were immediately withdrawn. Eventually, the Ministry of Information found out about the problem, and Jameson found her copy of her letter of resignation dated March 1939, and was able to show that she had ceased to be a PPU sponsor. She expected that the incident would merit a black mark on her file, but at least the permits were now restored. She concluded: 'It was an odd thing for VB to do. I don't intend to tell her that I know.'

Indeed, she continued to work at the friendship. Brittain noted in her diary for 9 September 1940 that Jameson had rung and told her to leave London, as she couldn't possibly write her book under the bombing. On 17 September, she went to stay with Jameson in Mortimer, and made a series of cheerful entries on their walks together. But Jameson soon found Brittain's presence wearing, especially with her sister away in America. Dorothy had taken the children over in August, and United States regulations required her to stay for six months. In October, Jameson told Irene Rathbone:

Vera Brittain has been here now since September 17. You know I was always very sorry for her, but I have for the first time—since she was almost always away when I stayed in her house that time—seen her at close quarters. For your ear only, I will say that she is a monument of self-pity, vanity, unconscious malice. I have never before understood why people dislike her. In her last Peace Letter she described herself as 'homeless and a refugee'. It was written here, and her Chelsea house is still intact and she still has an expensive service flat near the Langham! Is that your notion of a homeless refugee? [...S]he causes so much trouble in the house, and her complaints of her unparalleled suffering are so unbelievable and almost endless, that I am exasperated beyond decency. Except that I do behave myself, at least outwardly. The Government clearly will not ever give her a permit to go to the States, and my only hope now is that her husband will come back and take her back with him as his wife.[44]

Everyone was feeling the strain. The same letter reported that Whitby had been bombed twice, and that Jameson would be going there the next day to see her father and her aunt, and assess the damage. Jameson's latest novel, *Cousin Honoré*, dedicated to Irene, had been bombed in the binders' warehouse, some stock had been destroyed, and it might not be possible to publish it within the year. (In the event, it came out in mid-November.) Jameson's club in Pall Mall had been bombed. And—she added in a postscript—the arms factory visit had been done, and had taken up a fortnight. She had however given up on the pamphlet. She had written an article for *Atlantic Monthly*, and had notes 'for a heavy sort of article to be written after the war'.[45] Otherwise, it had been a waste of time, though the visits themselves had been 'passionately interesting'.

The following week, Vera was infuriating her again:

She is always talking about suicide now, and comes in from her lonely walks having sobbed her way round the lanes. I truly think she is what the people so usefully call 'mental'. I think she is almost despicable and yet has a kind of blindworm honesty, and is pathetic. And—this is something you would do, too—I recognise in her form of despicableness all my own worse faults. Guy will leave me soon, of course. [46]

Guy had notoriously little patience with the pathetic. But until George Catlin came home from the United States, Jameson hadn't the heart to turn Brittain out; London was certainly no place to send even a treacherous friend. Jameson closed with a warning to Irene to stay well away from the capital:

There is no water or gas from Whitehall to Piccadilly, a bomb has wrecked St James's church in Piccadilly, and a cinema in Leicester Square—not the same bomb, 200 people were drowned in the cellars of Morley College, Macmillan's office has a 1000lb time bomb outside it, all the lavatories in the War Office or is it the Admiralty are choked, that amuses me, every single night some other part of London is crumped and you never know when you go up whether your office is standing.

But on 1 November, Brittain noted in her diary, she and Jameson drove round London for five and a half hours, looking at the damage in the blitzed areas described in *England's Hour*, in the chapter 'The Ruins of Troy'.[47]

In December, Brittain's third application for a visa to the United States was refused. In January, Jameson wrote to Irene that she was now staying in Mortimer as a paying guest, exasperatingly patronising in consequence, and even with Dorothy back home, the situation had become untenable. She had taken an expensive flat in Piccadilly looking over Green Park, 'with the best air-raid shelter in London', for two weeks, while George Catlin was back in England, and even if he wasn't permitted to stay, she would not be allowed back to Mortimer. The letter ended: 'At any time this would not be a house for a delicate-minded duodenal ulcer, but now...!' [48]

Jameson's ulcer was probably less of a problem than the fact that Guy had just left for a week's training at Brockenhurst, in the Army Education Corps, and she was hoping he would be stationed near Mortimer on his return. This certainly required the absence of Vera. On 30 January 1941, Brittain recorded in her diary an 'annoying letter' from Jameson asking her to 'move my things'.

A later entry on 6 February 1941 notes a fulsome letter of thanks from Jameson for her copy of *England's Hour*, and its dedication. Jameson must have found especially irritating the frequent references to the delights of life in a friend's house in a Berkshire village. But she said nothing of that in the letter she wrote to Lovat Dickson regretting her initial churlishness: 'I wrote her a brief note to thank her for the dedication, and then was so ashamed of my ungraciousness that I wrote again, giving all the praise I possibly could, and more than I ought. It is not a good book, and will do her reputation little good.'[49] On 26 February, Brittain was finally dislodged, and Jameson was gleeful: 'She behaved very badly the three days she was here, and no one is sorry she has gone!'[50]

The split widened. On 15 May 1941, Brittain declared in her diary that she was leaving Jameson almost completely out of her will, except for a small legacy: 'Don't want someone who disagrees with my views on most vital points to be in charge of either children or books.' Later in the year, Jameson published her PEN pamphlet, *The End of This War*, in which she tried to give an honest account of her reasons for abandoning her pacifist position. There was, she argued, a dilemma that could not be resolved, a choice between two forms of guilt and two prices to pay, for pacifists and non-pacifists alike. On the one hand, there were the camps, people bent on killing the weak for their own pleasure, and the corruption of humane discourse; on the other, the prospect of millions of dead and cities in ruins. There was no easy choice.[51] Brittain responded at once. Jameson reported to Hermon Ould:

Vera, Rose Macaulay tells me, is 'running a campaign against The End of This War'. The nice woman who was Dick Sheppard's secretary told her so. Her long letter of explanation etc to you is just what she always does. After planning or achieving some trick or meanness, she hastily guards herself by a long explanatory letter, putting all and herself in a reasonable and noble light. By the time she has finished it, she believes everything she has written. I used to watch the process at work when she was with me.[52]

She was pleased with Ould's supportive response:

Your letter to Vera seems perfect to me. I fully expected we should hear from her. My spiteful mind thinks that since she cannot dazzle America she would like to prance a little in the PEN. So far as it rests with me, I won't have it. The 'Queen *cannot endure* it'. I have an idea of myself as a person who does not feel injuries. It is an illusion. What really happens is that they take a long time to sweep through my soggy nature, but once the process is complete, I feel an irrational antipathy for the injurer, such as some people feel for snakes. [...]

She would like to be entrusted with the organisation of a joint deputation to Churchill. I think that at any cost she must be prevented from interfering, and her offer, tentative or otherwise, refused. I hope she will take the hint of your brief first paragraph to keep out, but if she persists, she must, I think, be politely but plainly rebuffed. [...]

Damn. That's enough of her.[53]

Not quite. Brittain's diary entries for 21 and 24 February 1942 noted the receipt of 'angry' and 'furious' letters from Jameson, saying Brittain had 'spoken ill' of her and accusing her of disloyalty. The origin, Brittain thought, was in some 'hostile' information passed on by Middleton Murry. Jameson referred to the issue, without explaining it, in a letter to Lovat Dickson dated 21 February:

Vera has written me a long maddeningly foolish letter, to which I thought I'd better reply kindly. I hope she will soon begin to write a book, since that will absorb her mind. I saw last week a half-dozen letters from her, written to a fortunately discreet person, any one of which, if it got into the hands of M.I.5, would land her and George in a flat in Holloway. She'd be not only happier but safer writing a book.[54]

In July, Jameson asked for the return of all her letters. Brittain made arrangements to have them copied first:

When I send them back and she has used them for her autobiography she will certainly destroy them, & this is the kind of literary massacre from which the perpetrator should be prevented. They couldn't be published in her or my lifetime any more than mine to her could, but the correspondence (extending for nearly ten years— longer if the first two letters, wh. I am not going to return, are counted) could be left among my literary 'remains' and published eventually by John & Shirley as my literary executors.[55]

Whatever else went on in private, the two ignored each other in their subsequent work. Jameson's autobiography makes no mention of Brittain. Brittain's *Testament of Experience* makes one named reference to her former friend, noting that she was reading Jameson's *Europe to Let* on the ship home from an American tour, in April 1940, and two unnamed references, one to a fellow PEN member commiserating over the refusal of a permit for Brittain to lecture in America, and another to 'an old friend' who invited her to her home, where she stayed for ten weeks.[56] Jameson nursed her grievance. She refused to take part in Olaf Stapledon's initiative in spring 1943 for a PEN collection of essays on 'Fundamental Values' if Brittain's husband George Gordon Catlin was going to be involved, saying he was untrustworthy, derivative, and dreary.[57]

She wrote to Irene Rathbone in October 1947 about a piece on Brittain written by Rosalind Wade, and tore both author and subject apart:

She [Wade] must know that it is all lies about Vera's war work, and the picture of Vera writing an article with one hand, cooking with the other, and rocking a cradle with her foot is so near caricature that I half wondered if R. [sic] had meant it so. Vera who can't even boil a kettle, who had expensive nurses for both children, who always cursed me for consenting to do any domestic work because it was slavish and let down the feminist side. What a monument of sycophancy and cynical lying.[58]

13

1941: Fighting with the French

The Romains Affair

In July 1941, the International President of PEN began his self-imposed exile in New York.[1] He immediately mounted an exercise that alarmed and angered the officers of the London Centre and the European refugee writers regrouping under their aegis. Jameson's published account in *Journey from the North* of his initiative for a 'European PEN in America', which gathered together exiles such as Thomas Mann, Maurice Maeterlinck, Somerset Maugham, and Stefan Zweig, and his subsequent removal from the International Presidency, is short and not very precise.[2] Her original draft was longer, full of comic abuse of Romains himself and the secretary of his Centre, attacks on Romains's friendships with certain French politicians, and the likes of Abetz and Ribbentrop, and an accusation garnered from a friend in the Foreign Office that he was probably writing speeches for the Vichy ambassador.[3] Romains's critics and historians are fairly silent on the episode. It is referred to on the Russian website of PEN, which presents the English, led by Wells (Jameson's role, and her Presidency, are not mentioned), as antagonistic to Romains partly because of their long-standing rivalry with the French and partly because Wells had his pacifist cause to press, and presents Romains as a defender of democracy.[4] Romains, contrary to Jameson's presentation, appears there as an advocate of intellectual *ralliement* to the war against Hitler, though his 'friendly contacts with the German youth movement, which was National Socialist inspired' are conceded, as well as his opportunism (termed 'his desire to please everyone').

There is a startling contrast between the salon politicking of the writer in New York, and the harsh realities of life on the cultural Home Front. The London officers, whatever axes they were grinding, were certainly naive in their failure to register the implications of Romains's activities, and too restrained in their first responses to them. They were also occupied with other matters. Romains for his part took full advantage of his distance from the battlefield to engage in good old-fashioned career-advancing manoeuvres.

The first shot came from Romains, in a letter of 15 December 1940 to Ould, as International Secretary, saying that he and other refugee writers in the States were thinking about setting up a PEN Club in New York to combine the writers of various nationalities.[5] On 18 February 1941, Ould wrote in reply: 'that if after studying the question with his colleagues M. Romains thought that it would be the most useful way of preserving continuity of European Centres, the international Executive Committee would no doubt approve his plans'. To this diplomatic formulation, reminding the President discreetly that the International Executive must make the final decision, he added a personal rider, expressing his scepticism about the project and saying that he thought the separate groups in England were happy working together as they were. The discretion was wasted. Romains wrote back to Ould on 14 March, on headed notepaper from 'The European PEN in America', which gave himself as President and listed a Permanent Council that included many of the most important refugee writers in America, with Somerset Maugham as London Honorary Member. He sent a copy of the new Centre's Statutes, spoke of the 'former' PEN in Europe, and regretted that he had only just received Ould's February letter. On 9 May, he cabled information about an inaugural dinner to be held on 15 May. The London Executive Committee meeting on 30 May considered a letter sent on 16 May by Madame Romains with the text of her husband's speech at the dinner. Parts of it they deemed defeatist, although the general tenor was held to be acceptable. A number of the more prominent refugee writers in the UK had already expressed their disapproval. The Committee cabled to Romains on 4 June an unambiguous statement of their common position: 'Undermentioned European Centres domiciled in England strongly disapprove proposed European PEN in America. Nomenclature misleading. Propose name be changed to Group of European Refugee Writers in America. English Czechoslovak Polish Norwegian Catalan Austrian German.' Two days later, on 6 June, a furious cabled reply from Auernheimer Goffin, one of Romains's American supporters, insisted that London had agreed to the new enterprise. Ould returned that his answer had been misconstrued, and that in any case Romains had made his move before receiving it. A letter dated 13 May from Robert Nathan, president of the American PEN Centre, describing Romains's election as President of the new Centre as a putsch, would seem to bear out the London interpretation.

Romains, the June meeting was told by an Executive Committee member, was known to the Foreign Office, and had been making anti-British speeches in America. It was noted that the International President could be deposed at the AGM during the Annual Congress. Jameson and Ould had already proposed at the Executive meeting of 25 January that a conference should be held in London on the contribution of intellectuals to the post-war world that would, they hoped, attract support from the Ministry of Information and the British Council, and planning was well advanced. The Committee formally approved arrangements for an International Congress, to be held in the Autumn on the premises of the Institut Français, in London, and the title was settled as 'Literature and the World after the War'.

Copies of the correspondence attached to the Committee Minute of 23 June include a letter from Romains dated 14 March 1941 with a justificatory postscript arguing that a European group was needed in the States, partly because the representatives of individual nations gathered there were too few to make effective groups, but mostly because the aim must be to preserve the distinctive European culture which transcended national cultures, both from the barbarism in Europe, and from the overwhelming difference of the American culture by which it was surrounded. Rather tactlessly, Romains spoke of the need there would be to bring back the European heritage, after the war, to countries that would by then have forgotten it. And Ould's answer was an angry one: it was wrong to talk as if a free Europe no longer existed. He cited the active English, Scottish, Irish Centres, and the Centres in exile in London— Polish, Czech, Norwegian, Catalonian, the Polish Centre of Yiddish PEN and the anti-Nazi and Austrian Groups. None of these saw any need for a European PEN, but if there was one, 'its seat must be in England, which remains free and is, after all, Europe'. Putting a European PEN in America was, he said, an unjustifiably defeatist gesture.

In a BBC radio broadcast to America on 4 July, for American PEN members, Jameson herself settled the 'defeatist' President's hash. It was, she began, a pity that she could not have spoken to them a year ago, and assured them that Britain was not going to be defeated:

The famous French writer who is the International President of PEN, M. Jules Romains, took—then—a poor view of our chances. After the surrender of France, he says, in an article I have been reading, 'for everyone or almost everyone, in France and elsewhere, the defeat of England was only a question of days, or of weeks.' If only we had been able to talk to him at that time, we could perhaps have convinced him that there are moments in history when logic and intelligence are less reliable weapons than plain stupidity. The English were too stupid to see what was clear to the rest of the continent.

Not, thank God, to all of it. Soldiers wearing the uniform of half a dozen nations landed on this island—on a corner of Europe which knows more about human liberties than about logic. So did writers talking as many languages, Czechs, Poles, Norwegians, Belgians, French. We welcomed eagerly these survivors of European freedom. Our sole regret was that the International President of the PEN had gone to New York.[6]

Turning the knife with evident pleasure, she listed the PEN Centres that had settled in London for the duration of hostilities—the Czech, Polish, Norwegian, Catalan, and the anti-Nazi Germans and Austrians, and continued:

I must say we took a poor view of the speech M. Romains delivered the other day in New York at the first dinner party of the group of writers sitting in the name of the European PEN in America. He said they were going to speak for Europe because Europe can no longer speak. Really? You should hear our Czechs, our Poles, our Norwegians, our Catalans, our Germans and Austrians—not to make too much of the Scotch and the Irish we have always with us. And not forgetting the English. And, he said, he and his colleagues had left us in order to speak, in our name, in a free land. It was a kind thought—but we speak for ourselves, thanks—in more than six languages, in this free land, in England. Still, at this moment, pleasantly situated in Europe. You can believe me, it *is* Europe.

Writers in Freedom

Resentment against Romains was strongly marked in a number of the addresses delivered at the International Congress of September 1941, on 'Literature and the World after the War.'[7] Robert Neumann devoted his whole speech to an attack on Romains's *Seven Mysteries of Europe*, Romains's seven strange accounts of his contacts with the crowned heads and leading statesmen of Europe, attempting to persuade them to the cause of peace, and his boasts in that text of his connections with Henri de Man, Daladier, Otto Abetz, and Ribbentrop. The delegates from the smaller countries were especially irate. Rebecca West joined the queue at the pillory, referring also to *The Seven Mysteries of Europe*, and asking for sympathy for someone who was, she mused, clearly not quite sane: 'I do think that when we are dealing with M. Romains we are dealing with what is called "a sad case"; it is more like the case of Poor

Aunt Emily, who thought she was a poached egg and wanted to sit down, than an international tragedy, and I would beg of you not to start witch-hunting.'[8] There were a (very) few voices to speak out for the International President, but the general feeling was that his copybook had been thoroughly blotted.

Personal animosity was not allowed to mar the larger aims of this important conference: to draw together the fragments of European culture (the national PEN Centres of writers in exile, established in London, and Europe's allies, the United States and Canada, China and India), and to discuss the writer's role in post-war social reconstruction. This meant confronting the issue of social justice and providing the soldiers of this war, and their children, with the better share of society's goods they had been promised and then denied in 1914–18, as well as addressing the question of European co-operation. Jameson's presidential address, 'The Duty of the Writer', laid out the need for socialism and European unity. She reiterated the themes that had driven her writing in the 1930s, declaring the writer's responsibility to declare for the side of reason, humane values, and social justice: 'We [Allies] have a great many things we do not want to preserve—the dole, the outrageous wastage of child life. The force that really opposes the Nazis is [...] the need, the only half-conscious impulse, of Western civilization to renew itself.'[9] It was the duty of English writers to persuade their compatriots of their responsibilities to Europe:

Only a fool would try to minimize the immense difficulties of creating a new European order. Only Englishmen who are ignorant, or who are tired and discouraged, will refuse to make the effort. Here we touch the root of the problem. A disillusioned and mistrustful people will refuse, passively or actively. It is an old root. It has been growing in us for a very long time. Unless we realize that scepticism and despair are latent in us with the other microbes, of influenza or unemployment, we cannot judge of our chances of escaping a worse disaster than the war.[10]

She argued for an end to the nationalist mind-set:

In 1919 the men responsible for making the peace started off several young nations into the future. Not enough of us understood then that a team of sovereign national States is not the only possible or natural, or the most viable political order. That in fact it ran counter to the hope of a peace based on reason.[11]

Europe was a contentious subject. Wilhelm Keilhau, from a recently occupied Norway, argued provocatively for 'The Non-Existence of Europe', noting the difficulty and danger of putting boundaries to such a complex geographical, racial, cultural, political concept. This was, he pointed out, Hitler's project.

He moved on to attack isolationism, and urged delegates to think in larger terms of world reconstruction based on 'the new axis Washington–London–Moscow–Chungking and the common interests of the Atlantic powers.'[12] But Jameson's lead was followed by most others. Europe represented a common heritage, shared intellectual values, the ideal of the free mind. From Catalonia, Batista I. Roca and Carles P. Sunyer, defending nationalism, nevertheless argued passionately for such a community of culture, in which, they said, individual national differences could flourish. André Labarthe, editor-in-chief of *La France Libre*, defended the honour of recently defeated France, which had set the ideal of freedom, and the values of the mind, at the core of European culture.

As the Congress drew to a close, H. G. Wells, for the International Executive, put a proposal to elect a new International President. Romains, he said, had failed to turn up, and had given no good reason why. It was finally agreed that the Presidency should be declared vacant, and its functions be fulfilled by an International Committee: Wells himself, Thomas Mann, Thornton Wilder (who, like his fellow-delegate John dos Passos, had managed without difficulty to find a plane from New York), and Jacques Maritain (whom failing, Denis Saurat).

The conference was important for the agreement it confirmed among intellectuals and politicians, and made known to the wider public, on the importance of a European orientation for the post-war world. For Jameson herself, it was a marker of national and international recognition of her status in the domain of cultural politics. She was no longer, as in the 1930s, hesitating on the edge of other people's meetings, trying out uncomfortable, borrowed rhetorics. She had a platform and a language of her own, speaking out for liberal solidarity and European renewal in the world of urgent practical action.

Fighting with the Free French

For the September Congress, all Jameson's skills of organisation and entrepreneurship had been called into play to secure funding and support. The cultural arena had provided a unique opportunity to draw together like-minded people who would be major players in post-war Europe, from John Winant, the American Ambassador, who became Jameson's personal friend, to the editors of *La France Libre*.[13] PEN's connections with the French were at this point closer than they had ever been before, or would be again. The politics, for once, were right—that is, liberal left—on both sides. The key figure was the Director of the Institut Français du Royaume-Uni, Denis Saurat.

A passionate Anglophile, Saurat occupied his post at the Institut Français, which was under the control of the Universities of Paris and Lille, from its inception in 1924 through to 1945. He was a highly respected scholar, and also held a Chair of French in King's College, London, from 1926 to 1950.[14] He had been in contact with Hermon Ould, with whom he shared an interest in mysticism, as far back as May 1932, when he invited Francis Carco over to give a lecture, at Ould's request, and in 1935, Ould sent him an Honorary Membership card for the London Centre of PEN.[15] In March 1939, Saurat was writing to thank Jameson for an invitation to Pagani's to attend an event to honour his old friend.[16] In June 1941, Saurat accepted with pleasure Ould's invitation to take part in the conference, which chimed opportunely with his own enthusiastic political activities on behalf of General de Gaulle.[17] He was put down to chair a session, and to speak himself. He offered the Institut, then in Cromwell Gardens, as the venue. An air raid blew out all the windows the night before the conference opened, but Saurat's staff mopped up, and everyone carried on.

Before then, Jameson had joined Ould in Saurat's confidence, and both her own writing and her work for PEN benefited from his wide-ranging network of insider connections among French and English writers and, especially, politicians. She invited him to lunch at the Café Royal with Ould and herself, on 6 July 1940, as Romains was leaving for New York.[18] This was four days before the deputies in Vichy convened to vote full powers to Marechal Pétain (10 July) and the British War Cabinet met to decide what action to take against French exiles in Britain.[19] Saurat's conversation was illuminating. In her autobiography, Jameson said only that he made discreet references to the embattled Prime Minister Reynaud and to Romains, was very positive in his support for de Gaulle, and had a lot to say about the response of French writers to the Occupation—basically, that they would keep their heads down. She wrote with fuller details of what seems to have been another meeting to Valentine Dobrée:

Yesterday I had lunch with Denis Saurat, and he was full of stories that made me weary and despairing. He spoke of the layer of rottenness that had spread right across French society, and seeped down. He said Reynaud was not a strong character, that at the end he was playing the politician's game in the usual French way, expecting that Pétain would be forced to reject the German terms and then he, Reynaud, would come back stronger, and retreat with a tamed cabinet to Africa—but 'he didn't know his Pétain'. That if Reynaud had told Pétain, when he threatened to resign if an armistice was not asked for, to resign and be damned he could have carried the day. But he hadn't the strength for that. He said that Pétain is really and truly gaga, and thinks he is Joan of Arc. That de Gaulle begged again and again for tanks to invade Germany, where he could have created an equal havoc and confusion as the German tanks were creating in France. (Incidentally, Gillies, the secretary of the international Federation of Trade Unions, told me last week that it was the French who held the English back from bombing the concentrations of troops and arms in the Rhineland between September and March.)

Saurat said a lot more, but I have forgotten it, but the most alarming thing he said was that there is a strong Foreign Office movement to try to make a deal with Pétain and Mussolini—not even Halifax, but the permanent officials still playing grande politique. He had this from de Gaulle, but whether it is true or not—how can one know, except that it sounds likely to be true?[20]

De Gaulle had left France for London on 17 June in disgust at the armistice and Pétain's defeatism. On 18 June he made his famous BBC broadcast to his countrymen, urging them to fight on. A month later, on 17 July, Saurat, who had offered his services to the General as soon as he arrived, introduced him to the English public at Queen's Hall London, where he set out his intention to continue the fight for France from England. Having set up his Free French Headquarters in Carlton Gardens, in easy walking distance of Whitehall and Westminster, the General consulted with Saurat regularly. In August 1940, he supplied a letter to serve as Preface to Saurat's book, *Regeneration*, in which he expressed his support for Saurat's thesis (which was also Jameson's) that what the world needed for its transformation was a return to respect for ideas, and signed himself 'votre ami dévoué'.[21]

The recruitment of English writers to the consolidation of Franco-British relations in 1943 is well documented. The PEN connection with the French who were regrouping in London in 1940, assisted by the friendship of Jameson, Ould, and Saurat, is a less familiar story. This was a personal alliance, in which both sides were following paths of their own, but it reflected a need recognised at the highest government levels. A joint report on how press reporting of the Franco-British war effort should be conducted had been drawn up on 1 January 1940 by R. E. Balfour, of the Ministry of Information, working with the British Embassy in Paris and the Commissariat Général à l'Information. He acknowledged there was a superficial difference of temperament between France and Britain, but argued that below that surface, unlike Britain and Germany, the two countries believed in 'the same fundamental values'.[22] It was certainly more difficult to sustain that position after France's capitulation and Pétain's Armistice, and in August 1940 Mass Observation reported extremely hostile comments from the general public on the 'Bleeding French'.[23] The version of those 'fundamental' values that Saurat, Jameson, and Ould stood for—a common humanist culture, but even more, a humane society—was probably the only one capable of closing the rift.

Their collaboration would not of course get very far, given the right-wing orientations of the political leaders on both sides. But it contributed to the growing recognition, across the political spectrum, that after the war something would have to be done to recognise popular pressure for social change. For a moment, the attachments to the Gaullist cause of intellectuals in London with a socialist bent were strengthened. Saurat especially would suffer for that, though he would have suffered anyway for his repeated attempts to impress on de Gaulle the need to consolidate his base by expressing a commitment to social reform. A substantial number of the many conservative French exiles in London, attached to the Pétainist camp and believing in the legitimacy of the Vichy government, were already deeply, if unreasonably, suspicious that de Gaulle had connections to the Popular Front. In addition, Saurat was notoriously a friend of the English, and rejoiced in his access to English politicians—Lord Asquith, Sir Robert Vansittart, head of the Vansittart Committee, which in June–July 1940 had primary responsibility for French matters, and Lord Lloyd, Director of the British Council. He hoped to turn the Institut into a powerful instrument for drawing together de Gaulle's circle and the English.[24]

Lord Lloyd was especially forthcoming. Saurat's note dated 20 September, which seems to be quoting Lord Lloyd, reports frank discussions of the perceived shortcomings of de Gaulle's headquarters, a warning of an imminent new action against the French (probably the unsuccessful West Africa Expedition, Operation 'Menace', conducted by Anglo-Free French forces)[25] and agreement on the greatness of de Gaulle; the General must, said Saurat, be built up into a myth. He was promised £12,000, to run the London Institute and help create Institutes in Edinburgh, Glasgow, Leeds, and Cardiff, and assured of continuing independence; and Lloyd urged the Director to come and see him frequently with his advice.[26]

Saurat in his turn spoke frankly to the General, passing on to him, for example, in September 1941, in a spirit of helpfulness, Philip Noel Baker's comments about his dictatorial ambitions.[27] Tact was not his strong point.

On that same occasion, he pressed to become a member of the General's new *Comité national* (National Committee). He was bitterly disappointed to be cut out in favour of his rival René Cassin, a law professor, who was given the brief for Public Education and Justice.[28] Nevertheless, he continued his efforts to encourage the British to take the General to their hearts. He introduced de Gaulle's Albert Hall speech on 20 November, and told him afterwards that he should have made more of the social reforms that were planned for France after the war.[29] The tone of the publications coming from the Institut at that point was increasingly overtly socialist. In February 1942, *La France Libre* drew to the attention of readers exiled in Britain, or turning the pages surreptitiously in Occupied France, an account of England's model for future reform: 'Affranchir l'homme de la misere', Walter Hill's account of the Beveridge Report.[30]

It should have come as no real surprise to Saurat when he saw by chance in August 1942 a report made by officials in de Gaulle's headquarters, drawn up while he was away in Africa on a mission for de Gaulle from February to May 1941. This report included his name on a list of people to be taken out of the movement, and described him as a freemason, unreliable, gamey, and a venal *arriviste*. Alongside him were listed Antoine, Cassin, and Dejean; the notes on them, he said, were pretty similar, and they were also designated Jews.[31]

The period from November 1940 to mid-1942 saw a fair amount of contact between PEN members and *La France Libre*. French contributors such as the novelist Ignace Legrand were familiar presences in PEN, helping translate English contributions into French, and some became, like Saurat, personal friends. With Legrand, Jameson made a slow start; she could read French with ease, but she had to ask Irene Rathbone, an ardent Francophile, to explain to him that she was tongue-tied when they met because of her bad spoken French.[32] *La France Libre* published a small but significant number of pieces by or about Jameson, which presented her to readers as one of the great contemporary English writers. Denise Amye, for example, discussing how few English people read French in translation, noted that many of the great English writers read French in the original, and mediate French writing to their public:

All today's great English writers speak French and read our authors in the original. They translate them and are influenced by them. It is probably through Huxley, Forster, Virginia Woolf and Storm Jameson that the insights of Gide, Proust and Giraudoux have reached the widest circles of English readers.[33]

In January 1941, *La France Libre* printed a long review by Irene Rathbone of *Cousin Honoré*, the novel that Jameson completed on 15 June 1940, the day after the Germans entered Paris.[34] Rathbone took the opportunity to introduce generally Jameson's work to a new public. She picked out the sharp realism of the novels written in the 1930s, praising Jameson's ability to evoke the emotions flashing across a character's inner landscape ('a frenzy of ambition [...] a wave of despair, sudden fear, an impulse of cruelty or love') with the same swift, concise images as she conjured up the reality of the external world ('a sunny garden path, a kitchen table, a woman walking, a man's hand, or smile'). She referred to *No Time Like the Present*, to explain Jameson's change of position on pacifism, and to the novel *Europe to Let*, to characterise the 'intense accumulation of fiery inner energy' that made Jameson the epitome of 'the civilised person'. Only then did she turn to an analysis of *Cousin Honoré*, which she conducted with no concessions to French readers' sensitivities.

Jameson's novel, she said, showed how the nation that had stumbled to the edge of destruction had lived in a world where humane values had almost vanished from sight. The First World War had stripped France of more than two million of its best, and those who were left lived in fear for the future, and for the safety of the nation. Fascism was spreading through the possessing classes. The debilitating divisions of the nation were represented in the conflicting interests and factions within the Alsatian ironmaster–winegrower Honoré's extended family of wealthy peasants and businessmen. France, the former leading light of Europe, clung to the service of old men, who in their turn clung to power. Yet, in Jameson's vision, 'eternal France' is an ancient fortress 'still young behind her old walls'. Her children will rally to resist the Nazi invader, and their fathers will acknowledge the mistakes and derelictions of their generation, which allowed evil to grow in Europe, and left war as the only solution.

Rathbone missed, or thought irrelevant in this context, the main aim of Jameson's novel, which was to explore the structural similarities in French and English society that had brought both countries to the edge of the same precipice. There is an unspoken parallel between Honoré Burckheim's peasant stock, with its roots deep in the vineyards of Alsace, and the men of the Yorkshire moors to whom William Lamb looked for refuge as the floodwaters rose. Both carry the same desperately nostalgic hope for the future which the youthful reader of Tawney would never abandon. Honoré himself is a composite of the leading men of the inter-war years in Germany, France, and England, mostly politicians, not so much wicked as selfish, committed to their class interests, pragmatic, and blinkered.[35]

The Hindenburg of Wheeler Bennett's biography, transposed to an Alsatian estate, generated a character that in turn merged into her idea of Stanley Baldwin, and the upshot was 'Cousin' Honoré, whose relations span several frontiers. Effectively, what Jameson's method produced was a mirror of the political and ethical options facing Europe between the wars, analysing their structures and their psychological context. This was family drama on a continental scale.

In September, Jameson wrote a piece for *La France Libre* to announce the forthcoming PEN Congress. It was an Anglo-French gesture of defiance, and a manifesto for the collective future of France, England, and Europe. She subsequently turned it into the speech with which she closed the Congress. It brought together culture and politics, combining a statement of her personal debt to the aesthetic innovations of the French avant-garde, the visionaries who showed how to make things new, with an invocation of a future where the old men would no longer rule.[36]

She opened with an evocation of London in 1941, 'the cultural centre of free Europe', functioning for the first time in its history as a European capital, rallying all the representatives of Europe's great humane heritage in defence of Europe's freedom. She defined what it was to be 'European', sharing a recognisably common culture and way of thinking that unites Erasmus and Voltaire: 'both are caught in the light of an intellectual impulse which is neither Greek, Roman, nor Judaeo-Christian, but a synthesis of the three. A Valéry, a Čapek, a Rilke, have one language in common even when each is working miracles in his own dialect.'

But most of all, she argued, Europe, since the Middle Ages, has followed the lead, and the vision, of France:

It is not only that nineteenth-century France is incomparably rich in great painters: without making any effort to do so they affected the eyesight and mental habits of three generations of painters in other countries. Simply by looking at nature with eyes that were determined to see the living anatomy of form and colour they changed the appearance of the world. Writers as well as painters see a tree, a room, a human figure, with eyes educated by Cézanne, Matisse, Picasso. Poetry? Europe without Baudelaire, Rimbaud, Laforgue, Mallarmé? These Frenchmen set us all down at new points of departure. The journeys we made on their advice were, it is true, not reassuring. Oftener than not, they left us with a nostalgia more of time than of place. [...] They dissolved the precise images we had inherited from our fathers, and we found ourselves without the wit to create another and secure world. But what riches in the discoveries we made! At the worst we have learned, and shall hand on to our children, a power to read in nature backwards, from the symbol to the image, from inner to outer.[37]

France offers the way of seeing the future, and also the way it must now be lived. France, uniquely, has found the way to breed individuals whose identifications and allegiances are threefold: to their region, to their national culture, and to Europe.

They are shaped by their childhood in a French province [...]. Yet by a trick of which the French provinces have so far kept the secret, these school-children often grow up to be Europeans while remaining as French as their choice of words.[38]

Jameson may frequently have complained of the distractions that wartime politics brought to her writing, but the insights formulated here, out of political need, into the scope offered by landscape to multiple forms of cultural and political allegiance were already creating the dynamic of the experimental novels, *The Fort* and *Then We Shall Hear Singing*, and her masterpiece, *Cloudless May*.

The rest of her essay struck a personal note, describing the shock, in June 1940, of walking into the Hachette bookshop in London and realising that the cultural links to France had been cut—a worse shock, she said, than the September 1939 invasion that had cut her off from the landscapes of France. She evoked lyrically the affection English writers felt for Paris, and all the provinces of France, in all their variety, the light, and the clear air. She admitted the nostalgia that tinged that delight, for a way of life resistant to mechanical civilisation, one that England had lost. In conclusion, she touched lightly on France's abandonment of Czechoslovakia, and linked it with Britain's failure to commit herself fully to war until France was defeated. The two countries had failed together, but would now survive together, allied as leaders of a new Europe.

14

1941–1943: Holding On

Plain Selfishness and Unpatriotic Conduct

Back in Mortimer after the PEN Congress, Jameson found their two maids had joined up. She was happy to deal with the washing and ironing, but the overall responsibility of running a house was anathema (though it was Dorothy who had borne most of it, and for a while, Barbara, who had done a painful stint as general factotum, treated more like a maid than a daughter-in-law). She decided not to renew the lease for the coming March, and let Dorothy go back to her house in Reading.[1] She took a small flat close to Broadcasting House at the end of October 1941 (Flat 19, No. 88 Portland Place). It was a bombing target, and therefore very cheap, but not at all comfortable.[2]

By that autumn, the stress of personal quarrels, activities on behalf of the refugees, committee work (now including the 191 Committee, the Books and Periodicals Committee of the British Council, the Editorial Committee of the Authors' National Committee, and the chairmanship of the Committee of Management of the Society of Authors), broadcasting, journalism, and her own creative writing, was taking its toll.[3] The ulcer that had first appeared at the end of December 1940 was growing much worse, and she was slow to recognise how serious it was.

There were bright spots. Her books were being published in the United States at the same time as in England, and getting a good reception, thanks to Carol Hill. On 24 January 1942, her grandson Christopher was born in Chubb Hill Nursing Home, in Whitby. The birth certificate gives the mother's name as Barbara Allin Clark, formerly Cawood, and the father as Charles William Storm Clark, Pilot, Railway Air Services, of 111 Elm Drive, Mossley Hill, Liverpool.[4] She had to write to help support this growing family, as well as further the war effort, and she was publishing a book every six months. A new short novel, *The Fort*, was published by Cassell's at the end of 1941.

215

Figure 18 Barbara Storm-Clark and Christopher in Liverpool, 1942.

Naomi Mitchison met her during a trip down from Scotland to England in early February 1942, and noted in her diary:

Storm Jameson extremely gloomy, owing to having dealt with refugees, especially Jews, since 1937 about, keeping alive people who would be better dead. Unable to see a tolerable new world. Eager for my news, just because I'm leading a good life and can put it across to her a bit. Has a gastric ulcer, very grateful for eggs, so was Dr Pirret. A fine story of the bourgeois of Tours going out and defending their town, led by the Bishop. Tours smashed, the bridge and hotel at Saumur, all the Loire country. I try to cheer her up.[5]

Such vigorous cheering-up must have been deeply irritating, but had Mitchison met her a few days later, Jameson might have been significantly less gloomy. The struggles on behalf of the refugees that Mitchison knew about, and the quarrel with Vera Brittain of which she was probably ignorant, had been exacerbated by the financial difficulties that had been accumulating since Guy's firm fell apart in the 1920s. These had been accelerated by the responsibilities she took on for her expanding family, and the Chapmans' tendency to live as extravagantly as they could. But in February 1942, Lovat Dickson helped her make an agreement with Macmillan to bring her into solvency. She had, she told him on 3 February, a debt of £2,000 in the form of a loan from the Midland Bank she had taken out after putting Bill through three years at Cambridge and two years at Hamble. A few days later, she proposed a strategy that should finally straighten out her finances. She had worked out she could manage to live without drawing on her English royalties, so if Macmillan were to lend her £1,000 to pay off half the bank loan, and then give her £100 on each new novel manuscript she submitted, they could keep all the royalties above that until the loan was paid off. For everything else, including income tax, she would make do with her (small) American royalties and odd earnings, and Guy could feed her.[6]

She had the bit between her teeth. She wrote again to Lovat Dickson, on the same day, in terms that would have shocked Hermon Ould had he seen them. She absolutely had to shed all the responsibilities that were getting in the way of her real work. She was desperate with exhaustion—and also, though she didn't say it, desperate not to lose yet another chance of making a success of her writing. She could leave PEN in November, when the normal election came round; the chairmanship of the Society of Authors was for one year only, finishing in August/September; at the same time she could resign from Kilham Roberts's committee, and the Council of the 191 Committee, which, she said, she was only on because Priestley had bullied her. She would stay on the Books and Periodicals Committee of the British Council until the end of the year, but it only met once a month. There was a book for the American Red Cross (*London Calling*) to be done, but it was a finite project. Moving house would help. Portland Place was too central, and everyone dropped in. Guy might be moved shortly to a command in the country. If he was kept at the War Office, they would move out to somewhere within reach of a tube station. She concluded plaintively:

I'm very much in your debt for all the trouble you have taken over my affairs. I think I'd be a better writer if I did nothing else. I have only a sense that perhaps no one has a right to be merely a writer in these times. Isn't it just plain selfishness and unpatriotic conduct? Ask Daniel Macmillan if he doesn't think so? And what do you think?[7]

But she really was ill. She wrote a couple of weeks later to Hermon Ould, telling him she had fainted twice, and must rest. At the beginning of March, she wrote again to tell him that Guy had mumps, and the doctor who came to him had also examined her and identified a potential heart condition. He had ordered her to reduce her commitments, which she thought might include the PEN Presidency; but she had to go on writing.[8]

Writing included a review of Denis Saurat's latest book, *Watch over Africa*, for *La France Libre*. She picked out for special attention Saurat's portrait of de Gaulle, his hopes for a renaissance of France, and his dream of an education that would teach every child its own national culture while also inculcating a European sense of freedom, conscience, justice, and humanity. This was the dream that de Gaulle and his Forces Françaises Libres would spread. Ironically, Saurat's discovery of the critical report on him from the Gaullist bureaucracy was only four months away.[9]

Guy went away at the end of March for a week's convalescence from his mumps, and she enjoyed the peace of quarantine. In April, she resigned from the British Council committee, telling Ould it was a relief to be free of everything except PEN.[10] She would have given up PEN too, but Ould was insistent that the Presidency needed the weight of her name. She told Lovat Dickson that according to her doctor, years of overwork had ruined her heart. Her present situation was excellent: she was allowed to write when not lying down, and it was an irrefutable reason for escaping from committees.[11]

For two months, she was reading, writing, and resting. In May, she finished *Then We Shall Hear Singing*,[12] returned to the writing of *Cloudless May*, and started work, with Macmillan's help, on *London Calling*.[13]

In December 1941, after the bombing of Pearl Harbour and the United States' entry into the war, the Ministry of Information had asked Jameson for suggestions what English writers might do to help cement Anglo-American relations. She volunteered to edit a book of stories, essays, and poems for sale in America for the benefit of American servicemen.[14] The account in *Journey from the North* includes an impressive list of contributions to *London Calling*, including poems from John Masefield, Walter de la Mare, T. S. Eliot, Edmund Blunden, Helen Waddell, Edith Sitwell, and C. Day Lewis. The list does not include the writers who produced essays of left-wing inspiration, which gave the collection a political edge that was reinforced by the bibliographical details on contributors. Harold Butler, it was noted, had been a leading official in the Ministry of Labour when it was created in 1917. At the Paris Peace Conference, he had taken part in discussion of the Labour Section of the Treaty, which gave birth to the International Labour Organisation, and was Secretary General to the first ILO Conference in 1919.[15] Butler's essay, 'The Issue', described the emergence of a desire for a new order, at home and abroad: '[People] are becoming aware that "democracy" in itself is not enough. [...] The next generation will want something more inspiring than the quest of money, comfort, pleasure. It is looking for a new faith to cast out the creeds both of violence and materialism.' Harold Laski's essay, 'Lincoln as America', followed up Butler's idea of a new faith by speaking of the world's dream of America, as a refuge for working men from oppression, insecurity, and failure, and appealed to America to live up to her best.[16]

Jameson's own Introduction, 'We Just Brought You This' or 'Ninety Times as High as the Moon', described itself as an attempt to explain the English to the Americans, express gratitude for America's coming into the war, and try to tell its citizens what the war, and especially the Blitz, had been like. She professed herself anxious about reports of anti-English feeling in the United States. The great men in both countries had their own interests, but she wanted a pooling of interests between 'the common people of your country and the common people of mine' and she added that:

[W]e can talk to each other past the Great Irresponsibles...you are not going to tell me that the appalling disasters—slums, crises, wars, not to speak of the enthusiasms of this century, are the work of responsible minds...

It is a pity that our voices the voices of the true America, the true England, without affectation, second thoughts, cleverness are not louder. The headlines—it is their speciality—ignore us.[17]

Figure 19 Noel Streatfeild in WVS uniform. An active participant in war work for PEN alongside Jameson, Streatfeild was also a part-time ARP warden, and in charge of shelter feeding for the WVS on American mobile canteens in Deptford. She wrote 'From My Diary: The Beginning of London's Blitz' for *London Calling*, and Jameson expressed admiration for her courage.

This book, her own writing, and her broadcasts to America, were building up a solid reputation in the United States, helped also by the articles and serialisations that appeared in the *Saturday Evening Post*. The friendships she made during the war, with Ambassador John Winant, her American PEN colleagues (especially Thornton Wilder and Dos Passos) and numerous journalists and academics would consolidate the link. She would complain bitterly after the war that Americans were always dropping in—but then, she always did complain of visitors, unless there were none.

On Saturday 9 May, at 10.30 p.m., a 50-minute radio version of *The Fort* was broadcast on the Home Service. She missed it, but Ould wrote to tell her the production had brought out the poetry of her language.[18]

She was one of the first to contribute to the new radio drama section that was being rapidly expanded by Val Gielgud, with the London BBC Repertory Company. The aim was to provide entertainment and access to national and European culture for traditional theatre-goers: 'to maintain interest in classic plays, British and foreign, and especially those of Shakespeare; to provide what may be termed recognizably theatrical entertainment for lovers of drama cut off by circumstances from the theatre itself; and finally—perhaps the most important of all—to encourage the writing of new plays specifically designed for the medium of broadcasting.'[19] Policymakers were also aware of their clandestine listeners, and the section 'Broadcasting to Europe' noted that 'many of the more cultured Europeans' listened to the programmes in English, the 'cultural appeal of the English language' being enhanced by the German Occupation.[20]

In his own later account of the development of radio drama, Val Gielgud described another, even larger potential audience, consisting of listeners forced by blackout and Blitz to become consumers of high culture:

[L]iterally thousands of listeners who had never bothered to give serious attention to that type of radio programme which must demand from the audience both attention and imagination found themselves making these necessary contributions to their own enjoyment simply because they had little or no alternative.[21]

Gielgud marshalled a wide range of offerings, including modern thrillers, early drama documentary, historical drama, and poetic drama. Much of it was unapologetic propaganda, concerned with raising morale, and dealing with such subjects as resistance, freedom, and suffering. Jameson's play, *William the Defeated*, which came later in the war, fell in this category, and she was listed by Gielgud among the important writers who had contributed to the new medium. Stressing that payments from the BBC to writers were not, whatever people said, unduly mean, he added:

Nor is it true that most established authors have withdrawn the hem of their garments from this so-called poor relation of the literary family. Clemence Dane, Dorothy L. Sayers, Peter Cheyney, Eric Linklater, Tyrone Guthrie, Richard Hughes, Cecil Lewis, Storm Jameson, Robert Gore-Brown, Louis MacNeice, Compton Mackenzie, are only a few of the contributors to the Theatre of the Air. No writer surely could feel ashamed, or even disinclined, to be numbered with such a company.[22]

Gielgud spelled out the challenges of the new form for dramatists used to working with visual effects and immediate audience reaction. But there were compensations:

The listening audience—just because it is not a mass audience, but one composed of individuals or small groups, for the most part in a domestic environment—is particularly susceptible to an intimacy of approach automatically denied in the theatre. The cramping boundaries of acts and scenes can be dispensed with. The imagination of the listener can be stimulated, by the use of words, of music, and of sound, to paint scenery, dress characters, even to establish the physical traits of such characters. The author can range through time and space at will. Radio has restored the use of the 'aside'. It has contributed, not without distinction, to the recent revival of drama in verse [...]. Last but not least, for the author who believes that he has anything worth saying, there must be the consoling reflection that his words are reaching the largest possible number of people.[23]

Ways of reaching larger audiences were what Jameson had been looking for since the 1930s. In January 1941, she had written from Mortimer to Hilton Brown, in the office of the Director of Talks, asking whether someone might read the play she was just finishing now. It might be too dark and too abstract to be appropriate for broadcasting, but an opinion would be useful to her.[24]

On Hilton Brown's advice, she sent *The Fort* directly to Gielgud, who wrote the next day to her agent, Nancy Pearn, that he found it 'quite absorbing and beautifully written', though it would need drastic adaptation.[25] The political implications were checked, which was standard procedure, and Gielgud wrote to the producer Barbara Burnham on 7 February, asking her to go and see Jameson in Portland Place to discuss the project. The play was broadcast on the Home Service, at 10.30 p.m., on Saturday 9 May.

The script preserved in the BBC's Written Archive follows the novel more or less verbatim. The adaptation was credited to Barbara Burnham, but the dialogue form of much of the original novel will have made it easy to translate to the new medium. The voices, all middle-class, are well heard, if stylised (a mixture of the poetic and the clichés of the wartime media). The introductory music behind the ghost voice speaking from the First World War ('Mademoiselle d'Armentières', cross-fading to 'Roll out the Barrel') situated the action within that lost world of shared values and national unity. Judicious cutting by the producer of what was originally an over-lengthy script to just under an hour produced a lucid analysis of the situation in defeated France (which had, implicitly, its analogue in England) and the prospects for the future. The play highlighted the dangers in the conflict between fascist defeatism and socialist idealism that had split the younger generation, the imminent disappearance of those few middle-aged idealists from 1914–18 who were still giving leadership, and the time-honoured antagonism between a France that was always collapsing and an England that always turned up late. But the closing moments, after the dramatic gunning-down of the English officers by the invaders in the cellar of the French farm, drew together the old ghosts of the past and the new ghosts in a lyrical promise of victory to come. The true fort is the landscape of memory, where the home places of England are fused with the shell-holes, trenches and roads of France:

Murray: (puzzled) When did you get here?
    Voice [Ghost]: Oh, I couldn't tell you that, it seems longer than I can remember. I know every shell-hole and every stone, almost every smell. I very much doubt if the natives know their roads as well as the English army knows them. [...]
    Murray: Good Lord, I hadn't realised we were holding this place.
    Voice: In my humble opinion, it does the holding. I feel what you might call at home here. [...]

In June, Jameson came back from Wales to the flat in Portland Place, prepared to try to live more sensibly. With her publishers' encouragement, she set about gathering up copies of her early work to be republished under the Macmillan imprint.[26] She also began planning for her replacement in PEN, someone internationally minded, who could consolidate her efforts to create a movement that was left-wing, and who would be prepared to act for free speech as well as write about it. She wrote to Ould that they must have John Lehmann as a member of PEN and put him straight onto the committee. He was, she had heard, endlessly patient and helpful with the refugees who haunted his office, and, an additional quality, he disliked Cyril Connolly.[27] Lehmann ought, in fact, to be the next President:

The election of such a president will change the colour of the PEN, I know. But it seems to me that the PEN has GOT to change, and that therefore it is better it should change with forethought.[28]

Co-founder of *New Writing*, with Isherwood, Spender, and Auden as his fellow-directors, and owner since April 1938 of the Hogarth Press, Lehmann would certainly have linked PEN's activities to a sharply focused radical politics. Whether he was ever aware of Jameson's ambitions for him is unknown, but if he was, they formed no part of his own ideas for his career.

By August, in any case, she was back in the chair at PEN Committee meetings, and planning the next Conference, on 'The PEN of the Future', to discuss how PEN should work in the world after the war, well aware that: 'The question of politics will come up. My own view is that we can no longer avoid politics, in the sense that we can no longer avoid expressing an opinion on certain fundamental questions. We should however stick to the word ethics or some other word which lifts it out of the region of parties inside a nation.'[29]

Relations with the French had taken a new turn. On 23 June 1942, de Gaulle had broadcast his manifesto of resistance from the radios of Brazzaville, Beirut, and London, condemning the Vichy regime and declaring 'While the French people is uniting for victory, it is assembling for a revolution'.[30] PEN threw its weight behind the rehabilitation of the French in the eyes of the English public. A new association for foreigners was mooted, she wrote to Ould in August, and Professor René Cassin and Dr Theodora Ohenberg had come to Portland Place to talk with her about it.[31] René Cassin's name appears frequently from this time in her correspondence with Ould, discussing the moves he was organising against their friend Denis Saurat (on behalf of de Gaulle, Ould thought). In September 1941, Cassin had been appointed to de Gaulle's *Comité national* as Commissioner for Justice and Public Education, the post Saurat thought should have been his. Ould admitted to liking Cassin, who seemed sincere, but noted signs of future problems: Cassin had apparently said that Saurat's Friday evening talks at the Institut Français did not represent Free French opinion, and that the Institut was not doing anything to spread French culture.[32] De Gaulle himself, in his *Memoirs*, in his one reference to Saurat, later said the opposite, placing the Institut at the top of his list of the centres of French life in London that he had made a point of frequenting: 'The Institut Français, which had rallied to me literally from the first moment in the person of its director, Professor Saurat, supplied our compatriots with valuable educational resources and an active intellectual circle.'[33] That was, however, a long time after and in another country, and the difficult Saurat, by then, was politically dead.

These were no longer Jameson's problems. She had told Ould in September that the specialist said she must rest or she would have angina or a leaky heart valve, and could only continue to work for PEN from a distance.[34] As news of her illness spread, Phyllis Bottome (Phyllis Forbes-Dennis), whom she knew only by reputation, offered the loan of her house in Cornwall for two months, as well as a barrage of comments: PEN should not have banned the discussion of politics, and should be listening to Phyllis's views, as a spokesperson for New Order and an expert on Central Europe, where she had spent ten formative years before the war. And there was some warm personal advice: 'I recovered once at your age from a serious TB attack by living entirely alone at the top of a mountain with a wolf-dog and a nice stout pony of a peasant to look after me.'[35]

Living in North Wales

Phyllis Bottome's Cornish house was politely refused, and before long the Chapmans were planning to move to North Wales. Jameson was in excellent mood when she replied from Portland Place in October to Macmillan's request for new autobiographical details:

I am furiously active in all the activities of foreign writers in this country, free French, Czechs, Poles, Norwegians, Belgians, Catalans, Germans, Austrians (there must be more). My name will, I hope be a thrice-told tale in all European countries after the war. I should say, I fear. It is bad enough to give them tea and counsel now. To keep up a correspondence after the war will be worse. This gossipy note is going all wrong, PLEASE edit it with discretion. I am on a panel formed by M.O.I. to help entertain and advise distinguished Americans visiting us. I am writing a play for the B.B.C. following the stunning success of the broadcast version of The Fort. My husband, Lt-Colonel Guy Chapman, is to command a new army school for officers in North Wales and I am tearing myself with groans from my comfortable London flat to accompany him and be a Commandant's wife. In any time I have left over, I am writing a long novel. I almost died of heart trouble following overwork this summer, but am recovering. (This ought to be worth a tin of orange juice from someone.)[36]

She was also an ex-officio member of a committee concerned with Young Writers and the War Effort, along with Arthur Calder-Marshall, Cyril Connolly, Tom Harrisson, Alan Thomas, and Hermon Ould. The idea was not to exempt writers from service, but give them periods of leave to do special writing jobs. From Wales, it was impossible to make meetings, but her fellow-members refused to let her resign.

At the end of October, the books and furniture went into store. Guy had obtained a posting to Harlech, as Commandant of the new Army Bureau of Current Affairs (ABCA) school for officers. He was living in at Coleg Harlech, and she settled into two rooms at the Oakeley Arms in the nearby village, Maentwrog, on the side of a hill facing Cardigan Bay and looking across the estuary to hills on the other side, 'a mole's retreat into obscurity'.[37]

The obscurity was relieved by Guy's visitors, such as their old friend Basil Liddell Hart, still out of favour with the War Office for his pre-war pronouncements on Britain's ill-preparedness for war, who came up to give a (disastrously bad) lecture. Among the neighbours was Thomas Jones, living in Harlech, a former secretary to Lloyd George and Baldwin, who in the 1930s had been in close touch with Ribbentrop.[38] Jameson wrote to Lovat Dickson of her pleasure in being so close to Dr Tom Jones, who in the days of Lloyd George had exerted considerable influence.[39] And below the hills was Portmeirion, a mixed blessing. The closeness of her old friend Amabel was very welcome, and Jameson found stimulus in the visiting crowds of cosmopolitan intellectuals and refugees.[40] She pursued the writing of *Cloudless May*, and read the negative reviews for *Then We Shall Hear Singing*.[41]

In November, as Jameson made her plans to attend and address the PEN conference, news arrived that her father was seriously ill. In the five years since her mother's death, he had lived alone in Whitby, in the Saxon Prince house at 3 Clent Hill, visited daily by an elderly housekeeper. Jameson wrote to him regularly, and had visited him twice, most recently in September that year.[42] From Whitby, she wrote an incoherent letter to Ould describing how she had been wired for on Friday, and had arrived the previous evening. Her father had had a stroke. She promised she would come to Conference if she could, and in any case would write a speech. There followed a stream of scribbled advice on current PEN matters, and then:

Forgive stupid letter. Two days' travelling—up all last night, pain over my heart.
  Oh my God I have no words to express what I feel that this should have happened now.[43]

A postscript added that the doctor had just been and said her father might last a week, so it must be assumed that she could not come to the Conference. The next day, she posted Ould a few words for the Conference address, and said she had written to Saurat and asked him to read them. The doctor said her father would not survive the day. The letter ends, in a tiny crabbed hand: 'He has just died.'[44]

In her autobiography, she was to indict herself for yet another 'failure to love', and give a vivid account of how she failed to respond to his calls in his last night, leaving him to the housekeeper, and was not there the next day in the nursing-home when he died.[45] It was her mother's fault, she said, that she ignored his calls, and her sister Do's fault that she burned his logbooks (a lifetime's diaries) and travel souvenirs, which the director of the local museum had hoped to take. But the tone of the passage indicates genuine affection, and recognises the limitations imposed on her father's generation by its training to self-discipline, and the repression of feeling. She must have rescued from his papers his indentures as a young merchant seaman; they were among her own when she died. Do's response was very different:

I have just been up north to my father's funeral. That is I did not go so much for this funeral as to help Storm clear up papers, clothing etc. I rather lost interest in him when he cut me off without even the proverbial shilling some fifteen years ago and never spoke to me since! The muddle of a lifetime of 88 years of papers etc. stored in a house with only three great lumber-rooms was terrific. I am sure the salvage figures for that week must have gone up. Everything is left to my unmarried sister [Winifred] who is now a censor in Bermuda.

It was wonderful to see the sea and moorland again and also interesting to go into a defence area. We really did feel as though we had had a holiday, though the place was hardly recognisable.[46]

There was no time for mourning. The letter in which Jameson told Lovat Dickson of her father's death also reported that she was working hard, and had finished a play for the BBC and written two-thirds of *Cloudless May*.[47] In January 1943, there were letters of a different import to be written, about Britain's double-faced responses to the revelations coming from Europe about the situation of the Jews.

On 17 December 1942, the Foreign Secretary, Anthony Eden, revealed to the House of Commons the mass executions of Jews by Germans in Occupied Europe, and read out an Allied declaration condemning 'this bestial policy of cold-blooded extermination'.[48] He said that the United Nations would try to give asylum to as many refugees as possible. Despite that, the Cabinet continued to drag its heels on the admission of Jewish refugees. Between 1933 and the Nazi take-over in Berlin, and the declaration of war by England in September 1939, only about 50,000 Jews were admitted into the UK, and that only because the Jewish community assured the Home Secretary in April 1933 that no Jewish refugee would become a charge on public funds. On 31 December 1942, 'Eden presided over a meeting of the Cabinet Committee on the Reception and Accommodation of Jewish Refugees at which it was agreed that Britain could not admit more than 1,000 to 2,000 further refugees'.[49]

On 4 January 1943, Jameson sent Ould a synopsis of a projected letter to the press on the Jews' situation, making it a larger protest against anti-Semitism, which she thought would make it more effective:

We might say, in effect, that it has been stated that there are fears in official quarters that any attempt to save Jewish children by bringing them to England would rouse anti-Semitic feeling here. That we think this is a slander on our people. But then add that ugly weeds do grow in a war atmosphere, and that we desire to express our loathing of the vulgar and hideous doctrines of anti-Semitism, and that it is the duty and privilege of every non-Jew in this country to stamp on it wherever they see any trace of it. And not simply for the sake of the Jews, but to prevent ourselves from becoming stupid and callous by indulging in inhuman deeds and thoughts. [50]

On 8 January, Ould sent her an advance copy of Victor Gollancz's pamphlet, 'Let My People Go,' which called for 'a full open door policy' to help save those Jews who were still trapped in Europe. The pamphlet included reference to a claim, which Gollancz attributed to the Home Secretary, Herbert Morrison, that there would be a public outburst of anti-Semitism if Jewish refugees were allowed into the country.[51] A letter from Sir Andrew McFadyean, published 6 January in the *Daily Telegraph*, indicated that Morrison had apparently been responding to a deputation of 23 September 1942, led by the Archbishop of Canterbury, Cardinal Hinsley, and the Moderator of the Church of Scotland, which asked him to allow entry to the United Kingdom for 2,000 French-Jewish children from Vichy France. Subsequently, said McFadyean, 'of 2,000 children, from two years of age upwards, deported from Vichy France in cattle trucks, half were dead on arrival at their destination and the rest were dying.'[52] On 9 January, Jameson forwarded her finished letter to Ould: 'It is my confession of faith about the Jews, as well as a letter from the Executive Committee of the PEN.'[53] The Executive appears not to have liked it, and even John Lehmann, by then a member, thought its tone too emotional and righteous.[54] In the end, Jameson allowed this version to be dropped.[55] The Minutes recorded that Jameson had drafted a letter to *The Times* concerning the admission of

Jewish children to the country, which was sent to *The Times* on 27 January but had still not appeared, that subsequently the Committee had agreed to ask her to draft a letter on the extermination of the Jews, and that she had passed that commission to John Lehmann.[56]

Ould's letter of 16 January had also brought unwelcome news about PEN colleagues in France. Accusations of collaboration were flying thick and fast. From the Belgian PEN, they had heard that Benjamin Crémieux was in hiding, with his beard shaved off, wanted 'not for his race but for his opinions'. Various painters were collaborating, going to Berlin and holding exhibitions, Corton was collaborating 'like mad', and there was immense anti-British propaganda everywhere.[57] She was in the thick of finishing *Cloudless May*, begun in 1940, which incorporated the whole gamut of French reactions to the prospect of Nazi rule. Herman Ould, reading her drafts, praised her ability to capture the panorama of people and events, in vivid and concentrated depth: 'It is almost a poem. Nobody is writing like this except you. It is an unending panorama of people and events, all alive, all significant.'[58]

From her Welsh distance, she commiserated with Ould on his continuing struggle with the factions of the French in exile: 'My poor Hermon, worse than Calais will be written on your heart—the cross of Lorraine is firmly round your neck.'[59]

In the following week, she responded very positively to an idea from Olaf Stapledon for a PEN Inquiry into Fundamental Values. She saw here continuity with Paul Valéry's initiatives for collaboration between European intellectuals; she had, she said, a copy of the Report of the Paris meetings of the Institut de la Coopération Intellectuelle, a collection of fascinating essays of a very high standard.[60] A committee was formed to implement Stapledon's project, and Denis Saurat agreed to be a member. It was not to be a successful undertaking. Jameson had misjudged the capacity of her colleagues to match the standards of Valéry and his peers, and Saurat was to return the proposed contributions to Ould in January 1944 saying that only the statements by Ould, Jameson, and Richard Church were up to scratch.[61] She also misjudged the public's growing boredom with discussions of 'values'; Stapledon couldn't find a publisher.

The project would however give her a chance to set out the understanding she had reached at this time of the relationship between writing and political and social commitment. She was now ready to declare that the writer's political impact came primarily from his effective use of language, which was a product of detachment:

A writer should carry the effort of detachment so far that everything—in this are included his own emotions and thoughts—becomes the object of contemplation. At the same time, the field of contemplation is widened to take in as many objects as possible, both within and without the writer, who notices how they are related to each other—how this emotion joins itself to many others, this object ressembles [sic] an infinity of objects—in a pattern as just as it is complex. 'Sensitive and intelligent aware-ness of the world, including oneself and other selves and human society as a whole' is the thing given, or its seed is given, to the writer: if he induces it in others, he does so by finding images, of emotions, actions, persons, through which his knowledge, the fruit of his conscious attention to himself and the world, becomes audible and visible.[62]

Conscious propaganda was not the writer's function, as writer. The greatest changes, she argued, had been effected by writers like T. S. Eliot. Eliot's impor-tance rested not so much in *The Waste Land*, influential though that was. The impact of his *Four Quartets* had been less noticeable, but the concentration there of thoughts and feelings, simultaneously personal and generic, must affect readers at far deeper levels. She had moved well away from her positions of the 1930s, and now declared that: 'A writer who wants to escape can do it just as well by rushing about to political meetings.'

In response to Stapledon's question about her own current aims, she said that when young, she had thought her ideas and feelings were supremely inter-esting. She was not quite like the primitives of the Vézère caves, who at least kept their eye on the object. She had been intensely influenced by Anatole France, Arthur Symonds's *History of the Renaissance* and Allen Upward's *The Divine Mystery*, but all she had of her own was her delight in words: 'I was a young ape with a paint-brush.' At a later stage, she had more genuine emotions, but still could not objectify them. The breakthrough in understanding came when 'my imagination began to be disturbed [...] by the fear in the world,' and her aim now was to try to understand and recreate her personal reactions to that fear ('the figures, the types, the emotions, which stalk through my brain'), to help others understand their own:

[T]o present to the imagination a shape of evil, in all its horror and with all its little-ness, a shape of good, with all its weakness, is the most potent thing a writer can do to change 'other selves and the human society as a whole'. But change will not be his intention.

His intention will be to communicate understanding, so that readers them-selves can identify and effect change. Writing should aim to create an 'active community between mutually aware and mutually respecting persons'.

229

Two days after she had agreed with Ould that Stapledon's project should go ahead, on 10 February 1943, as she was approaching the final chapters of *Cloudless May*, a German bomb fell on the civic kitchen in Reading where her sister Dorothy was working as a volunteer cook for the Women's Voluntary Service.[63] She wrote to Ould the following day, in tears,[64] and again a fortnight later:

The fact is that I relied on my young sister to provide me with all the colour, including the annoyances, of family life. A peculiar greyness has now invaded one patch of my mind—it doesn't incapacitate me, it's just there, and my opinion is that it will always be there.[65]

Dorothy had taken her two children over to America in August 1940. A friend of Jameson's, a Miss Hockaday, head of a girls' school, had found a home for them with a childless couple, Sam and Betty Leake. (Subsequently, during the time the Pateman children were with them, the Leakes had three children of their own.) Dorothy wrote regularly from Mortimer to Betty and the children, long, lively letters scattered with war news, anecdotes of her recently resumed career as a journalist (a general freelancer, and then a cookery editor), and accounts of her volunteer work in the community kitchen run by the WVS. She devoured news of the children—Judy's leg braces, recommended by the paediatrician, Dr Perkins, Nick's tonsil operation, chickenpox, Judy's birthday parties, the electric cleaner she got as a birthday present, starting school. She noted the vivid contrast of their lives in America with the dangers and privations of their English home:

Though I'd give ten years of my life just to see them now I wouldn't have them back again. [...] Thanks to you and Sam we don't regret having brought them into this world. If they were here we should.[66]

Dorothy's letters reported the stringencies of clothes rationing and food rationing. By September 1941, children were reduced to half a pint of milk a day, and adults less (though she was able to buy extra milk from a local farmer), and there was a two pounds a head onion allowance for the whole winter (though they had grown some in the garden). Then the two maids had left for war work:

It was inevitable, but it leaves me with a fourteen room house and nobody to help me. It is a very old house and the kitchens have brick floors that must be scrubbed each week, there is no gas, only paraffin and coal fires to light—I think I would prefer the war work! Still what does it matter, one gets through anything somehow and can still laugh at the funnies.[67]

As the bombing got heavier in the spring of 1942, she had confronted the possibility that she and Robert might die, and made plain her preference that the children should make their permanent home with the Leakes. She wrote to Betty:

We have learned to take happiness as and when it comes and no regrets and no remorse and without reserve. <u>At this moment</u> we are especially glad to hear of your affection for the children, and would like to feel that you have not set a time limit on your trust. It would be sad if they ever had to become a rich woman's protégées [sic] and not someone's family—do you understand what we are trying to say? God grant that this may never be but we must be prepared.[68]

She added a postscript telling Betty to keep the letter in case she might want this paragraph some day, and then another postscript saying not to, it was asking too much.

After Dorothy's death, Jameson did her best to fill a maternal role for which she was clearly not best suited. She took up the correspondence with the Leakes, writing a frantic letter from Gwynedd on 13 February to describe what had happened to Dorothy, to say how happy Do had been that the children were safe and happy with the Leakes, and that when the war was over she wanted Robert and the children to live with her, so she could help bring them up. The letter went astray for a while, so she had to write again on 16 April. On that occasion, she said firmly that Robert, about to go into the RAF as an Armaments Officer, would be registering herself as the children's guardian in the event of his being killed in action. And she wanted to discuss with Betty how best to tell the children about their mother's death. Betty Leake returned a long letter dated 3 May saying how the children had taken the news. Judy was particularly anxious at the idea that she now had no Mummy, and referred to her aunt as 'Mummy in England'—but she had assured Betty that she didn't think she would go back to England after the war.[69] The two women agreed to exchange regular letters so that both sides could get to know each other.

Settled back in Wales after Dorothy's death, Jameson finished *Cloudless May* by the end of March 1943, and posted the typescript to Macmillan.[70] The *Génie Française* project was now taking off, and she discussed the proposed committee membership with Ould. She respected Raymond Mortimer, she said, liked Charles Morgan, and disliked Cyril Connolly—who had, however, since January 1943, been the establishment's nominee to lead the recruitment of writers and the public, through French culture, to the cause of France.[71] Had she been less busy, she might have spared time for an expression of annoyance at the usurpation by Connolly of a role that previously had been amply fulfilled by writers—not journalists—such as Charles Morgan and herself. Their political views were presumably too radical, and too independent, for Churchill to trust them with such high-profile propaganda responsibilities.

In the United States, the *Saturday Evening Post* had just published a short story she had written in connection with a massacre perpetrated by the Germans in the previous year, in the Czechoslovakian village of Lidiče. In revenge for the assassination of Reinhard Heydrich, deputy leader of the SS, in May 1942, the Germans had selected at random the little village, north of Prague, sealed it off, shot all the men over 16, and sent the women and children to separate concentration camps.[72] The British public was shocked. War records declassified in January 2006 show that Churchill, five days afterwards, advocated that the RAF be sent to bomb small German villages 'on a three-for-one basis'. He abandoned the plan reluctantly in the face of opposition from Cabinet colleagues, who saw in it a needless risk to the lives of aircrews, and Clement Attlee advised against entering into 'competitions of frightfulness with the Germans'.[73] Jameson's story received considerable attention.[74] 'The Last Night' probed the thoughts and feelings of a young crippled German soldier, a late-recruited member of the occupying troops in Czechoslovakia, brought up to unquestioning obedience of authority. Through his naïve eyes, she presented the kindness as well as the cruelty of his compatriots, and—somewhat implausibly—produced a conclusion in which he was spared by the Czechs when they took back their country, and treated with kindness. The unexpected plea for forgiveness for the ignorant German rank and file, victims of a system, struck a note in sharp contrast to the prevailing national mood.

In April, Ould and Jameson were both elected to the Executive Committee of the *Génie Française*.[75] She didn't attend any meetings, but she was one of the very few people who actually paid a subscription. In June, Ould reported on the shambles of the foundation meeting, due partly to Cassin having been removed from de Gaulle's *Comité national* just before it began, but mostly owing to the lack of supporters.[76] She replied expressing her despair at the internecine wars of the French, and the increasingly visible antagonisms between the French and the English.[77] She nevertheless went on to make practical suggestions about how the project might be made to work, either attached to the British Council, as Ould suggested, or, as Harold Nicolson suggested, with the backing of the French Ambassador once one was appointed again. She still thought that French civilisation and culture was worth propagating in

England, and a body that could do that would be very worthwhile. The matter dragged on, as did the sparring between Cassin and Saurat.[78]

In the middle of July, Jameson suggested the English offer an ultimatum: either the scheme should be dissolved, or Cassin must produce a written promise of official French support and agree that the Director of the Institut Français be co-opted to the Committee.[79] By the end of the month, she was desperately anxious about the future of the Saurats, and asking Ould to alert Nicolson and the Foreign Office to Cassin's wheelings and dealings.[80]

Throughout the arguments, she kept on writing. Everybody had their own collaborative schemes, and they all wanted contributions. In May, she told Irene Rathbone she had written 'a feeble and pessimistic piece' for Arthur Koestler's projected PEN Anthology—the idea of writing about the post-war world had not inspired her.[81] When his scheme collapsed, she sold the story to *Modern Reading* for eight guineas, and gave the money to the PEN Fund.[82] And she had sent Ignace Legrand a chapter, she told Irene, presumably for him to forward to Henri Bosco's literary journal, *Aguedal*, based in Casablanca. Bosco wanted to devote a number to English writers, and Jameson wrote round asking her friends for contributions.[83] In September, Max-Pol Fouchet was looking for people to write for an English issue of his review *Fontaine*, published from Algiers.[84]

And between 1941 and 1943, she published three novels.

15

Fortifying the Nation: Narrative, Memory, and Culture

Jameson's two major novels of 1940, *Europe to Let* and *Cousin Honoré*, written on the edge of war, had explored the collective sensibility that made war inevitable: the inertia of self-interest, the pettiness of local perspectives joined with nationalist prejudice, and the possessive individualism that was the dark side of peasant resilience. This sensibility operated within the lethal political conditions created by a long culture of revenge, and the inability of England and France to make an honest peace in Europe. Carelessness of other people's right to safe boundaries, and retrenchment inside one's own, had created a new Europe whose distinctive landscape was that of exile. The questions of what European identity, and European values, now meant, and how to hold on to what was left of them, had urgently to be addressed. Jameson's next novels looked to the refuge and rallying-point that was the European cultural heritage, and explored ways to turn cultural memory into a culture of resistance.

Between 1941 and 1943, the collapse of the little nations of Central Europe, followed by the fall of France, inspired Jameson to write three very different novels on the same themes: national identity, national differences, cultural heritage, and cultural memory. She attributed the inspiration for two of them (*The Fort*, 1941, and *Cloudless May*, 1943), to conversations in June and July 1940 with Denis Saurat and Elie Bois, the latter the former editor of *Le Petit Parisien*. Both men passed on the scandals circulating about Prime Minister Paul Reynaud and his mistress, Hélène de Portes, and tales of the weakness and incompetence of the French Government in retreat at Bordeaux.[1] Writing to Lovat Dickson in August 1940, she told him: 'There is a marvellous novel in the Reynaud–Mme de Portes story, about which I've collected enough information to invent the rest.'[2] And a few days later, she indicated to Valentine

Dobrée other sources of information she had found, and the anxieties she was developing, not least about the chances of Britain going the same way as France. She had been re-reading J. C. Bodley's book on France, and expressed her amazement at the extent and depth of the present decay:

But Werth's books, and the things that were said to me by a professor at the Lycée Montaigne I saw a lot of when I was staying in Paris [André Buffard], and the newspapers during the Cagoulard episode which was still going on when I was there, had prepared me for the possibility of trouble. But I would never have believed that it would happen so quickly or so thoroughly. [...] I talked to General de Gaulle's propaganda aide de camp, and he professed that he didn't see what form the new France would take. But all these people are very Right Wing, too, though not rotted by the sort of false international of finance and the Great Interests. What makes me afraid, when I am afraid, is the fear that our Government is itself so opposed, or at best so reluctant, to face the <u>necessity</u> of social revolution that might (in the event of a prolonged war or a partial defeat) be faced by a Pétain move here. That devil Sir Horace Wilson is still there spinning his threads. He is secretly active on the Swinton Ctte [sic], he is partly responsible for the internment scandal.[3]

Then We Shall Hear Singing. A Fantasy in C Major, published in 1942, and set in occupied Central Europe, dealt with issues that were also of urgent relevance to France. All three books advanced together, and very quickly. By May 1941, Jameson was telling Macmillan that she had an 'immense' novel on the stocks [*Cloudless May*], had finished *The Fort*, and was writing a 70,000-word story called *The Stones Cry Out*.[4] The publication of the sequence established her reputation as a major novelist of the war, an accomplished and innovative stylist—and a best-seller. *The Fort* sold modestly well (helped doubtless by the radio version discussed in the previous chapter). *Then We Shall Hear Singing* sold very well, earning £650 in its first week.[5] The first edition of *Cloudless May* sold out immediately, cleared all Jameson's debts with Macmillan, and was nominated as a Book Society choice.[6]

The Fort

The Fort was composed quickly between November 1940 and January 1941 in two versions, a short novel and a play. It was an attempt to understand the collapse of the Allies before the German advance, to restore British morale, and to maintain, with difficulty, some sense of the humanity of the German nation.[7] The action is set during the evening of 13 June 1940, in north-eastern France, in the cellars of a farmhouse that are all that is left of the original building, razed in the First World War. A representative collection of soldiers has been swept together by the German advance: two middle-aged officers, one English and one French, two young French soldiers, and one young Englishman, in flight from the defeat at Cambrai. Their peasant-farmer host, a sergeant in the previous war, is refusing to abandon his land for a second time. A young German prisoner, devoted to Hitler, completes the tally. A series of stylised dialogues dramatises the ideological conflicts represented within the group: differences of national identity, and differences within nations and between generations.

The *TLS* reviewer, R. D. Charques, appreciated 'a touch of the poetically symbolical in the taut and incisive dialogue that invests Miss Jameson's contrasts with a quality of luminous justice'.[8] Some of it is a pastiche of Jean Giraudoux's popular and much-admired poetic drama of ideas, *La Guerre de Troie n'aura pas lieu*. But the best comes from long meditation on the style evolved by English writers of the First World War, at once symbolic and direct, to convey the intensity of experience at the front. Jameson had written in 1932:

I think that the only literature of value my generation (which began to write in 1919) will have to leave is its War books. None of us has written anything so well worth writing as *The Middle Parts of Fortune*, *Undertones of War*, *The Spanish Farm Trilogy*, *In Retreat*, *These Men Thy Friends*, *The Memoirs of an Infantry Officer*, and some few others. The final value of these books is that the experience they convey is one that involved the whole self—the events, physical and emotional, of that time in the writer's life when he was most sharply alive. [...] It is by these books and not by a *Good Companions*—to make one bustling book stand for a regiment—that my generation will speak, for itself and perhaps for the one nearest after it.[9]

Tolstoy and Barbusse were interesting too for her in terms of form;[10] and the painfully spare prose of Guy Chapman's war reminiscences was always an inspiration. She quoted for a correspondent, after Guy's death, the final lines of *A Passionate Prodigality*, which, she said, 'I shall recall as I die':

Beyond, a dark grey morning, windless with a hint of drizzle, colourless trees and hedges, and no sound but the steam from the engine. The train jerked into movement. We passed over into Germany. No trumpets sounded.[11]

The contrasts Charques admired are strongly drawn. There are the long-standing, debilitating antagonisms between France and Britain, intensified by the tensions of defeat, and a mutual incomprehension that between the two older men at least settles finally into a mutual understanding that each of them will sacrifice himself in the name of resistance. There is a major class divide between the two young Frenchmen, one an impoverished socialist, hostile to fascism, and the other a defeatist, aristocratic ultra, fanatically anti-Semitic and an admirer of Nazi energy. Frenchmen, at this moment, can only turn against each other, or at best follow through ill-conceived orders to their hopeless end. Effective resistance is left to the two Englishmen, who transcend generational differences in the defence of their shared idea of England. But as in Giraudoux's play, the search for common ground between so many antagonists comes too little, and too late. The story collapses swiftly to its end. Sedan falls, the armies are evacuated from Dunkirk, the French are driven back across the great rivers of the North, Paris falls, France surrenders, and the two Englishmen die together in the cellar.

In this symbolic drama, the one note of hope for the future resides in the landscape, where personal and national identities are embedded. The French farmer complains of the devastation wreaked in the First World War by soldiers clearing the line of sight between his farmhouse and the Channel, that left only one poplar still standing, of the long line on the horizon that he planted for his wife. The Impressionists' iconic image has gone; but in the process, France and her ally across the water can see each other more clearly. And the landscape, apparently empty, is crammed with ghosts, traces of the people who have gone before and the relationships of loyalty, obligation and affection they created together. The French officer who is heading back to join his compatriots falling back on the Loire first renews his compact with the English comrade he fought alongside in 1914. The peasant and his daughter leave for safety in a surrendered area, but the daughter's flirtation with the young English soldier binds her to the struggle, and her father declares himself forever indebted to the unknown English soldiers who saved his life in 1914. As in the radio version, the novel closes with the ghostly dialogue of two generations of English war dead rising in the cellar, linking the landscapes of home and France, and conjuring up a visionary landscape of collective memory, and trans-national community, that could yet reclaim Europe from the enemy.

Then We Shall Hear Singing

In the early 1960s, with science fiction and fantasy entering the cultural mainstream, Jameson described the novel that followed *The Fort* as 'a proof that even a minor writer is able, now and then, to overhear the future', and pointed out in *Then We Shall Hear Singing. A Fantasy in C Major* an allegorical dimension that was highly relevant to the present, where human beings were still being conditioned 'to be apathetic or docile atomies in a dangerously over-crowded world, no nuisance to their betters...'[12] In November 1942, Vera Brittain's diary was contemptuous: 'Review of M.S.J.'s latest novel by Philip Toynbee in the *New Statesman* suggests that it is completely sterile (another of her obsessive studies of Nazi frightfulness).'[13] But Nazi frightfulness was less than half the story, which was much more about the human capacity to resist the destruction of individual personality and the resources to be tapped in the common cultural heritage. Naomi Mitchison made a very different diary entry: 'Read Storm Jameson's last book, rather good'.[14]

The book was first conceived in April 1941.[15] It was dedicated to Líba Ambrosová and her country, Czechoslovakia, 'a country with the longest memory in the world for freedom'. It was also, implicitly, written for the ordinary English women Jameson had met in her visits to armaments factories, and women like her sister Dorothy, and Toni Stolper's sister, Anna Jerusalem, holding together homes and families across wartime Europe.[16] In *The Fort* and *Cloudless May*, armed resistance is men's business. In an occupied country, the weapons for resistance are in women's hands. The narrative voice-over tells the reader:

> At whatever moment you choose to come into Europe, you are able to hear a woman talking to her neighbours about invasion or some sort of everyday violence. The voice is the same, the look of patience and contempt is the same, the words are almost the same. One moment is being played over and over again [...].
>
> History, accurate history, is an affair of poor women, in spring, in summer, in autumn, in winter, in a country which has been invaded and conquered, talking. Defeat and hope in their wombs, they scrape with their fingers a rim of dirt on the inside of a pan, and talk. It's not of much account, what they say.[17]

The review in the *TLS* appreciated Jameson's choice of the symbolic mode for her war novel. If an author has no direct experience of fighting, then invoking 'the imaginative perception which crystallizes [sic] the event in the symbols of history' was the next best thing. But the reviewer was unhappy about the 'nervous feminine intensity' with which she identified the spiritual issues of the war, her 'all-embracing compassion', and what he thought was simultaneously an over-simple and over-subtle treatment of the power of human memory to resist evil.[18] The mood and tone he criticised, quite unlike the conventional English coolness of *The Fort*, would later become familiar currency in the fantasies of writers such as Doris Lessing, Ursula Le Guin, and Margaret Atwood. But even at the time, Jameson could have defended the accuracy of the notes she was striking, by pointing to the letters she had received from Oscar Vočadlo describing Nazi attempts to wipe cultural memory from the Czechoslovakian landscape, and the passionate declarations of national resistance that had struggled through to London from Jiřina Tůmová and her PEN colleagues.

The novel is set in an unnamed country, five years after fighting has ended, with a populace just beginning to tolerate the presence of their occupiers. The normal slow processes of post-war assimilation are not enough for the leaders of the conquering State, who have found a scientist who can destroy minds without damaging bodies, and turn individuals into docile servants. He is sent to experiment on a remote village. First the men and then the young women are taken away and transformed. The old peasant women are considered to be harmless. In fact, they are the ones who prepare the ground for resistance, preserving memories and traditions, sustaining hatred, refusing to forgive, hiding rifles, ready for the repressed violence of the men to make its inevitable return. After the occupying soldiers have left the village they think is pacified, old Anna comes out of the shadows to become the centre round which the disrupted community is recreated.

The issue is whether, and how, cultural memory can revive in a nation where it has been systematically obliterated.[19] Culture in its most significant form, as the title of the novel indicates, is the culture of everyday life. The singing that returns in triumph at the end of the narrative, with the liberating army, is pitched in C Major, the basic, common scale. The creative relation an individual enjoys to public and private space, memorialised in the rituals and habitual practices of everyday life, is the experience that forms his identity.

Jameson's metaphors draw together 'high' culture and the creativity that is part of daily living. To work the landscape, the narrative voice declares, is to read it, to come to a bodily recognition of the history that past generations have embedded in it:

Turning over the soil of his country, the villager turns the pages of its life. Before the invasion, the country had had twenty years of freedom. Before then, three hundred years of conquest. In those three hundred years, the memory of freedom remained so near the surface that to come on it a man had only to thrust a spade into the ground. [...] Memory in the children of this country was a sixth sense, used as naturally and freely as the others.[20]

Words are central to cultural experience, and their acquisition is another bodily, not merely intellectual process, in which individual, culture and landscape are identified. This time, the narrative works with organic metaphors:

Wherever he learns it, a man's own language is grown in his soil and reaches him smelling of it and not of any other richer or dryer. He saturates it with his own blood. He nourishes it with his own life, in every moment, with every breath his mind takes. In the beginning—that is, in his beginning—a child hears it when he is still in the womb; as soon as he is born, the same voice, using the same language, goes on speaking to him or says, 'Give him to me.' When he uses it for the first time it separates him from things as familiar to him as the parts of his body. Later, he gives himself back again to things, when he describes them, when he takes them in his hand, when he thinks, This is my cup. He gives it, with his seed, to his fields or his children. When he dies and goes to his long home, in the last minute he dies from his own speech; and his words, his dear words, go to nourish the life past and future, the perpetual present.[21]

Words by themselves, written or spoken, are an easy target for the invader. Books can be taken away, songs can be banned, and the language of the invader can be imposed in the teaching practices of the schoolroom. The most resistant forms of identity are those lodged in the mundane sensuous practices of domestic space, where hands 'remember' long-established relationships of knowing and making. Baking bread, washing cups and plates handed down through generations, embroidering traditional patterns, growing scented flowers and herbs in the kitchen garden, may seem to the invader to pose no threat. But the rooms of home are treasure-chests, storing potent memories:

[The national language] was the only one understood by the things they had been forced to give up, and which now, without ears, tongues, eyes, passed from hand to hand among the invaders. Sometimes a woman would be called out of her cottage to work in her old house for one of the visitors, and then, feeling her hand on it, a chair, a wooden step, would come suddenly and thankfully to life and begin to tell all it knew.[22]

Objects mediate the forbidden words by which they were known, with the words come lost associations, and the memory of loss produces the anger that fires resistance. Old General Lesenow, the 'good' German forced to preside over this abuse of the victor's power, thrills in his nerves at the sight of 'lights deliberately placed by human hands in the dark', and wonders:

> Was there the chance of a memory, lodged in the country itself, in its stones, finding its way directly to the nerves of [the scientist] Hess's victims? He smiled. If, he thought, it happens, it will probably be through the most commonplace, the least exalted of memories. A line from a great poet never reaches your secret agony; it takes a shabby arm-badge or a vulgar catchword to do that.[23]

Cloudless May

In 1943, *Cloudless May*, exploring in epic scale and realistic historical detail the causes and unrolling of the fall of France, returned to the same question of what can survive in a culture subjected to enemy action, and produced the same answer. High culture, certainly, is resistant. France has led, aesthetically and philosophically, in the creation of the European cultural heritage, and the memory of that will be hard to erase. But of much more importance are the standards France has set for the culture of everyday life, and the values of life lived on the human scale: freedom, justice, and solidarity. Confronting the superior weight and technology of the German war machine, Bergeot, the local Prefect, is facetiously realistic:

> No nation has ever sold itself and its culture so successfully to the rest of the world. But this, my friend, is a crisis of shells and intelligence. It's really serious! Our guns, tanks, the General Staff, are all out of date. Perhaps our intellect is, too. We've constructed a moral Maginot out of our painters and writers—very impressive, but can we hold it? In any case, we can't frighten the Germans into submission by quoting Baudelaire to them. Only the English and Americans fall for that now. We really need more tanks—and a few better generals.[24]

The German advance spells out the imminent ruin of everything that is France—libraries, galleries, cathedrals, castles, the intellectual and the architectural heritage, the landscape, and the people. What will survive is not the products of culture, but how its people have chosen to live it.

The bulk of the writing took place between May 1941 and March 1943, as the Allies were preparing for the push back into Europe.[25] The British public

241

was still angry and resentful at the speed with which France had surrendered, and old antagonisms needed to be soothed. French Communists, who were proving to be a major element of the growing Resistance inside France, were particular objects of resentment and suspicion, even after the collapse of the Hitler–Stalin Pact and the signing in London of the Anglo-Soviet alliance in May 1942. A key figure over the period 1942–4 in the rehabilitation of France's cultural and military standing with the British public, and the restoration of confidence in the French Left, was the poet Louis Aragon, a leading member of the Communist Resistance in France.[26] His poems were seized on by reviewers who set aside his Communist allegiance to praise the poet, the Resistance fighter, the lover of Elsa, his wife—in short, the lyrical spokesman for the suffering and emotions of ordinary men.

Aragon's celebrated lament in *Le Crève-Coeur* for the betrayal of France provided the title for Jameson's novel, and its epigraph: 'Mai qui fut sans nuage et juin poignardé.'[27] Her hero Captain Rienne is part-modelled on Basil Liddell Hart,[28] but he also represents the spirit of Aragon. The austere soldier of peasant stock, who reads the poetry of Charles Péguy in his small barracks room, on the banks of his native Loire, is devoted to the landscape of France, loyal to its people, and loyal to leaders he knows are wrong, weak, and self-interested. He fights the invaders until the last hope is gone, and when defeat is certain he takes his loyalty to London, and rallies to de Gaulle's Free French. *Cloudless May* was published in September 1943. In the following month, General de Gaulle made his famous speech from Algiers, before an audience at the Alliance Française, rallying all who were struggling for liberty, invoking the poets, scientists, and artists, and quoting Aragon by name.

Jameson's novel helped to separate in the public mind the French who had followed de Gaulle's example from those who had remained on the wrong side of the Channel. Among the latter, it distinguished between those who had actively supported Pétain's refusal of Churchill's offer in June 1940 of union with Britain, and his signature on 22 June of the armistice with Germany, and those who stayed in France because there was nowhere else for them to go. The book was also an indictment of fascist cruelty (French, as much as German), and a call to resistance and hope in the face of apparent defeat. Reprinted in 1945, with a dust-jacket commendation from George Bishop of the *Daily Telegraph* as 'Perhaps the best novel that has been produced by the War', it would find yet another political role to play as European unification came onto the agenda.

Even before she finished *The Fort*, on 13 January, Jameson had been pursuing her researches, 'questioning Frenchmen and reading everything I could lay hands on that might help me to live in the France that had capitulated' and making careful notes of the smallest passing comment on 'the bridge at Saumur, a village—Montreuil-Bellay?'[29] She will have had long conversations with Guy, who lectured on the French defeat in Coleg Harlech in early 1943, presenting his analysis of the factors that had left the French unprepared for war, and defending them against charges that they were all corrupt—he had, he said, been doing that informally since June 1940.[30] Through her friendship with Basil Liddell Hart, she will have been familiar with the struggle of modernisers in the British army to mechanise battalions, and to update training and strategic thinking to support the changes.[31] That the British military mind-set at the start of World War two was not quite so backward-looking as that of its French counterparts was due in great part to Liddell Hart's long polemic struggle in his books, pamphlets, and articles in the national press, and to the private advice he gave to ministers. Rienne's anxieties over the backwardness of the French army command echo Liddell Hart's criticisms, and the technical precision and dramatic effectiveness of the scenes where the French tanks are finally, too late, called into action to defend the Loire bridges, owe much to the expertise of Jameson's friend and his new offensive–defensive strategies.[32]

Rich and detailed source documentation fed into an epic drama where Jameson analysed once again the interpenetration of public and private life, and the shaping of politics by personal ambition and desire.[33] The Loire Valley she had been cut off since the summer of 1939 had become a second mother-country; and she made it the stage for her most impressive evocation to date of the human energies invested in landscape, and their role in the creation and renewal of individual and national character.

The charting of history in the novel is precise. From the opening scene, the dates of France's collapse are carefully logged. On 5 May 1940, Captain Rienne leaves his barrack room to walk in the square of 'Seuilly', the composite town on the Loire, with a topography very close to that of Saumur, that is the heart of the action. On 19 June, young Lucien Sugny says goodbye to his mother as the Germans advance, unstoppable; eleven days later, spent mostly in a fishing-boat, he is met by Rienne on the station platform in London and takes up his role in the Resistance. Inside this precision, the characters struggle confusedly in their own little corners of the great French webs of personal and factional self-interest, until the arrival of the Germans makes all things perfectly clear.

Behind the dates, time is strangely elastic. One day charting the German advance can fill several chapters, while the eleven-day journey from the Sugny farm to La Rochelle, and on to Plymouth and London, is condensed into two paragraphs. The movement of time through the narrative matches the progressive, increasingly swift peeling of the layers of pretence from around the rotten core of France.

In Jameson's story, the leaders are the primary cause of the rot. Elie Bois's account (*Truth on the Tragedy of France*, 1941) instructed her in the motivations of those at the top:

> [W]hatever the motives of an old bewildered soldier like Marshal Pétain may have been, whatever he may have hoped to be able to do in the role of father of his people, the motives of a Laval and a Baudouin were ambition, greed for power, and fear of personal loss. Mr. Bois [...] has considerable sympathy for Daladier, a certain contempt for Reynaud in spite of admiring his gifts, and only hatred and bitterness for the men who saw in surrender to Hitler not the salvation of their country but rewards for themselves.[34]

But leadership, Jameson showed, operates at different levels, and failings at the highest level are most pernicious as they filter down into the decisions of those deemed by history to be 'minor' characters, but who have direct impact on the day-to-day lives of the nation. Pétain's example confirms the stubborn self-belief of old generals, who glimpse only in their nightmares the disasters their stubbornness brings, and who in the daylight are still sending men to their deaths. Prime Minister Reynaud is heard on radio in the early sections, encouraging the nation with lies and false hope, and failing to resist the forces of decay. His weaknesses are re-enacted on local ground by Emile Bergeot, the Prefect of Seuilly, Rienne's old schoolmate, once a good man, ruined by his ambition and his love for a greedy mistress. Bergeot's tragic love affair with Marguerite de Freppel follows closely in its narrative outline Reynaud's obsession with the countess de Portes. Here, though, Jameson introduces an important new twist. Whereas Hélène, passionately anti-British, apparently wanted Reynaud to surrender to Germany and become the dictator of France, with herself the power behind his throne, Marguerite's manoeuvrings to push Bergeot to greater power are driven by simpler and more commonplace financial motives.[35] The child of an impoverished family, with a brutal father, forced into prostitution to make her escape, Marguerite has clawed her way to security and lives in fear of losing it.[36] Jameson's leaders are ordinary people with a mirror-relationship to those they lead.

Self-seeking and corruption have become the common way of life in France, and the source of its inevitable collapse. Rottenness at the top doesn't exculpate the rest of the nation from its collective responsibilities, as Rienne recognises, for all his sympathy with 'the mob of ordinary people' applauding the platitudes of the Minister unveiling the bust of Foch in the Town Hall Square.[37] Waiting in the local hospital to see Louis Mathieu, the Jewish newspaper editor who has been beaten up by local fascists, Rienne listens to the local people abusing their leaders, and wonders how they would answer if he told them what he thinks of them:

The Republic you've begun to abuse isn't simply an affair of bribes and tricks, it was once the daily bread of a people satisfied to be anonymous. Except that they were Frenchmen. If you have let all that wither, what have you in the ground to take its place?...Some of them would smile ironically, and the others...there are only women and old men here, and children.[38]

Belatedly, he recognises that the voices he condemns are not the whole of France; the best are out there, fighting.

Not many contemporaries took Jameson's point. The Francophobe *TLS*, for instance, was less than half-convinced:

It is not a one-sided picture that Miss Jameson draws. Brave and honourable men have almost as numerous a place in it as the others, and even the others are seldom wholly without human virtue. Yet the doubt which the elaborate, skilful and passionately honest narrative raises, now that one is conscious of the enormity of France's malady of soul, is whether those who have loved her best have not also sentimentalized her greatness.[39]

But Jameson was quite clear that the derelictions that had brought France to the edge of ruin were not hers alone, and to deny France the possibility of recovery had grave implications for the future of Europe. A moral and social Renaissance, in the name of social justice, was what France and Europe should have been working for. The Prussian refugee caught in the French internment camp, Mathieu's friend, a socialist and a Jew, tells Rienne: 'France, the true France, is going to be defeated for a time. It's unfortunate for you French— and for Europe—that you are fighting a war when you ought to have been looking for a Renaissance. Which is overdue.'[40] The overdue Renaissance of the Common Man is also acknowledged by the local bishop ('we have not been common enough'), while the atheist schoolteacher has already joined with the local priest ('the two poles, the two clarities, the two idealisms, of the

French spirit') to admit their common failure to see through a dying bour-geois way of life.[41]

The battle for the Loire, the 'seam' of France, is also the battle for the seam of Europe. At the intricately linked levels of the sensuous culture of everyday life, and the high humanist culture that came to birth during the Renaissance in the valley of the Loire, France and Europe, Jameson argues, live in the same modes. The novel explores the distinctive French heritage, a long continuum in time and space. In a graphic image, the dead are pictured crammed into the shabby thirteenth-century houses along the river's edge in Thouédun, Rienne's home village, jostling comfortably with the living, making the houses 'tougher than the strong columns of the church. They, and not the church, were France's immortality'.[42] The bread and wine have the flavour of their own soil, imparted to those who consume them. Cultural allegiance, like national allegiance, begins in the experience of the individual in relation to his lived space. Rienne recognises that: 'All these great names, names of a town, a prov-ince, a poet, Racine, Ingres, Aquitaine, the Marne, are not France. France is some good little nothing each of us is protecting behind the names.'[43]

Meditating in a local twelfth-century church, Rienne makes the link between the lived knowledge accumulated in his ordinary home village and the larger world:

The word Ur, the word Mycenae, had fallen into silence, without the world being any the worse for it. But the word France must go on, since the whole world had been waiting for it, for this frail new point piercing a young branch, smelling of the leaf, of autumn, promising Chartres and Tours, and foreknowing or remembering Ronsard, Hugo, Péguy, the battle of the Marne, Verdun. All this, which was still hidden in the future, still wrapped in the fresh bud, must not be lost. Nor must a word be lost that hid in itself the poorest village—with its single dusty square, its single cafe, its poor and tremendous church, seeming so much too large for such a small village, and in fact scarcely large enough to accommodate so many dead. The word for Thouédun, for instance.[44]

The sensuous nature of culture, lodged in living experience, informs every line of Jameson's text. Bergeot leans on the stone sill of his house, and reads its history with his hands.[45] Language is rooted in the interaction of men and their landscape:

More than the smell of southernwood or garlic, more even than the sight of men argu-ing over glasses of cloudy yellow wine, [the Angevin accent] was the accent itself of [Bergeot's] childhood. When she was dying his mother had turned back into it, and so it was also the language that the dead of the province talked to each other with their faces against yews and poplars.[46]

The culture that counts is material, something accumulated in the landscape and the bodies of the people. France's rivers are the key to her survival. Jameson turns a historical fact of military strategy into a major cultural insight. The rivers are the distinctive local strands of the network that constitutes a nation, each carrying its own part of a heritage too rich and complex to be destroyed. The German tanks roll over the Somme, the Aisne, and the Marne, the Northern borders that have been France's sacrificial terrain since Roman times.[47] They are stopped briefly on the Loire, where the army, in the shape of Rienne and his friend Ollivier, the tank officer, belatedly makes a stand. Quiet and lazy in the earlier pages, heavy with the weight of the past, and swollen by tributaries that reach into every corner of France, the Loire by the end is the conduit to the future, a promise to the young peasant soldier of something that will survive on the other side of defeat: 'The benefits of the Loire—a light breeze smelling of seaweed, and the scent of young leaves, history, and Spanish broom—waited on Lucien Sugny.'[48] The light that shines on the Loire, the enlightening ray of French reason, is a motif that flickers through the whole text. In the stench and darkness of the internment camp on the banks of the river, where Rienne visits Mathieu's Prussian friend for the last time, unable to save him from the advancing Nazis, the light trembles on the edge of defeat; but even then, the novel promises, it will hold its place, in Uhland's mind, and Rienne's memory.[49]

The novel leaves the future of France, and Europe, in the hands of Rienne and Lucien, the soldier-peasant-intellectuals of two generations, who opt for resistance and exile, their womenfolk, sister and mother, holding on at home, and—breaking out of the familiar binary—the Jewish outsider Mathieu. Editor of the *Seuilly Journal*, Mathieu stands in direct contrast to the Cohen/Rothermere who in *The Mirror in Darkness* surrendered his voice to fascism. He is a history specialist, a patriot, a conservative, and a Republican, opposed equally to Right and Left for the damage they have done to his idea of France. As a Jew, Mathieu inhabits a place where France's professed values are constantly being tested, and he understands that values have to be asserted and fought for.[50] Modelled on PEN's Benjamin Crémieux, by then in hiding, he challenges the rooted anti-Semitism of both France and England. Mathieu, like his friend Rienne, understands that when nations collapse, responsibility reverts to individuals: 'For the present there is no France, there are only French-men.'[51] He can't be bought. He will fight to preserve France's culture, and he, or someone like him, will be ready when the soldiers return. He knows that it is the duty of those left 'to prepare a resistance. [...] Of all that the Germans will try to destroy—of the memory and habit of freedom.'[52] The historical irony of Mathieu's defiance is a knowing part of Jameson's text: in October 1940, Vichy abrogated the rights of Jews to French citizenship.

16

1943–1945: Struggling to the End

Combating Claustrophobia

Life in Wales in the spring of 1943 was increasingly claustrophobic, she told Ould, with nowhere to go in the evenings and noone to talk to.[1] Distraction came in the form of a new and difficult project, the *Journal of Mary Hervey Russell*.[2] This was an autobiographical text that Jameson had wanted to write since early 1940. She had written then to Macmillan that what she wanted to write was not 'straight autobiography', by which she simply seemed to mean an event-based narrative of her life, but studies of thoughts and feelings, the projections of subjectivity, for which the historical account of her life could provide the necessary supporting frames:

I cannot write straight autobiography—it always seems to me ridiculous for a writer, who is not a public person and does not lead a public life, to think that anyone could be interested in what he did, apart from what he thought or felt. I wrote all the straight autobiography I could in NO TIME LIKE PRESENT [sic] and it didn't take many pages. But one cannot write of what one has thought, felt, or seen, in vacuo—so that there has to be a personal thread running through such a book. If I am impressed by something Beneš has said to me, it is after all I who am impressed, although Beneš and what he said is the important thing. And if I spend hours or days in Rouen or Bordeaux trying to imagine where my Mother, who is dead, went when she was in those cities, it is I who am walking in that hot sun, though it is my Mother who is the real figure.

So it seems to me that there would be enough of what is hideously called 'personal interest' to carry the book.[3]

Three years later, on a more personal note, she wrote to Lovat Dickson that she needed to write this book to exorcise all her recent memories—of Paris and France, of deaths and of refugees—and the ideas about the new English poets that were thronging in her mind, before she could write another novel.

249

She still had no intention of writing what she thought of as conventional auto-biography. This was still going to be an aesthetic exercise in distilling feeling into symbolic event:

What I can try to do is to write a quite different sort of book, in which all these experiences and thoughts and feelings are concentrated down to their essences, so that you get not only the event or the feeling but its meaning—as you do in Rilke's 'Notebooks of Malte Laurids Brigge' (if I am remembering that book, read years ago, rightly). [...] I cannot get rid of the conviction that this is the next stage of learning to write and I must go through it, and if I bye-pass [sic] it I'll never be able to write the novels I want to.[4]

The book she was about to begin would give a major place to France, as her adopted landscape of home, and the nurturing space of a European cultural heritage that could take the European family and its ghosts towards a new future. It was an exercise in learning to write objectively about the emotions that had shaken her generation, while preserving all their intensity. From the recently discovered Paleolithic paintings in the caves of the Vézère, to the great Symbolist poets, France, the *Journal* noted, had led in the exploration of symbolic form, the means by which writing can crystallise and communicate the intensity of human experience.[5] In England, there might have been Auden, but his defection had left a poetic generation leaderless. Inside the framework of the aesthetic exercise, Jameson could begin to write up the cumulative tragedy of her family deaths—her mother, father, and youngest sister, and the brother who died twenty-five years before—and dissolve her grief in the harmonious light of the Loire at Saumur.

She was reading voraciously in French. To Irene, in early May, she sent a copy of Drieu La Rochelle's *Gilles*, which she recommended highly (making no mention of his reputation as a collaborator), and Saint-Jean Perse's new poem, *Anabasis*, with the comment: 'I loved that thing, without understanding it. But I get the same thrill from a lot of Claudel—especially the marvellous *Soulier de Satin*.' In the depths of Wales, she was still tuned to the latest cultural events. Claudel's spectacular epic, dramatising the conflicts of passion, loyalty, and duty that had fuelled the spread of European 'values' across the globe in the Spanish Golden Age, had just had its famous first production by Jean-Louis Barrault, before an audience in Occupied Paris that had picked up with delight on its promises of liberation 'for all captive souls'. She had taken out of the London Library all the volumes of Péguy. The Catholic soldier-poet of the First World War, and fiery advocate of social justice, holds pride of place in the closing pages of the *Journal of Mary Hervey Russell*: 'Lots of it is dullness itself, but he fascinates me.'[6]

Later in May, a great scandal was making its way into the columns of the newspapers. Hitler had made an offer to release substantial numbers of Jewish children from internment camps if places could be found for them in countries outside Germany and her satellites. Britain for no apparent reason was dragging her heels. Jameson was vastly agitated. She sent Ould a postcard on 20 May: she had no wireless, no newspapers had come, and she needed to know whether the promised statement in Parliament on the refugees had been made.[7] She wrote again on 22 May that she had read the report in *The Times*, and couldn't make out whether the government was doing its best or dragging its heels, and whether or not PEN must prepare to protest.[8]

Depression was setting in, despite the upward turn the war was taking. Her writing was bringing personal success, but none of that was unalloyed. Her play *William the Defeated* went out on the radio on 5 July, and she wrote fretfully to Ould that she had missed it:

I wish I had heard my William, because I want to complain about the choice of Ernest Milton, but feel I can't, not having heard him. I once saw him act—King John—he tore everything in sight to fragments and his eyes flashed green and red lights like a traffic signal.[9]

Securing a commission for the play had been something of a personal triumph. After *The Fort* was broadcast, in Barbara Burnham's adaptation, she had written to Val Gielgud expressing her wish to try writing directly for radio, and confessing her lack of experience:

I do not even know how much can be done in an hour. My ignorance is one reason why I should like to learn to tackle such a job. I'm more interested in experimenting in forms than in anything else.[10]

Gielgud advised her to consult the introduction to *How to Write Broadcast Plays* published by Hirst and Blackett, though she should not, he said, pay any attention to the three plays offered as samples, except as models of how not to do it.[11] She came up with two ideas, one for a reworking of the figure of William the Conqueror, another for a suspense-laden plot based on a group of people inside the border of Occupied France, or in Paris, running an underground newspaper. She was most enthused by her ideas for William, and the scope for exploring issues relating to invasion and collaboration:

William himself is a much subtler character than we learned when we were learning 1066 (the only date in history I remember). And then there are the pro-French fifth column who were the Bonnets of their time, and the English nobles who collaborated after he won, so as to keep their estates. And as protagonist to William, I invented a cultured Englishman (they existed) who preferred to lose his lands rather than submit to William, and whom William liked, almost loved, in spite or because of their arguments. He got involved in a crazy conspiracy, he couldn't not get involved in it, because the English conspirators were his friends and his former peasants. So he had to be killed by William in the end. But what is not killed is the Great English Idea—of Justice, which he has always told William will be stronger than the conquerors in the end, and in the end, William knows it.[12]

Barbara Burnham too liked the historical drama: 'We have had so much about France lately, both in plays and features, that we would really prefer the other.'[13] Settled by then in the grim flat in Harlech, where Guy was teaching at his Officers' College, Jameson promised the script would be ready by January, 'provided we have not perished of cold. I seem to remember a broadcast play—it must have been in the primitive days—in which the wife of a whaling boat went mad and played the harmonium muttering about "the cold, the misery, the brutality". Have you a harmonium handy? There ought to be one in this Welsh home but there isn't.'[14]

Despite the death of her father, the script was ready only a few days late, on 5 January 1943.[15] A fee of 75 guineas was arranged, and Gielgud professed himself very pleased with the content, though the construction needed improving for broadcasting, not least because Jameson had written it in scenes, like a French play. He asked Barbara Burnham to help knock it into shape.[16]

Jameson asked for sample scripts to follow, and was sent one adaptation by E. M. Forster (*Celestial Omnibus*), one by James Hilton (*Lost Horizon*), two plays by Patrick Hamilton written specially for broadcasting, and Tyrone Guthrie's *The Flowers are Not For You to Pick*.[17] Her sister's death was another shock, but as she explained to Barbara Burnham, grief was, for her, always relieved by hard work, and she wanted to learn: 'And what I am most anxious to be made to understand is <u>why</u> such and such changes are necessary. So that I can begin to get an idea of audible drama.' She added tactlessly: 'Perhaps it is less necessary than it was a few years ago though? I suppose television will shift us back to visual drama again?'[18]

Initially the play was scheduled for forty minutes, but even with Burnham's help it was impossible to get it below fifty. Jameson was struggling to manage without the help of narrative description, and complained of the awkwardness of the dialogue she had to produce to convey what characters were doing.[19] But when the play was transmitted on the Home Service on Monday 5 July 1943 at 9.25 p.m. Burnham and Gielgud were both pleased.[20]

There was nothing in *William* to set the airwaves on fire in the way Dorothy Sayers' *Life of Jesus* or Louis MacNeice's plays had recently done. Set in 1066–7, from autumn through to spring, just after William's invasion of England, it was a timely exploration of Englishness in the context of invasion, and of concepts of freedom and servitude, resistance and collaboration. The script printed by PEN in 1950 is cut across with idiosyncratic representations of the class relationships of the time (the friendship between William and a Saxon earl, and the easy relationships of the Saxon lord and his serfs), reminiscent of the relations of officers and ranks in Guy's versions of military life.[21] How much of all this survived in the broadcast version is unknown. Burnham promised Jameson she could hear a recording to reassure her of the acting quality, but neither recording nor script remains in the BBC archives. The book version has the tone of the day, and the voice of the rabble is straight out of RADA, but the characters are simple and likeable, if stereotypes, and the dialogue is lively, humorous, and easy. The storyline has the ferocity that was Jameson's trademark. William, unable to win the collaboration of his friend Lucius, has him hanged before his own home, with his eyes put out so he can't look his last on it. This was not an easy scene to write for radio, and Jameson struggled to put together for Sweyn, the loyal serf, a speech to make it 'visible' for listeners. Sweyn is the common Englishman, closely related to the lovable Cockney corporal, who whistles and sings an unlikely pastiche of soldiers' songs from the First World War ('Send out the silly English bowmen, | They'll face the danger with a smile. | Send out me muvver, me sister and me bruvver, | But for Gawd's sake don't send me').[22] Lucius is the English commander, whose first thought is for honour, and the lives of his men. Through the clichés, from which Jameson never shrank, pierces an interesting idea of how Englishness was first formulated as resistance to attack. This is coupled with praise of England's 'mongrel' antecedence, and her capacity to absorb and incorporate successive waves of invaders. Lucius tells William:

You pride yourself on your culture. Our English culture is Roman and ancient Egyptian and pre-Roman and Celtic. And Saxon and Danish. The last were a tough lot. There were people here before the Celts [...]. But we've done more than kill each other across these centuries. Believe me, stubborn as we are, we've found ways of living together. It's the supreme human art![23]

From Harlech, the Chapmans moved back at the end of July to the Oakeley Arms, at Tan-y-bwlch, Blaenau Festiniog. Jameson was in heaven again, in the small hotel was situated where the estuary narrowed to a stream, surrounded by hills and valleys, close to a little slate village.[24] She promptly started writing her *Journal of Mary Hervey Russell*.

Things were moving at last, especially the Chapmans: a rumour first heard in the summer became fact, and at the end of October Guy was posted to Northern Command, in York.[25] London suddenly became so much more accessible.

On the PEN front, the Russians had to be welcomed back to the fold, and she prepared herself to make one of the speeches she so detested, especially nervous after her long absence from duty.[26] Her article on 'Literature Between the Wars: The Tyranny of Things' had appeared that month in the *TLS*, and to Ould, she defended her claim that the generation of Priestley were smaller men than Wells and his contemporaries, and regretted the time spent on political activity that prevented PEN from discussing literary issues. The same letter worried over recent attacks on Thomas Mann, and agonised over the heavy responsibilities facing PEN's officers in recreating networks of intellectual friendship at the end of the war:

[I]t seems to me that at the end of the war we shall be left with tasks far exceeding our energy, wisdom, goodwill. Even the PEN offers a terribly difficult task. It is practically, to rebuild from the ground in Europe. (I have drafted several notes for a letter to go out when the time comes that there are any safe—I mean living—addresses to send it to. [...] And it will be necessary to speak at length and plainly at Stockholm or wherever. And perhaps we shall not feel so tired then.)[27]

Anglo-French solidarity was beginning to wear thin in some quarters. She was shocked by the review of *Cloudless May* in the *TLS*:

I don't a bit mind, cursing France myself, but I'm shocked when the Lit. Suppl. implies, as this review does, that even the greatness of French civilisation is a myth. Connolly's boot-licking shocks me, this review's sneer shocks me (I shouldn't wonder if it was Murray himself)—I am very unreasonable. And yet when one reads about de Gaulle saying to Giraud, 'You have stolen my Corsica!' one wonders whether it is possible to despair too much about the French. But perhaps all these comic-opera tragedians will be swept away by le peuple—if there is a peuple.[28]

The move to York in October was a not unwelcome distraction, despite the loss, once again, of books and papers to store. It had one very positive outcome, in the discovery in those papers of an unused folder of notes for *The Mirror in Darkness*, which reawakened her interest in the figure of David Renn.[29]

A Yorkshire Purgatory

Guy had immense trouble finding lodgings for his wife in 'an overcrowded city. At length, out of all patience, she came, and lived for some time in slatternly lodgings.'[30] But she didn't lose patience until Christmas, and for two months the two were separated.

In October 1943, she came up to Leeds from Wales to be presented for an honorary doctorate of letters by their old friend Bonamy Dobrée, who in 1939 had presented T. S. Eliot for the same honour. The *TLS* noted the occasion. R. D. Charques praised first and foremost her writing skills, but also her commitment to European cultural politics:

Through the mounting disharmony of European politics her peace-lover's instinct found expression in the internationalist cause, above all in the service of intellectual cooperation between the nations of Europe and in practical testimony to the cultural unity of European society. Her internationalism found fullest scope when she was elected President of PEN, and it was again in practical enough fashion, amidst the persecution of thought in a dozen lands, that she sought to translate her belief in the common cultural inheritance of a Europe on the brink of catastrophe.[31]

In the *Journal of Mary Hervey Russell*, with the help of a quotation from Péguy, she would acknowledge the futility of honours with no family to share the joyful news. But to Ould she wrote more cheerfully, a characteristic mixture of self-deprecating pleasure in her success, protestations of overwork, and delight in the scope and variety of her current projects, including the *Journal* itself.[32]

This book, finished at the end of 1943 but only published in May 1945, was to be one she always numbered among her favourites. It was not well liked by her publishers, and didn't sell well, but it was well reviewed on first appearance.[33] The anonymous reviewer in *Time and Tide*, who came nearest to understanding fully what Jameson's aims had been, reviewed the text alongside Edmund Wilson's *Note-Books of Night*, under the title 'Minds at Work', and emphasised that this was neither a *journal intime* nor a personality display; the discontinuities of form generated a sense of the stress of the times but also a sense of remoteness, which put the period into perspective.[34] And R. D. Charques's

255

review in the *TLS* was one of the last positive accounts of her work she would receive from that journal for some years.[35]

If work was going well, family matters continued difficult. After recording in *Journey from the North* the move to York, she took a page (cut from the published version) to bewail the blunders she felt she had made over the two subsequent years, until the end of the war, in her personal relationships. Even in the cut section, she gave no detailed account of what these were.[36] In her correspondence, the shapes of conflict slowly emerge, first with her brother-in-law Robert, and then with Bill and Barbara. For the moment, though, there was an uneasy peace. In November she wrote an apologetic reply to a letter from Betty Leake reporting the birth of the Leakes' son, David. In it, she repeated her intention to look after the children after the war, and included a significant comment on her relationship with her own son:

> I want so much to look after Nick and Judy that I'm hoping I'll do better than I did with my Bill—I spent everything on him but time. So he had everything on earth, but not the unreserved attention of his mother. He has turned out all right, but maybe that is no thanks to me. Do always said that I spoiled him.[37]

She reported general optimism in England that the war might be over after one more winter, and her high hopes for the current negotiations in Moscow. Guy was keen to come over with her if possible to fetch back Dorothy's children from Dallas.

Family must still take a back seat to the work for PEN: money-raising, as always, and meetings and speeches to strengthen alliances. On 14 December, Pierre Maisonneuve, one of de Gaulle's Free French colleagues, arranged for her to address the French Chamber of Commerce in London. In *Journey from the North*, she tells how a Frenchman in the audience came up smiling afterwards to tell her that an old gentleman with white hair had been standing approvingly behind her chair as she spoke; she recognized her grandfather, George Gallilee.[38]

From Gwynedd, she wrote to Betty Leake that she was about to go to York to spend Christmas with Guy, and then find somewhere for them to live—though she would have preferred to stay in Gwynedd for the duration of the war—and the following day she sent a Christmas letter to Nick and Judy telling them about the monkey she had had made as a present for their little cousin Christopher.[39] Immediately after Christmas, she wrote to Betty again to tell her that York was impossible, and she was looking for a small furnished flat near London. She spun fantasies of what they might do after the war for the children, if only Guy and Robert knew where they'd be. They might all go to Canada, less poisoned than England and Europe, and with more sunshine ('Five years living only in England makes me realise how much one depended on getting into the sun in France at least once a year'). Nick could go to engineering school (but not Oxford), and she'd teach Judy to dance and ride 'so that she doesn't go one-sidedly intellectual'.[40] She was still flat-hunting the following month when she wrote again to Betty to tell her that Robert wanted the children to stay in the States until the war was over, and she had made a note in her diary to make sure she wrote to them every four weeks.[41]

In January, she was making plans to go to Moscow to help the link with the Russian Centre, and discussing plans for a new PEN Headquarters in London.[42] Then the doctor intervened to say her heart was bad again, and her blood pressure dangerously low; he suspected another operation might be needed.[43] She wrote to Irene Rathbone in March from Crawford Cottage, Berkhamsted, Herts (where she was staying with Wyn Griffith), to say that she had agreed to go in for treatment after 30 March. But she was so busy:

SUCH a refugee high tide—I've finished L. Linke's book, but I have to write a preface to Kuncewiczowa's soon, and to read and correct her second MS, which has been quite abominably translated.[44]

The previous day, she had written reassuringly to Betty Leake:

I'm just going into hospital for four weeks. My heart has gone bad, and has to have treatment to prevent it getting worse. They say it can be made as good as new in time, and you can be sure I want it to be made new and intend that it shall be. It is just overwork and over-strain, nothing serious unless it is let rip. I'm not letting it rip any further.[45]

She was still spinning plans for a visit to Dallas after the war to see the children, but there was no more house-hunting at the moment, as Guy might be moving to London. When she wrote from Crawford Cottage, Wyn Griffith's home, on 3 May to Nick and Judy, she was still talking about them coming over to England to live.[46] But by April 1944 it was clear that she was very ill.[47] She dated her resignation letter from the PEN Presidency on 8 April as from Crawford Cottage; her autobiography, oddly, doesn't mention it.[48]

In May, she was still with Guy in the 'slatternly lodgings' in York, at 55 Monkgate, writing to Irene that it was a horrible set of rooms, and she was weak and ill.[49] In June, with pernicious anaemia and nervous exhaustion, and under instructions to rest for three months and not to write, she moved down to Hove to be nursed at 24 Hove Street by Leonora Eyles, wife of the editor of the *TLS*, D. L. Murray, and an admiring reviewer of her work.[50] She complained to Betty Leake of the doctors' slowness in diagnosing her pernicious anaemia:

But now they have found it out, I am getting better. I'm not allowed to work, or even write letters, and I can't walk far. Mental age, about three, and backward at that. But they have sworn that if I obey them and do rest completely, I shall be much more normal in three months' time and in six absolutely all right. You can be sure that, with the thought of the children coming back next year, I am obeying all right.[51]

The same letter contained very exciting news: the invasion of Europe had begun, Cherbourg had been taken, the race for Berlin was on, and Robert might be sent out to the States. The following month, she described to Betty the planes going over Hove:

The planes go out and come back like a gigantic quadrille across a blue blue Channel—on y danse dans le rond over there today. Sometimes this house shakes from something very heavy going up or coming down over there.

We haven't had any visitations from the flying bombs here yet. They pass over our heads, usually at night. I hate the sound of them, it is a most odd sound, like a lunatic motor-cycle engine going very fast. I guess I'd hate it much worse if I were where they have a habit of coming down.[52]

She was going to forget about finding a flat for the next six months, and settle instead into a country hotel. Guy had been given four months' special leave to write a book, and a professor from Chicago University who had read *Culture and Survival* wanted to meet him. Her own writing was taking a new turn, and she had scrapped all the novel plans she had on the stocks:

I realised suddenly that there was a deep gulf now between pre-war and post-war, and only those writers willing to try to jump across would be any good. But it's awfully difficult to get the immediate present, not to speak of the immediate future, into focus. Sometimes I think the only way to do it would be to write about the time when the Roman Empire was breaking up, and barbarians coming down on Roman villas in South France! [...] But who wants to read about Roman Gaul?[53]

In August, she moved to Thierry's Imperial Hotel in Tenby for a week, and then to the Oakeley Arms. Guy had joined her, and Leonora Eyles, she told Irene, hated him at first sight: 'Of course he is exhausting, he has a genius for freezing one up or stabbing one to the heart at the most unexpected moments. But he doesn't bore me, and most men do. And I am pretty tough.'[54]

Counting the Cost of Freedom

The Allies entered Paris on 25 August, and David Murray asked her to write the editorial celebrating the liberation of the city.[55] He gave her two hours to do it, she told Irene, and then altered a phrase about her beloved Giraudoux.[56] Cultural life in France came out from under cover. In September, Hermon Ould wrote that the PEN Centre in Paris had begun to hold meetings again. He had a cutting about it from *Les Lettres françaises*. He thought the article too adulatory of the achievements of French writers under the Occupation; it was, he said, easy enough to write when you weren't also fighting a war.[57] Jameson wrote back from the Oakeley Arms, demanding he bring her new books from Paris (Giraudoux, Camus, Sartre, Malraux) and collected editions of old favourites such as Péguy, Stendhal, Balzac, and Laforgue.[58]

Not all the news from France was good. In the same letter, she enclosed a cutting from *Vendredi* for November 1944, giving the blacklist that had been drawn up of French writers accused of collaboration, and an article in an October *Time and Tide*, sent to her by Irene, G. Turquet-Milnes's 'Midnight Books'.[59] Turquet-Milnes's historic revelations of what had been happening in French publishing during the Occupation brought the first intimation of the deaths of some admired PEN friends: Decour, Crémieux, Max Jacob, Saint-Pol-Roux. She was deeply shocked.

In her Christmas letter to Betty Leake, Jameson spoke of her plans to leave North Wales in January, go to London and start looking for a big house in Berkshire, near enough Reading for Robert to travel to his job in the factory. She and Robert had tried to book passages to America for May, but it hadn't been possible; in any case, she added, the V2s were too dangerous to bring the children back yet.[60]

The Oakeley Arms was losing its charm, becoming, it seemed, a collection point for displaced writers. She reported to Irene that the Robert Neumann had moved in first, and then Arthur Koestler had turned up in November, looking for a cottage in Wales. He was back again in December 'with a charming child called Paget, he says he adores her, but I think he is rather a corruptor of youth. [...] He goes to Palestine on the 20th, that's tomorrow. Perhaps he'll settle there!'[61] Two years later, she would be reporting to Irene a row between Neumann and Koestler, who had snapped up a house Neumann had his eye on, and installed himself there 'with his Mamaine (such a pretty creature, and somehow quite immoral in a wellbred way, which is all wrong and half shocks me).'[62] In February 1945, her family started to arrive. She told Irene:

My brother-in-law is going to Canada for 3 months (for the RAF), and coming here next week, Bill is coming for a week on the 19th, Barbara is here until the 27th, when I have arranged for her to go to the Pengwern Arms, since I hope by then to be in Oxford. I might as well take over the Oakeley for my relations—meantime I can't get on with my new book, which is needed, to pay for all these excursions. It is very bad, and arid, but I believe that it is better to go on struggling to write, even if it means destroying it later.

A previous letter to Irene had expressed concern for the effects of the Allied invasion in France, and the impact of the bombing round Chartres. Now she added:

When I think of the French, I cry tears that corrode my inside. I don't think that the Germans will be deliberately built up again by us, but I do think that they still have a power of recovery that the French, so tortured and starved, won't have. Pray God I am wrong.[63]

As the end of the war approached, scores were being settled, and tales began to spread about 'the ugly face of Liberation'.[64] Some of the score-settling came very close to home. Ould reported that Denis Saurat had been sacked from the Institut Français, for having made disrespectful references to de Gaulle's totalitarianism. The French Government was anti-British, Ould added, and Saurat was *persona non grata* because of his links to the Foreign Office through the British Council.[65] Jameson was concerned to know whether Saurat still had his job in London University to fall back on. It was, she felt, all a great shame; he was no more careerist than the next Frenchman, he didn't have his fingers in the pot, and he liked the English. She hoped de Gaulle would soon be done with: 'It seems a pity to spend years and destroy Europe to pull down one dictator, and set up another in Paris.'[66] Ould wrote shortly afterwards that he was working with Saurat to start a discussion of how French and English intellectuals could best cooperate. Eluard was coming over. Indeed, 'there are all sorts of Frenchmen coming over now, including Vercors. We shall soon know more about French poets of the Resistance than about English airmen in the Battle of Britain.'[67] The end of hostilities seemed to mean that the old Anglo-French cultural war was being resumed.

She was eager to go to Paris. Her American agent had just toured Europe with some of her writers, and had said that France was the country it was most important to understand, and to explain to the rest of the world. She encouraged Ould to continue his work rebuilding bridges to France and Europe:

The PEN is the most important thing you could do, as important as any Relief. Call it Intellectual Relief Work. This isn't a joke. Everything depends on what we think of each other. The Centres will be terribly difficult to handle. Someone has got to tell them things, and get them started off on the right roads. [...] We'll need a book about it—about what the clercs have been doing all this time.[68]

PEN seemed increasingly set to play an important role after the war, especially if Labour was elected. But family commitments were beginning to set obstacles in the way of Jameson's participation. In May, she had stretched her finances to pay for Winifred to go into a nursing home in Sussex after an operation.[69] House-buying had proved another expense, though not in the way she had anticipated. She was stunned in January, as she later told Betty Leake, when Robert said he didn't want any of the houses she'd been looking at, and wanted instead to go to America. He had gone to Montreal, where he had met Betty, Judy, and Nick, and gone with them to Dallas. She wondered if she should go to Dallas and help Robert get started there; she hoped he would remarry, and didn't want to do anything that might prevent that. Instead of buying the projected big house for Robert and herself, she had bought a smaller one for Bill, and his wife and baby. Bill had now transferred to the Air Ministry, since he was starting to be afraid when flying.[70]

In July, she reluctantly refused her invitation to the All India PEN Conference. Her brother-in-law might be bringing the children home, and Guy, who had just refused a job in the University of Chicago, had been short-listed for a job at Leeds University. She told Ould he had little chance of it, but if he got it she knew she would have to move to play her wifely supporting role—and lose, yet again, the chances that might take her somewhere.[71]

The worst happened. Guy was appointed to the Chair of Modern History, and the headship of the department. All her own plans were in ruins, and there were now terrible divisions of loyalty. She wrote to Betty Leake to say she would leave Guy to look after Robert in Dallas if needs be, but felt since Do's death and his RAF training he was probably much more self-reliant than he used to be.[72] Betty ignored the hints; she wanted her to come over, even if Robert were to remarry soon, and create a tie the children knew they could rely on. Jameson promised to come, but foresaw problems in getting, and paying for, a passage before summer of 1946:

I don't make any money in the States. I get marvellous reviews for my books and then they sell about what would keep two growing children in shoes for a year. I can't expect to sell anything else to the *Saturday Evening Post*—that was a fluke. And if they won't let me have any of my English money sent out, it's not going to be anything but extremely difficult to set up house, buy furniture, get help, and the rest of it. Maybe my American publisher would lend me some money, though he has never shown any signs of being weak in the head.[73]

Three days later, she wrote to Betty that Robert had written in extreme distress at the disruption Guy's job had brought to their plans. She had assured him she would come when there was a passage available. In the meantime, however, she had to fly to Poland in the following week on a snap invitation, for a ten-day visit.[74]

In her autobiography, she describes the excursion in detail, arranged by the Polish Embassy in London ('not then the embassy of a wholly communist government'), to a Conference on Polish Culture.[75] There were four English passengers on the plane going over, including Val Gielgud, and a group of Poles, considering the possibility of returning for good, including the poet Antoni Slominski. She carried messages from her friends in exile, she looked down from the plane and out of her hotel window at the ruins of Warsaw ('ossuaries of fractured stone and brick'),[76] she was entertained to a lavish dinner of caviar and smoked salmon supplied by the Russians who ate in the same hotel, and she admired the indomitable energy of a people and a culture who had defied the systematic attempts of the Germans to destroy them, after the Ghetto Rising of 1943, and were determined to rise again from the ruins. She learned that there was no love left here for her Polish friends in London, the self-exiled. A young film group showed the delegation an 'almost unendurable' film of Auschwitz and Majdanek, made out of photographs.[77] But Antoni Slominski confirmed her feeling that though much in Warsaw was very wrong, not least its persistent anti-Semitism, many good new things were also happening. And in Cracow, she met the poet Czeslaw Milosz, whose admiration for Eliot bridged the ruined cultural past of Europe and the future which his generation would build; but whose vengeful hostility to the Germans, understandable as it was, confirmed for her the great obstacles that lay in the way of the wish of the Allies to negotiate a lasting peace in Europe. She returned to London with a different kind of insight into the nature and function of cultural memory. The only habit children need to be taught, she decided, was 'the habit of loss'. With that gift, they might survive the collapse of civilisation and start again 'without resentment or self-pity'.[78]

Figure 20 Warsaw's old market square (1945). A note on the back dated 30/XII/45 (not in Jameson's hand) ends: 'The quarter of the old town of Warsaw has been completely destroyed during the Warsaw insurrection as the Poles there had on their lips the words: fight till death.'

Figure 21 One of the collection of photographs from the camp at Terezin, dated May 1945, which Jameson kept in her papers (see n. 77)

263

After her visit to Prague in November 1945, a meeting with her old friend Jiřina Tůmová, shattered by her husband's death under torture, and a visit to the prison where Jiřina had been held, she was less sanguine.[79] To Irene, she wrote: 'Germany will be built up over my dead body. I hate the brutes! Have you read a book called Assize at Arms by a Brig-general [sic] Morgan? Do.'[80] And she sent Irene a copy of a letter she had just written to the *Manchester Guardian* (which doesn't seem to have been published), angered by the gap in understanding between her English compatriots who had experienced the Blitz, but not Occupation, and her Czechoslovakian friends who were now holding Germans in the same internment camps where they, and their families and friends, had suffered.[81]

Sir,

I expect anything of the MG except to be shocked by an illiberal and obtuse comment. Your letter of December 4th on the expulsion of the Sudeten Germans from Cchekoslovakia provides it. 'The Czechs,' you say, 'shd [sic] have thought of that (the possibility that the expelled men will be very useful as skilled workers in Bavaria) before they let racialism interfere with business.' The Czechs have an acquaintance with the Germans of a closeness and a nature which makes it difficult for them to remember that 'Business as usual' is a sacred doctrine. They have no reason to trust the loyalty in the future of people whose leaders were on Hitler's payroll in 1933, and no reason—if they were to trust it and were again betrayed—to suppose that this country would help them more effectively than in 1938 at Munich. It may be difficult for a country which has not been occupied by Germany to understand the hatred which Germans have earned in Czechoslovakia, as in Poland—well and truly earned. Wuth [sic] the exercise of a little imagination it should not be impossible. And not more impossible to realise that if the Czechs, who are rational people, prefer losing skilled workers to keeping Germans among them, there are reasons which have as little to do with racialism as with business.

A continuing feeling of guilt for England's abandonment of Czechoslovakia to Hitler was part of her response, as well as her sense that the Czechs, unlike the Poles, had been hurt at a psychological level that left them more violent, less confident in their own resources, and more vulnerable to the influence of Russia. There was not very much she could do, except write about them, and help them maintain contact with their friends in the West. It must have seemed to her very inadequate, but it was appreciated.

PART IV

Going Home

17

1945–1949: Clearing Up

A Yorkshire Haven

Guy took up his Chair, and for six years they lived in 'temporary' accommodation in Ghyll Court Hotel in Ilkley. She wrote all day, walked the moor, and managed her PEN duties with ease. She agreed with Ould that they should invite the French over—Membré, the Secretary of the Paris Centre, and Schlumberger, who had succeeded Paul Valéry as President—and prepare to revisit old documents and mend fences.[1] She continued to resist moves to punish writers who had collaborated with the Germans: 'Some time ago I signed a petition for Ezra Pound, which had Eliot's support, so I am sure he would support anything we cared to do for [Knut] Hamsun.'[2] Towards sympathisers with Russia, she was less tolerant: 'You must, yes, must take Calder-Marshall's communism seriously. It is serious, in so much as he is never a free mind. And this business of the party line is the most sinister bar that lies over the future. You know I'm not an anti-Soviet hound, so take me seriously about this, do.'[3] She was fearful about the ambitions of the Russians in Europe, and the clumsy revanchism of post-war negotiations, as she wrote to Irene:

I'm afraid I'm pro-German if thinking it crazy to take away the Ruhr is pro-German. I'd internationalise it, and have it working like hell to supply Europe. But as for taking it away, and leaving inside it about 600,000 Germans (as the French propose) longing for their fatherland, it's asking for trouble. It's also making Russia a present of Germany—my private nightmare. I loathe Germans, I'll never touch one that came out of Germany after 1933, but I do see that to keep Germany as a sort of poor Balkan country isn't possible. If we can't teach them manners, there is no hope. And we don't seem even to be trying.[4]

Basil Liddell Hart's latest book had been reviewed in the *Observer*, and she agreed with him wholeheartedly, she added, about the folly of requiring unconditional surrender, and the saturation bombing: 'What happened to Dresden is horrible.'

In May 1946, she and Irene attended the first PEN Congress since the war, in Stockholm, where she did her best, alongside Ould, to resist the attempts from occupied countries to impose a blacklist of writers. She commented after they got back:

The real villains, as usual, are safe in other countries, Argentina or Switzerland, and the only people who will suffer are little people who just weren't very brave. [...] It wasn't to be expected that the French and the others would take up Mauriac's attitude (see his *Le Baillon Denoué*), but I wish they had been less bitter and revengeful, and satisfied themselves with just writing a letter to any Centre where a real villain might present himself—in Zurich or Buenos Aires.[5]

There were some personal successes to record. *The Other Side*, completed in play form in November 1944, and then as a novel in February 1945, had been well reviewed. It was a timely exploration of the personal suffering and rivalries, obscured by nationalist ideology, that develop in a situation of defeat and Occupation. Set in the French zone of the Rhineland, in the first few months of French military occupation, it studied the interactions of a German aristocratic family and the young French girl who had married into it in 1942. Stock bought it for translation into French, along with *The Journal of Mary Hervey Russell* (Jameson was disappointed that no one would buy Felix Rose's translation of *Cloudless May*, though anyone but the author might have recognised that this was not the moment for the French public to read of their collapse before the German advance).[6] The play version was staged in Scarborough on 8 August, and part was broadcast on BBC radio on 20 August.[7] By the end of the year, the novel was sold to America, though not, Jameson insisted angrily, on the strength of the play version, and she begrudged the royalties she had to pay the theatre manager and the principal actor.[8] Translations of *Europe to Let* and *The Journal of Mary Hervey Russell* were coming through in Czechoslovakia.[9]

Catastrophes and Quarrels

She had taken a flat in Scarborough at 2 Granville Road from 3 July to 2 October.[10] It was uncomfortable, and there was no domestic help to be had. She moved out long before the tenancy finished, but she had to be back in

Scarborough in September to look after Winifred, who had her own flat there, and was confined to bed with a poisoned leg.[11] The following week, back in the Oakeley Arms, she wrote to Irene out of an exhaustion that spilled over into intense pessimism about the future of Europe's post-war settlements:

Europe is finished, the French are to blame for their hostility to us (NOT the French, but their politicians), we are to blame for 'unconditional surrender' and for our many other sins, the Americans are what they always were, and Stalin is probably preparing a preventive war. It's gone too far. What is happening now is a despairing effort to build up Europe, not just Germany—and it will fail, short of a miracle.[12]

Even the Oakeley Arms was providing no consolation. It was rainy, she said, there was no food, and Arthur Koestler was always horribly drunk and had quarrelled with almost everyone.

But far harder to deal with was the crisis that broke between Bill and Barbara in July.[13] Barbara had already forgiven her husband once, for an affair with an air hostess. This new affair was infinitely more serious. The crisis built to nightmare intensity through the autumn, with Jameson seeming to bear the brunt of Barbara's anger in place of Bill. By the end of November, which was the worst month, divorce was on the cards.[14]

In PEN, there were developments of varying interest. She was now on the Provisional Executive Committee of Les Amis du Génie Français.[15] The organisation, as she had prophesied, was doing little, and would shortly collapse. Links with UNESCO, reported by Ould on his return from Paris in December 1946, were a more exciting prospect, and Lilo Linke, by now working with UNESCO, was helping to further PEN initiatives. Jameson was back in a prominent position as delegate to the International Committee of PEN, and raring to join the intrigues ('I'll come earlier in the week by a day at least, so that you can tell me where to avoid stepping on snakes in the grass (speaking French probably, Nous sommes trahis!').[16] The Committee's first job, in January 1947, was to find a new International President, preferably neither French nor British. The intrigues came up to expectations; at the end of the month, Jameson responded to Ould with ironic amusement at the revelation of Membré's apparent Communist connections.[17]

At the International PEN Congress in Zurich in the first week of June 1947, the second Congress after the war, there was conflict over a request by German writers, including Thomas Mann, to restart the German Centre dissolved in 1934 when its members refused to protest against the Burning of the Books.[18]

269

Jameson was personally unhappy to be supporting the Germans rather than the French, but her political instincts were on the side of re-admission. The German and Austrian Centres were both reinstated. Her report of the conference in the *Manchester Guardian* noted the bitterness the debate had provoked, and cited Vercors's intervention to the effect that 'only the strongest guarantees could meet the mistrust of men who feared to find themselves sitting beside the torturer of a friend'.[19] At the end of the month, she wrote to Ould declining his suggestion she should come back in a Presidential role, eager to avoid the appearance of International PEN being run by a triumvirate of the two of them and Saurat.[20]

She was now sharing in the demoralisation of a nation caught in economic crisis, strikes, and food supply problems.[21] She praised a recent article by Irene on the situation in France, but thought she had understated England's suffering:

I feel more and more that this country suffered, in every way, even in sheer physical suffering, more than France, more than anyone except Poles and Russians. It doesn't show, the women and children burned alive in their East End streets have no one to lament them as the women of Oradour (or Lidice) are lamented, the endlessly weary women in our towns and cities now are still paying for the war, but the world outside sees nothing.[22]

She was even more depressed by the family problems to be dealt with. From Budock Vean Hotel, in Falmouth, she wrote to Irene in July that she was helping with the exorbitant costs of the divorce, and the cost of Bill's buying a boat to live in, and that she was 'cleaned out'.[23] Her novel *Before the Crossing* had been a failure, and next year's income was in jeopardy. In her autobiography, she made only very brief reference to this period.[24] It was a terrible summer, as her letters to Irene indicate, postmarked mostly from Ilkley. She was forbidden, she said, to see her grandson, and made complicated arrangements to catch glimpses of him in his taxi from her hotel window. She was asked to take him for the week of the divorce hearing, in October, and then, she claimed, the arrangement was rescinded. (Christopher Storm-Clark told the present author in conversation that he recalled going to Ilkley and attending a nursery school there briefly. But he also remembered spending three months while the divorce was before the courts with his other grandmother, Mrs Cawood.) She complained to Irene of neurotic letters from Barbara.[25] But Barbara's distress was understandable; even before the divorce, plans for Bill's second marriage were going ahead, and by the end of November, the wedding date had been fixed for 18 December.[26] The divorce came through on 12 December, with the respondent (Bill) found guilty of adultery, and on 18 December Jameson wrote to tell Barbara that Bill and Ruth were married.[27]

Jameson made a £200 per year settlement on Barbara, and with that security, and the prospect of Barbara getting a part-time job, relations calmed down for a time.[28] They would however regularly explode into acute resentment on both sides. In correspondence at least, both women made efforts to maintain friendly relations for the sake of the child, but Jameson's desire to organise Barbara's life, as well as provide support, was oppressive. Her grandson recalls snide and hostile comments about Barbara when he came to visit on the annual holidays that were part of the formal divorce settlement; but he also recalls the readiness with which she came to sit with her daughter-in-law in the Purey Cust Nursing Home in York for a week, during Barbara's last illness.[29]

Deeply partisan towards her son, she also displaced onto Barbara much of her guilt for her neglect of Bill as a child. Her last novel, *There Will Be a Short Interval*, written twenty-five years after the divorce, just after Barbara's death, refers to the attempts of the narrator's son, Simon, to come to terms with the suicide of a lover whom he had left, an older woman, who refused to accept that their affair was over. The portrait of the woman is edged with hostility: 'with all her thirty odd years in her face [...] the body of a grown woman, with the hint of inflexibility that overtakes a sedentary woman after first youth [...] uncommonly large eyes, dark and wide-set—easy to imagine them blazing, *Venus [sic] toute [sic] entière à sa proie attachée.*'[30] The father feels 'a cold anger—why need she have sunk her claws in a schoolboy?'[31] But Jameson had recognised by then the intemperance of her feelings. One turn in the plot charts the father's efforts to recover embarrassingly revelatory letters the woman had sent to Simon; Simon's grandmother, a famous novelist, intends to use them in her current book. As the grandmother-novelist refuses to hand the letters back to her son, 'The movement of her tongue across her lips started in him the atrocious idea that she was enjoying fingering the younger woman's entrails.'[32] This deep-rooted streak of violence and cruelty in herself was something of which Jameson, increasingly, after the war, became only too well aware. It both frightened and intrigued her.

As the divorce was played out in the courts in October, the quarrel between Jules Romains and the officers of the London Centre surfaced yet again. This time, Ould reported to Jameson from Berlin, on 20 October, Romains was claiming, among other things, that Benjamin Crémieux's death in a concentration camp was due to indiscretion on the part of Jameson and Ould. Fortunately, Ould had a copy of a joint statement issued by Romains, Crémieux,

Jameson, and himself, that gave the lie to Romains's accusations of English disloyalty, but he was resigned to the fact that at some point there would need to
be a confrontation.[33] Jameson was less sanguine:

I take a more serious view of Romains's attack than you do. Perhaps because being a
constant reader of French newspapers and periodicals, I know just what an appalling smell of skunk he has attached to us. To hint that we were collaborators in soul,
that you were responsible for Crémieux's death, that we held the Germans to be no
worse than the Allies—he could not possibly have said more frightful things about
us. If he had said that we murdered, robbed, lived by brothels we ran in Pimlico, his
French hearers (because we can be sure he doesn't confine this line of talk to Membré
and Duhamel, or indeed to French people) would have been comparatively unmoved.
Romains is doing two things of course, avenging himself for having lost the presidency,
and covering up his own flight to America AND his work there for a Vichy ambassador.
But most terribly at our expense.[34]

In December, Jameson reported to Ould an unexpected telephone call from
Valentine Dobrée, consisting of a fifteen-minute monologue. Valentine had
apparently been brooding for a year about *Before the Crossing*, and had decided
she no longer wanted to know the writer of such a book. Jameson professed herself bewildered, since Valentine had praised the book when she first read it, and
had been perfectly friendly when they met only a few days before.[35] Two pages
describing the incident in the original typescript of *Journey from the North*, and
the subsequent break with a friend she called 'Leah', were completely cut from the
published version.[36] To Ould, she later wrote that 'the Valentine stroke went in
very deep. [...] I made myself look through *Before the Crossing* again last week—
you know she made this book and its "hatred and evil" the starting-off point for
the appalling fantasy she had been evolving for so many months. And I could
not see that it was so evil as that.'[37] And to Irene, she spoke of a letter she simply
couldn't understand, and her suspicion that there was more to do with what
Valentine called 'all the chatter in London' about *Before the Crossing* than she was
admitting; although 'What chatter, and who chattered, is a complete mystery.'[38]

Before the Crossing and *The Black Laurel*

Before the Crossing and *The Black Laurel* are among Jameson's best books.[39]
They present a truthful and unsparing vision of the England of 1939, on the

brink of war, self-interested, shallow and self-serving, and the country that in 1945 emerged unchanged into the ruins. There is indeed deep hatred in both books. But its targets are well chosen, the author does not spare herself, and the indictment is tempered by compassion and hope for the future. None of these things could have been seen by the metropolitan chatterers, who appear in Jameson's pages among the primary offenders—not so much for what they did, as for what they allowed to be done, in England's name. Reviews were poor, including the short notices in the *TLS*.[40] But Jameson knew the writing was good, and so did Guy. He read the typescript of *The Black Laurel* on 21 May 1947, in Ilkley, while she was briefly away, went to bed after finishing it at 1.30 a.m., and wrote in her diary a page that she copied out and kept in her own copy of *Journey from the North*: '[I]t is the finest work you've ever done. It has quite outstanding intensity, and the real wisdom of the artist. [...] The ideas are stretching the skins of the people.'[41]

The single novel Jameson originally envisaged turned into two: *Before the Crossing* (finished in July 1945 and published in 1947), and *The Black Laurel* (finished in April 1947 and published in 1948).[42] Between these two volumes and the trilogy covering the 1920s, there is some continuity in the names and history of the characters, but nothing as marked as in Romain Rolland's great *roman fleuve*, *Jean-Christophe*, or Jules Romains's *Les Hommes de bonne volonté*, or even Balzac's *Comédie Humaine*, all of which Jameson had had in mind as models; and there are many new figures to explore, as Jameson looks hopefully to the next generation, the children paying for their parents' derelictions, for some promise of a better world. Between the dream of social justice that collapsed with the General Strike and the opportunism of Ramsay MacDonald, and the purging by fire that was the Second World War, great cracks had opened in the world and Jameson's understanding of it, and of herself. Hervey Russell, the mother-figure, well-intentioned and powerless, gave way to David Renn, the socialist activist turned soldier, self-sacrificing, incorruptible—and driven to action by the same sadistic force he condemns in the capitalist enemy. Like his creator, Renn is forced by the necessities of war to recognise in himself an active love of cruelty and the will to dominate. This was to be a theme that obsessed Jameson for the rest of her writing career. The war revealed the cruelty that had been bred in the bones of all her generation, and in her own case, she came to feel, by the abusive mother of her childhood. It seemed to confront all of them with the same imperative: choose to be torturer, or victim.

Before the Crossing was the book Jameson was writing while convalescing with the Murrays on the South coast in April 1944. David Renn, a novelist and a spy, is asked in the summer of 1939 to investigate the murder on a wharf in East London of his old friend Henry Smith, the solitary socialist in the Parliamentary Labour Party, who, it turns out, had uncovered evidence of illicit arms shipments from England to Germany. Renn tracks the crime from the London dockside to Paris, the city waiting for the Nazi invasion that English venality has made possible.

The novel shows the deep undercurrents of National Socialist sympathy in the English establishment: the metropolitan media, scientists and arms dealers, politicians, and the parents whose own children will never be sent into battle. Julian Swan, now a famous writer, runs a neo-fascist review, *Order*, funded by Berlin and by his ageing mistress, Evelyn Lamb. Evelyn is its literary editor, and the author of an article on 'My friend Hitler'.[43] Swan sets out for Renn the ideology of a generation of meritocrats:

I want to see a united Europe. This time, united not by the Catholic Church for the benefit of the great landowners as it was in the Middle Ages, but by scientists and technicians for the great administrators. My dear fellow, you can't, you're intelligent, avoid seeing that democracy is a corpse. Look at it! Look at its woman-ridden culture. Look at the impotence of socialists clinging mildly and genteelly to capitalism in the very moment when it, too, is arthritic and flatulent. Look at the common man and tell me whether he's happy. Or even alive?[44]

The craving for violence that drives Swan's choice of clichés shows through at every point. Swan beats and humiliates his promiscuous wife, the former Georgina Roxby. Captain Tim Hunt, now 60, is Swan's pilot and bag-carrier. Bred for violence, Hunt helped Swan form a Civil Guard during the General Strike and flew bombers for Franco in Spain. The official dossier says his wife was 'a bad lot', who died in 1920.[45] The reader might remember from *Company Parade* Hervey Russell's blowsy but well-intentioned friend Delia, bruised and bedridden after her husband's return from the front. Louis Earlham, now a successful Labour MP, has investments in an armaments firm. T. S. Heywood, Evelyn's husband, Georgina's lover, and Hervey's old friend, the former iconoclast, has become an armaments scientist. Behind the scenes, emerging only briefly to protect or break his many dependents, is the great puppet-master, the international financier William Gary, who controls the world market in arms.

Understanding comes not only through listening to what these people have to say, but by looking at the spaces in which they operate: constellations of past and present, with the future waiting to be read within them. The great public space is Paris, the mirror and working horizon of London. Paris frames the action. The novel opens in a Paris cafe in summer, 1939, with the city already under the eye of the barbarians. The brittle, superficial city revives in Renn memories of his youthful promise, as the soldier and student of Class 1914, and renews in him an energy that he carries back to a London waiting for war. The end of the tale takes him in pursuit of Hunt back to a Paris mobilised for battle, wondering whether the English will let France down yet again. In this city of light, only one street is dark; that one street hides the English murderer, and mirrors the dark wharf in London where the shells manufactured by Gary, and sold by Swan and Hunt, have been shipping to Germany since 1929.

The other key site, a private space, is Renn's dead mother's house in Hitchin, where he returns in the final pages. She is not Jameson's mother, though circumstantial details are borrowed from that relationship. Acknowledging the sacrifices he and his mother made for each other, Renn accepts his own responsibility for the next generation. The account with the past is closed, and Jameson writes a luminous ending. Renn walks down the path, abandoning the old house, and crossing into the sunlight of the unknown future, ready for the fight.

Jameson began writing *The Black Laurel* immediately her first book was finished, and completed the last chapter in North Wales, with the 5-year-old Christopher asleep in the next room.[46] Her anxiety over Christopher's situation, between two divorcing parents, explains some, though by no means all, of the emphasis in both books on the need to save the children. The epic dimension of the catastrophe that now constitutes the spectacle of Europe made it hard to separate one form of personal wretchedness from another. A photograph she saw in the *Daily Mail* on 3 April 1945, of a 16-year-old German captive walking to his prison cage in tears, reminded her of her 17-year-old brother, saying good-bye in an earlier war.[47]

Jameson had never visited the ruined Berlin of August 1945 where the novel is set, though, she told Ould, she saw it from the air, and she had walked among the ruins of Warsaw.[48] Certainly, her visits to Warsaw and Prague just after the war produced the surreal overviews in the novel of a broken Europe seen from the air, the graphic descriptions of a population scrabbling to survive and rebuild in the ruins of their city, glimpses of faces in the streets, phrases and anecdotes, snapshots of German atrocities. To her personal experience of Central Europe she added her own research and reading, help from one of Guy's old military comrades and from a member of British Intelligence she met on the boat to the United States, and information from a relative of Irene Rathbone's, who was a Colonel in the Legal Division at Main Headquarters of the Control Commission for Germany (British Element) at Luebbecke, BAOR. He knew intimately the workings of the military sectors, and especially the system of military jurisdiction over civilians that was important for her denouement.[49]

Describing later the writing of the book, she gave its theme as 'the problem of justice versus expedience'.[50] The rough justice of the military world is expressed at the beginning, in the British prisoner-of-war camp in Scotland, close to William Gary's estate, where two German prisoners are being executed for murdering two of their fellows who had betrayed an escape plot (an episode based on recent history),[51] and again at the end, in Occupied Berlin, where the well-intentioned Kalb, a former Jewish refugee returned from London, is set up for charges of murder and looting, and is sentenced to execution by a military court. In between, the text is riddled with hangings, shootings, suicides, and executions. The Nuremberg show trials of 1945 had ended in 1946, with the death of most of the accused.

Jameson's conviction of the political folly of revanchism, and her critique of its injustices, might of itself have explained the near-unanimous hostility of reviewers. She pushed her ideas to the limit, as Guy had seen, and asked questions no one wanted to hear about England's collective responsibility for the devastation of Europe, and the slender prospects of saving the next generation from the ruins her bombers had left. She absolved the young pilots (Bill's generation) from ultimate responsibility for their actions, and reserved her most devastating shots for the rich old men who sent the planes and took the profits.

The narratives emerging from the ruins of Berlin, London, and Europe are many and complex, but it is this positive thread that eventually dominates. William Gary, it seems at the outset, holds all the reins of power, and seems set to impose his own benevolent version of fascist order on the world. But the young can see through him. The ex-bomber pilot, Arnold Coster, employed to fly Gary's personal plane, comes slowly to realise that the price of his protection is uncritical obedience, and collusion in his readiness to sacrifice the weak and vulnerable to his own idea of progress. Arnold resigns and walks away; and the novel and the future, it turns out, in reality belong to him.

Arnold, a good and kindly man, is also the agent of wholesale murder and destruction. Jameson created in this novel some of her most effective symbolic landscapes, to represent the catastrophic damage to Europe's places and people for which Gary and Arnold are jointly responsible. As the airman sees it, flying over Berlin, this is a civilisation bombed back beyond the Stone Age:

Sprawling pyramids of dust, of shattered brick; the skeletons of buildings leaning over ossuaries of splintered stone and dust. A single column erect in acres of reddish dust. Carcasses of tanks, burned-out cars. The torn-out megalithic bones, corroded by fire, of a railway-station. Perspectives, beyond those he could see, only of ruins.[52]

The world's ending in water, fantasised by William Lamb before the war began, has been worked out in real history in fire and thunder. The apocalyptic and artistic references are discreetly hinted, as David Renn looks on Prague, and its great fortress-palace and prison, Hradcany. Unmarked by the invader, the fort is nevertheless, like the ruined architecture of Berlin, a monument to a civilisation whose time is almost done. Renn meditates: 'those who come after us will have to content themselves with something a little more modest in the way of history—a broken cup or page 18 of *The Waste Land* found in a cellar.'[53]

But at the same time, this corner of Prague is crammed with intimations of new beginnings:

A light the colour of silence, the colour of warmth, the colour of forgetfulness of tortures, fell on [the fortress] from a young sky. A great many youths and girls walked, hurried, along the embankment: it struck him that nowhere else had he seen so many of these: they moved with a brusque energy and lightness, as though they knew for certain where they were going. Is it true? he wondered. Is there really one city which has memories of a future?[54]

Arnold carries far heavier burdens than the young people of Prague. But as he looks on the ruins he has made, he feels only 'a detached curiosity'.[55] Flying Gary to his meetings in Berlin, over the skeleton of Hanover, he makes no attempt to disown what he has done. Only by acknowledging his role in what, from one perspective, was a necessary murder, can he take up the responsibility and the power that in the process have become his. There can be regret, and dismay, but no crippling guilt; it was History, and the greed of his elders, that laid on him his part. The new Europe belongs to him, he and his generation have paid for it with their own bodies, and its possession is source not just of dismay but delight. The future of Europe lies with the planes Gary has paid for, but which Arnold has, by use, made his own. Through the young body of Arnold, the future, in language that echoes Auden's in its imagery and twisting syntax, is 'making itself hands and a voice':

The hangmen had done their work thoroughly, the body of Europe, flayed while still living, was stretched below him in the sunlight, the nerves exposed and torn, the fractured bones, the nails rotted, decomposing flesh, a death terrible, sordid, poisoned. He had an instant of dismay. Yet—why regret it any more than anyone regrets the Middle Ages? The composite death—made up of a million obscure deaths—stretched out down there had been those ages' future: somewhere to right or left of the strong wings grown through the nerves of his own hands into his body the future was making itself hands and a voice. With a rapidly suppressed excitement, he thought: 'I shall live in it'.

He had almost forgotten Gary's presence.[56]

Jameson is uncompromising. The new world belongs rightly to those who fought for it, and the common British soldier Hervey turned to for salvation at the end of *None Turn Back*, and the French captain holding the line in *Cloudless May*, now find in the airman their latest avatar.

Between Moscow and Washington

For the moment, there were still problems that Jameson's own generation must deal with. In an England crowded with unemployed soldiers, determined this time not to be cheated of change, and a Europe where Stalin was strengthening and extending his borders, Communism presented a growing threat. On 24 February 1948, Jameson finished her play about an imminent Russian invasion of England, *The Moment of Truth*, begun the previous October, and immediately set about turning it into a short novel.[57] A few days later, responding to Ould's complaints that the Communists, especially Jack Lindsay, were playing with PEN, she expressed her fury at Lindsay and her conviction that if there was to be economic breakdown in Britain, the country would go Communist.[58] She appreciated Arthur Calder-Marshall's favourable review of *The Black Laurel* in *Reynolds' News*, but was still asking if he was a Party member. She passed on to Ould Willa Muir's warning that Vanček was a Communist, and the PEN Committee must be careful what it said in front of him, to avoid involving their Czechoslovakian friends in some indiscretion.[59]

In May, she had another breakdown, due to the accumulated pressure of the quarrels with family and friends, and the strain of writing *The Black Laurel*.[60] The shattering of her carefully built-up self-confidence brought back childhood memories of the wounding ridicule from her mother that had destroyed it in the first place:

I never had any confidence in meeting people properly, in being able to, I mean. I've trained myself to do it as well as I can, but there are always times when such a show as I can put up is knocked down by a sort of black wave of diffidence ('You are the laughing stock of the neighbourhood.') [...] (I guess that was why Valentine's dismissing me had such an effect was that it touched off a lot of buried memories of being laughed at. People shouldn't laugh at children.)[61]

She was still determined to work for the construction of a Europe on which she now pinned all her hopes:

It is far more than kindness to let me think I'll be able and allowed in Rome (Venice, Florence) to work for the thing I care about very deeply—the idea of Europe. The international p.e.n. [sic] seems a frail thread, but it has outlasted two wars, it isn't so frail as that, indeed it's stronger than anything else I see. It's the only international web that holds. What is more, I begin to see very clearly where and how S. America is important to the Idea of Europe itself. We might have talked of this in Copenhagen if I were not the deflated creature I am.[62]

In June, Guy's mother had to be certified, and Jameson went to clear up her filthy and neglected house. Back in Ilkley, she wrote to Ould of the coming fights PEN must prepare for. Freedom of expression in Europe was one, and PEN must take care not to condemn any one country—by that she meant Russia's satellites in Central and Eastern Europe. Rebuilding relations with Germany was another, and she expressed continuing exasperation at the selfishness of the French.[63]

Jameson desperately needed a break. The Chapmans' visit to Pittsburgh, in planning since the previous autumn, was imminent, and she and Guy were due to sail for the United States on 24 July. Pleasure was not unalloyed. The Berlin airlift had begun the previous month, and Bill initially took part in it (it would continue, without him, until September 1949).[64] But there was much to look forward to. Phyllis Bottome had offered introductions to Eleanor Roosevelt, F. P. Adams and his wife, and to Alexandra Adler, daughter of the renowned psychologist Dr Alfred Adler.[65] There would be good friends to meet in the American PEN Centre, and her agents Carl and Carol Brandt had plans for tours to promote her writing. Friends made during the war, such as the wealthy Henry Steele Commager, whom Guy had met in Harlech, were eager to offer hospitality. Winifred was in New York, and Dorothy's children in Dallas. Guy had university duties associated with his exchange post, and she had agreed to teach Creative Writing, though she had no idea what that entailed. But there should still be ample time for thinking, writing, and resting.

The lengthy account of her visit to the United States given in *Journey from the North* begins on a negative note.[66] By the end, her criticisms are tempered by positive comments on the vitality of America's cities and people, and the role beginning to be played by the numbers of émigrés brought there by the war. Here, it seemed, was another space for European culture to develop, in a distinctive new form. She was ready to go home, but she had enjoyed her stay. This polite farewell was of course written in the 1960s, for publication, with her American friends and contacts in mind. Letters dated 1948–9 to Ould and Rathbone tell a more varied story.

Family came first. Winifred was living in New York, in a flat at 171 West 12th Street, and she stayed with her for a few days. She wrote to Irene Rathbone that she had been 'coping with my sister—who baffles me completely', and becoming acquainted with post-war America:

There is no doubt now in my mind that this is The Future, and I loathed it with all my heart and soul. [...] I so hated the richness, and more than that the awful mechanical nature of it—the fact that there is a machine to do everything. [...] America is still struggling to be born [...]. And I am European to my smallest bone.[67]

Before leaving, reading with admiration John Wheeler Bennett's *Munich*, with its emphasis on the joint responsibility of France and England for the war, she had told Irene that the two countries needed to work together to resolve Europe's real problem, which was America: 'It's our weakness, our dependence on the Americans that matters, not the original sin of Germans.'[68] And on the boat coming over, she had lectured French fellow-voyagers on their politicians' refusal of union with England in 1940:

It makes me cry when I think of it, because only Union of us, the French, and the other northern European nations can save Europe from being overwhelmed by this great American wave. The wave doesn't even want to overwhelm us. It will just do it in the course of nature—unless we are a rampart, all of us together.[69]

In November of the previous year, her view of Europe's American connection had been rather different:

Europe is doomed to be overrun by America or the USSR. I prefer, eyes open, America. We have a chance of recovering our soul from America in time. From the communists we shall recover neither soul nor body. They are coldbloodedly murdering France at this moment. [...] And when I hear people like Ed Murrow talking, I feel that we can trust America.[70]

But though Communism made rapid advances during her time in the United States (in August 1948, the Republic of Korea was proclaimed, and in September, after the long triumphant march of Mao's Red Army, would come the establishment of a North China People's Republic), that threat seems to have paled against her own first-hand experience of American capitalism.

After New York in August, came a visit to 1185 Hill Top Road, Kansas City, where her brother-in-law was living with his children and his second wife, Louise. Louise was the daughter of the Montreal family, friends of the Leakes, who had taken Dorothy to live with them for a few days while she was waiting for the return convoy to England, and had looked after Robert when he first came to Canada. Dorothy had liked her very much,[71] and she was a kind and loving stepmother to the children. Jameson's immediate reactions were more mixed than those recorded in her autobiography. Later, from Pittsburgh, she wrote to Ould of her pleasure at seeing them and her horror at the gangster comics that seemed to be their only reading matter.[72] She told Betty Leake that meeting Judy had been a shock ('she is so like and so unlike Do').[73] It was saddening to find she no longer remembered the mother who had furnished her doll's house. There was to be another visit to Kansas the following year, for a week in May, which also went fairly well.[74] But it was the visit to the Leakes in March 1949, recorded in detail in her autobiography, which brought Jameson closer to her sister, who had been a much-loved and well-remembered member of the household.[75]

Pittsburgh was another shock. The Chapmans moved into 419 Fairfax, Fifth Avenue, Pittsburgh 13. The city soon caught her imagination, especially by night, but she remained struck by its noise and filth.[76] (In later years, she would tell her grandson that Pittsburgh was exceptionally clean, unlike Leeds or Sheffield.) The same letter records an imminent flight to New York for a weekend to attend General Eisenhower's inauguration as President of Columbia University, where Guy was the official delegate from Leeds University.

Her moods swung wildly. In October, she was pleasantly surprised by America's positive feelings towards England, especially as expressed in the generosity of food parcels, which she was able to send to a number of friends in London and Cambridge, struggling with rationing.[77] In November, she was again railing at the filth of the city, its provincialism, the difficulties of her teaching job, and the people:

It is awful to be compelled to feel that the only people worth meeting are bankers and steel and glass kings and their consorts. I am about to meet Heinz. Shall I ask him to put me on his free list?[78]

She was missing the excitement of PEN. She responded eagerly to Ould's accounts of the much-publicised first World Congress of Intellectuals for Peace, convened in Wrocław, Poland on 6 August 1948, where the British contingent had been mostly from the Left. Jack Lindsay and his wife, Ould reported, were the only PEN Communists among the writers, but among the scientists, including Haldane, who was also a PEN member, a number were either Communist or fellow-travellers.[79] She replied wistfully:

I wish I'd been with you in Wrocław, there are people in Poland I'd like to have seen, and I enjoy being with Poles, mad as they are. Also, I'd really like to have seen the communist team in action. Olaf Stapledon is plain silly, I think, not wicked. Haldane is a fool, and as for Kingsley—but you know my opinion of Kingsley. I shall treasure your letter to use against fellow-travellers everywhere.[80]

She reported on the party in the United States (a minority, she said) that was agitating for war with Russia. If there was war, she thought, America would win it and go fascist in the process, but the impression she had gained in Washington was that most people saw war as unlikely.[81]

She was clearly sorry to be missing the rapid development of the links between PEN and UNESCO, especially the new project on translations, and the signing of a one-year contract for a grant of 2,500 dollars.[82] In the small hours of the morning, she pondered PEN issues and sent Ould advice on who might be the next International President, and received from him exhortations to ginger up the New York PEN Centre, inveterate diners, who could, he thought, for a start, protest against McCarthy's Un-American Behaviour campaign.[83] In May 1949, Guy's friend Henry Steele Commager accepted to be President of the American Centre, and in June she reported that he had personally protested, in speech and in writing, against McCarthy's campaign.[84]

They left Pittsburgh on 7 June for New York, to stay with Winifred—or rather, use her flat as a postal address while they visited friends—before returning from Montreal on 15 July, to arrive in Liverpool on the 22nd or 23rd of the month.[85] In her last letter from Pittsburgh, she told Ould she had written to ask Thornton Wilder to be International President, as he had suggested, in preference to his other suggestion, Thomas Mann, who, she believed, was a cryptocommunist.[86] Wilder quickly refused, saying he hadn't the negotiating and diplomatic skills Jameson seemed to deploy so effortlessly.[87] The last few weeks in America were spent mostly with the Commagers in Vermont, and a last week in July in Ida Wylie's house, joined for two nights by Noel Streatfeild.[88]

Summing up, in *Journey from the North*, she decided that by and large, it was a new kind of European collaboration that was needed to oppose Stalin's USSR. But America was a good place, and certainly a better place for writers than England's *panier à crabes*.[89] It had been very hard work, but she had been appreciated, to an extent she wasn't in England, they had made good new friends in Pittsburgh, and stayed with old ones, all wealthy and well-connected, family matters had been satisfactorily resolved, and there had been enough engagement with PEN issues to keep her happy but not overwhelmed. Her American reputation would continue to grow. To Irene, she wrote from New York that she was returning to England 'A haggard aged woman, a stone and a half lighter, a decade greyer and more lined'.[90]

18

1949–1953: A European Future

Jameson left America reinforced in her conviction that the nations of Europe must unite to secure their own future, or each would independently decline. She wrote in *Journey from the North* of the insight that came to her on 3 July 1949, on the shores of Lake Minnewaska. The one enterprise that might motivate them all was the construction of a single European nation, with a new ideal:

Oppose, to the new Russia, a new Europe, a new intellectual inspiration, a new plan of living—voilà tout ce qu'il faut....[1]

Family problems engaged her again. As soon as they got back, Jameson went down to Chichester to see Bill and the new baby, only to discover, as she wrote to Lovat Dickson, that he would be out of work on 18 August. He had left British South American airlines during his divorce and joined a charter firm that was now, she explained, finding itself in difficulties and laying off its more experienced and expensive people. In the following months, Lovat Dickson was provided with a copy of Bill's curriculum vitae and roped in to help him find a new job.[2]

Meetings at the PEN Congress held in Venice in September 1949 were more enjoyable, and Guy took pleasure in snubbing the renegade Auden, met during a sightseeing trip.[3] But the respite was brief. She visited London at the end of the month to see Barbara, who was rocked by the insecurity into which she had been plunged by Bill's abrupt ending of financial support. She came back feeling, she told Irene Rathbone, like 'an old old woman' after a devastating confrontation that severed connections between the two for some time.[4] She told Irene she was determined not to see Barbara again, but was not at all sure whether she was doing wrong or right by her grandson.[5]

She plunged into work. In September, she wrote a 12,000-word story based on a tragic incident she had seen reported in a newspaper while they were in

Pittsburgh—she needed the money, with so many people depending on her.[6] Then at the end of November, she began writing *The Green Man*, which would be completed two years later, in June 1951.

The Writer's Situation: Writing for Europe

Whatever family problems there might be, she still had public responsibilities. *The Writer's Situation*, published by Macmillan in 1950, organised essays written over the last ten years, and posed the questions she thought all writers must now confront, about the values they upheld in the present, and the future they wanted to write.[7] The rebuilding of Europe was beginning, in the shadow of Hiroshima and behind the battle-lines of the Cold War, and Class 1914 must again fight to be heard. The collection is striking in its coherence and energy, and as one reviewer commented, very much in the spirit of the age.[8]

The future, Jameson declared, was European, and it was French writers who were showing the way to win it. She reprinted her wartime essays from the *TLS*, which had set out the values for which the war was fought. 'Writing in the Margin', from October 1939, defended the free speech on which European civilisation must rest; 'Paris' (26 August 1944), celebrated the liberation of the city of light. 'A Crisis of the Spirit', written in October–November 1941, held up the anti-industrial, humane culture of France as the just measure for the civilisation of the future. The message was confirmed by the two addresses with which she had opened and closed the PEN International Congress of September 1941. 'The Responsibilities of a Writer' were to make a new order of social justice in Europe, beyond nationalisms, and in this, writers and readers must be 'Creditors of France', to whom Europe had always turned for the renewal of the heritage.

The first pages of the collection renounced the fellow-travelling and even the liberal humanist fervours of the 1930s. Dignity and freedom, she argued, were already long gone by then, though the writers fighting for them could not see it, and the tyranny of the machine over civilisation was already irreversible. The questions asked by writers in 1939 were no longer relevant.[9] The language in which to ask them broke now in a writer's hands, emptied of meaning or distorted by censorship and hypocrisy ('The Novelist Today', May

1949). Language no longer provided the means to assert shared values within a common cultural landscape, and the collapse of a common cultural language meant the death of human relationships. What Jameson had written of Europe in October–November 1941 was even truer in the post-war context.

Words no longer mean the same thing to men of equal intelligence in different nations—or to two men of the same nation. The word for justice, the word for pity, the word for truth has a different meaning according as it is spoken by a Russian or a German or a Frenchman. Or by two Englishmen, one of whom is a party communist and the other an old-fashioned liberal. [...] The crisis extends to all human relationships. To whom does a man owe his final loyalty? To his brother, to an all-powerful leader, to the Party?[10]

The essay 'The Writer's Situation', dated May 1947, made much of the cultural ferment of newly liberated France, which focused, she said, on the Communists around Aragon and the existentialists around Sartre; but greater than either, she thought, was André Malraux, the only one whose commitment to the restoration of Europe might yet raise the cultural heritage from the ruins. [11]

She found much to criticise in Sartre's ethics of action, attacking what she saw as an excessive emphasis on the individual's responsibility to find his own meaning, and the temptation to 'romantic despair'.[12] Sartrean freedom, she asserted, generated conflict between men, not solidarity and community. Sartre's atheistic existentialism was packed with inconsistencies, and the novels he made out of his philosophy were unreadable: 'The first two volumes of *The Age of Reason* are an animated thesis [...].'[13] Ten years later, when she began to write her autobiography, she would keep back direct criticism of the man whose thought and politics were in many respects not so far removed from her own, and point her attack at his crasser disciples.[14] For the moment, it was probably his fellow-travelling sympathies, politically unacceptable, as well as her intellectual rivalry, that pushed her to distance herself from him.

André Malraux, her PEN colleague since the 1930s, could be praised unreservedly. *La Lutte avec l'ange* wrestled with the great issues of the age. Malraux had no illusions about the cruel depths of human nature, but he still believed in 'the divine in man' and in the future ('not piously in any future, but in the future of men in Europe, in the resurrection and everlasting life of Europe').[15]

Two years later, when Malraux astounded contemporaries by crossing to the side of General de Gaulle, she was confident that he had done so because he saw in de Gaulle the one person who could save Europe, and she continued to trust in his driving faith in Europe's future. Jameson drew her account of 'The Novelist Today' to a close with an (humanist) act of faith in the need to have faith:

We believe something, or we die. For this very good reason I believe in the future of mankind. And of Europe. And, at the last, of England.[16]

In the early 1960s, Jameson would finally regret the loss of Malraux to the French cultural establishment.[17] She added no details, but from 1959, as de Gaulle's Minister of State for Cultural Affairs, he was engaged in disseminating nationally and internationally an elitist version of humanist culture which she will have considered deeply one-sided. But in 1950, she identified herself completely with his ambitions for Europe to become a power in the world, and in October of that year, she was delighted to hear from Harrison Salisbury, Moscow correspondent of the *New York Times*, that her name figured together with that of the great Frenchman in the 'Book of Death'—the list of anti-Soviet activists proposed by the *Literary Gazette*.[18]

In 1943, Jameson had told Olaf Stapledon that form was paramount in the novel. In 1949, what mattered was a storyline, and a way of writing, that could introduce readers to new experiences, and make them think.[19] But she was clear that writers should not be expected to make socially significant statements. Form remained the writer's way of making a political intervention. The strongest challenge to society's commitment to the fast-moving machinery of capitalism and consumerism had come from the poets: Eliot, Mallarmé, Aragon, Edith Sitwell, and Paul Valéry ('Between the Wars'). The long meditation that had produced the pure poetry of 'La Jeune Parque' had equipped the poet to think past the tyranny of things towards 'the deep note of life itself', and create a unique, objective vision of the relations of things. The great writers, she declared, were both great stylists and children of their age: Tolstoy, Stendhal, Proust, Dostoevsky, Murasaki.

The landscape of culture, for Jameson, was now more than ever that of France, shot through with the clear light of rationalist order and organically rooted in an invincible faith in its own past and future: 'I believe that the French concept of man—a being who needs bread, wine and leisure more profoundly than he needs speed and efficiency—is a living concept. From it civilisation could be re-grafted.'[20] 'Culture' for Jameson was still equally a force embedded in the landscape of everyday life and the creation of high artistic endeavour, and in France, she believed, the two could still be found.

The Moment of Truth

At the end of the 1940s, Jameson was still interested in hearing her work broadcast on the radio. But she seemed to have recognised her inability to write dialogue that could communicate as effectively to the listener's ear as it did to the reader's eye, and proposing texts for adaptation by others was to be her way forward. Regional radio was being developed, so living in Leeds was for once an advantage. A proposal from North Region for an adaptation by Anthony Gittings of her recently-published novel, *The Moment of Truth* (1949), was approved by BBC London and the play was scheduled for broadcast on 11 September 1950 as a 90-minute drama in the Home Service's Saturday Night Theatre series.[21] The dramatic storyline was ideal for radio, as was the central group of strongly drawn characters. Three young people, all RAF pilots, one of whom is a pregnant woman, and their middle-aged Yorkshire mechanic, are waiting on a North of England airfield for a plane to take them to America. The third world war, an atomic war, is almost over. The Russians are winning, and Britain is about to be invaded. Six VIPs turn up at the last minute to demand their seats, among them two generals, a famous writer, and a famous physicist. Who should stay and organise the resistance, and who should go, is one issue. Cold War or not, Jameson's play expresses her strong feeling that America is not the place to lodge the best hopes for the world's future.

As in *William the Defeated*, Jameson affirmed her faith in the capacity of England's people, and Western European civilisation, to 'corrupt' and assimilate the invader, over time. Collaboration is always a possible option, if by it a people can survive to make their own future. In a dramatic climax, the pilot turns out to be a Communist, who declares he would be happy to stay and work with the Russians and will not help a resistance committed to restoring capitalist values. He is threatened with shooting, on the pretext that he might denounce the rest of them. His response expresses Jameson's loathing of all authoritarian regimes:

'I've denounced no one. You've no reason to suppose I would. You want to shoot me for something you think I *might* do, some day.' He hesitated, and said in a strangely weak young voice, 'You'll do it because, politically, I'm on the other side—nothing more.'[22]

The physicist, who has already fled once from a Europe at war, sets out stumblingly the principle that must direct their decisions at this moment of truth:

'We should reflect whether the idea of justice, and the idea of people being innocent when they have not yet done their crime—perhaps I should say, the passion for justice, perhaps it is not only an idea—whether it isn't part of the human estate, so to speak—and ought to be saved.'[23]

Unfortunately for Jameson, her drama was too timely, and her understanding of the tensions of the post-war world far too acute. In January 1950, Klaus Fuchs had confessed to the British authorities that he had passed atomic and hydrogen bomb secrets to the USSR, and President Truman issued his State-ment directing the Atomic Energy Commission to continue its work on all forms of atomic weapons. In June, North Korean forces invaded South Korea, and in July, United Nations forces, under a bellicose Douglas MacArthur, were sent to repel them. It was decided that the play could not be broadcast. The Controller of the Northern Region wrote to Jameson on 3 August that:

At a time of very grave international tension, the BBC would be open to very serious and justifiable criticism if it broadcast a programme of which the background was the defeat and occupation of this country by (unambiguously) Russia, with particular reference to the inadequacy of our Allies etc.[24]

The performance was recorded, and some hope was held out that it might be broadcast on the Third Programme. This was considered the following August during a lull on the international scene, but it didn't happen. BBC administra-tors had to engage in lengthy correspondence with an irate Jameson, annoyed less by the censorship of her play than by the realisation that she had signed the standard BBC contract stipulating that no performance would result in no fee, and would not be receiving money that she needed very badly.[25]

In August 1950, Hermon Ould, who had recently retired, was diagnosed with cancer and died shortly afterwards. Her sense of loss is clear from her autobiography; the original draft commented at even greater length on his selfless work for PEN, and his quiet resistance to Jameson's best efforts to exhort him to make time for his own work.[26] In August too, Bill, Patchen, and a 2-year-old Frances set off in the yacht for Australia. They returned in Octo-ber, beaten back by gales and having been badly let down and endangered by the professional sailor they had hired to crew for them.[27] After that, Bill went into a flying job with an independent airline, but October was still a desperate time financially.

In her letters to Lovat Dickson, Jameson was increasingly upset at the demands she forecast she had to meet over the next two years, including a

£1,600 bill for income tax.[28] Relief came with a substantial advance from Macmillan. The terms of that advance were not, in her view, generous; the first £1,000 was a loan, and the firm had her insure her life in their favour for two years and deducted the premium from the amount they handed over.[29] Sheets put together by the accounting department at the time the loan was agreed, in October 1950, certainly show considerable fluctuations in her annual sales and earnings from 1939, which might well have justified their caution. Jameson herself was shocked by the firm's losses on her books, although, from *Cloudless May* onwards, there was clearly an upward turn.[30] The Chapmans could no longer afford to stay at Ghyll Court Hotel, and they moved in December 1950 to an unfurnished flat at 12 North Hill Court, Leeds 6.

Jameson wrote to Irene Rathbone at the beginning of 1951 that the flat was wearing her out. It was a terrible place, with black greasy dust that settled back as soon as she cleaned it, she hated all the domestic chores, and she couldn't write—though she had to, the money was more needed than ever, as Bill had lost his job again. And with Hermon gone, replaced as International Secretary by his old friend David Carver, the PEN connection was increasingly irritating:

I'm bored [...] with PEN. David [Carver] writes for advice or help, I answer with great care and at once, and get no reply for days and days to my own questions, or I find they have just ignored my advice but expect me to help just the same with their international troubles—about which I don't care a bit. Take no notice of this sour remark, I am a pig.[31]

In the middle of her tribulations, success finally arrived.

A Career Takes Off

In 1951, she found a new agent. She had written to A. D. Peters in 1947 expressing regret she could not, in decency, abandon Nancy Pearn.[32] A few months later, however, she told Lovat Dickson that her patience was exhausted, and she had given Pearn Pollinger and Higham notice that *Black Laurel* would be the last book of hers they would have.[33] She tried to save money for a while by acting for herself, but as the fiasco with the BBC indicated, the cost in time and temper was not worth it. In February 1951, she replied to a discreet enquiry from A. D. Peters about her current position:

I will come and see you since you say I may. [...] It's necessary you should take a look at me before anything. I'm not the brash young woman you knew, and were kind to. I haven't her confidence [this sentence added by hand]. I don't want the same things she wanted. I'm a much better writer, but that's nothing to the point.[34]

Realising perhaps that this might be her last chance to make a career as a writer, Jameson began to shed more committees and society memberships. In May, she resigned from the SCRSS (the Society for Cultural Relations between the peoples of the British Commonwealth and the USSR).[35] PEN, however much she grumbled, still had a claim on her conscience. She would, she told Peters in June, have already finished *The Green Man* had she not been shanghaied into attending a PEN International Committee meeting in Paris (her fare had been paid by UNESCO under the co-operative agreement negotiated with Hermon Ould).[36] Effectively, she was, as she designated herself, a reformed rake, and her writing was at last taking precedence.[37]

There was some transitional struggle over rights with PPH, but the small embarrassment it caused her was worth it. She posted off to Peters two short stories, the original play version of *The Moment of Truth*, and a list of which publishers owned which of her titles, and the ones she would like best to see back in print.[38] Peters acted quickly to put her chaotic affairs in order, and to concentrate her publications into Macmillan's hands. He made a list of the foreign rights to her work that were scattered haphazardly throughout Europe, and with the help of his well-organised worldwide network of agents, gathered them together and sorted out new ones. On the American side, Jameson strengthened her agency links and her friendship with Carl and Carol Brandt in New York.

At the agency, Margaret Stephens and John Montgomery joined in the diligent search for outlets for the short stories Jameson was writing with increasing facility for the expanding popular magazine sector. In the beginning, sales were slow. Her writing did not fit easily into the conventional categories. Jack Hargreaves, at *Lilliput*, turned down 'This Is It', offered with a £400 price tag, on the grounds that it was too womanly to suit his preponderantly male readership, by which he meant, he said, that the heroine was annoyingly hysterical.[39] For other editors, Jameson was not womanly enough. In 1955, *Women and Beauty* would reject 'The Custom of the Country', saying it was absorbing reading, but as its main preoccupation was political, it was not suitable for a woman's magazine, and there was not enough human interest.[40]

Back in 1951, *Good Housekeeping* paid 50 guineas for 'Very Clever People', which *Woman's Own* and *Woman* had hesitated over; two 'damns' had to be cut.[41] 'This is It' was rejected in the course of 1951 by *John Bull*, *Good House-keeping*, *Woman's Own*, and *The Star Weekly* (Toronto); eventually the Cornhill Press bought it in the summer of 1952.[42]

Macmillan took *The Green Man*, and offered initially to sell it at 21 shillings, with a royalty of 20 per cent.[43] The final agreement was for 15 shillings, with a royalty of 10 per cent on the first 5,000, and 15 per cent thereafter.[44] Its success on publication in July 1952 was to be another watershed in Jameson's writing career.

But at the end of 1951, Peters was still disentangling his client's chaotic finances. Macmillan had advanced £1,300, they told him, since December 1950 and Jameson's royalties to date were £116 0s.6d.[45] In March 1952, Jameson herself was pessimistic about the prospects of her writing ever providing a reasonable living.[46]

March had brought another trip to Paris for a meeting of the International Executive Committee of PEN, and a welcome reconciliation with Henri Membré, secretary of the French Centre. Membré's death six weeks later brought her personal sadness, as well as the realisation that it meant the end for her plans for a PEN future based on Anglo-French cooperation.[47]

It must have been a blow to her financial hopes as well as her self-confidence when at the end of May she finished a political novel set in a small, impoverished South American Republic, and decided immediately to scrap it. *The Gamble* started from a well-conceived situation (a reforming Minister of Works, attempting to secure jobs and land for the exploited Indians in his country, is caught between the intrigues of conservative and Communist factions, is arrested, and commits suicide). Its politics were contemporary, and she may have benefited from the advice of Sydney Harland, who had some knowledge of the area.[48] But she was right to abandon it: the dialogue is excruciatingly trite, the relations between characters sentimental and far-fetched, and there is an artificial tone to it all.

Jameson was now keen to try her hand at television drama. John Montgomery proposed 'A Common Place Heart' to Cecil McGivern at the BBC, on 3 July 1952. Michael Barry, Head of Television Drama, wrote to Montgomery on 7 August to suggest a story treatment that would keep the plot framework while identifying pages that would generate strong and simple visual images, and developing or inventing minor characters to strengthen the main theme. A meeting was arranged between Jameson, Barry, and Sir Basil Bartlett, Drama Script Supervisor for television. On 9 October 1952, Sir Basil sent her a suggestion for a script treatment. She returned her script after a fortnight, without the new characters, the Braithwaites, Sir Basil had suggested would help amplify the theme, with a note indicating that: '<u>With</u> Braithwaites the whole act went frightfully slack, so slack you could have strangled a mule with it. If you absolutely insist, I'd try again to push them in. At least I think I would. Maybe I'd leave the country instead.' She included a poem in the manner of T. S. Eliot:

> Braithwaite addressed full length to shave,
>   Broadbottomed, pink from nape to base,
> Knows the female temperament
>   And wipes the suds around his face.
>
> The lengthened shadow of a man
>   Is history, said Emerson
> Who had not seen the silhouette
>   Of Braithwaite straddled in the sun.[49]

She was cavalier in her response to Sir Basil's polite request for changes, which were eventually made by Nigel Kneale and George Kerr. They had to do a lot of work, since Jameson was not available for further consultation, but even so, Sir Basil asked that she be paid as much as possible. She eventually received a total fee of 130 guineas, in addition to which she negotiated a return rail ticket from Leeds to London and a night in a London hotel. The play was scheduled to be produced by John Fernald on 13 January 1953, and Jameson accepted an invitation to attend a rehearsal, asking if she could bring her friend Mrs Williams (wife, she name-dropped, of the Arts Council Secretary), with whom she was staying in Westbourne Terrace.[50]

An immediate follow-up attempt by John Montgomery in February 1953 to offer 'This is It', just out in *The Cornhill Magazine*, received short shrift from the BBC's readers, including, not surprisingly, Nigel Kneale. It was turned down again in 1956, and then again in 1963, by which time, as one reader pointed out, *Z-Cars* had set new standards for plots and characterisation in crime drama. With this, as all other proposals that the agency sent in over the 1950s and 1960s, Jameson supplied only the story, and abandoned the adaptation to others. As A. D. Peters wrote to the BBC in August 1959, forwarding Jameson's synopsis for 'Plain Annie', a contribution to a drama series called 'Personal Column' that he was seeking to put together: 'She does not pretend to understand television drama technique.'[51]

The Chapmans agreed to drive a wealthy American round the Loire for two weeks in July 1952; that, Jameson told Irene, was the only way they could afford a summer break in France that year.[52] After that, her letter continued, she would try and get a job in London. Leeds and the flat were wearing her out:

Imagine a city this size without a single restaurant where one could take the poorest Frenchman without being ashamed, and probably poisoned by vinegar poured over everything, even into the coffee. There is NOWHERE to eat. That's why I have to cook every single day. Having also to clean every single day is an added wearying corvée, due to my faithless daily.[53]

She sank into self-recrimination:

You must not blame Guy for my miseries. He is a victim, too, of my idiocy in spending, wasting, all my money, over years and years and years, when I ought to have been putting by, as they say. It is utterly impossible for him to support us both at Ghyll Court, whence follows the misery of this flat.[54]

In August, there was more misery. She had rheumatism in her shoulder, possibly, she thought, fibrositis, and Guy, to her annoyance, insisted she was in too much pain to go to the International Conference of Artists in Venice (though in the event, they did).[55] On their return, they took 10-year-old Christopher to a hotel in the New Forest for two weeks. This was Jameson's first meeting with her grandson for three years.[56]

An old PEN quarrel sprang into new life. In his address to the Nice PEN Congress in 1952, Jules Romains had attacked the officers of the London PEN Centre for what he called their failure to support his wartime rallying call for writers' engagement. The text of the address was published in the August–September issue of the widely read European journal *Preuves*, a pro-American production of the liberal Centre and Right, founded by the *Congrès pour la liberté de la culture* (Congress for Cultural Freedom) and boasting a prestigious list of associates (Madariaga, Croce, Dewey, Jaspers, Maritain, Russell, Denis de Rougemont).[57] Old documents were dug out, old wounds reopened, and Jameson helped David Carver compose a dignified rebuttal. Romains responded, and the quarrel was finally laid to rest.[58]

By October, money was again a great anxiety. Guy was unhappy in his job and they both longed to leave Leeds, but they needed his salary.[59] But by December 1952, *The Green Man* had been reprinted four times since its appearance in July.[60] There were good reviews in *The Listener*, *The National and English Review*, *The Observer*, *The Sunday Times*, and *The Spectator*.[61] This book, with its closing note of hope for the revival of England and Europe's fortunes, was about to make Jameson's own.

An Epic for the Future: *The Green Man*

Two years' work, from 1949 to 1951, had gone into Jameson's epic text, in which the *TLS* reviewer saw nothing but 'an enormously long chronicle', charting a relentless sequence of events from the 1930s to the present.[62] *The New York Herald Tribune* was to be much more welcoming to 'a panorama' in which it saw 'a story of our times, and of the inter-relation between private lives and public events; men make events and events make men' and also 'the story of the intellectual earth tremors which over the last twenty-five years have rocked our Western World; the great depression, anti-Semitism, the rise of Hitler, World War II, the moral guilt of Hiroshima, the growth of Communism, the new problems of labor and capital, the estrangement between men and women, parents and children, the search for faith.'[63] The review was accompanied by a particularly bad photograph of Jameson with her hair plastered flat.

The novel was a personal as well as a national retrospective. It justified Jameson's own voluntarism in the face of historical contingencies, and brought to light her views on some key aspects of the 1930s (the Spanish Civil War, the role of fellow-travellers in establishment circles) on which she had made little comment in her own name. Richard Daubeny, owner of the old English manor, was another character part-drawn on Tawney.[64] His career path had come to the same crossroads as Jameson's, and he had made the same life-defining choices: commitment to the European cultural heritage, defence of refugees, rejection of fascism, refusal to climb on feminist bandwagons. In his son Andrew, she figured the limits of her sympathy for the underdog, her capacity to be charming to the point of dishonesty, and her streak of repressed violence.

The themes of the novel were all familiar: loathing of the ruling establishment of businessmen, arms manufacturers and politicians, faith in the individual, and faith in the young and the masses, both so easy to impose on and both capable of going so far, with so little encouragement. In them she placed her short-lived post-war hopes that what she and Guy saw as the best of France and England, re-energised by wartime resistance, might secure a separate future for Europe, at a proper distance from American capitalism and Stalinist Communism. The novel's edge of heroic nostalgia is palliated by sceptical insights into the complexities of the present, and the ambiguities of the futures on offer. Hoyt Bradley, the millionaire from St Louis, may indulge in nostalgic longings for the old country, but he will take no risks for it and withdraws his offer to buy the manor house as war draws near. If such as Richard Daubeny are preparing to fight Hitler, then England is a dangerous place to lodge one's cash. 1930s Communism is shown spawning violence and corruption and destroying the weak, at the same time as it sows the seeds of good. Richard's younger son, Paley, rejects his father's values in its name, but carries them despite himself into a teaching career in the London slums.

The novel renews the questions that Jameson asked in *The World Ends*: what is the core of the English and the European cultural heritage, and what of it can be preserved to produce the most hopeful future? More cynically, it asks how much can be surrendered (the panelling, the books, the house itself) before everything is lost? The answer is an existentialist one. The weight of history can't be shrugged off, but there are always different places to make new starts. The manor and estate are only the sheltering space where individuals grow and leave, to carry its values elsewhere.

Richard Daubeny's house, quintessentially old England, has acquired a new role as the heart of a network of European relations: 'Richard, the most intransigently and narrowly English of Englishmen, was a passionate European. He fed one passion from the other.'[65] Richard, like his creator, is shackled to the cause of the European mind. He edits a journal, the *European Quarterly*, he is writing a history of eighteenth-century Europe, he is devoted to workers' education, and he writes countless letters:

He worked unbelievably hard, a day of eighteen hours, not less than three of them devoted to the vast web of letters passing between scholars and scientists which he more than any other person had woven into the torn fabric of Europe since the end of the War. The fabric was handed to us by Erasmus, and what have we done with it? This part of his work took more out of him than any other, his immense unfinished book, the *Quarterly*, the lectures to workers—but he would not hear of letting it go.[66]

Family and friends, the nice and the noxious, are all made equally welcome in his house. He takes in those the rest of society has no time for—the Czech refugee Adamek; Pearson, the working-class lad who left Oxford with a chip on his shoulder and a virulent form of Communist ideology; Egill, the incompetent worker. Behind Richard stands Troy, the cook–housekeeper, archetype of the unsung women who nurture the generations; the creation of a culture is a process of many levels, including the rituals of everyday living.

Not all tables are as open as that of Richard and Troy. This novel looks at the inside of the way of life that the outsiders of the 1920s, Hervey Russell and Class 1914, and working men in their trades unions, had failed to bring to an end. Parties and dinner parties make and maintain the networks of Left intellectuals in inter-war Oxford and London (Auden's generation), link them to the intellectual leaders of Europe (Monsieur Santenac, for example, at Andrew's London dinner-table, carries traces of Jules Romains),[67] and create the bonds that lead young men to sacrifice themselves on Spanish frontlines, in bombing raids over Germany, or in covert Resistance operations in Occupied France. But they also consolidate the links of a corrupt establishment that controls, unchecked and unseen, the highest levels of education, industry, business, and politics.

English politics is in the hands of Richard's twin brother Matthew, a former Cambridge economics professor with expertise in international finance and politics, chairman of Cassler Chemical Industry, and a skilful manipulator. He is contemptuous of the League of Nations, but he understands the need to appear to support it. For him, Russia, not Hitler, is the enemy of Europe, and at the end of the war he recruits the socialist MP George Dean, to defuse revolution in England by offering minimal social reforms. Dean thinks he can manage Matthew; Jameson knows he cannot. This branch of the family corrupts the future.

Landscape in this novel has even more significance than in earlier texts. In the early sections of the novel, Eliot is mentioned twice, briefly.[68] Auden, heavily criticised, in the character of William Acker, for his destructive influence on others, is no longer Jameson's designated model for understanding the moral and political function of place. Both poets, however, have left their mark on a text where landscape, caught in the changing lights of history, plays a major part in the evolution of both societies and individuals.[69] England is defined by two great interacting spaces: the northern moors, where the Daubeny manor-house sits alongside the old Daubeny colliery and the new Daubeny chemical plant, and the Oxford–London axis. The latter reproduces the corrupt circles of power of a culture whose time ought to be done, while the former represents the self-regenerating heart of England, the frontier of past and future created by the energies of working men. London, the place of the power-brokers, is the place that has to be conquered and reconfigured by Andrew's generation if the exploitation of the North is to end.

Among that generation, familiarity and self-interest blunt the perception of inequitable distributions of power. Through the motif of changing light in the landscape, Jameson tracks the enlightenment that slowly comes to Andrew with experience. Fresh from Oxford, taking his first career steps as a bag-carrier for his uncle, he registers nothing of the city that is shaping him. Only in 1938, with London drawing closer to war, on his way to meet Robert, who has been flying for the Republic in Spain, does he become aware of the tensions of the capital. As he walks down Piccadilly, the young, natural light of his own energy reveals the disjunctive syntax of a body politic dragged down by its own weight, cut through with stark contrasts of excess and deprivation, equally blind to its present dangers and future possibilities:

Andrew hurried along Piccadilly towards the Circus. A light the yellow colour of jonquils, too strong for the electric signs: darker side-streets: pavements clotted with strollers: an immensely solid and discreet wealth: on the edge of the Circus, gaping at it, a very young soldier, arm in arm with a sluttish girl …. [...] An old dilapidated woman drowsed, knees wide apart, over her piled newspapers with their sinister headlines—bought and casually read. Who can believe actively in a danger which has become only another nerve twisted in with the others, as constant as the rumour of the traffic, confused, obscure, endless? [70]

As Andrew walks back with Robert after their meeting to his friend's lodgings behind the British Museum, a different kind of light, harsh and violent, presides over the transformation of London's life into the terrifying unity of a city under threat of destruction:

It was dark, cloudy. Searchlights, crossed knives, had caught and were playing with an aeroplane at no great height. The rumour of London covered the noise of the engines. It rose, this rumour, from the thousands of streets, squares, wharves, alleys, of the old city, a deep confused vibration of life, rolling together the last faint fall of dust in an obliterated grave with the youngest weakest cry of the living: all present on the edge of darkness, and all threatened.[71]

The young man's powerful but narrow allegiance to the landscape of London contrasts with his father's mature understanding of how many other places link to London's life, for all of which an Englishman, who is also a European, must be answerable. In September 1938, just after Munich, Richard walks back to his brother Matthew's house from a dinner party he has disrupted with his declaration that he is on the side of the Czechs, rather than Chamberlain and

Hitler. The streets vanish as he falls into a meditation on the past and future of England and Europe, and the clouds of rain hanging over them turn into the darkness of the cruelty that is about to swallow up all culture, love, and freedom. The deadly weight of history on this time and place seems irresistible. But Richard's vision of history has perspectives of its own, and freedom is still its determinant. In his meditation, London and France stand at the beginning and end of Europe's history, and they bracket and contain the barbarity of modern Germany and old Russia. And London's streets lead to many different destinations. Waking from his reverie, Richard decides he must 'do something' for the German refugee whose plight his fellow-diners have cynically dismissed.[72]

In 1943, as the sirens sound, coming out of the Underground at Piccadilly to meet Robert one last time, Andrew, in uniform, has his London at last in perspective. Here is a different kind of darkness, with a natural light and energy that puts the trivia of the capitalist world in their place. Andrew, like his father, has chosen his own version of his own landscape for living and fighting. Englishness, the novel declares, will find its own modes of regeneration, in the minds and bodies of successive generations:

Cleared by a strong north wind, an immense sky, immensely deep, brimming over with stars, made as little of the city and its millions of lives scratching behind walls as if all of it, not simply a few streets, were a trickle of dust, millennial dust, but dust. He waved his arm. 'You can keep it,' he said aloud. He was madly happy to be living. Happiness was the black-out, the frosty December stars, the intense cold, equalling the energy of his body. Tuppence for an eternity without a café.[73]

19

1953–1959: Understanding Exile

Learning to Enjoy Life

From the beginning of 1953, horizons were brighter. In January, Jameson accepted an invitation to the Dublin Congress in June, and for once looked forward to an occasion free of onerous duties: '[I] am practising how to behave like W. H. Auden, Cecil Day Lewis et al—that is, take no notice of the Congress but just sit about drinking.'[1] In the event, May and June saw her entangled in long negotiations with French colleagues over votes to change cumbersome administrative structures, and the distribution of the money coming from UNESCO. In Dublin, she found herself intriguing to secure the International Presidency for her friend Charles Morgan, and head off a rival candidacy from André Chamson. Congress was also enlivened by the antics of the East German delegate, Tralow, keen to be everybody's friend, fearful of committing gaffes that would put him in danger back home, and quite out of his depth—she began to feel sympathy for him, and made use of him later in a novel.[2]

In May, Guy's mother died.[3] Guy resigned his university post in June. By then, almost all Jameson's unearned balance with Macmillan was cleared, and she was showing signs of turning into a profitable proposition. By the end of 1953 and during the first half of 1954, there was enough money coming in to take them to France, where they spent three weeks with Christopher in Brittany. After taking him back to England, they returned to France, driving back by a leisurely route to Bordeaux. Guy needed to work in university libraries on his monograph on the Third Republic, and she had various things to do, including rewriting *The Hidden River* for a serial version in the *Saturday Evening Post* which would earn her 30,000 dollars.[4]

They spent the whole of October in Bordeaux, which she loved, and where Guy had university contacts, lodging with Madame Beaumont at 31 rue

300

Nicolas-Beaujon. They had travelled there by way of Brittany, the Riviera, Arles, and Aix-en-Provence. In November, they were in Vence, at the Nouvel Hotel, making ready to move to the Hotel Helios, in Nice-Cimiez, so that Guy could have more company.[5] They were there over Christmas 1953, welcomed by Denis Saurat and his wife. Saurat was now shunned in French circles, because of his hostility to de Gaulle, and his Anglophilia.[6] They visited Paris for a PEN conference in March 1954, stayed four weeks at the Maison internationale des PEN Clubs, in rue Pierre Charron, and saw Paul Claudel's 'magnificent' new play, *Christophe Colomb*.[7] She was alarmed by David Carver's report of the activities of Naomi Mitchison and Jack Lindsay at the Congress in Amsterdam in March, trying to set up an AWPA meeting (Authors' World Peace Appeal), and wrote back asking him to try to head it off; PEN in the United States, she said, was under constant threat from the McCarthyites, and such activities were dangerous.[8] There were dangers on both sides for PEN; the 1950s and 1960s were also a period during which the CIA, working through the Congress for Cultural Freedom, was trying to turn International PEN into a vehicle for American government interests. David Carver would seem to have leaned most readily to the views of the Congress and its supporters (such as Silone, Koestler, Spender, Milosz).[9] Jameson, never very fond of such as Koestler and Spender, protective of her friends in Central and Eastern Europe, and equally hostile to McCarthyism and Stalinism, seems to have worked to preserve PEN's reputation for defending freedom of expression irrespective of the sources of attack.

After Paris, it was back to Provence, the Lascaux caves, then Bordeaux again, and back through the Loire. And after 22 April, the wanderer reported with pleasure, there would be no address until they returned on 23 May.[10] They were in Holland for ten days in mid-June. On their return, they set out on an abortive bout of house-hunting.

Jameson's fiction was now sought after world-wide. By 1954, translation rights were under discussion for *The Green Man* in Portugal, and throughout that year, enquiries after various texts were coming in to the agency from Germany, France, Israel, and Holland.[11] *Cloudless May* was scheduled for reprinting in Macmillan's Modern Fiction Library. Harper's wanted permission to publish her forthcoming novel, *The Hidden River*, in the States, under the unsubtle title adopted by the *Saturday Evening Post* (*House of Hate*).[12] *Housewife* magazine offered 700 guineas to serialise the novel in four instalments, January to April, 1955.[13] Jameson wrote to her agents: 'It really is extraordinary

301

how people go on buying *The Hidden River*. I shan't even be surprised now if you write to tell me that Levers have bought it to advertise soap.'[14]

The *Cornhill Magazine* commissioned an article on France for the issue of Autumn 1954.[15] The account Jameson wrote for her old friend, John Murray, offered a sharper vision than the idealised versions she had produced in wartime. The France she had just visited, she said, had nothing in common with the familiar images produced by English nostalgia for a lost world of docile servants and good cooking. It was a country of glaring contradictions: alongside the peasant vitality that was the base of its fundamental stability, and its unchallenged intellectual integrity, ran political corruption and social misery. The energy of post-war reconstruction and house-building had suddenly disappeared. There had been some achievements through the Monnet Plan, but industry was still weak and underdeveloped. Since the war, popular cynicism, and lack of respect for politicians, had increased. There was widespread hostility among the older generation to America's wish to rearm Germany, and a strong preference for Russia over the United States. A wine-grower friend in the Dordogne had told her that:

A French government with the moral courage of any poor devil of a soldier [...] would order America to withdraw its occupying troops, and invite the rest of Western Europe to join us in a neutrality pact which would satisfy the Russians that they had nothing to fear in Europe. If Mr. Eisenhower felt compelled to go on issuing his challenges, it would be his funeral, not ours. [...] There are moments when I believe that nothing will save France except a Russian occupation. If it doesn't last more than five or six years. Longer would be the death of us.[16]

Young Frenchmen, less intransigent, wanted reconciliation with Germany. Internal splits were marked; she cited the vengeful atrocities that had marred the moment of Liberation, and the lingering divisions between Catholics and secularists. In her closing paragraphs, she reminded readers again of the debt of European civilisation to France, and recalled from *Cloudless May* her praise for a culture that contrived to be both a high and ancient heritage and the property of the common man. But before these luminous conclusions rolled out, she had made it clear that the dream of France that saw her and her compatriots through the past ten years of war and its aftermath had at last been punctured. The amazing popular success that would shortly greet *The Hidden River* was due at least in part to the same cold honesty.

The summer saw a string of temporary addresses: Burningford Hall Hotel, in Dunsfold, Surrey; Glendorgal, close by Newquay, Cornwall; the Lansdowne

Club; Portmeirion, in Wales; and back to Burningford Hall Hotel. The pleasures of being in transit had to be foregone in the autumn, and Jameson took a flat in SW1 at 3 Halkin Place on 4 October, on a six-months' lease.[17] On 12 October, she flew to Cyprus for three weeks, lodging at 3 Irene Street, Nicosia. Bill was stationed there, with his wife and two children, the younger less than a year old. It was a happy time, before, as she put it, the madness began in earnest.[18]

The Hidden River, published in January 1955, received some bad reviews in *The Listener*, the *TLS*, and *The Times*, but they had no effect on sales. The novel was named as the Book Society Choice for January 1955, the first in a series of Book Club nominations.[19] Ten years after the war, readers still needed to engage with the drama of Occupation, collaboration, betrayal and retribution, conflicting loyalties, and families tearing each other apart. Requests came in for the stage rights.[20] By January 1956, the book had earned royalties of £2,500 from Macmillan, and an additional £268 from Book of the Month Club sales in Canada. Jameson's dollar earnings were such that she had to ask Macmillan to hold back payments, so that she could spread liability for her income tax.[21]

The Hidden River brought a more sophisticated understanding to the ferocious simplicities of wartime ethics. Just before travelling to France in July 1952, Jameson had found the key idea for her novel. It was to centre on the anguish of a man who secretly shoulders the guilt of an act of retributive justice, and thereby provides closure for a family deeply damaged by the war. In both France and England, Jameson had identified a desire for retribution—the primitive bloodlust that was as European as the high cultural heritage—that must, it seemed, be satisfied before civilised values could be restored. During the journey, she had noted a shocking item in a local newspaper, expressing a complex of emotions generated by the tensions of Occupation and collaboration, which went straight into her novel. One mother had been forced to pay compensation to another, whose son had been denounced by the first woman's daughter and subsequently died in a concentration camp. Jameson was struck by the malice of neighbours' responses, but in England, she thought, it would have been just the same.[22]

The plot of *The Hidden River* involves an Englishman, Adam Hartley, a former Special Intelligence officer assigned to work with the Resistance. He returns after the war to the family living on the Loire, beyond Saumur, who had sheltered him in 1943, in order to find out who had denounced one of their members, Robert Regnier. Hartley is committed to creating a future driven by a union between England and France, but a condition of that future must be to acknowledge and resolve the unpalatable truths about both, that wartime necessity had revealed:

Could it be helped that mistrust, cruelty, violence, lying, had to become the second nature of a determined resister? Hartley learned that anything is possible. And that things which are not humanly permissible have in some circumstances to be permitted. No one who learns this lesson remains innocent.[23]

His wartime comrade, Jean Monnerie, now head of the family, wants to repress the dark history of Occupation and Resistance. The truth emerges that it was Jean's younger brother, François, who betrayed Robert, out of youthful selfishness and thoughtlessness. That might be forgiven but, though older now, François feels no remorse, and is simply afraid of being punished. Jean poisons him and passes off his death as suicide, since men like him have no part in the new France.

The final impression the novel leaves with its readers is curiously mixed. There is celebration of an Anglo-French European future: Adam and Elizabeth, the daughter of the French house, are clearly destined to marry, and live in England. Elizabeth's respect for the continuity of the home and the family, like Jean's coldly rationalist sense of justice, and pragmatic readiness to act in the name of progress, are qualities England needs, and England will temper the extremes of French reason with her traditional patience and tolerance (what Jameson would earlier have called apathy). But this Anglo-French future has been secured at a price, and it is France that is paying it. Murder in the name of the future, Adam thinks, is still murder. Jean must leave his home, and live the rest of his life outside the society he has helped create, wrestling with the meaning of what he has done, 'to *think* his act. To wrestle with his angel—or devil'. The language is taken from Malraux; for Jameson too, the hero of the post-war world is also of necessity a criminal.

If the French must kill for England and Europe, they must also live for them. Adam muses that lives only have a meaning in the stubborn attachment to one place, and decides that the commitment of the family to the traditional life of their valley 'drew [the] bitterness' from Jean's act.[24] Again, commitment comes at a price. Listening to the hidden river in the valley, that now carries the scent of the sea and the rumbles of distant change, Elizabeth glimpses the long tradition of self-sacrifice by which the women of her family have secured the continuation of the valley's life. Part of a new order, she can escape to England, but Marie, mother of the murdered Robert, remains, unable to forget or forgive. A luminous ending in which Marie opens a window to let in 'the valley, the Loire itself, solitude, and the light' can't disguise the dark undertones in Jameson's vision of the valley of tradition.[25]

What she says here is in stark contrast to the praise she had given ten years before to Kate Roberts's short story collection, *A Summer's Day*, which celebrated the modest lives of a hidden Welsh valley.[26] At the heart of the new Europe, it seems, there must be a dazzling vision of an iconic landscape of origins, a synthesis of light, community, and cultural tradition, but it will be a vision fixed in amber, created also of centuries of frustration and resentment. Jameson reinscribes in the landscape of France her formative perception of the northern communities of her childhood, Whitby and the moors behind it, closed and unchanging, the dream of home whose other face is nightmare. Few contemporary readers registered the political implications of this drama of family feeling. Understanding the valley of one's making is the precondition of the journey to a better future. But such understanding can also lead to a deep pessimism. Jameson continued to dream of a new Europe, while recognising the forces of old habit and feeling that worked against the prospects of change.

In April 1955, she fell seriously ill. She went into University College Hospital in the middle of the month for ten days' observation, and was still there on 6 May. She told Betty Leake, much later, that she had been in hospital for two months, and almost died of a lung embolism.[27] She was out by the beginning of July 1955, declaring herself still half-crippled and likely to be so for a long time.[28] Her leg was hugely swollen (for years, according to her grandson, she referred to it as 'Jumbo'), due to a botched operation for varicose veins. But she went on working. She attended the PEN Congress, and helped the divided Poles and the Germans begin talking to each other again. She was writing *The Intruder*, which she had begun in hospital. Not one of her best books, though it became another Book Society Choice, it revisits to no new effect old personal wounds that illness had perhaps reopened (the young wife, humiliated by a philandering and sadistic husband). It includes a gratuitous cameo based on Jules Romains, with sniping references to his visit to Goebbels in 1935 and his flight to New York to set up European PEN. The best of the novel is in the repeated sketches of the dry, bony landscape of the Provençal village in which it is set, and the set-piece evocation of the archaeological layers of its past. Jameson reiterates her act of faith in the enduring powers of the Greek humanist inheritance, and the European peasant, to absorb the barbarian conquerors. The intruder, history shows, always loses in the end, and humane values will triumph. She had the book ready for Peters to read by the end of the year, but it took another year to revise and complete it.[29]

In August, a Swedish publisher had paid a £75 advance for *The Hidden River*, and Italian sales of *The Green Man* produced royalties of £600 from the first six months—better, her agent wrote, than any other recent English book in Italy.[30] Commonwealth sales of the Book of the Month Club edition of *The Hidden River* (mostly in Canada) had earned royalties of £637 0s. 2d, and she received half of that.[31] By December 1955, the balance of her account with A. D. Peters was just over £1,800.[32] Burningford Hall Hotel was a welcome and affordable refuge that summer, and she also enjoyed a three-week break with Christopher in Scotland, in August, in a borrowed house (Innes Cottage, by Elgin, rented from the Tennant Estate, reputedly the destination of Hess's flight to England in 1940), where she engaged in a flurry of cooking and cleaning.[33] Her links with Barbara were being slowly remade. Her grandson was taught fishing and shooting by the estate gamekeeper in an attempt, he says, to make him a gentleman in spite of his West Riding antecedents. One afternoon, in the cottage garden, he almost shot his grandmother by mistake.

But by the end of the year, overwork and illness had again left her exhausted. She was struggling with Lovat Dickson at Macmillan, who was depressingly insistent that she was incapable of writing long novels, and with Carl Brandt, who was asking for major rewrites. She was, she told Peters, so easily discouraged, and the persistent lack of recognition was wearing: 'You know, I'm awfully bored with my position as the invisible aunt of English letters. No—I mean that I'm living through one of those pockets of being bored by it. I'd have been worse bored, I know, by a life spent making friends and influencing people.'[34] She scolded Irene Rathbone: 'You shouldn't have taken time off to write to John Lehmann. These people have no use for either of us, we are not IN anything, we don't give charming dinner parties, we don't exist.'[35]

In the New Year, there was an unpleasant moment when her first husband resurfaced, and David Carver reported to her that he had applied for membership of PEN. She wrote back from Burningford Hall Hotel on 18 January. He made up stories, she said, about his friendship with Churchill, and jobs he had carried out for the Privy Council and the Secret Service:

He will be silent for years and then out of the blue write me four or five immensely long letters, full of these fantastic stories, horribly facetious and vulgar, and often downright obscene. (He was brought up by strict Quaker parents, and the obscenity is a sort of reaction, I think.) [...] I shudder when I think that stories about me may be circulating, of a fantastic, vulgar or obscene kind, which naturally I shall never hear about.[36]

Carver sent her a copy of the bizarre letter Clarke sent to him a couple of days later, on 20 January.[37] The family, he claimed, was descended on the wrong side of the blanket from a fighting Bishop of Durham and the illegitimate son of a Duke, and Clarke confessed himself a bit of a lad. Jameson, he thought, would bear him out, even though he had been forced to divorce her.

In February 1956, the *Manchester Guardian* accepted a feature on the Chapmans' house-hunting problems. 'Somewhere to Live' was ideally pitched for middle-class sufferers from the current housing crisis. In April, she was looking for a good tax accountant, and writing to Peters that she had just set up a trust for her grandson's education at Westminster, Guy's old school, and was going to build a house.[38] The house was never built; owning her own house was always the least of Jameson's ambitions. Her lack of interest in cooking and cleaning was extreme to the point of loathing; Guy liked to be comfortable and eat well, and catering for his requirements interfered with her work. The two moved around a lot, following his various jobs as well as her PEN commitments. They liked to travel—weeks at a time in France, a year in the States. They got easily bored by most places in England, except London, which was expensive. Nevertheless, Jameson toyed regularly with the idea of buying a house. She had had the Whitby house in 1929, with its inspiring view onto the moors, which she sold when they moved back to London (with relief) for Guy to study at LSE. At the end of the 1930s, wartime exigencies had prompted them to move together with Do and her family to Mortimer, and for some time after the war it wasn't clear how big a house would be needed; she might have had to take in her sister's family. Choosing a house was, as it still is, a great bother, and buying was a big single expense she would rarely have been able to cover before 1956. Hotels, on the contrary, were not particularly costly at that time, and a very practical option. According to Christopher Storm-Clark, 'in an era when maids and waiters were paid very little, it was common for people to live permanently and at moderate cost in hotels (which is why many were so easily converted into care homes), and during and after the war, hotels offered some respite from rationing and queues. [...] plenty of American writers lived in hotels during the same period.'[39] When the Chapmans did eventually buy their retirement home in Cambridge, they regretted it bitterly.

At the end of July they were back in a London flat: Flat 2, Clive House, 5 Connaught Place, London W2.[40] 'Schweppes Towers', sited in a terrace facing the Marble Arch corner of Hyde Park, in a block for Schweppes executives, was provided at a very low rent by Sir Frederick Hooper, a fellow-member of Guy's in the Savile Club.[41] Their windows looked out across the Park, a notorious haunt of prostitutes, and a coffee stall; there was occasionally a skiffle band, and the barrage of noise from the London traffic prevented them from sleeping. But there was a hall-porter, formerly at the Savile Club, to look out for them, and Jameson loved it. '"I have never," said my wife, "known until now what it is to be a member of a well-found well-liked London club, or a company commander watched over by a discreet and experienced C.S.M."'[42] The delight was short-lived. Jameson returned from a two-week trip to Sweden with Christopher to see Guy into St Thomas's Home on 20 August for an operation for cancer that removed part of his left lung and left him better, but weak.[43] She took him to convalesce in the Parkhill Hotel, Lyndhurst, Hampshire, and then, over Christmas, to Portmeirion.

A dispute between Macmillan and A. D. Peters over the division of royalties for cheap Pan paperback editions of Jameson's novels, spilled over into January 1957. The agency dug in its heels, and the project was shelved.[44] The new market was enormous, but there was an important principle at stake, for both authors and publishers.

There was some consolation to come in the continuing success of *The Hidden River*, now adapted for play production in the United States by Ruth Goetz. It opened in New Haven on 2 January, and in New York on the 16th, and Peter cabled from New York on the 25th that it had an excellent reception, with good reviews in the *New York Times* and the *Tribune*.[45] The English version produced by David Pelham two years later was to be less successful, and Jameson's revision of the original script antagonised Mrs Goetz, who in her turn antagonised the actors, including Leo Genn and Catherine Lacey, and the production staff.[46] The novel went on selling throughout the year.

August 1957 was mostly spent in Switzerland. On 11 September they went to Princeton, where Guy enjoyed his association with the Institute for Advanced Study, and she decided she hated everything about the new America: the country seemed less stable, and more meretricious.[47] There was however the bonus of a meeting with two young academics, the critic and philosopher George Steiner and his wife Zara, a historian, with whom the Chapmans immediately struck up a friendship that was to last a lifetime.

'The Face of Treason': *A Cup of Tea for Mr Thorgill*

A Cup of Tea for Mr Thorgill came out in October, while they were in Princeton. Jameson had begun the novel at the end of 1955, and sent in the typescript to Margaret Stephens at the beginning of 1957.[48] In August, The American Book of the Month Club made it their November choice.[49] The *Sunday Times* and *Daily Mail* both liked it, as did the reviewer in the *TLS*—who didn't however see the relevance of Mr Thorgill, and missed, Jameson noted, the real significance of the book.[50] She was stupefied by its reception by some journalists, who only saw a slander on Oxford.[51] Mary Dilke, of Warner Brothers, had asked in the summer to see the novel with a view to assessing its potential as a film, but told the agency the material was too inflammable for them to handle.[52] Two years later, television drama producers were bolder. Associated Rediffusion broadcast 'The Face of Treason' on Tuesday 10 March 1959, at 8.30 p.m.

A Cup of Tea for Mr Thorgill was Jameson's most extensive discussion of Communist ideology and its implications for English society. When she began it, 'the doctrinal split of our time—between a militant communism and a liberalism gone in the tooth' seemed to her deep and incurable, a form of religious war that echoed that between early Christians and educated Romans in Roman Gaul.[53] By 1956, the larger force of the quarrel was gone. She should, she mused, have written it years before, and set it in France or Central Europe, with their murderous doctrinal passions. A version written in the first person, from the perspective of Gurney, the decent liberal Senior Tutor of the Oxford college where the action is set, was finished in April 1956. She began rewriting it in October in the third person, and finished it 23 December.[54] The shift of narrative perspective is crucial, leaving readers freer to choose whose perceptions they will embrace.

Even in the 1930s, rallying to the front against fascism, she had refused uncritical support of the Communist Party and its doctrines. She set out her indictment of Communism in the foreword she wrote in 1951 for the paperback edition of *The Diary of Anne Frank*. But she made reservations in particular cases. Arthur Calder-Marshall, for example, had always been a dear friend, and, she told David Carver, should be encouraged back into action in PEN: 'he is one of the most honest, decent men I know and very intelligent (and an ex-communist who knows their ways).'[55] In *Thorgill*, she was concerned only to assess how, in present-day England, different people had operated within and around the ideology, and what their experience meant for her own generation's ambitions for social change. She watched neither her back nor her tongue. In the original draft of her autobiography, she was explicit about one particular real-life resonance to her account:

I had written a novel, based on the religious split in our day between allegiance to a doctrine and a blind clinging to the past, which showed first of all the forms a religion can take in the human mind and heart, and secondly a vague memory of Csezlaw Milosz's experience here—how little understanding a renegade communist is likely to get from some of the persons he expects to applaud his repentance.[56]

Setting her novel in 1952, she drew the different kinds of Communist sympathisers to be found in the middle-class networks of Oxford and London: the fashionable fellow-travellers, the childish and naive, and those who see an opportunity for money and notoriety. Shockingly unkind and self-serving, all are simply butts of Jameson's acerbic satire, until suddenly an 'innocent' is hurt, and the story takes a different turn. Thomas Paget, an eminent Fellow of the College and the Party's undercover representative in Oxford, sets a sexual trap baited with an idealistic woman student, in order to discredit the Master's cousin, Miles Hudson, who has recanted his Party membership in a best-selling book. The harsh reality of Hetty's rape opens up dark perspectives the game-players could never see. Behind the gesturing comedians of the Oxford scene, and behind the national leadership of the Party, all stooges, stand the faceless men who organise Communist activity in the UK, and they link an unsuspecting England to the darkest forces of Eastern Europe.

Both the Oxford establishment and the Communist string-pullers are shown abusing their positions of authority to take advantage of the young, the underprivileged, and the weak. Nevil Rigden, the son of Frank and Sally, victims of the failure of the General Strike in *None Turn Back*, is the solitary working-class Fellow of the College. Musing on the reasons why people turn to Communism, he confesses that he himself was moved by anger at his own servility: 'Communism is a great many powerful things, not one. Among the rest, it's a religion for freed slaves.'[57] For the thug who was sent by the Party to murder him, the Party, he thinks, was also a means of regaining self-respect: 'All he wants, of course, is to be respected, and if he can't make himself valued, can't earn respect and admiration any other way, he'll do it by being as toughly ready to kill in private life—call it that—as he was when he was killing under licence as a commando.'[58]

Communism, the novel shows, feeds on social injustice. As long as working people are denied access to educational opportunities at every level, including the highest (Rigden, unlike the Master's cousin, is thrown out of the College when his former membership of the Party comes to light), the chances of social change without violent revolution are thin. With the death of Mr Thorgill, the old Yorkshireman and devoted WEA organiser, who makes two brief appearances and is paid off with his patronising cup of tea, the ambitions of Jameson's socialist generation seem to have run into sand.

Throughout the novel, Jameson's brilliant evocations of the sharply contrasting landscapes of England show the signs of a class war long since won, and the near-impossibility of challenging the limited scenarios of birth.[59] Against all odds, Nevil Rigden, who has travelled through all these places, engages himself at the end to return to the struggles of his origins, and heroically shoulders responsibility for cleansing the stinking slums he discovers in London:

He had to walk cautiously down the narrow uneven stairs. Here and there light of a sort came from a half-open door; various smells, quiescent at night, had stirred, rising from cracked rotten wood impregnated with dust, soot, the river damp in the walls, sweat, ash bins, an acid smell which seemed the breath itself of a house impossible to clean. He thought: what a place to begin thinking that life may possibly have a meaning.[60]

Rigden is persuaded to move to the North, still for Jameson the bastion of workers' freedom, to train and work, like the generations of Thorgill and Chapman, in the WEA. The miners he will teach there will presumably be those who will later engage in the resistance of the 1970s, and the last battles of the 1980s. In the meantime, the hopes of an England 'with only lower-middle-class ideas and wants' are left in the hands of a few decent administrators and educators, who know nothing of the plight of the English working class, or its consequences for the future of a country sliding none-too-gently into economic and political decline.[61]

Exile: The European Condition

The one person in Oxford capable of understanding the machinations of the Communist networks, and providing support for its victims, was the exiled Czech mathematician Vančura. Marginalised and barely tolerated in the College that had given him asylum, his insights into the operations of the international politics that pull England's strings are beyond the comprehension of his parochially-minded colleagues. The likes of Vančura, the exiles from fascism, and later Stalinism, who for over two decades had been part of England's social and cultural scene, began now to represent for Jameson sources of knowledge and understanding that might yet rescue England from its decay. In the process, they might also establish new horizons for England's internal exiles, Rigden, Hetty, and Jameson herself. Eastern Europeans, as Jameson commented in 1963, had learned to live in a far more dangerous world than that of middle-class England: 'Reality in England, even in the sixties, is not edged.'[62]

In her next important novel, *A Ulysses Too Many*, Jameson addressed the dilemmas of those refugees from Central Europe who were finding that the end of war by no means spelt an end to their troubles. Intellectuals who had escaped an antipathetic regime had to work through their feelings of responsibility, or guilt, towards the mass of their countrymen for whom leaving had not been an option. The tensions between those who left and those who stayed became more acute as the lines of the Cold War were drawn more tightly. Writers in exile, deprived of their audiences, and cut off from their native inspiration, found their creativity dry up.[63] The novel was an opportunity to make a statement not only about the politics of Europe but about the larger state of European writing—where exile, it would seem, was now the common condition.

The novel is the story of Nadzin, one of a group of Polish exiles who fought their way out of Warsaw and engaged in the wartime resistance. When the story begins in 1953, they are gathered in Nice to start up a political-literary journal to keep alive the flame of Polish nationalism in Europe, oppose Russia, and restore the Poland they knew before the war. Uniquely among the group, Nadzin returned to Poland straight after the war to help reconstruct his country. He exiled himself again in 1949, unable to countenance life under Russian domination. In the process, he now realises, he cut himself off from those who remained. He may once have been the best writer of his generation, but now his words are mere 'rhetoric', and he can say nothing to the new Poland: 'I found, yes, that I was beginning to write in the past—and why tell them less about their past than they know?'[64]

With a working title of *The Exiles*, the novel was begun in 1956 at Portmeirion, where the Chapmans spent two months shortly after Guy's illness.[65] Jameson started writing the day after 14-year-old Christopher left them, after a week's visit, and it is important that the novel is dedicated to him, of the generation that inherits this new world of exile. The first draft was finished in 1957, a month after Jameson, chairing an International Executive Committee of PEN, had helped block the abolition of the London Centre for German-speaking Writers Abroad, founded in 1933.[66] She acted, she said, out of pure sentiment; there was no real reason why, in 1957, Germans should be allowed to pose as exiles just because they preferred to live in London. The second version was sent to Macmillan in March 1958.[67]

Friendships with two very different kinds of exiles provided the insights out of which the novel was written. Of the many Poles who fled to London in wartime, the short story writer Maria Kuncewiczowa, who became a close friend, had tried to return to Warsaw—presumably against the advice of Jameson, who had been struck on her own post-war visit by the hostility of Poles who had stayed for those who had fled.[68] Back in London, she had asked Jameson in the summer of 1951 for help in finding funding to set up a PEN Centre for Exiled Writers. It included Poles, Czechs, Slovaks, Estonians, Catalans, Castilians, Hungarians, Russians, and Yugoslavians, and the definition of the exiled writer was generously cast: 'One who, were he to return to his country, would be in grave danger of denial of his human rights.'[69] The leadership of the Centre was later taken up by Paul Tabori.

When Tabori later put together a PEN anthology of writing from England's exiles, Jameson took the opportunity of the address she gave at the launch, broadcast on BBC radio, to emphasise the uniqueness of the present moment of cultural history, when exile was the commonest fate of European writers.[70] It was difficult, she argued, for an English writer to appreciate the pain of linguistic as well as geographical disjunction, which could, however, be of great value to the exile's adopted country, as a source of intellectual and aesthetic renewal. Young writers could develop new habits of mind, as did Joseph Conrad, 'young enough to be able as he was to force ancestral and childhood memories into an alien tongue without losing any of their depth'. Older writers, unable to transplant their poetic inspiration into new soil, must be translated, and their new public must listen to the sharp insights they give into the past before the war, in order to see the hazards of their own future more clearly. The voices of writers 'from the other side of Europe, the dark side' were warning of the emergence of a new issue in the world, the 'almost religious fear of freedom', and 'the religion of the closed mind'.

Of those many voices, the one that at this time concerned Jameson most was the poet Czeslaw Milosz. Milosz, who had stayed to fight in the Polish Resistance, and after the war tried initially to work with the Communist regime, was a late self-exile who encountered suspicion from all camps. It was his position that Jameson found most sympathetic, and his struggles to resituate himself both as poet and as citizen of a new global community, that must have helped inspire her new book.

What most appealed to Jameson in Milosz, from the moment of their first meeting in Cracow just after the war, was the enthusiasm of his newly liberated generation, and their determination to snatch a future from the ruins.[71] During the Occupation he had taught himself English, and translated Eliot's 'The Waste Land', with the aim, she noted with approval, not of imitating Eliot, but finding his own way of saying something new, for ruined Poland.[72]

They met several times after that, once in London, as he passed through with his wife Janka to take up a post of cultural attaché in Washington, and then again during her year in Pittsburgh, in Washington, in 1948, where she was visiting Maxine Davis and he was asked to dinner.[73] She put him in touch with other friends, and they remained in correspondence. In July 1951 she wrote about his tribulations to Lovat Dickson, expressing her hope that Macmillan would publish *Murti Bing*, and offering to send drafts: 'My firm belief is that he is an extremely important weapon in the hands of the West, if the West likes to use him.'[74] *Murti Bing*, she told Lovat Dickson, had already appeared in the July issue of *Twentieth Century*, and was the second chapter of the book Milosz was currently writing, which was a major attack on the doctrine of historical necessity.[75] She wrote again a few weeks later, describing the book as 'a psychological etc study of the communist faith, an effort to destroy it for intelligent young men'.[76]

They met again, in London, in spring 1952, when Milosz was sponsored to lecture by the Society for Cultural Freedom, and in January 1953, when they had lunch together.[77] In Paris, in March 1953, Milosz took her to dinner in the Place de l'Odéon, and told her he had left Warsaw for Paris, and was now trying to obtain a visa to go back to America and his family. She records having written many letters to American writers and politicians on his behalf, none of whom would intervene in the current (McCarthyite) political atmosphere.[78] In April, she asked David Carver to help get money from the States to get Milosz's poems published in *Kultura*, the monthly revue of free Poles published in Paris.[79] Their next recorded meeting was in July 1956, at the London PEN Congress, as Jameson was finishing *Thorgill*. She took pleasure in engineering a reconciliation between Milosz, over from Paris, and Antoni Slonimiski, the poet and friend of long standing, who had returned permanently to Warsaw.[80]

In the novel, she attacked the wartime exiles who thought they had truths to teach to those who stayed. There was no likelihood of a revolution against

Communism in Poland, and if any arose, they couldn't lead it. They were caught in a time warp with their 'fossilised nationalism', fighting old battles and confusing national with personal interests.[81] The best their journal could do, according to Nadzin, would be to 'try and discover and make maps of the new Poland forming below the ice—now'.[82] The people who stayed will free themselves.

Commendation is reserved for the man who is trying to find the words to write in exile. This is a process of creating a new country, working entirely in the present, for the future, together with other exiles from countries all across Europe, out of whatever arid landscape you may find yourself in. Of the past, Nadzin decides, only one thing is worth memorialising, the suffering of the victims:

There is only one thing worth repeating, he thought, one pattern, the common pattern of our time: broken houses, fear, the torn bodies of children, the piles of women's dresses and shoes neatly docketed in the sheds of death camps, the mass graves, deportations, exile, exile....[83]

Exile is not just an accidental geographical positioning but a moral choice, the recognition that to be human is to be in exile:

We're all exiles, being pulled backwards to a void—and those of us who crowd into the rotten holds of ships, to be turned back from the safety of harbours and to sink in a dark sea with the little bodies of terrified children slipping through our fingers, are simply living at the limit of the situation. How long before I can write about it clearly, in exact words—so exact that they force the attention of boredom and ignorance—and without bitterness?[84]

The exiled Poles safe in Nice can afford to express scepticism about the future of Europe, and the hope that a new kind of politics, transcending nationalism, might offer their country. Nadzin, speaking for the people living in Central and Eastern Europe, on the edge of disaster, sees a transformed, united Europe as the only hope:

I hope for Europe, for the death and resurrection of Europe. You—and all like you—if you get the chance, will accentuate the divisions in Europe, inflame all its mortal nationalisms. You'll do it even though the only chance—chance, not certainty, not even probability—for us is a Europe with one mind, one purpose, one dream.[85]

Even at this stage of the Cold War, and for all the hostility she expressed in *Thorgill* to the operations of the Stalinist machine, Jameson remained clear that the kind of Europe she had in mind was still fired by the anti-capitalism of Class 1914. Nadzin makes his allegiance equally plain:

I loathe Communism. I loathe a Russian official worse than any other sort, I loathe the whole police knife-machine [...] But that doesn't make me love *your* Poland, the Poland of the landowners, of the dead past.[86]

In July 1958, the month after the Russian invasion of Hungary, there was a pleasant visit to Portmeirion, unchanged except that it was 'more and more cluttered with the haut monde of Edgbaston and Birmingham and Liverpool and Manchester'.[87] In the late summer, the Chapmans went out to Las Palmas to wave off Bill, Ruth, and his family on their yachting trip across the Atlantic to Barbados—an absence that became protracted into stormy months without news.[88]

Writing through her anxiety, Jameson completed *The Road from the Monument*, which went to Macmillan in January.[89] There was an abortive period of flat-hunting in Brighton at the beginning of 1959, followed, after the triumphant return of Bill and family, by the dismal prospect of going to live in Portmeirion.[90] But at the end of the year, she was still in Clive House, and happily engaged in finishing *Last Score*.[91]

By the end of the 1950s, she seemed set for continuing fame, at home and internationally. Then the 1960s began, and she joined the exiles.

20

1960–1968: Letting Go and Settling Up

Finishing with PEN

Jameson's position in PEN after resigning the presidency was ambiguous. She was the English member of the small committee of international vice-presidents, whose powers were undefined. She was still attached to the interests of the exiles (Robert Neumann, according to his wife Rolly, said it was out of a sense of guilt).[1] She kept a hand in PEN's Central and Eastern European business. In 1960, there were letters from the General Secretary of the Hungarian PEN Club, in connection with a resolution from the Hungarian Centre, in which he expressed his hopes for an end to the isolation of his country since 1957, and gently took her to task for the fear of Communism and the Soviet Union expressed by the characters of *The Hidden River*.[2] On 10 June, Jameson wrote to David Carver supporting the renewal of links with the Russians, and arguing that they should be allowed in as observers, to help current moves to encourage them towards the West and away from China.[3] In May 1961, she was asked to chair the International Finance Committee.[4]

But the pressures of writing, and family problems, weakened her PEN connections. In June 1959, she couldn't make a trip to Frankfurt because she needed the money for Bill, who had job problems.[5] In 1960, she couldn't go to Brazil, partly because of the expense, partly because Winifred was coming on 1 May to stay for four months.[6] A month later, she wrote ruefully: 'I am nearly as distracted by my sister as if she were a score of Brazilians. Incessant cooking, incessant chatter, breakfasts in bed (but that is easy), Sunday Times, preparations or the bungalow project [...] Americans with letters of introduction, I feel like a merry-go-round that someone has forgotten to switch off.'[7]

In 1961, Rome was out, because she had to look after the youngest grandchild in October for three weeks so Bill and Patchen could go to Bermuda for a rest.[8] In 1963, she couldn't come to Reims because Winifred had had a nervous breakdown and she had paid her New York doctor's bills.[9] She gave up the job of permanent delegate to the International Committee in October 1962. She remained however on the Prisoners Committee and the translations project, and in 1966, she was still receiving audited accounts from David Carver, reporting how well PEN was doing with money from the UNESCO connection.[10] She and Guy were both guests of honour at the Oslo Congress in 1964.[11]

It was her choice, but she was still disconcerted by the speed with which she slipped from public sight. Beginning the chapter of *Journey from the North* dated 17 November 1961, she recorded that on the previous day she had taken the chair at the fortieth anniversary dinner of International PEN, listened to the speaker toasting the distinguished women writers present and naming Veronica

Figure 22 Bill's second wife, Patchen, and their daughters Frances and Troy, on holiday in the New Forest, one summer in the early 1960s. 'We enjoyed picnics and outings in the Dormobile but were much less keen on camping overnight. The parents slept in the body of the van, while Troy and I were stretched on racks under the hinged roof: cold, with condensation dripping on us!' (Frances Storm-Clark).

Wedgwood, Rebecca West, and Rosamund Lehmann, and was for the first time forced to deal in public with 'my own invisibility'.[12] Relations between herself and the young men of London letters were reaching their nadir. For a decade, a number of *TLS* reviewers had produced short, often waspish accounts of her novels.[13] Another generation had new interests, and the stylistic subtleties Jameson brought to the realist mode were by and large invisible to those who were keener to demonstrate their affinity for the elitist games being played in the *nouveau roman*. The fortnightly novel reviews she produced for the *Sunday Times* between April and September 1960 demonstrate how far she was drifting away from contemporary fashion. She accepted the contract out of financial necessity, just before hearing of a lucrative serialisation offer from the *Saturday Post*, and bitterly resented being tied to reading books she considered deeply bad.[14]

The lease on the Clive House flat ended in June 1960, and the usual long struggle to find suitable accommodation ended with the Chapmans settled in a totally uncongenial bungalow with inadequate room for books. Tiberias Lodge, where they moved in November, was situated in Prinsted, near Emsworth, in Hampshire, and its only advantage was its closeness to Bill's yacht. She wrote at length to Phyllis Bottome, lamenting the cold, all the cooking, and the loss of London's life:

This place is an error—but then, if I had said so before we came, Guy would always have thought of it as a paradise I cheated him of, poor Guy. Now, alas, he realises that life without the London Library, the Reading Room of the BM, theatres, French films, concerts, is no good to him. [...] We shall have to move again, an effort I do really dread, coward that I am. [...] I am cooking seven dinners every week—and seven luncheons. Now, I have made myself a good cook, and I hate it so fantastically that I cannot understand why my soufflés and casseroles don't poison the people who eat them! Also, which is serious, I no longer have enough energy for two lives, that of cook and writer. I think we must quickly find a flat in London which I can afford to buy—rents are far far beyond me—where at least there is a hope of a cook. Now and then Guy says: Why not Cambridge? But all those dons' wives alarm me.[15]

Last Score: The Imperialist Charade

1961 saw the publication of *Last Score*, which, thanks to Carol Hill, had already earned 30,000 dollars for serialisation in the *Saturday Evening Post*.[16] But it had had some rather poor English reviews. Jameson had mentioned earlier in the year to Phyllis Bottome how hurt she felt by the 'unkind' criticism that now followed all her books: 'At a deep level I do not mind, but there is quite a long way to go before I reach that deep level and all the way I feel disgraced.'[17]

She had started writing on 14 August 1959, soon after Britain agreed the future independence of Cyprus (February 1959) and allowed Archbishop Makarios to come back from exile (March). The third and final draft was finished in January 1960.[18] On August 16 1960, Makarios became first President of the independent Republic of Cyprus, and several reviewers assumed that the novel was set there.[19] Lovat Dickson certainly thought the setting was obvious, though he dismissed the idea that there were any similarities between Jameson's Governor, Ormston, and either Sir John Harding or Sir Hugh Foot, or between her fictional rebel leader and George Grivas, who led the Greek Cypriot terrorist organisation EOKA during the 1950s.[20]

But the novel's epigraph is clear. The colony is an imagined space, in which Jameson has represented the generic shapes of oppression: 'All revolts against what can be represented as an occupying force follow the same unhappy pattern and take the same disconcerting shapes.' The same applies to the characters: 'The events related are a vehicle for an account of the workings of that strange organ, the human heart.'

For the dust jacket, Jameson suggested something innocuous and discreet: 'A simple line drawing of an Algerian city?'[21] The revelations by a young French recruit of the use of torture by the French army in Algeria had appeared in France in February 1957 (*Le Dossier Jean Muller*). Henri Alleg's *La Question*, with Sartre's Preface, was published in 1958, in both French and English. But Britain's own treatment of her colonial subjects was wide open to criticism. In 1943, when Gandhi was arrested, Jameson had written to Ould:

Gandhi is going to survive, I hope and pray. I think we ought to have let him out the first day, just to prevent his becoming a rallying cry for ever. But I suppose it is just impossible to give way to him whenever he adopt [sic] this method. The whole India business is another nightmare. I do wish we didn't beat people, I can't think of any excuse for that sort of horror. The Indians are as impossible as the Irish, and we are mishandling the whole business. I think the British Empire is doomed—hubris.[22]

As recently as May 1952, she had tried, unsuccessfully, to deal with the aftermath of decolonisation in South America in *The Gamble*. She knew far more of the hearts and minds of the men and women who maintained British rule in Cyprus, and on her holiday with Bill and his family in 1954, she had been filled with excitement by the landscape:

I've seen the coast of Turkey, but not yet the mountains of the Lebanon. This is further East than I've been before, and I never smelled jasmine so strongly before, or saw so much old dust and bones of hills, or minarets against a blazing blue sky.[23]

In this exploration of the interactions of politics and the human heart, Jameson's main theme is the shaping force of cruelty within Western imperialism, and within that, the particular role of torture, and its repercussions for both torturer and victim. *Last Score*, subtitled *The Private Life of Sir Richard Ormston*, evokes the arrogance with which the representatives of the Western powers use the countries they occupy as stages for their private dramas. Jameson sets aside the historical specificity of the military and economic interests of the occupier, and the local motives for terrorist challenges. The situation is generic. The Governor represents an empire in decline, that since the First World War has lost its power to act to new Great Powers—America, Russia, and on the horizon, China—but still pretends to play a protective role in relation to the smaller countries it has colonised.[24] Gouraud, the old Frenchman, a rich amateur archaeologist, has seen the self-repeating structure in many times and places:

Often when I wake up—I wake early, old people do, you know—I don't recall at once whether I'm in Greece, Cyprus, North Africa. It could be any country where the dust is less mineral than human, dust of the uncounted generations of the dead [...]. You English are merely the latest invaders, the latest carriers of ideas which the sun and the poverty will rot. You won't be the last.[25]

Freedom and exploitation are here studied in terms of the psychology of competition and private ambition. Even the local revolt is a product of personal rivalries within the occupying power. Its leader, Tony Boyd, is an old rival of the Governor, and the Governor is sleeping with Boyd's wife.

In the race to make the last score, the local population is reduced to at best a side-show, individual faces glimpsed only briefly, expressing impotent hate; at worst, all individuality vanishes into a backdrop of darkness or decomposition.[26] In the landscape of colonisation, marked everywhere by brutish violence, the space of power is reduced to the claustrophobic cell in the depths of police headquarters, where the Governor who has given the order for torture confronts his victim. In the end, both men have lost, and in the process the charade of values by which Western imperialism has imposed its authority—

freedom, justice, humanity—is exposed. The son's contempt for his father, as he leaves the family home ('You order other people to act like—like animals, and you, you keep your gloves on. It…it's the most contemptible thing I've ever heard'),[27] spells the end of a world that has outlived its time—and the hope, perhaps, of some new start to be made.

Journey from the North: Writing a Substitute for Life

In the April of 1961, the Chapmans went on holiday to Greece for the first time.[28] In July, they were staying in Cambridge with the Commagers, and making plans to go for three weeks in Austria at the beginning of September with Christopher, who had just finished his first year as an Exhibitioner at Peterhouse. But a new edition of *The Journal of Mary Hervey Russell* that Macmillan had finally been persuaded to reprint was not well received. The following year, *The Road from the Monument* was published to very bad reviews and, after the poor reception of *Last Score*, that was a blow that shattered Jameson's confidence in her ability to write long and difficult novels.[29]

The disappointment must have been greater because of the new layers of autobiographical confession she had built into the character of Gregory Mott. The admired writer, respected for his leadership of one of London's most important cultural institutions, who suddenly realises how much he has lost of his youthful ideals and ambitions, and how many loved ones he has betrayed in his struggle for fame, is Jameson herself. He shares her feeling of hollowness, left with nothing but writing and memories to justify an existence, and no way apparent to get off the monument, forward or back:

He did not want to see Danesacre again. Certain moments, certain fragments of the little town—the level rays of a setting sun embracing the old grave-stones, wrinkled by the sea wind and salt, their names obliterated, on the cliff-top; [...] the bare north-ward-curving cliffs of the coast—were caught in his mind like leaves frozen into the ice of a lake. They existed nowhere else now. If, hoping to find them there, he returned to Danesacre, the reality would efface a gleam, a salt air, a curve, all the fragments that he hoped, when his time came, to take with him into the dark.

[...] A man may suddenly become aware that he is mortally ill, he has a cancer: in exactly the same way Gregory knew, in his body, in the cells of his brain, instantly, that his existence was a silly cheat.[30]

Private misery was compounded by unending public disasters. In April 1961, the US-backed invasion by right-wing dissidents of Castro's Cuba, at the Bay of Pigs, ended in serious embarrassment for the Kennedy administration, and the world became immensely more dangerous. The American newspapers Jameson picked up at the Commagers in July terrified her with their assumption that war was imminent and inevitable.[31] In the autumn of 1962, the confrontation between the US and the USSR over the Russian missile bases discovered in Cuba was indeed to put the world on the brink of war. In July 1961, Harold Macmillan announced that negotiations were under way for Britain's entry into the European Economic Community, a step towards European unity; in 1963, de Gaulle's veto would bring about Britain's rejection.

This was the context, a period of immense personal and public anxieties, in which Jameson wrote the first draft of her autobiography, *Journey from the North*, begun in 1960, and finished some time in 1965.[32] Life was going very wrong. In the uncut typescript, a reference to the 'business of living' that was holding up the finishing of one of James Hill's novels provoked a marginal addition:

As things have fallen out since, this business of living has become infinitely more difficult. Today—May 20 1964—I am living and driving myself to write this book without help of any sort. It is no one's fault but my own. This should console me a little—and does.[33]

And Jameson wondered how, now in her sixties, she could continue to find the energy to live three lives in one. There was, she concluded, no option, since one couldn't live a life without other people.

In its first draft, *Journey from the North* was an attempt to exorcise returning childish fears of humiliation and rejection. The cool meditation on memory that opens the published work was in the original a highly personal confession. The first chapter opened:

Can I write about my life without giving away a great many things I have spent a lifetime concealing, my fear of being laughed at, or being thought emotional, of boring people, and the humiliation (replaced by 'momentary disgrace') I feel when, as happens now every time I publish a book, I am damned by critics as accomplished or as a professional?[34]

Conflict between personal desires and ambitions, and family responsibilities, was always going to be a central, and painful theme. She dwelt on the conflict between her own unspeakable instincts (presumably her violently selfish ambition, as much as her craving for sexual freedom) and the sense of responsibility imposed by her mother; and she played with the notion of how much less treacherous she might have felt had she not taken on new responsibilities to a husband and a child.[35]

The personal is still balanced with the political, but the politics at this point have a slightly different emphasis. America's dangerous games with the stability of the world, cut to a passing phrase in the published version (a vague reference to the problems of living 'in a world so sharply menaced by destruction as ours') merited in the original a page-long meditation on America's phobia of Communism, and the urgent need to write against that:

The nicest Americans are nuts about communism.

A letter I received today, Monday 14th August, has lessened my qualms about this book. Written by an American woman, the kindest in the world, generous, warm-hearted, sensible, it runs: 'I think we should make a stand now, before communism takes over the whole world. If you study it and find out what it is, you feel that you are confronting the Devil himself, undiluted evil. I myself prefer death to communism. And I feel that way, too, about my children and grandchildren. Would you want to live in a world dominated by Russians?'...[36]

Jameson's answer was no, but, she went on, she was horrified by a mentality that could condemn children and the unborn to death, rather than let them take their own chance for happiness. If America's ruling powers thought the same, what hope was there for the world?[37]

But it is the future of Europe, and the nature of European influence in the world, that emerges in both drafts, coming to the foreground as the narrative moves through and beyond the Second World War, and poses the options: should Europe unite, be Americanised, or go over to Communism, and which of these might be most, or least, bearable? In the last analysis, the option is a united Europe, and the second volume ends with a flurry of European places and people, from the burning white light of Greece, the oldest part of the common heritage, to France and the best of the moderns, Stendhal, Valéry, Malraux, the great advocates of Europe.

Those closing pages confirm in one sense the emptiness in which Jameson now feels she finds herself ('The raw nerve-ends of our time are all outside England'),[38] but she had come to terms, in writing at least, with who she was, and who she might yet be. The autobiographical journey ends in one of the earliest, and best, memories of place from her Whitby childhood: the narrow passage of Park Terrace, opening onto the road out to the harbour. Gregory Mott made the same decision. He abandoned his stale present because he no longer understood how he had got there, or what he was doing, denouncing

'The sediment of life in this house possessed by the past as a savage by his fetish', and went back to Danesacre to fulfil a need for judgement and, perhaps, to let his future find itself afresh.[39] By the time Jameson had finished the second draft of her autobiography, published at the end of the decade, the problems of the past, personal and public, were rewritten as the challenges of the future. In July 1965, she told Irene Rathbone, she was turning out her papers so as to destroy as many as possible before she died.[40] This must, though she didn't say it, have felt like a beneficent settling of accounts with the past.

What began as a text for herself turned inexorably, like all her work, into a communication to others. She sent the first typescript draft of the first volume to friends to read. She told Basil Liddell Hart that George Steiner, A. D. Peters, and Elizabeth Crawshay-Williams had been the first to comment.[41] She sent it to Liddell Hart on 2 August 1965, and both he and his wife Kathleen liked it immensely.[42] The comments from the first set of readers provoked from her a vexed paragraph in the second volume (cut from the published version) on her determination to finish what she had started, despite others' lack of understanding. Of the four friends who had seen the first volume, one, a woman, had liked it, but:

The others were profoundly shocked. Not one of these three men has so much as a suspicion of the gulf that separates the effort to be truthful from the easier effort of writing to make a pleasant impression. It is frightful—I am surrounded by English gentlemen. Perhaps I should leave the manuscript to a great-grandchild.[43]

There followed immediately a lengthy quotation from a letter written by Maria Kuncewiczowa, giving her own view of Jameson, who couldn't, she said, recognise that version of herself at all. That section was also cut.

The readers were fairly unanimous in identifying Jameson's obsessive self-flagellation as an obstacle to the reader's engagement; as Liddell Hart pointed out, it could become wearisome.[44] The confessions of guilt were toned down in the rewritten version, as were the charges of sadism she levelled against her mother and first husband, to which she attributed her lifelong sense of inferiority. Titbits of scandal, with names attached, were cut, acid comments on the likes of Jules Romains were trimmed, and problems with Barbara and Bill, and Valentine Dobrée, were treated with more discretion. The personal question was still posed: what's the truth about myself? But the reduction of so much specific detail and personal observations played down the importance of the private self, and left the stage freer for Jameson's two other lives, as political activist, and writer. Autobiography turned towards memoir. Slight structural changes shifted the long opposition of France and Germany to the foreground, and the timeline of writing in the 1960s, threaded through the narrative of remembering, resituated that opposition into its contemporary context: the making of a new European polity. Most important of all was her concern with modelling the creative process—a special kind of writing—which is the formation of selfhood.

The chief truth about myself, this autobiography says, is what I write about myself: what I remember, by choice or perforce, where I remember it from, and how I write it out. I am many persons, and personas: mother's daughter, wife of two husbands, mother and grandmother, Daisy Jameson and Margaret; Storm Jameson the novelist, William Lamb and James Hill; Hervey Russell and Gregory Mott; the admirer of Orage and Malraux, the opponent of Jules Romains and the young men who write for the London papers; the President of PEN, whose personality vanished into committees and letter-writing, and the friend of Central Europe's refugees. I am the old woman of the last pages who merges with the child of the first, so that everything always begins again, and holds together.

The published account opens with a chapter on writing a life, which puts forward remembering, or rather, recalling, piecing together, summoning back, saying again, and saying it differently, as the process that is the origin of perceived identity. These are the operations of cultural memory that Jameson had evoked in her novels from *The World Ends* to *The Green Man*, and they had been the constituting characteristic of all her fictional characters from *The Pitiful Wife* to *The Road from the Monument*. They are also the familiar techniques of autobiography, practised and explained at length by writers from Montaigne to Gide (both evoked in *Journey from the North*), and Jameson had herself exploited them in her first autobiography, and pointed out their operations to her reader.[45] Neither reviewers nor readers seem to have recognised the highly modern, and modernist, representation of subjectivity that shapes the work. Both, however, were to acknowledge it as a consummate synthetic account of what it was to live through the first half of the twentieth century. Jameson here achieved her parallel, in writing, to what the musician-hero of *No Victory for the Soldier* had achieved in his form, transforming personal experience into the generic.

The plethora of literary references in the epigraphs to each section and in the text itself is a key part of the machinery that turns Jameson's life into a mirror for others. The everyday personal experience of a lived half-century is embedded in a cultural heritage assumed familiar, at least as much European as English, and most of all, French. Significantly, the closing pages of her narrative find room to mention one of the most important of her French counterparts, Sartre, the contemporary whose likeness to herself she is least willing to recognise.[46] Hard after the section in which he appears, she embarks on a discussion of her own lifelong passion for words, and its consequences. The 'masks' that words constitute, as they create the 'Doubles' of feeling, eventually become a substitute for the writer's own personality.

This double self, the subject dissolved into words, and the problem of its good or bad faith, which is the leitmotif of her autobiography, is the Sartrean subject that he evoked in his own much shorter autobiography, *Les Mots*, published in French in 1963, and translated into English in 1964—though Jameson needed no translation. She had no need of Sartre's example to recognise the double-sided nature of the writer's personality. The relation between experience and the words of its representation were her own long-standing preoccupation, and she could as easily have referred to her older love, Stendhal, for his handling of the same problem.[47] But the acknowledgement given here to the Sartrean subject renewed her own insights in a language another generation could hear:

The struggle in which I have spent my life is a substitute for living—my writing a substitute for life. And since there is no such thing, I don't live. I am among those present.

Nor did I guess that I had begun to use words as a defence, setting up, in front of the alien hostile 'real' world, another, more submissive, more tolerable, made entirely of language.

The mere act of writing, of turning pain, grief, joy, and the rest, into words, creates the doubles of these feelings, so that with enjoyment and pain the writer continually places between himself and reality another, a charming or dreadful mask.. [...] Between me and 'my' words, there is an empty space of dissatisfaction, failure, absence, nostalgia for a lost unseizable living self. And this regret is as near as I shall ever get to it.[48]

In *No Time Like the Present*, the autobiographical voice had also spoken both for itself, and for others. Bonamy Dobrée described how the directness of the address demanded from the reader a response to the ideas that were expressed:

For that is one of the qualities of this book, the sense she gets into it that what she talks about affects you profoundly; you have got to react, you have got to sit up and ask, 'And what am I doing?' Damn her! Here was I thinking I was going to pass a few happy hours enjoying vicarious pleasures, and vicarious suffering, in reading about her life.

327

But no; her life is in a sense my life, and your life, too, ungentle reader! It is because it is an amazingly vivid, astonishingly honest autobiography that it has this effect. [...] It is literature because it is life seen through the lens of a mind intensely alive.[49]

For the average reader of the early 1930s, literature and life were not separate realms, and Dobrée could characterise that written voice as entirely 'natural', and praise 'the impression of a person speaking to us in a living voice, the voice natural to a person of her knowledge and insight; it is as well the voice of her own generation, the generation that grew up just in time to be given the war by its proud parents.'[50] In complete contrast, the *Journal of Mary Hervey Russell* was composed as an exercise in creating distinctively aesthetic 'truths'. In a section cut from the published version of *Journey from the North*, Jameson contrasted the treatment she gave in both books to the same incidents. In the *Journal*, she hadn't been trying 'as now I am, to be nakedly truthful, [...] ruthlessly sceptical about myself [...]. I took up a position in the middle distance and let myself speculate about events <u>not</u> as if I were responsible (guilty), heart and soul, but as if I had the right to guard myself: protected like a fencer, I made gestures in the direction of the truth.'[51] In the published text, she describes how she wrote the *Journal* like one might write a poem. The words and the images rose to the surface and created their own connections, and her function as writer was to recognise their 'consanguinity': 'I did not let myself go, and my mind was invaded by phrases like a torrent of swifts fighting for a claw-hold in the ruins of a house.'[52]

Beyond both texts, *Journey from the North* acknowledges that what a reader will call a living, natural voice is always an effect of art. The publication of the first volume of the book, in October 1969, would be greeted by a deluge of admiring reviews as a writerly tour de force,[53] as well as a flood of private letters from long-lost family members, and friends past and present from Yorkshire and from London, all saying yes, that was exactly how it was, and how they remembered it too.

Hanging On

Before that moment came, there was the rest of an unforgiving decade to endure.

In August 1962, the hated Tiberias Lodge was sold, they had chosen a home in Cambridge, and they were waiting for it to be built.[54] It took however more than the year originally expected before it was ready.[55] It was the spring of 1965 before the Chapmans were installed at 11 Larchfield, in the Barton Road. It was a fourth floor flat, right at the top of the building, and there was no lift; the rooms were small, and it was not well-proofed against Cambridge cold and damp. But Guy would have dining rights at Churchill and Peterhouse, and there were the libraries, well-placed for visitors and visiting.

The house was the least of their worries. Jameson wrote her autobiography against a background of personal tragedies and writing flops. At the beginning of 1963, she published *A Month Soon Goes*, little more than a potboiler. She was suffering acutely from the rheumatism in her hands. She went to Dax, the French spa, in May 1963 to get her hands sorted out (and put the town into *The Early Life of Stephen Hind*). On her return, news was filtering through of the death of Lilo Linke, who had reinvigorated her political vision in the early 1930s, introduced her to the socialists of Berlin and Paris, and been a loyal and honest friend throughout the war years. Working as an important member of UNESCO, making regular visits to South America, Lilo had died on a plane between Athens and London. It took a long and anxious time to unravel the exact circumstances of her death. In the summer of 1963, Macmillan refused to reissue *No Victory for the Soldier* under Jameson's real name, and she was angry and disappointed.[56] Money was a perennial problem, partly because of the cost of waiting for the Cambridge house to be finished; but even when current income was healthy (US serialisation, for example, helped a lot in 1963), she was always anxious about the prospects for the following year. In October 1963, she had offers to purchase her manuscripts, and with Peters' help and advice, she eventually sold the large collection of manuscripts that is now lodged in the Harry Ransom Humanities Research Center, in the University of Texas at Austin.[57] *The Aristide Case* appeared in the spring of 1964, and was noted by reviewers in passing. In 1965, Bill was diagnosed with angina and lost his flying licence, and the following year, he had a coronary thrombosis.[58]

A visit to Portugal just before Christmas of 1965 was a welcome break[59] Back in England, Jameson's popularity was as low as ever. In the summer of 1966, Marigold Johnson reviewed *The Early Life of Stephen Hind*, and tore the novel apart. She praised its ingenious plot twists, lively characters, and varied social scene, but condemned its tidiness, its assiduous disposal of loose ends in the plot, and its general failure to observe the current fashions of form. It was a work out of time, impervious to the little shocks of reality which it has become almost a necessity for the novelist to convey: however up-to-the-minute the material may be, what is striking is the irrelevancy of Miss Jameson's novel to the experience even a Stephen Hind is likely to live through here and now.[60]

Friends wrote consolingly. She kept a letter from Margaret Lane, who said she and Elizabeth Jenkins had had the same problem. It seemed to be a necessary stage on the way to becoming one of the Grand Old Men of writing—and in any case, brutality nowadays was the critical fashion.[61]

Jameson was not herself above enjoying brutality when it was applied to others. The following year, 1967, David Carver wrote to her about the scandal exposed in the *Washington Post* concerning CIA money which had been channelled into International PEN in 1965. The International Writers' Fund, he said, had received money from tainted sources, though neither Paul Tabori nor he himself had known about it, and PEN itself had not been involved.[62] She wrote back joyfully, expressing her pleasure that Stephen Spender and Frank Kermode had been frustrated in their attempt to use the similar scandal with *Encounter* to get control of the journal. She thought the influence of the CIA still lingered on there, but much reduced, and added ironically that she thought the Agency should be thanked for enabling one good English journal to survive.[63]

At the other end of the political spectrum, a very different kind of action caught her attention. Letters from André Buffard, who taught at the Ecole des Mines and was the Chapmans' oldest French friend, introduced long ago by Lilo Linke, kept her in touch with the doings of a rising student generation whose rage matched that of the Eikonoklasts. In June 1967, he drew to her attention the rising feeling in France over the events in Berkeley. In May 1968, he wrote with excitement of the young people who were breaking through the old bourgeois interests and hypocrisies, enclosing a copy of the letter he had written to *Le Monde* denouncing police brutality to students, and an extract from *Le Canard Enchaîné*.[64]

21

Final Recall

The year 1969 began well, with a fairytale holiday over Christmas and the New Year in a country house thirty miles from Palma, spent with Henry Steele Commager and, she told the Liddell Harts with glee, a lot of other rich people.[1] But there was unhappy news in the summer, when a telegram came from Christopher in York that his mother was dying. Barbara was buried on 11 June. Jameson shared Christopher's grief, and he for his part always remembered that she came and sat with his mother during her last illness.[2]

The Chimney of Ambition

Journey from the North was published in September 1969. The reviews pleased Jameson, as did the television interview she recorded for half an hour on 1 October.[3] A colleague who had worked for her at Knopf in the inter-war years wrote to say she had seen Jameson on television in *Late Night Line Up*, and remembered that after an illness Jameson had bought her a warm coat with a fur collar, sent her fruit for lunch, and sent her for artificial sun baths.[4] She received many letters from people who had lost touch over the years: Gallilee relatives, old friends from student days in Leeds, and old writing friends (Frank Swinnerton, Noel Streatfeild). Archie White wrote, wondering how Winifred would feel at being so little mentioned, and Sydney Harland, who was still living in Snainton.

In the spring of the following year, there were two radio interviews. On Radio 4 on 3 March 1970, the presenter was a man of the West Riding, keen to swap clichés about Yorkshire common sense.[5] He asked about personalities discussed in the autobiography—Tawney, Nevison, and Priestley. The latter Jameson described as bumptious in a West Riding way, but she had a great regard for him, she said, although he was too like herself for the two of them to be friends. She was not at all bumptious about herself. Writing, she said, quoting her own text, was only a chimney for her blazing ambition: 'If *The Pot Boils* hadn't been taken I would have done something else. Found another chimney.' She had said that in the autobiography, and it was probably true. She ended by emphasising what a struggle writing and publication had been: 'I haven't been enormously praised. Nothing has been very easy. You write a novel, you put as much into it as you've got. It's terribly cursed. You begin again.'

The interview with Janine McMullen the following day was pitched at a less chatty and more thoughtful level.[6] McMullen wanted to explore personal themes of not loving enough, of guilt, and its childhood roots, but encouraged her to talk also about politics. Jameson spoke with regret of the current situation in Czechoslovakia (the aftermath of the Prague Spring and the Russian invasion of 1968, and continuing attempts by the USSR to crush dissent). It was difficult now to talk to Czech friends. Again, she was self-deprecating: she was, she said, merely intelligent and talented, no kind of genius.

Several reviewers had struck that particular note, which was, after all, received wisdom among the young literary men of London, and they were probably beginning to wear Jameson down. Ray Gosling, for instance, declared she was not a great novelist, but 'what makes *Journey from the North* so tremendous is that she has captured honestly the magic of a good but not great mind; the portrait of a very human intellectual, a sympathetic and civilized human being. [...] She has exposed the nerve ends that outcrop through all our life, those few key feelings that, in this age of free expression, are written of so rarely, and hardly ever so accurately as here.'[7] The reviewer in *The Economist* said the book had in it 'the stuff of history and humanity'. He was however more interested in the conceit with which he opened his review, declaring Jameson a loner, who couldn't be classified alongside any other women writer; if you wanted to play literary snap, you couldn't pair her up.[8] Jameson's reviewers were hardly ever up to the job.

This time, the quality of the work made its way through, but yet again circumstances prevented her enjoying her success. Guy was ill. In August, he had a slight stroke, and after that his missing lung pained him if he had to walk any distance, and he was soon out of breath. Her instinct was that they should take things gently.[9] At the end of November, the pains turned out to be angina.

In September 1970, Jameson published her last essay collection, *Parthian Words*. Dealing with the writer's situation in the 1960s, it tackled all the major fashionable talking-points: pornography, contemporary critics and criticism, and the effect of film and television on the role of the novel. Her key message was still that the writer's situation is European. The English novel is in decline. There is no 'towering presence' behind anyone's words, perspectives are 'parochial', no one dares address the complexities of the present through their own original, individual vision, and English culture has been disabled by the revolt against reason. This time, however, it isn't contemporary French writing that she thinks will provide the lead. Genet only wrote one good novel, and has been repeating himself ever since. The *nouveaux romanciers*, Sarraute and Robbe-Grillet, are arid intellectuals, and far less innovative in their language than Joyce and, especially, Beckett, whom she greatly admires. No one is asking the important questions, about what the relationship of writer, reader, and text nowadays needs to be, what the novel can do with the reader that film can't (since it involves a different relationship to time, and the processes of understanding), and what kind of language the novel should be using to engage its readers, at all levels, as co-producers of culture and society. The great Europeans—Stendhal and Proust, Tolstoy, Dostoevsky—are still the best models. These writers (especially Stendhal, with his lucid objectivity) ask the questions readers want to ask, giving no final answers, because it's not the novelist's job to do so. Instead, they offer instruments for understanding. She pins her stylistic flag to Stendhal's mast:

The little I was capable of learning from him I learned badly. But it sharpened my innate distaste for certain forms of writing, for exaggerated eloquence, wilful obscurity, botched slipshod language. It hardened me in my obsessive belief that a writer's first duty is to be clear.[10]

In June, pre-publication, *The Times Saturday Review* printed four extracts to illustrate her view of the character of the contemporary novel and her suggestions for a way forward. The choice of extracts demonstrated understanding of her call: to find a way of writing lucidly from the heart of chaos, to combine interior and exterior realities, to learn to sculpture language, and in sum, to aspire to write 'a traditional novel from a ruthlessly modern point of view'.[11] Robert Nye's review for *The Scotsman* mocked the author's retrograde stances, her 'windy fulmination' against Picassos and Pollocks, and her 'abuse of those filthy female writers who insist on mentioning periods, etc.' But he nevertheless agreed with her on the state of the contemporary novel, enjoyed her criticisms of Robbe-Grillet and Nathalie Sarraute ('here is a member of an older generation who can tell which Emperors are in the altogether'), and endorsed heartily her declaration that writing novels was primarily a question of condensing meanings into language, 'more meanings than can be broadcast or televised or filmed'.[12]

An End to Ambition

At the beginning of 1970, in January, Basil Liddell Hart had died. At the end of the year, in December, Bill had a second coronary.[13] Guy had been growing weaker through the year. In January 1971, while they were in Cornwall, he fell ill and his lung began to degenerate; in April, Jameson had a thrombosis in one leg.[14] Friends rallied round. Zara Steiner, Jameson wrote to Irene, came and talked history to Guy every ten days, and was 'a tower of strength'.[15]

Living on the fourth floor was proving difficult, and she would have liked to buy a small ground floor flat so Guy could get out and sit outside. By February of the following year, he was much weaker,[16] and by June she was exhausted:

Figure 23 Guy Chapman, at the Larchfield flat, Cambridge, 1971.

Guy's long long illness has passed into what his doctor politely refers to as its termi-
nal stage. Since I do not want him to die in hospital if I can help it, I have turned this
flat into a hospital, in which I am nurse most of the day and at night, and ward maid
during the very few hours when a real nurse takes over.[17]

To their joint pleasure, advance copies of the French edition of his last book,
on the fall of France in 1940, were flown over specially, and reached him a
little time before he died, on 30 June 1972.[18] Christopher had been summoned
down from York to Cambridge two days beforehand, and witnessed his quiet
death in bed. Jameson refused at first to believe that he had died, and then
became totally silent as they gathered up the soiled bed-linen. It was a dreadful
time of grief and self-recrimination.[19] In September, Christopher drove her
up to Scotland to scatter Guy's ashes.[20] She planted a birch tree for him in the
National Trust Garden at Inverewe, Poolewe, Ross-shire, and in the summer of
1975 Christopher took her to see it.[21] She spent months typing out and order-
ing the handwritten pages of the memoirs Zara Steiner had encouraged him
to write. She checked names, dates, and quotations, she later told Irene, and
filled in gaps using his letters to her (she had kept them all, from 1924), or his
unpublished essays. She would have liked to put material of her own in, about,
for example, his first wife's treatment of him, but she didn't.[22] His old friend
Rupert Hart-Davis advised on her draft. Getting a publisher wasn't easy, and
she was grateful to Livia Gollancz, who finally accepted it.

The memoirs were published in April 1975, and received good reviews from
Michael Howard in the *Sunday Times*, Robert Nye in *The Scotsman*, and Paul
Scott in *The Times*.[23] Jameson gave Guy's books and manuscripts to Churchill
College for a Guy Chapman Collection.

Her last major book came out shortly after Guy's death. She had begun
There Will Be a Short Interval at the end of 1970, when he first fell ill.[24] It took a
year to find a publisher. Eventually Harvill Press took it, and it was deservedly
well-reviewed when it appeared in 1973.[25] Jameson no longer cared much, telling Irene: 'In some queer way I wrote my books for Guy, and now he has gone
there is no point in it, no point in anything.'[26]

The short interval of the title is, in the opening pages, an image from the
theatre: the point between the acts where the audience can think about the
progress of the spectacle: how the characters are lining up to each other, and
what kind of ending they are moving towards. The most important questions
have to do with Simon, the grandson of the family under the spotlight, who is
the quietest and most mysterious, and the narrative wants to know, what is he

Figure 24 Jameson and Christopher, with Elizabeth Crawshay-Williams, eating in the yard of the Crawshays' cottage in Snowdonia, in the early 1970s.

like, and why is he who he is? As always with Jameson, the family is the microcosm, and the generator, of the larger collective; the novel is about the future of England, and Europe.

As a child, Simon was neglected by his father, SJ, who was obsessed by his French wife and went to live with her in France, because she was sick, needy, and couldn't stand London. The parallels with Jameson, Bill, and Guy are obvious. SJ came to see the child and brought him presents, but wouldn't give him the time he gave to his wife, and refused to have him to live in France. He was brought up by his grandmother, Dame Retta Sergeant, an internationally famous novelist. Retta was identified by some reviewers (and West herself) with Dame Rebecca West.[27] But she is also what Jameson saw as her own worst self, the vicious sadist modelled on her mother that marriage to the Texan might well have brought into being: ready to turn her own and others' experience into grist for her novelist's mill, putting career and honours before her family. *Short Interval* is one of Jameson's most interesting experiments in the prismatic creation of characters from different aspects of the people around her. SJ and Retta are herself, split.

The short interval is also the few days in which SJ has to decide whether he will have a dangerous operation. Confronted with the prospect of his death, he is forced to assess what his life has been worth. All that is left now is the son he produced. A sequence of confrontations with the young man reveals nothing. He is polite, distant, and friendly, especially at their last meeting, where SJ is introduced to his son's new girlfriend, Marina, equally polite, charming, and apparently miles away. Both have left their parents, to live together on their own terms. In a long conversation, SJ comes to acknowledge the irrelevance to this generation of his own liberal ideals, his sense of responsibility, and his imperative commitment to practical action. He begins to recognise also the guilt of his own generation in burdening them with two world wars, Hiroshima, and a society of organised greed. But there is no way to know for sure what the old have passed on, and what the young have absorbed. The best that can be hoped for is mutual consideration, and the flicker of understanding that runs beneath conventional exchange. Jameson catches it in beautifully measured language:

'Before I forget,' he said, 'David Salaman's brother Francis is the head of a firm of estate agents, and if you decide to sell the house you should go to him. You might do better to keep it—since you seem to have as little sense of money as your father. Or as mine had. [...].'

'I shan't need to do anything,' Simon said. 'You'll see to things yourself when you come out of hospital.'

Something as intangible and clear as the sound left behind in the air when a pianist lifts his hands from the keys hung for a moment between them, as though his son had made a tentative attempt to reach him. It vanished at once.[28]

Between mother and son, however, there can be no reconciliation. The last thing SJ recalls before slipping into unconsciousness before his operation resolves a mystery: who caused Retta's fatal heart attack. He, effectively, murdered her, entering her bedroom while she was asleep to take back the embarrassing private letters she had stolen from Simon, which she planned to use in her next novel. What SJ destroyed was the crazed monster of selfishness that drives the creative persona:

The grunt sound came from the bed before he had picked up [the bundle of letters]. [... H]e turned to see her hand throwing aside the sheet and her thick body roll out of bed as an animal rolls all in one piece. It ran between him and the open drawer.[29]

Jameson's animosity towards Bill's first wife is behind the letter sequence, but it also stands symbolically for all the acts of selfish cruelty that constitute most individual lives. Ironically, the referent is not abolished but reconfirmed, in as much as the recollection is inscribed into this latest novel, but how the memory

337

Figure 25 Christopher Storm-Clark, who was recording recollections
of life in mining communities, after an underground visit to
a colliery in South Wales in the early 1970s.

is written is what makes the difference: the short interval SJ has been allowed is
filled with admissions of guilt and acts of penitence. Killing the phallic mother,
however, he has no sense of guilt, only 'a tranquil sensation of change'. This is
the necessary murder, clearing the decks of old hatreds and jealousies to give
a new world its chance.

Jameson soldiered on, and the children looked after her. In the spring of
1974 she was in hospital with broken ribs after being run over in the street by
a builder, and writing to Irene that she hoped to move out soon: 'The supply
of ministering grandchildren must run out. None are so good as Christopher, whose own job is much the most demanding.'[30] She was only in Addenbrooke's for a day or two before she was thrown out for rudeness to a nurse
who had refused to make her bed. She was signed out by a doctor who had
not examined her, and Christopher picked her up, still in her night clothes, at
the entrance to the hospital. A young ward sister ticked him off angrily about
her behaviour, which in later years might have been better understood as an
early symptom of dementia. Sydney Harland, back in Peru, wrote to com-
miserate on the accident, offer thoughts about the body, wisdom, and beauty,

and suggested she write a third volume of her autobiography about old age, as Simone de Beauvoir had just done.[31] Her reply isn't on record. Paul Tabori also wrote, and took the opportunity to express his pleasure at the Silver PEN award she had just received.[32]

Another kind of recognition seemed to promise at the end of 1974, when *The Early Life of Stephen Hind*, adapted in three parts by Alexander Baron, was televised on BBC 2, in the 8.10 p.m drama slot. Michael Kitchen played Stephen Hind, and Beatrix Lehmann played Lady Renee Chalteney. The BBC reader had recommended it for serialisation as 'a brilliant, witty and sophisticated picture of the affluent society of the 1960s'.[33] Jameson wrote to Irene to tell her about it, saying she herself wouldn't be watching, and then wrote again to tell her she had been paid £750, minus her agent's 10 per cent, which was a welcome windfall for the children's Christmas presents.[34]

Jameson's success with broadcast versions of her work had been poor, despite her agent's best efforts. In 1962, *The Road from the Monument* had been deemed too literary and slow-developing to work in any other medium.[35] The script of 'Plain Annie', originally requested for Peters' series, turned up again in August 1962, but it was felt to be too lightweight, the characters too thin and the whole approach conventionally romantic.[36] In January 1963, the short story 'This Is It', a criminal thriller, was on the table, with two diametrically opposed reader's reports, the one noting it would need too much rewriting—the characters didn't match up to the standards of realism now set by 'Z-Cars'—and the other describing it as a deep and disturbing exploration of sexuality.[37] It was rejected. In January 1968, the BBC paid £175 (first instalment of £350) for the television rights, but never found a suitable dramatist.[38] Another project to televise a version of *A Day Off* collapsed shortly afterwards.[39] And *A Month Soon Goes* was dismissed uncompromisingly for television in January 1969 as thin, dated romance.[40]

But in 1973, after the publication of *Journey from the North*, and with the revival of interest in women's writing and politically-edged work, strong and well-argued readers' recommendations came through for *The Green Man* and *Cloudless May*. On the first, the reader noted, with obvious regret, that Jameson had fallen out of fashion, but nevertheless he saw good potential for serialisation in the historical sweep of the storyline, and living characters with attitudes as representative of their time as Aldous Huxley's *Point Counter Point* and *Eyeless in Gaza*, which had both just been successfully serialised, and feelings that were as deep though more circumspectly expressed. He acknowledged the difficulty of adapting work like hers where dialogue and narrative were so interdependent that her dialogue without her narrative risked seeming thin, but he still recommended following up the proposal.[41] The reader for *Cloudless May* was also positive, comparing it to *Clochemerle* and *Roads to Freedom*. It was, he thought, better than Sartre's books: '[T]here are comparisons with Sartre in the relationship between political philosophy and the bare fact of death and war. But I think that the intellectual agonies of Sartre's heroes are outdone by Miss Jameson's more down-to-earth provincials.' In fact, *Cloudless May*, in his view, was perfect television material:

It's a straightforward, fly-on-the-wall narrative, but done with great skill of timing and characterisation. The author has a gift for allowing her 'actors' to reveal themselves in unexpected ways. She also allows more than enough good mini-denouements to end at least half-a-dozen episodes.

Logistically: It's a fairly ideal television property with most of the talk going on at the dinner table, in the Prefecture, the Brothel, the Café etc., and a few action sequences in the open air (very definitely France).

Even the final battle as the Germans invade is fragmentary and quite easily filmed.

It's a cracking good story, and within the (I should imagine) limited demands for a series from this particular era has the makings of a damned good series.[42]

In the end, it was decided that for the moment *Cloudless May* would be too expensive to make.[43]

The history of the BBC's reception of Jameson's work says a lot about changing tastes and publics, as well as the BBC's rapid learning curve in radio and television drama as successive cohorts of self-trained scriptwriters and producers developed their craft, set themselves new limits, and broke through them. It shows too the limits of Jameson's capacity to move beyond the forms she had painstakingly developed for her novel-writing. For radio, she was handicapped by her inability to think herself into the place of the listener at the mercy of a fast, forward-moving soundtrack. Despite her best intentions, as the Reithian establishment lost its dominance, she, or her agents, could no longer think into the frames of 'popular' culture. She was very unlucky that her last fashionable moment came as television stood on the edge of new techniques and different funding priorities that could have opened up her historical epics to a wider audience.

Her best achievements as a novelist of the contemporary operated now to her disadvantage. The generation of the 1960s no longer responded to the subtle characterisation appropriate for the emotionally disciplined generations before them, for whom strong feelings were best communicated obliquely, in laconic dialogue. The director of 'The Commonplace Heart' in 1953 had made brilliant use of close-ups to focus the audience on flickers of reaction and feeling, but more directors and actors of that kind, as well as differently educated audiences, were needed to take the new media to the sophisticated levels the novel had taken centuries to master. (This would be Jameson's point in *Parthian Words*, comparing the subtleties achieved by language in Stendhal with the more limited possibilities of the filmic image.) The reader of 'This Is It' spotted its disturbing undercurrents of repressed sexuality, but offered no advice on how to script them for radio. Good storylines, and good narrative ideas, Jameson had in abundance, but their usefulness all came down to the capacity of broadcasters to provide appropriate scripts, actors and direction.

Honours and recognition were still trickling in. Her photograph was included in the exhibition of camera portraits by E. O. Hoppé at the National Portrait Gallery in 1978. Harrison Salisbury wrote to her in May 1978 that the American Academy and Institute of Arts and Letters had elected her to honorary membership.[44] At the end of the year, she refused the offer of a CBE in the Queen's New Year Honours List.[45] She was resentful that Rebecca West had been made a Dame while she was only offered a CBE, and told her grandson it conjured up visions of Widow Twankey; but she also thought that accepting honours from the State compromised the independence of writers and artists.[46] In 1980, Leeds University accepted with pleasure her offer of her head, sculpted by Anna Mahler, for their collection, and Christopher delivered it to the University in February of that year. PEN, in the person of Josephine Pullein-Thompson, offered her honorary membership in December, with a discreet reference to her health and financial problems, and a warm personal postscript expressing her admiration for the Minutes of the war years.[47] A practical and helpful letter came from New Hall, renewing her Dining Rights for as long as she lived in Cambridge.[48]

She published her last book, *Speaking of Stendhal*, in 1979.[49] It was a small book, chiefly focused on his life, but a good one to finish on, giving due recognition to the author whose influence throughout her writing career had given her writing such a distinctively different inflection from that of her English contemporaries. The *TLS* had made the point about the Frenchman in 1938, in an editorial commenting on how alien Stendhal was to English readers, as was Trollope to the French, and speaking of the 'nationalism of literary taste'.[50]

Speaking Across Generations: The Virago Imprint

In April 1981, Virago Press (Ursula Owen, Lenore (Lennie) Goodings, Alexandra Pringle, and Carmen Callil) approached her to ask about republishing the *Mirror in Darkness* trilogy.[51] Colin Walsh, book production consultants situated in Cambridge (The Book Concern Ltd), had also approached her, but she settled on Virago, whose plans seemed to offer less pressure—she had had enough of the treadmill. On the eve of the reissue by Virago in September 1982 of *Company Parade* and *Women Against Men*, she agreed to an interview with Janet Watts, which appeared in *The Observer Magazine* on 5 September, with a good photograph of her sitting in front of her bookshelves in Cambridge. Watts painted a portrait of an elegant, cool woman of 91, 'appalled to have lived so long'. Her current reading was Physics textbooks, and her last book had been on Stendhal: '"I don't think of him as a novelist. Nothing so disreputable." As what then? "A Frenchman."'

The publications brought renewed recognition. George Steiner wrote in the *Sunday Times* that: 'Storm Jameson belongs to the history of the breakthrough of women, particularly of women outside the sphere of privilege, into higher education, into journalism, into the public life of the mind. She is, with Dame Rebecca West, the embodiment of a formidable psychological and moral assertion.'[52] He noted the many people she had helped in her PEN capacity, without thinking of thanks, including 'one Nobel prize-winner whom she helped bring to sanctuary and kept whole, [who] failed to lift a finger on her behalf when she needed help later.' This was presumably Milosz. Naomi Mitchison, writing in the *TLS*, picked out from *Company Parade* Jameson's criticisms of the profit made from the war, and the scandal of the sloganising on Homes for Heroes.[53]

Bill died towards the beginning of 1983, just as Virago wrote to say they had sent her agent an offer to republish *Journey from the North*.[54] They would have liked her to write a Preface for the reissue, but in the circumstances, that was impossible. Publication date for the autobiography, and the two remaining books of the trilogy, was fixed for 23 January 1984, and they appear to have put as little pressure on her as possible for publicity. She agreed to an interview with Caroline Moorehead in *The Times*. She had, reported Moorehead, 'an expression of almost unbearable sadness', but managed nevertheless to 'underline everything she says with humour, however bleak'.[55] In her files, she kept the press cuttings sent by Durrants, which were numerous, and almost all warm and positive, from *City Limits* to the *Yorkshire Evening Post,* and the *Whitby Gazette.*[56] Once again, the journey from the North had come full circle.

Naomi Mitchison wrote to her on 25 January with a proof copy of her review for the *New Statesman.* She picked out Jameson's response to political torture, which was, she said, still an unusual and shocking phenomenon in the 1930s, and the chapters about the devastation left after the war, especially in Prague.[57] Jo Stanley, in the *Morning Star,* said she was in the inter-war years 'the nearest thing there was to a feminist novelist. A number of women now in their sixties have told me of how they reached for her books knowing that in them women would be doing independent things, thinking freshly. [...] Unfortunately, the novels feel sadly unradical now that women's literature is daring so much. But would this daring have been possible without Storm Jameson's tentative beginnings?'[58]

She felt now she could take on nothing else new. She could no longer cope with functions and interviews.[59] She declined invitations from BBC TV, and BBC Radio. She had had enough.

Living in Letters

In those last years after Guy died, she had lived most vividly through her letters. She destroyed much of her old correspondence after finishing *Journey from the North,* but she kept much that was written after that date. The three boxes left for her Executor give a picture of a Grand Old Lady of Letters, with many important and interesting British, American, and European (ex-refugee) friends and strong family relationships, often impoverished (or at least, anxious about money), and in frequent receipt of gifts of books and wine, and sometimes cheques for help with unexpected house repairs.

There were big bundles of letters from Americans, mostly friends of long standing. Alfred Knopf continued until the end of 1983 the correspondence they had begun in the 1920s. The substantial collection she kept of his letters, from May 1967 to December 1983, is a mixture of reminiscences and comments on current politics. They enjoyed slagging off to each other their respective governments (Knopf's word). On 28 April 1981, he sent her two typed pages with his views on Reagan's election and the switch of the Senate to

Republican control, and over the next few months firmly defended his increasingly left-wing stances on the American conservatives' attacks on abortion, the effect of Reagan's economics on the poor, women's rights, and job security for workers, and his government's attacks on human liberties in the name of defence against terrorism. Jameson refused to rise to his harder statements, though she was clearly uneasy with some of them.

Rache Lovat Dickson, a regular correspondent from Toronto, wrote as he reached the war years in his own memoirs, *The Lordless Man*, to praise the selflessness of herself and Hermon Ould, unique, he thought, among their literary contemporaries.[60] Another bundle of letters from Professor Henry Steele Commager (Felix) is covered by a note in her hand: 'A few letters from an enormous quantity running into thousands, received since 1943, when he came to England on some sort of official mission from America, and began a friendship with Guy and myself which has lasted strongly ever since. We stayed many times with him and his wife in America.' There is a fat bundle from Harrison Salisbury, written between January 1977 and May 1983. He too was writing his autobiography, and sent her a transcription from his journal of his wartime meeting with herself and Guy. There were new acquaintances too, including Professor Douglas Robillard, who delighted her with notice of his intention to write a paper on her, and his enquiry whether there were researchers contemplating writing her biography. She doubted it: 'Except for the five Second War years when I was foolish enough to let myself be talked into becoming President of the English PEN—thank goodness that most of my labours were for our exiles—I have never been a figure in literary circles. There is not enough time. One needs two lives, one in which to learn and one in which to look.'[61]

Among Europeans, there are many letters from Maria Kuncewiczowa, a close friend since she came to England as an exile in 1940, a few from Milosz, and some from Rolly Becker, who had eventually left Robert Neumann, but continued to help with the translation and publication of Jameson's work. From the Liddell Harts, there is a huge bundle, labelled 'A few of many many letters torn up.'

Other letters are sadder markers of illness and death among relatives and friends. Irene Rathbone died in January 1980. Winifred Jameson went into hospital in New York with congestive heart failure in 1980. Virginia Patterson, a wealthy friend of Winifred's, formerly with Cambridge University Press in the United States, wrote to tell Jameson Winifred was fine, but had walking, arthritis, and money problems. Jameson covered the last page of Virginia's letter with phone numbers for Winifred and Virginia, Winifred's address in Greenwich Avenue, and an injunction to herself to 'Write once a week,' underlined twice. At the end of the letter, she wrote: 'I ought to have taken her home to England after Guy died. I shall never forgive myself, never.'[62] Virginia, reporting on Win's progress in hospital, wrote with considerable common sense, describing her as a trial to everyone, demanding constant attention– the kind of person who, the more you did, the more she expected; she told Jameson that she must not consider taking her in, because she couldn't stand it.[63] This was the sister who even in their younger and healthier days had been more trouble than a horde of Brazilians. Winifred's doctor wrote in February 1980 to say that Winifred had had her cancer removed from her breast some time ago but now had a local recurrence, which radiation should deal with.[64] Winifred herself wrote in August, to discuss her will; the latest version, drawn up in 1972, shared everything equally between Jameson's grandchildren and Dorothy's children. She added that she wished the two of them lived nearer one another.[65]

News of Doreen Marston's death came in May, and in October 1982 Oswald Harland's daughter wrote to say that he was sinking fast.[66] Archie White had died long ago. Amabel Williams-Ellis died in 1984. But of them all, after Guy's, Bill's death in March 1983 was hardest to bear.

There were a few small moments of happiness still to come: seeing the cover design for a paperback edition of Guy's wartime memoirs, *A Passionate Prodigality*,[67] and visits, letters, and photographs from the grandchildren, who stayed in close touch. But old age was taking its toll on her faculties at last, and the clarity of her mind, and her memory, had begun to falter. From the beginning of 1985, Christopher took charge of her affairs, under the direction of the Court of Protection.[68]

The last letter in the collection to Irene is dated Monday 5 July 1976, and in it she thanked Irene for sending Guy's In Memoriam notice from the previous Wednesday's *Times*. She noted it was to appear on 30 June every year for ten years, and expressed the hope that she would not see the next.[69] She lived fourteen years without him, dying on 30 September 1986 in the Bethany Paxton Hall, near St Neots, Cambridgeshire. This was a newly opened nursing home specialising in dementia patients which Age Concern in Cambridge had recommended to Christopher just before she was discharged from a geriatric ward in Addenbrooke's, after a bout of food poisoning. The kindly woman consultant who looked after her had insisted she must go into care. Kitty Rokos, a friend whose parents she had rescued from Czechoslovakia, who visited her in Paxton Hall, reported to Christopher that in a brief moment of lucidity she had declared, 'I am in hell'. The death certificate showed bronchopneumonia, generalised arteriosclerosis, and old age.[70]

There were many obituaries. Brief, and not too well-informed, the *Guardian*'s contribution echoed the classic commentaries of London's literary young men of twenty years back, damning with faint praise 'a long run of generally decent, middle level novels'.[71] In contrast, the anonymous essay in *The Times* on 7 October 1986 ran to three half-page columns, and celebrated in thoughtful critical detail the long career of 'Miss Storm Jameson. Powerful writer with a bleak and brave eye.' It said she would be remembered best as an autobiographer, and that *Journey from the North*, written at the age of 78, 'overshadowed everything she had written since the Second World War'.

Jameson herself understood rather better what her life had been: not just one production, but many, as activist, autobiographer, novelist, traveller, Bill's mother, Guy's wife, and the last flag-bearer of Class 1914. The closing sequence of *There Will Be a Short Interval*, written many years before her death, represents her last and most successful attempt to find the words for who she 'really' was. The inspiration is Beckett, the best of the moderns, and his explorations of the point of perception that is generic human subjectivity, the capacity to know and create that resides in the interactions of reason, memory, and the senses. The words, and the unique experience they signify, are hers. The couple of the officer and the corporal, symbolising the relationship of the faculties, is an image chosen for Guy, but is also a motif that recurs in all her own thinking and writing, from *The Happy Highways* through to *No Victory for the Soldier*, and *The Green Man*. What remains to the last, as her persona SJ slides into oblivion, is the discipline of Class 1914, the army of volunteers in which responsible selfhood and commitment to others are both duty and choice. The child of history is still there, in the sound of the incoming sea, but all vision is gone, no light, no screams of children or birds, no names, nothing to see and nothing to speak of. All that's left at the end is all there was at the start: the insatiable curiosity of the human mind, and the old questions that might yet, this time, invoke something more than the old answers. In words, the text says, the matter of language, lie the endless recalls, and also the fresh beginnings:

Now he could not see. In front of him and folding round him was only a velvety blackness, he floated, weightless, in an absence of everything, no longer in touch with his body, neither dead nor living. Touch, sight, were both extinct. A single one of his senses—like a young corporal squatting beside his badly wounded officer—remained with him, and he *heard* the rise of the sea.

And summoned himself to recall … recall what?

When? Where?[72]

Figure 26 The view from Jameson's study window in Rydale House, Whitby, in the early 1930s. The moors begin where the garden leaves off.

NOTES

Introduction

1. Bonamy Dobrée, 'Views and Reviews. Autobiography Plus', *The New English Weekly*, Vol. III, No. 4, 11 May 1933, p. 90.
2. Virginia Woolf, cit. in Bonnie Kime Scott (ed.), *The Gender of Modernism* (Bloomington: Indiana University Press, 1990), pp. 642–5.
3. See e.g. my essay 'Beginning Again: Storm Jameson's Debt to France', *Critical Survey*, Vol. 10, No. 3, 1998, pp. 3–12.
4. *JN* I: 16–17.
5. *Love in Winter* (London: Cassell and Company, Ltd, 1935), p. 96.
6. Ibid., pp. 66–7.
7. *JN* I: 17.
8. James Hill, *No Victory for the Soldier* (London: Collins, 1938), p. 179.
9. *JN* I: 17.
10. Ibid.
11. Letter from MSJ to Peter (A. D. Peters), 23 Oct. 1963 (Jameson, Storm. Peters A. D. Literary Agent. (Correspondence Files) 1963. The Harry Ransom Humanities Research Center, The University of Texas at Austin).
12. Alan Bishop and Y. Aleksandra Bennett (eds), *Wartime Chronicle. Vera Brittain's Diary 1939–45* (London: Victor Gollancz, 1989), Entry for Tuesday 7 July 1942, pp. 160–1.
13. *JN* I: 163.
14. This paragraph is based on the cover note to Jameson's letter collection in the Private Collection of Christopher Storm-Clark (CSC), and information supplied in conversation by Christopher Storm-Clark.
15. *There Will Be a Short Interval* (London: Harvill Press, 1973), p. 195.
16. Frank Swinnerton, *Swinnerton: An Autobiography* (London: Hutchinson & Co., 1937), p. 366.
17. Anon., 'Life Intensely Lived', *The Economist*, 6 Aug. 1969.
18. Letter from MSJ to Basil Liddell Hart, 10 July 1965 (LH 1/408 PART 2- 409) Liddell Hart Centre for Military Archives, King's College London).
19. Letter from Dorothy Pateman to Betty Leake, Easter Monday [1942] (letter belonging to Judy Kistner, in CSC).
20. Letter from MSJ to Basil Liddell Hart, 17 Aug. 1952 (LHC: LH 1/408 PART 1).
21. *JN* II: 341.
22. *There Will be a Short Interval*, p. 191.

1. A Yorkshire Childhood

1. *JN* I: 17–18.
2. The family's pet name stayed with her all her life, and she hated it (information supplied by Christopher Storm-Clark).
3. From his Whitby studio, opened in 1894, the celebrated Frank Meadow Sutcliffe (1853–1941) brought social realism into turn-of-the-century photography. The collections published by The Sutcliffe Gallery, Whitby, give a lively evocation of the harbour, markets, alleys, and ramshackle houses of the Whitby of Jameson's childhood, and the families who thronged them.
4. *JN* I: 29.
5. *Company Parade*, p. 96.
6. Information in this section is drawn from Keith Snowden, *Whitby Through the Ages* (Pickering: Castleden Publications, 2000), pp. 40–1, referring to *Bulmer's Directory* (1890).
7. *JN* I: 25.
8. *Letters of James Russell Lowell*, ed. Charles E. Norton, 2 vols. (New York: Harper & Brothers, 1894), and *New Letters of James Russell Lowell*, ed. M. A. DeWolfe Howe (New York: Harper & Brothers, 1932), cit. Alan Whitworth, *Whitby as They Saw It* (Whitby: Culva House Publications, 2nd edn., 2003), pp. 40–3.
9. *JN* I: 27.
10. Snowden, *Whitby Through the Ages*, pp. 39–40.
11. *JN* I: 24.
12. MSJ, writing as George Gallilee, 'A Philosophy of Youth: Childhood *contd*', in *The New Commonwealth*, 16 Jan. 1920, n.s., Vol. 1, No. 3, p. 8.
13. Snowden, *Whitby Through the Ages*, p. 37, p. 41.
14. *JN* II: 320.
15. Snowden, *Whitby Through the Ages*, p. 37.
16. *JN* I: 21, 24.
17. *JN* I: 258; the papers are held in CSC.
18. *JN* I: 19.
19. TS of *JN* Vol. 1, p. 22, p. 31 (Jameson S. Works. HRC); *JN* I: 28. The anecdote is used in *Farewell Night, Welcome Day* (London: Cassell and Company, 1939), pp. 62–3, written shortly after her mother's death, and exploring the problems in bringing up a young family from the mother's perspective. The other accusations are hinted at discreetly.
20. *JN* I: 29.
21. *JN* I: 37.
22. *JN* I: 44; see also *Love in Winter*, p. 24.
23. TS of *JN*, Vol. 3, p. 275 (Jameson, Storm. Works (Autobiography) HRC); cf. *JN* I: 44.
24. *JN* I: 101.
25. *JN* I: 228.
26. Letter to MSJ from Archie White, 27 Aug. 1969 (CSC). She was however mentioned; she stayed with Jameson in Liverpool during the Great War, calm and unruffled when

her destitute sister sold her bed under her for cash (*JN* I: 106), and when the Chapmans passed through New York en route for Pittsburgh in 1946, staying (though Jameson doesn't say so) in Winifred's flat, Winifred's preference for New York over Whitby is noted briefly (*JN* II: 217).

27. After the war, MSJ wrote to Vernon Bartlett to ask his help in finding Winifred a job in the United Nations Organisation (Letters from MSJ to Vernon Bartlett, 10 and 20 Dec. 1945 (Letters from various correspondents to Vernon Bartlett, Vol. I, British Library, Add. Ms 59500, ff.161 and 162)).
28. *JN* I: 58.
29. *JN* I: 99–103.
30. A marginal note in Jameson's hand: 'On January 5 1917 he was shot down while directing artillery fire from his aeroplane from over the German lines. He was aged 20.' The photograph of the grave was sent by Tom Gudmestad, of Seattle, who began a correspondence with Guy having read *A Passionate Prodigality* in the 1970s, and visited the Chapmans every two years when he came to look at war graves in Europe. Jameson left a note saying he was to be notified when she died (CSC).
31. *JN* I: 102.
32. *JN* I: 330–1.
33. *JN* I: 99.
34. *JN* I: pp. 256–60.
35. In e.g. *The Voyage Home* (London: Heinemann), 1930, where Sylvia Hervey marries Captain Russell after a failed attempt at a runaway marriage to someone else, a vignette of the Captain standing lonely vigil outside her hotel in France suggests sympathy for his inarticulate devotion.
36. *Last Score*, pp. 214–19.
37. *JN* I: 47.
38. *NTLP*, p. 33.
39. *NTLP*, p. 17.
40. *NTLP*, p. 142; cf *JN* I: 43.
41. TS of *JN*, Vol. 2, p. 290 (Jameson, Storm. Works (Autobiography) HRC).
42. Note on the bundle of letters from the Harlands in CSC.
43. Sydney Cross Harland, *Nine Lives: The Autobiography of a Yorkshire Scientist*, ed. Max Millard (Boson Books, 2001), pp. 24–5. URL http://www.bosonbooks.com/boson/freebies/harland/harland.pdf. Cf. *NTLP*, pp. 48–51; *JN* I: 48–9.
44. Letter to MSJ from Sydney Harland, 27 June 1973 (CSC). Some elements of Sydney's hard-pressed childhood are echoed in the character of T. S. Heywood, in the *Mirror in Darkness* trilogy, the scientist who sells his pre-war socialist ideals for a lucrative contract to develop poison gas. Heywood's father was 'a small shopkeeper who died bankrupt, from incompetence, my mother kept me and herself alive by mending and washing for eight families' (*None Turn Back* (London: Cassell and Company, 1936; rpt. London: Virago Press Ltd, 1986), p. 75).
45. Harland, *Nine Lives*, p. 27.
46. *The Happy Highways* (London: William Heinemann), 1920, p. 23.

47. Harland, *Nine Lives*, p. 27.
48. Ibid., p. 28.
49. *JN* I: 49–50.

2. The Student in the North

1. *NTLP*, pp. 53–4.
2. *JN* I: 52.
3. *University of Leeds 8th Annual Report (1910–1911)*, pp. 46–9 (University Archive, Leeds University Library).
4. *University of Leeds 9th Annual Report (1911–1912)*, p. 38 (UALUL).
5. *University of Leeds Register of Students (1909–10)* (UALUL).
6. Her degree certificate, dated 29 June 1912, is held in CSC.
7. *JN* I: 58.
8. *NTLP*, p. 57; see also *JN* I: 54.
9. *NTLP*, p. 57.
10. *Parthian Words* (London: Collins & Harvill Press, 1970), p. 7.
11. *NTLP*, pp. 56–7.
12. Robert Scholes, General Introduction to the online version of *The New Age 1907–22*, 24 Aug. 1999, describes the range of Orage's journal, and points usefully to the distinctive variant it brought to the development of social realism, with its contributions from Sickert, and articles on Vorticism, Classicism, and the work of Fry and Bell on significant form (URL at 20 April 2008 http://dl.lib.brown.edu:8081/exist/mjp/show_series. xq?id=1158589415603817).
13. *JN* I: 56–7. On Clarke, see also *JN* I: 90, 118. In a letter to David Carver in 1956, asking for membership of PEN, Clarke designated himself C. Douglas Clarke. He claimed his family had travelled to Pennsylvania with William Penn, and his father, Dr Granville Clark, MD MA, had been a founder member of the Quaker Penn Club in Tavistock Square. Dr Clark, he said, was still a US citizen when he died in London. There was no 'e' in his father's name, but he himself, having been born in Ulster, was spelled with an 'e' (Letter from Charles Douglas Clarke to David Carver, 20 Jan. 1956, in PEN archive (London, uncat.), HRC). He is 'Clarke' on his birth certificate, which gives his date of birth as 15 June 1889, and his second name appears as 'Dougan' (CSC). Jameson's address book, inscribed to her from CD, with a date of 8 Jan. 1922, contains two addresses for Clarke, neither dated: one for London N7, and one in Welwyn Garden City (CSC).
14. *Leeds University Session Records. Sessional Entries of Students for 1905/6–1909/10, 1910–11* (UALUL).
15. *NTLP*, p. 53; *JN* I: 53.
16. *The Pot Boils* (London: Constable & Co., Ltd, 1919), Bk I, ch. 2.
17. *Leeds University Calendar 1910–11*, p. 590 (UALUL).

18. *Yorkshire College Women's Representative Council Minute Book 1902–1914*, Minute of 23 Jan. 1912, including letter from Michael Sadler to Margaret Jameson, 22 May 1912 (UALUL).
19. *Leeds University Calendar, 1910–11*, p. 592 (UALUL).
20. *The Gryphon: The Journal of the University of Leeds*, Vol. XIV, No. 2, Dec. 1910, p. 44.
21. *Leeds University Calendar 1910–1911*, p. 592 (UALUL).
22. *The Gryphon*, Vol. XI, No. 3, Feb. 1908, p. 45.
23. *The Gryphon*, Vol. XI, No. 4, March 1908, p. 49.
24. *The Gryphon*, Vol. XIII, No. 2, Dec. 1909, p. 25.
25. *The Gryphon*, Vol. XIII, No. 4, March 1910, p. 56.
26. *The Gryphon*, Vol. XIV, No. 2, Dec. 1910, p. 29.
27. *The Gryphon*, Vol. XIV, No. 2, Dec. 1910, p. 30.
28. SEE DEE, 'Scientific Essays in Modern Life. I. The Modern Maiden (For Male Readers only)', *The Gryphon*, Vol. XIV, No. 4, March 1911, p. 56.
29. *The Pot Boils*, p. 9.
30. Ibid., pp. 22–3.
31. *The Gryphon*, Vol. XV, No. 3, Feb. 1912, p. 47.
32. *The Gryphon*, Vol. XV, No. 4, March 1912, p. 57.
33. *JN* I: 57.
34. *The Gryphon*, Vol. XIV, No. 6, June 1911, p. 87.
35. *The Gryphon*, Vol. XIV, No, 4, March 1911, p. 53.
36. *The Gryphon*, Vol. XV, No. 6, June 1912, p. 84.
37. Tom Steele, *Alfred Orage and The Leeds Arts Club, 1893–1923* (Aldershot: Scolar Press, 1990), pp. 196–7.
38. Kandinsky's version of Abstract Impressionism, in which form and colour were not seen merely as means of artistic expression but vital elements of the cosmic organisation, was drawn from *Thought Forms*, written by Annie Besant and Cyril Leadbetter, which had originally inspired Orage and Holbrook Jackson, founders in 1903 of the Leeds Arts Club (Steele, *Alfred Orage*, p. 193). The Club had seen the introduction to Leeds of avant-garde ideas in art and in radical politics of all persuasions, with a special focus on the thinking of Nietzsche and Theosophy. Speakers included Yeats, Chesterton, Shaw, Belloc, Edward Carpenter, and Wyndham Lewis.
39. *The Gryphon*, Vol. XV, No. 4, March 1912, p. 54.
40. *The Gryphon*, Vol. XV, No. 6, May 1912, p. 66.
41. *The Gryphon*, Vol. XVI, No. 1, Nov. 1912, p. 10.
42. Steele, *Alfred Orage*, p. 190.
43. *The Gryphon*, Vol. XVI, No. 3, Feb. 1913, p. 40. Michael Sadleir quickly made a name for himself in London publishing, with Constable, and as a novelist (*Fanny by Gaslight*). His translation of Kandinsky's *Uber das Geistige* (*The Art of Spiritual Harmony*) appeared in 1914 (London: Constable & Co.).
44. Steele, *Alfred Orage*, p. 190.
45. *NTLP*, pp. 72–3.

3. London 1912–1918

1. Sydney Harland, *Nine Lives*, p. 32.
2. Ibid., p. 34.
3. Ibid.
4. Letter from Sydney Harland to MSJ, 27 June 1973 (CSC).
5. Harland, *Nine Lives*, p. 33.
6. *NTLP* pp. 63–4, *JN* I: 64.
7. 'Man the Helpmate', in *Man, Proud Man*, ed. Mabel Ulrich (London: Hamish Hamilton, 1932), pp. 105–36 (p. 124).
8. *JN* I: 66.
9. *NTLP*, p. 90.
10. *NTLP*, p. 67.
11. *JN* I: 65–6; *NTLP*, pp. 68–9.
12. *NTLP*, p. 64.
13. *NTLP*, pp. 78–9; *JN* I: 65.
14. TS of *JN*, Vol. 2, p. 207 (Jameson, Storm. Works (Autobiography) HRC).
15. *JN* I: 65.
16. *JN* I: 66.
17. *JN* I: 67. On Mrs Bridges Adams, see Jane Martin, 'An "Awful Woman"? The Life and Work of Mrs Bridges Adams, 1855–1939', *Women's History Review*, Vol. 8, No. 1, 1999. Her young married life may be the source of the section in *The Pot Boils* that describes a commune of young well-bred social revolutionaries established near London.
18. *The Happy Highways*, pp. 158 ff.
19. Ibid., p. 177.
20. *NTLP*, p. 58.
21. *NTLP*, pp. 80–2.
22. Letter to MSJ from Archie White, 27 Aug. 1969 (CSC).
23. *JN* I: 72.
24. Letter from MSJ to Hermon Ould, 1 May 1943 (PEN archive (London, uncat.), HRC).
25. *JN* I: 73–6.
26. Sydney Harland, 'Raving of an Immature Science Student', *The New Age*, 13 Feb. 1913, Vol. XII, No. 15, p. 395.
27. J. M. Kennedy ('Notes on the Present Kalpa: A Plea for the Parish Pump'), *The New Age*, 16 Jan. 1913, Vol. 12, No. 11, p. 249.
28. Morley Seymour, 'The Male Suffragist', *The New Age*, 20 March 1913, Vol. 12, No. 20, p. 475. Leading Labour politicians supporting feminist suffrage included Keir Hardie, George Lansbury, and Philip Snowden; Jameson came to know the last two well. The Men's League for Women's Suffrage had been founded in 1907 by left-leaning writers such as Laurence Housman, Henry Brailsford, and Henry Nevinson, Jameson's predecessor as President of PEN. The Men's Political Union for Women's Enfranchisement was established three years later. Frederick Pethick-Lawrence, a strong supporter of the Women's Social and Political Union, and Nevinson's wife

Evelyn Sharp, were also future colleagues of Jameson's on the London Executive Committee of PEN.

29. 'The End Thereof', *The New Age*, 20 March 1913, Vol. 12, No. 20, pp. 482–3.

30. 'New Statesmen. A Bill Providing for an Economic Basis of Marriage [Being a projected Fabian Tract, number 1001 (c.)]' *The New Age*, 2 April 1914, Vol. 14, No. 22, p. 682.

31. 'A Plea for the Arbitrary Limit', *The New Age*, 7 Sept. 1916, Vol. 19, No. 19, pp. 447–8.

32. Interview with Dora Marsden, *Evening Standard and St James Gazette*, 25 Oct. 1911, cit. Les Garner, *A Brave and Beautiful Spirit; Dora Marsden 1882–1960* (Aldershot and Brookfield USA: Avebury, 1990), p. 57.

33. See also Deborah Gerrard's account of the connections between Jameson's early fiction and Orage's and Marsden's journals, in ' "The Tempestuous Morning Energy of a New Art": Socialism, Modernism, and the Young Storm Jameson', in Jennifer Birkett and Chiara Briganti (eds), *Margaret Storm Jameson: Writing in Dialogue* (Newcastle: Cambridge Scholars Publishing, 2007), pp. 19–35.

34. Letter from MSJ to Dora Marsden, 1 Jan. 1914, cit. Garner, *A Brave and Beautiful Spirit*, pp. 165, 181 n. 47. See also *JN* I: 77–78.

35. Letter from Dora Marsden to Harriet Shaw Weaver, 3 April 1914 (Harriet Shaw Weaver Papers, BL, Add. Ms. 57354, f. 35 v.).

36. Letter from Dora Marsden to [Harriet Shaw Weaver], [?Oct. 1915] (Harriet Shaw Weaver Papers, BL, Add. Ms. 57354, f. 57).

37. *JN* I: 244. A translation of Gourmont's investigation of the New Woman phenomenon (*The Horses of Diomedes*) appeared in *The New Freewoman* (Aug.–Dec. 1913), and *The Egoist* (Jan.–March 1914), in some of the issues in which Jameson published her own first articles. On the same page of her autobiography, Jameson also indicates that she read the fragments of Joyce's *Ulysses* published in *The Egoist*, and found them, if not pleasurable, preferable to the standard productions of the 'bladder-novel' of the modern publishing market. Episodes II, III, VI, X appeared in *The Egoist* early in 1919 (Richard Ellmann, *James Joyce*, New York, London, and Toronto: Oxford University Press, 1959).

38. The autobiographical novel *That Was Yesterday* (1932) covers the period spent with Charles from Kettering up to her return to London in 1918.

39. *JN* I: 82.

40. *JN* I: 88. The period in Liverpool particularly is the source of the bitter comments in *The Pot Boils* about the trap of domesticity.

41. Letter MSJ to James Hanley, 26 Sept. 1935 (Papers of James Hanley, Correspondence from Storm Jameson to James Hanley, 920 HAN/4, Liverpool Record Office).

42. *JN* I: 114.

43. The reader at Duckworth & Co. found a lot to criticise in the author's shallow characterisation and the incoherence of his plot (constructed, he thought, in the French manner, 'throwing in jabs of light on a given character from many angles'); but he still thought 'the man' could write and was worth watching, and had recommended considering the book for later publication, when 'the Labour question will become acute, and reconstruction will be in the air' (*JN* II: 70).

44. Letter from Dora Marsden to [Harriet Shaw Weaver], 22 Jan. 1918 (Harriet Shaw Weaver Papers, BL, Add. Ms. 57354, f. 102).
45. Subscription List, Sixth Year (Harriet Shaw Weaver Papers, BL Add. Ms. 57362, f. 7 r.).
46. Letter from Dora Marsden to [Harriet Shaw Weaver], 22 Aug. 1919 (Harriet Shaw Weaver Papers, BL, Add. Ms. 57354, f. 112 v.). Grace is Grace Jardine, Editorial Secretary. Ten years later, just after her operation, and shortly after leaving A. A. Knopf, Jameson made great efforts to help Dora Marsden publish her book, *Definition of the Godhead*, and later to solicit favourable reviews for it (Garner, *A Brave and Beautiful Spirit.*, pp. 166–7).
47. Jameson described this as the only affair of passion in her life (TS of *JN*, Vol. I, pp. 143 ff.; PEN Archive (London, uncat.), HRC). She kept two signed photographs of Fry in her collection of family photographs (CSC).
48. *JN* I: 122.
49. *JN* I: 147–50.
50. TS of *JN*, Vol. I, p. 156 (PEN Archive (London, uncat.) HRC).
51. 'The Tale of the Solitary English Girl. The Pitiful Wife', *The New Decameron*, Vol. 3 (Oxford: Basil Blackwell, 1922), pp. 56–71. See also *The Clash* (London: Heinemann, 1922).
52. *Company Parade*, pp. 122–3.
53. Ibid., p. 123.

4. London 1919–1924

1. *JN* I: 137.
2. [George Herbert Cowling], 'New Novels', *TLS*, 6 Feb. 1919, Issue 890, p. 68.
3. *The Pot Boils*, p. 23, p. 38.
4. Ibid., p. 138.
5. Ibid., p. 189.
6. Ibid., pp. 75–6.
7. Ibid., pp. 85, 126.
8. Ibid., p. 244.
9. Ibid., pp. 190–2.
10. Ibid., p. 192.
11. Ibid., pp. 162–3.
12. Ibid., p. 247.
13. Ibid., p. 251.
14. Ibid., p. 1.
15. Ibid., p. 126.
16. *JN* I: 150.
17. Letter from MSJ to Ethel Mannin, 29 Dec. 1931 (MS (Jameson Storm) Letters, Mannin, Ethel 1931–2, HRC).
18. *The Happy Highways*, p. 47.

19. *JN* I: 161.
20. *JN* I: pp. 153–6.
21. Letter from MSJ to Alfred Knopf, 9 July 1981 (CSC).
22. See Allen Hutt, *The Post-War History of the British Working Class* (London: Victor Gollancz Ltd, Left Book Club Edition, 1937), pp. 25–7.
23. Annie Besant, 'The War and the Future' (15 Oct. 1919, 22 Oct., 29 Oct., 5 Nov.); G. D. H. Cole, 'Guild Socialism' (21 Nov. 1919); George Bernard Shaw, 'Socialism and Ireland' (12 Dec. 1919).
24. 'Divorce', *The New Commonwealth*, 1 Oct. 1919, Vol. 1, No. 1, p. 2.
25. See also the discussion of Jameson's contribution to *The New Commonwealth* in Catherine Clay, 'Storm Jameson's Journalism 1913–33: The Construction of a Writer' (in Birkett and Briganti, *Margaret Storm Jameson*, pp. 42–6), which points out the strong feminist dimension to Jameson's contributions, and the critical distance between the journal and organised feminism of the period.
26. 'America', *The New Commonwealth*, 15 Oct. 1919, Vol. 1, No. 3, p. 20.
27. M. I., 'A Woman's Thoughts. The Political Situation', *The New Commonwealth*, 22 Oct. 1919, Vol. 1, No. 4; 'Wages for Wives', 27 Oct. 1919, Vol. 1, No. 5.
28. See *Love in Winter*, pp. 37–8. In *La Chartreuse de Parme*, Hervey says, Stendhal is describing imaginative love throughout.
29. E.A.B., 'English Novels and the French', *The New Commonwealth*, 29 Oct. 1919, Vol. 1, No. 5, p. 37. EAB was probably Ernest A. Boyd, a well-known reviewer for *The New Age*, with a special interest in French literature. Jameson had on her bookshelves George Saintsbury's *A History of the French Novel (To the Close of the 19th Century)*, 2 vols (London: Macmillan, 1917).
30. Letter from MSJ to Mr White, 14 May 1952 (The Macmillan Archive at the British Library, 3rd Tranche).
31. *JN* I: 156. See e.g. 'Thro' Our Periscope', *The New Commonwealth*, 7 Nov. 1919, Vol. 1, No. 6, p. 3, for a short item on women and children starving in Austria (subheadings 'Austria's Agony', 'Living Skeletons'). The first leader on 14 Nov., headed 'Let Us Know the Truth About Europe?' with the sub-heading 'Starvation—Here and Elsewhere', blamed England and America for the situation.
32. 'The Author of Our Serial, "The Happy Highways". A Chat with Storm Jameson', *The New Commonwealth*, 7 Nov. 1919, Vol. 1, No. 6, p. 6. Weekly serialisation began on 14 Nov. 1919 and ended on 20 Feb. 1920.
33. 'A Cloke for Two', *The New Commonwealth*, 9 Jan. 1920, n.s., Vol. 1, No. 2, p. 11.
34. 'A Philosophy of Youth. Childhood contd', *The New Commonwealth*, 16 Jan. 1920, n.s., Vol. 1, No. 3, p. 8.
35. 'The Modern Novel', in 'Special Literary Supplement Containing Reviews of Current Literature by Thomas Moult and Storm Jameson', *The New Commonwealth*, April 1920, n.s., Vol. 1, No. 10, pp. 29–30. Parts of this piece were reprinted in *The Novel in Contemporary Life* (Boston, Mass.: The Writer, Inc., 1938), along with more recent essays on social realism. The book was part of a series advising writers how to write.

36. Anon., 'The Happy Highways. Miss JAMESON's remarkable novel', *The New Commonwealth*, October 1920, n.s., Vol. 2, No. 8, p. 15.
37. 'The Woman Doctor's Second Tale. A Player Perforce', *The New Decameron*, Basil Blackwell (ed.), (Oxford: B. H. Blackwell, Vol. 2, 1920), pp. 158–74.
38. Anon., Review of *The New Decameron: Second Day*, *The New Age*, 23 Dec. 1920, Vol. 28, No. 8, p. 95.
39. 'The Tale of the Solitary English Girl. The Pitiful Wife', *The New Decameron*, Vol. 3, 1922, pp. 56–71.
40. 'Monotony', *The New Decameron*, Vol. 4, 1925, pp. 178–93.
41. [Orlo Williams], 'New Novels: The Happy Highways', *TLS*, 16 Sept. 1920, Issue 974, p. 599.
42. *JN* I: 158.
43. Letter to MSJ from John Galsworthy, 1 Oct. 1923 (CSC).
44. *The Happy Highways*, p. 50.
45. Ibid., p. 127.
46. Ibid., pp. 127–8.
47. Ibid., p. 128.
48. Ibid., p. 240.
49. Ibid., p. 264.
50. Ibid., pp. 138 (cf. *NTLP*, pp. 72–3), 142.
51. Ibid., p. 281.
52. *JN* I: 79.
53. [Harold Hannyngton Child], 'The Modern Drama', *TLS*, 2 Dec. 1920, Issue 985, p. 792.
54. *JN* I: 160.
55. *JN* I: 160–3.
56. Jameson visited Walter de la Mare at home in South London, wrote a piece on him in the *English Review*, pub. early 1922, and maintained the contact carefully (*JN* I: 164–6). In a letter to MSJ dated 23 July 1953, Middleton Murry reported having found her last letter of 1923, written at a time of depression, regretted having lost contact with her, and asked whether, with her fame, she had also found happiness (letter in CSC; and see *JN* I: 192–3).
57. *JN* I: 162.
58. *JN* I: 166–8.
59. Clarke's Ulster origins are of interest here, but the impulse for her letter is more likely to have come through *The New Commonwealth*, which since Oct. 1919 had been running a series of articles on 'The Irish Problem', arguing that the Home Rule Act, passed in 1914 and which became law in Dec. 1919, was already out of date. Shaw's Supplement on 'Socialism and Ireland' had appeared in Dec. 1919.
60. Letter to MSJ from John Galsworthy, 2 July 1921 (CSC).
61. *JN* I: 171. Jameson noted the year in the margins of her personal copy of *Journey from the North* (CSC). On Sanger, celebrated author of *My Fight for Birth Control* (New York, 1931, London, 1932), see Alec Craig, *The Banned Books of England* (London: George Allen & Unwin, 1937).

62. *JN* I: 172–5.
63. *JN* I: 181–2.
64. Anon., 'New Books [...]. Fiction', *TLS* 11 May 1922, Issue 1060, p. 309. A positive notice appeared in *The Sphere*, written by Clement Shorter, and MSJ wrote to thank him (Letter from MSJ to Clement Shorter, 1 June 1922 (Storm Jameson Collection, LSC)). Grazia Deledda was awarded the Nobel Prize for Literature; James Hilton became the highly popular author of *Lost Horizon* (1933) and *Goodbye Mr Chips* (1934).
65. Letter to MSJ from Michael Sadleir, 11 May 1922 (CSC).
66. Letter of 17 Sept. 1922, cit. in Winifred Holtby, *Letters to a Friend*, ed. Alice Holtby and Jean McWilliam (London: Collins, 1937), pp. 125–6.
67. *The Pitiful Wife* (London: Constable and Co. Ltd, 1923). Either *The Clash* or *The Pitiful Wife* was the novel through which Guy Chapman first heard of Jameson; he read it with 'cold interest' (Guy Chapman, *A Kind of Survivor*, introd. and ed. MSJ (London: Gollancz, n.d.), p. 105).
68. [Orlo Williams], 'New Novels: *The Pitiful Wife*', TLS, 30 Aug. 1923, Issue 1128, p. 571.
69. *JN* I: 186.
70. *The Pitiful Wife*, p. 312.
71. *JN* I: 192.
72. *JN* I: 188. MSJ noted the year in the margins of her personal copy of *JN* (CSC).
73. *Lady Susan and Life: An Indiscretion* (London: Chapman and Hall, 1923); reviewed by [Marjorie Grant Cook], *TLS*, 24 Jan. 1924, Issue 1149, p. 52.
74. Letter from MSJ to Alfred A. Knopf, 5 Jan. 1924 (CSC).

5. London 1924–1928: Publishing, Passion and Politics

1. MSJ, Preface to *Survivor*, p. 14.
2. *Survivor*, p. 23.
3. Ibid., p. 225.
4. Ibid., p. 15.
5. Ibid., p. 105.
6. Ibid., p. 77; marriage certificate in CSC.
7. Ibid., pp. 85–6.
8. Ibid., p. 106; *JN* I: 231.
9. MSJ wrote in the margin to her personal copy of *JN* I: 207: '2½ years of acting as his representative in London when we were both young. I have a profound respect for Alfred Knopf, and I count these years as one of the pleasures and achievements of my life. My work for him ended in 1928. My respect and affection for him has lasted a lifetime' (CSC). Irving Kolodin, Knopf's biographer, told MSJ of Knopf's great respect for her work, especially in recruiting authors such as Warwick Deeping and Charles Morgan (Letter to MSJ from Irving Kolodin, 10 July 1984 (CSC)). To recruit Charles Morgan, she had to work hard to persuade Knopf of his potential, and the success of *The Fountain*, which helped the firm at a moment of near-bankruptcy, was

always recalled fondly by Knopf (Letter to MSJ from Alfred A. Knopf, 17 March 1975 (CSC)).

10. *JN* I: 192.
11. Letter from MSJ to Michael Baker, 27 March 1981 (CSC).
12. *JN* I: 202.
13. 'Recent Novels', *New English Weekly*, Vol. 1, No. 1, 21 April 1932, p. 14.
14. *JN* I: 209.
15. *JN* I: 220–3; the narrative in the autobiography is very close to the account in *Love in Winter*.
16. TS of *JN*, Vol. 2, p. 130 (Jameson, Storm. Works (Autobiography) HRC). Another incident is related in *JN* I: 210.
17. *JN* I: 204.
18. Letter from MSJ to Angela Bull, 21 Aug. 1981 (CSC).
19. *JN* I: 201.
20. *JN* I: 206.
21. 'A Recent Novel', *New English Weekly*, 7 July 1932, Vol. I, No. 12, p. 286.
22. *None Turn Back*, pp. 19–21.
23. Letters from Guy Chapman to MSJ, 6–9 Oct. 1924 (CSC).
24. *JN* I: 224.
25. *Survivor*, p. 111.
26. Ibid., p. 115; cf. *JN* I: 233.
27. Christopher Storm-Clark in conversation with present author.
28. *JN* I: 233–4.
29. Marriage certificate (CSC).
30. *Survivor*, p. 113.
31. Letter from MSJ to Irene Rathbone, 18 March 1944 (IR-CSC).
32. *Survivor*, pp. 116–17.
33. *JN* I: 236–8.
34. John Fothergill, cit. Humphrey Carpenter, *The Brideshead Generation. Evelyn Waugh and His Generation* (London: Faber & Faber, 1989), pp. 115–16; on Fothergill's tenure of The Spreadeagle, see Carpenter, pp. 113–19.
35. 'A Mingled Strain', *The Fothergill Omnibus*, introd. John Fothergill, R. G. Collingwood, and Gerald Gould (London: Eyre & Spottiswoode, 1931).
36. *JN* I: 248–51.
37. Naomi Mitchison, *You May Well Ask. A Memoir 1920–1940* (London: Fontana Paperbacks, 1986), p. 183.
38. Marjorie Watts, *Mrs Sappho: The Life of C. A. Dawson Scott, Mother of International P.E.N.* (London: Duckworth, 1987), p. 98. For a summary version of Jameson's PEN connections, see my essay 'Margaret Storm Jameson and the London PEN Centre: Mobilising Commitment', *EREA* Vol. 4, No. 2 (Autumn 2006), pp. 81–9. URL: www.e-rea.org.
39. Letter from MSJ to Hermon Ould, 1 May 1943 (PEN archive (London uncat.), HRC).
40. Four letters MSJ to Hermon Ould, n.d., then 1 Dec. 1926 to 29 Feb. 1927 (Storm Jameson Collection, Letters from Storm Jameson to PEN, Folder 1926–38, HRC).

41. See Amabel Williams-Ellis, *All Stracheys are Cousins. Memoirs* (London: Weidenfeld & Nicholson, 1983).

42. Clough Williams-Ellis, *Around the World in Ninety Years* (Penrhyndeudraeth: Golden Dragon Books, Portmeirion Ltd, 1978), p. 116.

43. [Marjorie Grant Cook], 'New Novels', *TLS*, 4 March 1926, Issue 1259, p. 160.

44. Letter from MSJ to Valentine Dobrée, 14 April 1927 (Dobrée/ Chapman Correspondence, Brotherton Collection, Leeds University Library).

45. *The Lovely Ship* (1927), *The Voyage Home* (1930) and *A Richer Dust* (1931) were published separately and then collected by Heinemann in one volume, *The Triumph of Time: A Trilogy* (1932). All page references are to the collected edition.

46. [Orlo Williams], 'New Novels: *The Lovely Ship*', *TLS*, 7 April 1927, Issue 1314, p. 248.

47. Vera Brittain, *Testament of Friendship* (1940; rpt. London: Macmillan, 1947), p. 273.

48. Vera Brittain, 'Portraits and Pastels', *Time and Tide*, 13 May 1927, p. 451. See for these early contacts Catherine Clay, *British Women Writers 1914–1945: Professional Work and Friendship* (Aldershot: Ashgate, 2006), p. 74.

49. Brittain, *Testament of Friendship*, p. 335. See also in that book p. 440, where Brittain uses a quotation from MSJ in defence of engaged writing for her discussion of Holtby's work.

50. *The Triumph of Time*, pp. 287–8.

51. Ibid., p. 295.

52. See *JN* I: 245–7 for MSJ's shrewd real-life negotiations with Constable and Heinemann.

53. *Love in Winter*, p. 21.

54. Ibid., pp. 18, 32.

55. 'Problem of Sex in Public Life', *Daily Mirror*, 28 March 1927.

56. 'Nothing Wrong with Modern Woman', *Daily Mirror*, 23 May 1927.

57. Letter from MSJ to Valentine Dobrée, May 1927 (Dobrée Correspondence, Brotherton Collection, Leeds University Library).

58. Biographical detail taken from *Valentine Dobrée, 1894–1974* (Leeds: The University Gallery, 2000).

59. Valentine Dobrée, *Your Cuckoo Sings by Kind* (London and New York: A. A. Knopf, 1927); see Letter from MSJ to Valentine Dobrée, 21 Feb. 1927 (DCBCLUL). T. S. Eliot praised the book warmly, and in the 1960s published Valentine's poetry with Faber.

60. Letter from MSJ to Valentine Dobrée, 14 April 1927 (DCBCLUL).

61. Letter from MSJ to Valentine Dobrée, 5 May 1927 (DCBCLUL).

62. Letter from MSJ to Valentine Dobrée, 23 May 1927 (DCBCLUL).

63. *JN* I: 240.

64. Letter from MSJ to Valentine Dobrée, 14 Feb. 1928 (DCBCLUL).

65. *Survivor*, p. 116.

66. A snap inserted by Jameson of herself, Guy and Bonamy in her personal copy of *JN*, between pages 248–9, marked 1928, is titled 'Staying with the Dobrées in Suffolk' (CSC).

67. Letter from MSJ to Valentine Dobrée, 17 Nov. 1928 (DCBCLUL).

68. Letter from MSJ to Valentine Dobrée, 3 Dec. 1928 (DCBCLUL).
69. The lecture was given to the Literary Circle of the National Liberal Club. Published by Heinemann in May 1929, it was described in the *TLS* as limited and trite. The reviewer preferred Rebecca West's suggestion 'that the modern novel must be regarded as essentially poetic in origin, deriving less and less at bottom from the outer life of the world and more and more from the inner-life of the poet-novelist' ([Geoffrey H. Wells], 'For Mr Robinson', *TLS*, 30 May 1929, Issue 1426, p. 433).
70. *Farewell to Youth* (London: William Heinemann Ltd, 1928).
71. Ibid., p. 10.
72. Ibid., p. 30.
73. Ibid., pp. 99–107. In 'The Soul of a Modern Woman', *The Evening News*, 7 Jan. 1929, Jameson wrote about her feelings of inadequacy before the men who went to war: 'My purse is full of spiders and my head is full of ghosts... young ghosts most of them... The women of my generation are so far behind its men that we shall never catch up. I feel less than two cents beside a man of my own age who fought through the war. [...] As beside them, we know neither terror nor pity nor endurance nor friendship nor relief nor courage nor the sharpness of living.'
74. *Farewell to Youth*, p. 99.
75. Ibid., p. 269.
76. Ibid., p. 290.
77. Ibid., p. 237.
78. Ibid., p. 296.
79. Ibid., p. 312.

6. London 1928–Yorkshire 1931: 'Trying to be Superwoman'

1. *The Evening News*, 1 Oct. 1928, p. 8.
2. Articles published Oct.–Dec. 1928; see Bibliography for details.
3. 'The Soul of a Modern Woman', *The Evening News*, 7 Jan. 1929, p. 11.
4. *Survivor*, p. 119.
5. Sally Cline, *Radclyffe Hall. A Woman Called John* (London: John Murray, 1997), p. 249.
6. Letter from MSJ to Michael Baker, 27 March 1981 (CSC). She checked her recollections with Alfred Knopf, who replied that with hindsight neither Cape nor Knopf had handled Radclyffe Hall's book well; but he didn't think her name could be attached to a period (Letter to MSJ from Alfred Knopf, 28th April 1981 (CSC)).
7. Letter from MSJ to Valentine Dobrée, 17 Nov. 1928 (DCBCLUL).
8. Letter from MSJ to Valentine Dobrée, 8 Dec. 1928 (DCBCLUL). For other accounts of the episode, see *Love in Winter* and *JN* I: 249.
9. Letter from MSJ to Valentine Dobrée, 2 Jan. 1929 (DCBCLUL).
10. Letters in MS (PEN) Recip. Jameson, Storm, 1897–, 2nd folder, PEN archive, HRC.
11. *Survivor*, p. 123.

12. Letter from MSJ to Valentine Dobrée, 4 May 1929 (DCBCLUL). Valentine's book was published by Faber and Faber in 1929.
13. *Survivor* 123; cf. *JN* I: 251.
14. Letter from MSJ to Valentine Dobrée, 22 Oct. 1929 (DCBCLUL). She kept photographs of her room and its view in her personal copy of *JN* I, between pp. 250 and 251 (CSC).
15. Letter from MSJ to Bonamy Dobrée, 13 Nov. 1929 (DCBCLUL).
16. [Marjorie Grant Cook], 'The Voyage Home', *TLS*, 30 Jan. 1930, Issue 1461, p. 76.
17. *The Triumph of Time*, p. 557.
18. Letter from MSJ to Bonamy Dobrée, 14 March 1930 (DCBCLUL).
19. *88 Short Stories, by Maupassant*, trans. MSJ and Ernest Boyd (London: Cassell and Company, 1930). Jameson had already translated Maupassant in 1924 and 1925, and this work provided a useful intermittent source of income (four tales were broadcast, for example, on the BBC Overseas Service, 1952–4).
20. *JN* I: 286–7, 305.
21. Letters to MSJ from R. H. Tawney, 18 Sept. 1930 and 20 Feb. 1931 (CSC).
22. *The Decline of Merry England* (London: Cassell and Company, 1930), p. 18.
23. Ibid., p. 249.
24. Ibid., p. 21.
25. *JN* I: 283–4.
26. Ibid.
27. Letter from MSJ to Hermon Ould, 12 Dec. 1930 (MS (PEN) Recip. Jameson, Storm, 1897–, 3rd folder, PEN archive, HRC).
28. Letter from MSJ to Valentine Dobrée, 3 March 1931 (DCBCLUL).
29. The novel was favourably reviewed by Marjorie Grant Cook in the *TLS*, 19 Feb. 1931, Issue 1516, p. 132.
30. Letter from MSJ to Valentine Dobrée, 19 June 1931 (DCBCLUL).
31. [Marjorie Grant Cook], *TLS*, 24 March 1932, Issue 1573, p. 216.
32. 'Man the Helpmate', in Mabel Ulrich (ed.), *Man, Proud Man* (London: Hamish Hamilton, 1932), pp. 134–5.
33. *Survivor*, p. 120.
34. Letter from MSJ to Valentine Dobrée, 21 Feb. 1931 (DCBCLUL).
35. *Survivor*, p. 128.
36. *JN* I: 285.
37. *JN* I: 286.
38. *Survivor*, 128.
39. *JN* I: 262.
40. TS of *JN*, Vol. 3, 'Eatage of the Fog', p. 203 (Jameson, Storm. Works (Autobiography), HRC).
41. *JN* I: 270. Ramsay MacDonald's Government resigned 24 Aug. 1931, after the Cabinet split on his proposal to balance the budget with a 10 per cent cut in unemployment benefit. On 25 Aug., he formed a National Coalition Government, pushed through his budget, and with Philip Snowden and J. P. Thomas was subsequently expelled from the Labour Party.

42. Hutt, *The Post-War History of the British Working Class*, pp. 209–13.
43. TS of *JN* , Vol. 2, pp. 56–7, p. 94 (Jameson, Storm. Works (Autobiography), HRC).
44. Letter to MSJ from Harold Raymond, 11 Dec. 1931 (MS (Jameson, S). Recip. Chatto and Windus (Storm Jameson Collection), HRC).
45. Letter from MSJ to Harold Raymond, 12 Dec. 1931 (MS (Jameson, S), Letters (Storm Jameson Collection), HRC).
46. Letter to MSJ from Harold Raymond, 14 Dec. 1931 (MS (Jameson, S). Recip. Chatto and Windus (Storm Jameson Collection), HRC).
47. Letter from MSJ to Ethel Mannin, 28 Dec. 1931 (MS (Jameson Storm), Letters, Mannin, Ethel 1931–2, HRC).
48. Letter from MSJ to Ethel Mannin, 29 Dec. 1931 (MS (Jameson Storm) Letters, Mannin, Ethel 1931–2, HRC).
49. Letter from MSJ to Ethel Mannin, 30 Dec. 1931 (MS (Jameson Storm) Letters, Mannin, Ethel 1931–2, HRC).
50. Letter from MSJ to Ethel Mannin, 5 Jan. 1932 (MS (Jameson Storm) Letters, Mannin, Ethel 1931–2, HRC).
51. Letter from MSJ to A. D. Peters, 5 Jan. 1932 (MS (Jameson S) Letters, HRC).

7. London 1932–1934: New People, New Politics

1. 'In the End', *Challenge to Death* (London: Constable & Co., Ltd, 1934), p. 328–9.
2. *JN* I: 405.
3. *JN* I: 293.
4. *Survivor*, pp. 129–30; *JN* says the visit began in February (*JN* I: 266).
5. *Survivor*, p. 130.
6. *JN* I: 268.
7. *Survivor*, p. 132.
8. *JN* I: 281.
9. John Lehmann, *The Whispering Gallery* (1955), rpt. in *In My Own Time. Memoirs of a Literary Life* (Boston and Toronto: Little, Brown and Company, 1969), p. 136.
10. Ibid., pp. 136–7.
11. *Survivor*, p. 137.
12. Naomi Mitchison, *You May Well Ask*, p. 185.
13. *The Gryphon*, Nov. 1936, p. 76.
14. *Survivor*, p. 129.
15. Tawney's famous account of the battle of the Somme, 'The Attack', appeared in the *Westminster Gazette* in Aug. 1916.
16. *Survivor*, p. 129; *JN* I: 285.
17. *Survivor*, p. 144. At Tawney's death, L. C. Knights wrote to thank Jameson for her angry public letter in response to Richard Cobb's snide obituary, and her expression of the respect and affection in which her generation had held him (CSC).
18. *Survivor*, pp. 141–2.

19. *Survivor*, p. 134.
20. See the essay 'Introduction and Apology for my Life', written in Sept. 1938, for *Civil Journey*.
21. *Survivor*, p. 138.
22. See article on William Casey by A. P. Robbins, rev. Marc Brodie, *Oxford Dictionary of National Biography* (URL http://www.oxforddnb.com/view/article/323210).
23. See article on Gerald Barry by Becky E. Conekin, *Oxford Dictionary of National Biography* (URL http://www.oxforddnb.com/view/article/30623?docPos=1).
24. See article on Clifford Norton by Peter Neville, *Oxford Dictionary of National Biography* (URL http://www.oxforddnb.com/view/article/65288).
25. *Survivor*, p. 136.
26. Jameson wrote that: 'The after-dinner gossip of foreign correspondents is the best in the world' (*JN* I: 318).
27. *Survivor*, pp. 136–7; cf. *JN* I: 323–5.
28. Martin Ceadel, *Pacifism in Britain 1914–1945: The Defining of a Faith* (Oxford: Clarendon Press, 1980), p. 108.
29. Ibid., p. 88.
30. Ibid., p. 102.
31. 'The Author of Our Serial, "The Happy Highways". A Chat with Storm Jameson', *The New Commonwealth*, 7 Nov. 1919, Vol. 1, No. 6, p. 6.
32. *JN* I: 307; TS indicates 1932.
33. Ceadel, *Pacifism in Britain*, p. 107.
34. Bonamy Dobrée, 'Views and Reviews: Autobiography Plus', *New English Weekly*, Vol. III, No. 4, 11 May 1933.
35. Sylvia Townsend Warner, 'This Book: Convincing as a Hailstorm', *Daily Worker*, 4 Dec. 1935.
36. *NTLP*, p. 94.
37. Ibid., p. 183.
38. Ibid., p. 213.
39. *Survivor*, p. 137.
40. *NTLP*, pp. 219–20.
41. Ibid., p. 237.
42. *JN* I: 282, 308, 320, 323.
43. Letter from MSJ to Vernon Bartlett, 2 March 1933 (Letters…to Vernon Bartlett, BL, Add. Ms. 59500, f. 157).
44. Letter from MSJ to Valentine Dobrée, 3 March 1933 (BC Dobrée correspondence, LSC).
45. *JN* I: 326. Jameson's article of 21 Oct. 1933 in *The New Clarion* ('Fifteen years ago—we said "Never Again!" ', Vol. 3, No. 71, p. 325, p. 327), referring to Hitler's withdrawal from the Disarmament Conference, demanded that the Socialist Party, as agreed a fortnight ago at the Hastings conference, engage in immediate debate on its position in the event of the threat of war; Jameson found herself unable to decide between war or the abandonment of the world to German militarism, but expressed her belief that if Hitler did re-arm, a socialist uprising in Germany against him was not likely. As positions in the

journal became increasingly pacifist, Guy Chapman published his own essay, 'Put Peace in its Place' (*The New Clarion*, 2 Dec. 1933, Vol. 3 No. 78, pp. 1–2), arguing that the current rise of anti-war propaganda was based on fear, not pacifist conviction, and the realisation that in the coming war civilians were as vulnerable to bombing as soldiers on the front line.

46. Clay, *British Women Writers*, pp. 75, 77.
47. Cit. Marion Shaw, *The Clear Stream: A Life of Winifred Holtby* (London: Virago, 1999), p. 220.
48. Letter from MSJ to the *New English Weekly*, 'Symposium or Law-Court?', 19 Oct. 1933, Vol. IV, No. 1, p. 24 (replying to reviews by C.H. Norman, 'Patriotism Ltd.' *New English Weekly*, 5 Oct. 1933, Vol. III, pp. 583–5 and Margaret R. B. Shaw 'Vera -Sed Non Veritas', *New English Weekly*, 12 Oct. 1933, Vol. III, pp. 618–19).
49. Vera Brittain, 'Can the Women of the World Stop War?' *Modern Woman* (Feb. 1934), rpt. in Paul Berry and Alan Bishop (eds), *Testament of a Generation. The Journalism of Vera Brittain and Winifred Holtby* (London: Virago, 1985), pp. 216–20 (p. 217).
50. *JN* I: 327. Brittain wrote a foreword for the American edition.
51. Letter to MSJ from Aldous Huxley, cit. in TS of *JN*, Vol. 2, p. 79 (Jameson, Storm. Works (Autobiography) HRC).
52. Letter from MSJ to Vernon Bartlett, 29 March 1934 (Letters [...] to Vernon Bartlett, BL, Add. Ms. 59500, f. 158).
53. Letter from MSJ to Vernon Bartlett, 13 June 1934 (Letters [...] to Vernon Bartlett, BL, Add. Ms. 59500, f. 160).
54. *Challenge to Death*, p. xi.
55. Ibid., p. 9.
56. Ibid., p. 19.
57. Ibid., p. 324.
58. Ibid., p. 329.
59. *JN* I: 328.
60. *JN* I: 320–1.

8. London 1934–1936: Expanding Horizons

1. *JN* I: 321–2.
2. *JN* I: 317.
3. Letter to MSJ from A. R. Orage, 8 Dec. 1933 (CSC). Catherine Clay has contrasted the readiness with which Jameson subsequently discussed her collaboration with Orage, and her failure to mention her contributions over the same period to the socialist weekly, *The New Clarion* (see Clay, 'Storm Jameson's Journalism 1913–33'). In this new series of the latter journal, which attracted contributions from George Lansbury, G. D. H. Cole, Harold Laski, and R. H. Tawney, Jameson's attacks on Britain's callous indifference to unemployment and poverty, especially child poverty, and her failure to follow France in legislating for free secondary education, were exactly in tune with the

radical tone (see e.g. 'The Christmas Snob', 3 Dec. 1932, Vol. 1 No. 26, p. 605; 'Salients', 31 Dec. 1932, Vol. 2, No. 30, p. 63); '"A Bad-Tempered Footnote" to Life in 1933', 10 June 1933, Vol. 3, No. 53, p. 11.

4. Letter to MSJ from A. R. Orage, 22 July 1934 (CSC).
5. Letter to MSJ from A. R. Orage, 5 Aug. 1934 (CSC).
6. Letter from MSJ to Irene Rathbone, 31 March 1937 (IR-CSC).
7. Letter from MSJ to Irene Rathbone, 5 Dec. 1940 (IR-CSC).
8. *None Turn Back*, p. 102.
9. G. D. H. Cole, 'Guild Socialism Twenty Years Ago and Now', *New English Weekly*, 13 Sept. 1934.
10. Philip Mairet, 'Patriots of Europe', *New English Weekly*, 15 Dec. 1932, Vol. II, No. 9, pp. 210–11.
11. Philip Mairet, 'Views and Reviews. A League of Minds', *New English Weekly*, 22 June 1933, Vol. III, No. 10, pp. 231–2.
12. Quintus, 'Germany and the Jews', *New English Weekly*, 13 April 1933, Vol. II, No. 26, pp. 610–11.
13. Letter from MSJ to Hermon Ould, 16 Jan. 1934 (MS [PEN] Recip. Jameson, Storm, 1897–, 3rd folder 1930–39, HRC).
14. Letter from MSJ to Hermon Ould, 18 Jan. 1934 (MS [PEN] Recip. Jameson, Storm, 1897–, 3rd folder 1930–39, HRC).
15. Letter from MSJ to Hermon Ould, 23 Jan. 1934 (MS [PEN] Recip. Jameson, Storm, 1897–, 3rd folder 1930–39, HRC); see also letter of 20 Jan., same source.
16. Letter from MSJ to Hermon Ould, 6 Feb. 1934 (MS [PEN] Recip. Jameson, Storm, 1897–, 4th folder 1930–39, HRC). Renn was eventually released in 1935. He took an active role in the Spanish Civil War, and subsequently followed an academic career in Mexico and, after the defeat of Germany, in East Germany.
17. Amabel Williams-Ellis, *All Stracheys Are Cousins*, p. 128.
18. Ibid., pp. 132–3.
19. John Lucas, 'An Interview with Edgell Rickword', in John Lucas (ed.), *The 1930s. A Challenge to Orthodoxy* (Brighton: The Harvester Press, 1978), p. 4.
20. Amabel Williams-Ellis, *All Stracheys Are Cousins*, p. 138.
21. H. Gustav Klaus, in Lucas, *The 1930s*, p. 17.
22. *JN* I: 294. See also Amabel Williams-Ellis, 'Soviet Literature', in *Britain and the Soviets: The Congress of Peace and Friendship with the USSR* (London: Martin Lawrence, 1936). It is not clear whether this is the same writers' friendship meeting where Jameson risked the organisers' disapproval by asking Alexander Fadayev, leader of the Russian delegation, what Boris Pasternak, then relatively unknown, was currently writing—eliciting coldly terrifying assurances that Pasternak had put aside his own work and was happily busying himself with translations (*JN* I: 295–6).
23. *JN* I: 320.
24. Ceadel, *Pacifism in Britain*, p. 153.
25. MSJ, cit. Colin Cross, *The Fascists in Britain* (London: Barrie and Rockliff, 1961), p. 114.
26. *JN* I: 328.

27. Richard Thurlow, *Fascism in Britain. From Oswald Mosley's Blackshirts to the National Front* (London and New York: I. B. Tauris Publishers, 1998), pp. 72–3.

28. T. R. F., *Jewish Chronicle*, 29 Oct. 1982, noted on the publication of the Virago reprints that *Company Parade* 'contains the detailed portrait of a Jewish newspaper-owner who has radical leanings which is, for its period, surprisingly sympathetic' (CSC).

29. Letter from MSJ to Henrietta Leslie, 8 Aug. 1934 (MS [PEN] Recip. Jameson, Storm, 1897–, 3rd folder 1930–39, HRC).

30. Marjorie Watts, *Mrs Sappho*, p. 198.

31. *JN* I: 332–3.

32. *Survivor*, p. 140.

33. Tossa was discovered fifteen years later by Rose Macaulay, who described it in *Fabled Shore* as a fashionable haunt of painters and writers before the Civil War, and picked out the Roman villa and the medieval town walls. She reported that the town was left relatively undamaged, though when she saw it the tourists were still frightened off by the discomforts and perils of war, by the inconveniences of bombing and starvation and the fear of anarchy (*Fabled Shore. From the Pyrenees to Portugal* (London: Hamish Hamilton, 1949; Readers Union Edition, 1950), pp. 58–64 (at p. 62)). Nowadays Tossa de Mar is a tourist hotspot at the heart of the Costa Brava, 100 km south of the French border and close to Lloret de Mar.

34. *New English Weekly*, 8 Feb. 1934, Vol. IV, No. 17, p. 408.

35. The Swiss was probably Walter Leonard, son of the singer Lotte Lenya. See extract from 'The Children They Sent Away', *Lookout*, Sept. 1983, on website 'Spanish Refugees and Basque Children: Faringdon Colony, Oxfordshire', URL http://www.spanishrefugees-basquechildren.org/C6-13-Faringdon_Colony.html (last consulted 8 August 2006, 16.53).

36. *JN* I: 333–5.

37. *The Green Man* (London: Macmillan & Co., Ltd, 1952), pp. 168–9.

38. Ibid., p. 169.

39. *JN* I: 316.

40. The portrait of the gluttonous writer-activist reappears in *No Victory for the Soldier* (London: Collins, 1938), published under the pseudonym of James Hill, which contains MSJ's only extensive treatment of the Spanish Civil War.

41. TS of *JN*, Vol. 2, p. 88 (Jameson, Storm. Works (Autobiography) HRC).

42. Roy Campbell, *Light on a Dark Horse. An Autobiography (1901–1935)* (London: Hollis & Carter, 1951), pp. 318–19.

43. *Survivor*, p. 145.

44. Letter from MSJ to Valentine Dobrée, 10 Aug. 1935 (DCBCLUL).

45. Letter from Barbara Cawood to Hilda Cawood, 15 Aug. 1935 (CSC).

46. Letters from MSJ to Hermon Ould, 25 and 27 Sept. 1935 (MS (PEN) Recip. Jameson, Storm, 1897–, 3rd folder, PEN archive, HRC).

47. *JN* I: 254–5.

48. *Survivor*, p. 150.

49. Letter from MSJ to Hermon Ould, 2 Nov. 1935 (MS (PEN) Recip. Jameson, Storm, 1897–, 3rd folder, PEN archive, HRC).

50. Letter from MSJ to Hermon Ould, 19 Dec. 1935 (MS (PEN) Recip. Jameson, Storm, 1897–, 3rd folder, PEN archive, HRC).
51. Letter from MSJ to Hermon Ould, 22 Feb. 1936 (MS (PEN) Recip. Jameson, Storm, 1897–, 3rd folder, PEN archive, HRC).
52. Letter from MSJ to Hermon Ould, 25 Feb. 1936 (MS (PEN) Recip. Jameson, Storm, 1897–, 3rd folder, PEN archive, HRC).
53. Letter from MSJ to Hermon Ould, 3 March 1936 (MS (PEN) Recip. Jameson, Storm, 1897–, 3rd folder, PEN archive, HRC).

9. Fiction and Form

1. *JN* I: 314. See also on this theme my essay, ' "The Spectacle of Europe": Politics, PEN and Prose Fiction: The Work of Storm Jameson in the Inter-War Years', in Angela Kershaw and Angela Kimyongür (eds), *Women in Europe* (London: Ashcroft, 2007), pp. 25–38.
2. *JN* I: 329.
3. Letter from MSJ to Valentine Dobrée, 27 April 1935 (DCBCLUL).
4. *Company Parade*, p. 19.
5. *None Turn Back*, p. 34.
6. *The Waste Land*, Jameson commented, 'gives the note of the 'twenties at its purest and strongest' (*The Writer's Situation*, p.174.) But both David Renn and Nicholas Roxby agree that its flaw is that Eliot never himself lived there, and they prefer the representations of Villon and Baudelaire (*Love in Winter*, pp. 222–4).
7. *Company Parade*, p. 286.
8. Ibid., p. 267. See Jameson's comments below in a review of 1932 on Dos Passos's novel, *Nineteen nineteen*.
9. *Company Parade*, p. 120.
10. Ibid., p. 305–6.
11. Ibid., p.167.
12. *None Turn Back*, p. 42.
13. Ibid., pp. 46–7.
14. Ibid., p. 306.
15. Ibid., pp. 124–5.
16. *Company Parade*, p. 106.
17. *None Turn Back*, pp. 26–7. The Zinoviev letter was a forgery, supposed to have been sent on 15 Sept. 1924 by Zinoviev, President of the Third International, to A. McManus, the British Communist Party representative, urging insurrection in Britain. The *Mail* published it on 25 Oct. 1924, and ended Ramsay MacDonald's chances of winning the 1924 election in the following week.
18. Ibid., p. 88. The same patriotism is attributed to the French Jewish newspaper editor in *Cloudless May*, who is totally uncorrupt—a mark of change in Jameson's attitude to Jews in the course of the Second World War.

19. Ibid., p. 132.
20. Ibid., p. 84.
21. *Love in Winter*, pp. 349–51.
22. *None Turn Back*, p. 102.
23. Ibid., p. 83.
24. *In the Second Year* (London: Cassell & Company Ltd, 1936); rpt. ed. Stan Smith, (Nottingham: Trent Editions, 2004). Page references are to the 2004 edition.
25. For an extensive identification of the real-life political and literary figures Jameson drew on for the characters in her novel, see Smith's Introduction and Notes.
26. *In the Second Year*, p. 62.
27. Ibid., p. 150.
28. See Jennifer Birkett, 'A Fictional Function: Storm Jameson and W. H. Auden', *English*, 2007, pp. 178–9.
29. *JN* I: 300–1.
30. Her influential essay on 'Documents' in *Fact* (No 4, 1937) is well-known and often (perhaps too often) quoted: 'Perhaps the nearest equivalent of what is wanted exists already in another form in the documentary film. As the photographer does, so must the writer keep himself out of the picture while working ceaselessly to present the *fact* from a striking (poignant, ironic, penetrating, significant) angle. The narrative must be sharp, compressed, concrete. Dialogue must be short,—a seizing of the significant, the revealing word. The emotion should spring directly from the fact. It must not be squeezed from it by the writer, running forward with a, "When I saw this, I felt, I suffered, I rejoiced. . . ." His job is not to tell us what he felt, but to be coldly and industriously presenting, arranging, selecting, discarding from the mass of his material to get the significant detail, which leaves no more to be said, and implies everything. And for goodness' sake let us get some fun out of it' (pp. 15–16).
31. Letter from MSJ to Valentine Dobrée, 3 March 1931 (DCBCLUL).
32. 'Recent Novels', *New English Weekly*, 4 Aug. 1932, Vol. I, No. 16, p. 379.
33. 'Recent Novels', *New English Weekly*, 21 April 1932, Vol. I, No. 1, p. 14.
34. 'Recent Novels', *New English Weekly*, 23 June 1932, Vol. I, No. 10, p. 235.
35. 'Recent Novels', *New English Weekly*, 15 Sept. 1932, Vol. I, No. 10, p. 525.
36. 'Recent Novels', *New English Weekly*, 26 Jan. 1933, Vol. II, No. 15, p. 350.
37. 'A Recent Novel', *New English Weekly*, 7 July 1932, Vol. I, No. 12, p. 286.
38. *JN* I: 300.
39. Letter from MSJ to James Hanley, 16 June 1933 (Papers of James Hanley (920 HAN/4 Correspondence from Storm Jameson to James Hanley), Liverpool Record Office).
40. Letter from MSJ to James Hanley, 29 June 1933 (Papers of James Hanley (920 HAN/4 Correspondence from Storm Jameson to James Hanley), Liverpool Record Office).
41. Letter from MSJ to James Hanley, 4 Dec. 1933 (Papers of James Hanley (920 HAN/4 Correspondence from Storm Jameson to James Hanley), Liverpool Record Office).
42. Letter from MSJ to James Hanley, 20 July 1934 (Papers of James Hanley (920 HAN/4 Correspondence from Storm Jameson to James Hanley), Liverpool Record Office).

43. Letter from MSJ to James Hanley, 6 Feb. 1935 (Papers of James Hanley (920 HAN/4 Correspondence from Storm Jameson to James Hanley), Liverpool Record Office).
44. Letter from MSJ to James Hanley, 26 Sept. 1935 (Papers of James Hanley (920 HAN/4 Correspondence from Storm Jameson to James Hanley), Liverpool Record Office). The unnamed author was Nelson Algren, the Communist activist and chronicler of the wild side of Chicago; *Somebody in Boots*, his ground-breaking novel of life among the dispossessed, was published in 1935.
45. 'Recent Novels', *New English Weekly*, 2 June 1932, Vol. I, No. 7, pp. 165–6.
46. 'Culture and Environment', *New English Weekly*, 9 March 1933, Vol. II, p. 21, p. 497.
47. Ibid., p. 498.
48. 'Recent Novels', *New English Weekly*, 12 May 1932, Vol. I, No. 4, p. 91.
49. 'Recent Novels', *New English Weekly*, 27 Oct. 1932, Vol. II, No 2, p. 41.
50. 'A Recent Novel', *New English Weekly*, 8 Dec. 1932, Vol. II, No. 8, p. 184.

10. 1936–1938: Waking up to War

1. TS of *JN*, Vol. 2, p. 95 (Jameson, Storm. Works (Autobiography) HRC).
2. *JN* I: 341–2.
3. TS of *JN*, Vol. 2, pp. 96–7 (Jameson, Storm. Works (Autobiography) HRC). The PPU is not mentioned in the published version of *Journey from the North*, though it figures at several points in the original typescript. Ceadel has a different date (22 May) for her attendance at the founding meeting of the PPU and acceptance to become a sponsor (Ceadel, *Pacifism in Britain*, p. 222).
4. TS of *JN*, Vol. 2, pp. 128–9 (Jameson, Storm. Works (Autobiography) HRC).
5. TS of *JN*, Vol. 2, pp. 178–9 (Jameson, Storm. Works (Autobiography) HRC). Jameson's anguish and embarrassment over her position, then and later, contrasts sharply with Ethel Mannin's account, in an autobiography published two years after Jameson's *Journey from the North*, of how she, like most people, cheerfully followed the fashionable road to pacifism. In 1935, Mannin said, the Jubilee year: '[P]acifism was all the rage. It really did seem like that—a craze, with a nation-wide Peace Ballot and the founding of the Peace Pledge Union in June. [...] I did not myself [...] join the PPU but all through 1935 I was strongly pacifist, and [...] became not merely anti-war but dedicated to the idea of non-violence generally. I am not being cynical when I say that in 1934 and 1935 pacifism was "fashionable", especially among the younger intelligentsia, along with what in the ILP we called "critical support of the Soviet Union". As Ronald Blythe says in *The Age of Illusion*, writing of the Thirties, "By mid-decade art talk and sex talk were out and political talk was in. It absorbed every stratum of society and the mass entertainers were obliged to note the trend and cater for it"' (Mannin, p. 165).
6. *JN* I: 344.
7. TS of *JN*, Vol. 2, pp. 101–2 (Jameson, Storm. Works (Autobiography) HRC).
8. *JN* I: 345.

9. I have discussed the knowledge of developments in Spain that Jameson acquired through Chalmers Mitchell and her journalist friend Philip Jordan in 'Margaret Storm Jameson and the Spanish Civil War: The Fight for Human Values', Special Issue of the *Journal of English Studies*, No. 5 (University of La Rioja, Logroño, forthcoming).

10. Editorial, 'A Popular Front?', *Time and Tide*, Vol. XVII, No. 21, 23 May 1936, p. 749.

11. 'A Popular Front', Letters to the Editor, *Time and Tide*, Vol. XVII, No. 23, 6 June 1936, p. 811.

12. Letter from MSJ to Hermon Ould, 18 June 1937 (MS (PEN) Recip. Jameson, Storm, 1897–, 3rd folder, PEN archive, HRC).

13. Letter from MSJ to Valentine Dobrée, 26 June 1936 (DCBCLUL).

14. P.B., 'The Writers of the World Plan an Encyclopedia,' *Time and Tide*, Vol. XVII, No. 26, 27 June 1926, p. 937.

15. Letter from MSJ to Hermon Ould, 16 May 1936 (MS (PEN) Recip. Jameson, Storm, 1897–, 3rd folder, PEN archive, HRC).

16. *JN* I: 347–9.

17. Letter from MSJ to PEN Secretary, 29 Sept. 1936; letter to Hermon Ould, 11 Oct. 1936 (MS (PEN) Recip. Jameson, Storm, 1897–, 3rd folder, PEN archive, HRC).

18. *JN* I: 350–5.

19. *Survivor*, p. 159.

20. Ibid., p. 160; *JN* I: 355–7.

21. *Survivor*, pp. 161–3.

22. Ibid., p. 179.

23. Letter from Dennis Bird to *This England*, *c*.4 Dec. 1992, in response to an article on MSJ published in Autumn 1991 (CSC).

24. Information supplied by Christopher Storm-Clark.

25. Ibid.

26. *JN* I: 358.

27. *JN* I: 408.

28. *Survivor*, pp. 164, 167.

29. Letter from MSJ to Valentine Dobrée, 26 Nov. 1937 (DCBCLUL).

30. *The Novel in Contemporary Life*, p. 20.

31. Letter from MSJ to Valentine Dobrée, 17 Dec. 1937 (DCBCLUL).

32. TS of *JN*, Vol. 2, pp. 131–2 (Jameson, Storm. Works (Autobiography) HRC).

33. William Lamb, *The World Ends* (London: J. M. Dent and Sons Ltd, 1937).

34. Guy Chapman, *Culture and Survival* (London: Jonathan Cape, 1940), p. 13.

35. Ibid., p. 243.

36. *The World Ends*, p. 78.

37. Ibid., pp. 153–7.

38. Ibid., p. 204.

39. Ibid., p. 40.

40. Ibid., p. 200.

41. Letter from Carol Hill to A. D. Peters, 3 May 1938 (Jameson, S., Misc., Peters (A D), Literary Agent (Correspondence files relating to Storm Jameson), HRC).

42. Letter from A. D. Peters to Carol Hill, 17 May 1938 (Jameson, S., Misc., Peters (A D), Literary Agent (Correspondence files relating to Storm Jameson), HRC).
43. Letter from MSJ to W. Roughead (ADP), 16 June 1938 (Jameson, S., Misc., Peters (A D), Literary Agent (Correspondence files relating to Storm Jameson), HRC).
44. *JN* I: 367, 370.
45. B. H. Liddell Hart, *The Memoirs of Captain Liddell Hart* (Cassell: London, 1965), II: 193.
46. *JN* I: 376.
47. TS of *JN*, Vol. 2, p. 143 (Jameson, Storm. Works (Autobiography) HRC).
48. There is a copy of Romains's speech, in French, in the PEN archive (London, uncat.), HRC.
49. *JN* I: 379–80.
50. *JN* I: 380–1.
51. *JN* I: 382–3, 415. The insight is the inspiration for *Then We Shall Hear Singing*....
52. *Survivor*, p. 176–8; *JN* I: 405.

11. 1938–1940: Crossing the Rubicon

1. Liddell Hart, *Memoirs*, II: 159.
2. *JN* I: 406.
3. Letter from MSJ to Valentine Dobrée, 5 Sept. 1938 (DCBCLUL).
4. *JN* I: 407.
5. Liddell Hart, *Memoirs*, II: 164–72.
6. *JN* I: 408.
7. For a full account of the treatment in the novel of the Spanish Civil War, see Jennifer Birkett, 'Margaret Storm Jameson and the Spanish Civil War: The Fight for Human Values'.
8. 'W. H. Auden: The Poet of Angst', *The Writer's Situation* (London: Macmillan & Co., 1950), pp. 83–101, was first written for publication in *The Gate (Das Tor)*, a short-lived small-circulation international review of literature and art in English and German, published in London and distributed mostly in Germany. Jameson's bookshelves (CSC) contained the following copies of Auden's poems (all with her signature on the flyleaf): *The Orators. An English Study*, 2nd edn (London: Faber and Faber, 1932); *Some Poems*, (London: Faber and Faber, 1940); *For the Time Being* (London: Faber and Faber, 1945); *The Age of Anxiety*, 2nd printing (New York: Random House, 1947); *The Enchafèd Flood* (London: Faber and Faber, 1951; *The Shield of Achilles* (London: Faber and Faber, 1955). For a full account of Jameson's Auden connections, see Jennifer Birkett, 'A Fictional Function: Storm Jameson and W. H. Auden', *English*, Vol. 56, No. 215, Summer 2007, pp. 171–85.
9. *JMHR*, p. 211.
10. *No Victory for the Soldier*, p. 63.
11. *JN* I: 408.

12. *JN* II: 372.
13. 'Introduction and Apology for my Life', *Civil Journey* (London: Cassel & Co., 1939).
14. Ibid., p. 14.
15. 'On Patriotism', *Civil Journey*, pp. 252–3.
16. *JN* II: 18.
17. The draft of *JN* included a 3-page tribute to Hermon Ould, the diplomatic skills he deployed to keep together acrimonious Centres throughout the world, and the extensive networks of correspondence he maintained with famous and obscure writers, all treated by him with equal impartial care (TS of *JN*, Vol. 3, pp. 138 ff.; Jameson, Storm. Works (Autobiography) HRC).
18. Minutes of Executive Committee, London PEN Centre, 28 Sept. 1938 (PEN archive (London uncat.), HRC).
19. Letter from MSJ to Hermon Ould, 5 Oct. 1938 (MS (PEN) Recip. Jameson, Storm, 1897–, 3rd folder, 1930–39, PEN archive, HRC).
20. *JN* II: 72–3. Copies of letters in red folder in PEN archive (London uncat.), HRC; see n. 38 below.
21. *JN* I: 413–15. Liddell Hart's *Memoirs* describe his continuing struggle as defence correspondent for *The Times* with an editor committed to appeasement, who refused to print, or watered down, his warnings of the weakness of Britain's defences. *The Times* relented only when he offered his resignation, and allowed him to write stronger pieces for other papers, such as his article for the *Evening Standard*, 'Britain is in Danger' (Liddell Hart, *Memoirs*, II: 180). In 1938, he associated himself with a movement proposed by Lord Sankey, 'The Hundred Thousand,' which would be devoted to 'the fuller development of the basic conditions of freedom in national life, to meet the challenging spread of totalitarian creeds'. Adherents eventually included Winston Churchill, Duncan Sandys, Vernon Bartlett, Richard Acland, Violet Bonham Carter, Ronald Cartland, Bob Boothby (ibid., II: 207). Liddell Hart backed out fairly quickly, suspecting that he was being bumped by Sandys, Churchill's nephew, into an anti-Chamberlain ramp. Jameson mentioned it in her autobiography, describing its aims as to broaden the government, begin urgent social reforms, and stop the retreat before Hitler (*JN* I: 414). Jameson was sympathetic, but concerned that it could easily turn into an English nationalist-socialist party.
22. Letters from MSJ to Hilary Newitt Brown, September-December 1938, in 'Margaret Storm Jameson: In her Own Voice [Correspondence of Storm Jameson with Hilary Newitt Brown and Harrison Brown]', Chiara Briganti and Kathy Mezei (eds), in Birkett and Briganti, *Margaret Storm Jameson*, pp. 181–7 (p. 186).
23. TS of *JN*, Vol. 2, pp. 214–15 (Jameson, Storm. Works (Autobiography) HRC).
24. Letter from MSJ to Hermon Ould, 13 Oct. 1938 (MS (PEN) Recip. Jameson, Storm, 1897–, Folder 1926–38, PEN archive, HRC).
25. Ibid.
26. See *JN* II: 19 for the brief account of this period MSJ gave in the 1960s. Walther Funk, a former financial and business journalist, was Hitler's personal economic adviser, and

his Minister of Economic Affairs from 1937 to 1945. Coal and steel interests, the big banks, insurance companies and business concerns channelled money to the Nazis through Funk. In 1939, he became President of the German Reichsbank.

27. Letter from MSJ to Valentine Dobrée, 23 Oct. 1938 (DCBCLUL).
28. *JN* II: 19.
29. Letter from Lord Eustace Percy to Sir Anthony Eden, 8 June 1937, PRO, FO 395/554, P 2485/138/150, cit. Frances Donaldson, *The British Council: The First Fifty Years* (London: Jonathan Cape Ltd, 1984), p. 56.
30. Cit. Donaldson, *The British Council*, pp. 57–8, from Colin Forbes Adam, *Life of Lord Lloyd* (London: Macmillan, 1948), pp. 284–5.
31. Minute of 26 Oct. 1938, Executive Committee Minute Book, London PEN Centre (Oct. 1937 to July 1943) (PEN archive (London, uncat.), HRC). On Olden, co-founder of the German Centre in Exile as well as Secretary, a highly-reputed defence lawyer from the 1920s (he conducted the defence for Carl von Ossietzky), see chapter 8 of Volkmar Zühlsdorff, *Hitler's Exiles: The German Cultural Resistance in America and Europe*, trans. Martin H. Bott, (London and New York: Continuum, 2004).
32. Letter to MSJ from Hermon Ould, 15 Nov. 1938 (PEN MISC., Refugee Writers Fund, N-O, PEN archive, HRC).
33. Letter from Doreen Marston to Rudolf Olden, 24 Nov. 1938 (PEN MISC., Refugee Writers Fund, N-O, PEN archive, HRC). An intimate friend of Jameson's, Marston was a reader for Collins, married to an army major and living in Belgrave Square.
34. Letter from Rudolf Olden to Hermon Ould, 26 Nov. 1938 (PEN MISC., Refugee Writers Fund, N-O, PEN archive, HRC).
35. Letter from Rudolf Olden to MSJ, 30 Dec. 1938 (PEN MISC., Refugee Writers Fund, N-O, PEN archive, HRC).
36. Letter to MSJ from Stanley Richardson, 14 Dec. 1938 (PEN MISC., Refugee Writers Fund, Arden Society Folder, PEN archive, HRC).
37. Letter to MSJ from Yvonne Foldes, 4 Jan. 1939 (PEN MISC., Refugee Writers Fund, PEN archive, HRC).
38. Letter to MSJ from the President of the Prague PEN Club, 1 Dec. 1938 (Red folder labelled: Interesting Archive. Early PEN. Keep for research purposes. PEN archive (London uncat.), HRC). My paraphrase of the original French. The red folder seems to have been collected by MSJ in answer to a request from Marjorie Watts. A covering note, dated 24 June, refers Marjorie Watts to statements Jameson made in *JN* II chapters 12 and 16; hence, this is material collected after 1969. The letter is mentioned *JN* II: 73.
39. *Survivor*, pp. 174–6.
40. Romains's speech in Toulouse had criticised Czechoslovakia for attempting to assimilate the Sudetenland Germans, rather than simply conceding them their autonomy, and complained of the difficulty alliances with countries like Czechoslovakia had caused France in reaching necessary compromises, and finding a way to talk to Germany (my paraphrase of extract in French from Romains's speech, in red folder n. 38 above, PEN archive (London uncat.), HRC).

41. Minute of 22 Feb. 1939, Executive Committee Minute Book, London PEN Centre (October 1937 to July 1943) (PEN archive (London, uncat.), HRC).
42. The following information is drawn from material in PEN MISC. Refugee Writers Fund, Arts and Letters Refugee Committee (PEN archive, HRC), *passim*. On 6 July 1939, the National Co-ordinating Committee was renamed the Joint Consultative Committee for Refugees.
43. Letters from MSJ to Miss Baylis, 12 March 1939, 13 March 1939 (MS (PEN) Recip. Jameson, Storm, 1897–, PEN archive, HRC).
44. Circular appeal of 20 March 1939 (PEN MISC. Refugee Writers Fund, PEN archive, HRC).
45. Letter from MSJ to Miss Baylis, 27 May 1939 (MS (PEN) Recip. Jameson, Storm, 1897–, PEN archive, HRC).
46. *JN* II: 15.
47. Letter from MSJ to Valentine Dobrée, 29 April 1939 (DCBCLUL).
48. TS of *JN*, Vol. 2, p. 192 (Jameson, Storm. Works (Autobiography) HRC).
49. Letter from MSJ to Hermon Ould, 13 June 1939 (MS (PEN) Recip. Jameson, Storm, 1897–, 3rd folder, 1930–39, PEN archive, HRC).
50. Ibid.
51. Letter to MSJ from Irene Rathbone, June 1939 (PEN MISC. PEN Congress, Stockholm, PEN archive, HRC).
52. *JN* II: 16–17; *Survivor*, p. 180.
53. Letter to Harrison Brown, 23 July 1939, in Briganti and Mezei (eds), 'Margaret Storm Jameson: In her Own Voice', p. 188.
54. Letter from MSJ to Miss Baylis, 4 Aug. 1939 (MS (PEN) Recip. Jameson, Storm, 1897–, PEN archive, HRC).
55. Minute of 24 Aug. 1939, Executive Committee Minute Book, London PEN Centre (Oct. 1937 to July 1943), (PEN archive (London, uncat.), HRC).
56. TS of *JN*, Vol. 2, p. 202 (Jameson, Storm. Works (Autobiography) HRC).

12. 1940: Vile Betrayals

1. TS of *JN*, Vol. 2, p. 212 (Jameson, Storm. Works (Autobiography) HRC). *JN* II: 28–31, 33, speaks only of asking him to help her find work for herself.
2. Letters from [?Janet Chance] to Rudolf Olden, 28 Nov. 1939, and Robert Neumann, 29 Nov. 1939 (PEN MISC., Refugee Writers Fund, PEN archive, HRC).
3. Letter from [?Janet Chance] to Rudolf Olden, 28 Nov. 1939 (PEN MISC., Refugee Writers Fund, PEN archive, HRC).
4. This and related information is based on information in the London Executive Committee Minute of 27 Sept. 1939 (Executive Committee Minute Book, London PEN Centre, Oct. 1937 to July 1943 (PEN archive (London, uncat.), HRC), and the red folder of material collected by Jameson for Marjorie Watts (see previous chapter, n. 38).
5. *JN* II: 73.

6. Folder for Watts, n. 4 above.

7. Jules Romains, 'Un essai d'une politique de l'esprit', *Preuves*, No. 18–19, Aug.–Sept. 1952, pp. 63–8. *Preuves*, the journal of the liberal-conservative movement for Europe, launched in Oct. 1951, was the house organ of the CIA-funded Congress for Cultural Freedom (Frances Stonor Saunders, *The Cultural Cold War. The CIA and the World of Arts and Letters*, New York: The New Press, 1999), p. 102.

8. 'Fighting the Foes of Civilization: The Writer's Place in the Defence Line', *TLS*, 7 Oct. 1939, Issue 1966, p. 571; see *JN* II: 27.

9. 'The New Europe', *The Fortnightly*, Vol. CXLVII, n.s., Jan. 1940, pp. 68–79 (p. 76). A 70-line extract (from pp. 75–9) was reprinted by Philip Bell in *History of European Integration*, ed. Walter Lipgens.

10. Ibid., pp. 76–7.

11. Ibid., p. 78.

12. *JN* II: pp. 13–14, 31–2.

13. Irene Rathbone, *The Seeds of Time* (London: Faber & Faber, 1952), p. 450.

14. *Europe to Let*, p. 75. See also my essay, 'The Spectacle of Europe'.

15. Ibid., pp. 236–7.

16. Ibid., p. 280.

17. Ibid., p. 281.

18. Letters from MSJ to Rache Lovat Dickson, 2 Jan., 8 Jan., 6 March 1940 (MABL).

19. Letter from MSJ to Rache Lovat Dickson, 28 Dec. 1939 (MABL).

20. Letter from MSJ to Mr Macmillan, 16 Jan. 1940 (MABL).

21. Letters from MSJ to Rache Lovat Dickson, Feb. and March 1940 (MABL). She still had three novels to write for Cassell, who published the UK editions of *Cousin Honoré*, *The Fort*, and *Then We Shall Hear Singing*.

22. Letter from MSJ to Rache Lovat Dickson, 29 March 1940 (MABL).

23. Letter from MSJ to Rache Lovat Dickson, 11 May 1940 (MABL). The contact with the Macmillan family lasted well past the war. According to Christopher Storm-Clark, Maurice Macmillan (Harold's son) told her that her name was prominent on the government's secret list of 'Premature Anti-Fascists' (as it was on the Gestapo's Black List) and that this was why she was never offered an honour until very late in life. Jameson first learned that she was on a Nazi blacklist in Berlin on 15 June 1939, the day she finished the writing of *Cousin Honoré*, from the Norwegian journalist Bjarne Braatoy, who had heard it from an American journalist who had seen the list (*JN* II: 61).

24. Letters to MSJ from André Gide, 29 Nov. 1939, 14 Jan. 1940 (CSC).

25. *JN* II: 36–8.

26. TS of *JN*, Vol. 2, p. 228 (Jameson, Storm. Works (Autobiography) HRC).

27. *JN* II: 48ff. Some of the following names and comments were cut from the published version: see TS of *JN*, Vol. 2, p. 244–5 (Jameson, Storm. Works (Autobiography) HRC).

28. Ceadel, *Pacifism in Britain*, p. 296.

29. Draft rpt. in *The Journal of Mary Hervey Russell* (London: Macmillan & Co., 1945), pp. 123–5. Appears in archive as "To the Conscience of the World", May 24 1940. Rallying call. International PEN Club. London Centre. "Statement Arising Out of the Present

Situation". 'Drafted by Jameson, Sept. 16–18 1939' (Folder marked PEN, 19.9. Jameson, Storm HRC in (London uncat.), PEN archive, HRC). The call is collected with other drafts of wartime PEN appeals for money for exiled writers, 1940, and a covering letter from MSJ to Marjorie Watts, 24 June 1981, says: 'Just to look at the last page (which is clean and legible) sends through me some feeling between weariness and a shudder, when I think of all the hours, days, months, I spent drafting these pitiful Appeals. To what purpose?'

30. Letter to MSJ from Rosa E. Hutchinson, 5 Sept. 1940, together with press cuttings ((London uncat.), PEN archive, HRC).
31. Programme put together by Dr J. K. Fragner, and read by him and Mrs Ficherova; broadcast Saturday 17 Aug. 1940, 6.15–6.30 p.m. (text in CSC).
32. Calder, *The People's War*, pp. 130–3.
33. Letter from MSJ and Hermon Ould to the Editor, *TLS*, 13 July 1940, Issue 2006, p. 339.
34. Letter from Robert Neumann to Hermon Ould, 8 Aug. 1940 (PEN MISC., Refugee Writers Fund, N-O, PEN archive, HRC).
35. Correspondence between Robert Neumann and Hermon Ould, 17 Aug. and 28 Aug. 1940 (PEN MISC., Refugee Writers Fund, N-O, PEN archive, HRC).
36. Telegram to MSJ from Robert Neumann, 25 Aug. 1940. MSJ had made numerous representations for Neumann's release. On 6 Sept. 1940, Hermon Ould wrote to the Under-Secretary for State, at the Aliens Department in the Home Office, on behalf of Mrs Lore Rolly Becker, interned on 27 May at The Hydro, Port Erin, Isle of Man. He pointed out that she was a former member of the editorial staff of the *Berliner Tageblatt*, an important democratic daily, and the author of numerous anti-Nazi books; she had not been on German soil since 29 June 1934; she had refused to have her German passport renewed in 1938, and the Home Office had granted her British travelling papers. All material in PEN MISC., Refugee Writers Fund, PEN archive, HRC.
37. See Rudolf Olden folder (PEN MISC., Refugee Writers Fund, N-O, PEN archive, HRC).
38. Letter from MSJ to Valentine Dobrée, 16 August 1940 (DCBCLUL).
39. In CSC.
40. *JN* II: 88. See also on Olden *JN* II: 64–7.
41. Minute of 31 Oct. 1940, Executive Committee Minute Book, London PEN Centre (Oct. 1937 to July 1943), in (PEN archive (London, uncat.), HRC).
42. Vera Brittain, *Wartime Chronicle. Vera Brittain's Diary 1939–45*, ed. Alan Bishop and Y. Aleksandra Bennett (London: Victor Gollancz, 1989), pp. 29, 32.
43. Letter from MSJ to Irene Rathbone, 28 Aug. 1940 (IR-CSC). Graham Greene, in charge of the authors section of the MOI, asked Jameson to write a book about Woman at War (Norman Sherry, *The Life of Graham Greene, Vol. II, 1939–55* (London: Jonathan Cape, 1994), p. 36). It was, she told Rache Lovat Dickson, a booklet of 30,000 words, to be published in a sixpenny series with Hutchinson. It would take two months and a lot of travelling, but after all the fuss she had been making about the Ministry not making use of writers, she felt she must do it (letter from MSJ to Rache Lovat Dickson, 7 Aug. 1940 (MABL)). In the end, she did not complete the project.
44. Letter from MSJ to Irene Rathbone, 15 Oct. 1940 (IR-CSC).

45. 'Women on the Spot', *Atlantic Monthly*, Feb. 1941, pp. 169–76. The 'heavy article' was never written. The material she collected, impressions and snatches of dialogue, from women workers in Birmingham and Nottingham, was vivid, detailed and politically tough, and would have made a good novel (preserved in CSC).

46. Letter from MSJ to Irene Rathbone, 21 Oct. 1940 (IR-CSC).

47. Brittain dedicated the first edition of the book to Jameson, but the dedication does not always appear in later editions.

48. Letter from MSJ to Irene Rathbone, 20 Jan. 1941 (IR-CSC).

49. Letter from MSJ to Rache Lovat Dickson, 19 Feb. 1941 (MABL).

50. Letter from MSJ to Rache Lovat Dickson, 27 Feb. 1941 (MABL).

51. *The End of This War* (London: George Allen and Unwin Ltd, 1941). See also *JN* II: 95–6.

52. Letter from MSJ to Hermon Ould, 2 Dec. 1941 (PEN archive [London, uncat.], HRC).

53. Letter from MSJ to Hermon Ould, 5 Jan. 1942 (PEN archive [London, uncat.], HRC).

54. Letter from MSJ to Rache Lovat Dickson, 21 Feb. 1942 (MABL).

55. Brittain, *Wartime Chronicle*, entry for 7 July 1942, p. 160.

56. Vera Brittain, *Testament of Experience. An Autobiographical Story of the Years 1925–1950* (1957; rpt. Paul Berry introd., London: Virago, 1979), pp. 247, 262, 265.

57. Letter from MSJ to Hermon Ould, 6 March 1943 (PEN archive (London, uncat.), HRC).

58. Letter from MSJ to Irene Rathbone, 2 Oct. 1947 (IR-CSC).

13. 1941: Fighting with the French

1. *JN* II: 74, 76.

2. *JN* II: 101–2.

3. TS of *JN*, Vol. 2, pp. 306–8 (Jameson, Storm. Works (Autobiography) HRC).

4. See URL http://www.penrussia.org/english.htm (consulted 9 June 2006 9.49 a.m.). The entry under History Information ends with the following account of the controversy over the European PEN Club in Exile and the ousting of Romains: 'When the German troops marched into France, Jules Romains fled via Spain and Portugal to the USA. In New York he took the initiative of founding a European P.E.N. Club in Exile. The international Secretariat in London sensed a threat to itself in this. Without consulting the international president beforehand, a congress was convened in London in the summer of 1941, at which Jules Romains was removed from office. From the outset one [sic] had reckoned on making H. G. Wells president of the international organization again. But he was prepared to accept only on one condition: namely, that he should have three vice-presidents to support him. Initially Thornton Wilder, Thomas Mann and Jacques Maritain expressed their readiness to stand for office. Mann and Maritain withdrew their candidacies, however, on learning that the meeting in London had expressed criticism of Jules Romains. After the conclusion of the London congress, Hermon Ould appointed two other candidates to these positions on his own responsibility. For this reason one can hardly claim that the P.E.N. Club had a formally elected leadership in the legal sense of that term, during those years.'

5. The Minute of 23 June 1941, Executive Committee Minute Book, London PEN Centre (October 1937 to July 1943) (PEN archive (London, uncat.), HRC) contains a long entry on 'The European PEN in America', described as the President's summary of the history. See also in the dossier prepared for Marjorie Watts (see above Ch. 11), the document 'Tombeau de Jules Romains', Jameson's account of the dispute. The account here draws on both sources, but chiefly the Minute Book.

6. MSJ broadcast to America, 'Britain Speaks', Thursday/Friday 3/4 July 1941 (BBC Written Archive, Caversham). The broadcast is mentioned briefly, and without information on its content, in *JN* II: 99.

7. The proceedings were published in *Writers in Freedom*, ed. Hermon Ould (London: Hutchinson & Co., 1942).

8. Ibid., p. 23.

9. Ibid., pp. 13–14.

10. Ibid., p. 16.

11. Ibid., p. 18.

12. Ibid., p. 112.

13. Letters from John Winant were preserved by MSJ (CSC). *La France Libre* (joint editors André Labarthe, former adviser to the Popular Front, and the philosopher Raymond Aron), which had its offices in the Institut Français, was avidly read by the exiled French in London, and circulated clandestinely in Occupied France. The first issue appeared on 15 Nov. 1940. The journal paid for a reception at the Congress.

14. For a biography of Saurat, see John Robert Colombo, *O Rare Denis Saurat* (Toronto: George A. Vanderburgh, The Battered Silicon Dispatch Box, 2003). Saurat was the one French academic of whom *The New Age* approved; a favourable review of his articles on Milton and Blake appeared there in Nov. 1920.

15. Letters from Denis Saurat to Hermon Ould, 28 May 1932, 9 Dec. 1935 (MS PEN RECIP Saurat, Denis, PEN archive, HRC).

16. Letter from Denis Saurat to MSJ, 24 March 1939 (MS PEN RECIP Saurat, Denis, PEN archive, HRC).

17. Letter from Denis Saurat to Hermon Ould, 14 June 1941 (MS PEN RECIP Saurat, Denis, PEN archive, HRC).

18. *JN* II: 74.

19. See Nicholas Atkin, *The Forgotten French. Exiles in the British Isles, 1940–44* (Manchester and New York: Manchester University Press, 2003), p. 194.

20. Letter from MSJ to Valentine Dobrée, 29 July 1940 (DCBCLUL). The details given here appeared in the first draft of *JN*, but were cut from the published version (see TS of *JN*, Vol. 2, pp. 275–6: Jameson, Storm. Works (Autobiography) HRC).

21. See Denis Saurat, *Regeneration* (London: Dent, 1940), and note by Saurat of the receipt of de Gaulle's letter on 16 Aug. at 10 p.m. (Dossier 35, Denis Saurat Archive, Archives of the Institut Français du Royaume-Uni-French Institute in London).

22. Atkin, *The Forgotten French*, p. 22. The official emphasis on 'fundamental values' provides the context for Olaf Stapledon's later initiative for a PEN investigation of the theme (see next chapter).

23. Atkin, *The Forgotten French*, p. 67.
24. The Saurat archive at the Institut Français contains foolscap notes of meetings in 1940, handwritten presumably by Saurat, beginning 13 Sept. 1940 (a meeting between Saurat, Lord Asquith, Sir Robert Vansittart, Lord Lloyd).
25. Campaign Summaries of World War 2. Amphibious Operations [...] Part 1 of 2, 1940–4 (http://www.naval-history.net/WW2CampaignsAmphibious.htm. Consulted 24 Feb. 2008).
26. Note on meeting by Saurat, 20 Sept. [1940] (Dossier 35, DSIF).
27. Note on meeting by Saurat, 9 Sept. 1941 (Dossier 35, DSIF).
28. Note by Saurat, 25 Sept. [1941] (Dossier 35, DSIF).
29. Note by Saurat, 20 Nov. 1941 (Dossier 35, DSIF).
30. Walter Hill, 'Affranchir l'homme de la misère', *La France Libre*, 15 Feb. 1942, Vol. V, No. 28, pp. 287–92.
31. Notes by Saurat on undated sheet of Institut Français headed notepaper (Dossier 35, DSIF).
32. Letter from MSJ to Irene Rathbone, 20 Jan. 1941 (IR-CSC).
33. Denise Amye, 'Echanges de Livres', *La France Libre*, 15 Oct. 1941, Vol. II, No. 12, pp. 541–3 (my translation).
34. Irene Rathbone, 'L'Alsace vue par une romancière anglaise', *La France Libre*, Jan. 1941, Vol. I, No. 3, pp. 275–80. Quotations in my translation. On the writing of *Cousin Honoré*, see *JN* II: 58–61.
35. See e.g. *JN* II: 58.
36. 'Le 17e Congrès International des PEN', *La France Libre*, 15 Sept. 1941, Vol. II, No. 11, pp. 395–9. English version reprinted in 'Creditors of France', *The Writer's Situation*, pp. 180–8.
37. *The Writer's Situation*, pp. 181–2. This is the beginning of the meditation that reached its final formulation in the *Journal of Mary Hervey Russell*, where Jameson set out the lessons she had learned from the French Symbolists and the stylised realism of Stendhal and Flaubert, in relation to the nature of poetic vision, the syntax of the image, and the web of relationships created in its production and consumption.
38. Ibid., p. 181.

14. 1941–1943: Holding On

1. *JN* II: 109–10.
2. Letter from MSJ to Rache Lovat Dickson, 30 Oct. 1941 (MABL).
3. Jameson had taken on a new responsibility 1941–2, succeeding St John Ervine as chairman of the Committee of Management of the Society of Authors (Victor Bonham-Carter, *Authors by Profession*, Vol. II (London: The Bodley Head and the Society of Authors, 1984), pp. 62–4, 301 n.). By late summer 1940, all the Society's business was being conducted in Mortimer, because of the bombing, where Denys Kilham Roberts had a house, so Jameson was conveniently placed. More to the point, Bonham-Carter

says, she and Guy Chapman 'were particularly well equipped to cope with the crises of the time. Both were "Europeans", primarily Francophiles, while Margaret had addition-ally a close knowledge of central European writers—anti-Nazi Germans and Austrians, Poles and Czechs—for whom she as President from 1938 to 1944, and Herman Ould as Secretary, of the English Centre of PEN, performed prodigies of service. [...] None of these achievements were publicly recognised; nor, I suspect, are they even remem-bered—except in PEN minutes—today.' She took the Chair again in 1954. The Editorial Committee of the Authors' National Committee was an initiative of J. B. Priestley's. Fellow-members were Priestley, Professor John Macmurray, and Denys Kilham Roberts. The aim was to publish a series of short books dealing with the problems of reconstruction after the war; only one appeared (Priestley's *Out of the People*), and the project collapsed because Priestley was too busy and too socialist for the others' taste (Bonham-Carter, *Authors by Profession*, II: 62).

4. Birth certificate in CSC.
5. Naomi Mitchison, *Among You Taking Notes,.... The Wartime Diary of Naomi Mitchison, 1939–45*, ed. Dorothy Sheridan (Oxford: Oxford University Press, 1985), p. 184.
6. Letter from MSJ to Rache Lovat Dickson, 9 Feb. 1942 (MABL).
7. Second Letter from MSJ to Rache Lovat Dickson, 9 Feb. 1942 (MABL).
8. Letter from MSJ to Hermon Ould, 17 March 1942 (PEN archive, (London, uncat.), HRC). See also letters of 23 Feb., 2 March.
9. Review of Denis Saurat, *Watch over Africa*, La France Libre, No. 18, 17 April 1942.
10. Letter from MSJ to Hermon Ould, 7 April 1942 (PEN archive, (London, uncat.), HRC).
11. Letter from MSJ to Rache Lovat Dickson, 8 April 1942 (MABL).
12. Letter from MSJ to Rache Lovat Dickson, 22 May 1942 (MABL).
13. The book had been commissioned by the Ministry of Information, to be sold in aid of the American Red Cross. Dates in the dossier in the PEN archive containing contribu-tors' drafts and biographical notes indicate that she began collecting material before March 1942 (MS (PEN) MISC (*London Calling* edited by Storm Jameson), PEN archive HRC).
14. *JN* II: 116–20.
15. The Note continued: in Geneva, Butler had been the first Deputy Director and then Director of the ILO. In 1938, he became the first Warden of Nuffield College, and when war broke out he was appointed one of twelve Regional Comissioners for Civil Defence. He had returned to Nuffield to help direct work relating to national and international reconstruction.
16. The Note on Laski described him as Professor of Political Science at the University of London, a member of various Government committees, and a member of the British Labour Party Executive Committee since 1937. His books included *Communism* (1927) and *The Rise of European Liberalism* (1936).
17. *London Calling*, pp. 5–6.
18. Letter to MSJ from Hermon Ould, 12 May 1942 (PEN archive, (London, uncat.), HRC).
19. *BBC Handbook 1942* (London: The British Broadcasting Corporation, Broadcasting House, 1942), p. 41.

20. Ibid., p. 24.
21. Val Henry Gielgud, *British Radio Drama 1922–56. A Survey by Val Gielgud. Head of BBC Drama (Sound)* (London and Toronto: George G. Harrap & Co., 1957), p. 85.
22. Ibid., p. 93. Ironically, Jameson would be one of those who gave a personal statement when the Society of Authors issued a manifesto of complaints on 29 May 1947 about the BBC's low fees, unreasonably wide rights, and high-handed behaviour with authors (Bonham-Carter, *Authors by Profession*, II: 224).
23. Ibid., p. 87.
24. BBC Internal Memo from Mr Hilton Brown to Mr Salmon, 27 Jan. 1941 (RCONT1, Storm Jameson Scriptwriter, File I 1941–61, BBC Written Archive, Caversham).
25. Letter from Val Gielgud to Nancy Pearn, 28 Jan. 42 (RCONT1, Storm Jameson Scriptwriter, File I 1941–61, BBC Written Archive, Caversham).
26. Letter from MSJ to Rache Lovat Dickson, 27 July 1942 (MABL). She told Lovat Dickson she was trying to get copies of *Delicate Monster*, and *A Day Off*. When Nicholson and Watson failed, she said, the one-shilling-and-under rights for *A Day Off* were sold to Wells Gardner, who put out a shilling edition with a pornographic-looking cover, which she had never seen.
27. Letter from MSJ to Hermon Ould, Wednesday 24 [June 1942] (PEN archive (London, uncat.), HRC).
28. Letter from MSJ to Hermon Ould, 22 July 1942, (PEN archive (London, uncat.), HRC). In March, Jameson had begun to try to persuade Ould that the Club should pass over to the young, and he should consider a Young Turk as the next President; she was prepared to hold on for a year or two until the PEN was ready to accept one (Letter from MSJ to Hermon Ould, undated [March 1942], PEN archive, (London, uncat.), HRC). Ould thought Young Turks too careerist; a PEN President must either be very venerable or someone like Jameson herself—young, famous, and still unassuming (Letter to MSJ from Hermon Ould, 2 March 1942 (PEN archive (London, uncat.), HRC)).
29. Letter from MSJ to Hermon Ould, 10 Aug. 1942 (PEN archive (London, uncat.), HRC).
30. Charles de Gaulle, *The Complete War Memoirs of Charles de Gaulle*, trans. Jonathan Griffin and Richard Howard (New York: Carroll & Graf Publishers, Inc., 1998), p. 275.
31. Letter from MSJ to Hermon Ould, 23 Aug. 1942 (PEN archive (London, uncat.), HRC).
32. Letter to MSJ from Hermon Ould, 19 Oct. 1942 (PEN archive (London, uncat.), HRC).
33. De Gaulle, *Complete War Memoirs*, p. 277.
34. Letter from MSJ to Hermon Ould, 14 Sept. 1942 (PEN archive (London, uncat.), HRC).
35. Letter to MSJ from Phyllis Bottome, 4 Sept. 1942 (PEN archive (London, uncat.), HRC).
36. Letter from MSJ to Rache Lovat Dickson, 11 Oct. 1942 (MABL).
37. *JN* II: 129; *Survivor*, p. 194.
38. *Survivor*, p. 197.
39. Letter from MSJ to Rache Lovat Dickson, 18 Oct. 1942 (MABL).
40. *JN* II: 130–2.
41. Letter from MSJ to Hermon Ould, 9 Nov. 1942 (PEN archive (London, uncat.), HRC).
42. *JN* II: 124–5.
43. Letter from MSJ to Hermon Ould, 16 Nov. 1942 (PEN archive (London, uncat.), HRC).

44. Letter from MSJ to Hermon Ould, 17 Nov. 1942 (PEN archive (London, uncat.), HRC).
45. *JN* II: 127–9.
46. Letter from Dorothy Pateman to Betty Leake, 3 Dec. 1942 (JK-CSC).
47. Letter from MSJ to Rache Lovat Dickson, 23 Dec. 1942 (MABL).
48. BBC ON THIS DAY for 17 Dec.. URL: http://news.bbc.co.uk/onthisday/hi/dates/stories/december/17/newsid_3547000/3547151.stm
49. Bernard Wasserstein, *Britain and the Jews of Europe, 1939–1945* (Oxford: Oxford University Press, 1979), pp. 345–8.
50. Letter from MSJ to Hermon Ould, 4 Jan. 1943 (PEN archive (London, uncat.), HRC).
51. Letter to MSJ from Hermon Ould, 8 Jan. 1943 (PEN archive (London, uncat.), HRC).
52. Letter from Sir Andrew McFadyean, former General Secretary to the Reparation Commission, cit. Vera Brittain, 'Letter from a Peace-Lover', 28 Jan. 1943, in *Testament of a Peace Lover. Letters from Vera Brittain*, ed. Winifred and Alan Eden-Green (London: Virago, 1988), p. 139.
53. Letter from MSJ to Hermon Ould, 9 Jan. 1943 (PEN archive (London, uncat.), HRC). The letter enclosed does not seem to have been preserved.
54. Letter to MSJ from Hermon Ould, 16 Jan. 1943 (PEN archive (London, uncat.), HRC).
55. Letter from MSJ to Hermon Ould, 20 Jan. 1943 (PEN archive (London, uncat.), HRC).
56. Minutes of 3 Feb., 3 March, 7 April 1943, Executive Committee Minute Book, London PEN Centre (Oct. 1937 to July 1943) (PEN archive (London, uncat.), HRC).
57. Letter to MSJ from Hermon Ould, 16 April 1943 (PEN archive (London, uncat.), HRC). Ould wrote later in the year with further news from Max-Pol Fouchet: Crémieux had been arrested and his son was rumoured to have been shot; Cocteau was equivocating; Dullin and Guitry were whole-hearted collaborators (letter to MSJ from Hermon Ould, 23 Sept. 1943 (PEN archive (London, uncat.), HRC)).
58. Letter to MSJ from Hermon Ould, 6 Jan. 1943 (PEN archive (London, uncat.), HRC).
59. Letter from MSJ to Hermon Ould, 1 Feb. 1943 (PEN archive (London, uncat.), HRC).
60. Letter from MSJ to Hermon Ould, 8 Feb. 1943 (PEN archive (London, uncat.), HRC). See account of Philip Mairet's review, Ch. 8 above.
61. Letter from Denis Saurat to Hermon Ould, 4 Jan. 1944 (PEN Recip. (2nd folder) 1940–51, PEN archive, HRC).
62. 'For Olaf Stapledon', MSS with Author's corrections, 4 pp. [1943] (Misc Jameson, Storm (Fundamental values), PEN archive HRC).
63. *JN* II: 132–4.
64. Letter from MSJ to Hermon Ould, 11 Feb. 1943 (PEN archive (London, uncat.), HRC).
65. Letter from MSJ to Hermon Ould, 24 Feb. 1943 (PEN archive (London, uncat.), HRC).
66. Letter from Dorothy Pateman to Betty Leake, 4 July 1941 (JK-CSC).
67. Letter from Dorothy Pateman to Betty Leake, 19 Aug. 1941 (JK-CSC).
68. Letter from Dorothy Pateman to Betty Leake, Easter Monday [1942] (JK-CSC).
69. Letter to MSJ from Elizabeth Leake, 3 May 1943 (CSC).
70. Letter from MSJ to Rache Lovat Dickson, 26 March 1943 (MABL).
71. Letter from MSJ to Hermon Ould, 2 March 1943 (PEN archive (London, uncat.), HRC). From spring 1942, Connolly had been literary editor of the *Observer* as well as editor

of *Horizon*. He began his propaganda on behalf of French culture in Jan. 1943, and his biographer mentions various projects, though not the *Génie Française* (Clive Fisher, *Cyril Connolly. A Nostalgic Life* (London: Macmillan, 1996), pp. 232–4). His important talk on 'French and English Cultural Relations', delivered in Edinburgh in March 1943, at the invitation of the British Council, was published in *Horizon* in June, and in the following months the magazine gave increasing prominence to French culture. Connolly's projects certainly overlapped with Jameson's, but their political dimension was much less sharp, and his presentation generally more superficial. There was obvious rivalry, which he dealt with by ignoring her. When the PEN Club convened 'a celebrated conference' in London, Connolly's biographer places him proudly at the same table as Stevie Smith, Arthur Koestler, and Guy Chapman (Fisher, *Cyril Connolly*, pp. 212–13). Jameson is never mentioned. For her part, Jameson drew on him for a few of her satirical portraits of London literary life (in *The Green Man*, for instance, the character who starts life as Auden merges into Connolly as the story progresses).

72. Peter Calvocoressi, Guy Wint, and John Pritchard, *Total War. The Causes and Courses of the Second World War* (Harmondsworth: Penguin Books, rev. 2nd edn, 1995), p. 289.

73. Ian Cobain, 'Churchill proposed "three for one" bombing of German villages in retaliation for the massacre of Czech civilians', *The Guardian*, 2 Jan. 2006, p. 10.

74. Jameson wrote to Ould that she had just been offered £100 for the story by an English editor, who had read it in the *Saturday Evening Post*, but she had given it away to the Czechs (Letter from MSJ to Hermon Ould, 17 March 1943 (PEN archive (London, uncat.), HRC)). It was reprinted in *Argosy*, and then in *Lidice: A Tribute by Members of the International PEN*, introd. Harold Nicolson (London: Allen & Unwin, 1944), pp. 50–84.

75. Letter to MSJ from Hermon Ould, 3 April 1943 (PEN archive (London, uncat.), HRC).

76. Letter to MSJ from Hermon Ould, 11 June 1943 (PEN archive (London, uncat.), HRC).

77. Letter from MSJ to Hermon Ould, 14 June 1943 (PEN archive (London, uncat.), HRC).

78. Letters to MSJ from Hermon Ould, 6 July and 24 July 1943 (PEN archive (London, uncat.), HRC). Saurat had been regularly shooting himself in the foot since the end of 1942 with public comments that challenged the pure Gaullist line. He published a letter in *The Times* on 18 Nov. 1942, as the Allies were trying to negotiate a ceasefire with the Vichyist Darlan in Algiers, and after the Albert Hall rally of 11 Nov. in which de Gaulle staked his claim to lead the French war effort. In it, he said that he wanted to see the laws of the Republic re-established, not just agreements between two generals, and while expressing pleasure that the French democratic system would soon be moving again, raised the unwelcome question of how to weigh the different claims to represent the popular will presented by the re-forming socialist party and the evolving resistance groups. On 10 Jan. 1943, the *Observer* printed his letter saying that at the Peace Conference France must be represented by 'competent democratic statesmen', not the military (Dossier 34, DSIF).

79. Letter from MSJ to Hermon Ould, 7 July 1943 (PEN archive (London, uncat.), HRC).

80. Letter from MSJ to Hermon Ould, 26 July 1943 (PEN archive (London, uncat.), HRC).

81. Letter from MSJ to Irene Rathbone, 3 May 1943 (IR-CSC).

82. Letter from MSJ to Hermon Ould, 11 Aug. 1943 (PEN archive (London, uncat.), HRC).

83. Letter from MSJ to Irene Rathbone, 3 May 1943 (IR-CSC); Letter from MSJ to Hermon Ould, 26 April 1943 (PEN archive (London, uncat.), HRC).
84. Letter to MSJ from Hermon Ould, 28 Sept. 1943 (PEN archive (London, uncat.), HRC).

15. Fortifying the Nation: Narrative, Memory and Culture

1. *JN* II: 75, 83; letter from MSJ to Valentine Dobrée, 29 July 1940 (DCBCLUL). Elie Bois, who had observed at first-hand the collapse of France's leaders at Bordeaux in June 1940, had already written about the scandal in the *Sunday Times* (*JN* II: 75), for which he later wrote weekly columns. He published subsequently a scathing account of Laval's defeatism (*Truth on the Tragedy of France*, (London: Hodder & Stoughton, 1940)), which Jameson recommended to listeners in a Home Service radio broadcast on 20 March 1941 (BBC Written Archive, Caversham). On Reynaud and Hélène de Portes, see Julian Jackson, *The Fall of France. The Nazi Invasion of 1940* (Oxford: Oxford University Press, 2003), pp. 126, 140–1.
2. Letter from MSJ to Rache Lovat Dickson, 7 Aug. 1940 (MABL).
3. Letter from MSJ to Valentine Dobrée, 16 Aug. 1940 (DCBCLUL). The Cagoulards were members of the Cagoule, the popular name for the group of clandestine right-wing terrorist organisations that formed after the victory of the Popular Front in the elections of May 1936 (Jackson, *The Fall of France*, p. 110).
4. Letter from MSJ to Rache Lovat Dickson, 20 May 1941 (MABL). The latter was to become *Then We Shall Hear Singing*.
5. Letter from MSJ to Rache Lovat Dickson, 13 May 1942 (MABL).
6. Letters to MSJ from Rache Lovat Dickson, 31 Aug. 1943, and from MSJ to Rache Lovat Dickson, 26 June 1943 (MABL).
7. *JN* II 92–3, 94; letter from MSJ to Rache Lovat Dickson, 19 Feb. 1941 (MABL).
8. [R D Charques], 'Novels of the Week. Men-At-Arms', *TLS*, 10 Jan. 1942, Issue 2084, p. 17.
9. *NTLP*, pp. 148–9.
10. 'The Craft of the Novelist' (1932), rpt. in *Civil Journey*, p. 66.
11. Letter from MSJ to Mrs Siv Lind, 6 Oct. 1983 (CSC). See also letter to MSJ from Agnes Headlam-Morley, 14 July 1960, in which the historian, an admirer of Guy's, commented on his manner of writing about war: he combined an objective account with inward-looking personal narrative, and glimpses of deeper levels of response (CSC). A review of *The Fort* in *La France Libre* (16 March 1942, Vol. III, No. 17, pp. 430–1) comments on Jameson's refusal to dress up war in rhetoric.
12. *JN* II: 120.
13. Brittain, *Wartime Chronicle*, 30 Nov. 1942, p. 196.
14. Mitchison, *Among You Taking Notes*, Thursday 31 Dec. 1942, p. 224.
15. *JN* II: 94.
16. *JN* I: 415.
17. *Then We Shall Hear Singing. A Fantasy in C Major* (London: Cassell and Company Ltd, 1942), pp. 82–3.

18. [R. D. Charques], 'Novels of the Week. The Indestructible', *TLS*, 31 Oct. 1941, Issue 2126, p. 533.
19. *JN* II: 94.
20. *Then We Shall Hear Singing*, pp. 29–30.
21. Ibid., pp. 53–4.
22. Ibid., p. 31.
23. Ibid., p. 156.
24. *Cloudless May* (London: Macmillan & Co. Ltd, 1943), p. 121.
25. *Cloudless May* was on the stocks in May 1941, with the research well advanced. Two-thirds was written by the time Jameson's father died in Dec. 1942, and the book was finished and posted to Macmillan in March 1943, just after Dorothy's death in Feb. (see letter from MSJ to Rache Lovat Dickson, 23 Dec. 1942 (MABL); and *JN* II: 134).
26. Aragon was slipped into British cultural discourse under the aegis of André Gide, much-admired by former fellow-travelling English liberals, including Jameson herself, and a leading figure in PEN. Harold Nicolson's praise of Gide in *The Spectator*, 26 June 1942, as the great representative of French individualism that would never give in to Berlin, referred to Gide's *Imaginary Interviews*, recently published in translation in Cyril Connolly's *Horizon* (May and June 1942). Nicolson also reproduced Gide's admiring quotation of Aragon's 'Zone Libre'. In his preface to Aragon's collection *Le Crève-Coeur*, published in Dec. 1942 by Curwen Press (co-edited by *La France Libre* and *Horizon*, with a preface by André Labarthe), the Resistance poets were presented as turning the 'tragedy' of the debacle in the direction of new victories. See for all this John Bennett, *Aragon, Londres et la France libre: réception de l'oeuvre en Grande-Bretagne, 1940* (Paris: L'Harmattan, 1998).
27. 'May without cloud and June stabbed to the heart'. Louis MacNeice's translation, in Hannah Josephson and Malcolm Cowley (eds), *Aragon, Poet of Resurgent France* (London: The Pilot Press Ltd, 1946).
28. Letter from MSJ to Basil Liddell Hart, 17 Aug. 1952 (LHC: LH 1/408 PART 1).
29. *JN* II: 93–94. The heroic defence of the bridge at Saumur on 18 June by the young cavalry cadets against the German tanks, which has passed into legend, may have helped inspire her account, dated 18 June, of the opposition to the German tanks by Ollivier's group, towards the end of *Cloudless May*. See Lormier, Dominique, *La Bataille des Cadets de Saumur. Juin 1940* (Honfleur-Saintes: Les Chemins de la Mémoire, n.d).
30. *Survivor*, p. 199.
31. Letter from MSJ to Basil Liddell Hart, 18 Sept. 1942 (LHC: LH 1/408 PART 1) mentions that she had enjoyed his latest book, *This Expanding War*; 11 Dec. 1942, she sent comments on *The British Way in Warfare*.
32. The first three chapters of Vol. II of Liddell Hart's *Memoirs* (Cassell, 1965) describe his close working relationship with Leslie Hore-Belisha, who became Secretary of State for War on 28 May 1937. On 31 May, Hore-Belisha asked Liddell Hart for a paper on how to modernise and mechanise an army that was profoundly resistant to change. His advice included bringing down the average age of the generals (reducing retirement age to 60), introducing more tank units (and more promotions for tank corps

officers), and motor vehicles and planes. He also advised that mechanisation required a changed mentality and different strategic thinking (the army leadership was still putting cavalry experts in charge of mechanised units, being interested in seniority rather than expertise), including new offensive–defensive methods based on surprise attack. Liddell Hart's acknowledged expertise as a moderniser and especially as a tank expert was of long standing, and had been influential throughout Europe. He claimed in his *Memoirs* that the French inability to respond to Hitler's March 1936 invasion of the Rhineland was due to: 'the French Army's lack of a mechanised spearhead of professional soldiers. I had originally urged the need for this in my 1927 articles on that army and in *The Remaking of Modern Armies*—an argument which had been taken up in the last two years by Lieutenant-Colonel de Gaulle in a striking little book *Vers l'armée de métier*, and by Paul Reynaud in Parliament' (*Memoirs*, II: 127). Guderian, the German commander, did however read and apply his analyses, with signal results.

33. *JN* II: 94 speaks of seeking '[to] uncover as many as possible of the relations between feelings, events, people'. Sending a copy of *Cloudless May* to Kathleen Liddell Hart, Jameson was however apologetic about some of the technical deficiencies of her book: 'Basil, I shudder to think will detect all the gaps and all the liberties I have taken with the proper conduct of a military region in France in war-time. I shall try to console myself with the remark made to me by a French officer I was questioning—"You cannot possibly take more liberties than the generals commanding certain of the regions took in the months before June 1940!" '(letter from MSJ to Kathleen Liddell Hart, 26 Sept. 1943 (LHC: LH 1/408)).

34. MSJ, 'What I'm Reading Now', BBC Home Service, Thursday 20 March 1941 (BBC Written Archive, Caversham). Shortly before the novel's publication, Lovat Dickson confirmed to Daniel Macmillan that the main story was based on Pétain and Laval, that all the minor characters were fictitious, and that the text had been checked for libel (memo from Rache Lovat Dickson to Daniel Macmillan, 21 July 1943 (MABL)).

35. Hélène was said, for example, to have blocked Reynaud's proposal to send the French fleet and the remnants of the army to North Africa, to support the British (Entry for 4 March 1941, in Harold Nicolson, *Diaries and Letters 1939–45*, ed. Nigel Nicolson (London: Collins, 1967), p. 150). This would have been an alternative to the conservative General Weygand's manoeuvrings towards a surrender that would leave the army in a position to support 'reconstruction' of the nation, ruined, in the view of his faction, by the doctrines of the Popular Front. Julian Jackson however attributes the failure of Reynaud's alternative, which he first mooted on 29 May 1939, to Weygand and the naval leaders, who made no preparations and constantly argued its impracticality. On 5 June, reshuffling his government, Reynaud brought in de Gaulle as Under-Secretary of State for War, and asked him to liaise with the British to transfer men and supplies to North Africa, but the rest of the reshuffle had not produced the will to resistance that would have made the policy effective (Jackson, *The Fall of France*, p. 134; *France, the Dark Years, 1940–44* (Oxford: Oxford University Press, 2001), pp. 121–2).

36. *Cloudless May*, p. 41.

37. Ibid., pp. 74–7.
38. Ibid., p. 359.
39. [R. D. Charques], 'Novels of the Week. The Downfall', *TLS*, 25 Sept. 1943, Issue 2173, p. 461.
40. *Cloudless May*, p. 392.
41. Ibid., p. 505, p. 437.
42. Ibid., p. 92.
43. Ibid., p. 438.
44. Ibid., pp. 173–4.
45. Ibid., p. 56.
46. Ibid., p. 52.
47. Ibid., p. 120.
48. Ibid., p. 393.
49. Ibid., pp. 389–92.
50. Ibid., p. 507.
51. Ibid., p. 373.
52. Ibid., p. 376.

16. 1943–1945: Struggling to the End

1. Letter from MSJ to Hermon Ould, 6 May 1943 (PEN archive (London, uncat.), HRC).
2. Letter from MSJ to Hermon Ould, 19 May 1943 (PEN archive (London, uncat.), HRC).
3. Letter from MSJ to Mr Macmillan [probably Daniel], 9 March 1940 (MABL).
4. Letter from MSJ to Rache Lovat Dickson, 10 May 1943 (MABL).
5. The cave-paintings of Lascaux were discovered on 12 Sept. 1940 by four schoolchildren, and first visited by the prehistorian Henri Breuil on 21 Sept. His report of 1940 was first published in Léon Laval, *La Caverne peinte de Lascaux* (Montignac-sur-Vézère, Périgord Noir, 1948), pp. 31–41, and in the years following the Liberation, they became an important point of reference for French writers and artists (see Douglas Smith, 'Beyond the Cave: Lascaux and the prehistoric in Post-War French Culture', *French Studies*, Vol. LVIII, No. 2, pp. 219–32). Jameson made the connection well in advance of the writers Smith discusses. She may have had in mind Eliot's meditations in 'Tradition and the Individual Talent' (1919) on how the poet should understand the 'mind of Europe—the mind of his own country [...] a mind which changes, [...] a development which abandons nothing en route, which does not superannuate either Shakespeare, or Homer, or the rock drawing of the Magdalenian draughtsmen'. See my essay 'Beginning Again: Storm Jameson's Debt to France'.
6. Letters from MSJ to Irene Rathbone, 3 and 5 May 1943 (IR-CSC).
7. Postcard from MSJ to Hermon Ould, 20 May 1943 (PEN archive (London, uncat.), HRC).
8. Letter from MSJ to Hermon Ould, 22 May 1943 (PEN archive (London, uncat.), HRC).
9. Letter to MSJ from Hermon Ould, 7 July 1943 (PEN archive (London, uncat.), HRC).

10. Letter from MSJ to Val Gielgud, 6 Aug. 1942 (RCONT1, Storm Jameson Scriptwriter, File I 1941–61, BBC Written Archive, Caversham).

11. Letter from MSJ to Val Gielgud, 7 Aug. 1942 (RCONT1, Storm Jameson Scriptwriter, File I 1941–61, BBC Written Archive, Caversham).

12. Letter from MSJ to Barbara Burnham, 20 Oct. 1942 (RCONT1, Storm Jameson Scriptwriter, File I 1941–61, BBC Written Archive, Caversham).

13. Letter from Barbara Burnham to MSJ, 21 Oct. 1942 (RCONT1, Storm Jameson Scriptwriter, File I 1941–61, BBC Written Archive, Caversham).

14. Letter from MSJ to Barbara Burnham, 23 Oct. 1942 (RCONT1, Storm Jameson Scriptwriter, File I 1941–61, BBC Written Archive, Caversham).

15. Letter from Nancy Pearn to Val Gielgud, 5 Jan. 1943 (RCONT1, Storm Jameson Scriptwriter, File I 1941–61, BBC Written Archive, Caversham).

16. Internal memo from Val Gielgud to Barbara Burnham, 23 Jan. 1943 (RCONT1, Storm Jameson Scriptwriter, File I 1941–61, BBC Written Archive, Caversham).

17. Letter from [Barbara Burnham] to MSJ, 5 March 1943 (RCONT1, Storm Jameson Scriptwriter, File I 1941–61, BBC Written Archive, Caversham).

18. Letter from MSJ to Barbara Burnham, 1 March 1943 (RCONT1, Storm Jameson Scriptwriter, File I 1941–61, BBC Written Archive, Caversham).

19. Letter from MSJ to Barbara Burnham, 9 May 1943 (RCONT1, Storm Jameson Scriptwriter, File I 1941–61, BBC Written Archive, Caversham).

20. Letter from Barbara Burnham to MSJ, 12 July 1943 (RCONT1, Storm Jameson Scriptwriter, File I 1941–61, BBC Written Archive, Caversham).

21. 'William the Defeated', *The Book of the PEN*, ed. Hermon Ould (London: Arthur Barker Ltd, 1950).

22. Ibid., p. 220.

23. Ibid., p. 195.

24. *JN* II: 134–5.

25. *Survivor*, p. 201.

26. Letter from MSJ to Hermon Ould, 20 Sept. 1943 (PEN archive (London, uncat.), HRC).

27. Letter from MSJ to Hermon Ould, 21 Sept. 1943 (PEN archive (London, uncat.), HRC).

28. Letter from MSJ to Hermon Ould, 28 Sept. 1943 (PEN archive (London, uncat.), HRC).

29. *JN* II: 136.

30. *Survivor*, p. 205.

31. R. D. Charques, 'Storm Jameson', *TLS*, 30 Oct. 1943, Issue 2178, p. 523.

32. Letter from MSJ to Hermon Ould, 3 Nov. 1943 (PEN archive (London, uncat.), HRC).

33. The book was remaindered. Jameson recriminated with Macmillan in 1960, asking for a reprint (letter from MSJ to Alan Maclean, 18 Aug. 1960 (MABL). A second edition was produced in 1961, which had more success.

34. Anon., 'Minds at Work', *Time and Tide*, 2 June 1945.

35. [R. D. Charques], 'Years of Crisis', *TLS*, 5 May 1945, Issue 2257, p. 212.

36. *JN* II: 136; TS of *JN*, Vol. 2, p. 350 (Jameson, Storm. Works (Autobiography) HRC).

37. Letter from MSJ to Betty Leake, 1 Nov. 1943 (JK-CSC).

38. *JN* I: 20.

39. Letter from MSJ to Betty Leake, 11 Dec. 1943, and letter from MSJ to Nick and Judy Pateman, 12 Dec. 1943 (JK-CSC).
40. Letter from MSJ to Betty Leake, 8 Jan. 1944 (JK-CSC).
41. Letter from MSJ to Betty Leake, 12 Feb. 1944 (JK-CSC).
42. Letter from MSJ to Hermon Ould, 10 Jan. 1944 (PEN archive (London, uncat.), HRC).
43. Letter from MSJ to Hermon Ould, 3 Feb. 1944 (PEN archive (London, uncat.), HRC).
44. Letter from MSJ to Irene Rathbone, 18 March 1944 (CSC). Lilo Linke's book was presumably *Andean Adventure: A Social and Political Study of Colombia, Ecuador And Bolivia* (n.p.: Hutchinson, 1945); Maria Kuncewiczowa's [*Cudzoziemka*] *The Stranger*, trans. B. W. A. Massey (London: Hutchinson's International Authors, [1944]). Jameson's Preface was rpt. in *The Writer's Situation*, pp. 118–25 (dated June 1944).
45. Letter from MSJ to Betty Leake, 17 March 1944 (JK-CSC).
46. Letter from MSJ to Nick and Judy Pateman, 3 May 1944 (JK-CSC).
47. *JN* II: 137; Jameson wrote the date in the margin of her own copy (CSC).
48. Letter from MSJ to Hermon Ould, 8 April 1944 (PEN archive (London, uncat.), HRC).
49. Letter from MSJ to Irene Rathbone, [10 May 1944] (IR-CSC).
50. Letter from MSJ to Irene Rathbone, 18 June 1944 (IR-CSC).
51. Letter from MSJ to Betty Leake, 26 June 1944 (JK-CSC).
52. Letter from MSJ to Betty Leake, 17 July 1944 (JK-CSC).
53. Ibid.
54. Letter from MSJ to Irene Rathbone, 19 Aug. 1944 (IR-CSC).
55. Jameson, 'Paris', *TLS*, 26 Aug. 1944, Issue 2221, p. 415, rpt. in *The Writer's Situation*, pp. 114–17.
56. Letter from MSJ to Irene Rathbone, 29 Aug. 1944 (CSC). Jameson had written 'the enchantments—alas that there will be no new ones—of a Giraudoux'; Murray replaced her aside with 'in the days before his name was a sign of controversy'. Giraudoux had died on 31 Jan. 1944. As a civil servant, with a long history of public and diplomatic service, he was asked by Daladier to form a Division of Information in Aug. 1939, and after mobilisation helped produce war propaganda. He moved to Bordeaux in a new post with the Ministry of Foreign Affairs, and there wrote *Armistice à Bordeaux*, a defence of France's capitulation (21 June 1940, not published until 1945). He was recruited into the government at Vichy, where he served briefly as director of historical monuments. His biographer argues that by the beginning of 1943 he was engaging in clandestine writing against the Nazis (collecting war crimes material, etc.), and that his son deserted on 19 June 1940 and made his way to London to offer his services to de Gaulle. See Laurent LeSage, *Jean Giraudoux. His Life and Works* (Pennsylvania: Pennsylvania State University Press, 1959), pp. 113–21. Jameson would have been as aware as Murray of the cloud over Giraudoux's name, but as she subsequently demonstrated in a number of contexts, discussed below, she was less eager than many to denounce collaboration in occupied countries, not least on the grounds that no one could know how they might have behaved under similar constraints.
57. Letter to MSJ from Hermon Ould, 20 Nov. 1944 (PEN archive (London, uncat.), HRC).
58. Letter from MSJ to Hermon Ould, 21st Nov. 1944 (PEN archive (London, uncat.), HRC).

59. G. Turquet-Milnes, 'Midnight Books', *Time and Tide*, 21 Oct. 1944, Vol. 25, No. 43, pp. 924–5 (p. 924).

60. Letter from MSJ to Betty Leake, 30 Nov. 1944 (JK-CSC).

61. Letters from MSJ to Irene Rathbone, 29 Nov. and 19 Dec. 1944 (IR-CSC).

62. Letter from MSJ to Irene Rathbone, 16 April 1946 (IR-CSC).

63. Letter from MSJ to Irene Rathbone, 6 Feb. 1945 (IR-CSC).

64. *JN* II: 139.

65. Letter to MSJ from Hermon Ould, 8 March 1945 (PEN archive (London, uncat.), HRC).

66. Letter from MSJ to Hermon Ould, 10 March 1945 (PEN archive (London, uncat.), HRC).

67. Letter to MSJ from Hermon Ould, 10 April 1945 (PEN archive (London, uncat.), HRC).

68. Letter from MSJ to Hermon Ould, 12 April 1945 (PEN archive (London, uncat.), HRC).

69. Letter from MSJ to Irene Rathbone, 18 [May 1945] (IR-CSC).

70. Letter from MSJ to Betty Leake, 16 June 1945 (JK-CSC).

71. Letter from MSJ to Hermon Ould, 16 July 1945 (PEN archive (London, uncat.), HRC).

72. Letter from MSJ to Betty Leake, 26 July 1945 (JK-CSC).

73. Letter from MSJ to Betty Leake, 18 Aug. 1945 (JK-CSC).

74. Letter from MSJ to Betty Leake, 21 Aug. 1945 (JK-CSC).

75. *JN* : II, 147–73 (p. 147).

76. *JN* II: 149

77. *JN* II: 168. Among her papers, Jameson kept a collection of all too similar photographs (CSC). The note in her handwriting wrapped round them says they were taken by a group of Czech doctors who had visited ?Terezin (word unclear) on 3 May 1945, with the International Red Cross, just before the SS guards fled. Over sixty people were killed while the doctors were there. The pictures were taken by the doctors when they got ?back (word unclear).

78. *JN* II: 172.

79. *JN* II: 174–97.

80. Letter from MSJ to Irene Rathbone, 5 Dec. 1945 (IR-CSC).

81. She later described at length and with horror her own trip to one of those camps (*JN* II: 189–94).

17. 1945–1949: Clearing Up

1. Letter from MSJ to Hermon Ould, 14 Jan. 1946 (PEN archive (London, uncat.), HRC); see *JN* II: 265–6 for her account of their meeting.

2. Letter from MSJ to Hermon Ould, 16 Jan. 1946 (PEN archive (London, uncat.), HRC).

3. Letter from MSJ to Hermon Ould, 29 April 1946 (PEN archive (London, uncat.), HRC).

4. Letter from MSJ to Irene Rathbone, 16 April 1946 (IR-CSC).

5. Letter from MSJ to Irene Rathbone, 1 July 1946 (IR-CSC).

6. Letter from MSJ to Irene Rathbone, 10 July 1946 (IR-CSC).

7. Letters from MSJ to Hermon Ould, 20 July and 10 Aug. 1946 (PEN archive (London, uncat.), HRC).

8. Letter from MSJ to Hermon Ould, 9 Dec. 1946 (PEN archive (London, uncat.), HRC). The translation into Polish earned 50,000 zlotys, which Jameson gave to the fund for rebuilding Warsaw (*JN* II: 209). The President of Warsaw sent her a certificate, which is still preserved among her papers (CSC).
9. Letter to MSJ from ?Jirina Tumova, 3 Sept. 1946 (PEN archive (London, uncat.), HRC).
10. Letter from MSJ to Irene Rathbone, 1 July 1946 (IR-CSC).
11. Letter from MSJ to Hermon Ould, 4 Sept. 1946 (PEN archive (London, uncat.), HRC).
12. Letter from MSJ to Irene Rathbone, 13 Sept. 1946 (IR-CSC).
13. Letter from MSJ to Hermon Ould, 29 July 1946 (PEN archive (London, uncat.), HRC).
14. Letter from MSJ to Hermon Ould, 30 Nov. 1946 (PEN archive (London, uncat.), HRC). The first draft of *JN* has one paragraph that was cut from the published version, but both versions treat this period with great discretion (TS of *JN*, Vol. 3, p. 71 (Jameson, Storm. Works (Autobiography) HRC)).
15. Letter to MSJ from Hermon Ould, 11 Nov. 1946 (PEN archive (London, uncat.), HRC), written on back of a sheet of the Association's headed notepaper. Headquarters were in La Maison de France, 3 Cavendish Square. Charles Morgan was President, Hermon Ould Secretary and Treasurer, and other names on the notepaper included Herbert Agar, Professor René Cassin, Sir Kenneth Clark, Dr Milan Grol, Ignace Legrand, Storm Jameson, Matja Kuncewiczowa, Raymond Mortimer, Harold Nicolson, Dr Theodora Ohenberg, and H. A. St George Saunders.
16. Letter from MSJ to Hermon Ould, 7 Dec. 1946 (PEN archive (London, uncat.), HRC).
17. Letter from MSJ to Hermon Ould, 29 Jan. 1947 (PEN archive (London, uncat.), HRC).
18. *JN* II: 206–7.
19. 'Writers in Conflict. Nationalism at PEN Conference', *The Manchester Guardian*, 12 June 1947. See also the report of the Congress drawn from this by *The Yorkshire Post*, 14 June 1947 (letter from MSJ to Hermon Ould, 14 June 1947 (PEN archive (London, uncat.), HRC).
20. Letter from MSJ to Hermon Ould, 24 June 1947 (PEN archive (London, uncat.), HRC).
21. *JN* II: 210.
22. Letter from MSJ to Irene Rathbone, 14 June 1947 (IR-CSC).
23. Letter from MSJ to Irene Rathbone, 12 July 1947 (IR-CSC).
24. *JN* II: 210.
25. Letters from MSJ to Irene Rathbone, 5 and 22 Sept. 1947 (IR-CSC).
26. Letter from MSJ to Irene Rathbone, 28 Nov. 1947 (IR-CSC).
27. Certificate of making Decree Nisi Absolute (Divorce), dated 12 Dec. 1947; letter from MSJ to Barbara Storm-Clark, 18 Dec. 1947 (both items in CSC).
28. Letters from MSJ to Irene Rathbone, 6 and 31 Jan. 1948 (IR-CSC). Jameson's statement about the settlement (apparently a court settlement, against which appeals were lodged) does not tally exactly with her grandson's recollections of his mother's finances, though she certainly supported Barbara financially while the divorce was being settled. Christopher Storm-Clark also recalls that in the years he became responsible for handling her financial matters in 1985/6 he found no evidence of payments she claimed to have made to Patchen and Bill, which often gave rise to recriminations on her part. She certainly paid school fees for her grandchildren.

29. Verbal communication.
30. *There Will Be a Short Interval* (London: Harvill Press, 1973), p. 47.
31. Ibid.
32. Ibid., p. 82.
33. Letters to MSJ from Hermon Ould, 20 and 22 Oct. 1947 (PEN archive (London, uncat.), HRC).
34. Letter from MSJ to Hermon Ould, 21 Oct. 1947 (PEN archive (London, uncat.), HRC).
35. Letter from MSJ to Hermon Ould, 4 Dec. 1947 (PEN archive (London, uncat.), HRC).
36. TS of *JN*, Vol. 3, pp. 79–81 (Jameson, Storm. Works (Autobiography) HRC).
37. Letter from MSJ to Hermon Ould, ?23 April 1948 (PEN archive (London, uncat.), HRC).
38. Letter from MSJ to Irene Rathbone, 6 Jan. 1948 (IR-CSC).
39. See also my essay ' "Waiting for the Death Wind": Storm Jameson's Fiction after the Second World War', in Birkett and Briganti, *Margaret Storm Jameson*, pp. 127–45.
40. [Mrs Michael Roberts], 'Which is the Victim', *TLS* 10 May 1947, Issue 2362, p. 221 [*Before the Crossing*]; [Maurice Lane Richardson], 'Partisans and Prisoners', *TLS*, 6 March 1948, Issue 2405, p. 133 [*The Black Laurel*].
41. Annotation by Jameson in her personal copy of *JN*, opposite II: 203 (CSC).
42. *JN* II: 140.
43. *Before the Crossing*, p. 87.
44. Ibid., p. 131.
45. Ibid., p. 19.
46. *JN* II: 201.
47. *JN* II: 140.
48. Letter from MSJ to Hermon Ould, 2 March 1948 (PEN archive (London, uncat.), HRC).
49. See Storm Jameson Collection, (Jameson, S.), Misc., Black Laurel: Research Notes, HRC. The member of British Intelligence was an E. C. King, from Sevenoaks (letter from MSJ to Rache Lovat Dickson, 10 Sept. 1948, MABL).
50. *JN* II: 203.
51. See David McKie, 'A Grisly Christmas Tale', *The Guardian*, 23 Dec. 2004, p. 20. McKie wrote his piece for the 60th anniversary of the death of Wolfgang Rosterg, an anti-Nazi murdered as a traitor and a spy by fellow-prisoners in a tough concentration camp in Comrie, Perthshire.
52. *The Black Laurel* (London: Macmillan & Co. Ltd, 1947), p. 36.
53. Ibid., p. 305.
54. Ibid.
55. Ibid., p. 36.
56. Ibid.
57. *JN* II: 210.
58. Letter from MSJ to Hermon Ould, 2 March 1948 (PEN archive (London, uncat.), HRC).
59. Letter from MSJ to Hermon Ould, 25 March 1948 (PEN archive (London, uncat.), HRC).
60. Letter from MSJ to Hermon Ould, 5 May 1948 (PEN archive (London, uncat.), HRC).
61. Letter from MSJ to Hermon Ould, [May] 1948 (PEN archive (London, uncat.), HRC).
62. Ibid.

63. Letter from MSJ to Hermon Ould, 14 June 1948 (PEN archive (London, uncat.), HRC).
64. Bill flew in the Berlin airlift May–July 1949, for Skyways Ltd (Personal Details for Clark, Charles William Storm, attached to letter from Rache Lovat Dickson to Colonel A. H. T. Chisholm, 4 April 1950, following up MSJ's request to help Bill find a job (MABL)).
65. Letter from Phyllis Bottome to MSJ, Oct. 1947, and reply from MSJ to Phyllis Bottome, 25 Oct. 1947 (Phyllis Bottome Correspondence, BL, Add. Mss., 78837, Nos 100, 101). Bottome's letter was primarily written to ask Jameson to become a patron of the Committee for Furthering Education in Psychology, formed to support the making of a film about Adler. She appears on the notepaper as 'Margaret Storm Jameson MA, President of International PEN Club, 1938–42; fellow-patrons included Daphne du Maurier, Sybil Thorndike, Professor John McMurray, Her Grace the Duchess of Hamilton and Brandon, and Lady Pakenham (Phyllis Bottome Correspondence, BL, Add. Mss., 78837, No. 30).
66. *JN* II: 211–49.
67. Letter from MSJ to Irene Rathbone, 10 Aug. 1948 (IR-CSC).
68. Letter from MSJ to Irene Rathbone, 8 June 1948 (IR-CSC).
69. Letter from MSJ to Irene Rathbone, 10 Aug. 1948 (IR-CSC).
70. Letter from MSJ to Irene Rathbone, 25 Nov. 1947 (IR-CSC).
71. Letter from Dorothy Pateman to Betty Leake's mother, 1 Nov. 1940 (JK-CSC).
72. Letter from MSJ to Hermon Ould, 10 Sept. 1948 (PEN archive (London, uncat.), HRC); see also *JN* I: 218–20.
73. Letter from MSJ to Betty Leake, 8 Oct. 1948 (JK-CSC).
74. Letter from MSJ to Betty Leake, 23 May 1949 (JK-CSC).
75. Letters from MSJ to Betty Leake, 27 Feb., 16 March, 4 April 1949 (JK-CSC); *JN* II 241–4.
76. Letter from MSJ to Betty Leake, 8 Oct. 1948 (JK-CSC); cf *JN* II: 227.
77. Letter from MSJ to Irene Rathbone, 5 Oct. 1948 (IR-CSC).
78. Letter from MSJ to Hermon Ould, 29 Nov. 1948 (PEN archive (London, uncat.), HRC).
79. Letter to MSJ from Hermon Ould, 26 Oct. 1948 (PEN archive (London, uncat.), HRC).
80. Letter from MSJ to Hermon Ould, 1st Nov. 1948 (PEN archive (London, uncat.), HRC).
81. Letter from MSJ to Hermon Ould, 29 Nov. (PEN archive (London, uncat.), HRC).
82. Letters to MSJ from Hermon Ould, 15 Nov. and 30 Dec. 1948 (PEN archive (London, uncat.), HRC).
83. Letters from MSJ to Hermon Ould, 19 March, 16 April 1949 (PEN archive (London, uncat.), HRC); from Ould to MSJ, 30 May 1949.
84. Letters from MSJ to Hermon Ould, 19 May, 3rd June 1949 (PEN archive (London, uncat.), HRC).
85. Letter from MSJ to Hermon Ould, 30 April 1949 (PEN archive (London, uncat.), HRC).
86. Letter from MSJ to Hermon Ould, 3rd June 1949 (PEN archive (London, uncat.), HRC).
87. Postcard to MSJ from Thornton Wilder, 7 June 1949 (PEN archive (London, uncat.), HRC).
88. Letter from MSJ to Hermon Ould, 19 July 1949 (PEN archive (London, uncat.), HRC).

89. *JN* II: 248–9.
90. Letter from MSJ to Irene Rathbone, 7 July 1949 (IR-CSC).

18. 1949–1953: A European Future

1. *JN* II: 248.
2. Letters from MSJ to Rache Lovat Dickson, 30 July 1949, April 1950 (MABL).
3. *JN* II: 250; *Survivor*, p. 225.
4. Letter from MSJ to Irene Rathbone, 23 Sept. 1949 (IR-CSC); see *JN* II: 250.
5. Letter from MSJ to Irene Rathbone, 1 Oct. 1949 (IR-CSC). Intermediaries, including Guy, were allowed to maintain contact with Christopher, and at this point the Chapmans took on responsibility for Christopher's education (letter to Rubensteins solicitors, 15 Nov. 1949, in CSC).
6. TS of *JN*, Vol. 3, p. 126 (Jameson, Storm. Works (Autobiography) HRC).
7. See also the discussion of this text in Birkett, ' "Waiting for the Death Wind" '.
8. *The Listener*, 28 Sept. 1950. On Sunday 22 Oct., two extracts were broadcast on William Plomer's radio programme, 'Books and Other Pleasures'.
9. 'The Writer's Situation', in *The Writer's Situation and Other Essays* (London: Macmillan & Co. Ltd, 1950), pp. 2–4.
10. 'A Crisis of the Spirit', in *The Writer's Situation*, p. 137.
11. The essay probably draws on a lecture she gave in 1947 at a women's college near Pittsburgh on Sartre, Malraux, and the future of Europe (*JN* II: 245). It may later have become the 'Lecture by Mrs M. Storm Jameson on "The Situation of the Writer Today"', advertised for 2 June, at the Lyceum Club, for the Ladies of the XIXth Congress of the International PEN Club, Zurich 2–6 June 1947 (programme, p.7) (Jameson's home file of PEN documents (Dr Storm Jameson, International Vice-President), labelled in her own hand 'Pen[sic] File (fragments of a monstrous mass)' (CSC)).
12. 'The Writer's Situation', in *The Writer's Situation*, p. 26.
13. 'The Novelist Today', rpt. in *The Writer's Situation*, p. 76. 'The Novelist Today', dated May 1949, was first published in *The Virginia Quarterly*.
14. *JN* II: 374.
15. *The Writer's Situation*, pp. 27–31.
16. Ibid., p. 81.
17. *JN* II: 372.
18. *JN* II: 254.
19. 'The Form of the Novel', in *The Writer's Situation*, pp. 39, 43.
20. 'A Crisis of the Spirit', p. 159.
21. Letter from D. L. Ross (Copyright) to Miss J. Leroy (Pearn Pollinger & Higham), 21 March 1950 (RCONT1, Copyright. Jameson Storm, File 1 1950–1954 (BBC Written Archive, Caversham)).
22. *The Moment of Truth* (London: Macmillan & Co. Ltd, 1949), p. 136. Quotations are from the novel; no radio script is extant.
23. Ibid., p. 138.

24. Letter to MSJ from Donald Stephenson, 3 Aug. 1950 (RCONT1, Copyright. Jameson Storm, File 1 1950–1954 (BBC Written Archive, Caversham)).

25. Letter from MSJ to Miss Ross, 3 Aug. 1950 (RCONT1, Copyright. Jameson Storm, File 1 1950–1954 (BBC Written Archive, Caversham)). The episode did not put an end to her attempts to write for radio. *JN* II: 262 records she is writing a commissioned comedy at the very end of 1950, though there are no references to it in the BBC Archives. In 1961, Val Gielgud, who had seen an over-cut television adaptation of *The Moment of Truth* in New York, proposed a full-length adaptation, with no success (Internal memo from Val Gielgud to Donald McWhinnie, 8 Aug. 1951: RCONT1, Storm Jameson Scriptwriter. File 1 1941–61 (BBC Written Archive, Caversham)). At that point, it was discovered that the radio recording was technically no longer up to standard.

26. *JN* II: 260–1. See also her contribution 'In Memory of Hermon Ould', to *Hermon Ould: A Tribute* (Slough: Kenion Press Ltd, n.d.), pp. 8–13.

27. *JN* II: 251–4.

28. Letter from MSJ to Rache Lovat Dickson, 11 Oct. 1950 (MABL).

29. Letter from MSJ to Rache Lovat Dickson, 30 Oct. 1950 (MABL).

30. Ibid.

31. Letter from MSJ to Irene Rathbone, 14 Jan. 1951 (IR-CSC).

32. Letter from MSJ to A. D. Peters, 16 Jan. 1947 (Jameson, S., Misc, Peters (A D), Literary Agent (Correspondence files relating to Storm Jameson), HRC).

33. Letter from MSJ to Rache Lovat Dickson, 22 Sept. 1947 (Margaret Storm Jameson, Folder 1947, MABL).

34. Letter from MSJ to A. D. Peters, 14 Feb. 1951 (Jameson, S., Misc, Peters (A D), Literary Agent, (Correspondence files relating to Storm Jameson), HRC).

35. Letter to MSJ from Judith Todd, 21 May 1951 (CSC).

36. Letter from MSJ to A. D. Peters, 2 June 1951 (Jameson, S., Misc, Peters (A D), Literary Agent, (Correspondence files relating to Storm Jameson), HRC).

37. Letter from MSJ to A. D. Peters, 22 June 1951 (Jameson, S., Misc, Peters (A D), Literary Agent, (Correspondence files relating to Storm Jameson), HRC).

38. Ibid.

39. Letter from A. D. Peters to Jack Hargreaves, and reply from Jack Hargreaves, 29 June and 6 July 1951 (Jameson, S., Misc, Peters (A D), Literary Agent, (Correspondence files relating to Storm Jameson), HRC).

40. Letter to John Montgomery from Anita Christophersen, 10 May 1955 (Jameson, S., Misc, Peters (A D), Literary Agent, (Correspondence files relating to Storm Jameson), HRC).

41. Letter from John Montgomery to MSJ, 31 Dec. 1951 (Jameson, S., Misc, Peters (A D), Literary Agent, (Correspondence files relating to Storm Jameson), HRC).

42. Letters of July and Dec. 1951 (Jameson, S., Misc, Peters (A D), Literary Agent, (Correspondence files relating to Storm Jameson), HRC).

43. Letter from A. D. Peters to MSJ, 13 July 1951 (Jameson, S., Misc, Peters (A D), Literary Agent, (Correspondence files relating to Storm Jameson), HRC).

44. Letter from Rache Lovat Dickson to A. D. Peters, 25 July 1951 (Jameson, S., Misc, Peters (A D), Literary Agent, (Correspondence files relating to Storm Jameson), HRC).

45. Letter from Macmillan to A. D. Peters, 12 Nov. 1951 (Jameson, S., Misc, Peters (A D), Literary Agent, (Correspondence files relating to Storm Jameson), HRC).
46. Letter from MSJ to Irene Rathbone, 20 March 1952 (IR-CSC).
47. *JN* II 263–7.
48. The manuscript of *The Gamble*, 273 pages, is in three notebooks (Jameson, Storm. Works (The Gamble), HRC). See also *JN* II: 263.
49. Letter from MSJ to Sir Basil Bartlett, 2 Nov. 1952 (T28/114, TV Scriptwriters. Jameson, Storm, File 1 1952–1953 (BBC Written Archive, Caversham)). Letters from Montgomery, Barry in same file.
50. Letter from MSJ to Sir Basil Bartlett, 20 Dec. 1952 (T28/114, TV Scriptwriters, Jameson, Storm, File 1 1952–1953 (BBC Written Archive, Caversham)).
51. Letter from A. D. Peters to Donald Wilson, 13 Aug. 1959 (T48/341, 1, Television Script Unit, Dramawriter's File, Storm Jameson). The 'Personal Column' project came to nothing, although it included a script from C. Day Lewis, writing as Nicholas Blake. 'Plain Annie' was better liked than the other suggestions, and there was an attempt to write it up as a one-off production. The young John McGrath tried his hand, but it turned out not to be the right subject for him.
52. Cf *JN* II: 271; Jameson claimed to have forgotten where the money for the trip came from.
53. Letter from MSJ to Irene Rathbone, 7 July 1952 (IR-CSC).
54. Letter from MSJ to Irene Rathbone, 9 July 1952 (IR-CSC).
55. Letter from MSJ to David Carver, 9 Aug. 1952 (PEN archive (London, uncat.), HRC).
56. *JN* II: 276.
57. Jules Romains, 'Essai d'une politique de l'esprit', *Preuves*, Aug.–Sept. 1952, 2nd year, Nos. 18–19, pp. 63–8. See also above, Ch. 12 n. 7.
58. Letters from David Carver and Jules Romains, *Preuves*, Jan. 1953, 3rd Year, No. 23, p. 106.
59. Letter from MSJ to Irene Rathbone, 2 Oct. 1952 (IR-CSC).
60. Letter from Rache Lovat Dickson to Frank Upjohn, 30 Dec. 1952 (Margaret Storm Jameson, Folder 1952–54, MABL).
61. Letter from MSJ to Rache Lovat Dickson, 11 Jan. 1953 (Margaret Storm Jameson, Folder 1952–54, MABL).
62. [Maurice Lane Richardson], 'Seabord to Shire', *TLS*, 1 Aug. 1952, Issue 2635, p. 197; see also *JN* II: 274.
63. Margaret Parton, 'Books and Things', New York Herald Tribune, 5 March 1953.
64. *JN* II: 249.
65. *The Green Man* (London: Macmillan & Co., Ltd, 1952), p. 67.
66. Ibid., p. 62.
67. Ibid., pp. 212, 368.
68. Ibid., pp. 21, 44–5.
69. In a letter to David Carver, 26 Aug. 1952 (PEN archive (London, uncat.), HRC), Guy Chapman commented on the treatment of light in this novel, and in *Cloudless May*, which reviewers, he said, never noticed.

70. *The Green Man*, p. 221.
71. Ibid., p. 226.
72. Ibid., p. 289.
73. Ibid., p. 317.

19. 1953–1959: Understanding Exile

1. Letter from MSJ to Maureen St John Gebbie, 22 Jan. 1953 (PEN archive (London, uncat.), HRC).
2. *JN* II: 278–80; TS of *JN*, Vol. 3, p. 167 (Jameson, Storm. Works (Autobiography) HRC).
3. Letter from MSJ to David Carver, 20 May 1953 (PEN archive (London, uncat.), HRC).
4. *JN* II: 290.
5. Letter from MSJ to Rache Lovat Dickson, 28 Nov. 1953 (MABL).
6. Letter from MSJ to Irene Rathbone, 23 Dec. 1953 (CSC); *JN* II: 298–302.
7. Letters from MSJ to Rache Lovat Dickson, 21 and 26 March 1954 (MABL).
8. Letter from David Carver to MSJ 26 March 1954, letter from MSJ to David Carver 27 March 1954 (PEN archive (London, uncat.), HRC).
9. See on the interactions of International PEN and friends of the Congress for Cultural Freedom in the 1950s and 1960s, with special reference to the role of David Carver, Stonor Saunders, *The Cultural Cold War*, pp. 362–8.
10. Letters from MSJ to A. D. Peters, 2 and 27 March 1954 (Jameson, S., Misc, Peters (A D), Literary Agent, (Correspondence files relating to Storm Jameson), HRC).
11. See letters Jan. 1954–Dec. 1954 (Jameson, S., Misc, Peters (AD) Literary Agent, (Correspondence files relating to Storm Jameson), HRC).
12. Letters from Carl Brandt to A. D. Peters, 7 Jan., 24 and 27 Aug. 1954 (Jameson, S., Misc, Peters (A D), Literary Agent (Correspondence files relating to Storm Jameson), HRC).
13. Letter to MSJ from John Montgomery, 1 July 1954 (Jameson, S., Misc, Peters (A D), Literary Agent (Correspondence files relating to Storm Jameson), HRC).
14. Letter from MSJ to John Montgomery, 15 July 1954 (Jameson, S., Misc, Peters (A D), Literary Agent (Correspondence files relating to Storm Jameson), HRC).
15. Letter to MSJ from John Murray, 25 Aug. 1954 (Jameson, S., Misc, Peters (A D), Literary Agent (Correspondence files relating to Storm Jameson), HRC).
16. 'A Note on France', pp. 446–7. Another version of the anecdote attributes the same views to a retired history professor she met through Saurat (*JN* II: 300–301).
17. Letter from MSJ to A. D. Peters, 29 Sept. 1954 (Jameson, S., Misc, Peters (A D), Literary Agent (Correspondence files relating to Storm Jameson), HRC).
18. *JN* II: 316.
19. Letter to A. D. Peters from Lovat Dickson, 17 June 1954 (Jameson, S., Misc, Peters (A D), Literary Agent (Correspondence files relating to Storm Jameson), HRC). The following year, it was American Book-of-the-Month Club choice for April 1955, involving a $1500 advance (letter from Rache Lovat Dickson to Bernice Baumgarten, 25 Jan. 1955 (MABL)), which was split between Jameson and Macmillan. The book was also

requested by Odhams Companion Book Club and considered by World Books (Note to Rache Lovat Dickson from Alan Maclean, 20 Jan. 1955 (MABL)).

20. Letter to MSJ from John Montgomery, 28 March 1955 (Jameson, S., Misc, Peters (A D), Literary Agent (Correspondence files relating to Storm Jameson), HRC).
21. Account statement for *The Hidden River*, 20 Jan. 1956, and letter from MSJ to Rache Lovat Dickson, 4 April 1956 (both MABL).
22. *JN* II: 270–3.
23. *The Hidden River* (London: Macmillan & Co., Ltd, 1955); Book Society edition, p. 19.
24. Ibid., p. 225
25. Ibid., p. 266.
26. MSJ, 'Foreword' to Kate Roberts, *A Summer Day and Other Stories* (Cardiff: Penmark Press, 1946).
27. Letter from MSJ to Betty Leake, 14 Jan. 1956 (JK-CSC); *JN* II: 308.
28. Letter from MSJ to John Montgomery, 2 July 1955 (Jameson, S., Misc, Peters (A D), Literary Agent (Correspondence files relating to Storm Jameson), HRC).
29. Letter from MSJ to A. D. Peters, 14 Dec. 1955 (Jameson, S., Misc, Peters (A D), Literary Agent (Correspondence files relating to Storm Jameson), HRC).
30. Letters from A. D. Peters to MSJ, 9 and 12 Aug. 1955 (Jameson, S., Misc, Peters (A D), Literary Agent (Correspondence files relating to Storm Jameson), HRC).
31. Letter from Macmillan to A. D. Peters, 14 Sept. 1955 (Jameson, S., Misc, Peters (A D), Literary Agent (Correspondence files relating to Storm Jameson), HRC).
32. Letter from A. D. Peters to MSJ, 13 Dec. 1955 (Jameson, S., Misc, Peters (A D), Literary Agent (Correspondence files relating to Storm Jameson), HRC).
33. Letter from MSJ to Margaret Stephens, 23 July 1955 (Jameson, S., Misc, Peters (A D), Literary Agent (Correspondence files relating to Storm Jameson), HRC).
34. Letter from MSJ to A. D. Peters, 30 Dec. 1955 (Jameson, S., Misc, Peters (A D), Literary Agent (Correspondence files relating to Storm Jameson), HRC).
35. Letter from MSJ to Irene Rathbone, 25 Dec. 1955 (IR-CSC).
36. Letter from MSJ to David Carver, 18 Jan. 1956 (PEN archive (London, uncat.), HRC).
37. Letter from Charles Douglas Clarke to David Carver, 20 Jan. 1956 (PEN archive (London, uncat.), HRC). See also above, Ch. 2, n. 13.
38. Letter from MSJ to A. D. Peters, 8 April 1956 (Jameson, S., Misc, Peters (A D), Literary Agent (Correspondence files relating to Storm Jameson), HRC).
39. Written communication to the present writer.
40. Undated change of address card, for correspondence after 27 July 1956, MSJ to A. D. Peters (Jameson, S., Misc, Peters (A D), Literary Agent (Correspondence files relating to Storm Jameson), HRC).
41. Information provided by Christopher Storm-Clark.
42. *Survivor*, p. 246.
43. Letter from MSJ to A. D. Peters, 4 Aug. 1956 (Jameson, S., Misc, Peters (A D), Literary Agent (Correspondence files relating to Storm Jameson), HRC); II: 324–6.
44. See e.g. letter from Rache Lovat Dickson to MSJ, 9 Jan. 1957 (Jameson, S., Misc, Peters (A D), Literary Agent, (Correspondence files relating to Storm Jameson), HRC).

45. Cable to MSJ from A. D. Peters, 25 Jan. 1957 (Jameson, S., Misc, Peters (A D), Literary Agent, (Correspondence files relating to Storm Jameson), HRC).

46. Pelham asked Jameson to revise the original script to make it suitable for an English audience. She was horrified to find it a melodramatic travesty of her novel, full of mistakes about France and the Resistance, and she made a number of changes. The play closed after a short provincial tour in March and a two-week run in London at the Cambridge Theatre, from 13 April. See TS of *JN*, Vol. 3, pp. 250–4 (Jameson, Storm. Works (Autobiography) HRC), and letters from Harold Freeman to MSJ, 10 Nov. 1938, and from MSJ to A. D. Peters, 9 Dec. 1958 (Jameson, S, Misc, Peters (A D), Literary Agent, (Correspondence files relating to Storm Jameson), HRC). There was another play production of *The Hidden River* in Vienna, in the autumn of 1959 (Letter from MSJ to David Carver, 1 Sept. 1959 (PEN archive (London, uncat.), HRC)).

47. Letter from MSJ to ?Alan Maclean, 1 Oct. 1957 (MABL).

48. Letter to Margaret Stephens from MSJ, 21 Jan. 1957 (Jameson, S., Misc, Peters (A D), Literary Agent, (Correspondence files relating to Storm Jameson), HRC). See also my account of this novel in Birkett, ' "Waiting for the Death Wind" ', pp. 133–5.

49. Letter to A. D. Peters from MSJ, 1 Aug. 1957 (Jameson, S., Misc, Peters (A D), Literary Agent, (Correspondence files relating to Storm Jameson), HRC).

50. [David Tylden-Wright], 'Scheming Spires' *TLS* 15 Nov. 1957, Issue 2907, p. 685.

51. *JN* II: 343; see e.g. review by Patricia Hodgart, *Manchester Guardian*, 19 Nov. 1957.

52. Letter from Mary Dilke to John Montgomery, 19 June 1957 (Jameson, S., Misc, Peters (A D), Literary Agent, (Correspondence files relating to Storm Jameson), HRC).

53. *JN* II: 319.

54. *JN* II: 326.

55. Letter from MSJ to David Carver, 11 April 1956 (PEN archive (London, uncat.), HRC).

56. TS of *JN*, Vol. 2, p. 236A (Jameson, Storm. Works (Autobiography) HRC).

57. *A Cup of Tea for Mr Thorgill* (London: Macmillan, 1957), p. 149.

58. Ibid., p. 204.

59. See for the expansion of this point my essay ' "Waiting for the Death Wind" ', pp. 134–5.

60. Ibid., p. 273.

61. Ibid., p. 255.

62. *JN* II: 358.

63. *JN* II: 329–30.

64. *A Ulysses Too Many* (London: Macmillan & Co., 1958), p. 49.

65. *JN* II: 329.

66. *JN* II: 331–2.

67. Letter from John Montgomery to Macmillan, 27 March 1958 (Jameson, S., Misc, Peters (A D), Literary Agent (Correspondence files relating to Storm Jameson), HRC).

68. *JN* II: 159.

69. *JN* II: 258.

70. BBC recording T2587, Prose and poetry from the PEN series *In Exile*, ed. Paul Tabori, n.d. (BBC Sound Archive, BL).

71. 'The Writer's Situation', pp. 9–13; *JN* II: 158–62.
72. *JN* II: 161.
73. *JN* II: 233–4.
74. Letter from MSJ to Rache Lovat Dickson, 15 July 1951 (MABL).
75. This was *The Captive Mind*, eventually published in 1953. *Murti-Bing* was also published in New York, in 1951, by the American Committee for Cultural Freedom (23 pp.).
76. Letter from MSJ to Rache Lovat Dickson, 15 July 1951 (MABL).
77. Letters from MSJ to Maureen Gebbie, 23 April 1952 and 22nd Jan. 1953 (PEN archive (London, uncat.), HRC).
78. *JN* II: 263–5.
79. Letter from MSJ to David Carver, 23 April 1953 (PEN archive (London, uncat.), HRC).
80. *JN* II: 321–2. The two stayed in touch sporadically after Milosz's story eventually achieved a happy resolution. Jameson preserved in her archive only three letters from Milosz: one reporting various family information, including his wife's illness, and two requesting that she look out for his son Peter, who undertook a brief postgraduate career in Cambridge in 1982. Aged 91, she was unable to help (CSC).
81. *A Ulysses Too Many*, p. 164.
82. Ibid., p. 182.
83. Ibid., p. 47.
84. Ibid., p. 304.
85. Ibid., p. 257.
86. Ibid., p. 274.
87. Letter from MSJ to Alan Maclean, 3 July 1958 (MABL).
88. *JN* II: 347ff.
89. Letter from A. D. Peters to Macmillan, 20 Jan. 1959 (Jameson, S., Misc, Peters (A D), Literary Agent (Correspondence files relating to Storm Jameson), HRC).
90. Letter from MSJ to Alan Maclean, 5 April 1959 (MABL).
91. Letter from MSJ to Lovat Dickson, 11 Dec. 1959 (MABL).

20. 1960–1968: Letting Go and Settling Up

1. TS of *JN*, Vol. 3, p. 133 (Jameson, Storm. Works (Autobiography) HRC); letter from MSJ to David Carver, 30 Aug. 1963 (PEN archive (London, uncat.), HRC).
2. Letters to MSJ from Laslo Kery, 20 May and 6 July 1960 (CSC).
3. Letter from MSJ to David Carver, 10 June 1960 (PEN archive (London, uncat.), HRC).
4. Letter from David Carver to MSJ, 30 May 1961 (PEN archive (London, uncat.), HRC).
5. Letter from MSJ to David Carver, 13 June 1959 (PEN archive (London, uncat.), HRC).
6. Letter from MSJ to David Carver, 2 Feb. 1960 (PEN archive (London, uncat.), HRC).
7. Letter from MSJ to David Carver, 10 June 1960 (PEN archive (London, uncat.), HRC).
8. Letter from MSJ to David Carver, 5 Aug. 1961 (PEN archive (London, uncat.), HRC).

9. Letter from MSJ to David Carver, 17 Aug. 1963 (PEN archive (London, uncat.), HRC).

10. Letters from MSJ to David Carver, 22 Oct. 1962, and from David Carver to MSJ, 21 Nov. 1966 (PEN archive (London, uncat.), HRC).

11. Letter from MSJ to David Carver, 2 April 1964 (PEN archive (London, uncat.), HRC).

12. *JN* I: 142.

13. See e.g. [Julian Symons], 'The Moment of Truth', *TLS*, 8 July 1949, Issue 2475, p. 441; [Maurice Lane Richardson], 'Seabord to Shire', *TLS*, Aug. 1 1952, Issue 2635, p. 497; [Erik de Mauny], 'Comédie Française', *TLS*, Jan. 21 1955, Issue 2764, p. 37.

14. Letters from MSJ to Rache Lovat Dickson, 29 March 1960, and Alan Maclean, 7 April 1960 (MABL).

15. Letter from MSJ to Phyllis Bottome, 28 Dec. 1961 (Phyllis Bottome Correspondence, BL, Add. Ms. 78861, ff. 60, 61).

16. Letter from MSJ to Rache Lovat Dickson, 21 March 1960 (MABL).

17. Letter from MSJ to Phyllis Bottome, 2 Jan. 1961 (BL, Add. Ms. 78861, f. 58 r.).

18. *JN* II: 364.

19. Gillian Tindall, *Time and Tide*, 18 May 1961; see also [Marigold Johnson], 'Topical Agonies', *TLS*, 19 May 1961, Issue 3090, p. 305.

20. Letter to MSJ from Rache Lovat Dickson, 8 Feb. 1960 (Jameson S., Misc, Peters, (A D), Literary Agent (Correspondence Files)).

21. Letter from MSJ to Lovat Dickson, 8 July 1960 (MABL).

22. Letter from MSJ to Hermon Ould, 2 March 1943 (PEN archive (London, uncat.), HRC).

23. Letter from MSJ to A. D. Peters, 22 Oct. 1954 (Jameson, S., Misc, Peters (A D) Literary Agent, (Correspondence files relating to Storm Jameson)).

24. *Last Score* (1961; London: The Reprint Society Ltd, 1962), p. 107.

25. Ibid., pp. 11–12.

26. See my discussion of the landscapes of *Last Score* in ' "Waiting for the Death Wind" ', pp. 137–9.

27. *Last Score*, p. 224.

28. *JN* II: 365–70.

29. TS of *JN*, Vol. 3, p. 248 (Jameson, Storm. Works (Autobiography) HRC). See e.g. the review by [Marigold Johnson], 'The Moment of Truth', *TLS*, 26 Jan. 1962, Issue 3126, p. 53: '[N]owadays it is a little embarrassing to be invited quite so bravely to share even the most banal cogitations about Life as it is lived between the covers of the traditional novel.'

30. *The Road from the Monument* (1962); (London: White Lion Publishers), 1974, pp. 287–8.

31. Letter from MSJ to Lovat Dickson, 13 July1961 (MABL).

32. The earliest date of writing noted in *JN* is 21 Nov. 1960, the date of the move into Tiberias Lodge (*JN* II: 370); the latest date for a segment heading is 24 March 1965 (*JN* II: 379). Jameson wrote to Margaret Stephens at A. D. Peters on 24 Aug. 1962, asking the cost of making a dozen copies of the script of an unrevised volume of memoirs, currently over 100,000 words—which she feared, she said, she would not have the courage to publish; on 31 Aug. 1962, she mentioned to Peters a second or even third volume (letters from

MSJ to Margaret Stephens and to Peters (Jameson, S., Misc, Peters (A D), Literary Agent (Correspondence files)). When Jameson sent Vol. 1 to Basil Liddell Hart on 2 Aug. 1965, she said she had just finished typing Vol. 2 (LHC: LH 1/408 PART 2– 409).

33. TS of *JN*, Vol. 2, p. 127 (Jameson, Storm. Works (Autobiography) HRC).
34. TS of *JN*, Vol. 1, p. 1 (Jameson, Storm. Works (Autobiography) HRC).
35. Ibid., p. 179.
36. Ibid., p. 7.
37. This last comment was reproduced in the published version (*JN* II: 344).
38. *JN* II: 372.
39. *The Road from the Monument*, p. 339.
40. Letter from MSJ to Irene Rathbone, 30 July 1965 (IR–CSC).
41. Letter from MSJ to Basil Liddell Hart, 10 July 1965 (LHC: LH 1/408 PART 2– 409). In fact, Alan Maclean and Lovat Dickson had also read it, and been too shocked to comment (letters from MSJ to Peters, 27 March and 6 April 1963 (Jameson S., Peters (A D) Literary Agent (Correspondence files)).
42. Letter from MSJ to Basil Liddell Hart, 2 Aug. 1965, and letter to MSJ from Basil Liddell Hart, 6 Aug. 1965 (LHC: LH 1/408 PART 2– 409).
43. TS of *JN*, Vol. 2, p. 255 (Jameson, Storm. Works (Autobiography) HRC). A similar segment appears in TS Vol. 3, p. 1.
44. Letter to MSJ from Basil Liddell Hart, 6 Aug. 1965 (LHC: LH 1/408 PART 2– 409).
45. 'Feelings and beliefs exist in the mind at different levels, and are more valuable at one time than at another. [...] I do not know what you are like, you whose pulse is close to this page. And you will know much less about me from what I say than (if you have time to listen to it) from the tone of my voice. [...] It is not certain either that what I say is what I wholly think. The words I use are the very texture of time, waver daily, momently, in my mind. The pattern repeats itself but the repetitions have nothing in common except the frame, the skeleton, on which each is created. The memory of single events appears again and again, in a compound of which a new event is the nucleus.' (*No Time Like the Present*, pp. 103–5).
46. In the published version, Sartre has only one brief mention (*JN* II: 374); in the uncut version, he also merits another short paragraph, in which Jameson attacks his atheistic view of life as 'an absence' (TS of *JN*, Vol. 3, p. 273 (Jameson, Storm. Works (Autobiography) HRC)).
47. Discussing Sullivan's autobiographical fiction in her review in the *New English Weekly*, 21 April 1932, she referred to Stendhal's *Amiel* to point to the impossibility of complete honesty in writing the self: 'even Amiel could not uncover to the skeleton'. She also refers in *JN* I: 36 to having read Stendhal's *Souvenirs d'égoisme* for the first time between the wars, and her delighted response to the writer's stated desire 'not to be seen into'.
48. TS of *JN*, Vol. 3, pp. 275–6 (Jameson, Storm. Works (Autobiography) HRC). The first paragraph is a marginal handwritten addition. In the published autobiography, the theme is written with a less negative inflection (*JN* II: 375).
49. Bonamy Dobrée, 'Views and Reviews. Autobiography Plus', *The New English Weekly*, Vol. III, No. 4, 11 May 1933, p. 90.

50. Ibid., p. 91.
51. TS of *JN*, Vol. 2, p. 348 (Jameson, Storm. Works (Autobiography) HRC).
52. *JN* II: 135.
53. John Barkham 'The Literary Scene', *The New York Post*, 17 Feb. (1971), described 'SJ, novelist, telling the story of Storm Jameson, human being, with the same candor that she would bring to any of her invented characters'.
54. Letter from MSJ to Margaret Stephens, 24 Aug. 1962 (Jameson S., Misc, Peters (AD), Literary Agent (Correspondence files relating to Storm Jameson), HRC).
55. Correspondence between MSJ and Peters, 27 March and 11 Dec. 1963 (Jameson S., Misc, Peters (AD), Literary Agent (Correspondence files relating to Storm Jameson), HRC).
56. Letter from MSJ to Peters, 27 July 1963 (Jameson S., Misc, Peters (AD), Literary Agent (Correspondence files relating to Storm Jameson), HRC).
57. Correspondence between MSJ and Peters, 22–29 Oct. 1963 (Jameson S., Misc, Peters (AD), Literary Agent (Correspondence files relating to Storm Jameson), HRC).
58. Letter from MSJ to David Carver, 5 Feb. 1965 (PEN archive (London, uncat.), HRC); letter from MSJ to Alan Maclean, 14 April 1966 (MABL).
59. Letter from MSJ to Basil Liddell Hart, 10 Dec. 1965 (LHC: LH 1/408 PART 2– 409).
60. [Marigold Johnson], 'Somebody Up There's Like Me', *TLS*, 9 June 1966, Issue 3354, p. 520.
61. Letter to MSJ from Margaret Lane, Countess of Huntingdon, 15 June 1966 (CSC).
62. Letter to MSJ from David Carver, 28 June 1967 (PEN archive (London, uncat.), HRC). See Frances Stonor Saunders, pp. 362–8; and see Chapter 19 above. Stonor Saunders says that David Carver was an 'unofficial agent' for *Encounter*, and distributed copies at PEN meetings (p. 363).
63. Letter from MSJ to David Carver, 30 June 1967 (PEN archive (London, uncat.), HRC).
64. Letter to MSJ from André Buffard, 16 May 1968 (CSC).

21. Final Recall

1. Letter from MSJ to Kathleen and Basil Liddell Hart, 13 Jan. 1969 (LHC: LH 1/408 PART 2– 409).
2. Letter from MSJ to Basil Liddell Hart, 2 June 1969 (LHC: LH 1/408 PART 2– 409); verbal communication from Christopher Storm-Clark.
3. Letter from MSJ to Kathleen Liddell Hart, 2 Oct. 1969 (LHC: LH 1/408 PART 2– 409). She also gave a 5-minute reading of the Whitby sequence of *JN* for the *Great North Road Show*, a BBC regional television programme transmitted from Newcastle on 4 Aug. 1970 at 10 p.m. (Memorandum from Jon Maplebeck to M. Herring, RCONT20, Solicitors and Copyright Registry, Storm Jameson, File III 1968– (BBC Written Archive, Caversham)).
4. Letter to MSJ from Freda Gibson, 9 Oct. 1969 (CSC).
5. J. Singleton, *Home this Afternoon*, Radio 4, 3 March 1970; recorded 12 Jan. 1970 (BBC ref LP33092, Sound Archive ref ILP 0196495 (BBC Sound Archive, BL)).
6. J. McMullen, *Books and Writers*, 4 March 1970; recorded 20 Jan. 1970 (BBC ref LP 35394, Sound Archive ref 1LP0195571 (BBC Sound Archive, BL)).

7. Ray Gosling 'The Formidable Girl', *The Times*, 6 Sept. 1969.

8. 'Life Intensely Lived', *The Economist*, 6 Sept. 1969.

9. Letter from MSJ to Basil Liddell Hart, 21 Nov. 1969 (LHC: LH 1/408 PART 2– 409).

10. *Parthian Words* (London: Collins and Harvill Press, 1970), pp.155–6.

11. 'Inside the Explosion', *The Times Saturday Review*, 27 June 1970.

12. Robert Nye, 'A few backward shots,' *The Scotsman*, 4 March 1972.

13. Letter from MSJ to Irene Rathbone, 21 Dec. 1970 (IR-CSC).

14. Letter from MSJ to Kathleen Liddell Hart, 26 April 1971 (LHC: LH 1/408 PART 2– 409).

15. Letter from MSJ to Irene Rathbone, 30 Dec. 1971 (IR-CSC).

16. Letter from MSJ to Irene Rathbone, 24 Feb. 1972 (IR-CSC).

17. Letter from MSJ to Alan Maclean, 3 June 1972 (MABL).

18. *Survivor*, p. 12.

19. Information supplied by Christopher Storm-Clark.

20. Letter from MSJ to Kathleen Liddell Hart, 7 Sept. 1972 (LHC: LH 1/408 PART 2- 409).

21. Letter from MSJ to Irene Rathbone, 17 June 1975 (IR-CSC).

22. Letter from MSJ to Irene Rathbone, 13 Feb. 1974 (IR-CSC).

23. Letter from MSJ to Irene Rathbone, 28 May 1975 (IR-CSC).

24. Letter from MSJ to Kathleen Liddell Hart, 24 Dec. 1972 (LHC: LH 1/408 PART 2– 409).

25. See e.g. Auberon Waugh, 'A Congenial Despair', *The Spectator*, 16 Dec. 1972; Alex Hamilton, 'Storm in a Nutshell', *Arts Guardian*, 3 Jan. 1973.

26. Letter from MSJ to Irene Rathbone, 15 June 1973 (IR-CSC).

27. A letter to MSJ from Macmillan 2 Feb. 1973, drawing this to MSJ's attention, is marked 'Not sent' (MABL).

28. *There Will Be a Short Interval* (London: Harvill Press, 1973), pp. 216–17.

29. Ibid., p. 222.

30. Letter from MSJ to Irene Rathbone, 6 May 1974 (IR-CSC).

31. Letter to MSJ from Sydney Harland, 5 June 1974 (CSC).

32. Letter to MSJ from Paul Tabori, 29 June 1974 (CSC).

33. Reader's Report by Douglas Allen, 11 Dec. 1968 (T48/341,1, Television Script Unit, Dramawriter's File, Storm Jameson, BBC Written Archive, Caversham).

34. Letters from MSJ to Irene Rathbone, 18 Nov. and 17 Dec. 1974 (IR-CSC).

35. Reader's Report by Lorna Hemingway, 13 Feb. 1962 (T48/341,1, Television Script Unit, Dramawriter's File, Storm Jameson, BBC Written Archive, Caversham).

36. Comments by Michael Voysey, 30 Aug. 1962 (T48/341,1, Television Script Unit, Dramawriter's File, Storm Jameson, BBC Written Archive, Caversham).

37. Reports by Denis Constanduros, Fred Watson, forwarded by Michael Voysey to Jon Warrington, 17 Jan. 1963 (T48/341,1, Television Script Unit, Dramawriter's File, Storm Jameson, BBC Written Archive, Caversham).

38. Memorandum from Jon Henderson to H. P. D. Tel., 17 March 1969 (RCONT18, Storm Jameson, Copyright, File II 1963–69, BBC Written Archive, Caversham).

39. Letter from George Spenton to Cedric Messina, 29 May 1968 (T48/341, 1, Television Script Unit, Dramawriter's File, Storm Jameson, BBC Written Archive, Caversham).

40. Reader's Report by Geoffrey Tetlow, 19 Jan. 1969 (T48/341, 1, Television Script Unit, Dramawriter's File, Storm Jameson, BBC Written Archive, Caversham).
41. Reader's Report by Arnold Hinchcliffe, 8 Sept. 1973 (T48/341, 1, Television Script Unit, Dramawriter's File, Storm Jameson, BBC Written Archive, Caversham).
42. Reader's Report by Hugo Martin, 1 Oct. 1973 (T48/341, 1, Television Script Unit, Dramawriter's File, Storm Jameson, BBC Written Archive, Caversham).
43. Handwritten note with above from Lennox Phillips, 24 Oct. 1973.
44. Letter to MSJ from Harrison Salisbury, 4 May 1978 (CSC).
45. Letters between MSJ and Kenneth Stowe (10 Downing Street) 24, 29 Nov. and 1 Dec. 1978 (CSC).
46. Information supplied by Christopher Storm-Clark.
47. Letter to MSJ from Josephine Pullein-Thompson, 17 Dec. 1980 (CSC).
48. Letter to MSJ from Rosemary Murray, 15 July 1980 (CSC).
49. She told Douglas Robillard that it was a shortened version of a Life for which she had been making notes for many years (letter of 21 Jan. 1980 (CSC)). In 1967, she told Kathleen Liddell Hart she had just finished a 10,000-word essay on Stendhal for a coffee-table publication by an American (letter of 25 Oct. 1967 (LHC: LH 1/408 PART 2– 409)). In 1973, she sent for inclusion in an Anthology to celebrate ten years of the Calabrian International Award a section of the long essay on Stendhal she had written to accompany an English translation of *Le Rouge et le noir* published three years before by private subscription (letter to Professor Morabito, 9 Aug. 1973 (CSC)). Her bookshelves contained three volumes of Stendhal's correspondence, in the Pléiade edition.
50. Editorial, *TLS*, 22 Oct. 1938.
51. Letter to MSJ from Carmen Callil, 21 April 1981 (CSC).
52. George Steiner, 'The Voice of a Free Woman', *Sunday Times*, 12 Sept. 1982.
53. Naomi Mitchison, 'An eye on the truth', *TLS*, 22 Oct. 1982.
54. Letter to MSJ from Ursula Owen, 15 March 1983 (CSC).
55. Caroline Moorehead 'Just killing time until death', *The Times*, 2 March 1984.
56. Deborah Philips, 'Autobiography/Fiction,' *City Limits*, 10 Feb. 1984; Barrie Farnill, 'Memoirs of a Veteran Writer,' *Yorkshire Evening Post*; S.W., 'Book of the Week,' *Whitby Gazette*, 3 Feb. 1984.
57. Letter to MSJ from Naomi Mitchison, 25 Jan. 1984 (CSC).
58. Jo Stanley, *The Morning Star* 21 Feb. 1984; see on the novel reprints Mikki Doyle, 'Storming her way into publishing', *The Morning Star* 21 Feb. 1984.
59. Letter from MSJ to Lennie Goodings, 28 June 1984 (CSC).
60. Letter to MSJ from Rache Lovat Dickson, 6 Feb. 1979 (CSC).
61. Letter from MSJ to Douglas Robillard, 2 Oct. 1980 (CSC).
62. Letter to MSJ from Virginia Patterson, undated (CSC).
63. Letter to MSJ from Virginia Patterson, 14 Feb. 1980 (CSC).
64. Letter to MSJ from Matthew Ferguson, 21 Feb. 1980 (CSC).
65. Letter to MSJ from Winifred Jameson, 17 Aug. 1980 (CSC).
66. Letters to MSJ from Adrian Marston, 19 May 1980; and letter from Margaret Harland Millan, 28 Oct. 1982 (CSC).

67. Letter to MSJ from Buchan and Enright Publishers, 27 Sept. 1984 (CSC).
68. Letter from Christopher Storm-Clark to Josephine Pullein-Thompson, 19 Feb. 1986 (CSC).
69. Letter from MSJ to Irene Rathbone, 5 July 1976 (IR-CSC).
70. Information supplied by Christopher Storm-Clark. Death certificate in CSC.
71. John Cunningham, 'Restless Spirit', *The Guardian*, 9 Oct. 1986.
72. *There Will Be a Short Interval*, pp. 222–3.

Select Bibliography

1. When Nicholson and Watson failed, the one-shilling-and-under rights for *A Day Off* were sold to Wells Gardner, who put out a shilling edition. A collection *A Day Off. Two Short Novels and Some Stories* was published in 1959 (London: Macmillan & Co.).
2. MSJ wrote a substantial amount of the copy for Frederick Thoresby's journal. The following list contains only those pieces she signed with her initials, and those where the pseudonym clearly indicates her authorship.

SELECT BIBLIOGRAPHY

A. Published Works by Margaret Storm Jameson

*Texts used for page references, if other than the first UK edition.

1. Novels

First US edition is given at the end of each sequence.

The Pot Boils (London: Constable & Co. Ltd, 1919).

The Happy Highways (London: William Heinemann, 1920; New York: Century, 1920).

The Clash (London Heinemann, 1922; Boston: Little, Brown, 1922).

Lady Susan and Life. An Indiscretion (London: Chapman & Dodd, 1923; New York: Dodd Mead, 1923).

The Pitiful Wife (London: Constable & Co. Ltd, 1923; Popular Edition Constable & Co.: London, 1926; New York: Alfred A. Knopf, 1924).

Three Kingdoms (London: Constable & Co., 1926; New York: Alfred A. Knopf, 1926).

The Lovely Ship (London: William Heinemann Ltd, 1927 (Popular Edition 1928, Uniform Edition 1935); Pocket Edition, Cassell and Company, Ltd, 1946; reissued William Heinemann Ltd, 1971; New York: Alfred A. Knopf, 1927).

Farewell to Youth (London: William Heinemann Ltd, 1928; New York: Alfred A. Knopf, 1928).

The Voyage Home (London: William Heinemann Ltd, 1930, reissued 1971; New York: Alfred A. Knopf, 1930).

A Richer Dust (London: William Heinemann Ltd, 1931; Leipzig: Bernhard Tauchnitz, 1932; New York: Alfred A. Knopf, 1931).

**The Triumph of Time: A Trilogy* (*The Lovely Ship—The Voyage Home—A Richer Dust*) (London: William Heinemann Ltd, 1932; Leipzig: Bernhard Tauchnitz, n.d.).

That Was Yesterday (London: William Heinemann Ltd, 1932; Leipzig: Bernhard Tauchnitz, 1933; New York: Alfred A. Knopf, 1933).

The Single Heart (London: Ernest Benn (Benn's Ninepenny Novels. No. 5), 1932).

A Day Off (London: I. Nicholson & Watson, 1933;[i] *London: Remploy Limited, 1980).

Women Against Men (*A Day Off, Delicate Monster, The Single Heart*); (Leipzig: Bernard Tauchnitz, 1933; London: Virago Press Ltd, 1982; New York: Alfred A. Knopf, 1933).

The Mirror in Darkness
   I. *Company Parade* (London: Cassell and Company, Ltd, 1934; *London: Virago Press Ltd, 1982; New York: Alfred A. Knopf, 1934).
  II. *Love in Winter* (London: Cassell and Company, Ltd, 1935; *London: Virago Press Ltd, 1984; New York: Alfred A. Knopf, 1935).
 III. *None Turn Back* (London: Cassell and Company, 1936; *London: Virago Press Ltd, 1984; New York: Alfred A. Knopf, 1936).

In the Second Year (London: Cassell & Company Ltd, 1936; *Stan Smith ed. and introd., Nottingham: Trent Editions, 2004; New York: The Macmillan Company, 1936).

Delicate Monster (London: I. Nicholson & Watson, 1937).

The Moon is Making (London: Cassell & Co., 1937; New York: The Macmillan Company, 1938).

[as William Lamb], *The World Ends* (London: J. M. Dent and Sons Ltd, 1937).

[as James Hill], *Loving Memory* (London: Collins, 1937; Boston: Little, Brown and Co., 1937).

[as James Hill], *No Victory for the Soldier* (London: Collins, 1938; *New York: Doubleday, Doran & Co., Inc., 1939).

Here Comes A Candle (London: Cassell & Company Ltd, 1938; *Pocket Edition London: Cassell & Company Ltd, 1945; New York: The Macmillan Company, 1939).

Farewell Night: Welcome Day (London: Cassell and Company, 1939; *4th edn, 1946); as *The Captain's Wife* (New York: The Macmillan Company, 1939).

Europe to Let: The Memoirs of an Obscure Man (London: Macmillan & Co. Ltd, 1940; New York: The Macmillan Company, 1940).

Cousin Honoré (London: Cassell and Company, 1940; New York: The Macmillan Company, 1941).

The Fort (Cassell and Company, Ltd., 1941; New York: The Macmillan Company, 1941).

Then We Shall Hear Singing. A Fantasy in C Major (London, Toronto, Melbourne, and Sydney: Cassell and Company Ltd, 1942; New York: The Macmillan Company, 1942).

Cloudless May (London: Macmillan & Co. Ltd, 1943; London: The Reprint Society, 1945; London: Panther Books, 1965; New York: Macmillan, 1944).

The Journal of Mary Hervey Russell (London: Macmillan & Co. Ltd, 1945, *2nd edn 1961, rpt. 1965; New York: The Macmillan Company, 1945).

The Other Side (London: Macmillan & Co. Ltd, 1946; Stockholm and London: The Continental Book Company, 1949; New York: The Macmillan Company, 1946).

Before the Crossing (London: Macmillan & Co. Ltd, 1947; New York: The Macmillan Company, 1947).

The Black Laurel (London: Macmillan & Co. Ltd, 1947; London: Panther Books, 1962; New York: The Macmillan Company, 1948).

The Moment of Truth (London: Macmillan & Co. Ltd, 1949; New York: The Macmillan Company, 1949).

The Green Man (London: Macmillan & Co., Ltd, 1952; New York: Harper, 1953).

The Hidden River (London: Macmillan & Co., Ltd, 1955; London: Remploy, 1979; New York: Harper and Brothers, 1955).

The Intruder (London: Macmillan & Co. Ltd, 1956; London: Panther Books, 1963; London: White Lion Editions, 1977; New York: The Macmillan Company, 1956).

A Cup of Tea for Mr Thorgill (London: Macmillan & Co., Ltd, 1957; *New York: Harper and Brothers Publishers, 1957).

A Ulysses Too Many (London: Macmillan & Co., 1958); as *One Ulysses Too Many* (New York: Harper and Brothers, 1958).

Last Score, or, The Private Life of Sir Richard Ormston (London: Macmillan & Co. Ltd, 1961; *London: The Reprint Society Ltd, 1962; London: White Lion Publishers, 1977; New York: Harper, 1961).

The Road from the Monument (London: Macmillan & Co. Ltd, 1962; *Frome and London: White Lion Publishers 1974; New York: Harper, 1962).

The Aristide Case (London: Macmillan & Co. Ltd, 1964; London: Panther Books, 1967); as *The Blind Heart* (New York: Harper and Row, 1964).

The Early Life of Stephen Hind (London: Macmillan, 1966; New York: Harper and Row, 1966).

The White Crow (London: Macmillan and Co Ltd, 1968; New York: Harper and Row, 1968).

There Will Be a Short Interval (London: Harvill Press, 1973; New York: Harper and Row, 1973).

The following titles were reissued in paperback by Berkeley Medallion Books (New York) in 1976: *Company Parade, The Lovely Ship, The Voyage Home, A Richer Dust, The Captain's Wife, That Was Yesterday, Love in Winter.*

Serialisations:

The Happy Highways, The New Commonwealth, 14 November 1919 to 20 February 1920 (weekly instalments).

Hate Dies Hard, The Saturday Evening Post, 30 June, 14 July, 21 July 1945.

House of Hate [*The Hidden River*], *The Saturday Evening Post*, 16, 30 October, 6, 13, and 20 November 1954.

The Hidden River, Housewife Magazine, January–April 1954.

A Month Soon Goes, Housewife Magazine, October–December 1955.

The Lion and the Dagger [*Last Score*], *The Saturday Evening Post*, 8, 15, 22 April 1961.

Works translated into other languages:

Drömmen och Verkligheten (*The Pitiful Wife*), trans. Linda Öberg-Oljelund (Uppsala: J. A. Linablads Förlag, 1925).

Elva och Tjugufem kvar 11.25 Kvar (*A Day Off*), trans. Karl Ragnar Gierow (Stockholm: P. A. Norstedt and Söners Verlag, 1933).

Auhourd'hui c'est fête (*A Day Off*), trans. Magdeleine Paz (Vendôme, Paris: Imprimerie des Presses universitaires de France; Paris: Rieder, 1937).

Le Cousin Honoré (*Cousin Honoré*), trans. E. H. Linger (London: Heineman et Zsolnay, 1944).

Ein Herrenhaus im Elsass (*Cousin Honoré*, American edn), trans. Lino Rossi (Zürich, New York, and Oprecht: Druckereigenossedschaft Aarau, n.d.).

Faestningen (*The Fort*) (Copenhagen: Schønbeigske Forlag, 1947).

L'autre rive (*The Other Side*), trans. Germaine Delamain, Pref. by Charles Morgan (Paris: Delamain et Boutelleau, 1948).

Maggio Senza Nubi (*Cloudless May*), trans. Beata della Frattina (Verona: Arnoldo Mondadori Editore, 1948).

Il Fiume Nascosto. Romanzo (*The Hidden River*), trans. Lidia Velani (Milan: Rizzoli, 1957).

Het Verborgen Verdad (*The Hidden River*), trans. Nel Bakker (Utrecht andAntwerp: Prisma-Boeken, n.d.).

O Incendio Romance (*Here Comes a Candle*), trans. Maria Franco and Cabral do Nascimento (Lisbon: Editorial Minerva, n.d.).

Dom nad Loara, trans. Kalina Wojciechowska (Warsaw: Państwowy Instytut Wydawniczy, 1970).

2. Short and long-short stories

'A Cloke for Two', *The New Commonwealth*, n.s., 9 January 1920, p. 11.

'The Woman Doctor's Tale: Mother Love', *The New Decameron*, Vol. 1 (Oxford: Basil Blackwell, 1919), pp. 78–102.

'The Woman Doctor's Second Tale. A Player Perforce', *The New Decameron*, Vol. 2 (Oxford: Basil Blackwell, 1920), pp. 158–74.

'The Tale of the Solitary English Girl. The Pitiful Wife', *The New Decameron*, Vol. 3 (Oxford: Basil Blackwell, 1922), pp. 56–71.

'The Bureaucrat's Tale: Monotony', *The New Decameron*, Vol. 4 (Oxford: Basil Blackwell, 1925), pp. 178–193.

'Splendid Days', *Argosy (UK)*, June 1930.

'A Mingled Strain', *The Fothergill Omnibus*, introd. John Fothergill, R. G. Collingwood, and Gerald Gould (London: Eyre & Spottiswoode, 1931).

'A Day at the Zoo', *Modern Reading*, No. 2, ed. Reginald Moore (London: Staples and Staples, July 1941), pp. 11–26.

'You Don't Speak French, Do You?' *Modern Reading*, No. 4, ed. Reginald Moore (London: Staples and Staples, April [1942]), pp. 47–64.

'The Last Night', *The Saturday Evening Post*, 30 January 1943; rpt. *Argosy (UK)*, February 1944; rpt. in *Lidice: A Tribute by Members of the International PEN*, introd. Harold Nicolson (London: Allen & Unwin, 1944), pp. 50–84.

'Very Clever People', *Good Housekeeping*, 1952.

'This is It', *The Cornhill Magazine*, February 1953.

'The Cost of Freedom', in *The PEN in Exile*, ed. Paul Tabori (London: The International PEN Club Centre for Writers in Exile, 1954).

'The Mask', *Winter's Tales No. 1*, ed. Alan Maclean (London: Macmillan & Co., 1955), pp. 128–66; *Argosy (UK)*, August 1955.

'The Friendly One', *Winter's Tales No. 5*, ed. Alan Maclean (London: Macmillan & Co., 1959), pp. 181–215.

3. Plays and adaptations

Full Circle (Oxford: Basil Blackwell, 1928; produced Liverpool, 1928).

The Fort (radio broadcast, BBC Home Service, Saturday 9 May 1942, 10. 30 p.m.).

William the Defeated, in *The Book of the P.E.N.*, ed. Hermon Ould (London: Arthur Barker Ltd, 1950), pp. 187–230 (radio broadcast BBC Home Service, Monday 5 July 1943, 9. 30 p.m.).

The Hidden River, adaptation by Ruth Goodman Goetz and Augustus Goetz (New York: Dramatists Play Service, 1957; produced in New York. With revised script by MSJ, produced in Scarborough and London).

The Commonplace Heart (BBC Television, 13 January 1953, 8. 30 p.m.,).

The Face of Treason (Associated Rediffusion, 10 March 1959, 8.30 p.m.) [*A Cup of Tea for Mr Thorgill*].

4. Other Books (autobiographies, criticism, essays, published letters)

Modern Drama in Europe (London: Collins and Company, 1920; New York: Harcourt Brace, 1920).

The Georgian Novel and Mr. Robinson (London: William Heinemann Ltd, 1929; New York: Morrow, 1929).

The Decline of Merry England (London: Cassell and Company, 1930; Indianapolis: Bobbs Merrill, 1930).

No Time Like the Present (London: Cassell and Company Limited, 1933; New York: Alfred A. Knopf, 1933).

[ed.], *Challenge to Death* (London: Constable & Co. Ltd, 1934; New York: Dutton, 1935).

The Soul of Man in the Age of Leisure (Pamphlets on the New Economics. No. 13) (London: Stanley Nott, 1935); coll. in [TSCP] (London: Stanley Nott, 1935).

The Novel in Contemporary Life (Boston, Mass.: The Writer, Inc., 1938).

Civil Journey (London: Cassell and Company Limited, 1939).

The End of This War (London: George Allen and Unwin Ltd, 1941).

(ed.) *London Calling* (New York and London: Harper & Brothers, 1942).

The Writer's Situation and Other Essays (London: Macmillan & Co. Ltd, 1950; New York: The Macmillan Company, 1950).

Morley Roberts: The Last Eminent Victorian (London: Unicorn Press, 1961).

Journey from the North, 2 vols (London: Collins and Harvill, 1969–70, *rpt. London: Virago Press Ltd, 2 vols, 1984; New York: Harper and Row, 1 vol., 1971).

Parthian Words (London: Collins & Harvill Press, 1970; New York: Harper and Row, 1971).

(ed). *A Kind of Survivor: A Memoir by Guy Chapman* (London: Gollancz, 1975).

Speaking of Stendhal (London: Gollancz, 1979).

'Margaret Storm Jameson: In her Own Voice' [Correspondence of Storm Jameson with Hilary Newitt Brown and Harrison Brown.], ed. Chiara Briganti and Kathy Mezei, in Jennifer Birkett and Chiara Briganti (eds), *Margaret Storm Jameson: Writing in Dialogue* (Newcastle: Cambridge Scholars Publishing, 2007), pp. 164–206.

5. Introductions to books by other writers

Cazotte, Jacques, *A Thousand and One Follies* (*Les mille et une fadaises*) and *His Most Unlooked-for Lordship* (*Le Lord impromptu*), trans. Eric Sutton (London: Chapman & Hall, 1927).

Linke, Lilo, *Tale Without End...* (London: Constable & Co., 1934).

—— *People of the Amazon* (London: Robert Hale, 1963).

—— *Andean Adventure: A Social and Political Study of Colombia, Ecuador and Bolivia* (n.p.: Hutchinson, 1945).

Brown, Hilary Newitt, *Women Must Choose: The Position of Women in Europe Today* (London: Gollancz, 1937).

Kuncewiczowa, Maria, *The Stranger* [*Cudzoziemk*], trans. B. W. A. Massey (London: Hutchinson's International Authors [1944]).

Roberts, Kate, *A Summer Day and Other Stories*, trans. Dafydd Jenkins, Walter Dowding, and Wyn Griffith (Cardiff: Penmark Press, 1946).

Legrand, Ignace, *The Land Within* (London: Phoenix House, 1948).

Frank, Anne, *The Diary of Anne Frank* (London: Pan Books, 1954).

Beyle, Henri-Marie, *The Red and the Black* (Geneva: Edito-Service [1969]).

6. Articles, contributions to books, reviews

'The End Thereof', *The New Age*, 20 March 1913, Vol. 12, No. 20, pp. 482–3.

'The Drama of Ideas since Ibsen', *The Egoist*, 15 January 1914, Vol. 1, No. 2, pp. 29–30.

'Modern Dramatists', *The Egoist*, 16 February 1914, Vol. 1, No. 4, pp. 74–5.

'Modern Dramatists', *The Egoist*, March 1914, Vol. 1, No. 6, pp. 116–17.

'New Statesmen. A Bill Providing for an Economic Basis of Marriage. [Being a projected Fabian Tract, number 1001 (c)]', *The New Age*, 2 April 1914, Vol. 14., No. 22, p. 682.

'The Theatre', *The Egoist*, 15 April 1914, Vol. 1, No. 8, pp. 155–6.

'England's Nest of Singing Birds', *The Egoist*, 1 November 1915 (extract in V. Kolocotroni et al. (eds), *Modernism: An Anthology of Sources and Documents* (Edinburgh University Press, 1998), pp. 321–3).

'A Plea for the Arbitrary Limit', *The New Age*, 7 September 1916, Vol. 19, No. 19, pp. 447–8.

'Reviews', *The Egoist*, September 1916, pp. 135–6.

The New Commonwealth[ii]

'Divorce', 1 October 1919, Vol. 1, No. 1, p. 2.

'Profiteering', 8 October 1919, Vol. 1, No. 2, p. 15.

'America', 15 October 1919, Vol. 1, No. 3, p. 20.

'The Author of Our Serial, "The Happy Highways." A Chat with Storm Jameson', 7 November 1919, Vol. 1, No. 6, p. 6.

'Shaking Hands with Murder', 14 November 1919, Vol. 1, No. 7, p. 2.

At the Theatres. 'Romance As You Like It', n.s., April 1920, Vol. 1, No. 10, p. 10; 'The Three Best Plays in London', May 1920, Vol. 2, No. 3, p. 13; 'Two Plays and a Novel', 20 June 1920, Vol. 2, No. 4, p. 15; 20 July 1920, Vol. 2, No. 5, p. 9; 20 August 1920, p. 7; 20 September 1920; 20 October 1920.

413

'The Modern Novel', in 'Special Literary Supplement Containing Reviews of Current Literature by Thomas Moult and Storm Jameson', April 1920, n.s., Vol. 1, No. 10, pp. 29–30.

(as George Gallilee), 'The Joy of Work', 5 December 1919, Vol. 1, No. 10, p. 9; 'A Philosophy of Youth', n.s., Vol. 1 ('On Fear', 2 January 1920, p. 12; 'Childhood', 9, 16, 23, 30 January 1920).

'Review of *Memoirs of a Midget*', *The English Review*, May 1922, No. 34, pp. 424–30.

'Problem of Sex in Public Life', *The Daily Mirror*, 28 March 1927, p. 4.

'Nothing Wrong with Modern Woman', *The Daily Mirror*, 23 May 1927, p. 6.

The Evening News

'Bored Wives', 1 October 1928, p. 8.

'The Only Perfect Match I Know', 13 October 1928, p. 8.

'Men', 23rd October 1928, p. 8.

'What are you going to do with your Boy ... ? A Modern Mother on the choice between the Day-School and the Public School', 7 November 1928, p. 11.

'Modern Morality Just Means Playing the Game', 13 November 1928, p. 11.

'The Best Wife I Know', 20 November 1928, p. 11.

'Which Would You Choose—?' 27 November 1928, p. 11.

'Who'd Be a Woman?' 10 December 1928, p. 11.

'The Love-Letter of a Modern Girl', 17 December 1928, p. 11.

'The Golden Age of Spinsters', 31 December 1928, p. 11.

'The Soul of a Modern Woman', 7 January 1929, p. 11.

'Autobiography and the Novel', *The Bookman*, February 1931, Vol. LXXII, No. 6, pp. 557–65.

'Man the Helpmate', in Mabel Ulrich (ed.), *Man, Proud Man* (London: Hamish Hamilton, 1932, pp. 105–36.

New English Weekly

'Recent Novels', 21 April 1932, Vol. I, No. 1, to 26 January 1933, Vol. II, No. 15 (fortnightly contributions).

'A Recent Novel', 7 July 1932, Vol. I, No. 12.

'Culture and Environment', 9 March 1933, Vol. II, No. 21.

The New Clarion

'Storm Jameson asks: Why do *you* read novels?' 11 June 1932, Vol. 1, No. 1, p. 12.

'Abolish Reviewers!' 9 July 1932, Vol. 1, No. 5, p. 109.

'Films the Opium of the People', 6 August 1932, Vol. 1 No. 9, p. 205.

'The Lost Generation', 10 September 1932, Vol. 1, No. 14, p. 321.

'No Escape: Two Books Which Keep to the Facts' [reviews of Chris Massie, James Hanley], 1 October 1932, Vol. 1 No. 17, p. 391.

'A Novel of Quality' [review of H. E. Bates, *The Fallow Land*], 29 October 1932, Vol. 1, No. 21, p. 490.

'The Christmas Snob', 3 December 1932, Vol. 1 No. 26, p. 605.

'Salients', 31 December 1932, Vol. 2, No. 30, p. 63.

'About the Next War: What are *You* Going to Do?' 28 January 1933, Vol. 2, No. 34, p. 144.

'This Vested Interest of Writers', 18 March 1933, Vol. 2, No. 41, p. 285.

'"A Bad-Tempered Footnote" to Life in 1933', 10 June 1933, Vol. 3, No. 53, p. 11.

'Fifteen years ago—we said "Never Again!"' 21 October 1933, Vol. 3, No. 71, p. 325, p. 327.

'The Dangers of Fiction', *Highway: The Journal of the Workers' Educational Association*, November 1932, pp. 8–10.

'The Cultivation of Values', *Highway: The Journal of the Workers' Educational Association*, March 1933, pp. 28–9.

'To a Labour Party Official', *Left Review*, 2 November 1934, p. 29.

'Crisis', *Left Review*, 4 January 1936, pp. 156–9.

'A Popular Front' [Letters to the Editor], *Time and Tide*, 6 June 1936, Vol. XVII, No. 23, p. 811.

'Socialists Born and Made', *Fact*, May 1937, No. 2, p. 87.

'Documents', *Fact*, July 1937, No. 4, pp. 9–18.

'[Response No. 3]' in *What is Happiness?* by Martin Armstrong, Gerald Bullett, et al. (London: John Lane The Bodley Head, 1938), pp. 33–41.

'Fighting the Foes of Civilization: The Writer's Place in the Defence Line', *TLS*, 7 October 1939, Issue 1966, p. 571; rpt. as 'Writing in the Margin', in *The Writer's Situation*, pp. 189–200.

'The New Europe', *The Fortnightly*, January 1940, Vol. CXLVII, n.s., pp. 68–79; extract rpt. in *History of European Integration*, ed. Walter Lipgens.

'Women on the Spot', *Atlantic Monthly*, February 1941, pp. 169–76.

'Le 17e Congrès International des PEN', *La France Libre*, 15 September 1941, Vol. II, No. 11, pp. 395–99; English version rpt. as 'Creditors of France', *The Writer's Situation*, pp. 180–8.

'The Writer's Duty', *Fortnightly Review*, October 1941; rpt. 'The Responsibilities of a Writer', *The Writer's Situation*, pp. 164–79.

Review of Denis Saurat, *Watch over Africa*, La France Libre, 17 April 1942, No. 18.

'Literature between the Wars: The Tyranny of Things', *TLS*, 18 September 1943, Issue 2172, p. 450; rpt. as 'Between the Wars', *The Writer's Situation*, pp. 126–35.

'Paris', *TLS*, 26 August 1944, Issue 2221, p. 415, rpt. *The Writer's Situation*, pp. 114–17.

'A Seeker After Value: Views in a War-Time Mirror', *TLS*, 9 December 1944, Issue 2236, p. 594.

'Writers in Conflict. Nationalism at PEN Conference', *Manchester Guardian*, 12 June 1947.

'W. H. Auden: The Poet of Angst', *The Gate*, November 1947, rpt. *The Writer's Situation*, pp. 83–101.

'The Novelist Today', *The Virginia Quarterly*, May 1949, rpt. *The Writer's Situation*, pp. 62–82.

'In Memory of Hermon Ould', *Hermon Ould: A Tribute* (Slough: Kenion Press Ltd., n.d.), pp. 8–13.

'A Young Girl's Diary', *Everybody's*, 19 April 1952. p. 10, p. 26.

'Inner & Outer Worlds' [Review], *TLS*, 26 September 1952, Issue 2643, p. 628.

'The Dualist Tradition', *TLS*, 6 August 1954 [Special Autumn Number: Personal Preference], Issue 2740, p. 508, xxxvii.

'A Note on France', *The Cornhill Magazine*, Autumn 1954, No. 1001, pp. 439–52.

'Somewhere to Live. A Long Search', *Manchester Guardian*, 25 February 1956.

'Can It Be Done? The Case for Providence', *TLS*, 7 August 1959 [British Books Around the World Supplement], Issue 2997, p. 464, xxviii.

'One Man in his Time', *Sunday Times*, Magazine Section, 31 January 1960, p. 15.

'Fiction of the Week', *Sunday Times*, Magazine Section (3 April 1960, p. 18; 17 April 1960, p. 17; 1 May 1960, p. 17; 29 May 1960, p. 18; 12 June 1960, p. 28; 26 June 1960, p. 28;

10 July 1960, p. 28; 24 July 1960, p. 24; 7 August 1960, p. 23; 21 August 1960, p. 23; 4 September 1960, p. 27.

'Portrait of a County: Yorkshire', *Vogue* (British edition), No. 14, Whole Number 1884, Vol. 116, Mid-October 1960, pp. 70–3, 138, 143; rpt. in 1962 edition of *Vogue's Gallery*.

'Morley Roberts: The Last of the True Victorians', *The Library Chronicle*, University of Pennsylvania, Philadelphia, Vol. XXVII, No. 2, Spring/Summer 1961, pp. 93–127.

'A Bolster to Young Mr X', *Books and Bookmen*, 1962, rpt. *Montreal Star*, and *Kultur* (Kurt Desch Verlag).

'The Writer in Contemporary Society', *The American Scholar*, Vol. 35, No. 1, Winter 1965–6, pp. 67–77.

B. Works by Other Writers

Reviews of individual works by Jameson are not included here, but can be found by searching the work's title in the Index.

Algren, Nelson, *Somebody in Boots* (New York: Vanguard, 1935).

Amye, Denise, 'Echanges de Livres', *La France Libre*, 15 October 1941, Vol. II, No. 12, pp. 541–3.

Anon. 'Miss Storm Jameson. Powerful writer with a bleak and brave eye', *The Times*, 7 October 1986.

Anon., *Valentine Dobrée, 1894–1974* (Leeds: The University Gallery, 2000).

Aragon, Louis, *Le Crève-cœur … et Les Yeux d'Elsa, etc.* (Londres: Édition Horizon-La France Libre, 1942).

Atkin, Nicholas, *The Forgotten French. Exiles in the British Isles, 1940–44* (Manchester and New York: Manchester University Press, 2003).

BBC Handbook 1942 (London: The British Broadcasting Corporation, Broadcasting House, 1942).

Bennett, John, *Aragon, Londres et la France libre : réception de l'oeuvre en Grande-Bretagne, 1940* (Paris : L'Harmattan, 1998).

Bennett, John W. Wheeler, *Hindenburg, The Wooden Titan* (London: Macmillan and Company, 1936).

Berry, Paul, and Alan Bishop (eds), *Testament of a Generation. The Journalism of Vera Brittain and Winifred Holtby* (London: Virago Press Ltd, 1985).

Birkett, Jennifer, 'Doubly Determined: the Ambition of Storm Jameson', in Jennifer Birkett and Elizabeth Harvey (eds), *Determined Women. Studies in the Construction of the Female Subject, 1900–90* (Basingstoke: Macmillan, 1991), pp. 68–94.

—— 'Beginning Again: Storm Jameson's Debt to France', *Critical Survey*, Vol. 10, No. 3, 1998, pp. 3–12.

—— 'Margaret Storm Jameson and the London PEN Centre: Mobilising Commitment', *EREA* Vol. 4, No. 2 (Autumn 2006), pp. 81–9. URL:http://www.e-rea.org/

—— '"The Spectacle of Europe": Politics, PEN and Prose Fiction: The Work of Storm Jameson in the Inter-War Years', *Women in Europe*, Angela Kershaw and Angela Kimyongür (eds), (London: Ashcroft, 2007), pp. 25–38.

—— 'A Fictional Function: Storm Jameson and W. H. Auden', *English: The Journal of the English Association*, Vol. 56, No. 215, Summer 2007, pp. 171–85.

—— '"Waiting for the Death Wind": Storm Jameson's Fiction after the Second World War', in Birkett and Briganti (eds), *Margaret Storm Jameson: Writing in Dialogue*, pp. 127–45.

—— 'Margaret Storm Jameson and the Spanish Civil War: The Fight for Human Values', Special Issue of the *Journal of English Studies*, No. 5 (University of La Rioja, Logroño, forthcoming).

—— and Chiara Briganti (eds), *Margaret Storm Jameson: Writing in Dialogue* (Newcastle: Cambridge Scholars Publishing, 2007).

Blunden, Edmund, *Undertones of War* (n.p.: Cobden-Sanderson, 1928).

Bodley, J. E. C., *France*, new revised edn (London: Macmillan and Co., Ltd, 1899).

Bois, Elie J., *Truth on the Tragedy of France* (London: Hodder & Stoughton, 1940).

Bonham-Carter, Victor, *Authors by Profession. Vol. II: From the Copyright Act 1911 until the End of 1981* (London: The Bodley Head & The Society of Authors, 1984).

Brittain, Vera, *Testament of Friendship* (1940, rpt. London: Macmillan, 1947).

—— *England's Hour* (London: Macmillan & Co., 1941).

—— *Testament of Experience. An Autobiographical Story of the Years 1925–1950* (London: Gollancz, 1957; rpt. with introd. by Paul Berry, London: Virago Press Ltd, 1979).

—— *Testament of a Peace Lover. Letters from Vera Brittain*, ed. Winifred and Alan Eden-Green (London: Virago Press Ltd, 1988).

—— *Wartime Chronicle. Vera Brittain's Diary 1939–45*, ed. Alan Bishop and Y. Aleksandra Bennett (London: Victor Gollancz, 1989).

Broch, Hermann, *The Sleepwalkers. A Trilogy* [*Die Schlafwandler*], trans. E. and W. Muir (London: Martin Secker, 1932).

Calder, Angus, *The People's War: Britain, 1939–45* (London: Panther, 1971).

Calvocoressi, Peter, *World Politics Since 1945*, 6th edn (London and New York: Longman 1991).

—— Guy Wint, and John Pritchard, *Total War. The Causes and Courses of the Second World War*, rev. 2nd edn (Harmondsworth: Penguin Books, 1995).

Campbell, Roy, *Light on a Dark Horse. An Autobiography (1901–1935)* (London: Hollis & Carter, 1951).

Carpenter, Humphrey, *The Brideshead Generation. Evelyn Waugh and His Generation* (London: Faber & Faber, 1989).

Caute, David, *The Fellow-Travellers : A Postscript to the Enlightenment* (London: Weidenfeld and Nicolson, 1973).

Ceadel, Martin, *Pacifism in Britain 1914–1945: The Defining of a Faith* (Oxford: Clarendon Press, 1980).

Cesarani, David, *Arthur Koestler. The Homeless Mind* (London: William Heinemann, 1998).

Chapman, Guy, *A Passionate Prodigality. Fragments of Autobiography* (London: I. Nicholson & Watson, 1933).

—— 'Put Peace in its Place', *The New Clarion*, 2 December 1933, Vol. 3 No. 78, pp. 1–2.

Chapman, Guy, (ed.), *Vain Glory. A Miscellany of the Great War, 1914–1918* (London: Cassell and Co, Ltd., 1937).

—— *Culture and Survival* (London: Jonathan Cape, 1940).

—— *The Third Republic of France.* Vol.1, *The First Phase, 1871–1894* (London: Macmillan & Co., 1962).

—— *Why France Collapsed* (London: Cassell, 1968).

—— *A Kind of Survivor: A Memoir,* ed. Margaret Storm Jameson (London: Gollancz, 1975).

Clay, Catherine, *British Women Writers 1914–1945: Professional Work and Friendship* (Aldershot: Ashgate, 2006).

—— 'Storm Jameson's Journalism 1913–33: The Construction of a Writer', in Birkett and Briganti (eds), *Margaret Storm Jameson: Writing in Dialogue*, pp. 37–52.

Cline, Sally, *Radclyffe Hall. A Woman Called John* (London: John Murray, 1997).

Cobain, Ian, 'Churchill proposed "three for one" bombing of German villages in retaliation for the massacre of Czech civilians', *The Guardian*, 2 January 2006.

Cole, G. D. H., 'Guild Socialism Twenty Years Ago and Now', *New English Weekly*, 13 September 1934, Vol. V.

Colombo, John Robert, *O Rare Denis Saurat* (Toronto: George A. Vanderburgh, The Battered Silicon Dispatch Box, 2003).

Connolly, Cyril, 'French and English Cultural Relations', *Horizon*, Vol. VII, No. 42, June 1943.

Craig, Alec, *The Banned Books of England* (London: George Allen & Unwin, 1937).

Cross, Colin, *The Fascists in Britain* (London: Barrie and Rockliff, 1961).

Cunningham, John, 'Restless Spirit', *The Guardian*, 9 October 1986, p. 24.

Danchev, Alex, *Alchemist of War. The Life of Basil Liddell Hart* (London: Weidenfeld & Nicolson, 1998).

Dobrée, Valentine, *Your Cuckoo Sings by Kind* (London & New York: Alfred A. Knopf, 1927).

Donaldson, Frances, *The British Council: The First Fifty Years* (London: Jonathan Cape Ltd, 1984).

Dudley Edwards, Ruth, *Victor Gollancz. A Biography* (London: Victor Gollancz Ltd, 1987).

Editorial, 'A Popular Front?', *Time and Tide*, Vol. XVII, No. 21, 23 May 1936, p. 749.

Ellmann, Richard, *James Joyce* (New York, London, and Toronto: Oxford University Press, 1959).

Fisher, Clive, *Cyril Connolly. A Nostalgic Life* (London: Macmillan, 1996).

Fothergill, John. *An Innkeeper's Diary* (London: Chatto and Windus, 1931; rpt. London: Faber and Faber, 1987).

Fothergill, John (ed.), *The Fothergill Omnibus*, introd. John Fothergill, R. G. Collingwood, and Gerald Gould (London: Eyre & Spottiswoode, 1931).

Freeman, C. Denis, and Douglas Cooper, *The Road to Bordeaux* (n. p.: The Cresset Press, 1940).

Furbank, P. N. and Mary Lago (eds), *Selected Letters of E. M. Forster*, 2 vols (London: Collins, 1983 and 1985).

Garner, Les, *A Brave and Beautiful Spirit: Dora Marsden 1882–1960* (Aldershot and Brook-field USA: Avebury, 1990).

de Gaulle, Charles, *The Complete War Memoirs of Charles de Gaulle*, trans. Jonathan Griffin and Richard Howard (New York: Carroll & Graf Publishers, Inc., 1998).

Gerrard, Deborah, '"The Tempestuous Morning Energy of a New Art": Socialism, Modernism, and the Young Storm Jameson', in Birkett and Briganti (eds), *Margaret Storm Jameson: Writing in Dialogue*, pp. 19–35.

Gielgud, Val Henry, *British Radio Drama 1922–56. A Survey by Val Gielgud. Head of BBC Drama (Sound)*, (London and Toronto: George G. Harrap & Co., 1957).

Giraudoux, Jean, *Bella: histoire des Fontranges* (Paris: Grasset, 1926).

—— *Pleins Pouvoirs* (Paris: Gallimard, [*c*.1933]).

—— *La Guerre de Troie n'aura pas lieu* (Paris: Grasset, 1935).

—— *Ondine* (Paris: Grasset, 1939).

Gollancz, Victor, *Let My People Go* ([n.p.] [n.d.], 1942).

The Gryphon: The Journal of the University of Leeds.

Harland, Oswald, *Yorkshire North Riding* (London: Robert Hale Ltd, 1951).

Harland, Sydney Cross, 'Raving of an Immature Science Student', *The New Age*, 13 February 1913, Vol. XII, No. 15, p. 395.

—— *Nine Lives: The Autobiography of a Yorkshire Scientist*, ed. Max Millard (Boson Books, 2001), pp. 24–5. URL: http://www.bosonbooks.com/boson/freebies/harland/harland.pdf

Hill, Walter, 'Affranchir l'homme de la misère', *La France Libre*, 15 February 1942, Vol. V, No. 28, pp. 287–92.

Hogben, Lancelot, *The Retreat from Reason* (London: Watts & Co., 1936).

Holman, Valerie and Debra Kelly (eds), *France at War in the Twentieth Century. Propaganda, Myth and Metaphor* (New York and Oxford: Berghahn Books, 2000).

Holtby, Winifred, *Letters to a Friend*, ed. Alice Holtby and Jean McWilliam (London: Collins, 1937).

Hutt, Allen, *The Post-War History of the British Working Class*, Left Book Club Edition (London: Victor Gollancz Ltd, 1937).

Hyams, Edward, *The New Statesman. The History of the First Fifty Years, 1913–63* (London: Longmans, 1963).

Jackson, Julian, *The Fall of France. The Nazi Invasion of 1940* (Oxford: Oxford University Press, 2003).

—— *France the Dark Years, 1940–44* (Oxford: Oxford University Press, 2001).

Josephson, Hannah and Malcolm Cowley (eds), *Aragon. Poet of Resurgent France* (London: The Pilot Press Ltd, 1946).

Leeds University Calendar.

Lehmann, John, *New Writing and Daylight* (London: The Hogarth Press, 1945).

—— *In My Own Time. Memoirs of a Literary Life* (Boston and Toronto: Little, Brown and Company, 1969), pp. 135–6. (*The Whispering Gallery*, 1955; *I Am My Brother*, 1960).

LeSage, Laurent, *Jean Giraudoux. His Life and Works* (Pennsylvania: Pennsylvania State University Press, 1959).

Liddell Hart, B. H., *The Memoirs of Captain Liddell Hart* (London: Cassell and Company, 2 vols, 1965).

Linke, Lilo, *Tale Without End*, introd. Margaret Storm Jameson (London: Constable and Co., 1934).

—— *Restless Flags. A German Girl's Story* (London, Constable and Co., 1935).

—— *People of the Amazon*, introd. Margaret Storm Jameson (London: Robert Hale, 1963).

Lormier, Dominique, *La Bataille des Cadets de Saumur. Juin 1940* (Honfleur-Saintes: Les Chemins de la Mémoire, n.d.).

Lovat Dickson, Rache, *The Ante-Room. Early Stages in a Literary Life* (London: Macmillan, 1959).

—— *The House of Words*, (London: Macmillan, 1963).

Lucas, John (ed.), *The 1930s. A Challenge to Orthodoxy* (Sussex: The Harvester Press, 1978).

Macaulay, Rose, *Fabled Shore. From the Pyrenees to Portugal* ([London]: Hamish Hamilton, 1949; Readers Union Edition, 1950).

Mairet, Philip, 'Patriots of Europe', *New English Weekly*, 15 December 1932, Vol. II, No. 9, pp. 210–11.

—— 'Views and Reviews. A League of Minds', *New English Weekly*, 22 June 1933, Vol. III, No. 10, pp. 231–2.

Mannin, Ethel, *Young in the Twenties. A Chapter of Autobiography* (London: Hutchinson, 1971).

Martin, Jane, 'An "Awful Woman"? The Life and Work of Mrs Bridges Adams, 1855–1939', *Women's History Review*, Vol. 8, No. 1, 1999.

Maurois, André, *Why France Fell*, trans. Denver Lindley (n.p.: John Lane, The Bodley Head, 1940).

Mitchell, Peter Chalmers, *My House in Málaga* (London: Faber and Faber, 1938).

Mitchison, Naomi, *You May Well Ask. A Memoir 1920–1940* (London: Gollancz, 1979; rpt. London: Fontana Paperbacks, 1986).

—— *Among You Taking Notes.... The Wartime Diary of Naomi Mitchison, 1939–45*, ed. Dorothy Sheridan (Oxford: Oxford University Press, 1985).

Morgan, J. H., *Assize of Arms. Being the Story of the Disarmament of Germany and her Re-armament, 1919–1939* (London: Methuen & Co., 1945).

The New Age. Available online through The Modernist Journals Project [Brown University and the University of Tulsa] (URL at 20. 04. 2008 http://dl.lib.brown.edu:8081/exist/mjp/show_series.xq?id=1158589415603817).

Nicolson, Harold, *Diaries and Letters 1939–45*, ed. Nigel Nicolson (London: Collins, 1967).

Norman, C. H., 'Patriotism Ltd.' *New English Weekly*, 5 October 1933, Vol. III, pp. 583 ff.

Orage, A. R. (ed.), *The New Age.*

—— (ed.), *The New English Weekly.*

Ould, Hermon (ed.), *Writers in Freedom. A Symposium Based on the XVII International Congress of the P.E.N. Club Held in London in September 1941* (London: Hutchinson & Co. [1942]).

—— (ed.), *The Book of the P.E.N* (London: Arthur Barker Ltd., 1950).

Select Bibliography

Oxford Dictionary of National Biography Online. URL: http://www.oxforddnb.com

P.B., 'The Writers of the World Plan an Encyclopedia,' *Time and Tide*, 27 June 1926, Vol. XVII, No. 26, p. 937.

PEN News.

Priestley, J. B., *Faraway* (Leipzig: Bernhard Tauchnitz, 1933).

Quintus, 'Germany and the Jews', *New English Weekly*, 13 April 1933, Vol. II, No. 26, pp. 610–11.

Rathbone, Irene, *We That Were Young* (London: Chatto & Windus, 1932).

—— *They Call It Peace* (London: J. M. Dent & Sons, 1936).

—— *The Seeds of Time* (London: Faber & Faber, 1952).

Romains, Jules, *Sept Mystères du destin de l'Europe* (New York: Editions de la Maison Française, 1940).

—— 'Un essai d'une politique de l'esprit', *Preuves*, 2nd Year, Nos. 18–19, August–September 1952.

Sadleir, Michael, *Michael Ernest Sadler* (London: Constable and Co., 1949).

Saintsbury, George, *History of Criticism and Literary Taste in Europe*, 3 vols (Edinburgh: William Blackwood & Sons, 1900–4).

—— *A History of the French Novel (To the Close of the 19th Century)*, 2 vols (London: Macmillan, 1917).

Sartre, Jean-Paul, *Les Mots* (Paris: Gallimard, 1963; Eng. trans. Irene Clephane, London: Hamish Hamilton, 1964).

Scott, Bonnie Kime (ed.), *The Gender of Modernism* (Bloomington: Indiana University Press, 1990).

Shaw, Margaret R. B., 'Vera—Sed Non Veritas', *New English Weekly*, 12 October 1933, Vol. III, pp. 618–19.

Stonor Saunders, Frances, *The Cultural Cold War. The CIA and the World of Arts and Letters* (New York: The New Press, 1999).

Shaw, Marion, *The Clear Stream: A Life of Winifred Holtby* (London: Virago Press Ltd, 1999).

Sherry, Norman, *The Life of Graham Greene*, Vol. II, *1939–55* (London: Jonathan Cape, 1994).

Smith, Douglas, 'Beyond the Cave: Lascaux and the Prehistoric in Post-War French Culture', *French Studies*, April 2004, Vol. LVIII, No. 2, pp. 219–32.

Snowden, Keith, *Whitby Through the Ages* (Pickering: Castleden Publications, 2000), pp. 40–1.

Steele, Tom, *Alfred Orage and The Leeds Arts Club, 1893–1923* (Aldershot: Scolar Press, 1990).

Swinnerton Frank, *Swinnerton: An Autobiography* (London: Hutchinson & Co., 1937).

Tabori, Paul (ed.), *The Pen in Exile. An Anthology* (London: International P.E.N. Club Centre for Writers in Exile, 1954).

Thurlow, Richard, *Fascism in Britain. From Oswald Mosley's Blackshirts to the National Front* (London and New York: I. B. Tauris Publishers, 1998).

Turquet-Milnes, G., 'Midnight Books', *Time and Tide*, 21 October 1944, Vol. 25, No. 43, pp. 924–5.

University of Leeds Annual Reports.

University of Leeds Register of Students.

University of Leeds Session Records.

University of Leeds Yorkshire College Women's Representative Council Minute Book.

Valéry, Paul, et al., *A League of Minds. Letters of Henri Focillon, Salvador de Madariaga, Gilbert Murray, Miguel Ozorio de Almeida, Alfonso Reyes, Tsai Yuan Pei, Paul Valéry*, International Series of Open Letters, Vol. 1 (Paris: no pub., 1933).

Watts, Marjorie, *P.E.N. The Early Years, 1921–1926* (London: Archive Press, 1971).

—— *Mrs Sappho : The Life of C. A. Dawson Scott, Mother of International P.E.N.* (London: Duckworth, 1987).

Wasserstein, Bernard, *Britain and the Jews of Europe, 1939–1945* (Oxford: Oxford University Press, 1979).

Whitworth, Alan, *Whitby as They Saw It* (Whitby: Culva House Publications, 2nd edn, 2003), pp. 40–3.

Williams-Ellis, Amabel, *All Stracheys are Cousins. Memoirs* (London: Weidenfeld & Nicholson, 1983).

—— 'Soviet Literature' in *Britain and the Soviets: The Congress of Peace and Friendship with the USSR* (London: Martin Lawrence, 1936).

Williams-Ellis, Clough, *Around the World in Ninety Years* (Penrhyndeudraeth: Golden Dragon Books, Portmeirion Ltd, 1978).

Zühlsdorff, Volkmar, *Hitler's Exiles. The German Cultural Resistance in America and Europe*, trans. Martin H. Bott (London and New York: Continuum, 2004).

C. Archives and Collections Consulted

The British Library Sound Archive (BBC Sound Archive).

BBC Written Archive, Caversham Park.

Correspondence and papers of and concerning P. Bottome and Capt. A. E. Forbes Dennis 1882–1972, British Library, Add. Ms. 78837 and 78861.

Centenary Archive of the *Times Literary Supplement* URL: http://www.tls.psmedia.com/

Denis Saurat Archive, Archives of the Institut Français du Royaume-Uni-French Institute in London.

Dobrée Correspondence, Brotherton Collection, Leeds University Library.

Dobrée/ Chapman Correspondence, Brotherton Collection, Leeds University Library.

Harriet Shaw Weaver Papers, British Library, Add. Ms. 57354 and 5732.

Papers of James Hanley (920 HAN/4 Correspondence from Storm Jameson to James Hanley, Liverpool Record Office).

Liddell Hart Centre for Military Archives, King's College London (LIDDELL: 1/408 1937–1973, 1986).

The Macmillan Archive at the British Library (3rd Tranche). [The Archive was uncatalogued at the time of consultation].

National Collection of Newspapers and Periodicals at Colindale, London (British Library).

PEN Archive, The Harry Ransom Humanities Research Center, The University of Texas at Austin. [To the original PEN deposit were added in 2004/5 the collection of items retained in the London PEN Centre, which I originally consulted there. These items were uncatalogued on my visit to Austin in April 2006, and references are given accordingly (uncat.).]

Private Collection of Christopher Storm-Clark.

Storm Jameson Collection, The Harry Ransom Humanities Research Center, The University of Texas at Austin.

Letters from various correspondents to Vernon Bartlett, Vol. I, British Library, Add. Ms. 59500.

INDEX

Index

439